SERVICE-LEARNING IN COMPUTER AND INFORMATION SCIENCES

SERVICE-LEARNING IN COMPUTER AND INFORMATION SCIENCES

Practical Applications in Engineering Education

Edited by

Brian A. Nejmeh

IEEE PRESS

A JOHN WILEY & SONS, INC., PUBLICATION

For general information on our other products and services please contact our Customer Care
Department within the United States at (800) 762-2974, outside the United States at (317) 572-3993 or
fax (317) 572-4002.

Wiley also publishes its books in a variety of electronic formats. Some content that appears in print,
however, may not be available in electronic formats. For more information about Wiley products, visit
our web site at www.wiley.com.

Library of Congress Cataloging-in-Publication Data:

Service-learning in computer and information sciences : practical applications in engineering education /
editor, Brian A. Nejmeh.
  p. cm.
  ISBN 978-1-118-10034-9 (pbk.)
1. Information technology—Study and teaching. 2. Service learning. I. Nejmeh, Brian A.
  T58.5.S467 2012
  004.071'1—dc23   2011052003

Printed in the United States of America.

10 9 8 7 6 5 4 3 2 1

This book is warmly dedicated to the two dear women who have taught me most of what I know about a life of service. My mother, Mary Nejmeh, for more than 86 years has lived an entire life of tireless and joyful service to others. Then, for the last 25 years, my remarkable wife, Laurie, has taught me on a daily basis what it means to unconditionally love and serve others as she cares for our children, Emily and Al, for our special needs daughter, Mary, and thankfully, for her needy husband.

With much love,

Brian

CONTENTS

CHAPTER 3   Ten Years of EPICS at Butler University:
Experiences from Crafting a Service-Learning Program for
Computer Science and Software Engineering
Panagiotis K. Linos

CHAPTER 4   The Collaboratory
David Vader

CHAPTER 5   The Humanitarian Free and Open-Source Software
Project: Engaging Students in Service-Learning through Building
Software
Ralph Morelli, Trishan de Lanerolle, and Allen Tucker

Part III—Service-Learning Projects in the Computer and Information Sciences

CHAPTER 6 Some Worked Better Than Others: Experience with a Variety of Service-Learning Projects
Ken Vollmar and Peter Sanderson

CHAPTER 7 EPICS Software Development Projects
William Oakes and Saurabh Bagchi

CHAPTER 8 HFOSS Service-Learning Case Study: The Bowdoin–Ronald McDonald House Projects
Allen Tucker, Ralph Morelli, and Trishan de Lanerolle

CHAPTER 9   Service-Learning and Project Management:
The Capstone Course in Information Technology Leadership
Charles Hannon

CHAPTER 10   Service-Learning and Entrepreneurship for Engineers
Lisa Zidek

CHAPTER 11   Teaching Information Systems Ethics through
Service-Learning
Thomas S. E. Hilton and Donald D. Mowry

CHAPTER 12   Computer Literacy Service-Learning Project in Brazil
Wen-Jung Hsin and Olga Ganzen

Chapter 13   Service-Learning through Agile Software Development
Joseph T. Chao and Jennifer B. Warnke

CHAPTER 14   Empowerment through Service-Learning: Teaching
Technology to Senior Citizens
Sally R. Beisser

CHAPTER 15   Hybridizing Virtual- and Field-Based
Service-Learning in Green IT
K. Branker and J. M. Pearce

CHAPTER 16   Engaging Engineering Students in a Development
Program for a Global South Nation through Service-Learning
Willie K. Ofosu, Francois Sekyere, and James Oppong

CHAPTER 17   Leveraging Local Resources to Implement
Community-Oriented, Sustainable Computer Education Projects
in Los Angeles
Rohit Mathew and Christine M. Maxwell

CHAPTER 18   Using Labdoo to Bridge the Digital Divide:
A New Form of International Cooperation
*Jordi ros-Giralt, Kevin Launglucknavalai, Daniel Massaguer, Julieta
Casanova, and Christine M. Maxwell*

CHAPTER 19   The CHARMS Application Suite: A
Community-Based Mobile Data Collection and Alerting Environment
for HIV/AIDS Orphan and Vulnerable Children in Zambia
Brian A. Nejmeh and Tyler Dean

**Part IV—Lessons Learned about Service-Learning in the
Computer and Information Sciences**

CHAPTER 20   Lessons Learned— Guidance for Building
Community Service Projects
Michael Werner and Lisa MacLean

CHAPTER 21   Assessing both the Know and Show in IT
Service-Learning
Rick Homkes

CHAPTER 22   From Kudjip to Succotz: The Successes, Lessons, Joys,
and Surprises from 25 Years of Service-Learning Projects
James Paul Skon and Doug J. Karl

CHAPTER 23   Educational Impacts of an International Service-Learning
Design Project on Project Members and Their Peers
Peter E. Johnson

CHAPTER 24   Is the Community Partner Satisfied?
Camille George

CHAPTER 25   Service-Learning in the Computer and Information
Sciences: Lessons Learned and Guidance for the Future
Brian A. Nejmeh

PREFACE

Service-learning (SL) is a pedagogical model that actively integrates community service with learning outcomes in a credit-bearing academic course or cocurricular project. In service-learning, students actively engage in an authentic service activity that meets the actual and real needs of a community served by a community partner. The community partner is typically a nonprofit organization. Such service-learning projects are designed and structured to promote and foster a mutually beneficial relationship. Students then critically reflect, examine, and converse about the service activity from both technical and nontechnical perspectives. As a result, students gain keen insights and a fresh perspective about the course content and its practical application. Service-learning also promotes a commitment for students to become active and socially responsible members of their communities [1].

Since its inception, service-learning in the academy has occurred predominately outside of the computer and information sciences [2]. Adams [3] noted that, "While service-learning is becoming more common in college curriculums, it is still noticeably absent from many computer science programs." Sanderson [4] also noted back in 2003 that "computer science is not very visible in the service-learning community." Of the more than 300 service-learning syllabi listed at the Campus Compact website in 2011 [5], only five entries exist for computer science.

Collectively, we refer to computer science, information systems, computer engineering, software engineering, and so on as the "computer and information sciences disciplines." The term "SL in CIS" is used throughout this book to refer to "service-learning in the computer and information sciences." The computer and information sciences disciplines offer significant opportunities for engagement in service-learning. This is due to the fact that many nonprofit organizations (NPOs) lack the expertise, capacity, resources, and time to leverage information technology to improve the overall efficiency, effectiveness, and value of the services they provide.

Students with skills and aptitude in the computer and information sciences disciplines have historically been in high demand and often rank among the most highly paid out of college. An important aspect of SL in CIS is that it exposes students to the opportunities and rewards of using their skills in the context of doing projects for NPOs. Perhaps by being exposed to such projects, students might more seriously consider career opportunities with such NPOs as part of their notion of community service upon graduation.

Curriculum and courses in the computer and information sciences disciplines have struggled to remain current and relevant in the academy [6]. Experiential learning, whereby students learn about information technology by applying it to real-world problems, is an emerging trend whose impact is just beginning to be understood [7, 8]. Service-learning is about the formalization of such experiential learning in the NPO realm.

There is an emerging and keen interest in service-learning in the computer and information sciences, as witnessed by the very recent increase (albeit still very small) in the number of published papers and sessions about this topic at computer and information sciences educational conferences. Although the recent activity in service-learning in the computer and information sciences disciplines is encouraging, it is still substantially disproportionate to such projects in other fields. The interest in SL in CIS spans faculty, students, higher education administrators (i.e., Deans and Department Chairs), and NPO leaders.

Despite the significant opportunities that nonprofit organizations represent for service-learning in the computer and information sciences, relatively little has been written about these opportunities. This book is the first known book on this subject. The purpose of this book is to introduce faculty members and administrators, as well as NPO leaders and the communities they serve, to the opportunities, benefits, and challenges of service-learning in the computer and information sciences.

The book begins by presenting a service-learning framework (Chapter 1) that defines various options for integrating service-learning into computer and information sciences courses and activities. The framework refines existing pedagogical models to fit the computer and information sciences disciplines. The following service-learning options are covered in Chapter 1:

- Training: focus on imparting computer and information sciences skills needed by the staff of NPOs
- Professional services: focus on providing advice in computer and information sciences issues facing NPOs
- Systems selection: focus on defining system needs of an NPO, identifying and evaluating candidate IT solutions, recommending a solution, and transitioning the solution to an NPO
- Support: focus on providing customer support related to IT systems for NPOs
- System projects: focus on developing an information system project for a specific NPO

- Products: focus on developing a common information system product used by multiple NPOs

The book is an edited collection of papers written by field practitioners actively engaged in service-learning in the computer and information sciences. In interacting with authors during the process of researching this book, it also became clear that there is much student/community engagement and service going on in the computer and information sciences outside the realm of a formal credit-bearing course. For this reason, the scope of the book includes noncredit-bearing student/community service experiences that occur in a cocurricular setting. The chapters in the book offer an in-depth look at the various forms of service-learning projects and structures in the computer and information sciences. The chapters discuss specific projects undertaken, how they were organized, and the challenges related to integrating service-learning into computer and information sciences curricula and cocurricular activities. The chapters place an emphasis on the unique lessons learned in doing service-learning engagements and on recommendations for those interested in conducting or encouraging such engagements. The book contains four main parts:

1. The first part of the book introduces the topic of service-learning in the computer and information sciences. It offers a framework for the various methods of integrating service-learning into computer and information sciences disciplines. The framework refines existing pedagogical models to fit the computer and information sciences disciplines and then illustrates service-learning options in the computer and information sciences. It also defines the range of service-learning activity across the continuum of research to assessment. The framework allows the reader to better understand the context for the various service-learning programs and projects discussed in the book.

2. The second part of the book focuses on organizational and pedagogical models for introducing SL in CIS. Chapters in this part of the book come from global field practitioners. These chapters discuss the organizational and pedagogical models for integrating service-learning into the computer and information sciences. Topics covered in this part of the book include how university initiatives around SL in CIS are organized and managed, curriculum integration concerns, accreditation concerns related to service-learning, capstone projects involving service-learning, and the use of open-source technologies in a service-learning setting.

3. The third part, and main body of the book, is a collection of chapters about service-learning projects in the computer and information sci-

ences written by global field practitioners. These chapters offer an in-depth look at the various forms of service-learning projects in the computer and information sciences.

4. The fourth part of the book focuses on lessons learned based on the experiences of field practitioners. It includes a chapter that synthesizes the lessons learned from the other chapters in the book. This chapter highlights best practices for successful integrating SL in CIS. This part of the book also includes chapters that discuss the impact of service-learning in the computer and information sciences.

For faculty and students in the computer and information sciences, service-learning offers significant benefits. Service-learning in the computer and information sciences directly addresses a chronic problem facing the computer and information sciences academic community—practical application. The technology industry has consistently criticized the academy for not equipping students for the workforce [6]. Furthermore, service-learning models whereby students learn about information technology by solving real-world problems are an emerging trend that is having a positive impact [8]. As such, SL in CIS offers much promise with regard to bringing practical applications to computer and information sciences education.

The book exposes faculty and students to many projects and different models for successfully executing them in both a service-learning class setting and a cocurricular, noncredit-bearing community service setting. It also exposes faculty and students to the nonprofit sector and how technology can be used by this sector to significantly impact the people and communities they serve. This will enable faculty to interact with local and global NPOs in a new way, leading to mutually beneficial project partnerships. Faculty will be introduced to a new teaching pedagogy in the computer and information sciences, enabling them to better understand the range of options for SL in CIS. The book is especially relevant to faculty teaching project-based courses or capstone courses. The book exposes faculty and students to the various ways service-learning can be integrated into the computer and information sciences disciplines. It provides a context within which student–faculty partnerships can occur in projects, learning, and scholarship. In summary, the book expands and enhances SL in CIS opportunities.

The current generation of students is very interested in active learning and in serving. This book will help students, faculty, the academy, and NPOs satisfy these interests. The book will allow students to more appropriately and successfully engage in SL in CIS as they learn from other successful projects.

Finally, many NPOs lack the expertise, resources and time to leverage information technology to improve the overall efficiency, effectiveness, and value of the services they provide. Service-learning projects can improve the overall efficiency, effectiveness, and value of NPOs. These projects lead to improved marketing, fund-raising, communications, service quality, and increased capacity to better meet the needs of the communities NPOs serve.

The book provides a framework, stimulus, and practical working models for promoting joint projects between the academy and the NPO community. It should serve to encourage NPOs to successfully engage with the academy in mutually beneficial partnerships. By doing so, NPOs will benefit in two direct ways. First, the SL in CIS projects they participate in will allow them to be better users of technology, leading to improved marketing, fund-raising, communication, and service quality, and increased capacity to serve their communities. Secondly, SL in CIS projects offer the possibility of increasing the technical workforce for these organizations as students are exposed to the opportunities and challenges NPOs face and may sense a calling to work in an NPO environment upon graduation.

BRIAN A. NEJMEH
February, 2012

REFERENCES

1. Messiah College, "What is Service-Learning," http://www.messiah.edu/external_programs/agape/servicelearning/about.html, retrieved October 12, 2011.
2. Droge, D. (Ed.) (1996). *Disciplinary Pathways to Service-Learning.* Washington: Campus Compact.
3. Adams, J. and E. Runkles, "May We Have Class Outside?: Implementing Service Learning in CIS Curriculum," *Journal of Computing Sciences in College,* Vol. 19, Issue 5 (May 2004), pp. 25–34.
4. Sanderson, P., "Where's (the) Computer Science in Service-Learning?" *Journal of Computing Sciences In College,* Vol. 19, Issue 1 (October 2003), pp. 83–89.
5. Campus Compact, http://www.compact.org/category/syllabi/, retrieved Oct, 12, 2011.
6. Ayofe, A. and A. Ajetola, "Exploration of the Gap Between Computer Science Curriculum and Industrial Skills Requirements," *International Journal of Computer Science and Information Security,* Vol. 4, Nos. 1 & 2, 2009, pp. 39–47.
7. Homkes, R. "Assessing IT Service-Learning," in *Proceedings of the 9th Conference on Information Technology Education, SIGITE 2008,* Cincinnati, OH, USA, October 16–18, 2008 (Joseph J. Ekstrom and Mark Stockman, Eds.), pp. 17–22, ACM, 2008.
8. Strom, S., "Does Service Learning Really Help?," *NY Times,* January 3, 2010, http://www.nytimes.com/2010/01/03/education/edlife/03service-t.html. Retrieved August 24, 2010.

ACKNOWLEDGMENTS

The author would like to acknowledge the contributions that many of his current and former CSC 333 and BIS 412 students at Messiah College have made to the ideas in this book. The author is grateful to Messiah College and its Collaboratory for Strategic Partnerships and Applied Research for the support it provided for this work. The author acknowledges the full support and encouragement he received from Ray Norman (School Dean) and Angela Hare (Department Chair) for this sabbatical project. He is also indebted to his many colleagues at Messiah College who have informed and influenced his understanding of SL in CIS; including David Vader, Ray Norman, Chad Frey, and Scott Weaver.

This book was a collective effort of many professionals and the author would like to acknowledge the authors of the individual chapters; as well as his long-time colleague Ian Thomas for Ian's review and editing of various chapters. Finally, the author would like to acknowledge the support and extensive editorial assistance he received from Laurie, his talented wife.

CONTRIBUTORS

Saurabh Bagchi, Electrical and Computer Engineering and EPICS Program, Purdue University, sbagchi@purdue.edu

Sally R. Beisser, Drake University, School of Education, sally.beisser@drake.edu

K. Branker, Department of Mechanical and Materials Engineering, Queen's University, brankerk@me.queensu.ca

Julieta Casanova, Ministry of Economy, Madrid, Spain, Labdoo.org, Madrid, Spain, julictacasanova@yahoo.es

Joseph T. Chao, Bowling Green State University, jchao@bgsu.edu,

Trishan R. de Lanerolle, Trinity College, trishan.delanerolle@trincoll.edu

Tyler Dean, Carnegie Mellon University, School of Information Systems & Management

Olga Ganzen, OTI Global Consultants, olgaganzen@gmail.com

Camille George, Program Director and Associate Professor of Mechanical Engineering, School of Engineering, University of St. Thomas, cmgeorge@stthomas.edu

Charles Hannon, Professor, Information Technology Leadership, Washington & Jefferson College, channon@washjeff.edu

Thomas S. E. Hilton, IS, University of Wisconsin–Eau Claire, hiltonts@uwec.edu

Rick Homkes, Computer and Information Technology, Purdue University, homkesrl@purdue.edu

Wen-Jung Hsin, Park University, Computer Science, Information Systems, and Mathematics, wen.hsin@park.edu

Peter E. Johnson, Associate Professor of Mechanical Engineering, Valparaiso University, Pete.Johnson@valpo.edu

Doug J. Karl, Project Consultant, Mount Vernon Nazarene University, doug@dougkarl.com

Kevin Launglucknavalai, Department of Mechanical and Aerospace Engineering, University of California, Irvine Labdoo.org, CA, klaunglu@uci.edu

Panagiotis K. Linos, Department of Computer Science and Software Engineering, Butler University, linos@butler.edu

Lisa MacLean, Department of Computer Science and Networking, Wentworth Institute of Technology, macleanl@wit.edu

Daniel Massaguer, Institute for Software Research, University of California, Irvine, Labdoo.org, CA, daniel.massaguer@labdoo.org

Rohit Mathew, Engineers without Borders—University of California, Los Angeles, rohitjm@gmail.com

Christine M. Maxwell, Engineers Without Borders, University of California, Los Angeles, California Institute of Technology, christine.lee@jpl.nasa.gov

Ralph Morelli, Trinity College, ralph.morelli@trincoll.edu

Donald D. Mowry, Social Work, University of Wisconsin–Eau Claire, dmowry@uwec.edu

Brian A. Nejmeh, Department of Information and Mathematical Sciences, Messiah College, BNejmeh@messiah.edu

William Oakes, EPICS Program and Engineering Education, Purdue University, oakes@purdue.edu

Willie K. Ofosu, Penn State Wilkes-Barre Lehman, wko1@psu.edu

James Oppong, Kwame Nkrumah University of Science and Technology (KNUST), oppongjk@yahoo.com

J. M. Pearce, Department of Materials Science and Engineering, Department of Electrical and Computer Engineering, Michigan Technological University, pearce@mtu.edu

Jordi Ros-Giralt, Engineers Without Borders, University of California, Los Angeles, Labdoo.org, Barcelona, Spain, jordi.ros@labdoo.org

Pete Sanderson, Department of Mathematical Sciences, Otterbein University, PSanderson@otterbein.edu

Francois Sekyere, University of Education, Kumasi Campus (UEW-K), fsekyere@gmail.com

James Skon, Professor of Computer Science and Department Chair, Mount Vernon Nazarene University, Jim.Skon@mvnu.edu

Allen Tucker, Bowdoin College, allen@bowdoin.edu

David Vader, Messiah College, dvader@messiah.edu

Ken Vollmar, Department of Computer Science, Missouri State University, IEEE Senior Member, KenVollmar@missouristate.edu

Jennifer B. Warnke, Bowling Green State University, jkbrown@bgsu.edu

Michael Werner, Department of Computer Science and Networking, Wentworth Institute of Technology, wernerm@wit.edu

Lisa Zidek, Academic Program Director and Associate Professor, Florida Gulf Coast University, lzidek@fgcu.edu

Carla Zoltowski, EPICS Program, Purdue University, cbz@purdue.edu

PART 1

A FRAMEWORK

CHAPTER 1

A FRAMEWORK FOR SERVICE-LEARNING IN THE COMPUTER AND INFORMATION SCIENCES*

Brian A. Nejmeh

ABSTRACT

There are substantial opportunities for service-learning in the computer and information sciences. To date, there has not been a comprehensive framework developed to provide a structure for understanding the breadth and depth of service-learning opportunities in the computer and information sciences. This framework delineates the range of options and opportunities for service-learning in the computer and information sciences disciplines. Its aim is to facilitate and broaden the practice of service-learning in the computer and information sciences among the academic and nonprofit organization communities by clarifying the options and choices open to stakeholders in these opportunities. This chapter proposes a three-dimensional framework for service learning opportunities in the computer and information sciences. The first dimension defines the *types of projects* to be performed in a service-learning engagement (i.e., training, professional services, systems selection, support/help desk, custom development projects, and product development projects). The second dimension defines the range of activity (i.e., research, analysis, design, implementation, test, transition, and assessment) to be performed in a service-learning project. The third dimension defines the *mode* (cocurricular, curricular, or hybrid) of performing the service-learning project.

*The original version of this chapter was authored by Brian A. Nejmeh and entitled "Faith Integration through Service-Learning in the Information Sciences." It appeared in the *Christian Business Academy Review,* Volume 3, No. 1 (Spring, 2008), pp. 12–25. Used with permission. This chapter is derived from this earlier paper.

1.1   INTRODUCTION

The mission of many colleges and universities includes some notion of service to the local, national, or global community. The incorporation of the service-learning model into the course curriculum and cocurricular activities can greatly enhance the service-oriented mission of many colleges and universities. Despite this fact, service-learning courses and cocurricular activities have only recently emerged in the computer and information sciences disciplines (i.e., computer science, information systems, computer engineering, software engineering, etc.). These disciplines, however, have significant opportunities for engagement in service-learning. Many community nonprofit organizations (NPOs) simply lack the ability, resources, and capacity to leverage information technology (IT) for the betterment of their organizations and the communities they serve.

The purpose of this chapter is to demonstrate that the computer and information sciences disciplines offer significant opportunities for meaningful service-learning engagement. This is done through the definition and presentation of a comprehensive framework for service-learning (SL) in the computer and information sciences (CIS). This framework outlines the breadth and depth of service-learning opportunities available within the computer and information sciences disciplines. We use the term "SL in CIS" throughout the chapter to refer to "service-learning in the computer and information sciences."

The service-learning framework for the computer and information sciences disciplines defined in this chapter will serve to inform its educators in these disciplines about the range of opportunities available to engage in service-learning. This is an important contribution to disciplines in which such a framework has yet to emerge and relatively little service-learning engagement occurs. This framework will serve to broaden the awareness of SL in CIS within the academic and NPO communities. As a result, a goal of this framework is to increase the volume and scope of SL in CIS as NPO leaders, deans, department chairs, faculty, and students become more aware of the vast array of possibilities for service-learning. The framework also provides a great planning tool for NPOs and academic partners as they consider how to best discover and articulate the IT needs of NPOs. The framework provides a lexicon or a vocabulary for beginning this discovery and articulation process. It allows NPOs and their academic partners to map out the evolution of their work over time across multiple projects.

1.2   BACKGROUND AND RELATED WORK

Historically, service-learning in the academy has been focused predominately outside of the computer and information sciences [1]; however, service-learning projects in the computer and information sciences have emerged over the past decade. Most of these efforts focus on the development of custom software to meet the specific needs of an NPO. For example, a service-learning project at Trinity College [2] involved students developing a system for managing disaster relief for an NPO. Another service-learning project focused on providing additional information technology (IT) support for school districts [3]. Another project [4] focused on the development of a course outline that incorporated service-learning into a computer science course. Similarly, another institution outlined a capstone project in information systems that focuses on community-based projects [5]. Finally, a panel session [6] outlined the opportunities and challenges for service-learning in the computer and information sciences. This review of the related work proved invaluable in the creation of the service-learning framework defined in this chapter. Consequently, each of the projects identified in the literature can be positioned within the framework.

Although the recent activity in service-learning in the computer and information sciences disciplines is encouraging, it is still limited compared to such projects in fields outside of computer and information sciences. Furthermore, no known service-learning framework exists for the computer and information sciences that outlines the breadth and depth of service-learning opportunities available to the disciplines.

From 2002 to the present, the author and others at Messiah College have been actively involved in service-learning projects in the computer and information sciences. Appendix A summarizes the wide range of service-learning projects being done in the computer and information sciences at Messiah College. In addition, the author participated in a multiyear task force funded by a Lilly Foundation grant, involving an interdisciplinary team of faculty focused on the definition of a service-learning framework. This project was informative regarding the essence of service-learning as practiced in disciplines other than the computer and information sciences. Collectively, these service-learning project experiences, as well as the interdisciplinary service-learning task force participated in by the author, provided the initial basis for the computer and information sciences framework defined herein.

The author began working on this book in March of 2010. Through his literature review and interactions with prospective authors, the need to enlarge the scope of the initial service-learning framework became apparent. In particular, the author realized the following:

- Project Mode. It became clear that much community service is being done outside the context of a formal course structure in a university setting. Such projects are happening in the context of service organizations on campus, such as student chapters of Engineers Without Borders [7] and student chapters of the ACM (Association for Computing

Machinery) [8]. Although such cocurricular activity is typically termed community service within the academy, such activities are going to be considered part of service-learning for purposes of this book.

- Multifaceted Projects. Projects that span more than one project type, activity range, and mode. It also became clear that many SL in CIS projects are difficult to pigeonhole into one project type, activity range, or mode. For this reason, the framework allows a project to be classified across multiple project types, activity ranges, and modes.

The framework for SL in CIS was modified to reflect these realities.

1.3   WHAT IS SERVICE-LEARNING IN THE COMPUTER AND INFORMATION SCIENCES?

At Messiah College, "service-learning is a pedagogical model that *intentionally* integrates academic learning with community service in a credit-bearing academic course. Students participate in an *authentic* service activity that *meets needs identified by the community* (designed within the framework of a mutually beneficial relationship), and critically reflect on that activity. Thus, students gain a *deep understanding of course content,* a commitment to *socially responsible citizenship,* and develop skills and understanding needed to contribute to civic well-being" (italics added) [9].

The critical elements of service-learning are *content, service,* and *reflection* [9]. In the context of the computer and information sciences, the author's experience is that *content* should be focused on readings, visuals, and class discussion that specifically relate service to the course objectives. A reading example could include excerpts from Bryant Myers' book, *Walking with the Poor* [10]. Visuals could include video, photographs or Web resources (blogs, twitter, etc.) that offer the students an opportunity to learn more about the communities they will serve and how their work can potentially impact the communities. Class discussion is used to amplify the relevance of service to the course in discipline-specific ways. This might also include an in-class discussion with a staff member from the NPO who is the partner for the service-learning project.

The author's experience is that *service* in the computer and information sciences should be oriented toward specific projects that address significant information technology needs of NPOs. Such needs cover a wide range of activities spanning the development of information systems to the installation of a computer network (see Appendix A and the chapters throughout the book). The range of service opportunities in the computer and information sciences is discussed in detail later in this chapter.

The author's experience is that *reflection* in the computer and information sciences should focus on guided journaling done by the students. Journal topics should relate the students' service experience to their vocation, community outreach, and responsible stewardship with the resources entrusted to them. In the author's experience, this is typically done via journal prompts that are provided to the students by the faculty member about every two weeks. Key issues that students should be challenged to ponder and reflect on include:

- What is the nature of the problems the NPO is facing and why do these problems exist?
- How can information technology (IT) be used to positively impact the NPO in order for it to better meet the needs of the community it is serving?
- How does indirect service through the application of information technology allow an NPO to better directly serve the needs of their communities?
- Comment on your understanding of how indirect service through an application of information technology to support an NPO can allow an NPO to better directly serve the needs of the communities they serve?
- How might someone be able to continue to serve NPOs and, in turn, the communities they serve beyond this service-learning project?

In one of the above questions, the phrase *indirect service* appears. This phrase has proven to be an important term to students. Most students in the computer and information sciences struggle to understand how their talents can be used in a community-service setting. They tend to see direct, hands-on community service as the only form of community service. The notion of indirect service is that you are serving an NPO indirectly by providing them with IT systems and assets they can, in turn, use to increase both their capacity and ability to better directly serve their communities of need. Hence, indirect service leads to IT systems that improve the overall operational efficiencies and effectiveness of NPOs, thereby allowing NPO staff and volunteers to have more time to directly serve their communities in need. In effect, this concept of indirect service and its linkage to direct service outcomes helps students better understand how their talents can be used to the benefit of NPOs and the communities they serve.

1.4 BENEFITS OF SERVICE-LEARNING IN THE COMPUTER AND INFORMATION SCIENCES

The author's experience points to several key student benefits of service-learning in the computer and information sciences. Student reflection journals confirmed the significant benefits that service-learning offered them. A summary of the key student benefits follow:

- Applied experience. Many students in the computer and information sciences long to engage in the process of solving practical problems with information technology. Service-learning experiences allow students to practice problem solving with an actual customer and organization. Such experiences also provide students the chance to apply the technology they have learned in theory, but have not had the chance to apply in practice.

- Ethics. Service-learning experiences also allow students to address ethical issues such as software licensing, pricing, and vendor claims of product functionality and performance. Such experiences offer the opportunity for students to practice clear and honest communication with a customer.

- Professionalism. Students performing service-learning projects get to practice professionalism in the form of meeting planning, presentation development, project deadlines, and trade-off analysis.

- Teams. Students are given the opportunity to work in teams as they perform service-learning projects. This is a critical skill that students must develop as they transition from college into the workplace.

- Trade-off analysis. Service-learning projects provide practical experiences for students to perform various forms of trade-off analysis. Such trade-off analyses include cost–benefit analysis, time–space analysis, design with change in mind analysis, cost–schedule–functionality trade-off analysis, and so on.

- Project management. Service-learning projects allow students to practice and develop project management skills related to project planning, estimation and scheduling as well as communication and coordination. In general, such projects allow for the development of key interpersonal skills students will need to succeed in the workplace.

- Diversity. Students often get to experience and see diversity as they work with NPOs. Diversity occurs as students interact with people that are different from themselves in terms of socioeconomic status, race, ethnicity, and location around the world.

- Compassion. Students can also come to appreciate the adversity that comes with being poor, disabled, or uneducated as they work with the NPOs that minister to people from such groups.

- Vocational exploration. Service-learning projects offer students the opportunity to explore their vocation, both in terms of the different types of organizations and the functional roles they would like to play within an organization.

- Culminating experience. Students often look at service-learning projects as the culminating or capstone project of their educational experience. These projects are often referenced to employers and others as a "rite of passage" into the workplace.

The author's experience also indicates that NPOs benefit from service-learning in the computer and information sciences. Such projects improve the overall efficiency, effectiveness, and value of NPOs. These projects lead to improved marketing, fund-raising, communications, service quality, and increased capacity.

1.5   A SERVICE-LEARNING FRAMEWORK FOR THE COMPUTER AND INFORMATION SCIENCES

Having established the relevance of service-learning in the computer and information sciences, a framework for service-learning in the context of these disciplines is needed to raise the awareness of the opportunities of SL in CIS for NPOs and academic partners. In turn, the framework can increase the scope and volume of practice of SL in CIS. Many disciplines in the academy have embraced service-learning for some time [1, 11]. Several generic frameworks have been developed to help inform the academy about the forms of service-learning. For example, Musil developed a service-learning taxonomy and maturity model around levels of engagement and authenticity [12]. As discussed earlier, service-learning in the computer and information sciences has emerged in this past decade; however, service-learning projects in the computer and information sciences are still in their formative stages and are still limited in number compared to such projects in fields outside of the computer and information sciences. Furthermore, no known service-learning framework exists for the computer and information sciences.

The framework refines existing pedagogical models to fit the computer and information sciences disciplines. The framework defined herein is based on:

1. Actual service-learning experiences (see Appendix A) performed in the computer and information sciences disciplines at Messiah College
2. An extensive review of the SL in CIS literature
3. The projects described in this book

The framework defines a three-dimensional space:

- Project Type. The first dimension defines the *types of projects* to be performed in a service-learning engagement.
- Activity Range: The second dimension defines the *range of activity* to be performed in a service-learning project.

- Project Mode. The third dimension defines the *mode* of performing the service-learning project.

1.5.1   Project Types

The first dimension of the framework is the *project type*. A project type defines the work to be performed in the context of a service-learning engagement. In terms of *types of projects* that can be to be performed, the framework defines the following service-learning options:

- Training. Focus on imparting computer and information sciences skills needed by the staff of NPOs.
- Professional services. Focus on providing advice in computer and information sciences issues facing NPOs.
- Systems selection. Focus on defining system needs of an NPO, identifying and evaluating candidate solutions, recommending a solution, and (potentially) transitioning the solution to an NPO.
- Support. Focus on providing customer support related to systems for NPO(s).
- System projects. Focus on developing an information system project for a specific NPO.
- Products. Focus on developing a common information system product used by many NPOs.

Table 1.1 more completely defines the project types for service-learning in the computer and information sciences. For each project type, the table:

- Defines the focus or nature of the project type
- Outlines the level of engagement typically required on the part of faculty–student teams to perform this project type
- Describes the key skills required to perform the project type
- Provides an example of the project type

1.5.2   Activity Range

The second dimension of the framework is *activity range*. Activity range defines the span of tasks completed in the context of a service-learning engagement. In terms of the activity range to be performed, the framework defines the following:

- Research. Spans the tasks of problem identification and concept definition.

Table 1.1.   Computer and information sciences service-learning project types

Project type	Focus	Engagement level	Key skills	Example
Training	Focuses on imparting knowledge or skill needed by the staff of NPO(s).	Low	Subject matter expertise (SME), training development	Microsoft Office® training for NPOs
Professional services	Focuses on providing expert advice on computer and information sciences issues facing an NPO.	Medium	Problem solving, SME	Strategic IT Advisory Board for a NPO
Systems selection	Focuses on defining the system needs of an NPO, identifying candidate solutions, evaluating identified solutions, recommending a solution and transitioning the solution to an NPO.	High	Requirements analysis, consulting, product research and evaluation, product installation	System analysis, selection and installation of donor management system for an NPO
Support/help desk	Focuses on providing customer support related to an application or system for NPO(s).	Medium	SME, listening, trouble-shooting.	Providing support for local area network for NPOs
Custom development projects	Focuses on the full life cycle development of a custom application for an NPO.	High	Software development, project management	Integration of bar-code system with asset-management system
Product development projects	Focuses on the full life cycle development of a product application that is common to several NPO(s).	High	Software development, project and product management	Impact-assessment portal for NPOs

- Analysis. Analysis spans the tasks of requirements discovery, documentation, and validation of a business process or system.
- Design. For the systems selection, custom development, and product development project types, design spans the tasks of architecture, database design, user-interface design, communications design, workflow design, and report design. For the training, professional services, and support/help desk project types, design involves outlining the solution strategy to be used to address the requirements established during the analysis activity.

- Implementation. For the systems selection, custom development, and product development project types, implementation spans the tasks of detailed design and implementation of a system. For the training, professional services, and support/help desk project types, implementation involves developing the actual solution outlined during the design activity.

- Test. For the systems selection, custom development and product development project types, test spans the task of integration of system and user-acceptance testing of a system. For the training, professional services and support/help desk project types, test involves internally validating that the actual solution developed during the implementation activity meets the needs of the NPO.

- Transition. For the systems selection, custom development, and product development project types, transition spans the tasks of installing a system and migrating from the old system to the new system. For the training, professional services, and support/help desk project types, transition involves delivering to the NPO the actual solution resulting from the testing activity.

- Assessment. Assessment spans the tasks of performance, usability, efficiency, effectiveness, and value/impact assessment of a system (i.e., the result of a system selection, custom project, or product development project type), for a training, professional services engagement, or support/help desk project. For training, professional services engagements, or support help-desk projects, assessment involves understanding the efficiency, effectiveness, and value of the services delivered by the project team.

Table 1.2 defines the activity range for service-learning.

1.5.3   Project Mode

The third dimension of the framework is *mode of project.* Mode defines the academic context and manner in which the service-learning engagement is being performed. In terms of the mode of project, the framework defines the items listed in Table 1.3.

1.5.4   Putting It All Together: The SL in CIS Framework

Structurally, the service-learning framework forms a three-dimensional space of project types, activity ranges, and project modes. A specific service-learning project is placed in one or more cells of the matrix. Table 1.4 follows and depicts the full computer and information sciences service-learning framework. This table has not been populated with sample projects, but simply demonstrates the skeletal framework. Table 1.5 has been populated with representative projects completed at Messiah College over the past

Table 1.2. Computer and information sciences service-learning activity range

Scope	Description
Research	Spans the tasks of problem identification and concept definition.
Analysis	Spans the tasks of requirements discovery, documentation, and validation of a business process or system.
Design	For the systems selection, custom development, and product development project types, design spans the tasks of architecture, database design, user interface design, communications design, workflow design, and report design. For the training, professional services, and support/help desk project types, design involves outlining the solution strategy to be used to address the requirements established during the analysis activity.
Implementation	For the systems selection, custom development, and product development project types, implementation spans the tasks of detailed design and implementation of a system. For the training, professional services, and support/help desk project types, implementation involves developing the actual solution outlined during the design activity.
Test	For the systems selection, custom development, and product development project types, test spans the task of integration of system and user-acceptance testing of a system. For the training, professional services, and support/help desk project types, test involves internally validating that the actual solution developed during the implementation activity meets the needs of the NPO.
Transition	For the systems selection, custom development, and product development project types, transition spans the tasks of installing a system and migrating from the old system to the new system. For the training, professional services and, support/help desk project types, transition involves delivering to the NPO the actual solution resulting from the testing activity.
Assessment	Assessment spans the tasks of performance, usability, efficiency, effectiveness, and value/impact assessment of a system (i.e., the result of a system selection, custom project, or product development project type). For training, professional services engagement, or support/help desk projects, assessment involves understanding the efficiency, effectiveness, and value of the services delivered by the program team.

several years. Some of the specific projects listed in Table 1.4 are further described in the Appendix A of this chapter. In addition, Table 1.5 is populated with several projects that are furthered described in chapters of the book. Brief names of the projects appear in the table along with a reference to the project (either Appendix A of this chapter or the chapter number in the book where a further description of the project can be found).

Several entries in Table 1.5 are now described in detail:

- The first entry in the table [MS-Office Training for Area NPOs (described in Appendix A)] was a project done in a business information

Table 1.3.   Project mode

Mode	Submode	Other attributes
Cocurricular. This mode of project is completed outside of a classroom setting as part of some community-service program.	*University-based.* This mode of cocurricular community service project is completed in the context of some university-based organization.	This might include campus organizations such as Engineers without Borders [7].
	Nonuniversity-based. This mode cocurricular community service of project is completed outside the context of a university-based organization.	This might include a student-organized project with an area church performing a community-service project on their own without any university affiliation.
Curricular. This mode of project is completed in the context of a course within the curriculum at a college or university.	*Common project course.* This involves the use of a common project course within which service-learning projects are completed. The course might be named "CIS Service-Learning Projects Course." Projects in a common project course could involve many sub-disciplines (i.e., databases, Web design, e-commerce, mobile development, etc.) within the computer and information sciences.	In some cases, project courses may be taken more than once by a given student. In such cases, the student (typically) plays a different role each time they take the course. For instance, the first time a student takes the course, they may play the role of documentation specialist. The second time they take the course they may play the role of software developer. The third time they take the course they may play the role of project manager.
	Subdiscipline-specific project course. This involves the use of a subdiscipline ourse within which service-learning projects are completed in that subdiscipline. Example subdiscipline courses include database development project course, Web development project course, mobile development project course, and so on.	
	Interdisciplinary course. This involves the use of multiple courses (typically offered at the same time) to complete a project. These courses might both be from the computer and information sciences disciplines (i.e., a Web design project course and database development course cooperatively developing a Web database application). Alternatively, one of these courses might come from the computer and information sciences disciplines and the other course might come from another discipline such as technical writing.	

Table 1.3.   Continued

Mode	Submode	Other attributes
Hybrid. This mode of project includes a cooperative style of completing a project that involves both a cocurricular component and a curricular or course-based component.	*Cocurricular led hybrid project.* For example, a cocurricular project team leading a community service project could subcontract with a project-based course to have some aspect of their cocurricular project completed for them by the project-based course.	
	Course-led Hybrid Project. A course-led service-learning project could subcontract to a cocurricular project team to do the field-trial work for a project.	

systems course as a student group project. The project involved analyzing the MS Office® training needs of area NPOs and developing a course to meet these needs. In turn, the course was offered and an assessment of learning outcomes for the course participants was also done. Thus, this project appears in the "training" project type with an activity range of "analysis to assessment." The project entry in the table is shaded in the ☐ pattern to reflect that the project was done in the context of a curricular course.

- A second entry in the table is the BOOTUP (Chapter 17) project. This project was done as a cocurricular project as part of the Engineers without Borders cocurricular group at UCLA. This project involves the creation of a custom development project in the form of a Web portal application and process to facilitate the collection, repurposing, and distribution of computers to those in need. The activity range ran the full spectrum from research to assessment. The project entry in the table is shaded in the ☐ pattern to reflect that the project was done in the context of a cocurricular group (Engineers without Borders).

- A third entry in the table illustrates a hybrid project. It is the Donor/Member Management System for MC Collaboratory (Appendix A) table entry. This project was originally conceived as a class project in an analysis and design project course. The results of the project from the course were then transitioned to a cocurricular group that did the final installation and ongoing maintenance of the system. The activity range ran the full spectrum from research to assessment. The project entry in the table is shaded in the ☐ pattern to reflect that the project was done in the context of both a course and a cocurricular group (Collaboratory).

Table 1.4. SL in CIS framework

Activity Range

Project Type	Research	Analysis	Design	Implementation	Test	Transition	Assessment
Training							
Professional services							
System selection							
Support							
Custom development projects							
Products							

▨ = project conducted by curricular group   ▫ = project conducted by cocurricular group   ▪ = project conducted by hybrid group

Table 1.5. SL in CIS framework with sample projects

Project type	Activity Range						
	Research	Analysis	Design	Implementation	Test	Transition	Assessment
Training			MS Office Training for Area NPOs (Appendix A)				
Professional services				Install LAN for CAPC (Appendix A)			
System selection	Research Select MIS for CAPC (Appendix A)						
	Donor/Member Management System for MC Collaboratory (Appendix A)						
Support							
Custom development projects	World Vision LEAP Impact Assessment Application (Appendix A)						
	CURE Intl Inventory Barcode System (Appendix A)						
	BOOTUP (Chapter 17), Labdoo (Chapter 10)						
Products	USDA NRCS (Chapter 6)						
	Volunteer Management System (Chapter 7)						
	Hometbase, Homeroom (Chapter 8)						

= project conducted by curricular group   = project conducted by cocurricular group   = project conducted by hybrid group

- A fourth entry in the table are the "Homebase and Homeroom (Chapter 8)" projects. These projects were conceived as open-source applications that could be used by any number of NPOs. Since these projects were designed to be used by multiple NPOs, we classify them as "Products." The activity range including the full set of activities from research to assessment. Finally, since the projects were completed in the context of a course, the project mode was "curricular."

1.6 CONCLUSIONS

The computer and information sciences disciplines afford numerous and unique opportunities for students to apply their gifts, skills, and knowledge via service-learning. Although the application of service-learning is emerging within the computer and information sciences disciplines, the framework defined in this chapter serves as a critical tool to encourage faculty to broaden the scope of service-learning within their disciplines. It outlines the types of activities that can be pursued as service-learning, such as training, professional services, systems selection, support/help desk, custom development projects, and product development projects. Furthermore, it outlines the scope of tasks that can be completed: research, analysis, design, implementation, test, transition, and assessment. Finally, it outlines the various project modes that can be used to implement service-learning projects, including cocurricular, curricular, and hybrid modes. It should aid NPOs, faculty, and students by helping them understand the key questions (and answers) they need to be able to choose SL in CIS projects wisely.

ACKNOWLEDGMENTS

The author would like to acknowledge the contributions that many of his current and former CSC 333 and BIS 412 students have made to the ideas in this chapter. The author also wishes to acknowledge the authors of the chapters in this book whose work has improved this framework. The author is grateful to Messiah College and the Collaboratory for Strategic Partnerships and Applied Research for the support they provided for this work. The author is also indebted to his many colleagues at Messiah College who have informed and influenced his understanding of SL in CIS. These colleagues include David Vader, Ray Norman, Chad Frey, and Scott Weaver. The author would like to thank Ian Thomas for his review of earlier drafts of this chapter. Finally, the author wishes to acknowledge Melissa Dobbins for her support and inspiration.

APPENDIX A: CASE STUDY APPLICATIONS OF THE SL IN CIS FRAMEWORK

Table 1.4 serves the dual purpose of depicting the overall service-learning framework and listing sample service-learning projects completed by Messiah College faculty and students. The projects listed in Table 1.4 are briefly described below.

- MS-Office Training for Area NPOs. This semiannual event offers the staff of Central Pennsylvania NPOs the opportunity to receive training on Microsoft Office™. This project happens in BIS 230 (Computer Applications) under the direction of a faculty member. Students, however, design and deliver the training, and NPO participants complete a feedback questionnaire at the end of the training.
- Install LAN for CAPC. This project involved a student–faculty team performing the professional service of designing, implementing, and testing a local area network (LAN) for the Capital Area Pregnancy Center (CAPC) [13]. The team also transitioned the LAN to CAPC personnel so they could administer the LAN.
- Research/Select MIS for CAPC. This project occurred in the 2006 Spring semester of BIS 412 (Systems Analysis and Design Applications), the BIS major capstone course. CAPC had a need for a Web-based distributed scheduling system to replace their manual scheduling method. The students formed a team under the direction of a faculty member and managed the complete life cycle spanning research through to testing and transitioning the application to CAPC staff. After extensive research and evaluation, the team selected the eKyros [14] application, a Web-based pregnancy center management information system (MIS) that included functionality far beyond distributed scheduling (client management, donor management, reporting, etc.). The students also raised $2000 so that CAPC could purchase the software. CAPC is fully operational with eKyros. The project is chronicled at [15]. Students completed reflection chapters that demonstrated the significant impact the project had on them.
- Donor and Member Management System for Messiah College Collaboratory. The Messiah College Collaboratory for Strategic Partnerships and Applied Research (see Chapter 4) had a need for a management information system to manage donors, volunteers, and members. This project was done in the 2007 Spring semester of BIS 412. The students formed a team under the direction of a faculty member and managed the complete life cycle spanning research through to testing and transi-

tioning the application to Collaboratory staff. After extensive research and evaluation, the team selected the CiviCRM open-source application [16], a Web-based constituent relationship management system designed specifically for NPOs. Upon completion of the project, student volunteer members of the Collaboratory (a cocurricular group on campus) took the project over.

- World Vision LEAP Impact Assessment Application. World Vision International [17] is the world's largest Christian relief and humanitarian organization, with over 25,000 employees in over 100 countries. World Vision had a need for a Web-based application for planning, designing, monitoring, and tracking the impact of field ministry activities. World Vision developed a formalized approach to field ministry known as LEAP (Learning through Evaluation with Accountability and Planning). World Vision provided a grant to Messiah College for faculty and students to develop a prototype system to support the LEAP framework. This project has been ongoing since 2005 in CSC 333 (Database Applications) under the direction of a faculty member, where students form teams and research and develop new features of the LEAP system every year. In addition, the World Vision grant provides funding for faculty and work-study student stipends so that work can continue on the project during the summer months. This aspect of the project was sponsored and done under the auspices of the Collaboratory, a cocurricular services group on campus. The funding also provides support for travel to Africa and related computer equipment. A paper that chronicles this project was recently published [18].

- CURE International Inventory Barcode System. CURE International [19] is a Christian organization that provides medical equipment and related services to needy areas of the world. The organization had a database of all of its medical equipment, but lacked the ability to track the equipment as it traveled throughout the world. In the 2004 Spring semester of CSC 333, a four-person student team under the direction of a faculty member, researched, designed, implemented, tested, and transitioned the integration of a barcode tracking system from Symbol Technologies into the CURE International medical equipment database. The project is chronicled at [20].

- Upper Allen Fire Department Purchase Order System. A local volunteer fire department desired a purchase order system to better manage and track purchase orders. In the 2003 Spring semester of CSC 333, a student-led team under the direction of a faculty member developed a Microsoft Access-based purchase order system custom application. This system has been utilized by the Upper Allen, PA Volunteer Fire Department since 2003. The project is chronicled at [21].

- Messiah College Summer Basketball Camp MIS. Messiah College runs a significant summer basketball camp program for several hundred young people. The director of the camp desired a system to manage the complete camp from registration through to team assignment and bank account management. In the 2003 Spring semester of CSC333, a student-led team under the direction of a faculty member developed a Microsoft Access-based basketball camp management system. The system has been in use by the camp since 2003. The project is chronicled at [22].

- Explore Impact Assessment Product. Several nongovernment organizations (NGOs) have expressed interest in a Web-based field ministry impact assessment system similar to the World Vision LEAP system described above. A team of faculty and students are beginning to research and explore how the existing LEAP system could be generalized into a product so that multiple NPOs could use the same software.

REFERENCES

1. Droge, D. (Ed.) (1996). *Disciplinary Pathways to Service-Learning.* Washington: Campus Compact.
2. Ellis, H., Morelli, R., de Lanerolle, T., Damon, J., and Raye, J. (2007). "Can Humanitarian Open-Source Software Development Draw New Students to CS?" In *2007 ACM SIGCSE Technical Symposium on Computer Science Education* (March 7–10, 2007), pp. 551–555.
3. Christensen, K., Rundus, D., Perera, G., and Zulli, S. (2006). "CSE Volunteers: A Service-Learning Program to Provide IT Support to the Hillsborough County School District," in *2006 ACM SIGCSE Technical Symposium on Computer Science Education* (March 1–5, 2006), pp. 229–233.
4. Rosmaita, B. (2007). "Making Service-Learning Accessible to Computer Scientists," in *2007 ACM SIGCSE Technical Symposium on Computer Science Education* (March 7–11, 2007), pp. 541–545.
5. Leidig, P., Ferguson, R. and Leidig, J. (2006). "Use of Community-Based Non-Profit Organizations in Information Systems Capstone Projects," in *2006 ACM SIGCSE Annual Conference on Innovation and Technology in Computer Science Education* (June 26–28, 2006), pp. 148–152.
6. Ferguson, R. and Liu, C. (2006). "Service-Learning Projects: Opportunities and Challenges," in *2006 ACM SIGCSE Technical Symposium on Computer Science Education* (March 1–5, 2006), pp. 127–128.
7. EWOB, http://www.ewb-usa.org/, retrieved October 17, 2011.
8. ACM, http://www.acm.org/chapters/students, retrieved October 31, 2011.
9. Messiah College (June 5, 2007). "What is Service-Learning at Messiah College?" Retrieved June 5, 2007, from http://www.messiah.edu/external_programs/agape/service_learning/

10. Myers, B. (1999). *Walking with the Poor: Principles and Practices of Transformational Development.* Maryknoll, NY: Orbis Books.

11. Heffner, G., Claudia D., and Beversluis, C. (Eds.). (2002). *Commitment and Connection: Service-Learning and Christian Higher Education.* Lanham, MD, University Press of America.

12. Musil, C. (2003). "Educating for Citizenship." *peerReview,* Spring 2003, pp. 4–8.

13. CAPC, http://www.lifechoicesclinic.org/, retrieved October 31, 2011.

14. eKyros, http://www.ekyros.com/Pub/, retrieved October 31, 2011.

15. CAPC Project, http://joshuaeverhart.com/bis412/, retrieved October 31, 2011.

16. CiviCRM, www.civicrm.org, retrieved October 31, 2011.

17. World Vision, www.wvi.org, retrieved October 31, 2011.

18. Nejmeh B. A. and Vicary, B. (2009) "Lessons Learned about Design, Monitoring and Evaluation Process Definition and Information Management for International Development Programmes," *Knowledge Management for Development Journal,* Volume 5, Issue 2, pp. 143–159.

19. Cure International, http://cure.org/, retrieved October 31, 2011.

20. Cure Project, http://home.messiah.edu/~bnejmeh/CSC33304/cure/DbApps/index.htm, retrieved October 31, 2011.

21. Upper Allen Fire Department System, www.home.messiah.edu/~bnejmeh/csc333b/bb1176/, retrieved October 31, 2011.

22. Messiah College Basketball Camp System, www.home.messiah.edu/~bnejmeh/csc333a/nr1157/index.html, retrieved October 31, 2011.

ORGANIZATIONAL/ PEDAGOGICAL MODELS AND APPROACHES TO SERVICE-LEARNING IN THE COMPUTER AND INFORMATION SCIENCES

There are many different approaches to incorporating the notion of service-learning into an institutional setting. The purpose of Part II of the book is to expose readers to the various organizational and pedagogical models for introducing service-learning into the computer and information sciences. The papers are written by global field practitioners who have been successfully applying the service-learning model for several years. A myriad of topics are covered by the chapters in this section, including the organization and management of university initiatives around service-learning in the computer and information sciences, curriculum integration concerns, accreditation concerns, capstone projects involving service-learning, and the use of open-source technologies and approaches in a service-learning setting.

The chapters in this section of the book were carefully chosen to offer readers exposure to a variety of ways of institutionalizing service-learning.

Service-Learning in Computer and Information Sciences. Edited by Brian A. Nejmeh
Copyright © 2012 John Wiley & Sons, Inc.

The papers come from diverse learning communities, ranging from a large public research university (Purdue University), to a medium-sized comprehensive private university (Butler University), to a small Christian liberal arts college (Messiah College), and, finally, to a group of small liberal arts colleges in New England (Trinity College, Connecticut College, and Wesleyan University). Thus, whether you find yourself at a large research university or a small liberal arts college, you will gain relevant insights about how to approach service-learning in the computer and information sciences.

Chapter 2, entitled "EPICS Program," is written by William Oakes and Carla Zoltowski of Purdue University. The paper chronicles the origins of the EPICS program at Purdue, arguably the most robust and long-standing service-learning engineering program in the world. As the authors state, "In the 2010-11 academic year, nearly 400 students participated each semester on the 30 teams from 74 majors, across engineering, computer science, technology, science, liberal arts, management and other colleges across campus." The success of the EPICS program at Purdue led to the formation of similar programs at many other institutions. More recently, they have started to explore the EPICS model in a high school setting. The EPICS program has focused on long-term partnerships with nonprofit organizations as a cornerstone of their approach. This chapter provides a case study of the EPICS program by examining the evolution of their partnership with the Homeless Prevention Network (HPN). The chapter describes the EPICS curricular structure that allows the EPICS courses to be taken for 1 or 2 credits per semester. The EPICS program curriculum includes course content that introduces students to key principles of design, project management, and community development. The paper overviews the four key areas of EPIC project engagement: education and outreach, access and abilities, human services, and environment. Finally, key foundational principles of the EPICS program are discussed, including a focus on software engineering, human-centered design, and multidisciplinary teams.

Chapter 3, entitled "Ten Years of EPICS at Butler University: Experiences from Crafting a Service-Learning program for Computer Science and Software Engineering," is written by Panagiotis Linos of Butler University. This paper does an excellent job of highlighting the formation and evolution of a service-learning program at Butler that was originally modeled after the Purdue EPICS program. The paper outlines how the EPICS program at Butler is integrated into their computer science and software engineering curriculum. The grading model for EPICS courses and the importance of long-standing community partnerships are also discussed. Various projects of the Butler EPICS program are discussed in detail and provide context and mini case studies. Summaries of student and client perspectives about various projects are also provided for the reader. The assessment model for the Butler EPICS program is discussed at some length, offering both qualitative and quantitative perspectives about the program. The chapter also offers a road map for those institutions wishing to embark on the formation of an EPICS program.

Chapter 4, entitled "The Collaboratory," is written by David Vader of Messiah College. This chapter chronicles a long-standing service-learning program at a small liberal arts college. It offers an excellent example of how institutional identity, in this case that of a Christian college, can greatly inform a service-learning program. The Collaboratory at Messiah College integrates curricular and cocurricular service-learning models. The author outlines the foundation of the Collaboratory and offers a rationale for the model. The organizational design and funding model of the Collaboratory is described in some detail, including the student-leadership model that guides the Collaboratory. The broad program areas of Collaboratory engagement (energy, water, disability resources, communications, transportation, education, and microeconomic development) are outlined in the chapter. Finally, Collaboratory results to date are discussed and the future directions of the Collaboratory are laid out.

Chapter 5, entitled "The Humanitarian Free and Open Source Software Project: Engaging Students in Service Learning through Building Software," is written by Ralph Morelli (Trinity College), Trishan de Lanerolle (Trinity College), and Allen Tucker (Bowdoin College). This chapter offers a fascinating look at a group of small liberal arts colleges in New England that are focused on service-learning in the context of the Humanitarian Free and Open Software Project (HFOSS Project). The chapter offers an overview of the open-source software model and details the relevance of this model to the service-learning approach. The chapter chronicles the origins of the HFOSS Project, including an early project focused on a disaster-management system. The major goals of the HFOSS Project are outlined along with the key concepts and methodologies. Descriptions of several HFOSS Projects that aid the reader in understanding the HFOSS approach are provided. The chapter also explores the application of the HFOSS model to K–12 education. Finally, the results of the HFOSS Project to date are described, along with some future directions and challenges for the HFOSS Project.

CHAPTER 2

EPICS PROGRAM

William Oakes and Carla Zoltowski

ABSTRACT

The EPICS (Engineering Projects in Community Service) program, founded at Purdue University in 1995, has been recognized for teaching multidisciplinary design through service-learning. EPICS is a curricular structure of design courses that support long-term partnerships with local or global community organizations. Students engage in the development of projects that span the engineering disciplines and often require multiple semesters or even years to complete. Software engineering has played a key role in the projects since its founding. Although most of the EPICS course divisions are paired with specific partners, the software divisions have been organized to work across partnerships and focus on similar technologies that can be shared with several community partners. The success of the Purdue EPICS program spawned similar programs at other universities and, more recently, high school programs.

2.1   INTRODUCTION

In the early 1990s, faculty in electrical and computer engineering at Purdue University were engaged in active discussions with industry about how to improve the preparation of undergraduate engineers to more effectively transition into an engineering career. The industry input was that they wanted graduates who were strong technically but also had a broader set of skills that allowed them to work in a global and rapidly changing economy. These discussions paralleled the national discussions that motivated the Accreditation Board for Engineering and Technology (ABET) to change its accreditation criteria to what became ABET 2000 (ABET 2002) and the subsequent reports by the National Academy of Engineer's report on the Engineer of 2020 (NAE 2004, 2005).

At Purdue University, these discussions evolved into a plan for a new set of undergraduate courses that became the EPICS program. The effort was led by Professors Leah Jamieson and Edward Coyle. The model was a design experience that spanned multiple semesters and even years, engaging students from the first through senior years. An initial curricular model was conceived using design problems from industry. However, an opportunity arose through the U.S. Department of Education's Fund for the Improvement of Postsecondary Education (FIPSE) Program to link technology with community needs and the model was shifted to address design needs within the local community and the EPICS model was born.

At that time, there were few if any models of engineering or computing engagement with the community. Professors Jamieson and Coyle saw an enormous opportunity as not-for-profit agencies, community organizations, and educational institutions were being asked to do more and to serve more people without significant increases in resources. To meet this challenge, organizations were pressed to explore using technology for the delivery, coordination, accounting, and improvement of the services they provide to the community. However, these organizations often possess neither the expertise nor the financial resources to acquire or design technological solutions that were suited to their mission. They needed access to people with technical expertise, and the model for EPICS could provide just that.

The different but complementary needs provided the opportunity for engagement between engineering, computing, and technology resources and the community. In the early 1990s, there were few if any models for this kind of engagement and it was up to debate if such approaches were viable. Professors Coyle and Jamieson presented their idea at a meeting of directors for local United Way organizations and the results were overwhelmingly positive. More than 20 project ideas came out of that one meeting, many of which required software solutions.

The EPICS courses were started in the fall semester of 1995 with five divisions and 40 students. Each division was called a team and was paired with a community partner or, in some cases, a group of community partners with a similar mission and need. Although most divisions of the EPICS courses had a single organization as their partner, one division had a consortium of agencies that were part of the Homelessness Prevention Network. This team linked the partners through their shared need of a software system that would allow the agencies to share data while protecting confidential information.

A hallmark of the EPICS program has been long-term partnerships. These partnerships are intended to be reciprocal partnerships, each bringing expertise and resources to address the community needs. The partnerships are also intended to be long-term, with EPICS teams working with their partner as long as appropriate projects could be identified and developed. Of those five original partnerships, four can be traced to active teams in 2011. Some of the agencies have been reorganized but the EPICS teams have remained engaged with that need. The one exception is the team that worked with the Homelessness Prevention Network, which is described below. (Coyle et al, 1997)

2.2 EARLY SUCCESS STORY: HOMELESSNESS PREVENTION NETWORK

One of the original EPICS partners was the collection of agencies that formed the Homelessness Prevention Network (HPN). The community need was to improve the coordination of services among the agencies addressing homelessness and to enable sharing of data. Collaboration across agencies would allow an assessment of their impact across the community; however, any collaboration system had to protect the privacy of those being served by the individual agencies. At the time, there was no commercial solution to meet these needs.

Under the direction of Prof. Edward Coyle, cofounder of EPICS, the HPN team took on the task of developing a customized software system. The team developed a database that allowed information to be entered by specific agencies and to protect or share specific fields. Six of the agencies deployed client machines that linked to a server on campus. The software system included security and encryption features, full report-generation capability, a duplicate client–file–merge algorithm on a server, and a custom, private email system to enhance interagency communications. In 2001, the county, in conjunction with the EPICS team, was awarded a Federal Department of Housing and Urban Development (HUD) grant to participate in a study of homelessness, because the county was one of only 19 in the United States that had a homelessness management information system that met their qualifications.

Their solution met the needs of the agencies so well that these agencies used it for their main means of data entry and management. Although this was a significant success, it also presented challenges of servicing and supporting the system. The agencies had no IT developers and relied on the student teams. During the semesters, students in the course rotated as the "on-call" contact. During the semester breaks, a rotation system was set up whereby students volunteered to be on call. Students were hired to support

EPICS for the summers and also provided the support contacts for the other EPICS software projects.

HUD took note of the benefits of the EPICS project as well as other pilots around the country and provided funding nationally for agencies and mandated linking to regional database systems to coordinate services. The result was the emergence of commercial products and regional databases managed by the companies. The availability of the commercial products and the HUD requirement eliminated the need for the student team. The HPN team was one of the early successes and was celebrated and retired.

2.3   EPICS CURRICULUM

The EPICS curricular structure was designed from the beginning to support diverse projects including software development, like the HPN project. Students can take the EPICS courses for 1 or 2 credits per semester and the credits count toward graduation in several majors. They are used as a substitute for either a required course (such as capstone design) or as a type of elective. How the EPICS courses count varies between departments and majors. Computer engineering, for example, counts EPICS courses as technical electives or as a substitute for capstone design. Computer science students can use EPICS courses as electives or as their senior project. The EPICS program provides a curriculum that introduces students to design, project management, community partnerships, communication, ethics, and social responsibility. These topics are introduced in lectures and readings and are practiced and learned in the design teams as they apply the ideas to their designs with the guidance of a faculty advisor. Design teams are grouped by lab divisions that are called teams. Each team may have two to five projects with eight to twenty students per division. The faculty use assessment tools that are provided by the EPICS program to track progress on the projects, assign grades, and certify mastery of outcomes where needed (e.g., capstone design students must demonstrate proficiency in the same outcomes as students in the traditional classes). EPICS has been through two sets of accreditation reviews and has been reviewed very positively as an example of multidisciplinary teaming. (Coyle, Jamieson, and Oakes, 2005)

Most of the courses that students use EPICS as a substitute for are three- or four-credit courses. That means that students must take EPICS for at least two semesters in order to substitute enough credits for the traditional course. This reduction in credits was done for two reasons. First, it provides a longer design experience for students. Second, it supports the development of projects that can have an impact, such as the HPN. Many students continue with an EPICS project for more than two semesters, with some staying on for seven or even eight semesters.

Having students on the project for multiple semesters is a cornerstone of the EPICS model, as it eliminates the restriction of the timing of a semester. This is very important with community engagement because the kinds of projects the community needs often take more than the traditional 10 week term or 15 week semester to develop. Software products, especially, can evolve over semesters and even years. When one considers the issue of supporting the projects delivered to the community organizations, such as the HPN, it becomes even more important that the curricular infrastructure support long-term participation.

Projects that last for more than one semester require a rethinking of the traditional timescales in courses (see Figure 2.1). In a project-based course, there are three synchronized timescales: student learning, project development, and the academic calendar (semester, quarter, or term). In this model, students begin a course with no knowledge, start a project that will enhance their understanding, and complete the project at the end of the semester when they demonstrate their mastery of their learning. Engaging in the community is not that simple and reduces the needs that can be met to those projects with a scope that can be developed in the semester. EPICS seeks to address the most compelling and appropriate projects for the community, which often do not fit into the timescale of a semester. The curricular structure insures that there are students within each division who are returning for the next semester and can carry the institutional knowledge about the project

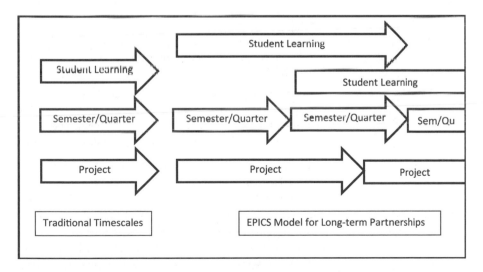

Figure 2.1.   Academic timescales.

into that next semester, thereby enabling multisemester projects as shown in the figure. It also requires faculty to accept that a student may not start or finish a project but would nevertheless have a meaningful design experience during their time on the team.

2.4   EPICS PROJECTS AT PURDUE UNIVERSITY

EPICS projects fall under four broad areas of impact within the community: human services, the environment, access and abilities, and education and outreach. In each of the areas of impact, projects involving different technologies are developed. Software projects span all four areas and Table 2.1 provides examples within each area. A complete list of projects at Purdue can be found at www.purdue.edu/epics under "Teams & Projects."

Table 2.1. Areas of impact for EPICS teams

Area of community impact	Example software projects
Education and outreach	• Games for middle schools to engage students in learning • Spelling quiz game for elementary school • Digital-image database for local historical society • Volunteer management system for school systems to match volunteers with teachers and track which volunteers have passed required background checks • Web-based weather station with real-time data
Access and abilities	• Interactive, multimedia voice recognition systems to help children with speech and language development • Simulation software to train audiologists • iPad apps to help students with disabilities communicate and learn
Human services	• Case management systems for agencies in the Homelessness Prevention Network • Case management systems for local probation department • Volunteer management systems for community meals on the holidays • Volunteer scheduling tools for local crisis center • Web-based volunteer and donor systems for not-for-profit organizations
Environment	• Energy modeling systems for low-income homes • Interactive educational games to teach about the environment • Web-interface allowing access to a constructed wetland and data from the wetland

2.5   CURRENT STATUS OF THE PURDUE EPICS PROGRAM

From the beginning, EPICS has been multidisciplinary but it has grown a great deal. In 1995, 40 students were distributed across five teams. EPICS has been recognized by many national and international organizations including the National Academy of Engineering (Coyle, Jamieson and Oakes, 2006). In the 2010–11 academic year, nearly 400 students participated each semester on 30 teams from 74 majors across engineering, computer science, technology, science, liberal arts, management, and other colleges across campus. EPICS has been designated as a separate academic program by the university, housed under the College of Engineering and supported by the provost. EPICS oversees a set of EPICS (EPCS) course numbers, from first-year to senior level and one- and two-credit options for each year. As an academic program, EPICS has a multidisciplinary faculty curriculum committee that oversees and approves changes to the curriculum. EPICS is housed in dedicated space with labs and offices in the newest of Purdue Engineering's buildings, the Armstrong Hall of Engineering. The labs are on the first floor behind glass walls providing enormous visibility. The tours for prospective students pass by the labs to showcase EPICS and talk about how learning engineering and computing design can be and is done while serving the community.

As EPICS has grown in size and scope, the support structures have developed and grown. Faculty continue to serve as advisors for the lab divisions, referred to as teams. However, the number of teams has grown faster than the faculty available to advise, so local professionals from industry in the area supplement the faculty by volunteering their time to advise EPICS teams. In addition, Purdue staff also participate as advisors. These professionals bring valuable skills and excitement to the projects. For example, IT professionals advise software-based EPICS teams.

Each division has a graduate teaching assistant (TA) who provides administrative and assessment support as well as technical guidance. Often, the TAs are from a discipline different from the advisor to provide a broader set of expertise for the students on that team. It is not unusual for more than one advisor to work with the teams, providing an even broader set of skills. The TAs are trained to support the curricular framework and the assessment tools. The intent is for the advisors (faculty, staff, or local professionals) to be able to focus on mentoring the students through their projects. This lowers the learning curve for the advisors and makes it easier for a larger number of faculty to participate. EPICS currently has 30 divisions with more than 40 active advisors.

EPICS students span all four undergraduate years. First-semester students have been engaged through the university's learning-community programs.

Students in the EPICS learning community take three courses together (EPICS, the first engineering class, and either English or Communications) and have the option to live on a learning-community floor in a residence hall. Currently, 96 students are in the EPICS learning community and the reaction has been very positive, with students able to be on a real design team in their first semester with the support of the learning community. The infusion of the first-year students provides opportunities for mentoring by juniors and seniors as well as opportunities for the first-year and sophomore students to rise quickly into leadership roles.

2.6   SOFTWARE ENGINEERING REORGANIZATION

For the first ten years of EPICS, the model held that each EPICS team was paired with the same community partner or group of partners with a common need. What we found is that almost all of the partners had some sort of software need. The teams that were not dedicated to software development would recruit students to address their projects as well as the software project. The result was that the software students were spread over all 30 divisions and students often felt isolated. It became hard to support so many projects being done in so many divisions and the interest of students from computing declined as the need for such projects increased. The response was to reorganize all of the software projects and concentrate them into three dedicated software teams. This allowed EPICS to partner with Computer Science, Computer Engineering, and Computer Technology to raise the interest and participation in EPICS and to focus the support from faculty and teaching assistants for the software development into these teams. The current needs were examined and grouped into common themes based on software technologies. The needs assessment showed that many of the needs were common and that core systems could be developed and then customized to meet specific agencies needs. This has allowed a larger number of partners to be served and increased interest among computing students. It has also enabled the EPICS program to respond to software needs more quickly since new projects are folded into the portfolios of existing teams.

2.7   HUMAN-CENTERED DESIGN AND EPICS

EPICS uses an approach to teaching design called human-centered design. Human-centered design makes the stakeholders central to the development of the design via frequent interactions with users and stakeholders. The community applications for EPICS designs are very well matched for this approach to design and software development. EPICS teaches a design process that encourages and supports frequent interactions with stakeholders. The design model used in EPICS is shown in Figure 2.2.

This approach is closely aligned with modern methods for software development. It involves early and regular interactions and engagement of users and stakeholders in the development process, early and frequent prototyping and testing with users; and a full understanding of the stakeholders. Students are supported and encouraged to understand the context of their users and their needs. This often involves students spending time with their community partners. It also means that students show prototypes and mockups of their ideas to users for feedback and discussion. Tools and techniques of human-centered design involve observations, interviews, focus groups, and personas (Dym and Little, 2004). Users are central to the designs and the software projects are developed with users in mind and with complete manuals and documentation.

The service-learning context offers a rich learning experience for this method of design. The users are not traditional software users and typically have little or no background in software development. This means that students must work with their stakeholders to elicit requirements. Spending

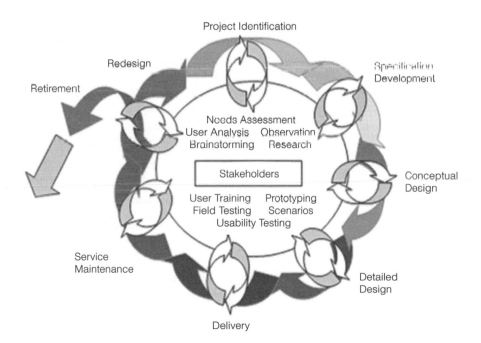

Figure 2.2. EPICS human-centered design process.

time with the users and stakeholders not only improves the designs, but since they are engaged in meeting needs of the community, students come away with a deeper understanding of the community needs and the social context.

2.8   MULTIDISCIPLINARY TEAMS

Students from outside of engineering and computing bring additional expertise that is needed in human-centered design. EPICS has intentionally recruited students from outside of engineering and computing and had over 70 majors in the last academic year. About 25% of the students are from outside of engineering or computing. Multidisciplinary teams add richness to the learning experience and produce more effective designs that can be used by a broad set of users.

However, bringing students from multiple disciplines presents many challenges. The wide net is an enormous positive but setting up multidisciplinary teams needs to be intentional and requires time and effort. EPICS has explicitly cultivated faculty from outside of engineering and computing to coteach sections of the course, lead design teams, and be engaged in the growth and development of the program. We have learned that to have multidisciplinary student teams, there needs to be a multidisciplinary leadership team to be able to provide voice to the important groups and to guide and critique the development of the curriculum and learning environment.

EPICS teams do team building at the start of every semester. Faculty, graduate students, and team leaders are trained to help facilitate a team environment that is open to multiple disciplines. The learning objectives for the class have been rewritten to make it open to all disciplines. The accreditation

Table 2.2.   Learning outcomes for EPICS students

1. Applies material from student's discipline to the design of community-based projects
2. Demonstrates an understanding of design as a start-to-finish process
3. An ability to identify and acquire new knowledge as a part of the problem-solving/design process
4. Demonstrates an awareness of the customer in engineering design
5. Demonstrates an ability to function on multidisciplinary teams and an appreciation for the contributions of individuals from other disciplines
6. Demonstrates an ability to communicate effectively with audiences with widely varying backgrounds
7. Demonstrates an awareness of professional ethics and responsibility
8. Demonstrates an appreciation of the role that their discipline can play in social contexts

criteria from ABET (ABET, 2002) were modified to take out the words "engineering" or "technical" and replace them with "discipline" and "disciplinary" as shown in Table 2.2. This has allowed the program to assess the contributions of many disciplines to the development of the designs.

2.9   DISSEMINATION OF THE EPICS MODEL

The approach taken by EPICS to teach design has proven to be effective in preparing students for careers in engineering and computing as well as a host of other fields. It has also been shown to change the way students view their own disciplines and its relationship to the needs of the world. Purdue University has invested in staff to allow EPICS to be implemented at other campuses and more than 20 universities and colleges have adopted programs modeled after EPICS. There is an increasing interest in adoptions internationally as well as opportunities for projects to be done for global communities.

In addition to other universities, EPICS has become engaged with high schools. Training programs have been developed for teachers to guide design teams to address needs within the community. The model is for teachers to guide the student projects and partner with computing or engineering professionals to provide the content expertise. IEEE has partnered with EPICS to establish partnerships whereby IEEE professionals mentor teams within the United States and internationally.

An example project in computing is the one done in Harbor Beach, Michigan, a rural town of less than 1500 people. The EPICS project was done through the calculus class in the local high school. The mission was to provide software support for the food pantries in the county. All of the food pantries were housed in country churches with no internet connections. The students worked at the food pantries to learn about their operation and modified commercial software to allow the pantries to coordinate services and allow members of the community to see what was needed. The team that did this had one young man and six young women. The team was seeing firsthand how computing can be used to address hunger in their community. The idea that engineers and computer scientists can make a difference with their work is the kind of messaging that has been cited to increase interest in engineering and computing. EPICS High has expanded to schools in ten states and abroad through IEEE. There are over 2000 students engaged; 44% are female and over 30% come from ethnicities that are traditionally underrepresented in computing and engineering. The EPICS High is proving to be a method to attract students who are interested in making a difference in the world to engineering and computing.

2.10   CONCLUSIONS

When EPICS was created, there was an open question whether engineering and computing could effectively engage in community-based design work. The resounding answer is yes! Not only can we meet community needs with software solutions, but students can gain the valuable experiences needed to be leaders in today's global economy. Community-based design education and its necessary engagement of users who are not technically savvy creates a rich learning opportunity for developing user-centered or human-centered design skills that have been cited an vital for today's designers and developers. The EPICS model for curricular integration has been proved successful at Purdue and other universities. The dissemination to high schools has proved that there are opportunities to engage the next generation of software engineers by showing them how software is a path to make the world, or their communities, a better place. EPICS has grown to a large program and has resources to help faculty (https://engineering.purdue.edu/EPICSU/) and teachers (https://engineering.purdue.edu/EPICSHS/) adopt a similar approach. The key to starting a class or program is to start small and successfully, and build as resources and experience allow. Teaching by engaging the community is fun, rewarding, and leaves an impact, on the students, on the community and on ourselves.

REFERENCES

ABET (2002). Engineering Criteria 2002–2003, Accreditation Board for Engineering and Technology, http://www.abet.org/criteria.html, May 2002.

Coyle, E. J., Jamieson, L. H., and Sommers, L. S. (1997). "EPICS: A Model for Integrating Service-Learning into the Engineering Curriculum," *Michigan Journal of Community Service-Learning,* Vol. 4, Fall 1997.

Coyle, E. J., Jamieson, L. H., and Oakes, W. C., (2005) "EPICS: Engineering Projects in Community Service," *International Journal of Engineering Education,* Vol. 21, No. 1, Feb. 2005, pp. 139–150.

Coyle, E. J., Jamieson, L. H., and Oakes, W. C., (2006). "Integrating Engineering Education and Community Service: Themes for the Future of Engineering Education," *Journal of Engineering Education,* Vol. 95, No. 1, January 2006, pp. 7–11.

Dym, C. L. and P. Little (2004). *Engineering Design: A Project-Based Introduction.* Hoboken, NJ: Wiley.

National Academy of Engineering (2004). *The Engineer of 2020: Visions of Engineering in the New Century.* Washington, DC: The National Academies Press.

National Academy of Engineering (2005). *Educating the Engineer of 2020: Adapting Engineering Education to the New Century.* Washington, DC: The National Academies Press.

CHAPTER 3

TEN YEARS OF EPICS AT BUTLER UNIVERSITY
Experiences from Crafting a Service-Learning Program for Computer Science and Software Engineering

Panagiotis K. Linos

ABSTRACT

This chapter describes lessons learned and challenges faced while crafting a service-learning program called EPICS at Butler University. Drawing from such experience, the chapter presents a road map to anyone who is interested in creating a similar EPICS program. Emphasis is given on how a service-learning pedagogical model can be incorporated within a computer science and/or software engineering (CSSE) curriculum successfully. Finally, some qualitative assessment data collected from our students and community partners are discussed that validate the success of EPICS at Butler.

3.1 INTRODUCTION

The idea of EPICS (Engineering Projects in Community Service) started at Purdue University in 1995 as an engineering design project [1]. Since then, it has evolved to be a multidisciplinary service-learning program that has been adopted successfully by several universities [2,3]. In August 2001, the Computer Science and Software Engineering (CSSE) department at Butler University attempted to create an instance of EPICS [4,5]. Ten years later, EPICS is a successful and endowed service-learning program at Butler [6], a private institution with approximately 4000 undergraduate and graduate students located in central Indiana.

This chapter explains how our EPICS program was built based on an effective service-learning pedagogical model whereby students earn academic credit by collaborating with various not-for-profit organizations. The chapter also discusses how EPICS is incorporated within our CSSE curriculum. After that, it presents briefly various EPICS partnerships with a focus on a specific project with the WFYI public radio/TV station. The following section presents an assessment of some qualitative data that demonstrate success and key challenges of EPICS at Butler. Finally, the chapter concludes by recommending a road map to help any institution that wishes to establish an EPICS program such as Butler's.

3.2   THE EPICS MODEL

In this section, the author discusses how the CSSE department at Butler University has incorporated, and now requires, service-learning within its own curriculum. In addition, he explains how and why EPICS provides a unique opportunity for creating an effective pedagogical model within the context of a University-wide and multidisciplinary education.

3.2.1   Curriculum

Currently, the CSSE department at Butler has four full-time faculty members and approximately fifty majors and several minors. Since 2001, the department offers two separate undergraduate degrees in CS and SE, respectively. Also since then, it has incorporated EPICS as a sequence of courses, which are now required by both majors. Students can register for these courses during any year of their studies (they may also repeat such courses for additional credit). More specifically, the EPICS courses offered include CSSE 282/283: EPICS I, described in our course catalogue as a "supervised team software project for a local charity or non-profit organization. May be repeated for credit. Prerequisite: Concurrent registration in CSSE 248 [Introduction to Programming] or permission of the department." This course is designed for first/second year students. The CSSE 382/383: EPICS II course has a similar description with different prerequisites: "concurrent registration in CS 351 [Algorithms and Data-Structures] and SE 361[Software Engineering I] and either CSSE 282 or CSSE 283 [EPICS I], or permission of the department." Our third-year students usually take such course. Finally, our fourth-year students can take the CSSE 482/483: EPICS III, which requires SE 461 (Software Engineering II) and either CS 382 or CS 383 (EPICS II).

The rationale behind offering each course as two or three credit hours (e.g., CSSE 482 or CSSE 483) is simply to provide some schedule flexibility to students. For instance, some students only need two hours to graduate, or wish to fill their schedule during a specific semester. Initially, we expected less workload from students who registered to the two-credit course. However, it quickly became apparent that such distinction was not necessary and was never an issue.

When we first created the EPICS course sequence, we decided to only provide elective credit to any registered student. At that time, the rationale was that service-learning should be elective in nature and not required. Since 2010, however, we started requiring all CS and SE majors to take at least one semester of EPICS for graduation. This decision was made based on the strong recommendations coming from our CSSE advisory board, the positive feedback from our students, as well as the suggestion of an external reviewer. It is worthwhile mentioning that despite the one-semester of EPICS requirement for graduation, we have observed that most of the students tend to register for our EPICS courses for several semesters (some students use the additional hours as elective credit for graduation and some simply accrue extra hours). Once students register for EPICS, they soon recognize the opportunity to gain valuable experience and balance their technical and soft skills. Also, by taking EPICS during consecutive semesters they become experienced and build momentum on a specific project, which allows them to become leaders of their teams.

On the average, approximately 10–15 students enroll every semester in our EPICS courses. They are supervised by a CSSE faculty member who is scheduled to teach EPICS that semester. Also, all of our EPICS teams are guided by at least one designated external mentor from the corresponding client site. Typically, before we launch a new EPICS project (with a new client) we make it clear from the beginning that clients are expected to commit the necessary time to mentor our students on a regular basis. In order to facilitate such mentorship, regular meetings are planned both on the client's site and on the Butler campus. Such meetings have proved to be very valuable learning experiences for our students, who are given the opportunity to sharpen both their technical and soft skills. For instance, one former client had set up a regular seminar for our students so that they could learn Joomla (a content management system) used to create the client's website and eventually our own EPICS website [6]. During another past meeting, the author remembers some helpful comments made by our clients to the students on the importance of business attire during their project presentations and client meetings.

3.2.2 Course Structure

Our EPICS courses are scheduled based on either twice- or three-times weekly class meetings (like every other course). The specific logistics of conducting the EPICS class really depend on each individual instructor.

The author has found that meeting twice a week throughout the semester typically works well. During the first weekly meeting, the team leader describes the status of the project and the progress of each individual team member to the instructor. In order to facilitate that discussion, the team leader is expected to prepare a Weekly Status Report (WSR) and to discuss it with the instructor. The author has used similar WSR templates as a consultant to industrial SE projects. Appendix A contains an example of a WSR template used by EPICS teams. As you can see in Appendix A, the WSR comprises important project information such as the date of the meeting, the names of all members involved, any red flags (i.e., critical problems that may change the direction of the overall project, such as the loss of a client or a team leader). Also, in the WSR the team leader describes any other technical and/or nontechnical issues such as the need for some specialized software or expertise. Finally, the WSR entails a list of dated project accomplishments during the past week as well as a brief description of the action items and goals for the upcoming week. So far, the WSR has proved to be a very simple and practical tool that helps everyone involved to stay focused. Both our clients and students have provided positive comments about the effectiveness of this practice.

Occasionally, during the first weekly class meeting various external or internal speakers may be invited (e.g., experts on a specific technology), technical workshops might be held (e.g., a jump-start workshop on smart-phone apps development), and/or other related educational activities can take place. On the other hand, during the second weekly meeting, the team leader is in charge and works directly with the team. He/she is responsible to keep the team focused and ensure that everyone is on task and making progress on their work. At all times, of course, the instructor is also available for answering any questions or to provide assistance if needed. That gives an opportunity for the team leader(s) to exercise their management and leadership skills. The author has also allocated separate time outside the classroom in order to mentor the team leaders on an as-needed basis.

Most of our EPICS projects follow the typical start-to-finish software development life-cycle process (i.e., planning, gathering requirements, designing, implementing, and testing, or providing maintenance to an existing software system). Depending on the nature of each specific project, the team (in consultation with its supervisors) selects the most appropriate software development process model. In particular, the students who have taken SE361 (our introductory software engineering course) have already been exposed to and have used agile software development methodologies such as Scrum©. More specifically, they are familiar with modeling tools and languages such as the UML (Unified Modeling Language), Use-case diagrams, and so on. Typically, these students undertake the technical lead of the project and teach others the necessary tools and related processes. They also understand the incremental and iterative nature of the software development process and apply it effectively to their project. Normally, the team starts by selecting a small subset (usually about 10%) of the agreed-upon requirements, proceeds to the design and implementation of such a subset of requirements, and then demonstrates a prototype implementation to the client for feedback. The team also designs and executes various test cases to detect and fix any defects before the first incremental release of the software system. This whole process is repeated in increments until all requirements are implemented.

Throughout the semester, every EPICS team is expected to produce various project artifacts and deliverables. Depending on the type of project and its stage, various related deliverables may include a requirements specification document, architectural/design diagrams, prototypes, code, test cases, project plans, timelines, project display posters, presentation slides, videos, and websites. Most of these deliverables are uploaded on our CMS (Content Management System), which is implemented on our EPICS website as they are produced. Every registered user to our CMS may access such artifacts and use them. This practice has proved to be an effective mechanism for project continuity. For example, when new team members are joining an ongoing project they can find and download any project-related items from our website. This way we avoid reinventing the wheel every time a new team undertakes an ongoing project.

Every EPICS group also prepares and submits a comprehensive report at the end of each semester, along with a final presentation given to the client and any other interested stakeholders. The expected content and format of the final report and the presentation are given to the students at the beginning of each semester. The report (or dossier) typically entails the problem statement; detailed requirements specifications; both short-term (i.e., for the semester) and long-term project goals; a project plan with timeline and milestones; any design, implementation and testing artifacts; and various technical manuals, tutorials, and other related documentation. In addition, the dossier describes each member's role, goals, and accomplishments for that semester. Also, it contains copies of all weekly status reports with individual member's detailed contributions, and a copy of the final PowerPoint presentation.

In addition, all teams are typically expected to prepare and give two separate presentations at the end of each semester: one for the client team (usually nontechnical) and another (which is technical in nature) for the faculty advisor. In some cases, both presentations are combined into a single one (when the client has the necessary technical background).

Finally, all EPICS teams are required to create a signature poster that includes information about the client, all team members, and a brief description of the project (it also includes pictures, photographs, and/or various graphic images). All of these posters are prominently displayed (along with project dossiers) in our computer teaching lab. This becomes our EPICS showcase for anyone who visits our department (e.g., prospective students and their families, potential clients, sponsors, and so on). Such displays have been an effective marketing tool for attracting new students and/or new clients to our EPICS program.

3.2.3   Grading

All students enrolled in an EPICS course receive a final letter grade (like any other CSSE course). Again, the grading scheme depends on the particular instructor who teaches EPICS that semester. The author (when he teaches EPICS) typically calculates such grades based on a formula that entails the following criteria: peer reviews, the client's performance evaluation of the team, all project deliverables produced, and, of course, the instructor's ratings. More specifically, during the peer review process every member of the team is expected to evaluate everyone's contribution, including their own, their leaders, and the performance of the team as a whole.

Such a grading approach strives for a balance between the amount of progress made on a task and the degree of learning new technologies. In particular, the author's grading scheme takes into consideration the importance of peer and mentor evaluations to assess the quality of the student's work and his/her overall performance (as in real life). So far, the students have responded positively to such a grading model (note that other EPICS supervisors may use a slightly different grading scheme).

It is the author's experience that students like the idea of peer reviews and see them as opportunities for them to provide constructive feedback to help their fellow team members (and the team as a whole) improve their performance (especially their leader). They also appreciate the fact that they are expected to participate in the performance assessment process. The following is an example of a student's midsemester peer evaluation comments about the team leader's performance.

> Our leader] does a really good job letting people know what their jobs are, and what tasks are needed to be done, but doesn't motivate everyone on completing their jobs. Our group is progressing, but if the team leader would motivate everyone we could have a much more productive semester.

The author has made some interesting observations when it came to students' self-evaluation (the hardest part of peer evaluations). Typically, some students tend to be hard on judging themselves, whereas others tend to glorify their work and a few provide several excuses for not performing well. Below are some quotes from such self-evaluation reports.

I feel I have brought a lot to the group this semester, compared to the last. I have completed most of the GUI's and updated the last one from the previous semester. I am learning a lot of JavaScript, which is becoming very useful with all of the GUI's. I hope to bring more to this project, but its taking some time to learn some of the material.

I feel that while I have been successful in keeping the team focused on their work, I have been less than successful in guiding the direction of the project. Once version 1.0 of the software system is finished, however, I am confident that the project's future will become that much clearer to me.

Also, below you can read some comments from students evaluating their own team as a whole.

This semester we have made huge strides. We all have come together to advance together. Some haven't brought enough to the group, but the others have picked up the slack and have really made some huge progress with the project. Hopefully, this semester will make a huge impact with the client and show them that we are getting a lot done.

We have a lot of intelligent minds, just not the organization to truly develop software in both an effective and rapid manner. As a new member, I find it's easy to not get as much done as I maybe could, because there's not much sense that leadership holds the team accountable for holding the group up or not delivering. If there were more of a culture of daily forward progress, more of the team might be compelled to kick start their performance, myself included.

During the middle of the semester, the EPICS instructor calculates an "estimate grade" for all students (based on the midsemester peer and client review process). The midsemester grade has proved to be useful in the sense that it gives the students an idea where they are standing with respect to their grade. Along with such an estimate grade, the instructor also recommends a list of areas for improvement so that the students know what they need to do in order to secure a better grade. (An example of a midsemester trial-grade and accompanying recommendations is included in Appendix E.)

Finally, it is important to mention the EPICS University website, an excellent source of various practical pedagogical tools (e.g., a repository of forms, questionnaires, evaluation surveys, assessment criteria and so on) [3]. These tools are available and they can be customized and used by any other EPICS site. Occasionally, we have borrowed, customized, and used such templates in our EPICS courses (and we are thankful to the EPICS University for their generosity). For example, the author has used such guidelines and questionnaires for conducting student peer reviews and for soliciting evaluation feedback from clients (see Appendices B and C, respectively). It is worth mentioning that during the process of customizing and fine-tuning the peer evaluation criteria, the author has found that it is important to involve the team leaders and take their input into consideration (see Appendix B). Below, is an example of such a partial questionnaire used to solicit feedback from one of our EPICS clients.

Did working with the EPICS team enable you to improve your business process? If yes, how? *"While the process seems to be moving slowly at times, the end product should be stronger thanks to the thorough work. The final product will likely be something we are all proud of!"*

What would you like the students to know about your organization? *"We are grateful for the work being done by the EPICS team and are looking forward to continuing the partnership."*

What three things could be done to improve the team and their project? *"The team is doing a great job of taking client input and applying it to the project. Since we come to the classes and are pretty open and informal, it may seem strange to say it would be a good idea for the students to dress nicely when they are making their presentations, especially the final one. They'll be glad to have heard this from a 'test' client versus in an actual job setting. Since we are not the "typical" client it would be good practice for them to step back and see how the team does when they are communicating with the nontechnical parts of the client team."*

What would you like the class instructor to know? *"I personally appreciate the fact that he is in touch with the project and can act as liaison between the client and the team. He helps manage the expectations for all of the players."*

Finally, the author typically shares and discusses such comments (using discretion) with all EPICS team members as constructive feedback from the clients.

3.2.4   Signature Features

This section describes some of the unique characteristics of the EPICS program at Butler University. Most of these features are inherited (and customized to our CS and SE majors) from the national EPICS program [3].

First, EPICS entails student-focused and student-driven team projects under faculty supervision and client mentorship. In other words, our students wish to engage with EPICS because they expect to experience something different from the typical lecture-based classroom model. More specifically, they want to have the freedom to choose and drive their own learning experiences by selecting, owning, and managing their preferred projects, clients, and teams. To accomplish that, at the beginning of every semester, we go through a matching process that allows the students to engage with a project of their choice. We have seen that such freedom makes our EPICS students more self-motivated and they tend to learn on their own and from others. In a later section, we provide some assessment data that supports such claims.

In real life, the duration of software engineering projects tend to span a few months to a few years. Our EPICS projects typically provide an opportunity for our students to engage in similar multiple-semester projects. This is a valuable experience for our students because they become familiar with various project management issues such as the moving target problem (i.e., continuously changing requirements) as well as project continuity issues (e.g. nonreturning team members, poor team leadership, change of mentors or supervisors, and so on) At the end of the day, everyone involved in EPICS benefits from interacting with actual clients, conducting real projects, meeting strict expectations, and facing rigid constraints.

Our EPICS teams are vertically integrated to include second-semester freshmen to seniors. They earn required (or elective) academic credit that counts toward their graduation. Such teams are also multidisciplinary and are open to students in any major. Although typical CSSE students tend to work and eventually learn on their own, we have observed that EPICS provides a platform that promotes and facilitates learning from each other.

In addition, EPICS appears to be an effective vehicle for attracting underrepresented groups (e.g., women in CSSE). It is worthwhile mentioning that our first EPICS student team at Butler consisted of five females and one African-American male.

Another signature feature of EPICS is that it promotes a project-focused learning model in which the type of selected project drives the educational content of the course. For instance, some EPICS projects may require our students to learn how to use a specific technology. Moreover, the EPICS model entails various self-motivated, engaging, and self-directed learning activities. For example, we have observed our EPICS students becoming resourceful and learning from various sources. Specifically, they might be learning new things on their own, from their instructor, an industry mentor, other students within vertical teams, other faculty members, or from taking other courses. On one occasion, the author had a student who located and took a course outside the CSSE department in order to learn how to use Macromedia Flash© to develop game animations for an EPICS project. Another example would be for students to take short courses on how to develop applications for smart phones (e.g., iPhone© or Android© apps), which are typically not offered by the CSSE department as regular courses.

Although our EPICS program is interdisciplinary, it is autonomous and managed solely by the CSSE department. It maintains its own website wherein anyone interested can find related information. The EPICS program has also been institutionalized within Butler University. More specifically, all EPICS courses are endorsed by Butler's Center for Citizenship and Community (CCC), and they are annotated by the Service-Learning (SL) course indicator [7]. Finally, some of the non-CSSE students who have taken EPICS courses so far include foreign-language and society and technology majors. They usually take the courses in order to satisfy elective credit for their major.

All students and instructors involved with EPICS are expected to engage in various external activities such as participating in conferences, competitions, and other related professional events. For instance, they have participated in and given various presentations and poster displays in several academic conferences and related workshops, including the National EPICS Conference [8], the Frontiers in Education Conference [9], the SENCER Summer Institute [10], the SIGCSE Conference [11], and the Computing Conference for Small Colleges [12]. In addition, EPICS teams have participated in various student competitions such as the ASEE Idea2Product competition [13]. Also, our EPICS teams have visited various centers and universities such as the Virtual Reality Center at IUPUI [14], the Electronic Visualization Lab at the UI–Chicago [15], and, of course, Purdue University, where they attended various EPICS projects presentations [3].

Finally, our EPICS teams have also been awarded various monetary (and nonmonetary) prizes due to their participation to various competitions, including the I2P 2004–2005 and the ISSAC 2002 [16]. Such awards earned by our EPICS teams have had an important impact on our students' self-esteem and professional development as well as their personal growth. Also, our EPICS program has been endowed by a generous gift from the Sallie Mae Corporation [17].

3.3 COMMUNITY PARTNERSHIPS

During the past ten years, our EPICS program has established numerous partnerships with various not-for-profit organizations in the Indianapolis Metropolitan area. Some of these collaborations have been more successful than others. One of the lessons we learned is that maintaining such healthy partnerships requires a serious commitment from all parties involved, which is key to the success of EPICS.

Typically, in order for an organization to qualify as a viable EPICS client, it has to be strictly a not-for-profit organization. To date, we use a simple process for selecting promising clients for our EPICS program. Most of the times, we receive calls and/or visits from various interested organizations from the local community. We first meet with them in order to understand their needs and see if there is a good match with our EPICS program at Butler. If indeed there is such a match, we ask them to write up a brief description of any possible projects for our EPICS students. These descriptions are then discussed with all teams and their advisors. As a result, the appropriate matching of students with the right project is accomplished. Although initially there was a concern about how we would attract and sustain EPICS clients, it quickly became apparent that the demand for engaging with our EPICS program was (and still is) much greater than its capacity. Today, we maintain a waiting list of interested potential EPICS clients.

Among others, some of our current or former EPICS customers and community partners include schools such as Crispus Attucks Middle School and the Oaks Academy [18], the Indianapolis Legal Aid Society [19], the POLIS Center [20], the Butler Undergraduate Research Office and Conference [21], the Crohn's and Colitis Foundation [22], WFYI Radio/TV Station [23], the Association for Software Testing (AST) [24], the Center for Urban Ecology at Butler [25], Lutheran Child and Family Services [26], and the nuAfrica Water–Education–Life Organization [27].

Some of these partnerships have resulted in projects such as the "Language-In-Action" (LIA) project with Crispus Attucks Middle School of Indianapolis. The LIA project started in 2001 and entails a Web-based suite of educational software for teaching Spanish and Greek (extendable to other languages) to middle school students. One interesting component of LIA is the "QuickDrop" software application, which helps students with practicing their Spanish and Greek vocabulary by playing fun animated computer games while they are doing their homework. Appropriate implementation technologies used during that project include Macromedia Flash© for its Web interface and animation as well as mySQL and php for the database back-end support. The LIA project is actually the inaugural EPICS project at Butler University. The author was the first faculty supervisor of LIA and the team consisted of six motivated CSSE students—five women and one African American male.

It is the author's opinion that LIA still represents one of the most successful EPICS projects he can remember. During that project, the EPICS team conducted many visits at Crirpus Attacks Middle School, helping students and Spanish teachers incorporate the LIA software into their curriculum successfully. The author remembers the students of the first LIA–EPICS team being extremely excited and self-motivated. They used to spend numerous late-night hours in the computer lab working on their project. Because of that, at that time, the author had introduced (with humor) the term "EPICS addiction." Among others, the LIA team won our first EPICS award in the Indiana Student Software Awards Competition (ISSAC) in 2002 (more about LIA can be found in [4 and 5]).

Another example of a long-term and successful partnership is our collaboration with the POLIS center at IUPUI in Indianapolis, which started in

2002 [20]. This effort resulted in work accomplished for the SAVI (Social Assets and Vulnerability Indicators) project [28,29]. SAVI is a dynamic community information system hosted by POLIS. During that partnership, our EPICS students were involved in the development of a .NET Web application that facilitates the process of searching the SAVI database. More specifically, the team developed a prototype query-builder back-end that parsed any textual user-entered string (like any search engine) and converted that string to a meaningful SQL query. That query was then compiled and executed on the SAVI database in order to locate and display the desired information. During that project, our EPICS students benefited tremendously from working with experienced SAVI personnel and learned the .NET platform. It is also worth mentioning that after that project, the author incorporated the .NET platform in his software engineering courses as a vehicle to introduce object-oriented design concepts and techniques (more details about this EPICS project are described in [5]).

More recently, in 2010, we have started an ongoing EPICS project aimed at the development of a set of smart-phone native applications called IndianApps for the Urban Ecology Center at Butler University [30]. More specifically, our EPICS team was tasked to develop a GPS-based pilot smart-phone application that would enable the citizens of Indianapolis to report and track environmental data such as information about injured birds, sick trees, rain barrels, and so on. In particular, the rain barrels are scattered all over the city, and citizens may enter their locations and their water volume using smart-phones (or other mobile devices) connected to the Internet. The initial high-level architecture of IndianApps designed by our EPICS team is shown in Figure 3.1.

As you can see in Figure 3.1, The GUI layer was developed using Dream Weaver©, the application algorithms used JavaScript and php, the database connectivity was done using phpAdmin, and the database used MySQL. The data then was exported into a spreadsheet and then geocoded (i.e., translated coordinates) so that they could be represented on a map. For more information on the IndianApps project see [25].

Finally, the WFYI Assets Management System (AMS) represents the result of another recent partnership with the WFYI Public Radio/TV Station in Indianapolis [31]. During that project, our students were engaged with various activities that spanned the complete software development life cycle. We will describe this project in the next section in more detail as an example of a successful EPICS project.

3.3.1   WFYI–EPICS Partnership

This section describes our partnership with the Indianapolis WFYI Public Radio/TV Station [23]. We believe that this particular EPICS project repre-

Figure 3.1. High-level architecture of the IndianApps system.

sents an example of a very successful partnership with a not-for-profit organization that has provided a positive learning experience for our students.

The rest of this section starts with an overview of the project and its history. Then it briefly explains its technical landscape, goals, and challenges. In addition, it discusses the contributions of our students to the project and the impact it has had on their education. This section concludes by describing some comments from the technical project manager of WFYI, including some important lessons learned.

The WFYI–EPICS partnership started during the spring of 2008 semester when an upper management team from WFYI visited Butler University to discuss a possible collaboration with our EPICS program. This project ended in 2010 when a beta version was released and installed at the client's site. Three different teams were engaged in this project, which lasted five consecutive semesters. The author of this chapter was the primary faculty supervisor since the inception of the project.

At first, our client expressed the desire to automate the process of storing and managing all their video production elements and related material. Such material included an estimated 4000 tapes containing approximately 2000 hours of video for more than 40 productions over a 10-year period. Based on that, we established an initial list of requirements for crafting an Assets Management System (AMS) for WFYI. It was decided from the beginning that the AMS would need to entail a Web-based interface with a typical relational database back-end. Such a database management system utilizes multiple connected tables to store all related information, which is optimized in order to provide a more effective query facility for searching and retrieving desired data. Figure 3.2 shows the main login Web interface of the AMS.

At the beginning of this project, our students experienced first-hand that gathering requirements can be a lengthy and challenging process (as was the case here). More specifically, the EPICS team conducted several meetings with various people from WFYI and devoted many hours discussing the requirements for the AMS. During such meetings, the EPICS team utilized various modeling tools (e.g., use-case diagrams learned in our software engineering courses) in order to model the system's functionality from the user's perspective. Also, simple use-case scenarios, user stories, and feature lists were found to be practical tools for collecting and specifying the requirements for the AMS. Such requirements started as high-level and evolved to be long, refined, and very detailed.

After the establishment of the final requirements, the EPICS team created a high-level architectural design for the AMS. Figure 3.3 depicts such an architectural diagram. As you can see in the diagram, the proposed system had to facilitate the process of online data entry as well as to handle an already existing large amount of related data that was stored in several scattered spreadsheets. In addition, the AMS was expected to provide some functionality for the database administrator (DBA) in order to create and manage new accounts for AMS users.

Figure 3.2. Main login window of the AMS. (The WFYI logo is copyrighted by WFYI Radio/TV of Indianapolis.)

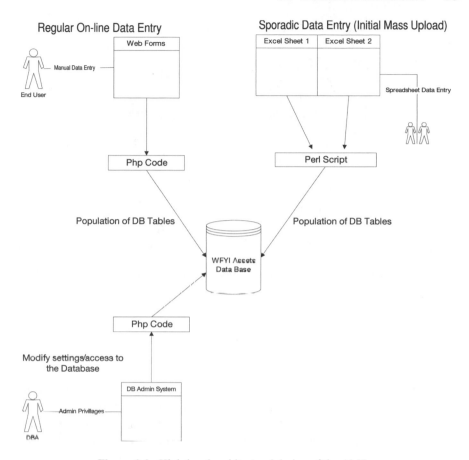

Figure 3.3. High-level architectural design of the AMS.

During the detailed design phase of the project, our EPICS team was divided into three separate focus teams. Each team was tasked with the completion of one of the above-mentioned subsystems of AMS. More specifically, the first focus team was responsible for the automation of the initial mass upload of existing data, the second team focused on the future online data entry and database management features, and the third team aimed at providing the system administrator functionality. Figure 3.4 depicts a simple data-entry form developed by the EPICS team for entering new information online. Figure 3.5 shows the main window implemented for the AMS administrator for creating and managing accounts for new users.

It is the author's experience that decomposing the initially proposed system into separate cohesive units (such as the ones described above) was critical to the overall success of the project. Based on such logical decomposition of the new system, the EPICS team was organized into smaller

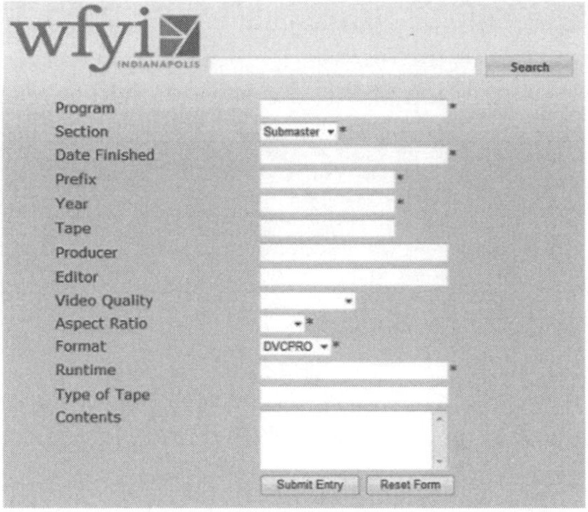

Figure 3.4. Online data-entry form of the AMS. (The WFYI logo is copyrighted by WFYI Radio/TV of Indianapolis.)

subteams. Such division was done based on various criteria such as the background of each team member. For instance, the students who were familiar with (or wanted to learn) the Perl scripting language undertook the implementation of the mass-data upload functionality. On the other hand, anyone who wanted to work with php and MySQL technologies worked on the online new-data-entry part. Therefore, it is important to discuss with the students the various options and allow them to choose which part of the sys-

Figure 3.5. System administration main window of the AMS. (The WFYI logo is copyrighted by WFYI Radio/TV of Indianapolis.)

tem they wish to engage with. (The author has found that such an approach has been effective most of the time.)

During the implementation phase, our students had to learn and use typical Web-based software development tools, languages, and platforms, including HTML, CSS, JavaScript, php, phpAdmin, PerlScript, and MySQL (some of these tools are taught in CSSE courses but others are not).

During the final phase, our EPICS team conducted various software testing activities (led by the students who had taken our Software Testing and Quality Assurance course). During that time, our students designed, generated, and executed several test cases. Based on that, some defects were detected and resolved before the final release and delivery of the AMS.

In addition to the technical challenges, our EPICS team learned some unique project management lessons during this project. For instance, it is worth mentioning that the team made an impressive effort to embrace a blind student who participated in this EPICS project for several semesters. With the support of all team members and the faculty supervisor, the blind student eventually played a central role and made an exemplary contribution to the project (mostly on designing and implementing the database back-end of the AMS). Moreover, the team learned how to survive a high turnover of various project constituents such as different team leaders and new members (also multiple users, developers, testers, business people, etc.) Another important lesson our students learned during this project is how to deal with frequently changing requirements. It took the team quite some time in order to understand what needs to be accomplished and eventually help the users/clients to realize what they really wanted (something typical of any real software engineering project).

Another experience worth mentioning is related to computer ethics. Although it was the end of the semester (and student grades were due), the team was reluctant to release the final version of the AMS prematurely (i.e., with known bugs). During a meeting at that time, it was stressed by the team leader that it would be unethical to release a buggy version to the client, which would go against everything that they had learned from our Computer Ethics course. The author (being the supervisor of that team at that time) was impressed by the way the EPICS students handled this situation on their own and made appropriate decisions. This incident represents an example of a case in which our students exhibited the ability to make mature decisions and effectively apply (nontechnical) knowledge (learned from the Computer Ethics course) to a real-life situation.

The rest of this section presents some feedback provided at the conclusion of our project. Such feedback mostly comes from the technical lead of our WFYI client as well as from some of the students involved. All this information was collected during an interview conducted by Butler's public-relations personnel in order to write a related article published in *Butler Magazine* [31]. The responses from that interview are described below (with permission), followed by the author's comments. It becomes evident from such praise that our EPICS students produced high-quality deliverables and exhibited a remarkable work ethic during that project. In addition, they made a great impression and impact on the WFYI personnel (especially the upper management). Finally, from the students' own comments we can see that they have appreciated such a realistic experience.

3.3.2 Students' Perspective

The overall feedback we received from all our students about their involvement in the WFYI–EPICS project was very positive. Below, we share related comments from some students involved, particularly the ones who worked all five semesters and had completed a summer internship at WFYI working with their personnel on the AMS.

> We got to design the solution. The professor stayed out of the project as much as possible. This removed the crutch that most students rely on, making us grow as developers.

Another, commenting on "soft skills," states:

> I learned how vital it is to communicate effectively with people that might approach the project or the organization as a whole from a different perspective.

3.3.3 Client's Perspective

The responses below describe the client's viewpoint of the initial project requirements and related logistics (e.g., real constraints and limitations, project duration, number of teams, final deliverables, etc.). As you can see, this represents a real, complex, and challenging project with actual constraints.

> The EPICS team was tasked with creating an Asset Management System to catalog and describe a series of tapes containing various video elements. The video elements were created for many different video productions that WFYI Productions did. These tapes comprise the raw camera footage from locations and the various "takes" created during production of documentaries, TV advertising spots, short information pieces, and television programs. The Asset Management System would store descriptive data called metadata about each tape that would describe the contents, when it was created, who created it, for what client, and the location of the tape among other information.
>
> There was an internal resistance to changing the way things were being done. There existed a varying degree of organization with regard to "raw

tapes" and that the "system" (used loosely) seemed to be working well enough. Few people were willing to devote time to build something new since they were too busy managing other production-specific projects, often tied to income for the station. There is also a very limited staff with the skill set needed to undertake a software project like this and that staff was already overstretched managing the development and maintenance of four websites.

The project design and implementation took five semesters and had three distinct teams during that time frame. [The students developed] a MySQL- and php-powered tool that WFYI Productions can use to catalog its production tape library. Each time a new tape is created by a videographer, they log the tape into the system and store it in a designated room with organized shelves.

An important accomplishment of this project is that the end-product is in fact utilized by the client (as the response below indicates):

The system is being used currently as intern and staff time is available to "backlog" the extensive preexisting tape inventory. I also believe the system is being used as new material is produced and cataloged.

It is fair to say that other EPICS projects, although developed for real customers, have not been in actual use due to various reasons (mostly nontechnical). On the contrary, the WFYI project is a good example of a project in which students developed a robust prototype application rather than an academic exercise used as a learning playground.

The following responses demonstrate that our EPICS students did impress our client due to their exceptional work ethic and enthusiasm to learn. Therefore, the client has expressed a genuine interest in continuing such collaboration with EPICS (the author is already being discussing such possibility with WFYI personnel).

I am a computer science graduate myself and understand the difficulties involved in learning the nuances of computer programming. I felt that the Butler students involved with EPICS were intelligent, easy to work with, and eager to learn. Also, given the enormity of this project, I think they were all brave and showed great determination to see the project to completion.

This was WFYI's first collaboration with EPICS, although I was aware of the concept of EPICS from my time at Purdue University. I will likely ask Butler EPICS to assist WFYI with future projects, since there will always be the need for the skills that computer science students possess and WFYI is unable to hire. There is always more work for me than I am able to complete.

Our EPICS students had a great opportunity to spend a summer at WFYI getting their hands dirty and, thus, being able to earn a deeper understanding of the end users real needs (as the response below indicates):

"When the team came in during the summer of 2009 and shadowed the staff and interns tasked with managing and organizing the tape library, they were able to clarify and refine the design goals of the project to closely match the actual need."

Finally, our EPICS students had an impact even on the WFYI upper management as the following important response indicates:

"The collaboration was beneficial to many upper management and staff here at WFYI. It forced many to realize that their broad and not clearly defined project requests don't clearly translate into a workable solution. A great deal of work is needed to define and specify the broad ideas and requests into solid foundations for a project to accomplish."

3.4   ASSESSMENT

This section describes how our EPICS service-learning program is being assessed internally. It also explains why we believe it has proved to be successful at Butler. The focus is on the reasons why EPICS has flourished at various levels (i.e., departmental, College, and University levels) within Butler.

First, it becomes evident that our EPICS program has been successful within the CSSE department due to various reasons. One such reason is that with EPICS, throughout the multiple-semester software engineering projects, our students have the opportunity to experience something beyond a typical internship or a capstone project. Moreover, via EPICS they can apply classroom knowledge and skills in a realistic environment by starting early in the curriculum (as mentioned above, EPICS can be taken as early as the second semester of the first year). In addition, they are given the chance to balance their technical and soft skills (dealing with real customers and project management issues). Finally they understand what it means to act as a professional during client meetings. Based on all of the above reasons and the feedback we receive from our students (see survey responses in the next section), it becomes evident that EPICS aligns very well and complements our own CSSE curriculum.

Second, we have watched EPICS flourishing within a liberal arts and sciences (LAS) college (compared to a typical engineering college). Some of the reasons include the fact that LAS students usually come to EPICS with a broader education and a solid understanding of how to be useful citizens and the need to help their community. Therefore, they have a positive attitude toward service-learning. They also know how to think outside the box and appreciate diversity and multiculturalism. Finally, we have seen that many LAS students that take EPICS are double majors (e.g., music and CS). In other words, a home such as the LAS College appears to be an excellent place for an EPICS program to flourish.

Third, we provide some reasons why we believe that EPICS has been successful as a viable program within a small private university such as Butler. The main reason is that the University's mission statement mentions, and clearly stresses, the importance of community involvement, service-learning, and outreach activities. In addition, Butler has institutionalized service-learning via the CCC (Center for Citizenship and Community), which manages and coordinates all service-learning courses and volunteerism as well as ensures a sense of community awareness and responsibility among students [7]. Finally, it is worth mentioning "The Butler Way" mentality that characterizes the spirit of Butler University, namely, a family-oriented environment with small-size classes where students receive (and expect) personal attention and, therefore, develop a caring behavior for others and their community. So it is the author's opinion that this justifies the success of EPICS at the University level.

3.4.1 Qualitative Data

During the past few years, the CSSE department has been collecting assessment data from our students regarding their experiences with EPICS. Such data are typically collected using surveys and they are depicted in Appendices G and F. As you can see from those surveys, the students are given two separate groups of questions: one related to learning new technologies on their own and the second about team work. Below are some students' responses regarding their ability to learn new technologies on their own (for more details see Appendix F).

> I have been able to become very familiar with php and SQL. Something else that has been a great learning experience is dealing with clients that don't know exactly what they need, but they know what they want to be able to do. This gave me the opportunity of coming up with multiple ways to solve a problem, and presenting them with their options. This helped embrace that there is always more than one way to solve a problem.

From the overall comments shown in Appendix F, we can clearly see that most students indicate that they have been able to learn new technologies on their own and apply them to their project successfully. Also, some students claim that they feel confident enough (with what they have learned) so that they can teach it to other incoming EPICS students (i.e., they feel that they have mastered such new knowledge).

Regarding project management experiences, most students state that their teamwork skills have improved greatly and some feel ready to lead their own teams (again, a more detailed description can be found in Appendix G). Here is an example of such comments:

> Although there were some issues with communication within the team, this was a great learning experience since not all groups will have good communication. I learned a lot about how to work with the conditions, as well as how to adapt to them. This was a very stressful semester. I learned far more than I have in previous semesters.

Finally, it is worthwhile pointing out some particular comments mentioned in Appendix G of a student admitting that he/she has regretted the fact that he/she was disconnected from the rest of the team. Another student also is confessing that he/she was not very happy with the work accomplished as a leader of the team and wanted to gain more experience.

3.4.2 Key Challenges

Although we have collected promising qualitative data that demonstrate the success of EPICS, it is the author's opinion that there is still room for improvement and fine-tuning of our EPICS program at Butler University. The main key challenges can be classified in the following categories: project management, assessment of learning, faculty involvement, and sustained funding. Below the author discusses each of these categories separately.

Managing vertically integrated and multidisciplinary teams is an ongoing challenge. Helping students to form and manage effective teams, selecting their leaders, and assigning appropriate roles to each team member are not easy tasks (especially in an academic environment). In the past, the author has tried to assign to each team member typical and specific roles (e.g., technical lead, customer liaison, recorder, historian, etc.) but has found that such roles do not always work (the students tend to prefer to create their own roles within each team, which make sense most of the time).

The author believes that we need to strive for a better mechanism that ensures balanced team structures and effective conflict management among team members. Moreover, we must look for better ways to deal with the team fragmentation phenomenon. For instance, some students tend to disconnect themselves from their team, preferring to work alone and/or with someone they know and trust, thus resulting in fragmented teams due to personality issues.

In addition, we need to improve our long-term project continuity mechanism. Such a mechanism may include an effective way of introducing smoothly new students in an ongoing project, to select and match appropriate software engineering projects with the right teams, and to synchronize in-class and on-the-job learning. Also, we have learned that it is important to know when it is a good time to bring a project to closure (e.g., a milestone has been reached and there is a consensus that this project must be brought to closure). Within that context, the author has observed that there is a difference between managing long-term projects (e.g., with a secure client commitment) versus short-term projects (e.g., with nonreturning or inattentive clients). For instance, the author had to terminate some projects in the past due to inadequate attention and lack of commitment from a client. Another reason for closing a project has been the lack of interest and motivation from the students.

Also, a key challenge is how to provide a good balance between ensuring student progress on a project while learning something new. For instance, in some cases, lack of progress can be due to a steep learning curve on a specific project. However, students need to understand that in real life you are expected to do both (i.e., learn new things and demonstrate satisfactory progress at the same time). Also, we must take a closer and more careful look at what we should evaluate and how (e.g., Do we measure how much students learn? What progress they accomplish? How happy have they made their customers?) In other words, it is solely the author's opinion that we still need a better way to measure service-learning effectively (at least within our own EPICS program).

Another important issue with EPICS is faculty engagement. More specifically, it is essential that any faculty member who wishes to teach EPICS courses receive credit equivalent to teaching any regular course. In general, teaching a service-learning course such as EPICS should provide credit that can be counted towards academic tenure and/or promotion. We have found at Butler that supervising two or three (sometimes more) EPICS projects is equivalent to teaching a regular semester course. Moreover, faculty members who are expected to teach EPICS courses should be given the opportunity for professional development. For instance, travel funds should be made available to them on a regular basis. Such support will allow faculty members to attend related professional events for preparing to teach service learning courses as well as to keep up to date (e.g., the EPICS annual conference, SENCER summer institute, etc.).

Finally, although we have established an endowment for our EPICS program at Butler, we still believe that it is essential to continue seeking funding from various sources (both internal and external). Such sources may include the university, corporate sponsors and alumni as well as various community foundations.

3.5 A ROAD MAP

This section is intended to provide some assistance to anyone who wishes to create a new EPICS program at their institution. It describes a plan and proposes a road map that entails a sequence of path points to be visited in order to craft such a program.

Path Point 1: Viability Study

The goal here is to assess the overall feasibility of establishing an EPICS program at your institution. You can begin by asking some fundamental questions such as: What is Service Learning (SL)? What does SL mean to you? Can EPICS be an actual implementation vehicle of SL? How can EPICS be implemented at various levels within your university (e.g. college, department) effectively? How would it affect your program? How can you integrate it in your curriculum? How would your students and your faculty benefit?

The above questions will hopefully provide a better understanding of EPICS and how it can be incorporated into your institution. At the same time, you may gather common goals from all stakeholders involved and define the future desirable state of your EPICS program. Then specify all necessary steps to get to that state. With this in mind, you can create and include a project plan of the overall effort. Finally, this viability study will entail a cost/benefit analysis in order to determine all necessary resources required to create a service-learning program and its long-term benefit to your institution.

Path Point 2: Establish Awareness

Here, the goal is to socialize the concept of EPICS at your institution. Begin by communicating your short- and long-term goals effectively to everyone involved (including students). At the same time, make sure you establish internal and external visibility of your efforts. Some recommended ways to accomplish that may include the formation of a service-learning committee within your department and/or college. Also, you may create an advisory board with members from your community and alumni. Such board will not only advocate for your EPICS service-learning program but it will also be able to help you secure some external funding. Moreover, at this point it is crucial that a level of some commitment is secured from your institution's upper management or administration.

Finally, you will need to start devising an effective mechanism for creating (and sustaining) meaningful partnerships with not-for-profit organizations in your community. You can start by asking for help from anyone inside your institution who works closely with your community. For instance, many universities have an office that coordinates student volunteerism, service-learning, and/or other similar outreach activities (at Butler we have the

CCC [7]). It is the author's experience that sustaining such healthy relationships with community partnerships is essential for the success of your EPICS program and it requires some effort from everyone involved. For instance, during the first few years of our EPICS program we organized an annual dinner and appreciation evening, and invited all of our community partners and students at the end of every semester. Such a social event gave everyone an opportunity to get to know each other at a personal level and eventually created a sense of bonding. This dinner usually took place at an outside restaurant or inside our department.

Path Point 3: Incorporate EPICS into Your Curriculum

Now you can start creating a course (or a sequence of courses as we did at Butler) that count toward your major. Since it is common at academic institutions to engage with a lengthy process for approving new courses, we recommend that you begin by using your special-topics course to offer a section on EPICS (until the formal course is approved) for any interested students (so you do not lose momentum). Also, remember to allow for flexibility in the number of credit hours that students can take. As mentioned in an earlier section, at Butler we found that our students sometimes prefer to take fewer credit hours to fill up their schedule in a particular semester (or to simply graduate). In addition, your course structure should be vertical in nature, allowing for freshman, sophomore, junior, and senior students to register for different courses (e.g., 200-level course for freshmen/sophomores, 300-level for juniors, and 400-level for seniors).

Finally, you may allow your students to register for EPICS over several semesters for additional credit. At Butler, students are required to register for the 200-level EPICS course during their first year (second semester). If they wish to continue taking the EPICS class (which they do most of the time), they register for the 300-level course, and, finally, during their senior year they may register for the 400-level EPICS course. Every semester when they complete an EPICS course, they earn additional credit. For the 300- and 400-level courses, we usually count such credit towards our upper division elective courses. Overall, we have seen many students repeating EPICS two or three times (especially the ones motivated to become the leaders of their teams) during their studies at Butler.

Path Point 4: Secure Resources

At this point, you are ready to launch your program. The key to success here is to identify the right faculty member(s) to teach your new EPICS course(s). The selected individual(s) must be enthusiastic about service-learning and have a genuine interest in engaging with the community and helping others in need. Typically, such enthusiasm and excitement is passed to the students who eventually will be advocating for EPICS and suggesting it to other motivated students. Also, based on the author's experience, the faculty member(s) who are about to teach EPICS need to understand that this is not a typical lecture-based course but is student-driven (i.e., students develop a sense of project ownership). Therefore, EPICS supervisors need to demonstrate some flexibility and act more in a mentor/coach role rather than as a traditional instructor.

During the first year, it is also recommended that you advertise your new EPICS classes to all your students. At Butler, at the beginning of every semester, our EPICS students visit other courses in order to attract interested students to join their own projects (i.e. students recruiting other students appears to work well for us). Also, at Butler University we offer various EPICS related scholarships and awards. For instance, we have established an annual EPICS-honorary award (i.e., an EPICS pin and pen) for senior students who have exhibited exceptional leadership during EPICS. Also, during 2001–2005 our EPICS students were eligible to receive an NSF scholarship for continuing their studies in computer science or software engineering. Such honors and awards can typically help you to attract, recruit, reward, and retain motivated and hard-working students for your EPICS program.

Finally, during the first year you will hopefully receive positive feedback from the first group of students that took your EPICS courses and you will start generating momentum. This is a great time to look for some seed money from your administration. Since you can demonstrate some early signs of success, hopefully you will be eligible for some financial support.

ACKNOWLEDGMENT

The author wishes to thank everyone who has contributed in making EPICS a successful service-learning program at Butler University. In particular, I would like to thank my CSSE colleagues at Butler for their continuous support and participation in EPICS. Also, I am grateful to all the students for recognizing and believing that EPICS has great potential to enhance their educational experience. In addition, the author would like to acknowledge the contribution and commitment of our community partners to our EPICS program. Special thanks go to the original creators of EPICS at Purdue University, including Ed Coyle, Leah Jamieson and Bill Oakes, for their initial encouragement. Finally, our EPICS program is appreciative of our Center for Citizenship and Community at Butler and the Sallie Mae Foundation for their generous support.

REFERENCES

1. E. J. Coyle, L. H. Jamieson, and W. C. Oakes, "EPICS: Engineering Projects in Community Service," *International Journal of Engineering Education,* pp. 139–150, Vol. 21, No. 1., 2005.

2. "The EPICS Program," Purdue University [Online]. Available at http://engineering. purdue.edu/EPICS. [Accessed October 2011]

3. "The National EPICS Program," EPICS University [Online]. Available at http://engineering.purdue.edu/EPICSU. [Accessed October 2011]

4. P. Linos, S. Herman, and J. Lally, "A Service-Learning Program for Computer Science and Software Engineering," in *Proceedings of the 8th Annual Innovation and Technology in Computer Science Education Conference,* ACM Press, 2003.

5. J. Sorenson and P. Linos, "EPICS: A Service Learning Program at Butler University," in *Proceedings of the Frontiers in Education Conference,* Indianapolis, 2005.

6. "EPICS at Butler University" [Online]. Available: http://epics.butler.edu. [Accessed October 2011]

7. "Center for Citizenship and Community," Butler University [Online]. Available at http://www.butler.edu/centerforcc. [Accessed October 2011]

8. "EPICS National Conference" [Online]. Available at https://engineering.purdue.edu/ EPICSU/Conference. [Accessed October 2011]

9. "Frontiers in Education Conference" [Online]. Available at http://fie-conference.org. [Accessed October 2011]

10. "SENCER" [Online]. Available at http://www.sencer.net. [Accessed October 2011]

11. "SIGCSE Conference" [Online]. Available at http://www.sigcse.org. [Accessed October 2011]

12. "CCSC" [Online]. Available at http://www.ccsc.org. [Accessed October 2011]

13. "ASEE" [Online]. Available at http://www.asee.org. [Accessed October 2011]

14. "IUPUI Informatics" [Online]. Available at http://informatics.iupui.edu. [Accessed October 2011]

15. "EVL," University of Illinois at Chicago [Online]. Available at www.evl.uic.edu. [Accessed October 2011]

16. "TechPoint" [Online]. Available at htpp://www.techpoint.org. [Accessed October 2011]

17. "Sallie Mac" [Online]. Available at http://www.salliemae.com. [Accessed October 2011]

18. "Oaks Academy" [Online]. Available at http://www.theoaksacademy. [Accessed October 2011]

19. "Indianapolis Legal Aid Society" [Online]. Available at http://www.indylas.org. [Accessed October 2011]

20. "The POLIS Center" [Online]. Available at http://www.polis.iupui.edu. [Accessed October 2011]

21. "Undergraduate Research Conference (URC)" [Online]. Available at http://www.butler.edu/undergrad-research-conference. [Accessed October 2011]

22. "Crohn's and Colitis Foundation" [Online]. Available at http://www.ccfa.org. [Accessed 2011].

23. "WFYI Public TV/Radio" [Online]. Available at htpp://wfyi.org. [Accessed C 2011].

24. "Association for Software Testing" [Online]. Available at http://www.the associationfor-softwaretesting.org.

25. "Center for Urban Ecology" [Online]. Available at http://butler.edu/cueb. [Accessed 2011].

26. "Lutheran Child and Family Services Center" [Online]. Available at http://lutheranfamily.org. [Accessed October 2011]

27. "nuafrica Water-Education-Life Website" [Online]. Available at http://nuafrica.org. [Accessed October 2011].

28. "SAVI Interactive" [Online]. Available at http://www.savi.org. [Accessed October 2011]

29. S. Kandris and K. Frederickson, "The Development of the Social Assets and Vulnerabilities Indicators (SAVI) Database," in *Proceedings of ESRI User Conference,* Indianapolis, 2001.

30. "IndianApps" [Online]. Available at http://indianapps.butler.edu. [Accessed October 2011]

31. "EPICS and WFYI," *Butler Magazine,* [Online]. Available at http://butler.edu/newsroom/resources/publications/butler_magazine. [Accessed October 2011]

APPENDIX A

WEEKLY STATUS REPORT (WSR)
Monday, April 6th, 2009

TO: All team members, advisors, mentors etc.
FROM: The EPICS-WFYI team leader
SUBJECT: Status of the Asset Management System (AMS)

I. RED FLAGS: None.

II. ISSUES: None.

III. ACCOMPLISHMENTS:

March 30th, 2009
- Based on the discussion from the March 23rd meeting with WFYI, the EPICS team continued to make improvements on their data model in order to better understand how the AMS operates with different asset types.

April 1st, 2009
- The EPICS team finished the latest version of their data model. This model will be used to create the new version of the AMS that the team will present to WFYI at their next meeting.

IV. PLANNED ACCOMPLISHMENTS (4/15/09 to 4/27/09):

Future meetings will be planned as follows:
- The EPICS team will meet with WFYI on April 13th to update them on the progress they have made on the AMS.
- Depending on how much progress is made before their April 13th meeting, the EPICS team will meet with WFYI on April 20th and/or April 22nd.
- On April 27th, the EPICS-WFYI team will have their last meeting of the semester. At the meeting, the EPICS team will follow their presentation of the AMS with a Q&A session. Pending approval from their faculty advisor, the EPICS team may also invite other students and faculty from the Computer Science department to watch their presentation.

APPENDIX B

EPICS Peer Evaluation Form

Please rate the performance of your team and its members including yourself by using a number between 1 and 5. For this evaluation, you can use the assessment criteria described at the bottom of this form. Please e-mail this completed form to your instructor no later than (due date goes here).

INDIVIDUAL TEAM MEMBER RANKING

1. NAME of team member: _____ **Rate (1–5):** _____
COMMENTS: please use the space below to provide some helpful suggestions and constructive comments on what this person needs to do to improve his/her performance this semester.

2. NAME of team member: _____ **Rate (1–5):** _____

3. NAME of team member: _____ **Rate (1–5):** _____

4. NAME of team member: _____ **Rate (1–5):** _____

5. NAME of team member: _____ **Rate (1–5):** _____

TEAM RANKING

Rate the overall performance of your team so far this semester (1–5): _____
COMMENTS: please use the space below to provide some helpful suggestions and constructive comments on what your team needs to do to improve its performance this semester.

PEER EVALUATION RATING SCHEME

1—Unsatisfactory
- Team member does not recognize his/her role in the team
- Functioning below what is expected
- Minimal or no initiative shown
- Often misses meetings
- He/she makes no commitments and/or sets no goals

2—Needs development
- Team member understands his/her role
- Has difficultly setting goals for him/herself
- Needs help identifying future tasks and stay focused
- Occasionally takes initiative
- This person is not as effective as other team members

3—Meets expectations
- Team member has a good understanding of his/her goals
- He/she schedules tasks to meet established goals
- Apply basic knowledge/experiences to accomplish his/her tasks
- Takes initiative sometimes
- Follows instructions and completes his/her tasks

4—Exceeds expectations
- Sets his/her own goals and demonstrates significant progress toward those goals
- Analyzes and tests options, questions actions when appropriate
- Provides constructive feedback to the team when necessary
- Regularly takes initiative and is very dependable
- Does at least his/her share for the team

5—Outstanding
- A key member of the team
- Consistently shows initiative
- He/she has a clear understanding of the team's long-term goals
- Makes consistent progress toward his/her own goals
- Takes responsibility for a major share of the team's work
- Helps the whole team make significant progress
- Assesses options, advocates for the most effective solutions

TEAM EVALUATION RATING SCHEME

1—Unsatisfactory
- Team does not have a well-defined goal
- It does not have a well-defined team structure

- Functioning below what is expected
- Shows no progress

2—Needs development
- Team understands its goal
- Team needs help identifying future tasks and staying focused
- Team structure needs improvement
- Team needs better coordination

3—Meets expectations
- Team has a good understanding of its goals
- Team schedules tasks to meet established goals
- Team demonstrates satisfactory progress
- Team structure is well defined and works well

4—Exceeds expectations
- Team demonstrates consistent progress toward its goals
- Team structure is well defined and very effective
- Team has a well-thought-out plan
- Team conducts regular meetings to discuss progress and future action items

5—Outstanding
- Team shows exceptional progress toward its goals
- Team has an excellent team structure and works effectively
- Team conducts additional meetings outside the regular class meetings
- Team assesses options, follows the most effective solutions
- Team is exceptionally productive

APPENDIX C

Project Evaluation Questionnaire (for EPICS Clients)

Please provide some feedback about your work with the Butler EPICS team. You may respond to the following questions by writing your answers in the spaces below.

- Name of your organization or agency _____

- Semester and year of working on this project _____

- Please rate the degree to which you are satisfied with the following:

	Very Satisfied		Neutral		Very Dissatisfied
a. Communication with student team	1	2	3	4	5
b. Responsiveness of team to customer's needs and interests	1	2	3	4	5
c. Professionalism of the team	1	2	3	4	5
d. Amount of time required to manage the team	1	2	3	4	5
e. Skill level of team	1	2	3	4	5
f. Quality of the work	1	2	3	4	5
g. Overall experience with Butler students	1	2	3	4	5

1. Did working with the team help you to improve your business process? If yes, how?

2. What 1–3 things could be done to improve the team and their project?

3. What would you like the students to know about your organization?

4. What would you like the EPICS faculty supervisor to know?

APPENDIX D

EPICS Final Project Report (Format and Content)

Cover page (course name, team name, team members, semester, project name, etc.)
Table of contents
Summary/Abstract
Chapter 1: Introduction
- Problem statement and objectives
- Motivation and rationale
- Description of the customer and developers

- Your overall approach and process model
- Glossary and terminology
- Organization of the report

Chapter 2: Requirements Specifications
- Description of functional (e.g., features) and nonfunctional requirements (e.g., performance)
- Assumptions and constraints

Chapter 3: Architecture
- Overview of high-level system architecture to include:
  - System services and/or features
  - System structure (logical components and their relationships)
  - System communication (interaction between components)
  - System functionality (responsibilities of each component)
- Architectural decomposition and style (client/server, Web-based, three-tier, etc.)
- System platforms (hardware and software)

Chapter 4: Design
- Description of the user interface (include screen shots)
- Features/operations
- Layout and aesthetics
- Organization of window displays, dialog boxes, and menus
- Print out report formats
- Navigation and browsing options
- Error message dialogs
- Data model

Chapter 5: Implementation
- Selection of implementation language(s)
- Coding standards and comments used
- Implementation process and distribution of work
- Organization of the code base (e.g., directories, files, packages, classes, etc.)

Chapter 6: Quality Assurance and Testing
- Describe the selection of your testing objectives
- Explain your basic testing approach and method(s) used
- Describe related checklists and/or templates used for testing purposes
- Explain your defect detection, reporting, and management process
- Include some documented sample runs of the code (using several test-data cases, a list of defects detected, and how they were fixed)

Chapter 7: Project Organization and Management
- Describe your team's organizational structure
- Explain the role and detailed contribution of each member in the team

- Clearly describe how the overall work was divided and carried out by different members
- Describe your project's management process (e.g., conducting meetings, scheduling, communication, planning, reporting, conflict resolution, etc.)
- Describe any related technologies and tools selection and use
- Include all Weekly Status Reports (WSR)
- Provide a detailed user's manual (e.g., instructions on how to operate your system)

References/bibliography (include all references and/or websites you used)

Appendices (complete source code, presentation slides, customer and peer evaluation forms, etc.)

APPENDIX E

Mid-Semester "Trial" Grade and Evaluation Feedback (Example Letter)

Team member name,

After calculating the averages of the peer evaluations data collected, the client's feedback as well as my own assessment, I am sending you an estimated grade so far for you and your team.

I am also including some brief recommendations on how to further improve your work during the rest of the semester.

Your grade: B plus (score received 3.6/5.0)
Overall team grade: A minus (score received 4.4/5.0)

RECOMMENDATIONS:

I can see that your team has accomplished a lot of work with establishing a solid connection with the customer, already selected an enabling technology (Joomla), and are getting to a point where you can start using it to develop the website.

Here are some recommendations on how to further improve your work during the rest of the semester:

1) Document well all the mini specs and features-list agreed upon
2) Finalize the design of the website and start implementation as soon as possible
3) Engage with your customer in regular meetings as frequently as possible

Other than that, keep the good work up!

Best,
Your EPICS instructor

APPENDIX F

EPICS survey (student responses)
Learning New Technologies

Question 1: **While taking EPICS, did you learn and use any new technologies for your project (i.e., something you have not been taught in other CSSE classes)? Please briefly explain.**

"I have been able to become very familiar with php and SQL. Something else that has been a great learning experience is dealing with clients that don't know exactly what they need, but they know what they want to be able to do. This gave me the opportunity of coming up with multiple ways to solve a problem, and presenting them with their options. This helped embrace that there is always more than one way to solve a problem."

"Actionscript III, Flash 9, some Photoshop."

"I learned to use Flash so as to create a game for the CCFA. Admittedly it was rather brief but I did get to learn about the technology. "

"I learned about Joomla, a little php, and some SQL. I also learned more in depth about perl. It helped doing this because I was able to learn how to connect outside programming languages into an SQL database (perl to sql)."

"No. Our project required that I deal primarily in developing the back end of a database-driven Web application. It was great practice, to be sure, but I already had significant experience with these technologies prior to Epics."

"I learned Macromedia Flash and Actionscript for making the game."

"I worked with database design that I haven't had to work with before."

"Yes, I learned several new technologies that have been integral to the success of my project. Those technologies are Joomla, MySQL, and php. I used the first to help update my project's website while using the second and third for contributing to its development."

"I learned how to use php, myadmin, and how to create databases. I also learned how to program in perl script and connect perl code to sql tables and fill them."

"I was familiar with all the technologies I worked with (PHP, SQL, Apache, and PHPMyAdmin) but I certainly know them better now because of doing this work with them than I did before."

"Joomla, little php, myAdmin/php."

"Well if you consider Chief Architect new then yes. However, I used the software last semester for the same project."

"I learned how to use Actionscript. I have never used this program before, so it took quite a bit of time to learn on my own. I have become familiar with creating and editing graphics, movie clips, and buttons. I also have a brief understanding of how the computer coding is handled."

"Learned how to create a website using Joomla 1.5"

"I learned a lot about php and got a lot of firsthand experience in Dreamweaver."

"Yes, I have gotten some experience with Joomla."

"With this project, we learned Joomla, which is a content management system for designing websites. Once set up, it allows for easy updating of the content, as well as management."

"Joomla is a dynamic CMS. It's a very nice system that has high potential."

"For this project, I learned how to use Microsoft Visio to create use-case and entity-relationship diagrams. As software engineering is the field that I would like to gain some experience in, this is an application that I will be using well in the future."

Question 2: To what extend do you feel that you have successfully learned this new technology? Rate using the scale 1–5 (1 means not successful and 5 means very successful)

"Though I have learned much regarding the aforementioned technologies, there is still a lot that I would like to know. These include designing a custom template in Joomla, adding user privileges to a website using php, and creating sophisticated databases using MySQL."

AVERAGE (5-point scale): 3.95

Question 3: How confident do you feel about helping new incoming EPICS students learn this new technology? Rate using the scale 1–5 (1 means not confident and 5 means very confident)

"I am certain that between now and the fall 2009 semester that I will have learned so much regarding the aforementioned technologies that I can help any new EPICS student learn a technology that they can use in their project."

AVERAGE (5-point scale): 3.89

APPENDIX G

EPICS Survey (Student Responses)
Team Work

<u>Question 1:</u> **Do you feel that your group worked as a team effectively? Rate using the scale 1–5 (1 means not effectively and 5 means very effectively)**

AVERAGE (5-point scale): 3.52

"Although my team worked effectively as a group, there is still much for them to learn about collaborating on a technical project."

<u>Question 2:</u> **How actively did you participate and engage with the team? Rate using the scale 1–5 (1 means not actively and 5 means very actively)**

AVERAGE (5-point scale): 4.02

"Though I actively participated with my team, I did not engage them as much as I should have. This is one of the mistakes that I hope to correct next semester as well as in the future with other projects."

<u>Question 3:</u> **How much do you think you have benefited from working as part of a team? Rate using the scale 1–5 (1 means not benefited and 5 means very benefited)**

AVERAGE (5-point scale): 4.15

"Although I benefited from working as part of a team, I did not benefit as much from leading it. I still have much to learn about what it means to be an effective leader in EPICS as well as other capacities."

"Although there were some issues with communication within the team, this was a great learning experience since not all groups will have good communication. I learned a lot about how to work with the conditions, as well as how to adapt to them. This was a very stressful semester, however, I learned far more than I have in previous semesters."

CHAPTER 4

THE COLLABORATORY

David Vader

ABSTRACT

The Collaboratory for Strategic Partnerships and Applied Research at Messiah College is students working with mentors and clients to conduct research and undertake development projects that foster justice, empower the poor, promote peace, and care for the earth through applications of their academic and professional disciplines. Through service today, participants increase their academic and professional abilities, vocational vision for lifelong servant-leadership, and courage to act on their convictions. This chapter explores the origins of the Collaboratory, presents an organizational model, and discusses internal processes and mission results.

4.1 INTRODUCTION

The Collaboratory for Strategic Partnerships and Applied Research is a center for service and scholarship at Messiah College that enables participants to apply academic knowledge and live out their Christian faith through imaginative, hands-on problem solving that meets the needs of clients in our region and around the world. Clients of the Collaboratory invest in the educational mission of the College through their interactions with students, and we produce professional and sustainable results for them by leveraging long-term partnerships and intergenerational volunteerism that enables projects to span multiple generations of students. Collaboratory projects enable students to engage classroom fundamentals in an authentic client-centered environment. Students lead and manage the Collaboratory in partnership with the educators and volunteer professionals who mentor them.

This chapter describes the mission, strategy, and tactics that organize people and their project activity in the Collaboratory, and how the Collaboratory organizational model developed over time in the context of Messiah College. It also explores the status and scope of Collaboratory activity and presents examples of projects and project outcomes.

4.2   BACKGROUND

4.2.1   Context

Founded in 1909, Messiah College* is a private Christian college of the liberal and applied arts and sciences with a student body approaching 3000. The College mission is to educate men and women toward maturity of intellect, character, and Christian faith in preparation for lives of service, leadership, and reconciliation in Church and society. Founded by the Brethren in Christ Church, the College is no longer legally owned by the Church but continues to emphasize its Anabaptist, Pietist, and Wesleyan theological heritage. This heritage informs longstanding commitments of the college to academic excellence and community service and engagement.†

The idealization of service at Messiah College is further shaped by the life and scholarship of the late Dr. Ernest Boyer. Among the College's most notable alumni, Boyer served as Chancellor of the State University of New York (SUNY) system, President of the Carnegie Foundation for the Advancement of Teaching, and President Jimmy Carter's Commissioner on Education. Boyer worried that overspecialization and compartmentalization of faculty research was contributing to a growing public association of *academic* with *irrelevant*. "Increasingly," Boyer (1997b) said, "the campus is being viewed as a place where students get credentialed and faculty get tenured, while the overall work of the academy does not seem particularly relevant to the nation's most pressing civic, social, economic, and moral problems." If we are to succeed in making whole persons and in engaging the pressing issues of our day, then the "most fundamental challenge confronting American higher learning is to move from fragmentation to coherence" (Boyer, 1997a). Boyer argued that in a few short decades at the close of the twentieth century the scope of what academics acknowledged as

---

*www.messiah.edu.

†The Carnegie Foundation for the Advancement of Teaching has named Messiah College to its Community Engagement Classification for Curricular Engagement and Outreach and Partnerships. Service to disadvantaged youth in our region put Messiah College on the President's Higher Education Community Service Honor Roll, with Distinction. *Washington Monthly* magazine says the College's commitment to community and public service is fifth in the nation among baccalaureate colleges. The Institute of International Education places Messiah College seventh in the nation among all undergraduate institutions that send students to study abroad. *U.S. News and World Report* consistently ranks Messiah College among the top 10 "Best Regional Colleges" in the northeastern United States.

scholarship had narrowed to center on what he called the scholarship of discovery. Discovery, said Boyer, was the search for knowledge for its own sake disseminated through journals and conference presentations to an audience of peers.

Boyer criticized the academy for having too many conversations that failed to engage outside the academy or even across disciplinary lines within, but he did not blame *discovery* research; he encouraged it. The university structure promotes depth of inquiry by organizing knowledge into territories called departments, and departments divide further into domains of research, often under the direction of individual faculty members. Boyer's response to academic isolation was to define and recommend three modes of scholarship in addition to discovery. His scholarship of *integration* underscores "the need for scholars who give meaning to isolated facts, putting them in perspective." Integration "seeks to interpret, draw together, and bring new insight to bear on basic research." It makes each discipline accountable to questions that might be asked of it by another. The scholarship of *application* asks how knowledge can be "responsibly applied to consequential problems," and be "helpful to individuals as well as institutions." Such service is often rejected as scholarship at many colleges and universities founded on promises to serve public interests. We no longer think of service as scholarship, we think of it as doing good. "To be considered *scholarship*," Boyer (1990) said, "service activities must be tied directly to one's special field of knowledge and relate to, and flow directly out of, this professional activity." Finally, Boyer 's scholarship of *teaching* is the work of recognizing effective pedagogical methods and processes, and of making them understandable to others. This is scholarship to advance the important task of equipping and inspiring future scholars. Of Boyer's four modes of inquiry, discovery and integration value the intrinsic worth of knowledge, whereas service and teaching value the instrumental worth of knowledge and seek to return that value to the public.

Although Messiah College lacks of some of the organizational infrastructure and the money for scholarship found at major research universities, ideals derived from the theological heritage of the College and the influence of Ernest Boyer's typology of scholarship* support an academic community that encourages interdepartmental and interdisciplinary collaboration and alternative modes of scholarly dissemination and review at levels often not possible at research universities. In this milieu, scholarship connects across

---

*Boyer's scholarship types are affirmed in the *Community of Educators Handbook* at Messiah College in the section for ranked faculty on term-tenure and promotion processes. The Schools of Humanities and of Business, Education and Social Science, moreover, are housed in Boyer Hall. Boyer Hall is also home to the Boyer Center, which promotes innovative educational practice and scholarship.

disciplines to provide meaning, serves pressing needs outside the academy, and innovates in the classroom to equip the next generation of holistic scholars. Term-tenure and promotion processes at Messiah College, moreover, reward excellent classroom teaching and pedagogical innovation,* and this has promoted the integration of scholarship projects into the curriculum to mutual advantage. The Collaboratory model for service and scholarship is not specific to Messiah College, but the ethos of the College community was certainly favorable for conceptualizing and nurturing the Collaboratory. Resources of institutional identity perhaps proved more important to beginning the Collaboratory than the organizational infrastructure or money for scholarship found in greater abundance at some research universities.

4.2.2 Rationale

What need does the Collaboratory satisfy? Although the Collaboratory serves many stakeholders, its purpose at Messiah College is to serve the educational mission of the College. Like many colleges and universities, we anticipate for each student a growing intellect informed by commitments of character and belief that, when mature, is manifested in fruitful action for the public good. Such commitments to attend to more than just cognitive education, but affective and behavioral education as well, are severely challenged today by the principles of scientific reductionism that organize much of higher education. The Collaboratory is one way that Messiah College overcomes such difficulties to make good on our promise to educate whole persons.

Tension in the academy between the purposes of making citizens and advancing human knowledge dates at least to Greek antiquity. Debate over which is preeminent has shaped and reshaped higher learning as one purpose routinely falls out of favor and is replaced by the other. Plato's (424–328 BC) educational vision, drawing from the Socratic belief that knowledge necessitates virtue, focused on the pursuit of knowledge through dialectic. Education for the pursuit of knowledge held forth in the Scholasticism of the Middle Ages and survived the Renaissance to find in the Enlightenment a catalyst that would propel it to renewed prominence in the modern research university. The alternative educational vision of Isocrates (436–338 BC), Plato's contemporary, emphasized the necessity of making citizens in post-Hellenistic Greece. This approach grew to full maturity in the writings of the

---

*Promotion to Associate Professor at Messiah College requires an evaluation by the Term-Tenure and Promotion Committee of meritorious in teaching and satisfactory in scholarship and service. Promotion to Full Professor requires an evaluation of meritorious in teaching plus either scholarship or service, and satisfactory in the remaining area.

Roman orators Cicero (106–43 BC) and Quintilian (35–100 AD), fell with the Roman Empire, and was revived by the Renaissance humanists and Protestant reformers, only to be compromised by the moderns of the Enlightenment (Kimball, 1986).

Higher education in America first was informed by Renaissance Europe, where the rediscovery of ancient voices such as Cicero and his *De oratore* (*The Orator*) favored breadth in education and spoke against specialization. Renaissance European scholars like Erasmus (1469–1536) bolstered this view. His *De ratione studii* (*The Program of Studies*) and concept of *humanitas* (humanity), "the program of scholarship and virtue by which one seeks to form the good citizen," did much to advance the humanist ideal as normative for education in Renaissance Europe (Kimball, 1986). This tradition of civic learning crossed the Atlantic to the American liberal arts college, initially mitigating the scientific reductionism of Enlightenment philosophy and its press toward specialization and professionalization in the academy. Well into the nineteenth century, most scientific inquiry was conducted by private individuals in workshops and homes. Instruction in scientific inquiry was likewise offered privately and apart from the work of the academy. By 1835, however, young faculty members returning to Harvard from advanced study at German universities were promoting change to make American universities more amenable to scientific inquiry (Kimball, 1986). With their promises of material return from scientific research, these calls for change fell into the fertile soil of American industrialization and Yankee utility (Kimball, 1986).

The German influence restructured the university, dividing knowledge into parts for examination by specialists and separating academics into departments for the oversight of inquiry into the various domains. The departments became guilds for members who became increasingly concerned with credentials, credentialing, and preventing the uninitiated from practicing their craft. As language specific and internal to each discipline emerged, the language of everything from literature to engineering was soon equally inscrutable to the uninitiated. Scholars began to disdain public acclaim for their work, viewing public accessibility as a sign that the work lacked sufficient rigor. Academic discourse was thus increasingly a conversation between guild members with diminishing accountability to other guilds let alone to the public (Kimball, 1986).

Faculty members necessarily became less versatile educators as the demand for them to specialize grew. Curricula also adapted to meet these new demands, enabling most college teachers today to be specialists charged with planning and executing a sequence of learning exercises to foster the focus and depth of inquiry needed to make new specialists in their field. Each faculty member contributes his or her part, attaches an evaluation, and sends the student on through the curriculum. The curriculum is responsible for the outcome, and a committee for the curriculum. Curricula, "however draped with rationales of breadth and depth, are often products of balancing the political interests of entrenched departments and programs," treaties negotiated to give everyone the right to teach a specialty (Kimball, 1986). Highly scripted classroom instruction offers educators the control they want to prevent the intrusion of messy personal concerns. A cadre of additional specialists, including residence directors, ministry staff, and councilors, are hired to tend to students' personal needs. We still care about cognitive, affective, and behavioral education, but have organized and compartmentalized each into relatively autonomous curricular and extracurricular structures. Students move freely between these structures, but collaboration between educators is limited.

If this sounds too negative, we must remember that specialization is important. We depend on specialists for a great many things, and we expect them to be competent in their fields. Specialization serves us in the classroom, moreover, by narrowing attention to foster depth of inquiry. It focuses time and work, enabling us to develop competencies. Difficulties begin only when the specialist ceases to inform or be informed by others. "Consider the separation assumed in the university between economics and politics," propose Stanley Hauerwas and William Willimon (1996), "a separation attributable to the capitalist presumption that economics is a 'science'. This science has its own laws and is subject to no theology beyond production and distribution of wealth.... We do not believe that our money can be separated from our politics." Mark Van Doren (1943) observes that technical education has likewise suffered "because it is willing to accept students whose training has not been general enough to make them recognize principles when they appear."

Words and facts must "return to their objects in the world," says Wendell Berry (1987). This "describes one of the boundaries of a university" and points us toward the educational purpose of the Collaboratory. C. S. Lewis (1970) once described walking into a darkened shed and spying a shaft of light streaming through a window. Examining the beam, he noticed the motion of dust particles carried along by air currents, and the way the particles scattered the light. With the right instruments, he might have measured the electromagnetic spectrum of the beam and variations of intensity with position in the shed. As Lewis stepped into the beam, however, he peered along it and reality was transformed. He now saw a tree in a meadow with blue sky and clouds overhead, and the sun 93 million miles distant. From the darkened shed he could dissect the beam, reduce it to its most elemental parts, but only when he entered into it did he discover the English countryside encoded in the beam. Trying to educate whole persons from within an essentially reductionist educational framework is like trying to see along Lewis' beam of light while standing apart from it in the darkened shed.

The Collaboratory exists to contribute to the mission of Messiah College to educate whole persons by helping students to advance and connect their cognitive, affective, and behavioral learning. Persons maturing in intellect, character and Christian faith must strive to comprehend both "What must I know?" and "What does it mean?" Those who would live lives of service, leadership, and reconciliation must also seek to understand "What is required of me?" The first task of the student seeking to earn a degree within a particular academic discipline is to answer "What must I know?" and gain ability to practice that discipline with exceptional ability. The educated graduate, however, must also answer the question "What does it mean?" in order to understand how the truth and methodologies of their major area of study intersect with the truth and methodologies of other disciplines, and how these disciplines speak collectively to the pressing problems of our day. Knowing "What does it mean?" is a prerequisite for all who would live and work with exceptional care for others and the earth as well as exceptional professional skill. Knowledge not appropriated in life, however, can become self-indulgence. Finally, therefore, the educated college graduate is called to seek and live out an answer to the question "What is required of me?" in order to graduate with a deep sense of vocation and the courage to act on convictions.

First, the Collaboratory adds value to classroom learning that advances professional practice in the learner. Thankfully, we already know much of what must be done to help students develop excellence in practice, a worthy vision for their lives, and the courage to act. Works like David Kolb's (1984) *Experiential Learning* and Donald Schön's (1983) *The Reflective Practitioner* were the first to point to the importance of contextualization and engagement to education for excellence in practice. These works launched decades of related scholarship, resulting in entire new fields of pedagogical inquiry, including experiential learning, collaborative learning, problem-based learning, and service-learning. This body of work posits a learning cycle that includes (1) a concrete experience that leads to (2) reflective observation on the experience and (3) the abstract application of theory to the experience or the conceptualization of new general rules. Theory then leads to (4) active experimentation in new ways to approach the situation of the previous experience, leading, in turn, to the next concrete experience. A typology of learning styles associates to the four steps; these are the activist, reflector, theorist, and pragmatist. The literature further connects the first and third steps of the learning cycle to two ways of knowing: knowing by "apprehension" (know-how) results from concrete experience, and knowing by "comprehension" (know-that) results from abstract conceptualization. The second and fourth steps represent two ways of transforming knowledge: reflective observation (dialectic) transforms knowledge by thinking, whereas active experimentation (empiricism) transforms knowledge by doing.

Excellent classroom instruction is foundational to students acquiring knowledge and methodologies in their field of study, even if they do not recognize how these relate to professional practice they have yet to experience. We have all experienced, however, how difficult it is to give proper attention and effort to mastering anything whose significance remains a mystery. Some of us have been astounded when, years later, a seemingly irrelevant, and therefore "incredibly dull," subject from school suddenly emerges at the center of our lives. It is not always possible for the student to know why something matters on this side of learning, making classroom learning without context difficult. Yes, it is the student's job to trust that the teacher is competent to construct a curriculum that matters, and the educator's job is to inspire and, when inspiration fails, to use grades as the carrot and stick to help students slog through to the discovery of why classroom content matters. Kolb, Schön, and many others, however, have shown that we have been far too optimistic about the capacity of classroom instruction alone to foster vision or engender action, and too optimistic about the capacity of students to connect, sometimes years later, their academic knowledge to the challenges of life. We all know there is a kind of on-the-job learning by experience that often does not begin until after college and proceeds at the employer's expense. This is why so many new graduates are left wondering how they are to satisfy the 3–5 years of experience that are prerequisite to many jobs.

Second, the Collaboratory adds value to classroom learning by helping students discover a worthy dream for their lives. Daniel Levinson (1978) was the first developmental theorist to recognize the power of the dream and that the novice phase of adulthood is the crucial time for forming a dream for one's life. He and Judy Levinson (Levinson and Levinson, 1996) have contended that an essential function of a mentoring relationship is the development and articulation of the dream. Sharon Parks (2000) calls the dream "an imagined possibility that orients meaning, purpose, and aspiration." The formation of a worthy dream is a critical task for young adults. Unfortunately, as Parks observes, the Western mind equates imagination with fantasy. "Fanciful in its common usage connotes 'the unreal.' Fancy takes the images already in the memory and arranges and rearranges them associatively or aggregatively. The task of imagination, and particularly religious imagination, is to compose the real" (Parks, 2000). It has been said there are two great days in a person's life: the day we are born and the day we discover why. The Collaboratory helps students move toward that second great day by enabling them to both gain and reflect on experience. Through this reflection, they obtain a better understanding of their individual gifting and how their gifting relates to and depends on the gifts of others. Finally, reflection helps them imagine a dream for their lives that is worthy of them—worthy because it seeks to do good that is larger than them each individually.

We encourage generosity in service to others to be part of everyone's dream. Recently in the academic world, much has been made of service and its potential to shape citizens. Regretfully, service is too often located with student affairs in the cocurriculum or, at best, in general education, and is infrequently connected to a student's major area of study. Some disciplines, such as teaching or nursing, are assigned the status of service disciplines by the nature of the work. Lawyers and physicians have fostered a culture within their disciplines of giving back some professional time through volunteerism. What about the rest of us? Are there no worthy causes that could benefit from what we do every day to make money, causes that would never access our help through the markets? Yes, a cross-cultural service experience of any kind is beneficial, but must we always insist on being paid for everything we do related to our profession, limiting voluntary service to opportunities outside of our day-to-day workplace expertise? Markets are wonderfully efficient at bringing needs and resources together, unless the ones with the need are too poor and, therefore, invisible to the market. The Collaboratory enables educators and students to volunteer their time in service to people and communities who have the same needs as everyone but have resources so small that their needs rarely attract help through market mechanisms.

Finally, the Collaboratory adds value to classroom learning by engendering hope and courage in students to act on convictions. We must acknowledge that knowledge and vision are not the same as results. Nearly everyone knows someone of ability who may even have a worthy dream for accomplishing some public good with their life but is unable to act on their knowledge or dream. Nevertheless, young adults are searching for something worthy of their life's work. Many young patriots see in military service something that is worthy, and for that they are even willing to risk their lives. Pacifists Stanley Hauerwas and William Willimon (1996) observe that "War is incredible moral competition for the Church. It brings out the best in people, requires incredible sacrifice, and draws people together against a common foe." Other young adults from affluent families, anesthetized by the consumption of ever less rewarding experiences, turn to ever more extreme sports and other risk taking to feel alive again. Meanwhile, we educators find ourselves competing with popular culture for our students' attention and have lost the courage to ask for too much lest they go elsewhere, and so we have nothing to offer young men and women searching for a worthy cause.

The Collaboratory is both demanding and attractive to students. It is attractive because it is demanding about things that matter to them. The U.S. Marines are demanding and know how to help their recruits learn to live out the ideas of the Marines: they put recruits in a group, move them through a perilous ordeal, teach them a new language, and give them skills to analyze what is wrong with their former lives. Marines often become uncomfortable with the culture of their former lives and are reluctant to go home because what once was comfortable is no longer home (Hauerwas & Willimon, 1996). The Collaboratory likewise places participants in community, moves them through a life-changing challenge, teaches them new ways of thinking and conversing about the purpose of their lives, and gives them skills to analyze what is wrong with a career of instrumental problem solving that leaves the value decisions about what should be done to others.

A dean of Messiah College said that to know is to think deeply, feel deeply, and act deeply. These are the marks of an educated person (Heie, 1993). How do university students today connect knowledge to values and move from values to action? Accomplishing this is the aim of the Collaboratory. To this end, Ernest Boyer (1997a) asked, "Why not have all incoming students join with faculty right away as young scholars in the discovery of knowledge, in the integration of knowledge, in the application of knowledge, and in the communication of knowledge? Why not have these four dimensions of scholarship become the four essential goals of undergraduate education? ... Rather than having freshmen and sophomores take a grab bag of courses of general education for two years ... why not offer all undergraduates a series of cross-disciplinary seminars that would run vertically from the freshman to the senior year, running parallel to and perhaps interweaving with the major? ... And, rather than have all undergraduates spend all their time on campus, engaged only with theory, why not have all undergraduates engaged in a field experience or a community project as a requirement for graduation, introducing them to the scholarship of application?" Boyer's vision has contributed much to the organizational and program design of the Collaboratory.

4.3 ORGANIZATION

4.3.1 Design

The Collaboratory* is a center at Messiah College for applied research and project-based learning in partnership with client nonprofit organizations, businesses, governments, and communities in our region and around the world. Current areas of engagement include science, engineering, health, information technology, business, and education. Our vision is to increase hope and transform lives through education, collaboration, innovation, and service. The twofold mission of the Collaboratory is:

*www.messiah.edu/collaboratory.

- To foster justice, empower the poor, promote peace, and care for the earth through applications of our academic and professional disciplines.
- To increase the academic and professional abilities of participants, their vocational vision for lifelong servant-leadership, and their courage to act on convictions.

Participants include students, educators, and volunteers. In the language of our community, we are Christians who aspire to obey the teachings and example of Jesus to love neighbors as ourselves, and to share the good news about God's work in the lives of people and creation.

Collaboratory participants have two weekly responsibilities. The first is to complete an assigned weekly task. Complex multiyear projects are accomplished in the Collaboratory when many people each faithfully complete a weekly work assignment. Participants are trained in and given the option of using either traditional project management with work-breakdown structures, timelines, and Gantt charts, or the newer Agile approach to project management developed by software engineers. Student leaders and their advisors participate in a week-long workshop in August, just prior to the fall semester, at which they receive training and participate in guided planning for the new academic year. The second responsibility of Collaboratory members is to participate in a weekly chapel that offers a recurring curriculum on a four-year timeline. The intention of this curriculum is to develop in each new generation of Collaboratory participants the ethos of the Collaboratory and to enable them to reflect on their experience in view of their studies and future plans. Although much of our work is cross-cultural and international, the Collaboratory's mission success is accomplished primarily by people working week-by-week throughout the year on campus in Grantham, PA. Although the work accomplished by teams that travel to partner communities, many in West Africa and Central America, is often the most visible and celebrated work of the Collaboratory, the number of members who travel for the Collaboratory is a fraction of the total workforce as the non-traveling members perform the bulk of the work. Site teams usually travel during the three-week January term of the College or over the summer to gain cross-cultural understanding, build trust relationships, conduct background research, test prototypes, and implement results. Travel in the Collaboratory is a means of bringing months and sometimes years of on-campus work to fruition, and it is how we prepare for future work.

A Director and Student Director provide executive leadership of the Collaboratory, while a Program Manager and Student Staff Group Manager provide leadership of day-to-day programming and execution of organizational strategy (Figure 4.1). The Director and Student Director create, assess, and refine organizational structures, programming, and services, both curricular

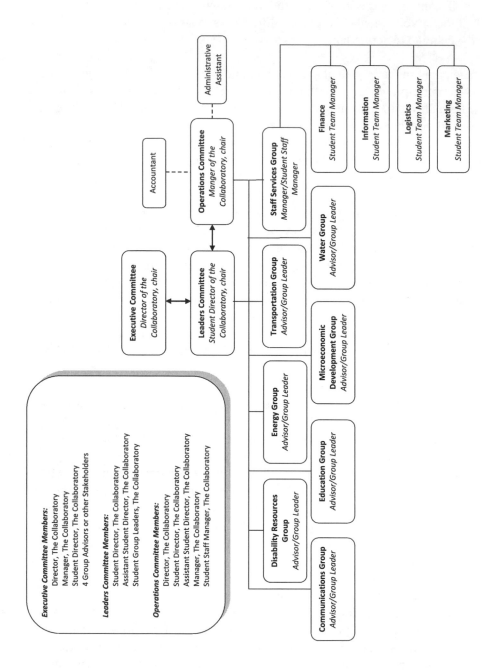

Executive Committee Members:
Director, The Collaboratory
Manager, The Collaboratory
Student Director, The Collaboratory
4 Group Advisors or other Stakeholders

Leaders Committee Members:
Student Director, The Collaboratory
Assistant Student Director, The Collaboratory
Student Group Leaders, The Collaboratory

Operations Committee Members:
Director, The Collaboratory
Student Director, The Collaboratory
Assistant Student Director, The Collaboratory
Manager, The Collaboratory
Student Staff Manager, The Collaboratory

Accountant

Administrative Assistant

Executive Committee
Director of the Collaboratory, chair

Operations Committee
Manger of the Collaboratory, chair

Leaders Committee
Student Director of the Collaboratory, chair

Staff Services Group
Manager/Student Staff Manager

Communications Group
Advisor/Group Leader

Disability Resources Group
Advisor/Group Leader

Education Group
Advisor/Group Leader

Energy Group
Advisor/Group Leader

Microeconomic Development Group
Advisor/Group Leader

Transportation Group
Advisor/Group Leader

Water Group
Advisor/Group Leader

Finance
Student Team Manager

Information
Student Team Manager

Logistics
Student Team Manager

Marketing
Student Team Manager

Figure 4.1. Collaboratory organization chart.

and cocurricular, that enable the Collaboratory to succeed in its mission. They also assist departments and faculty seeking to achieve teaching, scholarship, and service goals through the Collaboratory. The Director is a faculty member who teaches half-time and reports to the Dean of the School of Science, Engineering, and Health (SEH). The Student Director first serves one year as the Assistant Student Director, a part-time employee during the academic year, followed by a year as Student Director. The Student Director is a full-time paid intern in the summer immediately following service as Assistant Director. During that summer, the Student Director develops a Leaders' Workshop and chapel program for the new academic year, and partners with the Director on current organizational development projects. The Program Manager and Student Staff Group Manager recruit, equip, and oversee paid and volunteer staff members who provide public relations, finance, information management, and logistics support to Collaobratory projects. The Manager also organizes training for individuals and teams pursuing off-campus work in cross-cultural settings. The Manager is a paid nonfaculty educator, and the Student Staff Group Manager is a part-time employee during the academic year.

Collaboratory structures for organizing work are groups, projects, and teams. A group is the organizational unit of the Collaboratory, containing personnel who sponsor and manage projects related by a common purpose or theme. Groups maintain a knowledge base in addition to the material and personnel resources to support present and future projects in the group's area. The two types of groups in the Collaboratory are:

1. A *staff group* that manages the operations side of the Collaboratory and provides services in public relations, finance, information management, and logistics to internal clients, which include other Collaboratory groups, projects, and teams.
2. *Application groups* house projects and personnel organized around a common theme, presently including energy, water, disability resources, communications, transportation, education, and microeconomic development. The clients of application groups are primarily external to the Collaboratory.

A project is a time-oriented activity in the Collaboratory with specific goals and tangible client deliverables, such as starting a business, implementing a solar power plant, or publishing a newsletter. Projects are the building blocks of Collaboratory programming and the means of organizing day-to-day activities. Participants work on teams to complete projects. A project's duration may be hours or years, but all projects have a beginning and an end. The five project types are:

1. *Staff* projects that provide internal support services that enable other Collaboratory groups and projects to serve external clients.
2. *Exploration* projects are undertaken to study and plan future research or application projects, or to develop a group's internal resources.
3. *Equipping* projects provide consultation or workshop services to a client.
4. *Research* projects are undertaken to develop the internal knowledge and expertise needed to support future application projects in new areas of engagement.
5. *Application* projects are applied research and development that generate specific deliverables for an external client within a specified time frame.

A team is all of the students and educators who collaborate to complete a project. For the duration of the project, the team members serve the team and measure success by the quality of the team's work and service to the client. There are three types of teams in the Collaboratory:

1. *Staff teams* are permanent structures of the staff group that manage projects in the areas of public relations, finance, information management, and logistics.
2. *Project teams* are nonpermanent structures within an application group that are formed to deliver specific project outcomes on time and then dissolve.
3. *Site teams* are nonpermanent structures within the Collaboratory that may draw people from multiple staff and project teams for travel to implement projects, research future projects, or develop personnel for future work.

The Collaboratory is organized around nine program strategies or best practices that have been identified, tested, and refined over a span of more than a decade of organizational development to enable us to live our identity with integrity and to realize our vision and mission. These are:

1. Our projects enable students to act on their Christian faith and value commitments through excellence in their academic and professional disciplines.
2. Our students share project leadership and administration responsibilities with educators and learn by seeing their teachers in action.
3. Our educators connect their scholarship directly to student learning by making hands-on professional contributions to projects as mentors and members of project teams.

4. Our project teams include students from multiple years of study to enable peer mentoring and sustain team-member and leader transitions.

5. We reflect on our service through intentional Christian discipleship that invites God to transform our lives as he teaches us and speaks to us through the people we serve.

6. We engage multiple academic disciplines and partner organizations with their various modes of thinking and analysis for comprehensive solutions.

7. We commit to projects that can span multiple generations of students when needed to attain tangible and sustainable results.

8. We publicly document best practices and processes for continuous organizational improvement and the equipping of each new generation of student leaders.

9. We connect our projects to faculty loads and student graduation requirements to facilitate participation and increase academic engagement.

The first of these strategic best practices is included in our vetting process for potential new projects in order to require that the work involved in the project can enable participants to act on Christian faith and value commitments through excellence in their academic and professional disciplines. The Collaboratory is not prescriptive in defining characteristics of projects that satisfy this requirement: there will always be more opportunities to respond to faith than we yet know. What is required in every project proposal is a statement from participants of why and how the proposed work satisfies the requirement. Project initiators who reflect on the integrity of the work in view of faith and value commitments remind themselves that not everything that can be done should be done, and that professionals have an obligation to the public to participate in making the distinction. Education must do more than make careerists, and a graduate must consider more than salary, location, and personal enjoyment when pursuing work opportunities.*

A second strategic best practice in the Collaboratory is shared student leadership. Leadership in the Collaboratory is understood to be influence

---

*A guest lecturer from Sandia Laboratories once gave a fascinating lecture in my graduate program on the propagation of compression waves through porous media but was silent on the motivation for this work. In the Q&A time following his lecture, he revealed his system was a detonator for a nuclear weapon. People will judge differently on whether or not this is work that ought to be pursued. What is unacceptable is to pursue the work as an instrumental problem solver, an opportunist and careerist who does anything interesting for pay, with no consideration for the character or effect of the work and whether it should be done. Collaboratory participants practice the difficult work of making such distinctions.

that enables others to be fruitful in doing good. This is leadership resourced first by humility, not power, for the benefit of others. Shared advisor–student leadership is a core programmatic and educational strategy in the Collaboratory for mentoring and building up new generations of servant-leaders. In the traditional classroom, educators serve as the final authority on the content and direction of a course. Advisors in the Collaboratory are also educators, but their role is that of a player–coach, developing student leaders while also making hands-on contributions in their field of expertise. A primary task of advisors is to work themselves out of a job by developing student leaders to assume responsibility, and by transferring authority and responsibility that is commensurate with students' maturity and ability. Early in the relationship, the advisor will generally be prescriptive in directing the leader's work to protect the long term interests of other students and clients from rookie errors, but the goal for an advisor is to transition from the role of boss to coach, and from coach to delegator, because in the Collaboratory obligations to clients are equal to but not more important than educational goals for students. For this reason, advisors will sometimes give student leaders the freedom to choose their own course and to learn from mistakes. Student leaders are also servant-leaders with obligations to learn from their advisors and peers, relying on them to assess areas for personal growth. Advisors and students together lead by nurturing a humility in team members that anticipates not just serving clients and communities, but also being taught and served by those clients and communities. The great work in every discipline is almost always the work of a student, one who is able to pay attention and learn from others.

Consider next the fifth strategic best practice of the Collaboratory. Just as projects must look ahead to generous service as a condition for Collaboratory sponsorship, and as educators and students share leadership that looks around to foster both project success and participant growth, so also are Collaboratory participants challenged to look back to recognize and reflect on what they have learned through their work and from the people they have served. Reflection on service through intentional advisor and peer mentoring relationships is the fifth strategic best practice. When the Collaboratory began, participation was so demanding that shared vision motivated nearly all of it. Today participation is motivated by many things. People still come because of the vision, but also for résumé building, making friends, or just for the novelty of the experience. Experiences have become the objects of consumption today, perhaps even more than material goods, and the Collaboratory experience has become popular on the Messiah College campus quite apart from the idea of sacrifice for something greater than oneself. Poet T. S. Eliot (1963) observed that it is possible to have the experience but miss the meaning. We do not care that people come to the Collaboratory as consumers, so long as they do not leave that way. Advisors who mentor and share leadership with students contribute to the work of helping students discover meaning in their experiences, as do a new member orientations, weekly chapels, annual retreats, prayer breakfasts, leader classes and workshops, and equipping curricula for site teams.

The third strategic best practice is educators who, in addition to advising and mentoring, connect their scholarship directly to student learning by making hands-on professional contributions to projects. Some worthwhile faculty scholarship projects do not find a home in the Collaboratory because they are too advanced to engage students. The best Collaboratory projects engage students, but also include elements that are professionally challenging to the faculty members and volunteer professionals who are our advisors. The advisors are player–coaches; they coach but also contribute professionally to the project such that the project could not succeed without them. Classroom problem solving is highly scripted for efficiency, but when the answers are known in advance, problem solving appears to students to be the linear application of one known and apparently obvious step after the other. That is wrong. In the Collaboratory, students get to see their professors and other mentors at work on real problems with unknown answers, and they find out that real problem solving is a highly nonlinear process of making educated guesses about what to do next, with much backtracking when an action taken proves to be a dead end. This practice provides faculty members with scholarship projects that keep them current and advance their tenure and promotion objectives while also leveraging faculty scholarship for the benefit of student learning.

The fourth strategic best practice in the Collaboratory is forming project teams that include students from multiple years of study to enable peer mentoring and sustain transitions between team leaders and members. This practice enables the seventh strategic best practice, commitment to projects that can span multiple generations of students to attain tangible and sustainable results, and frees us for the ninth, connecting projects to faculty loads and student graduation requirements. Faculty and student academic loads are the local currency at a college or university, so bridging Collaboratory work to the formal curriculum helps pay for the work. Some students who begin in the Collaboratory as volunteers receive course credit by this mechanism, whereas others who perhaps used their time outside the curriculum to engage in athletics, music, or other worthwhile endeavors are able to also partially engage Collaboratory educational programming through the curriculum. The Collaboratory, moreover, resources courses with authentic client-centered projects. Students are highly motivated to engage project work when they know their work has purpose beyond satisfying course requirements and have the opportunity to interact with those who will benefit.

Authenticity offers significant pedagogical benefits over project work that is cooked up for, and has little basis in reality outside of, the classroom. Student projects that reside entirely in academic coursework also suffer from a lack of continuity. It is nearly impossible to transition partially completed projects from one course-based team to an entirely new one, so course-based projects must spring up *ex nihilo* at the beginning of a semester or, in the case of two-semester capstone projects, a new academic year and be brought to completion in a matter of months if not weeks. Not many real projects of consequence are amenable to such brief timelines, especially when each project team is largely comprised of beginners.

The Collaboratory engages academic curricula, but relies on volunteerism and a few employees who work outside of the curriculum to shepherd projects between academic semesters and years. To sustain work within the Collaboratory between generations of students, upper-division students are charged with the task of peer mentoring their own replacements, and they are motivated to perform this task with excellence because, by the time they graduate, they care deeply about the success of their projects and know that the work will not be completed by the time of their graduation. Incoming students, rather than traveling through the college experience in the bubble of their incoming class, are immediately put into a mentoring relationship with upper-division students, and when they are juniors and seniors they are asked to give back to the incoming class. Each new generation of students inherits the work of the last and depends on the next to sustain it. All student participants in the Collaboratory are part of a team that includes those journeying with them as they shepherd the work, as well as all those who came before and those who will come later. Member identification with a team and the success of the team is essential. Individuals who identify with their team's success over their own are freed to perform the many often humble individual tasks that, in aggregate, accomplish something great.

Placement of the Collaboratory within the academic structure of the School of Science, Engineering and Health* but outside of any particular academic curriculum helps us to achieve the sixth strategic best practice, to engage multiple academic disciplines and clients and their various modes of thinking and analysis for comprehensive solutions to problems. Departmentalization and compartmentalization of academic knowledge enables scholars to go deep in Boyer's scholarship of discovery. To the extent that the departments have become political domains that pursue rights and resources

---

*The Collaboratory is a department in the School of Science, Engineering, and Health. The Director of the Collaboratory is a faculty member who reports to the School Dean and serves with the chairpersons of academic departments on the Dean's leadership team for the School.

for the department, reductionist organizing of the academy has proven less amenable to this scholarship of integration and application because those activities are a kind of mutual composing that must necessarily cross disciplinary lines. Service, moreover, is understood to contribute to affective and behavioral education, and is, therefore, often organized in the academy under student affairs or some other nonacademic structure, creating greater distance between a life of service and the life of the mind than exists between the academic disciplines. For too many, the gifts and abilities we spend years developing through formal education and hone through daily professional practice are what we do to make money, whereas service is volunteerism unrelated to our professions that sometimes even takes paying work away from those we set out to help. The Collaboratory connects service to academic and professional activity, and gathers voices and expertise from all relevant academic disciplines around a need. We help people in the academy talk to each other across disciplinary boundaries, and give students a problem-solving experience like what they will encounter outside the academy. This helps us move toward deep understanding and comprehensive problem solving.

Finally, the eighth strategic best practice of the Collaboratory is public documentation and real-time updating of our internal practices and processes. The constant departure of graduates is our product, but it is also a tremendous challenge. We must have world-class documentation of internal practices and processes to enable the Collaboratory to survive and thrive each year through the loss of the twenty-five percent of our members with the most knowledge and experience. We cannot tolerate a breaking-in period of a year or more for new members because turnover rates are too high. A wiki* has thus become an essential tool for documenting practices and processes. A wiki is a Web page that any member with an account may contribute to at any time, so that documentation may be developed asynchronously by as many people as want to contribute. Positions, like the Student Director, Group Leaders, and Project Team Leaders, have e-mail accounts attached to their positions rather than to the persons occupying the positions, and each e-mail address is also attached to a wiki membership. Anyone who finds an error or recognizes the need for an update or improvement may edit any wiki page, but pages are watched by those with primary ownership over their content so that an e-mail notification of edits is sent to the primary owner. The wiki saves the current and all previous versions of every page indefinitely so that a page may be rolled back to a previous version should an incorrect edit be made. The editing rights of persons who edit irresponsibly or vandalize the wiki may be immediately revoked. In addition to document-

*www.thecollaboratoryonline.org/wiki

ing processes for joining the Collaboratory, becoming a leader, and initiating a project, the wiki includes a calendar of recurring tasks for each student leadership position to help new leaders know, immediately and throughout the year, the nature of their responsibilities. The wiki also includes event-planning guides to direct planning for recurring Collaboratory events such as the chapel program and leaders' workshop.

4.3.2 Ethos

The Collaboratory's approach to service is key to understanding the organization's work. We understand service to be something that is mutually composed by all participants, both members and clients, acknowledging that all have something to share and that everyone receives. Too often, service has been viewed as something that those with knowledge and material wealth do for those without those resources. Such thinking can and has quickly become paternalistic because those who think they hold all the resources also tend to believe that they know best what to do with them and even that it is their responsibility to direct the use of their "gift." Those enslaved to poverty, oppression, or other injustice then soon find themselves in further bondage to the good will of their benefactors. We seek to avoid creating such mutually damaging dependencies in the Collaboratory.

Mentoring and equipping in the Collaboratory teaches participants, instead, that the Collaboratory vision statement looks both outward and inward. When our Christian community thinks about "increasing hope and transforming lives," we have in view the hope and transforming power of the Gospel, good news for the bodily and spiritual sufferings of people in every community and culture and for all of creation. Motivated by the desire to live in obedience to Jesus, many have made sacrifices to serve others through the Collaboratory. But we are deeply aware that each one of us who sets out to serve is also on a journey toward hope and transformation. Those of us who possess much knowledge and material wealth often live with different kinds of poverty, perhaps the poverty of faith, or the poverty of self-centeredness that comes from fear that our wealth will not be enough to keep us safe, or the poverty of loneliness experienced by many living in our western culture of extreme individualism. We live with the burden of stewarding knowledge and material wealth for a good greater than the satisfaction of our own wants and fears.

Our community believes that God made all human beings in his image, and that God is at work in every culture, community, and person long before any relationship is forged with Christians in the Collaboratory. We also recognize that it is possible to set out for good and to do harm instead. Because our desire is to do more good than harm, Collaboratory work always begins in humility and with anticipation that before we do anything we will work hard to gain understanding and build trust relationships, to see all that is good and valuable that must be protected from damage by our attempts to serve. Our service is decidedly not a linear transferal of goods or knowledge from those who have to those who do not; it is a mutual sharing of material, knowledge, faith, and cultural resources that enables us together to accomplishing something for one another that neither of us could do on our own. For us, true service is almost always done with someone, and never to them. It does not demand gratitude, but it is a mutual sharing nonetheless. We challenge ourselves both to share sacrificially out of what we have and to embrace the humility needed to receive from others. In receiving the sacrifices born from the faith, hope, and love of others, we give perhaps our most precious gift, the satisfaction experienced by others that they are living lives of significance for having made a positive difference in our lives. What begins and very much feels like a sacrifice of generosity in the Collaboratory is often experienced as among the most rewarding experiences of our lives.

4.3.3 Funding

Although the material costs of project work and a majority of personnel costs of the Collaboratory are externally funded,* cost support from the operating budget of Messiah College is also significant. The cost of a half-time Director, who is also a faculty member with a half-time teaching load, is almost entirely† covered out of the operating budget of the College. A part-time‡ administrative assistant to the Program Manager is also internally funded. The Collaboratory is included in the Information Technology budget of the College, through which the large majority of our computing, audio–visual, and communications technology costs are paid. Space, utility, and liability insurance costs are also paid for through the College operating budget without charge-back to the Collaboratory. Collaboratory infrastructure and processes are also supported at no cost to its external funds budget by many offices of the College. These include the Dean of the School of Sci-

---

*Exceptions sometimes occur when the Collaboratory "subcontracts" a portion of a larger Collaboratory project to students working on a class project, thereby resourcing the course with an authentic project and a client outside of the classroom. In such cases, departmental money allocated from the College operating budget to cover course project costs are sometimes expended to the benefit of Collaboratory projects.

†Revenue from a small Collaboratory endowment funds a little more than 10% of the Director's half-time compensation. The endowment was capitalized using funds from a major gift to the College in support of the Collaboratory.

‡15 hours per week during the academic year and 4 hours per week over the summer.

ence, Engineering, and Health for strategic planning; Development for fundraising and grant writing; Business for account and payroll management; Human Resources for hiring and supporting personnel; Publications for newsletters and other print media; Public Relations for press releases and event organizing; and Information Technology for support of computational, communication, and audio–visual technology. Finally, and perhaps most significantly, a majority of the time educators give to advising and scholarship work in the Collaboratory is paid for through the operating budget of the College because their activities in the Collaboratory are also satisfying their responsibilities in the areas of teaching, scholarship, and institutional service.

The balance of Collaboratory costs are externally funded. These include the material costs of projects, the cost of travel for project research and implementation, the cost of personnel, the material costs of events to train members and develop leaders, and the material costs of marketing. Personnel costs include the full-time Program Manager, a summer internship for the rising Student Director, and work-study wages during the academic year for the Student Director, Assistant Student Director, Student Staff Group Leader, and Assistant to the Program Manager. Material costs for member equipping and leadership training include supplies, printing, food, sometimes lodging for the chapel program, a fall members' retreat, prayer breakfasts, an annual class for new leaders, and an annual week-long workshop for project planning. Material costs of marketing include printing of newsletters and other literature, Web hosting, postage, and hospitality to prospective members, clients, and investors.

Sources of external funding have included individual investors, churches, private foundations, government-funded grants, clients, and gifts-in-kind. Four categories of individual investors support the Collaboratory. The travel costs of students and some advisors for project research and implementation are often supported by friends and family who give to the Collaboratory while someone they know is participating. A second category of individual investor is those who first give to the Collaboratory because they know a participant and continue to give, even after that participant has moved on, because the investor likes our work. A third category of individual investor is persons who have made a major gift, often one-time but sometimes recurring, to fund operations costs or capitalize endowment. The fourth and final category of individual investor is future giving to the Collaboratory through estate planning.

In addition to gifts from individuals, significant project funding has come through private and government grants and from clients. Although clients have also funded research and travel costs, a common arrangement has been for the Collaboratory to fund research and travel and the client to fund capital costs associated with implementation.* Corporate friends of the Collaboratory have also made important gift-in-kind investments, particularly when the project deliverables fall within the geographic region where the business operates.[†] Churches also support the Collaboratory, usually when members of their congregations are doing service through the Collaboratory. One congregation supports the Collaboratory through its annual budget. In addition to funds given for the work of the Collaboratory as a whole, the Collaboratory receives funds given in support of, and therefore restricted in use to, specific project activities. All project budgets, however they are funded, include a 7% indirect charge to direct funds back into the unrestricted reserve assets of the Collaboratory. These unrestricted assets pay for the support services of the Staff Group to projects, investment in new project initiatives, and development of new Collaboratory organizational or equipment infrastructure.

Finally, some unrestricted money assets of the Collaboratory have been used to capitalize a small endowment that presently generates a revenue stream that covers approximately 10% of the compensation cost of the half-time Director and, at this writing, approximately 3% of operating expenses. Endowment growth is a strategy of the Collaboratory for long-term fiscal sustainability.

4.4   IMPLEMENTATION

Although the Collaboratory at Messiah College is still under development, the organization's model for service learning and scholarship has features sufficiently well-formed and proven to have attracted the attention of others with similar goals. As project opportunities have outpaced growth in capacity, participants in the Collaboratory at Messiah College have likewise recognized the opportunity to expand their mission success through partnership with other Collaboratories housed elsewhere. Particulars in design and operation will inevitably depend on the mission, culture, and resources of the host institution. A review of the origins, status, and direction of the Collaboratory at Messiah College may be helpful to those seeking to implement features of the Collaboratory elsewhere and to those shepherding continued development of the Collaboratory at Messiah College.

---

*Collaboratory investors might, for example, fund the design and travel costs of implementing a solar power plant, while the development staff of the client organization raises funds for the capital costs of system hardware.

[†]Local businesses, for example, provided very generous architectural design and construction support for an on-campus solar power installation that showcases a green technology and is a resource for training new generations of students to do solar design work.

4.4.1 Origins

The Collaboratory began with the scholarship agendas of individual faculty members in the Department of Engineering at Messiah College. Later, the project teams of those faculty sponsors began to adopt common administrative processes, project support structures, and quality standards. The purpose of organizing existing project activities was to increase quality assurance to clients and visibility to prospective volunteers and funding partners, and to provide more shared support services for less money to each project. These grass-roots rather than top-down origins of the Collaboratory have been both an asset and a limitation to organizational development. No one who worked on the first Collaboratory projects thought they were beginning a research center or an organization of any kind, and no institutional funding was sought. Requests to organize and for budget came after the first projects had produced results of value to the College, including service-oriented scholarship opportunities attractive to students, positive public visibility, and new external funding. Faculty sponsors volunteered their time in that they received no release from their teaching load or compensation for time worked in the summer. Term-tenure and promotion processes at the College did, however, reward faculty members by recognizing various contributions to teaching, scholarship, and institutional service. The first Collaboratory activities, therefore, required permission and resources that could be readily granted at the Departmental level without committing other institutional resources. Although this made it easy for willing volunteers to gain permission to begin their work, the Collaboratory eventually succeeded to the point of requiring internal policy and procedural accommodations, and, eventually, resources that the College had not committed in advance.

When Collaboratory cofounders Dr. Donald Pratt and Dr. David Vader were offered the opportunity to join the Department of Engineering at Messiah College in August of 1993 they were attracted by the Department's commitment to the idea that shared Christian faith among the faculty should inform the Department's teaching and scholarship program. The founder's first projects, though important to beginning the Collaboratory, were motivated by the example of colleagues also seeking to live out their faith commitments. Dr. James Scroggin, founding Chairperson of the Department of Engineering, and colleague Professor Carl Erikson, who served as the third Chairperson of the Department, also encouraged and gave much of their time and talent to support the formation and early development of the Collaboratory.

In December 1993, Vader began networking with Christian mission and international relief and development organizations in search of a project that would engage him and his students professionally and serve a humanitarian cause in a community that lacked the resources to attract engineering services through the market mechanism. At that time, the organization Serving In Mission (SIM) was also seeking to build stronger relationships with Christian colleges and universities. Mr. Mark Bruner of SIM visited Messiah College to explore partnership opportunities, and at his invitation Drs. Underwood and Whitmoyer joined Vader in visiting SIM in Charlotte, NC to continue the conversation. SIM leadership proposed that their work in West Africa was most likely to yield a project opportunity and recommended that Messiah College personnel visit SIM offices in West Africa to gain understanding, build relationships, and explore project opportunities. Messiah College personnel weighed concerns about their lack of ability to communicate in languages common to the region and travel cost and time relative to closer venues. In the end, they determined to trust the recommendation of SIM, their potential client. In January 1996, Bruner led a team from the College that visited SIM work in Niger, Côte d'Ivoire, Benin, Liberia, and Burkina Faso. Joining Vader on the Messiah College team were Dr. John Eby, Professor of Sociology and Director of Service Learning; Ms. Cindy Blount, Director of Student Outreach; and two engineering students, Mr. Sam Blanchard and Mr. Ben Claggett. The support of Dr. Eby and of Dr. Dorothy Gish, Academic Dean, was instrumental in the success of this exploratory trip. The Messiah College team members either self-funded or raised funds to pay for travel by inviting friends and family to invest in their vision for service in response to Christian faith.

Following this, SIM Burkina Faso invited the Department of Engineering to develop a solar power plant for a medical clinic in the rural village of Mahadaga. The Mahadaga solar project was chosen from among other options precisely because the technical requirements were interesting but straightforward. Project management, working on teams, funding, system testing, and installation were additional challenges that students faced infrequently in the classroom. The need, moreover, was compelling. The clinic staff provided basic health care in the region and specialized in obstetric care. Over 100 births that might have been life threatening to mother or child took place at the clinic every month. Infant mortality in the region was less than 1%, whereas the national average was 12%. For many years a diesel generator had been used to provide electric lighting between the 6:00 and 9:00 PM. Deliveries and minor surgeries after 9:00 PM were conducted with the assistance of flashlights. Fuel was expensive and shortages common. This and the increasing cost and frequency of repairs motivated the clinic staff to seek alternatives to the generator. Senior engineering students Mr. Greg Holmes and Mr. David Owen led the design effort in the 1996–1997 academic year, with administrative support from sophomore Mr. Ben Claggett and advisor support from Engineering staff members Vader and Mr. John Meyer. SIM USA raised capital funding to purchase solar panels and other equipment. A team of students, recent graduate and design team member Owen, and two advisors again used personal mailing lists to raise money for travel to install the system in January 1998. More than 20 students participated in the design and implementation work.

Student team members Claggett and Mr. Matt Walsh learned of additional project opportunities in engineering and many other disciplines. With Vader, they dreamed of organizing the people and resources needed to engage these projects, while also processing difficult but instructive lessons learned from the first project. The team's failure to become sufficiently motivated early in their work culminated in delays in the arrival of solar panels and batteries in Mahadaga. Having little time to negotiate with customs officials, SIM eventually had to pay half the value of the panels in import tax. Inadequate testing resulted in the lack of a relay switch for the low-voltage disconnect. The part was sent later, but battery damage was suspected. The team also failed to anticipate or provide adequate protection against lightning strikes. Meyer spent the next several years responding to service calls from SIM, until Walsh and three other Collaboratory alumni moved to Mahadaga to work full time in the community and assumed responsibility for the system. Clearly, future projects would require better project management, teamwork, and system testing. As new project opportunities were considered, so were the importance of nurturing professionalism and of limiting the scope of project activities to fit with the advisor, student, and funding resources at hand. The success of the first solar project led to projects in low-cost pump design and the design of personal mobility devices for persons living with disability. There were also additional solar design projects for the newly formed *Handicapés en Avant*, a center for the advancement of persons living with disability in Mahadaga, and for a hospital in Zimbabwe. To accomplish quality objectives and provide a single point of contact to the projects for the Development, Business, and Academic offices at Messiah College, Vader worked with student leaders and advisors to organize the projects under a common project management and support structure they named *Dokimoi Ergatai** (DE).

The Genesis Solar Racing project begun in 1993 by Pratt also proved instrumental to forming the Collaboratory. Genesis was formed out of a desire to develop earth-friendly transportation technologies while also equipping engineering graduates of Messiah College for excellence in professional practice. The team competed in its first Sunrayce,[†] a national intercollegiate solar car competition, in 1995. Many who show up with cars to race are unable to pass the inspection process. The Messiah College car passed inspec-

---

*Approved Workers.
[†]Sunrayce is now known as the American Solar Challenge.

tion and finished 22nd out of 38 challengers in a race from Indianapolis, IN to Golden, CO. The team also received the Missouri Mule Award for teamwork and determination and the race's Technical Innovation award for their solar array design. The 1997 team also raced from Indiana to Colorado and finished 12th in a field of 36 challengers, beating all other entries from Pennsylvania including Drexel University and the University of Pennsylvania. The 1997 car earned the Renaissance Innovation Award given for a motor optimization system that was deemed the most innovative technical achievement from among all entries. Genesis returned to competition in Sunrayce 1999 with a new vehicle sponsored exclusively by the Harsco Corporation. Genesis placed seventh out of 29 competitors in a race from Washington, DC to Orlando, FL. The Genesis team's success brought regional and then national media attention to Messiah College, and helped the project enjoy strong campus-wide support, including critical support from senior administrators of the College.

By 1997, Vader was serving as Chairperson of the Department of Engineering. Twice he and Pratt approached the Provost of Messiah College, Dr. Donald Kraybill, to propose the formation of a center to house Genesis, the DE projects, and other service scholarship activities emerging at that time. The goals of the center would be to uphold quality, provide administrative support to project teams, and promote the work of the center to prospective students, clients, and investors. Provost Kraybill thought the idea had merit but was competing with too many high-profile initiatives at the College at that time to gain approval. In 1999, following the success of Genesis that year, Harsco shared their willingness to consider repeat sponsorship of Genesis in 2001. Pratt thought Harsco might be interested in the other projects and saw an opportunity to share the vision for a center. In the fall of 1999, Pratt and Vader took Pratt's idea to Provost Kraybill who affirmed a plan to take an alternative proposal to Harsco and proposed that we call the center a Collaboratory. In 2000, Harsco made a generous lead grant to the College to begin the Collaboratory with Pratt serving as Director. Those funds enabled the Genesis team to build their 2001 car for the American Solar Challenge, a 2300 mile race along historic Route 66 from Chicago to southern California. The team finished 13th in a field of 30 competitors, and again was awarded the top honor for technical innovation of any car in the race, the Technical Innovation Award, for their solar array and battery pack design. The balance of the funds given by Harsco was used to advance DE and other founding projects of the Collaboratory, and as they matured those projects began to produce results that attracted new clients and additional funding.

For several years, the Collaboratory remained an informal confederation of faculty-sponsored projects and their student teams, plus the DE organization comprised of an administrative staff group and several application groups. The DE application groups maintained a knowledge base in their area and sponsored teams to complete projects with external partners. A staff group set quality standards, provided administrative support to project teams, and promoted DE to prospective students, clients, and investors. DE thus developed support structures and services needed throughout the Collaboratory. In 2002 Dr. Ray Norman began service as Dean of the newly formed School of Mathematics, Engineering, and Business (MEB). Norman brought to the School a vision for service in the MEB disciplines and experience with organizations such as World Vision and the African Development Bank. In his first semester, he formed a Collaboratory Expansion Task Force comprised of himself, his department chairs, and the Director of the Collaboratory. The task force was to develop organizational and management structure, material resources, and off-campus contacts to serve the entire MEB School. A major private gift received at this time enabled the expansion and began an endowment. New partnerships emerged with organizations such as World Vision, Hope International, the Brethren in Christ Church in Zambia, and Cure International; and there were new projects in areas that included database development, internal financial auditing and controls, math literacy for children in the developing world, and water access for persons with disabilities. In 2004 Dr. Kim Phipps, Provost and then Interim President* of Messiah College, authorized a half-time position for Director of the Collaboratory with quarter-time administrative assistant support. Vader began service as Director in August of 2004. In 2006, he asked DE members to merge their structure and support services into the Collaboratory, and to extend their identity and ethos as approved workers throughout the larger organization. This loss of identify was a very difficult sacrifice for committed DE members, but the transition brought DE back to its founders' vision of connecting scholarship and learning to service in many disciplines. Although DE is no longer an organization, the ideal of stewarding the resources of our academic disciplines and professions for the good of others continues as a motivating principle throughout the Collaboratory and a goal of our members. Dokimoi Ergatai is now the name of the Collaboratory newsletter.

By the mid-2000s, the Collaboratory was pursuing a strategy of curriculum integration to connect noncredit-bearing scholarship and service within the Collaboratory to the credit-bearing academic programs of the College. In 2006, the Collaboratory received a three-year grant from the W. M. Keck

*Dr. Kim Phipps was appointed President of Messiah College in December of 2004. She was followed by Dr. Randy Basinger in the role of Provost. The support of Drs. Phipps and Basinger has been instrumental to the development of Collaboratory programming and sustainability.

Foundation to integrate Collaboratory programming into academic curricula in the MEB School. One goal was for the Collaboratory to resource courses that have a project component with an authentic project and a client, enabling students to experience the motivation of working for results that would matter and could be implemented outside the classroom. Real projects resourced by volunteers that could span multiple generations of students were key to providing this service to courses. Another goal was to provide Collaboratory workers, both students and advisors, already committed to working in the Collaboratory with an opportunity to earn academic course credit or faculty-load credit for part of their work. To provide marketing, finance, IT, and logistical support to an increased amount of project activity, the grant funded a Program Manager position at 100% in the first year of the grant and less in subsequent years as the Collaboratory developed new sources of revenue to fund the position. For a year prior to this, Collaboratory graduate and former student leader Walsh served as a part-time Program Manager. Recent graduate and former student leader Ms. Lindsay Reilly served as Interim Program Manager for the first months of the grant. Ms. Deborah Tepley, the first full-time Program Manager, was instrumental in developing the position and growing the project support infrastructure of the Collaboratory.

The centerpiece of the Keck-funded expansion of Collaboratory programming into the academic curriculum was an Integrated Projects Curriculum (IPC) designed to provide every graduate of the Bachelor of Science in Engineering program with an opportunity to work on a Collaboratory project as a requirement for graduation. The IPC comprises three basic elements. The first element is two one-credit seminar courses to orient students to prevailing cultural assumptions about engineering and technology, explore how culture contextualizes technology, understand how client communities might think differently and emphasize different cultural values than we do, and examine where Christian faith commitments intersect and conflict with these realities. This seminar conversation runs parallel to project engagement, both informing the projects and drawing from them for reflection. It ends by providing students with an opportunity to assess their own life commitments and by encouraging them to engage those commitments in their life's work. A second IPC element is a one-credit Group Orientation (GO) course that orients students to the culture and history of the project teams they will join and includes project-specific technical content. GO also prepares students to work on teams, define project goals, and manage projects. Finally, the third IPC element is a sequence of two one-credit and two two-credit project courses wherein students participate in project work. Students may be admitted to GO as early as their second semester, particularly if they have already volunteered in the Collaboratory. This would permit them to take the first project courses in their sophomore year. The two-credit project courses must be taken sequentially in the senior year. Students may opt to continue project work in semesters when they are not in enrolled in the IPC by volunteering or by taking a practicum course.

The brand value of the Collaboratory has continued to increase, attracting new participants, clients, and investors. As many as 150 participants volunteer their time annually, including students, faculty and other educators, alumni, and other professionals. Additional students and faculty engage through academic curricula. In 2010, a restructuring of the academic schools that make up Messiah College placed the Collaboratory in the School of Science, Engineering, and Health, creating new opportunities to engage with students and educators in the health and science disciplines. The Collaboratory continues to engage Management and Business majors and Education majors in the School of Business, Education, and Social Science, and is exploring new opportunities to connect with students and faculty members in the Social Sciences.

4.4.2 Status

Today, the Collaboratory is succeeding even as it is continuously developing and refining structures and processes to achieve mission success. Three current organizational goals of the Collaboratory are to deliver more project results on time, to increase fiscal sustainability, and to be more effective in serving students and faculty members who engage the Collaboratory through a course.

The first organizational goal at this time is more project results on time. Increasing advisor resources is one strategy toward accomplishing this goal. In a healthy Collaboratory, people, projects and money resources will be in equilibrium. As recognition and trust in the Collaboratory brand has increased so have all of these resources, but growth in project opportunities has outpaced people resources. It is tempting to think that with enough money we could hire people to do the work, but that approach would fundamentally alter the mission and ethos of the Collaboratory. Among the people working in the Collaboratory there is a greater shortage of advisors than students in that more students could participate if we had more advising capacity. If student and advisor resources were in balance, we would simply take advantage of a surplus of projects to choose the best possible projects for the organization.

Several factors limit the engagement of faculty members as advisors. The value proposition of the Collaboratory to faculty members is their time given to activities in return for two things: help fulfilling teaching, scholarship, and institutional service requirements for term tenure and promotion; and an opportunity to do voluntary service using the same gifts and abilities they have been privileged to develop through years of access to higher education and professional practice. There are much easier ways to get promoted, however, and some who give their time generously in church and elsewhere in voluntary work unrelated to their profession object to giving away the thing they do to earn money. There is little the Collaboratory can do about the second difficulty, but it can and must find a way to enable people who want to advise to be able to give what they are able. Right now, the gap between not advising and giving the minimum amount of time needed to get started is too great.

Current tactics for achieving a manageable advisor workload are increasing the number of advisors by going to new sources, and dividing the tasks now undertaken by one advisor into multiple responsibilities that could be shared by several advisors. In addition to faculty advisors, the Collaboratory has secured funding that presently supports three nonfaculty educators who manage the day-to-day operations of projects and frees faculty members to focus their time on coaching students and making direct project contributions in their area of their expertise. Two of these positions, however, are grant funded. Not all worthwhile projects can secure such funding. A second source of additional advisor resources has been volunteer professionals from our community, many of them alumni of the Collaboratory. Online collaboration tools are assisting this effort. Finally, a graduate program in international development is under consideration. This program would be resourced by the Collaboratory with research projects and an internship experience, and graduate students would help guide the work of undergraduates. Most current advisors do three things in partnership with their student leader: they manage the project, they contribute from their area of academic and professional expertise to the project, and they mentor students. Some also lead site teams for field work, and a few write grants, articles, or other project-related documentation. A second tactic for increasing advisor resources, therefore, is to form advising teams wherein several people share these responsibilities according to their strengths and interests.

Additional strategies for getting more project results on time are increasing the effectiveness of our teams and helping individuals and teams to set and track performance goals. The idea that people serve teams and teams serve clients has been fundamental to the success of the Collaboratory from its inception. When the Collaboratory comprised twenty or thirty people and was not as well-resourced or organized, it was harder to work in the Collaboratory and few stuck around unless they identified strongly with other people on their team. Now it is easier for students to get involved for many reasons other than the team. Whether students come to the Collaboratory to hang out with friends, gain professional experience, or build their resume does not matter so long as they connect with their team. The cause and client one sets out to serve, even when motivated by faith, can seem distant when homework and exams pile up, but most of us find ways to not disappoint our closest friends no matter how busy we are. So the Collaboratory is working on team building, which at a minimum includes shared high expectations for project success, having fun together, and a graceful way for noncontributors to exit. The Information Management team of the Collaboratory has also developed a Member Achievement Portfolio (MAP) software application that tracks things like member participation and on-time job completion, and generates performance metrics based on this data. Individuals and teams in the Collaboratory will use MAP to establish performance goals and track success. MAP will also generate a cumulative report of a member's activity to help graduates build their resumes with information like volunteer hours worked, workshops completed, and positions held.

The second organizational goal of the Collaboratory is fiscal sustainability. Two strategies toward this goal have already been mentioned: a 7% indirect charge against all new funds to partially offset the cost of support services, and an endowment to reduce the dependence of support services on external funding. Some projects can leverage knowledge and infrastructure resources of the College and academic departments and generate results with very little cash, but there are always indirect costs for things like recruiting and equipping members. With an endowment, the Collaboratory could readily survive downturns in cash investments by continuing internal support to projects. A third strategy for fiscal sustainability has been the design of a system to attach all revenue and expenses to a specific activity in the Collaboratory. When the Collaboratory was one, two, or even three projects, the Director could keep all money resources in one budget account and manage them equitably. As the number of projects grew, this became impossible, and to further complicate matters it soon became important to distinguish between funds attached to a specific group or project and funds not so attached. These unrestricted assets are the funds available to the Director to pay for the Program Manager and internal support services provided by the Staff Group, to invest in existing or new projects, or to add to the endowment. The Finance Team worked with an Accounting faculty member to develop processes for tracking and assigning all revenue and expenses and we hired a part-time accountant to support execution. A fourth strategy for fiscal sustainability has been the creation of a financial-health dashboard that communicates metrics to the Director such as months of cash in reserve, which is the number of months the Collaboratory would be able to continue business as usual if no new funding were received. The financial-health dashboard will enable the leadership team to be responsive to shifts in revenue and expenses as they steward resources to maximize mission success.

The third organizational goal of the Collaboratory is to be more effective in serving students and faculty members who engage the Collaboratory through a course. The Collaboratory is pursuing two strategies to accomplish this goal. The first is assisting the previously mentioned IPC program to develop effective assessment strategies. The IPC course sequence in the Department of Engineering is an alternative to traditional capstone courses. IPC leverages volunteerism in the Collaboratory to sustain projects between academic years, thereby enabling capstone projects of greater depth and complexity in a client-centered environment because they need not be completed within a semester or academic year. We hope this model can be adopted by other departments, but student performance in the IPC has unexpectedly diminished since Engineering transitioned from a standalone capstone course. Although they rarely succeeded in completing a project, students pushed hard in the old capstone course because their assignment was to give a public presentation on a completed project on a specific date. They still give a public presentation, but now inherit last year's results and pass whatever they get done to next year's students. What is passed on is sometimes not enough. Grade inflation, which makes it possible for students to advance with minimal project productivity, is rampant in many course projects because a project cannot be assessed like an essay or exam and many faculty members lack the tools and experience to hold students accountable for results. We tolerate this too often when the project is a small part of a course grade, but in IPC, the project is the basis for the entire course grade. The Collaboratory is partnering with the Department of Engineering to research and propose best assessment practices for student project work in the IPC.

A second strategy for accomplishing the goal of greater effectiveness in serving those who engage the Collaboratory through a course is to partner with faculty members who have course-contained projects and to design workable processes for the Collaboratory to support them. A professor in Computer and Information Science has developed world-class service-learning curricula in several courses but would like to facilitate better transitions between classes of students to succeed with bigger and longer-term projects. Bridging the academic calendar to sustain long-term projects is what the Collaboratory does, but our model assumes projects that reside with volunteers in the Collaboratory and subcontracts work to resource courses with projects. Our support structures are not optimized for sustaining projects that reside first within a course. The Director of the Collaboratory is partnering with this colleague to develop strategies for supporting course-based projects, again in anticipation that this model will be attractive to other faculty members.

Finally, a conversation just now emerging in the Collaboratory is about the Collaboratory's future relationship to Messiah College. The Collaboratory is and has always been a department under an academic dean of Messiah College. The mission, identity, and people of the College, moreover, have proven essential to beginning and growing the Collaboratory. Even so, success has also challenged both the College and the Collaboratory. The needs of the Collaboratory have often clashed with necessary institutional practices and policies that were not designed to account for the existence of anything like the Collaboratory. As the Collaboratory has begun to attract larger grants, moreover, there has been concern expressed by faculty members responsible to deliver on those grants that College purchasing and student wage practices may be an impediment to their satisfying obligations to funding entities. There is a desire that grant-funded purchases not be driven by college policies on price and preferred vendors but by what is best for the requirements of the grant in the opinion of the research team and client. Past reviews and denials of purchase requests have caused delays that some faculty members have deemed unacceptable in a grant setting since their accountability for grant funding is ultimately to the grant-making agency. There has also been concern that student wages not be artificially constrained by a work-study rate schedule when competing to hire summer interns in disciplines that command much higher salaries in the marketplace. Some centers that have originated within a college or university have become an independent 501c3 that continues to partner with the parent institution. While this would provide greater freedom for the Collaboratory to optimize its internal policies, a significant increase in revenue would be required to replace the substantial support provided to the Collaboratory, often by those same departments that sometimes impose difficult policies. Although space is marginal for the work of the Collaboratory, it is paid for by the College, as are utilities, insurance, and compensation for the Director and Administrative Assistant. This is a challenging but important current discussion.

4.5   RESULTS

The two products of the Collaboratory are tangible project outcomes delivered to clients and graduates who practice their professions with excellence and generosity. Any number of Collaboratory projects could justify an article on their work and outcomes. More such articles can and should be written. To date, the Collaboratory has focused on dissemination through implementation, such as delivery of a technology, creation of a community savings association, or delivery of a workshop. This section will share briefly a sampling of project and student outcomes sufficient to help readers understand the nature and scope of the work of the Collaboratory.

For more than a decade, the Collaboratory has partnered with *Handicapés en Avant*, a ministry of SIM that is run for and by persons living with disability in Burkina Faso, West Africa. The ministry reaches one of the most marginalized populations in one of the world's poorest countries. *Handicapés en Avant* helps all people living with disability, physical or cognitive. Services include physical rehabilitation, assistive technologies, education, and employment assistance. The project also works with family members and the public to raise awareness about the potential and the needs of persons living with disability. The Collaboratory first partnered with *Handicapés en Avant* to provide solar electric power and water pumping for the center. A second project has been the development of personal transportation technologies. These low-cost, adult-sized, hand- and electric-powered, three-wheeled vehicles developed by the Collaboratory provide freedom and empowerment for persons living with physical disability. They provide mobility to farm, care for family, and commute to school or work over paths and dirt roads unnavigable in a wheelchair. A third-generation prototype developed with feedback from clients is in testing. The goal is a low-cost design that can be locally fabricated, maintained, and improved. A third project, partially funded by Joni and Friends, has been the research and development of instructional curricula and teacher-training resources to promote abstract thinking skills among children living with disability. Finally, building on our experience in partnering with persons living with disability in Burkina Faso, the Collaboratory secured funding from the Conrad Hilton Foundation to partner with World Vision, Water Aid, and Handicaps International to study and improve access to water and sanitation among people living with disability in Mali. A second phase of this work was recently funded through World Vision, with the Collaboratory acting as a partner, to extend the work into the West African region. The Collaboratory has partnered with Joni and Friends to accomplish the Water and Disability project work and to advance disability awareness and support in the Messiah College community.

The Collaboratory has engaged in technology projects in the areas of water, communication, energy, and transportation. An ozone-based water disinfection system was designed by a team in the Water Group in partnership with CURE International and has supplied water to a school and community for several years in Honduras. Teachers and students at the school have packaged water to sell for money to maintain the water treatment system and fund school projects. Low-cost PVC pumps have been developed and tested in Burkina Faso. A current water project aims to provide pumps and wells to individual households in Burkina Faso to enable dry-season gardening and animal husbandry businesses. Wireless Enabled Remote Co-Presence (WERCware) is a project of the Communications Group. WERCware connects one or more persons with a cognitive disability to a remote coach who can see and hear the same as their clients and help them to perform in a school, the workplace, and other settings. In addition to the many solar electric design projects completed worldwide, the Energy Group has developed small-scale bio-diesel processing technology. They are currently partnering with the Office of Sustainability at Messiah College to grow sunflowers on College land, press the sunflowers for oil, use the oil in cooking at the college, and convert the waste cooking oil to bio-diesel for use in College-owned equipment. They are also exploring opportunities with several Collaboratory clients to use small-scale bio-diesel production from nonedible feedstock to create jobs in disadvantaged communities. The Genesis Solar Racing team established the Transportation Group of the Collaboratory and is developing a two-seat Light Sport Aircraft (LSA). An LSA can develop lifting capacity and air speed suitable for moving people and material in and out of difficult locations to service disaster relief and community development needs and could also serve as an air ambulance. A goal of the project is to provide these services at a fraction of the cost of aircraft used for these tasks today. The design also includes folding wings and enables short distance take-offs and landings so the aircraft can be transported in a trailer by road and take off and land from a field.

From the Department of Management and Business, a business professional and alumnus of Messiah College advises students who have partnered with the Brethren in Christ Church Zambia (BICCZ) to create jobs and promote economic welfare among AIDS orphans and survivors in the BICCZ Simaubi Economic Development Zone. Collaboratory workers first partnered with a professor of art and her students to teach local people how to make paper and to help launch a papermaking business. They then developed protocols for helping local church leaders start community savings associations and have facilitated the start of several such associations. Savers have received very attractive rates of return on the money they placed on account, and the associations have made loans to individuals who used the money to increase family income, expand businesses, and create jobs. An accounting faculty member worked with accounting alumni and students to develop a week-long workshop for finance officers on fraud prevention and detection. The team spent two weeks in Ghana delivering a workshop for thirty World Vision finance officers from eighteen African nations. The team also worked with the Ghana National Office of World Vision to develop internal controls. This work led to additional workshops organized for World Vision and Hope International.

The Collaboratory has helped fund and provided support to projects in computer and information systems. One project funded by the Collaboratory enabled faculty and students to assist central Pennsylvania nonprofit organizations with their information technology needs. A faculty member and students have also developed a prototype database application to enable program managers in World Vision to track activities and assess outcomes (Nejmeh & Vicary, 2009). This work led to a follow-on project to develop a cell phone application that facilitates the collection of data, such as the availability of food and medicine, by World Vision staff visiting the homes of persons living with AIDS (Nejmeh & Dean, 2010). The goal was to expedite the mobilization of material help when needed. Additional projects in computer and information systems serve the Collaboratory. One project was a partner management database to help the Collaboratory communicate with alumni, investors, and other friends. Another was the development of the previously mentioned MAP application for helping members and teams to set and track performance goals.

Student outcomes, particularly the excellence and generosity with which they pursue their work after graduation, are equally important to project outcomes as a product of the Collaboratory. The Collaboratory must do more to track student outcomes and assess its success relative to this goal and is seeking to do so through a website and with social media. Anecdotal evidence, however, suggests that the Collaboratory is succeeding in serving our students.

- An alumnus now pursuing a PhD on a National Science Foundation (NSF) Fellowship says, "The Collaboratory gave direction and purpose to my college career. Here at Messiah College we hear a lot about 'vocation' from the administration, from faculty, and from student government, but to me the members of the Collaboratory embody vocation without even needing to mention the word."
- A nutrition major who went on to study nursing writes, "Through the Collaboratory I learned leadership and organizational skills that enabled me to get and succeed in a job not usually offered to recent graduates. I learned how to listen to people, and direct my compassion for them in a way that meets their perceived needs rather than merely fulfilling my expectations."
- An accountant and alumnus who advised a project says, "I was personally challenged and encouraged by World Vision's leadership and enthusiasm. It was thrilling to find myself standing in the middle of the intersection where my professional skills in accounting overlap with the Christian mandate to go to the corners of the earth and spread the Good News."
- A graduate who served on the same accounting project team writes: "Working with so many talented people in World Vision provided me with the opportunity to gain practical knowledge that is sometimes dif-

ficult to obtain in the classroom setting. I especially enjoyed the opportunity to use the knowledge I've gained through my courses at Messiah to serve others. That was incredibly rewarding and provided me with a better understanding of the world around me and a greater appreciation for all I have."

- An alumnus now advising an engineering project says, "The Collaboratory taught me to handle responsibilities that seemed out of my reach, like leading a team of engineers to do a technology project in Zimbabwe. My experience helped me to develop my understanding of global issues and put in perspective my role as an American Christian, and helped me develop the ability to apply my engineering major as worship to God through partnering with those who have been marginalized."

- A business graduate writes, "My time serving as Staff Manager brought out new talents that I didn't know I possessed, and because of it I changed my major to better align with my gifts." She says, "In essence I was the chief operating officer of an organization, which was incredible experience that most students never get."

- Finally, an alumnus who is now a Collaboratory client writes, "My experiences in the Collaboratory influenced every part of my life, including my graduate studies in leadership and management and my career as a long-term missionary in Burkina Faso. I look forward to working with the Collaboratory from Africa and hope I can help influence others in the same way I was influenced."

4.6   SUMMARY

Today, the Collaboratory enhances curricular and cocurricular learning in the School of Science, Engineering, and Health, and across our campus at Messiah College by implementing pedagogical innovations that enable students to express value commitments and disciplinary knowledge through creative, hands-on problem solving in real-life settings. Our goal is to more fully embody the College's identity and holistic mission: "to educate men and women toward maturity of intellect, character, and Christian faith in preparation for lives of service, leadership, and reconciliation in Church and society." The mission of Messiah College reflects a growing commitment in higher education to the unity of cognitive, affective, and behavioral learning; a commitment that is essential to making graduates into citizens. But making citizens is more difficult than making graduates. It requires that multidirectional connections be made between academic knowledge, vision and passion for a positive future, and the active response of the learner.

In the Collaboratory, students engage the knowledge content of their discipline in the context of a specific problem or need and reflect on the experience in view of their Christian faith commitments. As Donald Schön recommends, we propose to "reverse the figure and ground between academic work and the practicum." It is normative today for the practicum to come last in an undergraduate curriculum. Theory and technique are developed first in the core of the curriculum and followed by a capstone application. Contextualization of theory and technique comes almost as an afterthought, and problem-solving is approached more or less as a linear application of fundamentals learned in the core curriculum. Real problem solving, though, is messy. It is highly nonlinear and iterative, requiring constant interplay between theory and application such that each is informed by the other. The Collaboratory is where our students put theory to work, and where the work informs theory.

ACKNOWLEDGMENTS

The Collaboratory is the result of dedication and sacrifice by many who could not possibly all be named here, but you know who you are and so does the author. Heartfelt thanks to each one of you, especially to the Student Directors and Staff Group Managers who have enriched my life so generously.

REFERENCES

Berry, W. (1987). The Loss of University. In *Home Economics*. New York, NY: North Point Press.

Boyer, F. (1990). *Scholarship Reconsidered: Priorities of the Professoriate*. Princeton, NJ: The Carnegie Foundation for the Advancement of Teaching.

Boyer, E. (1997a). A Community of Scholars. In *Selected speeches: 1979–1995*. Princeton, NJ: The Carnegie Foundation for the Advancement of Teaching.

Boyer, E. (1997b). The Scholarship of Engagement. In *Selected Speeches: 1979–1995*. Princeton, NJ: The Carnegie Foundation for the Advancement of Teaching.

Eliot, T.S. (1963). The Dry Salvages. In *Collected Poems: 1909–1962*. San Diego, CA: Harcourt Brace Jovanovich, p. 194.

Heie, H. (1993). *Orientation for New Professors*. Speech presented at Messiah College, Grantham, PA.

Hauerwas, S., & Willimon, W. H. (1996). *Where Resident Aliens Live*. Nashville, TN: Abingdon Press.

Kimball, B. (1986). *Orators and Philosophers: A History of the Idea of Liberal Education*. New York: Teachers College Press of Columbia University.

Kolb, D. (1984). *Experiential Learning: Experience as the Source of Learning And Development*. Englewood Cliffs, NJ: Prentice-Hall.

Levinson, D. (1978). *Seasons of a Man's Life*. New York: Knopf, Inc.

Levinson, D. and Levinson, J. (1996). *Seasons of a Woman's Life*. New York: Knopf, Inc.

Lewis, C. S. (1970). Meditation in a Toolshed. In W. Hooper (Ed.), *God in the Dock: Essays on Theology and Ethics*. Grand Rapids, MI: William B. Eerdmans Publishing Company.

Nejmeh, B. & Vicary, B. (2009). Lessons Learned about Design, Monitoring and Evaluation Process Definition and Information Management for International Development Programmes. *Knowledge Management for Development Journal*, 5(2), 143-159.

Nejmeh, B. and Dean, T. (2010). The charms application suite: A Community-Based Mobile Data Collection and Alerting Environment for HIV/AIDS Orphan and Vulnerable Children in Zambia. *International Journal of Computing and ICT Research*, 4(2), 46-63.

Parks, S. D. (2000). *Big Questions Worthy Dreams: Mentoring Young Adults in Their Search for Meaning, Purpose, and Faith*. San Francisco: Jossey-Bass, Inc.

Schön, D. A. (1983). *The Reflective Practitioner: How Professionals Think in Action*. London: Temple Smith.

Van Doren, M. (1943). *Liberal Education*. New York, NY: Henry Holt.

CHAPTER 5

THE HUMANITARIAN FREE AND OPEN-SOURCE SOFTWARE PROJECT
Engaging Students in Service-Learning through Building Software

Ralph Morelli, Trishan R. de Lanerolle, and Allen Tucker

ABSTRACT

Begun in 2006, the Humanitarian Free and Open-Source Software Project (HFOSS Project) is an educational initiative whose goal is to engage undergraduates in computer science by building free and open-source software (FOSS) that benefits humanity, both locally and globally. During its short lifetime, the Project has inspired increasing numbers of students and instructors to make significant contributions to several humanitarian open-source software development projects. Contributions to the HFOSS Project come from professionals in academia, IT organizations, and nonprofit organizations who together engage undergraduate students in courses, research projects, and summer internship experiences. Its curriculum is accessible to a wide range of undergraduates, since it includes courses for nonmajors as well as computer science and engineering majors.

This chapter will discuss the origin, goals, curricular and cocurricular activities, accomplishments, and future challenges of the HFOSS Project. We emphasize the HFOSS Project's service-learning components, its pedagogical organization, its impacts, and its potential as a catalyst for initiating similar activities across a broad range of undergraduate programs in the information sciences.

Service-Learning in Computer and Information Sciences. Edited by Brian A. Nejmeh

5.1   INTRODUCTION

What if undergraduate students saw computer science as a discipline that, among other things, designed and built free software to help one's friends and neighbors in need? Would that attract more women and underrepresented minorities to the discipline? Would it help revitalize the computing curriculum?

The HFOSS Project has been addressing these questions since 2006. The goal is to help revitalize undergraduate computing education by engaging students in developing FOSS that benefits the community. The HFOSS Project started at Trinity College as a small independent study. Today the Project includes students from a dozen or so U.S. colleges and universities engaged in a variety of FOSS development projects, both global and local.

The Project has been supported since September 2007 by the National Science Foundation's CPATH program. Its overarching goal is to build a collaborative community of individuals, academic computing departments, IT corporations, and humanitarian organizations (local and global) dedicated to the development of socially useful software (Morelli, Tucker, de Lanerolle, 2010). In general, the Project aims to answer whether getting students involved in humanitarian FOSS indeed also helps revitalize undergraduate computing education.

5.1.1   FOSS, HFOSS and Service-Learning in Computer Science

Free and open-source software, in contrast to proprietary software, is software that is licensed to be studied, shared, modified, and redistributed. The "free" in "free software" refers to the freedoms associated with its use and reuse. In order to make these freedoms possible, it is necessary that the software's source code, that is, the code that is written by programmers, be open and accessible. Although most FOSS is also free in the sense of free of charge, the software's price has nothing to do with the concept of FOSS. Many proprietary software products, for example, Web browsers such as Internet Explorer, are distributed free of charge. But they are distributed in binary form, a form not accessible to programmers, and there are copyright restrictions that prevent users from sharing or revising the software. As Richard Stallman, the founder of the free software movement puts it, free software is "a matter of liberty, not price"; it is free as in free speech and not (necessarily) as in free beer.

The modern FOSS movement began in 1983 when Richard Stallman defined "free software" as the freedom to use, study, copy, change, and redistribute software "so that the whole community benefits" (http://www.gnu.org/philosophy/free-sw.html). Following the spectacular success of the

GNU/Linux project (http://www.gnu.org/), the free-software movement has grown in scope and importance. Today, there are literally thousands of free software products and free software makes up the lion's share of the software infrastructure that runs the Internet, the World Wide Web, and the e-commerce industry.

In addition to the software itself, there are currently over 100 copyright licenses that protect the freedoms embodied in the FOSS definition. Stallman's GNU General Public License (GPL) was the first such license to stipulate how the software can be freely used and shared.

The FOSS movement is also characterized by an open development process, a highly distributed, agile, nonhierarchical, peer-based activity. The FOSS approach stands in sharp contrast to the top-down, hierarchical, legacy-based model of traditional commercial software development. FOSS programmers collaborate in loosely organized communities, freely working, often as volunteers, on the projects and problems that are of most interest to them. The FOSS development process is also closely tied to the user community and marked by frequent releases closely monitored and tested by end users.

Thus, to use a familiar analogy, free and open-source software is to proprietary software as Wikipedia is to Britannica. Wikipedia's content is open for all to study, revise, and share. The content is protected through licenses that grant users these freedoms and is produced through highly democratic, peer-based collaborative processes. By contrast, Britannica's content is proprietary and protected by prohibitive copyright provisions and is produced through a hierarchical, top-down process that depends on experts who restrict access to the production process.

Despite its tremendous worldwide success within the software industry and its obvious influence on projects such as Wikipedia and others, the study of FOSS has been largely absent from formal computing education. As noted by David Patterson in his March 2006 President's letter in the *Communications of the ACM* (Patterson, 2006), "The open source movement is growing rapidly and has become an important component of the software industry. Yet it has received relatively little attention as an object of study in undergraduate computing curricula. Many schools use open-source software in their labs, but few schools teach about open-source methodology in their classrooms."

Although the ideas of sharing and collaboration are inherently humanitarian in the broad sense of that term, FOSS applications run the gamut of computer software, from operating systems, to word processors, to file-sharing programs, to Web browsers. By contrast, HFOSS (Humanitarian FOSS), as we define it, is software that serves society in some direct way. This definition is deliberately broad and is meant to be inclusive of a wide range of socially beneficial projects and activities.

The humanitarian potential of computing is something that was acknowledged by David Patterson in another of his columns in the *Communications of the ACM*. In November 2005, following the Katrina disaster, in a column entitled "Rescuing Our Families, Our Neighbors, and Ourselves" Patterson urged computer scientists to become more involved in disaster relief and other humanitarian efforts saying that "perhaps it is our civic duty to do so" (Patterson, 2005).

These two ideas—free and open-source software and its use to serve humanitarian purposes (in the broad sense of the term)—have served as the guiding principles of the HFOSS Project since its inception. Together, they constitute a form of service-learning that is unique to the computer science.

5.1.2   Sahana and the Beginning of the HFOSS Project

Because it provides such a clear illustration of the activities and outcomes of the HFOSS Project, we begin by describing how the project got started. In January 2006, a small group of students and faculty at Trinity College downloaded the open-source Sahana disaster management system, installed it on a department server, and began studying the source code. Sahana was developed in Sri Lanka by a group of volunteer programmers in the immediate aftermath of the 2004/5 Asian Tsunami. Over the next several months, the Trinity group designed and implemented a Volunteer Management module that was incorporated into the Sahana code base in December 2006. This collaborative development effort also gave birth to the HFOSS Project itself.

Following the initial success of the Sahana experience at Trinity, a group of computing faculty from Trinity College, Wesleyan University, and Connecticut College received a collaborative grant from the NSF under its Pathways to Revitalized Undergraduate Computing Education program (CPATH), whose aim is to revitalize interest in computing education. With NSF support, the project has engaged undergraduates from many schools in a variety of open-source development projects. The service-learning model is simple: undergraduates learn the principles and methodologies of the FOSS development process while at the same time contributing worthwhile software to their communities (Morelli, Tucker, Danner, de Lanerolle, Ellis, Izmirli, Krizanc, and Parker, 2009).

Although the HFOSS Project has collaborated with a number of other open-source communities over the years, Sahana continues to play a significant role in HFOSS's service-learning experiment. In 2008, HFOSS students worked with developers in Sri Lanka and with users and developers in China to help deploy Sahana in Chengdu, China following the devastating earthquake there (Morelli, de Silva, de Lanerolle, Curzon, and Mao, 2010). Students have also worked with Sahana team members on several activities ranging from disaster simulation exercises organized by the Naval Postgraduate School at Camp Roberts in California (http://www.star-tides.net/node/613) to instructional workshops organized by IBM in Washington, DC.

Students in software engineering courses have studied and worked on the code base and on Sahana issues as part of their class assignments. Students in introductory computer science courses helped test and report bugs for a Sahana deployment following the Haiti earthquake in early 2010. And HFOSS students are currently working on efforts to develop mobile tools that interface with Sahana.

Students who have engaged with Sahana in these ways have gained experience that is not normally available through the traditional undergraduate computer science curriculum. In addition to learning how to manage and use the tools and techniques of an open-source development environment, HFOSS students have also learned how large-scale, distributed FOSS development projects are organized. Over the course of the HFOSS collaboration with Sahana, two undergraduate students have earned committer status* in the Sahana project, thus becoming full-fledged members of the Sahana project team.

These students have learned how to collaborate with programmers and developers in the Sahana community, from diverse locations in Sri Lanka, Sweden, United Kingdom, India, California, and New York. They have learned the importance of well-designed and well-documented code by dealing with complex software systems that have been written by others, and they have seen first-hand that what matters in a FOSS meritocracy is whether or not your code solves problems that the development community considers important.

5.2 GOALS AND OBJECTIVES

As suggested above, the HFOSS Project's service-learning model addresses two distinct issues. The first involves undergraduate computing education. The second involves addressing the broader software needs of humanitarian organizations (where "humanitarian" includes any organization that serves the public good).

A major issue in computing education in the United States is that it is failing to prepare a workforce that will maintain the nation's global leadership

---

*A "committer" is a developer who has direct access to the code base. A "contributor" is a developer who must pass their code through some kind of review process before it can be added to the code base.

in computing, despite the continued and growing importance of computing in all sectors of society (Patterson, 2005). This crisis is characterized by sagging enrollments, out-of-date curricula, and underrepresentation of key demographic groups such as women and minorities. The dimensions of this crisis are four-fold:

1. **Curriculum.** Despite the rapid growth of computing technology, undergraduate computing curricula have changed very little in the past 20 years. New computing fields, such as agile software development and cloud computing, find little representation in undergraduate courses.

2. **Demographics.** The computer science discipline in the United States has done a poor job of attracting women and minority students. The percentage of computer science majors among these groups is sparse and has even declined during the past 10 years.

3. **Software Engineering Education.** Because of the growth of FOSS in government, industry, and other areas there will be a need for graduates familiar with FOSS development. Yet, to date, FOSS principles and practices have not been essential components of computer science or software engineering instruction at the undergraduate level.

4. **Service-Learning.** Despite the fact that many colleges and universities have service-learning programs, computer science programs have largely ignored this opportunity. Nevertheless, as HFOSS seeks to prove, there are many important ways that students in these programs can learn from and help their communities.

Among humanitarian organizations, the crisis appears in the form of a general absence of access to the quality computing and software resources needed to complete their missions. There are several reasons for this:

1. **Limited Budgets.** Software is often expensive and the budgets of humanitarian organizations are limited. Thus, their software budgets are inadequate to meet their needs.

2. **Lack of Technical Expertise.** Most humanitarian organizations lack expert IT staff that could help them address their technology needs.

3. **Absence of Custom Software.** Lacking a strong commercial market, traditional developers have produced few software products that address specific humanitarian needs.

The HFOSS Project addresses both the educational and the humanitarian problems noted above through an innovative program aimed at getting undergraduates engaged in building free and open-source software (FOSS) that benefits the public good. When the HFOSS model works, students learn the principles and practices of FOSS development and humanitarian organizations simultaneously gain access to quality software.

5.3   CONCEPTS, METHODOLOGIES, AND OUTCOMES

As a concept, HFOSS is clearly attractive to university computer science students and may help attract new students to computing. This is reflected not only in the interest that has been generated in HFOSS courses, independent studies, and summer HFOSS Institutes, where typically two to three times more students apply than can be accommodated, but also in the feedback we have received from students who have participated in HFOSS activities (Morelli et al., 2009).

There are three ways to implement the HFOSS concept.

First, FOSS and HFOSS content may be incorporated into undergraduate courses at the introductory level. We have developed pedagogical resources for courses at the CS0, CS1, and advanced levels that can be adapted and used at other schools. For example , in spring 2008 a general education course called "Open Source Software for Humanity" was taught (via videoconference) at Trinity College and Wesleyan University. Its "hook" was getting students to reflect on their own experience with FOSS products (such as Wikipedia and the Firefox browser) and then showing the connection to computer science education. Not surprisingly, the students were receptive to the ideals of sharing, community, and the public good. Students were also enthusiastic about discussing their experience with Wikipedia, blogging, open-source politics, and other aspects of the free and open culture they had grown up with. Students viewed the distributed FOSS model as an alternative means of producing culturally useful goods (Wikipedia) and services (SETI@home). Similarly, students generally saw elements of the FOSS ethic in their own experience with file sharing. They recognized that this is a time of change in public thinking about intellectual property and the common good. But despite their everyday use and enjoyment of FOSS products and their widespread acceptance of the freedom and openness characterizing the FOSS model, few students recognized the connections between the FOSS movement and the overall computing discipline. As one said, "Wow, I really got to look at how computer science can relate to humanitarian efforts. I now really understand [FOSS] and know why it came about."

Second. the FOSS development methodology and FOSS technology and tools are incorporated into upper-level software engineering courses. A substantial collection of pedagogical resources has been developed to support this type of activity (http://teaching.hfoss.org). For example in the Fall 2009, a high-level course, "Humanitarian Open Source Software Development," on the application of principles of programming to real-world problems was taught using the concepts and methodologies of HFOSS. This course was open to computer science students from Trinity College, Connecticut College, and Wesleyan University as a seminar/project course using video conferencing technology for weekly class meetings. The course involved analyzing, designing, and implementing open-source software. Students were expected to work in teams on one or more of the real-world projects supported by the HFOSS Project.

Third, students and faculty serve as contributors to Humanitarian FOSS projects in ways that are appropriate for their curricula. These may be independent studies, thesis projects, or capstone projects, summer and academic-year internships. A substantial collection of resources has been created to support this kind of change.

For example, students, under the supervision of a faculty member, have made contributions towards HFOSS Projects as part of their undergraduate capstone programs. As part of a program known as Undergraduate Capstone Open Source Projects (UCOSP) (http://ucosp.ca/), students from several Canadian universities have participated in collaborative mobile software development as contributors to the POSIT project, a mobile application developed at Trinity College (Asplund, de Lanerolle, Fei, Gautam, Morelli, Nadjm-Tehrani, and Nykvist, 2010). As testimony to student interest in mobile open-source development, the POSIT Project ranks amongst the most popular project selections for UCOSP students.

5.4   HFOSS IN PRACTICE

The HFOSS Project's approach engages students directly as practitioners in the humanitarian FOSS community. Its activities promote the study and practice of FOSS development in general, and its application to humanitarian needs in particular. Over the past five years, the HFOSS Project has contributed code to over 16 different active FOSS applications, varying in scope from international projects to locally based efforts. Applications developed by the HFOSS Project are used to benefit the public good in different domains, including disaster response, volunteer management, mobile applications, and educational/awareness tools, which provide students with real-world experiences to learn the principles, tools, and methodologies of FOSS development. Below we describe four exemplary HFOSS software projects.

5.4.1 POSIT-Haiti: Mobile Application to Manage Food Distribution Program

In July 2011, a Humanitarian FOSS Project team of faculty and students from Trinity College traveled to Haiti for 10 days to deploy POSIT-Haiti, a mobile data-gathering tool developed by HFOSS, and to train local staff on its use and maintenance. The Android-based smart-phone app supports beneficiary registration and monitoring to assist with a food aid distribution program for expectant mothers and infants in the Southeast Department of Haiti.

The humanitarian program is managed by ACDIVOCA, a private, non-profit organization that has been managing a USAID-funded Food for Peace program, the Multi Year Assistance Program (MYAP) in Haiti since 2008. It currently provides a food ration to over 10,000 registered beneficiaries and their families on a monthly basis.

ACDIVOCA currently uses a manual, paper-based system to serve its beneficiaries. However, due to transportation challenges, recording errors, and other issues, it is difficult to guarantee the accurate and timely updating of beneficiary data. In some cases, written records from a previous month's activities have not reached the headquarters in Jacmel soon enough to be entered into the central database where they are needed to generate the documents necessary to manage the next month's food distribution. In addition to the data's role in determining the amount of food needed for distribution, they are also important for monitoring, evaluation, and auditing of the aid program itself. As a result of the challenges faced by its manual-based program, AcdiVoca contacted the HFOSS Project in December 2010 to explore the feasibility of having HFOSS develop a version of its POSIT tool for use in Haiti. POSIT, which stands for Portable Open Search and Identification Tool, is an Android app that was designed to collect and share data in the aftermath of a humanitarian disaster.

A small HFOSS team developed a simple prototype version of POSIT for Haiti and traveled to Haiti in March to conduct feasibility tests. There is a growing cell phone presence even in remote rural areas in Haiti. Thus, it was determined that a mobile system based on the text-message protocol (SMS—Short Message System) would be feasible as a tool for supporting ACDI/VOCA's food distribution and monitoring programs and as a reference tool for field agents. During the next several months, HFOSS students and faculty developed a system that consists of data entry forms for registering both health and agricultural beneficiaries and for updating health beneficiary records. The system is fully localized, that is, its user interface can be presented in English, French, or Haitian Creole. The mobile app communicates through customized modem software, also developed by HFOSS students, to AcdiVoca's server in Jacmel. It supports both regular and admin users. Regular users are mostly auxiliary nurses who will be responsible for registering new beneficiaries and for updating records for existing beneficiaries during food distribution events. Admin users have the ability to add new users and are responsible for bulk SMS syncing operations.

During training and deployment exercises in July, ACDI/VOCA field staff appeared to have accepted the technology more quickly than expected. Some users who felt more comfortable with the phones, especially auxiliary nurses and agricultural extension agents, worked with their peers to explain features and how to use them more efficiently. This was particularly important during a food distribution event where speed and accuracy are key. Ongoing monitoring of the mobile app in the field will require close supervision during the roll-out period. The HFOSS Project will continue to monitor and maintain the system remotely during the coming months with of goal of having it achieve full deployment and integration with AcdiVoca's day-to-day operations.

The short-term result of this project will be to enhance beneficiary registration and distribution event monitoring to ensure timely and accurate delivery of services to the women and infants that are served by Acdi/Voca's program. Looking further into the future, discussions are underway to explore how POSIT-Haiti can be adapted and used in other countries to provide similar support for humanitarian activities. Given the ubiquity of cell service in poor and developing countries, it appears that there could be strong interest in this type of mobile application.

5.4.2   The Ronald McDonald House Project

In addition to participating in global FOSS projects, Humanitarian FOSS students have participated in a number of projects situated within their local or regional communities. In 2008, an instructor and a group of four students at Bowdoin College developed an on-line volunteer scheduling system (RMH Homebase) for the Ronald McDonald House in Portland, Maine as a one-semester software project (Tucker, 2009). It replaced a manual calendar system and is now used at the Portland Ronald McDonald House to manage the schedules of over 200 volunteers.

The RMH Homebase system was completed and installed at the House in May 2008 after a three-month development period, has been updated and improved several times, and is still in productive use today. Moreover, other Ronald McDonald Houses and nonprofits with similar scheduling challenges have inquired about adapting RMH Homebase to help with their scheduling needs. This is entirely possible since the software is open source and can be freely adapted by other developers to suit other related scheduling needs. Since 2008, RMH Homebase source code has been downloaded over 500 times from its Sourceforge repository.

A more detailed examination of this project and course can be found in Chapter 8, "An HFOSS Service Learning Case Study: The Bowdoin–Ronald McDonald House Projects."

5.4.3   The Collabbit Project

Collabbit is an open-source Web-based application that aims to increase emergency management efficiency through distributed asynchronous information sharing. The software is targeted to serve the needs of loosely coupled nonprofit disaster relief agencies that coordinate responses to disasters. Disaster relief agencies create a common operating picture of an emergency incident through remotely posted incident updates. Individual users subscribe to topics of interest and receive near-instantaneous updates on those topics. Where information is lacking, users may access a topically organized contact registry (De Lanerolle, Anderson, Morelli, Fox-Epstein, DeFabbia-Kane, and Gochev, 2010).

What is particularly interesting about Collabbit is that it provides the first example of the HFOSS Project's role as an incubator for a new FOSS product. The Collabbit project was begun during the 2009 HFOSS Summer Institute when a member of the New York City Office of Volunteers Active in Disaster (VOAD) who was familiar with the HFOSS Project's involvement in the Sahana effort requested that a simple collaboration system be developed for a table-top disaster recovery exercise. A prototype was developed in three weeks and used successfully at the exercise, providing a proof of concept that such software would be useful to VOAD and similar organizations.

During the remainder of that summer, HFOSS students worked closely with users from VOAD and the Red Cross and the Salvation Army to develop a full-fledged collaboration system. Collabbit is currently hosted on an HFOSS server and has been used by VOAD for similar table-top exercises. During the U.S. Thanksgiving holiday in 2009, it was used by the Salvation Army to help coordinate the distribution of 10,000 turkey dinners throughout the New York City metropolitan area.

Two of Collabbit's lead developers from Wesleyan University are in the process of creating a company to market and support Collabbit. As in many commercial FOSS enterprises, the software will remain licensed under its current LGPL license, and the development project will continue to be supported at http://collabbit.org/. HFOSS students and others will continue to participate in Collabbit's development community. At the same time, the students together with one of the principal designers from the VOAD community will form a corporation to oversee Collabbit's continuing development.

Although still in its infancy, Collabbit exhibits a completely unanticipated but welcome side effect of the HFOSS Project's educational effort, that is, a new project originating as an academic exercise can lead to the development of a mature and ongoing open-source software entity whose lifetime and impact are far larger than that for which it was originally developed.

5.4.4   Moving toward K-12: The App Inventor Experiment

App Inventor for Android is a new visual programming platform for creating mobile applications for Android-based smart phones. During the summer of 2010, the HFOSS Project participated in an experiment that used App Inventor to address the question: Can the HFOSS model be extended to K-12 education (Morelli, de Lanerolle, Lake, Limardo, Tamotsu, and Uche, 2010).

The App Inventor experiment was a collaboration among two high school teachers, two novice undergraduate students in computer science, a community outreach leader, and a computer science instructor. The HFOSS Project's component of this experiment explored the utility of App Inventor as a tool for engaging high school and early college students in the study of computer science by having them develop socially beneficial mobile applications. This focus can be particularly useful in attracting student interest from underrepresented groups, especially females, African Americans, and Hispanics, in computer science as a field of study.

In the fall of 2010, an application called "Work It Off," which was developed by the two students during the summer experiment, won a competition designed to promote nutritious food choices and physical activity for children as part of First Lady Michelle Obama's Let's Move! initiative. In the future, the Humanitarian FOSS project hopes to initiate more experiments like this one, aiming to extend to the K-12 cohort its effort to get students engaged in learning about and employing FOSS practices and principles and its service-learning model to benefit their communities. We believe that the potential for App Inventor to help improve public understanding of computer science is significant.

As a follow-up to this experiment, HFOSS is currently developing a new App-Inventor-based CS Principles course at Trinity College in collaboration with the Greater Hartford Academy of Mathematics and Science, a partnering high school in Trinity's neighborhood. This effort is part of a NSF-funded pilot project being run by the College Board with the eventual goal of developing a new advanced placement (AP) course that will take a breadth-first approach to teaching introductory computer science. Both courses will employ a mobile version of the HFOSS model to promote service-learning within the 9–12 cohort. Students will learn the principles of computer science by building apps that serve their local (or global) communities.

5.5   RESULTS AND OUTCOMES

Reactions from students participating in the HFOSS Project have been overwhelmingly enthusiastic. A typical sentiment expressed in course evaluations and questionnaires is: "After taking this independent study I realized that I can be in the lab, doing what I am interested in, and still make a humanitarian impact and help society." Thus, when humanitarian FOSS is developed in this way, everyone wins. Students gain either a course credit (as in the Bowdoin–Ronald McDonald House project) or a summer stipend (as in the HFOSS Summer Institute) by making a meaningful contribution to open-source software, a humanitarian organization gains a valuable software artifact, and computer science education adds a socially relevant dimension to its curriculum that can arguably make it attractive to a wider and more diverse range of talented students.

Our experiments with introductory and advanced courses, independent studies, and summer internships have shown that FOSS software and tools, including Apache, PHP, MySQL, Eclipse, PhpMyAdmin, and SVN, are quite accessible to today's undergraduates.

Similarly, working with local clients and international development communities has been an important motivator. For example, students learned that writing good documentation is as important as writing good code. The quality of student work improved as they recognized their increased level of public accountability. This message was constantly reinforced by mentors, peers, and clients. Depending on the specific course or project, students came with different levels of expertise, ranging from no prior programming experience for an introductory course to having nearly completed the major requirements for upper-level and software-engineering courses.

Engaging students through HFOSS must be done with sensitivity to their backgrounds and interests, but the projects themselves are rich and varied enough to accept contributions from students with different backgrounds. For example, students with no programming experience are still able to make significant contributions in requirements-gathering and documentation-writing. We have found that students are comfortable working in virtual teams and groups, having grown up with Facebook and Instant Messenger and interacting with friends through all kinds of electronic media. They also respond well to wikis for working collaboratively on documents and presentations and sharing their source code on public repositories, such as Google Code. One student said, "I now have a better understanding of what it is like to work with and contribute to a team of people, even when I may never meet them in person."

Computer science has not been broadly attractive at the undergraduate level, especially to women and other underrepresented groups. An April 2006 article in Computing Research Association Bulletin, based on data from the National Science Foundation and other sources, reported "[c]omputer science has the dubious distinction of being the only science field to see a fall in the share of its bachelor's degrees granted to women between 1983 and 2002" (http://www.cra.org/wp/index.php?p=83).

Attracting women and other underrepresented groups to computing remains a particularly challenging HFOSS Project objective. Only four women were enrolled in a 13-student introductory course in spring 2008, and for the summer 2008 internship program, only six out of 29 applicants were women. Of the 10 CPATH-funded summer interns only three were women, and two others were African-American. These numbers are not good, though they are somewhat better than the numbers in non-HFOSS computer science courses. For example, the fall 2008 CS1 courses offered at Connecticut College, Trinity College, and Wesleyan University included only 10 women and two African-American students out of a total of 69 students. Although these data are too sparse to support conclusions one way or the other regarding the appeal of HFOSS to women and other historically underrepresented groups, evaluations received from participating students suggest that the HFOSS approach has the potential to attract more women students to computing in the future.

Students' responses suggest that they speak positively about the project to their female friends. The HFOSS Project has made headway in addressing this challenge, and over the past three years on average two out of five HFOSS summer institute participants have been female. Moreover, there is a HFOSS Chapter established at Mt. Holyoke College, a women's college. But given the relatively small number of women and minorities who come to college with an interest in computing in the first place, the HFOSS initiative may not solve the problem altogether; the solution, if there is one, may ultimately extend beyond the academy.

A widespread misconception about computing is that it is all about programming or coding. At most U.S. schools, the introductory sequence focuses largely on teaching a programming language, further reinforcing this misconception. The HFOSS approach addresses this issue by contextualizing programming within a broader problem-solving and creativity-minded framework. Being engaged in real-world projects with teams of developers, students see that programming is just one part of a complex, team-oriented, creative process that produces software to benefit society.

Working closely with real clients, they see the need for transparent and secure code, extensive testing, and writing excellent user manuals and other supporting materials. They want to master these activities to improve their systems rather than step through mere academic exercises.

Another important HFOSS element is the ethic of sharing and collaboration. For this reason, the HFOSS Project teams students with one another as well as with mentors, IT professionals, and HFOSS community members. The HFOSS development process has no room for lone programmers working in isolation.

Student feedback reflects these observations. For example, one student said, "[this activity] shows how computer science can be a very helpful field of study than what we just know of it as programming in different programming languages." Another said, "[this activity] definitely changed my views of how effective software projects can be run. If we work collectively for the greater good, then we can get much more done."

The HFOSS Project has focused on individual courses and internships and has only just begun to address how its approach might fit into an undergraduate curriculum. Reinforced throughout our experience is the longstanding view that computer science must be presented as a creative problem-solving discipline, and the more this value is built into the computing curriculum the more attractive it will be to a wider variety of bright students eager to solve problems. Georgia Tech and other institutions have begun exploring curricular models that contextualize programming within broader applications of computing (http://www.insidehighered.com/news/2006/09/26/gatech). The HFOSS approach would clearly complement such a model.

A common software industry complaint is that new computing graduates are strong on theory but lack practical understanding of the modern IT workplace. A common complaint from academics is that IT professionals want colleges and universities to serve as training centers for their latest programming languages and software platforms. HFOSS addresses these issues by recruiting computing and IT professionals as advisers and mentors for its summer interns. For example, IT consultants from Accenture Corporation have helped to mentor HFOSS students and serve as advisers in project management and other areas. Students appreciate the mentoring as they begin to understand the complexity of software development. They see that challenging problems rarely yield to "textbook" solutions and that the design process is often a protracted interaction between programmers and end users. One student said, "[this activity] definitely helped me understand more options of the IT profession. Now I know one more aspect of it, and how exciting it can be."

5.5.1 Other Projects and Outcomes

Other projects to which HFOSS students have contributed include:

- *OpenMRS* (http://openmrs.org), an open medical record system that was begun by Dr. Paul Farmer's Partner in Health organization in conjunction with the Regenstrief Institute

- The *GNOME Accessibility Project* (http://accessibility.gnome.org), an effort to make the GNOME user interface accessible to handicapped individuals
- The *TOR Project* (http://tor.org), an open-source anonymizing system used to protect the identities of journalists and human rights workers

For more details about these projects, see http://www.hfoss.org.

Students in all these software projects have gained experience that is not normally available through the traditional undergraduate computer science curriculum.

Each of these is an example of FOSS being used to benefit the public good in different domains (disaster response, volunteer support, project management, and collaboration). HFOSS students have also made significant code contributions to these projects while learning valuable collaboration and software development skills and principles.

Source code from these projects has been studied and used in courses, independent studies, capstone projects, and summer research internships. In the case of the RMH Homebase project, the experience motivated the publication of a textbook in 2011 called Software Development: An Open Source Approach (Tucker, Morelli, & de Silva, 2011). This textbook is designed for use in any college-level software development or software engineering course that teaches FOSS development in a hands-on way.

5.6   HFOSS SUMMER INSTITUTES, CERTIFICATION, WORKSHOPS, AND SYMPOSIA

In addition to its efforts to get students engaged in open-source projects, the other main goals of the Humanitarian FOSS project are:

- To get faculty and students at other colleges and universities involved in similar activities
- To develop a certificate program to recognize student achievement in open-source software development

During the period 2007–2011, the HFOSS Project has introduced over 275 students, across a dozen different colleges, to FOSS concepts, methods, and technologies through project-supported summer institutes and courses. Project faculty have developed several new courses incorporating FOSS into the computer science curricula, ranging from the introductory level to advanced software engineering and special topics courses.

The Bowdoin activity described above was the first example of the potential for growing the Humanitarian FOSS community at schools outside Trinity College, Wesleyan University, and Connecticut College. The Humanitarian FOSS Project has since provided seed funding to start chapters at several other schools, including Mount Holyoke College in Massachusetts, Bergen Community College in New Jersey, Oregon State University in Oregon, and St. Johns University and Rensselaer Polytechnic Institute (RPI) in New York. Many other HFOSS-inspired programs and activities at universities have started across North America, including John Carroll University, University of New Hampshire, North Carolina State University, University of Wisconsin, University of Hartford, Drexel University, University of Pennsylvania, Western New England College, and University of Toronto.

The HFOSS Project has also organized and held several faculty workshops that provide hands-on introduction to teaching the FOSS development process, focusing on communication and development tools and practices and providing an introduction to several HFOSS development projects. Five different workshops have had over 100 attendees. Altogether, these HFOSS Project outreach efforts have reached over 300 faculty through five workshops, four symposia, and various other presentations.

5.6.1 The FOSS Certificate Program

The HFOSS Project has also developed a FOSS Certificate, a credential by which a student can demonstrate mastery of FOSS concepts and practice. The purpose of the FOSS Certificate is to recognize student achievement in FOSS development.

The certificate also helps identify the core software development curricular elements that belong in a modern undergraduate computing education. Thus, it can also raise awareness and interest in FOSS principles and practice among a wider range of computing faculty, students, and programs nationwide.

Applicants may prepare for FOSS certification by satisfactorily completing one or two college-level courses (or their equivalent) that have significant FOSS curriculum content and by having achieved contributor status in one or more FOSS projects. For the purpose of certification, contributor status means any active contribution to the code base, documentation, or other part of the software that affects the software's productive use. Certificate applications are reviewed by three-person teams consisting of academic computer scientists, FOSS project leaders, and professional software developers.

The HFOSS Project is currently in the process of implementing the certificate program. In addition to serving as a way to recognize student achievement, we are hoping the FOSS Certificate can also serve to stimulate thinking among academic computing departments about the place of FOSS in the undergraduate curriculum. The FOSS Certificate may also provide an additional credential for computer science graduates seeking employment in the software industry.

Further details about the FOSS Certificate can be found at http://cert. hfoss.org/.

5.7   FUTURE CHALLENGES: GROWTH OF HFOSS "CHAPTERS," CURRICULUM, AND SUSTAINABILITY

NSF support of the HFOSS Project runs through August 2012. The project is currently exploring ways to extend its model and sustain its activities. A suitable model of portability and sustainability would involve three elements: growth, curriculum, and sustainability:

1. **Growth: H-FOSS@NewSchool Chapters.** During the past five years, the HFOSS program has offered competitive internships and organized summer institutes. In 2011, the Summer H-FOSS Institute included activities at Trinity College, Wesleyan University, Connecticut College, Mt. Holyoke College, St. John's University and Rensselaer Polytechnic Institute. In 2010/11, we seed funded new HFOSS chapters at Mt. Holyoke, Bergen Community College, St. Johns University, and Oregon State University. Since its inception, HFOSS has grown from chapters at three schools to active chapters or projects at more than 15 schools. It is hoped that the HFOSS service learning model can continue to grow in the coming years in order to continue its impact on computing education and humanitarian service.

2. **Lightweight Curriculum.** The FOSS Certificate program was developed in consultation with our industry and FOSS community partners. This program provides an incentive to students and faculty at other schools to join the HFOSS community. The HFOSS Project will provide the infrastructure as well as pedagogical and instructional support, training and tutorial materials for faculty and students, and a directory of accessible FOSS projects (such as Sahana, Mozilla, etc.).

3. **Sustainability.** The HFOSS program has grown largely through personal face-to-face outreach among like-minded colleagues and it has been sustained through a funding model that depends almost entirely on writing grants. Obviously this hands-on approach will not scale. For long-term sustainability, it will be necessary to establish a financing model that would ensure the expansion and extension of this program. The project is currently exploring funding and sustainability

models with its partners and supporters. For example, in collaboration with a team of management consultants at Accenture Corporation, the project is currently looking at how similar organizations sustain their activities. This will be an important initiative going forward.

5.8 CONCLUSIONS

The primary outcome of the HFOSS Project has been to engage students and faculty with the broader community in a wide range of service-learning activities. Just as computer scientists and educators of an earlier age led to the establishment of the Internet, today's educators and students are at the forefront of articulating the FOSS model throughout undergraduate education and the broader society.

The HFOSS Project has made excellent progress toward its objective of stimulating interest among undergraduate computer science students. It has also brought together the computing departments in colleges, IT corporations, and the humanitarian community in an important partnership. The HFOSS Project has grown significantly since its inception in 2006 and we are encouraged by the impact its students have made in helping solve real-world problems that matter to global and local humanitarian organizations. HFOSS students have gained significant knowledge of the open-source development process. Local and global organizations have gained valuable software tools. Colleges and universities that have participated in the HFOSS experiment have gained new and practical dimensions that help connect their computer science programs to the professional and humanitarian world around them.

For more detailed discussions about the conduct and impact of a typical HFOSS Project, readers are encouraged to look at Chapter 8, "An HFOSS Service-Learning Case Study: The Bowdoin–Ronald McDonald House Projects." There, the questions of on-going project sustainability (maintenance and evolution) and impact on humanitarian organizations are addressed in more detail.

Readers who are interested in discussing starting an HFOSS Project at their school should feel free to contact any of the authors directly.

REFERENCES

Asplund, M, de Lanerolle, T., Fei, C., Gautam, P., Morelli, R., Nadjm-Tehrani, S., and Nykvist, G. (2010). Wireless Ad Hoc Dissemination for Search and Rescue. In *Proceedings of the 7th International Conference on Information Systems for Crisis Response and Management* (ISCRAM).

De Lanerolle, T., Anderson, W., Morelli, R., Fox-Epstein, E., DeFabbia-Kane, S., and Gochev, D. (2010). Development of a Virtual Dashboard for Event Coordination Between Multiple Groups. In *Proceedings of the 7th International Conference on Information Systems for Crisis Response and Management* (ISCRAM).

Morelli, R., de Lanerolle, T., Lake, P., Limardo, N., Tamotsu, B., and Uche, C. (2010). Can Android App Inventor Bring Computational Thinking to K-12? Unpublished.

Morelli, R., de Silva, C., de Lanerolle, T., Curzon, R., and Mao, X. (2010). A Global Collaboration to Deploy Help to China. *Communications of the ACM,* Vol. 53, No. 12, pp. 142–149.

Morelli, R., Tucker, A., Danner, N., de Lanerolle, T., Ellis, H.J.C., Izmirli, O., Krizanc, D., and Parker, G. (2009). Revitalizing Computing Education by Building Free and Open Source Software for Humanity. *CACM,* Vol. 52, No. 8, pp. 67–75.

Morelli, R., Tucker A., and de Lanerolle, T. (2010). The Humanitarian FOSS Project. *Open Source Business Resource,* Talent First Network, Ottawa, December 2010.

Patterson, D. (2005). Rescuing Our Families, Our Neighbors, and Ourselves. *CACM,* Vol. 48, No. 11 (Nov. 2005), 29–31.

Patterson, D. (2006). President's letter: Computer Science education in the 21st century. *CACM*, Vol. 49, No. 3, 27.

Tucker, A. (2009) Teaching Client-Driven Software Development. In *ACM CCSC2009 Proceedings,* Hammond, LA.

Tucker, A., Morelli, R., and de Silva, C. (2011). *Software Development: An Open Source Approach.* New York: CRC Press.

SERVICE-LEARNING PROJECTS IN THE COMPUTER AND INFORMATION SCIENCES

There are many different styles and types of SL in CIS projects that have been completed. The purpose of this section of the book is to offer the reader a broad exposure to a wide variety of SL in CIS projects. In part, these chapters were chosen for their diversity in terms of project types, application domains, institutional settings, and geographic location.

Chapter 6, entitled "Some Worked Better Than Others: Experience With a Variety of Service-Learning Projects," is written by Ken Vollmar (Missouri State University) and Peter Sanderson (Otterbein University). The paper chronicles their experiences in incorporating service-learning into a software engineering course. In particular, the authors analyze the probable causes of success and failure of SL in CIS based on specific project experiences.

Chapter 7, entitled "EPICS Software Development Projects," is written by William Oakes and Saurabh Bagchi of Purdue University. This paper describes various software development projects undertaken by the Purdue EPICS Program. It also identifies some best practices for conducting SL in CIS projects.

Chapter 8, entitled "An HFOSS Service Learning Case Study: The Bowdoin-Ronald McDonald House Projects," is written by Allen Tucker (Bowdoin College), Ralph Morelli (Trinity College), and Trishan de Lanerolle (Trinity College). This paper describes the details of two Humanitarian Free and Open Source Software (HFOSS) projects. It offers an in-depth look at the use of an open-source development model in a SL in CIS setting.

Chapter 9, entitled "Service Learning and Project Management: The Capstone Course in Information Technology Leadership," is written by Charles Hannon of Washington and Jefferson College. The paper chronicles a senior capstone course in information technology leadership taught as an SL in CIS course. The course has a strong project management orientation and offers a novel approach to SL in CIS.

Chapter 10, entitled "Service-Learning and Entrepreneurship for Engineers," is written by Lisa Zidek of Florida Gulf Coast University. She offers a unique look at service-learning done in the context of an engineering entrepreneurship course sequence. The evolution of the course sequence is discussed, along with the rationale for the course changes. Assessment data related to the courses are also presented for the reader.

Chapter 11, entitled "Teaching Information Systems Ethics through Service-Learning," is written by Thomas Hilton and Donald Mowry of the University of Wisconsin–Eau Claire. This paper explores how ethical issues in CIS can be taught and ethical behavior evoked in an SL in CIS senior capstone course for IS majors.

Chapter 12, entitled "Computer Literacy Service Learning Project in Brazil," is written by Wen-Jung Hsin (Park University) and Olga Ganzen (OTI Global Consultants). This paper describes a computer literacy service-learning project performed in Brazil. This project was done in the context of a computer networking course.

Chapter 13, entitled "Service-Learning Through Agile Software Development," is written by Joseph Chao and Jennifer Warnke of Bowling Green University. This paper offers an in-depth look at the use of Agile methods in the context of an SL in CIS software engineering course. It also describes the Agile Software Factory (ASF) concept they created to support the selection and ongoing sustaining engineering of SL in CIS project results.

Chapter 14, entitled "Empowerment Through Service-Learning: Teaching Technology to Senior Citizens," is written by Sally Beisser of Drake University. This paper offers an analysis of a two-year SL in CIS project focused on digital citizenship empowerment for senior citizens. The paper offers keen insights regarding the impact that this project has had on students and the senior citizens.

Chapter 15, entitled "Hybridizing Virtual- and Field-Based Service-Learning in Green IT," is written by K. Branker and J. M. Pearce of Queen's University (Ontario, Canada). This paper examines an SL in CIS course designed to promote IT energy conversation. Appropedia, an open-source education tool, was used to collaboratively develop and field trial the use of IT energy conservation measures. The chapter also examines the impact of the project on students upon completion of the course.

Chapter 16, entitled "Engaging Engineering Students in a Development Program for a Global South Nation through Service-Learning," is written by Willie K. Ofosu (Penn State–Wilkes-Barre), Francois Sekyere (University of Education, Kumasi Campus), and James Oppong (Kwame Nkrumah University of Science and Technology). This paper examines an SL in CIS project related to the design of providing Internet access over power lines (power-line communication) in Ghana.

Chapter 17, entitled "Leveraging Local Resources to Implement Community-Oriented, Sustainable Computer Education Projects in Los Angeles," is written by Rohit Mathew and Christine Maxwell of UCLA. This paper examines BOOTUP, an education and civic engagement project undertaken by the UCLA Chapter of Engineers without Borders. The focus of BOOTUP is to "design and implement a sustainable computer education project that provides value to both the local community as well as engineering students at UCLA."

Chapter 18, entitled "Using Labdoo to Bridge the Digital Divide: A New Form of International Cooperation," is written by Jordi Ros-Giralt (UCLA), Kevin Launglucknavalai (University of California–Irvine), Daniel Massaguer (University of California–Irvine), Julieta Casanova (Ministry of Economy, Madrid, Spain), and Christine Maxwell (UCLA). This paper describes Labdoo, a project originally conceived by the UCLA Chapter of Engineers without Borders. This paper describes Labdoo as a fascinating community portal and process model used "to provide laptops for every school on the planet so that children can gain free access to sources of education."

Chapter 19, entitled "The CHARMS Application Suite: A Community-Based Mobile Data Collection and Alerting Environment for HIV/AIDS Orphan and Vulnerable Children in Zambia," is written by Brian Nejmeh (Messiah College) and Tyler Dean (Carnegie Mellon University). This paper details a mobile-desktop–Web application project developed as part of two different SL in CIS courses (database applications and systems analysis/design applications). The project resulted in an application suite that was field tested in Zambia. The results of the field test and lessons learned from the project are summarized in the paper.

CHAPTER 6

SOME WORKED BETTER THAN OTHERS
Experience with a Variety of Service-Learning Projects

Ken Vollmar and Pete Sanderson

ABSTRACT

For a number of years, we have incorporated service-learning into our computer science undergraduate curriculum through software engineering course projects. Although students benefit from participation, project outcomes have been mixed. The number of causes of project failure is relatively small but difficult to recognize and predict at project start. Here we present and characterize a number of specific projects, relate project characteristics to subsequent outcomes, and draw conclusions.

6.1   INTRODUCTION

In this chapter we describe some of the service-learning (S-L) projects in computer software we have used in software engineering courses, and consider the effect of project characteristics upon project outcome. Although we firmly believe that the experience of the project is always professionally beneficial to the students, the outcomes of projects have been mixed. It appears that the number of causes of failure of S-L projects is relatively small, but that conditions that contribute to failure are difficult to recognize and predict at project start.

This chapter assumes the environment of S-L projects that exists at Missouri State University. In some courses, the S-L project is integrated into the course for every student, is not optional, and does not result in additional course credit. In other courses, including software engineering, an S-L project is an optional, one-credit-hour additional course component, to which students demonstrate their commitment through the corresponding tuition [1]. An S-L project is often a service performed on behalf of a customer who is a community partner organization. In software engineering, S-L projects are most commonly group projects in which the group is self-formed.

6.2   CHARACTERISTICS OF S-L PROJECTS IN STEM EDUCATIONAL ENVIRONMENTS

First we describe the three primary shareholders in a service-learning project: the students, the S-L customer or community partner, and educational administration, which includes the course instructor, S-L program administration, and university administration. These three groups of shareholders are associated through a triangular relationship and interactions. Goals and priorities differ for the three groups, as each group serves its own primary mission.

Students may expect to receive from an S-L project (in no particular order) course credit, including additional credit or hours where applicable; portfolio and resume building through the completion of a large or useful project; and the satisfaction through community involvement and contribution.

It should be expected that the customer or community partner, as a first priority, is primarily interested in project outcome to the benefit of their own clients. We have called S-L projects in the fields of science, technology, engineering, and mathematics (STEM) "all-or-nothing" projects [2], because the value of the project to the customer is wholly reliant on the successful completion of the project. Acceptance of an S-L project by an educational institution implies that the instructor and students have used professional judgment to determine that the project can be completed within the schedule.

Educational administration of S-L projects involves multiple actors. Instructors have a responsibility to approve and monitor an S-L project for alignment with course goals and outcomes, correctness, and appropriateness for the customer. Instructors and the S-L administrator facilitate interaction with the customer or community partner and verify compliance with university guidelines.

Critical considerations of an S-L project in an educational environment are

1. Completion of project in time available (semester, etc.)
2. Complexity of project compared to team size (extent of contribution expected from each team member)

3. The project's technical content and accomplishment of educational goals of the course that houses the project

4. Extent to which the project will fulfill the community partner need, including postcourse maintenance

The extent of maintenance and support after the initial delivery is an important consideration. In the worst case, an instructor may feel responsible for an accumulation of previous S-L projects after students have left the educational institution. Other considerations include the level of student commitment to the project, the availability of communication with the customer, and the extent to which the scope of the project is flexible [2].

It is often difficult to initiate an S-L project, as there are only a few weeks during which all involved parties must describe, understand, evaluate, negotiate or counterpropose, and agree upon the scope of a project that satisfies all considerations of an educationally aligned S-L project. At Missouri State University, the S-L project is optional, so the number of students who may simply be interested in any S-L project is unknown until the first week of the term, and students must make commitment to a particular project in the first weeks of the term.

6.3   DESCRIPTION OF TYPICAL SOFTWARE S-L PROJECTS

Any project for a software engineering course provides opportunity for typical workplace and professional issues and situations, such as use of a software development model, group dynamics and responsibility, estimating and scheduling, documentation, and recovery from unforeseen issues. An S-L project adds a dimension of reality to a project: interaction with genuine customers instead of the course instructor, whose specification of a project and scope may arouse suspicion of artificiality.

S-L projects in our courses have included original, ground-up development of software in some high-order language; databases; Web pages, including design layout; and spreadsheets. One type of project that we have not (yet) considered as a course project, S-L or otherwise, is that of maintenance or extension of an existing project. Although such a project is expected to occur far more often in industry, our projects have been original development.

Selected, typical examples of course projects at Otterbein University in software engineering for external customers are:

- The Warehouse Inventory System developed for the Greater Columbus Habitat for Humanity is a Windows application that provides a solution for large-scale asset management. Staff will be able to track tools as they are checked out either to a job site or maintenance, as well as update the available quantity of consumable assets. Managers will also be able to generate inventory reports based on numerous parameter combinations. It was developed using Visual Studio C#.NET with an underlying Access database.

- The Donation Pickup Scheduler developed for the Greater Columbus Habitat for Humanity is a Windows application to coordinate, track, and schedule the Build-It-Again-Center's donation pickup process. It will provide a monthly report of donors' names and addresses and other information. Upon entering the donor information, it will inform the user of the next available pickup dates. The system also prints a daily schedule for drivers of pickup vehicles. It was developed using Visual Studio C#.NET with an underlying Access database.

- The website developed for Dreams on Horseback is geared toward charitable groups, individuals, and other potential registrants or donors interested in learning more about equine educational programs. The website contains schedules, multimedia, brochures, pictures, and general information about the program. The user can download brochures and forms. The user can contact the Executive Director via e-mail on the contact page and make donations via regular mail. It was developed using Dreamweaver HTML and Flash.

6.4   CASE STUDIES (SOME SUCCESSFUL AND SOME FAILURES)

In this section we describe several S-L projects and the characteristics that we believe contributed to the project's success or failure.

6.4.1   USDA NRCS—A Successful Project for Image Storage

Project Description. The United States Department of Agriculture Natural Resources Conservation Service (USDA-NRCS) is a federal agency that supports soil surveys, watershed projects, water quality, outreach to elementary and middle schools (including development of materials), and resource conservation. Renowned for its technical expertise in conservation and land stewardship issues, the NRCS organization essentially "helps people help the land."

In August 2006 at the annual lunch event that matches community partners with university S-L instructors of courses that might meet S-L needs, Ken Vollmar met for the first time Steve Hefner, team leader for the USDA-NRCS South Missouri Water Quality Project. Mr. Hefner described and proposed a software project to support NRCS through standard digital photography operations, particularly indexing and storage. NRCS personnel rely upon digital images when communicating with private landowners regarding installation and documentation of conservation practices.

Project Benefits. The need for a simple and concise method of organizing, storing, tagging, and transferring digital images is essential for smooth NRCS operations. The number of digital images makes it imperative that some software be used for image archiving. Despite the widespread availability of image management software in a wide range of characteristics, capabilities, and usage licenses, federal regulations prohibit the installation or use on federally-owned computers of software that has not been properly certified. At the time of the project, no image archiving software had been submitted to USDA for certification, possibly because certification involves inspection of source code.

A project that provided basic image operations and that could be USDA-certified would satisfy fundamental USDA-NRCS image archiving needs.

Project Risks. Although the development team was aware of one federal regulation upon USDA-NRCS computers (that only certified software could be used), another regulation not apparent at project start was that only NRCS employees are allowed to use or access the computers. Typically, such a prohibition would have hampered typical installation activities. In this case, the access prohibition did not affect the outcome as the project was implemented in Java with only typical file operations required for installation. Certainly the certification process, which took several months, formed a much larger schedule risk

Progression and Results. The software development required the team of student computer designers to interview NRCS staff to learn which features were needed, write and debug large amounts of code, and develop a user's manual. NRCS users must be able to add or delete images and provide unique file names, descriptions, and key words for each image. The software, named PhotoStore by the student team, includes a search feature that will produce thumbnail images based on search criteria provided by the user. Once identified, the image will be accessible for transfer to other software utilities.

The software is not an invention of new capabilities, although the implementation of the software is not trivial. The critical characteristic of the software is that its source code is available for inspection to be certified for use by a U.S. federal agency.

The team submitted the software product to the National USDA Interoperability Lab in Washington, D.C. for certification. PhotoStore was nationally certified and approved by the State Information Officer in June 2007 and made available to USDA offices nationwide. The software has been installed and used at USDA facilities in several states.

Lessons Learned. We feel that this project was so successful because of the following characteristics:

- The project was well defined. The students and NRCS staff selected essential features by examining several freely available image management software applications. The selected features were conducive to implementation in Java with Swing components.
- The project was nearly an ideal size for a semester-long project of four CS upper-level students with typical skills. Serendipitously, the requested software features were well suited to the number of students and the time available.
- The customer was familiar with S-L projects. Mr. Hefner and his USDA-NRCS team had previously partnered with a different S-L course for linguistic translation of NRCS materials. As a result of that experience, Mr. Hefner had a good idea of the level of assistance needed by the S-L team to complete this project.
- One student was available after the end of the semester to complete lingering software tasks. Although it is entirely typical for industry projects to have a few tasks remaining at the end of the original schedule, university students often have obligations that prohibit extending the schedule. The customer was amenable to schedule extension and the student's additional effort was instrumental in project success.

6.4.2   King's Way Preschool—A Mixed-Outcome Project for Learning Telephone Numbers (Software Was Completed but Project Was an Operational Failure)

Project Description. One of Ken Vollmar's concerns with service-learning projects for the software engineering course has been the nature of projects proposed by community partners. Many community-partner computer-related needs are not bespoke, ground-up software development projects that are traditional to software engineering courses. More typically, partners propose Web pages, spreadsheets, or database projects, which, although worthy and needed by the community partner, are not well aligned with the course goals of the software engineering course of which service-learning is a component. Also, often projects are requested just prior to the course semester with little opportunity for exploration prior to the date for student commitment to the project. After a few consecutive unsatisfactory outcomes of projects that were solicited from community partners, Ken Vollmar decided to design an appropriate S-L project and find a community partner to accept it.

Ken Vollmar designed characteristics and a rough description of a game that would assist young children in learning a telephone number. In the proposed game, a child performed some reasonably entertaining game action to obtain each digit of a phone number, after which the entire phone number would be displayed visually and audibly. Only arrow keys and minimal mouse actions were required to operate the game. The game would have minimal competitive characteristics: no scoring, timing, or violence.

Ken Vollmar sought and found a community partner and obtained permission through MSU's Institutional Review Board for Research Compliance. University students in the software engineering class completed the game design: a maze to be traversed by a player image in search of the goal that is an image of the next digit of the phone number. Arrow keys move the player image toward the digit. As the digit is reached, that digit is added to the cumulative set of digits in the entire phone number and a new maze is generated with the next subsequent digit. When all phone number digits have been reached, the entire phone number is audibly announced.

Project Benefits. The project assists children in memorizing and understanding a contact phone number for use in emergencies. At the time of its development, cell phones especially designed for children were not yet available and phone calls were primarily made through dialing digits rather than menu or image selection. Therefore, memorization of a contact telephone number was an important component of a child's readiness for unexpected situations.

An aspect of the game advanced for its time is customized imagery and sound. The player image, which moves through the maze toward each phone number digit, may be an image selected on behalf of the user, such as a facial image created by the game administrator, a soccer ball, cartoon logo, and so on. The sound file used to announce the full phone number after successful game completion may be recorded in the familiar voice of a parent or caregiver.

Project Risks. Risks for this project were low, in that community partners had not initiated the project nor specified a needed schedule. After completion, the project would be made available to the general public or any community partner expressing interest. Software risks were minimal, as the project was developed in Java, whose libraries provided standard graphics and IO functions, and the students had substantial previous Java experience.

Progression and Results. A local private preschool agreed to allow the project to be piloted by their students. University protocols for privacy and safety of experiment subjects were followed in that university students or instructors had no access to personal information or physical access to the preschool or students. Critical information (e.g., phone numbers) was entered by preschool teachers in a role as system administrator, rather than the university students as developers.

University students implemented the project in a pleasantly satisfactory manner. Students researched, discovered, and corresponded with a musician whose hobby and specialty was retro Atari-style music, exactly suitable for the style of the game difficulty and technology level, and received permission for its use as background music. Administrator utilities were developed for input of user data: each preschool student's phone number, maze image, and recording of spoken phone number.

Initially, Ken Vollmar visited the preschool to demonstrate the project to the preschool teachers and assist with the use of administrator utilities so that the game would be ready for use by students. On the day of initial use, the university students visited the preschool to observe the students in their use of the game. Preschool teachers introduced the university development team to the preschool students, and selected the first two students to play the game.

The two preschool students sat down together and began to play. They immediately grasped the maze concept and were gratifyingly enthusiastic in their grasp of the game as they exuberantly began to collect the digits to hear the phone number upon completion.

Lessons Learned. However, the fatal flaw in the project concept became immediately apparent. In short, the preschool students loved the game, but they were learning their friend's phone number! The game failed to protect the confidentiality of phone number data during typical preschool computer usage in which computer viewing by multiple students is at least commonplace if not standard. The game was intended to assist in memorization of one instance of protected information. However, the game should not be accessed without confidence in privacy of access and view. That confidence is provided by a password, which is simply a memorization of a different instance of protected information.

This project did not include input or feedback from a community partner. During its design, biases of typical university-level computer usage patterns obscured the target customer's computer usage pattern, introducing a fatal flaw in data security. The program is suitable for use in a trusted environment where passwords are not necessary, for instance, in a home where all computer users are family members and have already been trusted with the phone number data.

6.4.3 Discovery Center—Mixed Outcome Project for Creating Kiosk Display Slides

In the Spring of 2009, we undertook a jointly developed service-learning project that involved one community partner, the two authors of this paper, four Missouri State University students, and five Otterbein University students, with 700 miles separating the campuses. This project was intended to duplicate the increasingly common industry environment of physically separated teams contributing to the same software project.

Project Description. The Discovery Center (www.discoverycenter.org), an interactive hands-on museum in Springfield, Missouri, had a large collection of PCs and touch-sensitive monitors that had been donated by a past commercial exhibitor. Discovery Center (DC) personnel had a vision of installing some of the systems in kiosks located throughout the center to provide information about exhibits as well as to answer frequently asked questions, such as "Where is the nearest restroom?" All interaction would be through the touch-sensitive monitors. Each full-screen image would include hotspots, each defined to transition to a different full-screen image.

Such presentations can be created using PowerPoint™ by defining image hotspots that link to other slides. Nonetheless, we determined that this could be a good student team software engineering project. The tasks of creating and displaying the presentations are simple and well-defined. Software dedicated to these tasks could be easy to use for people not trained in Power-Point. Discovery Center personnel could create presentations themselves and deploy systems appropriately in the museum.

This project also seemed well suited to an idea we had discussed previously: a software engineering project developed jointly by student teams from Missouri State University and Otterbein University.

Project Benefits. The Discovery Center would benefit by having a free software tool their personnel could use to create and display interactive touch-screen presentations in the museum. Such presentations would not only benefit their visitors by enhancing their interactive experience, but also reduce the time that personnel spend responding to routine frequently asked questions.

Our students would benefit by operating in a distributed team development environment more closely resembling one they may experience after graduation. The project could be implemented in Java, a language familiar to all team members from both universities. The application would be challenging to develop yet engaging and doable in the projected time frame. Students would also gain experience working with a real-world client and the personal satisfaction common to S-L projects.

Project Risks. This being our first attempt at such a joint project, we anticipated a number of risks but could not know their significance in advance. The most obvious risks are listed here.

- *Curriculum structure.* Missouri State students were developing this project as an integral component of the three-semester-hour software engineering course. Students had the option of selecting a one-hour companion service-learning course but were not required to do so. The software engineering course did not include a scheduled project meeting time. Otterbein students were developing this project as a stand-alone practicum course with a software engineering prerequisite. The practicum included four hours of scheduled meeting time per week. There was a mismatch in student prerequisite knowledge and team meeting opportunities.

- *Schedule.* The Missouri State software engineering course covered the spring semester, mid-January through mid-May, meeting on Monday, Wednesday, and Friday. The Otterbein practicum course was actually a two-course sequence covering the winter quarter and spring quarter, early January through early June, meeting on Tuesday and Thursday. Thus, there was a mismatch in course schedules and grading periods.

- *Combined structure and schedule.* Otterbein students started sooner, finished later, and, due to the previous fall's software engineering course, already had not only knowledge and experience with software development life cycle models and activities but also a team structure already in place at the start of the project period.

- *Instructor requirements.* The two of us needed to coordinate our expectations for project deliverables and schedules. Would deliverables be developed jointly? If so, how would they be evaluated and how would students feel about part of their grade being determined by the work of students at a different university 700 miles away? Also, both of us had other teams to consider as well as the joint team. This would require ongoing effort and communication.

- *Communication.* There were many means for Missouri State and Otterbein team members to communicate with each other: telephone, e-mail, text messaging, wiki, and social networking. Neither we nor the students knew which would be effective.

- *Client contact and commitment.* Missouri State students could have direct face-to-face contact with the project clients whereas Otterbein students could not. Client commitment to the project is always a risk, particularly with not-for-profit organizations with many needs and few personnel.

Progression and Results. Prior to the January 2009 formal joint project start, we communicated with each other regarding project possibilities, and a Missouri State student did some proof-of-concept game programming as an independent study to demonstrate that the touch-sensitive monitors were functional and programmable. At this point, one of the monitors and PCs was shipped to Otterbein for use by its team.

In the meantime, client commitment was beginning to falter. A planned exhibit for which they wanted to use the kiosks was being delayed and they were uncertain about alternative uses.

This uncertainty about the project mission continued into January. While this was being resolved through communication among the two of us and the Discovery Center, Missouri State students started their software engineering course and began project selection while Otterbein students started experimenting with the touch-sensitive monitor and game software provided by the Missouri State student.

We followed more or less a waterfall development approach for this project. Although not ideal, it can work in situations in which client time commitment is uncertain or inconsistent. This is frequently the case in service-learning projects. Community partners are often overwhelmed and understaffed. They can commit focused attention for the duration of a requirements analysis but not the consistent interaction over time needed for successful agile development.

Once the basic project scope and team membership were determined, the teams began to establish communication and document-sharing channels. Asynchronous channels were determined to be preferable due to the difficulty in scheduling a common time for all team members to meet and communicate via Skype or similar media. Social media such as Facebook proved difficult to configure properly to include all team members while excluding others. E-mail was satisfactory for person-to-person and team-to-team communication but inefficient for exchange of project artifacts.

The teams determined that a wiki combined with e-mail would be the best solution. The wiki would serve as a repository to which any team member could contribute to the exclusion of others. One of the Otterbein students analyzed free wiki-hosting services and decided on Wikidot (www.wikidot.com). An account and URL were established, members were added, and the basic wiki structure was created. In hindsight, Wikidot may not have been the best choice. It did not offer a WYSIWYG editor, requiring a markup language that was similar to but different than HTML. This is not a learning barrier for upper-division computer science students but it does slow down content addition and maintenance. The most useful feature proved to be the ability to add a comments section to any page. The most awkward aspect was the artifact repository. Uploading a document to the wiki does not make it visible; one must also explicitly create a link to it on the wiki page.

The wiki included pages for the Project Vision document; a week-by-week schedule, including timelines for deliverables; the document repository; a collection of project resources; and a discussion forum. All pages except the forum included a comments section at the end.

The greatest challenges involved developing a set of requirements and dividing the tasks between the Missouri State and Otterbein teams. Missouri State students had direct client access but Otterbein students were not to serve as hired hands, simply writing code as directed. Collaboration was proving to be a significant challenge.

As spring break arrived for both universities (fortunately, the same week), the project was floundering. During the break, we decided it was necessary to intervene and dictate a system design that would enable both teams to work more independently. The Missouri State team would develop the software that controls the kiosk presentations (MapDisplay) and the Otterbein team would develop the software used to create the presentations (MapMaker). The only common code was a Java interface (TouchMap) specifying operations for a presentation slide. MapMaker is the more complex of the two applications but the Otterbein team not only had more students but also an additional four weeks due to the quarter schedule. The situation is not ideal because MapMaker will be used by Discover Center personnel and Otterbein students do not have easy access to them.

Following spring break, the pace and productivity increased rapidly. One slight bump occurred in early May, when the Missouri State team was preparing to present their project to Discovery Center personnel. They needed both a prototype and a user manual for Otterbein's then-incomplete MapMaker application for their presentation. The prototype was already available for download from the wiki but the user manual had to be created. It was a revelation to the students that the user manual could be written before the software was completed! It was also a reminder that their code needed to be consistent with both of those specification-oriented artifacts. The user manual was easily written, incorporating screen shots from the prototype, and the presentation and demo went well. After some post-spring-quarter tweaking, the complete system was delivered in July.

The two of us paid a follow-up visit to the Discovery Center several months later for an additional demonstration, Q&A, and training. They expressed great satisfaction with the software and demonstrated an ability to use it. However, as of this writing they have not used it to create any presentations.

Lessons Learned. Although a functioning system was delivered to the client, this project can be considered only a partial success. Some of the risks described above were realized and affected the project to various degrees.

The semester–quarter mismatch caused some difficulty but that was predicted and manageable. The prerequisite mismatch between the two universities led to serious problems. At the start of the project, Otterbein students had already completed the software engineering course that the Missouri State students were only beginning. Although this was also known in advance, we did not plan for it as well as we should have. The Otterbein team spent its first month on project background activities that proved to add little value to the final product.

Although the two of us consistently communicated and collaborated on course requirements for deliverables, we could have improved this as well. Both of us had other teams working on different projects, and we had to assure that our adjustments to the Discovery Center project requirements maintained equity with the other teams.

It is not necessary for all team members to be involved in every aspect of a software engineering project, but in a collaborative project it is highly desirable for representatives from both teams to be involved in all development phases. Otherwise, it turns into a stereotypical outsourcing situation in which one group determines the requirements and designs and the other group implements them. This is difficult to achieve when the client is local to one and remote from the other. It is also difficult without synchronous communications between the groups. Skype was available at the time of the project, and we should have compelled students to schedule and conduct video calls using it. They would have been difficult to schedule due to student class and work schedules in addition to the Tuesday–Thursday versus Monday–Wednesday–Friday class meeting times.

We had some degree of control over all the above factors and now know how to mitigate them for future projects. However, we do not control our client, whose changing needs in this case affected the course of the project to an extent. This was a good experience for our students, who came to realize that projects do not always progress as smoothly as do the case studies in their software engineering textbooks!

6.4.4   Board Games on the Screen—A Mixed-Outcome Project (Software Was Completed but Project Was an S-L Failure)

Project Description. A student team in the software engineering course proposed a course project involving the graphic implementation of the familiar board games "Chutes and Ladders" (trademark of Hasbro Corp.) and "Hi Ho! Cherry-O" (trademark of Hasbro Corp.). One but not all of the students in the group wished to undertake an S-L project (the S-L component is a one-hour, 300-level course, which can be attractive to meeting university degree requirements of 40 hours at the 300-level or above). The student involved in the S-L component proposed, in addition to the baseline project, to prepare and tailor the implemented games for use by a local after-school program.

Project Benefits. According to the Hasbro website [3], referring to a similar game, "The game teaches color recognition and matching while reinforcing the lesson of taking turns and being a gracious winner or loser." Additional benefits of online game implementation are that game pieces cannot be lost, that a single player can be provided with one or more virtual opponents (eliminating the former benefits of social interactivity), and that a broader variety of games can be made available than would be expected through physical games.

Project Risks. Java was used for the implementation, and the primary risk was the animation of the game pieces and action. The students had originally planned more games, but during the initial planning stages chose to limit themselves to the more manageable number of two games.

A substantial risk was undetected during project design and ultimately doomed the S-L project: copyright and trademark issues of the board game appearance and use. All parties concentrated on software and technical risks and did not properly consider the intellectual property of the game itself.

Progression and Results. Although the project was divided into four purportedly similarly sized parts, the project design and implementation were dominated by two of the four group members with high levels of skill and self-confidence. By project end, all members had contributed to portions of the software and to the implementation of one of the games. The games were well implemented with smooth animation of game pieces. The quality of playing experience of the online version compared to the physical version is perhaps a matter of individual choice.

Lessons Learned. At the time it became clear that the S-L project would encounter substantial copyright and trademark issues, the S-L portion of the project was redirected. The S-L student completed the S-L portion by visiting a local elementary school to observe first-graders' computer usage habits and skills.

This project was our first experience of a project for which some members of a group participated in the S-L component and other members of the same group did not participate. We believe this to be an unworkable arrangement. The interaction with the customer should form a substantial portion of the project and all members of the group should expect to participate in all aspects of the project. At the same time, we have allowed students to be a group of one person, possibly with an S-L project.

6.4.5 Get-Well Notes for a Hospital—A Successful Project

A local hospital wished to have an e-mail mechanism through which to accept greetings and get-well notes for patients.

Project Description. E-mail is a fast and attractive alternative to traditional, postal-delivery greeting cards. However, legally mandated standards for patient privacy and health data prohibit the existence of a publicly accessible patient list, including an acknowledgement that a person is in fact a patient. Without a publicly accessible patient directory, e-mail cannot be sent directly to a corresponding individual e-mail address. Instead, all e-mails will be sent to a central location from which they will be printed and delivered by volunteers as hard copy.

The Web page that implements the project should be an implementation of an e-mail form containing both required and optional data. Required data includes patient name and sender's name and e-mail. (The user must have obtained knowledge from some other source than the hospital that a person is a patient. Receipt or delivery of messages is not acknowledged by the hospital so that there can be no phishing for verification that anyone is a hospital patient.) Optional data includes a message and selection of common phrases and imagery.

This project had remained on the hospital's to-do list as a low-priority item for some time. One of the students in the class was aware of the project because he was employed by the hospital in a software capacity. The student obtained permission to take on the project for the class.

Project Benefits. Existence of an e-mail get-well note system solves some problems of timely delivery and protection of health data. For instance, items arriving through U.S. mail addressed to former hospital patients should be either forwarded to the patient's home address or returned to sender. Either action is at least a time-consuming activity for hospital volunteers and in the worst case could improperly disclose protected information. Conversely, e-mail need not be either forwarded or returned. E-mail get-well notes will still result in some volunteer activity: printout, lookup of patient name and room, and physical delivery to rooms.

Project Risks. Many risks were eliminated by the circumstances of the project selection. Because the student was employed at the hospital in a computer role, he was familiar enough with the need and the expected operation that he could, in effect, act as the customer to describe the project to the rest of the S-L project team.

Progression and Results. The project progressed with no discernible issues. The project was probably somewhat smaller and less complicated than is preferable for the course, but was complicated enough that the hospital's own computer staff had not taken it up for some time. The project team members had not been familiar with the necessary Web programming techniques, and so acquired those skills during the project.

Lessons Learned. This project could be described as one that was developed by the class and then offered to a customer, without direct involvement by the customer during development. That environment is less damaging to the customer in the event that the project fails to materialize, but does not provide students with the level of interaction that the S-L experience is intended to provide.

6.5 CONCLUSIONS

It is important to separate the success of a project as an educational element of the course and as a solution to an S-L customer's need. A project may have been quite effective in reinforcing course goals, yet not meet the customer's need. Conversely, an S-L project could be successful to a customer but not meet the course goals. An ideal S-L project would succeed in both areas.

In our experience, genuine successes of S-L projects that are components of software engineering courses with a community partner have been few. It has rarely been our experience to be contacted after the delivery of the project, suggesting either that the software continues to meet the customer needs without modification, or that the software is no longer in use.

Failed S-L projects have been those in which:

- Some fundamental flaw was overlooked at project design, especially due to tunnel vision, focusing on schedule and technical details.
- An S-L project, typically proposed by a community partner, was accepted as a course project although not genuinely well-aligned to course goals. For example, a community partner may request a complex spreadsheet, which is a worthy project but not a typical project for a software engineering course.

Successful S-L projects have been those in which:

- The community partner representative is engaged and meets consistently with developers (that is, active communication between developer and customer).
- The project is either relatively simple or a representative of the community partner had the talent to maintain the system.

REFERENCES

1. Citizenship and Service-Learning at Missouri State University, Annual Report 2011. Retrieved August 29, 2011 from http://www.missouristate.edu/assets/casl/CASL_AR_080211_CMYK_Hcompr2.pdf.

2. Vollmar, K., and Sanderson, P. (2010). Checklists for an "All-or-Nothing" Service-Learning Project. In M. A. Cooksey and K. T. Olivares (Eds.), *Quick Hits for Service-Learning: Successful Strategies by Award-Winning Teachers* (pp. 158–159). Bloomington: Indiana University Press.

3, Hasbro Games—Chutes and Ladders Game. Retrieved August 29, 2011 from http://www.hasbro.com/games/en_US/play/browse/Chutes-Ladders/Both/_/N-3pZ1z/Ne-2l.

CHAPTER 7

EPICS SOFTWARE DEVELOPMENT PROJECTS

William Oakes and Saurabh Bagchi

ABSTRACT

The EPICS program, founded at Purdue University, has proved to be an effective model for university engagement with local communities. Software development has been a vital component of the portfolio of projects within the EPICS program since its inception. Initially, software projects were distributed across the program, with individual divisions supporting software needs for their particular community partner. EPICS restructured and concentrated the software development efforts into specific software divisions that serve multiple community partners. This chapter highlights the efforts of these divisions with examples of database projects that are used across multiple local applications.

7.1 INTRODUCTION

The EPICS program, described in Chapter 2, pairs teams of students with local or global not-for-profit agencies, educational institutions, or government organizations to develop solutions to meet the needs of the community (Coyle, et al., 1997, 2005, 2006). The opportunities for software projects are immense and span such a wide range of partners that the EPCIS program dedicated specific divisions of the courses to software development. Projects are grouped based on common needs so that common technologies can be shared with multiple community partners. Like all projects in EPICS, the software projects often extend across multiple semesters and the teams provide support to fielded projects from prior semesters.

7.1.1   Not-for-Profits as Contexts for Software Development

Local community organizations offer rich learning opportunities for students in software development. The community organizations provide real users who often do not know what can be done with software nor can they articulate all of the requirements for a software system. This means that the students must work to identify the specifications and the needs for their users. In today's globally competitive work environment, understanding users and creating robust and easy-to-use software is critically important. The community-based projects provide the kind of learning environment and experiences for students to gain just such skills.

In addition to student learning, these projects are compelling because of the tremendous needs within the community and opportunity to leverage software solutions to be able to meet these needs more efficiently. Not-for-profits, schools, and governmental organizations are being asked to serve more people with fewer resources. Software solutions can add the efficiencies needed to meet these needs. The problem is that these organizations have neither the technical staff nor the financial resources to take advantage of these capabilities. This gap is an opportunity for the software engineering education community (Jamieson, 2002; Oakes et al., 2002).

7.1.2   Purdue EPICS program and Software Development

This chapter provides experiences from selected projects developed within the EPICS program at Purdue University. Example partnerships, projects, and lessons learned are provided. Additional information on EPICS and the projects can be found at the EPICS website (www.purdue.edu/epics).

EPICS has concentrated software engineering expertise into a few specific lab divisions that can serve multiple community partners. These divisions were organized around technologies and the kind of partners they served. The specific software divisions include:

1. Advanced Design (APPS), which is developing apps for mobile devices, iPad, and Google Android that can benefit the community. This team works across multiple organizations to develop apps.

2. Web-based Interactive Software Engineering (WISE) team develops interactive Web-based data software solutions across multiple local community agencies in order to expand their ability to meet local needs (EPICS 2011a).

3. Database and Innovative Software for the Community (DISC), which is creating database applications and innovative solutions to help not-for-profit, educational, and service agencies. This team works across multi-

ple community organizations with similar software needs (EPICS, 2011b).

4. Information Management Systems for EPICS Teams (IMS) develops online, large-scale software applications for EPICS students and faculty. The team is the internal development team for EPICS course software that can be used across institutions to enable EPICS teams to serve their communities more effectively.

5. Greater Lafayette Area Special Services (GLASS) develops technological solutions that enable students with disabilities aged 3–21 to function more independently and enjoy a better quality of life. This team is the one that works across technologies, including hardware, mechanical, and software projects with its focus on children with disabilities. The software projects have been focused on developing apps for the iPad, specifically involving communication disabilities among the students they serve.

The WISE and DISC teams were created to develop software for their community partners, who in some cases have other EPICS teams developing other projects for them. Example community partners are shown in Table 7.1 and example projects, software and nonsoftware, are described.

7.2   EXAMPLE EPICS SOFTWARE PROJECTS

Three projects are highlighted that serve the needs of the partners listed in Table 7.1. A more complete set of projects can be found on the Purdue EPICS website at www.purdue.edu/epics. Each of these projects have been done within the EPICS courses and have spanned multiple years in the development and support of the projects.

7.2.1   Tippecanoe County Probation Department

The Tippecanoe County Probation Department serves the Tippecanoe County Courts through the preparation of presentence and predisposition investigations and the supervision of adult and juvenile offenders. The partnership with the Probation Department started in 2000 with the formation of the Judicial Database Systems (JDS) team. The team was advised originally by an industry volunteer who worked for a company in the Purdue Research Park and subsequently by a faculty member from Computer Science in 2007. Over that time, the team averaged about eight students per semester on the project. Like many of the software projects in EPICS, the team began to

Table 7.1. Example partnerships and projects

Community partner and mission	Software developed	Other EPICS projects developed for the partner
Tippecanoe County Probation Department serves the Tippecanoe County Courts through the preparation of presentence and predisposition investigations and the supervision of adult and juvenile offenders.	Create a secure and reliable Web access for parole officers to retrieve and modify information on the parolees from any computer connected to the Internet.	N/A
The Lafayette Crisis Center is a resource center for suicide prevention, rape, and other forms of crisis. They have a 24-hour hotline as well as walk-in services at their location.	Create a scheduling system that will automatically generate a schedule based on volunteer's preferences.	Information kiosks allowing community members to identify and locate community services and call or print information about the resource
University Place Retirement Community is a retirement community near Purdue's campus.	Create a volunteer management system to efficiently identify and link volunteers with events.	Design of a closed-circuit TV, communication and information system, computer coaching for residents, and optimization of acoustic environments.
Community and Family Resource Center serves the community through after-school programs for school-aged youth, Head Start, a food pantry, and counseling, and sponsors community dinners.	Create a volunteer management system to efficiently identify and link volunteers with events.	Model Mars rover for a after-school program, donation-management system to organize and distribute donations.
Lafayette School Corporation is the school system for Lafayette, Indiana, serving preschool through 12th grade.	Create a volunteer management system to efficiently identify and link volunteers with events.	Recycling system for the school, demonstration models for physics classroom, traffic flow analysis, and model customized traffic signals for school parking lot.

struggle to recruit and retain a critical mass of students and the interest waned. In 2009, the project was folded into the newly created Database and Innovative Software for the Community (DISC) team, which is advised by one faculty member from computer science and another from computer engineering. The DISC team averages about 12 students and has multiple partners. This project had four to six students in a given semester.

This project was to create a secure and reliable Web access for parole officers to retrieve and modify information on the parolees from any computer connected to the Internet. The previous team (JDS) had developed two versions of the software for the Probation Department. When the project moved to the DISC team, a new version was developed that would be compatible with the previous versions. The look and feel of some of the screens needed to be similar to the look and feel of the corresponding screens in their current system. Further, the software needed to work with the Probation Department's other software, which included Windows Server, ASP.NET, IIS, and Microsoft SQL Server, and it had to support Firefox 3 and up, as well as IE 7 and up. The team created the front end, the middle tier, and the back end to support the functionality. This involved creating multiple tabs for different requirements, such as reading a parolee's information and updating the information. The team put various security measures in place so that only authorized users could make modifications. There was a mandatory federal requirement for the strength of the encryption (128 bit) and the different categories of users that had to be supported (general user, privileged user, super user, etc.). The team encountered several persistent and common bugs in various functionalities, such as data entry causing the site to crash (due to too long a data field), validation issues with user input, and cross-browser display problems. However, with the appropriate software-building expertise, the students were able to overcome these problems and delivered a new working version to the partner. Improvements are being developed as part of the next version with additional features.

Among the lessons learned by the team over the past decade of engagement was to maintain contact with the community partner. The initial software deliveries were successful and met the needs at the time but as time passed, the needs changed and these changes needed to be addressed in subsequent versions. It is very important to be clear about the expectations of the community partner on a project. It was important to acclimate new members both to the technologies that were used by the team but also about the community partner's environment and needs. The EPICS program learned several lessons while working on the project.

7.2.2 Lafayette Crisis Center Scheduling

The Lafayette Crisis Center (LCC) fills a major need in Tippecanoe and White Counties by providing round-the-clock crisis intervention, suicide prevention, and information and referral 24 hours a day, 365 days a year. The Crisis Center was one of the first partners for EPICS in 1995 with initial projects involving a network of interactive kiosks for referrals to community services. That project was successful and ended. The Crisis Center had been a good partner and EPICS sought to fill other needs and that involved software.

The need for a software system to manage their volunteers was identified and the project was included in the portfolio of the DISC EPICS team. The DISC team has two faculty advisors and an average of 12 students per semester. The DISC team managed multiple projects at once, so about four students would work on the scheduling project each semester.

Creating the volunteer schedule with all of the volunteer's schedule preferences is time-consuming when done by hand. The team was tasked to develop an automated system to improve efficiency. The goal of the system was to have the volunteers enter their schedule preferences and automatically produce an optimized schedule. The system would allow the crisis centers to manage the volunteers efficiently, freeing the staff to concentrate more time on the core elements of the center. Confidentiality and security were key requirements of the projects.

The design has two parts: Visual Studio has a database/graphical user interface (GUI) and a Python script that contains the scheduling algorithm. Visual Basic was chosen so that future versions could implement an online ASP application if the partner desired. All of the community partner's requests are accounted for in the GUI. The program simulated, as close as possible, the manual process of creating the schedule, capturing as many of the benefits from the manual method, and meeting the partner's requirements. The user can input all the data of the volunteer's schedule and submit the data in the GUI. The data is then written to a formatted file that maintains the information and preferences of each volunteer. The program is created to save the previous month's data file to allow access to previous schedule information. The formatted files can be reloaded into the GUI and modified as needed.

The Python script contains a working-scheduling algorithm that takes the formatted file and generates a working schedule. Variations of algorithms to optimize the matching of volunteer preferences and available shifts were developed and tested with sample cases provided by the partner. The optimized algorithm produces a schedule that is output in an iCal format file that can be opened up in several different calendar viewers. The program automatically opens the created schedule in Microsoft Outlook for the community partner to view and manually edit if he/she desires. The project was developed over two semesters and the first version delivered to the partner in December of 2010. A sample of the GUI is shown in Figure 7.1. Newer versions with added features are under development.

One of the biggest lessons that were learned from the project was truly understanding the user and his/her needs and constraints. The initial proto-

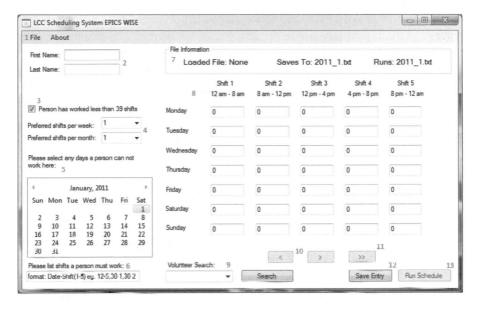

Figure 7.1. GUI for volunteer scheduling software.

types that were being developed missed aspects of the user's needs. Ideally, the team would spend time with the user or stakeholders. The Crisis Center presented particular challenges with their issues of privacy. The team wanted to observe the center but there is a policy of privacy and confidentiality of the staff. The students could not be in a place where they might overhear a call if it came into the center, which pretty much eliminated opportunities to observe and talk with the staff. The team did some observations and discussions with the partner and they also developed prototypes that the center could react to. The early ones were not viewed as intermediate prototypes but attempts at the solution. The users would react and provide meaningful feedback after seeing a version and this lead to satisfactory iterations on the designs that produced the final product. The lesson learned was to prototype early and often to get the information from the users.

7.2.3   Volunteer Management System

Many of our community partners manage large number of volunteers but lack the technical support to create and manage software systems. The result is that the volunteers are managed manually or using simple tools such as spreadsheets that are manually coordinated. Events such as the Community Christmas Day Dinner that serves over 3000 meals to area residents and engages nearly 800 volunteers require a great deal of staff time to manage volunteers. Although many partners have the common need to manage volunteers, each has a set of unique requirements that necessitate customization to meet their respective needs. The school systems, for example, needed a feature to screen volunteers who had been approved through criminal background checks before they were allowed to be school volunteers. A community center needed a way for families to sign up together for their community events rather than just as individuals. The solution was to develop a core volunteer management system that could be easily modified to meet the specific needs of several partners.

The project is part of the portfolio of the WISE EPICS team that has two advisors and an average of 15 students per semester and four to six students dedicated to this project in a semester. The team began by surveying partners and developing a common set of requirements for those needing a volunteer management system. The overall concept of the design is to allow for the staff of the organization to create forms for the volunteers to use the World Wide Web to sign up for events online. Administrative functions would be available for the staff to manage volunteers and to track them as needed.

A common SQL database was designed using a classes approach. For example, if you wanted to connect to the database, you would just call the connect to database class. This would help with reusing code, for the present and the future. You could also call these classes APIs. Classes are implemented based on the tables in the database. account, family, admin, event and jobs are the classes used in the system. Creating a new account class gives functionality to create, read, delete, and update an account by the user. The other classes have similar functionality. A user signing up for an account on the system is automatically added to the family table in the database. For an admin account, the admin will be added to the account table and the admin table, similar to the family account. For a guest account, the admin will enter the user into the database under the account table. For events, an event is added to the database, and then jobs are added that point to the database. When somebody signs up, that person is added to the signedup database table.

The team took the concept and developed use-case diagrams and ER models. They visited community partners to critique the ideas. The partners provided positive feedback and were extremely excited to see the diagrams and were able to easily understand the processes so the design proceeded.

The team used ASP.NET and C# inside of visual studio to develop the applications. The main reason for using visual studio was the autogenerated code. ASP.NET was easy to learn and all members on the team could be brought up to speed quickly. C# required knowing classes, which is taught in the first year for computer science students, and taught in the sophomore year for computer engineering students.

The core system was developed over four semesters. The system has been customized and delivered to three partners within the community and is expanding to other partners while the team supports the fielded versions. The results have been very positive with the agencies reporting significant time savings on the part of their staff. This time saving is critically important as current budget and economic conditions are putting more pressure on the nonprofits.

The team learned that understanding the user's needs and their capabilities, in terms of computer knowledge and physical infrastructure, was critically important. They have also learned that to manage multisemester projects requires effective transition planning and execution. The documentation must be done well and the codes well commented, to make the transition to the next semester effective. Tutorials were prepared by returning students to get the new students up to speed quickly so that they could participate in the code development.

7.3 BEST PRACTICES

Facilitating the development of software projects for nonprofits places faculty in the role of advisors or coaches to students as they learn how to develop their own projects. In this role, we can guide students and we have learned several best practices for the student teams. This is a different kind of teaching from traditional lecture and exam courses. Some of the key best practices we have experienced include:

1. Understand the requirements of the software, including the environment in which it will be operated and from what kinds of devices. For example, is it going to be used from a desktop or a hand-held mobile device? Over what kind of network (what speed, what reliability, etc.) will it run? Many of the organizations use hardware that students would consider obsolete, whereas others have the latest technologies. Students need to be aware of the environment and to design their software appropriately.

2. Understand the users. Students need to spend time with the users to understand them. What is the need they are addressing with the software? What is the technical expertise level of the people who will be operating the software? Are there users with any physical or mental challenges? We have to keep the usability of the software pegged to

the technical level of the people who will be using it. We have to ensure that user interfaces are appropriate for the users. The students must understand whether there is in-house expertise to maintain the software, even at the most basic level, such as updating the underlying software platform (such as the Microsoft .NET framework).

3. Gather the right team. There should be a proper mix of expertise needed on the project. For example, in the project for the Tippecanoe County Probation Department, described above, we needed several students with expertise in C# and a fewer with expertise in HTML and Cascading Style Sheets (CSS). There are also places for students who are not software engineers but can add skills and experiences to do usability studies, research on the users, or generate good manuals that are appropriate for the users.

4. Create a time line with enough time for integration and testing. Testing should not be left until the end and should be part of the development process. Early testing includes storyboards and screenshots of mockups. Component testing and user testing is as important as testing the final code. Make sure that the students leave time for beta testing at the nonprofit's premises to test for system issues. Have internal milestones in the timeline at a granularity of two weeks early on and more frequently closer to delivery.

5. Have some members of the team be responsible for maintenance of the software once it has been delivered. This is understandably a nonglamorous part of the project, but critically important for the long-term adoption of the project. Ideally, some of the developers will stay with the project long enough to be able to maintain it. In the nonideal scenario, the developer team should leave a detailed troubleshooting guide that will aid others in maintenance. Pay careful attention to recruit students who will have the skill to maintain an existing project. It would be ideal to train some personnel at the nonprofit's site to ultimately take over the task of maintenance. This is keeping in mind the transient nature of the student population.

6. Train new students for the projects. The most successful EPICS software teams have developed transition processes for new students. These include mentoring and tutorials to orient students to the software. Provide opportunities for the students to learn the development tools and review the prior work to becoming oriented. This can be instructional as well, as attributes and deficiencies can be identified as they review the prior work. Schedule times for the students to meet, see, and interact with the community partners to begin to understand their context, needs, and capabilities.

7.4 DEFINING REQUIREMENTS: UNDERSTANDING THE USERS

Developing software for the community requires the development team to truly understand the community partner. Visit and talk to the personnel from the nonprofit organization who will use or be impacted by the software. This should include personnel at different levels of the management chain: people who will be operating the software, those who will be maintaining it (the local IT people), those who will be making purchasing decisions (what kinds of machines, cooling, furniture, etc.), as well as those who may be indirect users or who will be impacted by the designs.

Once a team has had an initial discussion, go back to the drawing board and come up with a sketch of the design of the software. It should show different screens, including the buttons that will go on the screens. Show these to the partners and listen for their reactions. Do not just ask for a blessing of your ideas but rather use the sketches as a communication device to learn more about their needs.

Explain to the partner the software and the hardware platform that you are planning on using. Make sure that these platforms are either already available or can be acquired at the partner site. Also check that your platform requirements do not clash with any software platform that they already have. For example, if they are using the iPad as the rendering device, do not rely on Adobe Flash for your animations.

Repeat the process of visiting the community partners. At the second meeting, you may have more sketches or screenshots of mock ups. Collect another round of feedback from a variety of persons at the partner organization, again preferably at different layers of the management chain. Expect the requirements to change during the process. It is important to keep the conversation going with the partner to be aware of when the requirements have changed. The partner may not feel the requirements have changed but your understanding of their needs may change. Once they see your ideas, they may want to go in another direction, which is why frequent interactions are key.

Ground the partner's expectations in reality—one cannot develop a robust software system if the requirements change continuously. There is a trade-off. It is prudent to fix the requirements before the design begins and then stick to these requirements. Real projects often require changes. Small changes to the requirements can be accommodated through minor releases of the software, but no more than that. The key is to learn as much about the partner and the requirements early so that major changes are not needed at the end.

7.5 CONCLUSIONS

The model for EPICS of creating partnerships with local and global community organizations is an excellent model for software development. The ability of the program to respond to needs within the community has been increased by concentrating the software engineering capabilities within specific divisions of the EPICS courses. This model has allowed the faculty with expertise in software development to concentrate on these divisions and provide appropriate mentoring for the teams. It has also increased interest among software students.

The community provides many opportunities to challenge students to develop innovative approaches to software designs. It also provides real users that students can interact with and learn from. The community users are not always technically savvy and often require students to be creative to extract the requirements for the software. This provides excellent learning opportunities for the students in user-centered design approaches.

The opportunity to make an impact within the community is significant but care must be taken to ensure that we add value to the community. Simply developing a software package for a community context is not enough. We have seen over and over that issues arise after delivery of software. Sometimes, bugs are found. Other times, features are identified that could lead to another version. Creating curricular structures that allow students to participate and lead in the support as well as the development creates learning experiences that can prepare our students to become leaders in software development and meet the needs of the community. The EPICS approach is one approach that has proved successful in both areas.

REFERENCES

Coyle, Edward J., Jamieson, Leah H. and Sommers, Larry S. (1997). "EPICS: A Model for Integrating Service-Learning into the Engineering Curriculum," *Michigan Journal of Community Service-Learning,* Vol. 4, Fall 1997.

Coyle, Edward J., Jamieson, Leah H., and Oakes, William C., (2005). "EPICS: Engineering Projects in Community Service," *International Journal of Engineering Education* Vol. 21, No. 1, Feb. 2005, pp. 139–150.

Coyle, E. J., Jamieson, L. H., and Oakes, W. C., (2006). "Integrating Engineering Education and Community Service: Themes for the Future of Engineering Education," *Journal of Engineering Education,* Vol. 95, No. 1, January 2006, pp. 7–11.

EPICS program, (2011a). WISE Team, Retrieved October 31, 2011 from http://epics.ecn.purdue.edu/wise/.

EPICS program, (2011b). DISC Team, Retrieved October 31, 2011 from http://epics.ecn.purdue.edu/disc/.

EPICS program, (2011c). Past Teams—JDS Team, Retrieved October 31, 2011 from https://engineering.purdue.edu/EPICS/Projects/PastTeams/viewTeam?teamid=17.

EPICS program, (2011d). Past Teams—LCC Team, Retrieved October 31, 2011 from https://engineering.purdue.edu/EPICS/Projects/PastTeams/viewTeam?teamid=20.

Jamieson, Leah, (2002). "Service Learning in Computer Science and Engineering." in *Proceedings of the 33rd SIGCSE Technical Symposium on Computer Science Education.*

Oakes, William, Duffy, John, Jacobius, Thomas, Linos, Panos, Lord, Susan, Schultz, William W., and Smith, Amy, (2002). "Service-Learning In Engineering," in *Proceedings of the 2002 ASEE/IEEE Frontiers in Education Conference,* Boston, MA, Nov. 2002.

CHAPTER 8

HFOSS SERVICE-LEARNING CASE STUDY
The Bowdoin–Ronald McDonald House Projects

Allen Tucker, Ralph Morelli, and Trishan de Lanerolle

ABSTRACT

This paper discusses two service-learning projects that were taught by the first author as one-semester computer science software development courses at Bowdoin College. It identifies how these projects were inspired by the HFOSS Project (see Chapter 5), their service-learning components, their pedagogical organization, their impacts, and their usefulness as a model for similar activities within other undergraduate programs in the information sciences.

8.1 INTRODUCTION

Prior to 2007, the software development course in the Computer Science Department at Bowdoin College (called CS260 hereafter) had been offered in a rather traditional way. The course is a junior–senior level elective open to CS majors and minors. Although it included a team software project, the course was based on a rather traditional approach to software engineering (the waterfall model) and it also included formal methods.

In 2007, however, the instructor in this course had become concerned about the growing evidence that the traditional ways of teaching software engineering and conducting software projects had a very poor record of accomplishment. For example, the 2004 CHAOS Report [1] reported that the percentage of software projects that were completed on time and on budget with complete functionality was a mere 34% (The 2009 CHAOS Report showed even worse results). That report also found software project waste to be $55 billion, out of a total annual project spending of $255 billion. Moreover, other software engineering literature is filled with stories about failed projects. The instructor concluded that the traditional ways of teaching about software engineering in colleges and universities had most likely contributed to this record of failure. In particular, many such courses (though not all) have been teaching outdated software methodologies, have discouraged collaboration, and have neglected to treat the user community as full-fledged participants in the software process.

Since 2007, several substantial efforts have begun to move the software engineering curriculum away from these outdated practices. At Trinity College, for example, Morelli and coworkers [2] defined a model that uses the goal of Humanitarian Free and Open Source Software (HFOSS) to teach the principles of software development. The HFOSS Project's approach is to use collaboration, agile programming, education–industry partnerships, and live humanitarian open-source projects as cornerstones for teaching students about the principles and practice of software development. An important outcome of the HFOSS Project is that its approach improves computer science enrollments by making the discipline interesting to a broader audience of capable students than the traditional curriculum model.

In 2007, however, the CS260 instructor was not familiar with the principles, methods, and goals of open-source software development. But a serendipitous conversation between the instructor and Ralph Morelli (co-Principal Investigator of the HFOSS Project) led to a series of meetings through which the HFOSS Project's successful efforts with students at Trinity College could be applied to create a version of the CS260 course. The HFOSS Project provided the instructor with crucial guidance about how to integrate the key practices of open source development—collaboration, code synchronization, and agile development—into a software engineering course.

Another serendipitous event led to the identification of a live software project that subsequently became the driver for the new CS260 course. The instructor's spouse had been volunteering at the Ronald McDonald House (RMH) in Portland, Maine.* One afternoon, she noted how awkward and error-prone was the process of volunteer scheduling—it used a paper-and-pencil calendar for scheduling over 200 volunteers into four three-hour shifts, seven days a week. The process was clearly ripe for replacement by a Web-based calendar and volunteer database that could be accessed and updated by the House Manager and any volunteer who had Web access and a brows-

---

*The Ronald McDonald House (RMH) is a nonprofit organization that provides no-cost temporary housing for families whose children are undergoing medical treatment at a nearby hospital. There are currently more than 300 RMHs in major cities throughout the United States and abroad.

er. This was exactly the kind of project that would be ideal for the CS260 course at Bowdoin!

In 2007, it turned out that Bowdoin was also reemphasizing its commitment to service-learning by establishing a new "Center for the Common Good." This new center was designed to help faculty and students find new ways for integrating service learning across the College curriculum. Service-learning activities had traditionally occurred within social science and humanities curriculum, but the Center for Common Good was now reaching out to the sciences to find new initiatives in which students would be able to supplement their studies with service-learning activities. Thus, the timing for this new approach to CS260 was ideal and the College was eager to provide IT staff and other support that the course would need.

Inspired by these three events—the HFOSS idea, the availability of a natural HFOSS project at the Ronald McDonald House, and Bowdoin's new service-learning initiatives—the instructor developed and taught the CS260 course for the first time in the spring semester of 2008. In this course, four students developed and delivered a complete Web-based volunteer scheduling and database system called Homebase. This system has been in productive use at the Portland RMH ever since. Because the software is open source, and thus freely reusable, it has since been adapted for use in at least two other nonprofit organizations of which we are aware.

Due to this success, the CS260 course was reoffered at Bowdoin in spring 2011 in a similar format, but with a different open-source software project called Homeroom. Students in this course developed and delivered a Web-based room-scheduling system for the Ronald McDonald House in Portland, Maine. These two projects' designs and goals are summarized below in some detail. Later sections describe their pedagogical content, their service-learning components, and their potential for use in similar courses in other undergraduate computing programs.

8.1.1 The Homebase Project

In fall 2007, the instructor prepared for the CS260 course by developing, in consultation with the Ronald McDonald House Manager, an initial design document for Homebase. This design document was intentionally developed in advance of the course in order to jump-start the remainder of the implementation process when the students joined the project. While this decision truncated the level of student participation in the initial design process, it had three major benefits:

1. The project reflected a more realistic setting for students to contribute to the project (rarely does an actual software project start from scratch).

2. Students had a chance to complete a substantial software project by the end of the semester, rather than becoming bogged down in the details of design as often happens in this type of course.

3. It may be argued that students encountering a software project whose design is (partially) complete still have ample opportunities to make substantial design contributions, especially at the user interface level.

This activity uncovered the essential nature of the current volunteer scheduling system as a baseline:

- The existing system was 100% paper-and-pencil-based. A blotter-sized calendar at the front desk showed who was scheduled to work each shift during the month. A Rolodex file provided contact information for each volunteer.
- Since the existing system was used by all volunteers and staff, it was error-prone and required constant attention by the House Manager and others working at the front desk. For instance, when a volunteer cancelled a shift, her entry on the calendar was manually erased and a substitute call list of other volunteers who might be available for that shift was built by hand, in order to help find a substitute.

The design document for the new system [4] provided the major guidelines for the tasks that students would need to complete in order to implement the Homebase software. This document had five major elements:

1. A narrative description of the current manual scheduling system, including scanned images of schedules, calendars, and other key forms and pieces of information
2. A requirements analysis for the new software
3. Nine use cases that described the key user–system interactions supported by the new software
4. A list of desired technical characteristics for the new software
5. A sketch of the initial domain classes that would be used to anchor the software itself

Specifically, these use cases described how volunteers and RMH staff would use the software to:

- Update applicant profiles
- Update volunteer profiles

- Update a substitute call list
- Generate a weekly calendar from a master schedule
- Change the master schedule
- Change a calendar
- Find a substitute
- View their future scheduled shifts
- View a list of volunteers

The design document identified three different types of users (actors) who would be using the software: guest, volunteer, and house manager (administrator), each with a different level of access to the system.

To illustrate the style of a use case, Figure 8.1 shows the use case FindA-

Actors—the House Manager or a Volunteer
Goals—to locate a sub to fill a vacancy in the calendar
Preconditions—
    1. There is a vacancy on the calendar.
    2. There is a Sub Call List for that vacancy.
Postconditons—
    1. The vacancy is filled.
Related Use Cases—ViewAList, ChangeACalendar
Description—the House Manager or a Volunteer on Duty may fill a calendar vacancy by calling people on the Sub Call List.
Sequence Diagram—

Actor	System
1. Log on to website	2. Ask for id and password
3. Enter id and password	4. Verify and display outcome
5. Locate a vacancy on the calendar and access the sub call list for that vacancy	6. Display outcome
7. If there's no "Yes!" on the Sub Call List, view all subs available on the list for that vacancy. Call as many of these as time permits and enter result of each call on the sub call list	8. Validate each entry and display outcome
9. If there's a "Yes!" on the sub call list, add that Sub to the Calendar (ChangeACalendar)	10. Validate the replacement and display outcome
11. Log off website	12. Terminate Session

Figure 8.1. The FindASubstitute use case.

Substitute, which describes how a volunteer or house manager can find a substitute to fill a vacant shift on the calendar. The desired technical characteristics that the new software should possess were described in the design document as follows:

1. The system should be easy to learn and use.
2. It should be platform-independent and accessed through a Web-based browser.
3. It should be secure, ensuring privacy of personal data.
4. It should be computationally efficient, reliable, and available 24/7.
5. It should allow easy maintenance, backup, and recovery.
6. It should be free and open source.

This last characteristic is key to ensuring open access, adaptability, and portability by developers (students and professionals) to fit similar needs in other organizations.

Finally, the design document's identification of an initial set of domain classes and their instance variables provided an initial name space and vocabulary for students developers who were engaging and communicating about different aspects of the software. This allowed the student developers to begin with a common set of the key domain classes and their instance variables, to which they made substantial refinements (mainly by adding methods and other supporting classes) during the early part of the project. Throughout the life of the project, this document was revised four times; the fourth version [4] describes the final system.

The CS260 course ran from January to May 2008. A team of four Bowdoin CS students and the instructor developed Homebase from scratch during this one-semester course. The software was installed in May 2008 at the Ronald McDonald House in Portland, Maine (rmhportland.org/volunteers/homebase) and has been in use ever since. The software carries a Gnu Public License, and its current code base is downloadable at sourceforge.net/projects/rmhhomebase. The software was recently adapted for use at the Ronald McDonald House in Wilmington, Delaware (rmhde.myopensoftware.org). Further discussion of the challenges of adapting and reusing open-source software appears in Section 4 of this paper.

With the idea that this hands-on approach to teaching software development would be valuable to other undergraduate courses in software engineering, the instructor, with help from Ralph Morelli and Chamindra de Silva, developed a new textbook, Software Development: An Open-Source Approach, which was published by CRC Press in January 2011 [7]. The textbook and its accompanying lab support (available at the website http://myopensoftware.org/textbook) can be used as a basis for a one-semester course in software development at other institutions. The book includes many examples from the Homeroom code base to illustrate the various principles of open-source development. Further discussion of the book and its use in a software development course appears in Part 4 of this book.

8.1.2 The Homeroom Project

The second offering of CS260 took place in spring 2011. It was organized similarly to the 2008 offering, except that students undertook the development of a different open-source software project. This new project, called Homeroom, was designed by the instructor during the summer of 2010, again with help from the Ronald McDonald House Manager. That design document [5] is at sourceforge.net/projects/rmhhomeroom, and its details are also discussed in Chapter 11 of the aforementioned textbook [7].

The Homeroom design document was structured similarly to that of the Homebase design document, but with one exception: it did not have a complete set of use cases. Instead, the project's use cases evolved through weekly discussions between the student developers and the House Manager during the course of the semester. This process is known in agile circles as the elicitation of user stories. The developers found that user stories were an effective tool for understanding, designing, and implementing the user interface for Homeroom.

So the spring 2011 offering of CS260 required weekly design discussions among the two Bowdoin CS students, the instructor, and the House Manager. These discussions took place using a four-way Skype video conference, since the four participants were in four different physical locations throughout the semester. The software was completed and installed for staff training and field testing in June 2011. The test site is hosted at http://homeroom.myopensoftware.org, and the GPL-licensed code base can be downloaded from the Mercurial repository at http://code.google.com/p/rmh-homeroom.

Beyond user stories, a second major difference between the first project and the second was the fact that the second project borrowed much from the experience that had been gained from the first. For example, the layered client–server software architecture of Homebase carried over almost directly as a framework for the architecture of Homeroom. Moreover, many code snippets from Homebase were used as exemplars when student developers wanted to design a similar database or user interface module in Homeroom. In short, using predeveloped and pretested code provided valuable resources and examples because the code could be freely accessed from an open-source repository. The educational value of open-source software in this particular regard cannot be overstated.

A third major difference between the two projects was the existence of the textbook [7] and accompanying website for the second project. The textbook provided a point of reference for students to use in two different ways. First, the principles of software development are thoroughly covered in the textbook, with illustrative examples taken from the Homeroom and Homebase projects. Second, the practices of open-source software are also covered in detail in the textbook and its accompanying website. These supporting materials were not available for the first project, so that students had to rely on outside readings and tutorials for all background information and hands-on support, and these were often difficult to find.

The next section describes the pedagogical elements of the CS260 course in greater detail, emphasizing its curricular content, unique features, and service-learning components.

8.2   PEDAGOGY

From an academic standpoint, a course using either the Homebase or the Homeroom project can provide a complete introduction to software engineering principles and practice. For example, students in both offerings of the CS260 course learned the principles that would occur in a traditional software engineering course, as well as the practices that would occur in an actual software project.

The particular software engineering principles that are covered by such a course include the agile and test-driven development models, software licenses, domain class design, client–server architecture, database design and normalization, software security, and user interface design (including the model–view–controller framework). The course also requires that students learn the following software engineering practices: using a version-control system (VCS), setting up and using an integrated development environment (IDE), contributing to a collaborative discussion forum, conducting unit tests, code reading, refactoring, and videoconferencing.

These practices are directly related to the service-learning components of the course: engagement with a real client, developing a real software artifact, and leaving a code legacy that other students can reuse in subsequent courses that have service-learning components. These components are not normally included in a traditional software engineering course.

With modest guidance from the instructor, this course requires students to develop and test all the software components—the classes, modules, database interfaces, and integrated help tutorials—that are implied by the requirements document.

The remainder of this section will describe the organization of each project within the framework of a one-semester (13-week) academic course. Drawing on the essential collaborative nature of FOSS itself, such a course requires students to participate in team formation, collaborative task assignment, code reading and writing, unit testing, milestone setting, and review and client feedback activities.

8.2.1 Team Formation and Collaboration

When the 2008 offering of CS260 was publicized in December 2007, four seniors registered up for it. Three were computer science majors who had already completed an introductory course in software design and the fourth was a math/economics major with a lot of interest and skill in programming.

In January 2008, the complete development team was formed. It included the instructor as team leader, these four students, four RMH staff members who would use the system, the Bowdoin CIO, two Bowdoin IT staff members (for technical support), and two observers from Trinity College who had experience with student-based HFOSS software development.

As the team dynamic began to take shape, a strategic decision about collaboration was made. Responding to a recommendation by Bowdoin IT staff, the team began using a collaboration tool called Basecamp (see http://www.basecamphq.com/). This tool organized the team's discussion threads, project milestones, to-do lists, and a repository for tutorials and documentation as they evolved.

Although most team members had never used such a medium before, Basecamp proved to be an invaluable project tracking device and communication medium for developers, clients, and others as the project unfolded. Using this new medium alongside the good will that had developed among the team members, we quickly learned how to communicate effectively.

The 2011 offering of CS260 took a different approach to team formation and collaboration. This time, the team consisted of the instructor, two students, and one RMH staff member. The need for technical support from Bowdoin IT staff had disappeared, since new tools—specifically Google Groups, Google Projects, and Mercurial VCS repositories—had now become available and could be easily maintained by the instructor for this type of project. We found that these tools, along with a new website whereby we could manage and discuss the test versions of the software as it developed, obviated the need for ongoing IT support from the College.

8.2.2 Milestones

A semester is about three months long, so the project's timeline had to be configured with that as a firm constraint. Working backward from a target delivery date of May 9, the 2008 offering of CS260 divided the project into five major phases, or milestones:

1. One week was spent reviewing the HFOSS software, called Sahana, that had inspired this project.
2. Three weeks were reserved for domain-class development and testing.
3. Three weeks were reserved for studying database principles and developing the database tables and related modules.
4. Four weeks were reserved for user-interface development from the nine use cases.
5. Finally, two weeks were reserved for integration testing, on-line documentation development, two RMH staff training sessions, and final debugging.

During the domain class and database development phases, students designed a unit test for each of the classes and modules that they developed. During the user-interface development phase, the domain classes and database modules thus became relatively stable and reliable. Client involvement picked up significantly during the fourth and fifth phases, and RMH staff provided valuable feedback about particular features as the system became more coherent and potentially useful.

The development team reviewed elements of the working software with RMH staff at two key points in the project. One review came early, when the first PHP form was developed for adding a new person to the database. The other review came later, after several of the user scheduling and calendar functions had been implemented. Several new features were suggested by RMH staff and added to the system as a result of these reviews.

The 2011 offering of CS260 had about the same set of milestones. However, the first milestone was spent reviewing the software that had been developed during the 2008 offering, alongside the general principles of agile and open-source software development that are covered in Chapters 1 and 2 of the textbook [7].

Unit testing and client feedback were just as essential in the 2011 project, which also benefited from the existence of a tractable code base that provided many models of good code that could be essentially reused in the current project.

Finally, the 2011 project did not include a staff training session because there was less of a need for staff training in the case of room scheduling as there was in the case of volunteer scheduling. That is, Homebase allows any or all of the 200 volunteers to schedule themselves into or out of a shift on the calendar, so that some training is required to introduce them to the new software. Homeroom, on the other hand, is used only by the house manager and social workers at the hospital who are referring families to the house when their children are scheduled for surgery. Thus, the training requirement for Homeroom is much more limited than that for Homebase.

8.2.3   Collaborative Activities, Self-Selection, and Grading

In the spirit of agile programming, the users (RMH staff and volunteers) were full-fledged members of the development team. Thus, the users were comfortable interjecting their thoughts and answering questions from the student developers throughout the development process. The students were equally comfortable collaborating with users when questions arose that they could not answer. This particular collaboration between developers and users was a key ingredient for the success of both projects. By the time each system was delivered, users had gained a very clear idea about what kind of software tool they would receive and how it would replace the existing manual system.

It is important to point out that the student team members often exchanged assigned tasks on a week-to-week basis. That is, although the discussion threads and the design document provided a clear picture of what tasks had to be done at each milestone, the actual assignment of tasks by the team leader was often accompanied by self-selection into and out of tasks by team members according to how well the tasks were matched with individual skills and preferences.

Variations in task assignments were greater during the first project than during the second. That is, at later stages in first project, students who were keen to do more programming assumed the bulk of the programming tasks, whereas other students assumed the bulk of the online help-page development and user training tasks. Each one was thus contributing to the project in a way that utilized his/her particular strengths. However, in the second project, each student was willing to do an equal amount of programming, and also to develop an equal portion of the online help pages.

The lessons learned as a result of these two experiences are significant. Whereas it is important that every student member of a software development team contribute significantly to the code base, it is also important to recognize and reward individual student differences. The grading system at the end of the course must, in turn, be suitably flexible to evaluate student work on more or less of a portfolio basis rather than a one-size-fits-all traditional final exam format. In particular, a student who contributes more to the user documentation and training than to the code base should have no less access to an A grade in the course than a student who contributes more to the code base.

With a larger class and more than one project, the instructor would have used a grading rubric to gather student feedback and arrive at a fair grade for each student participant. For example, the instructor taught a software development course in 2005 with 18 students and 4 project teams. In that course, each student was required to fill out a form like the one shown in Figure 8.2 and submit it confidentially to the instructor at the end of the course. With

Team Member's Name	Score (1–4)	Comments
Teena	2	Good performance on coming up with (specially) login and other class diagrams.
Andrew	1	Excellent on the way he led the team.
Blaire	1	Excellent on coming up with the design of the project.
George	2	Good at explaining the strategy of "first-come first-serve."
Mohammad	2	Good at writing JML specifications and drawing the sequence diagrams to reflect how objects of different classes interact in real time.

Figure 8.2. Sample scoring form.

feedback from each student about the performance of all the students on the team (including him/herself), the instructor can be better informed about the assignment of final grades.

In the case of the Homebase and Homeroom projects, the numbers were small enough and the relationships and roles were clear enough that this sort of grading rubric was not needed.

8.2.4 Software Architecture and Security

Since the system was to be open source and Web based, the number of choices for programming language, database, and server technology were automatically narrowed, though not completely prescribed.

Both projects chose the PHP/MySQL platform because it would support all the goals in the design document. Although the students did not have PHP experience, they did have programming experience, so moving to this platform presented few obstacles. Development work was done using an Eclipse IDE and a local-host installation of an Apache server with PHP and MySQL, thus enabling the developers to write and test their software modules locally before committing them to the VCS repository.

During the first two or three weeks of each project, the students spent as much time reading PHP tutorials and code snippets as they did writing and testing the core domain classes. This learning went quickly, and they soon began to appreciate some of PHP's unique strengths for this sort of application: associative arrays, treatment of dates as first-class data types, web-based interactive forms, and integration with MySQL.

Security and privacy are key requirements for this sort of system. In the case of Homebase, security is needed because only RMH staff members should be able to update the volunteer database and the master schedule. Privacy is needed to protect sensitive information about each volunteer from being read or modified by other volunteers or curious outsiders.

The Homebase architecture ensures security and privacy by associating one of three levels of access with a login session: guest, volunteer, or manager. Each level views the system through different a different set of functional menu bars, as shown in Figure 8.3. Guests can learn about the system by viewing an "about" page and the on-line help tutorials (see below). Volunteers can view and manage the calendar by changing their own or others' scheduled shifts, and view and edit their own personal database entry. Managers can perform all these functions, as well as edit the master schedule, generate new scheduled calendar weeks, edit a volunteer's personal database entry, and add new people to the database.

8.2.5 User Support and Evaluation

During the early weeks of the Homebase project, we expected only to produce a working prototype that later courses could refine for delivery and productive use. Toward the end of the project, it became clear that we would be able to implement a complete working system that could be used right away.

Thus, the need for excellent usability to encourage RMH staff buy-in became an increasingly important goal. To maximize system usability, the student team members wrote a set of integrated help pages and conducted two training sessions so that RMH staff and some volunteers would become comfortable using the software prior to delivery on May 9. A sample personal home page for Homebase is shown in Figure 8.4.

Although each page by itself is very intuitive to use, the supplementary help pages provide tutorial support for new users. For example, the help page for learning how to use the personal home page is shown in Figure 8.5.

Armed with on line documentation, students conducted two user training workshops during the last week of the semester. Eleven persons attended the two workshops: four RMH staff members and seven volunteers. Workshop

Guest access:
>   home | about | apply | logout

Volunteer access:
>   home | about | calendar : house, family room | people : view, search | help | logout

Manager access:
>   home | about | calendar : house, family room | people : view, search, add
>   master schedule : house, family room | log | help | logout

Figure 8.3. Three levels of secure access.

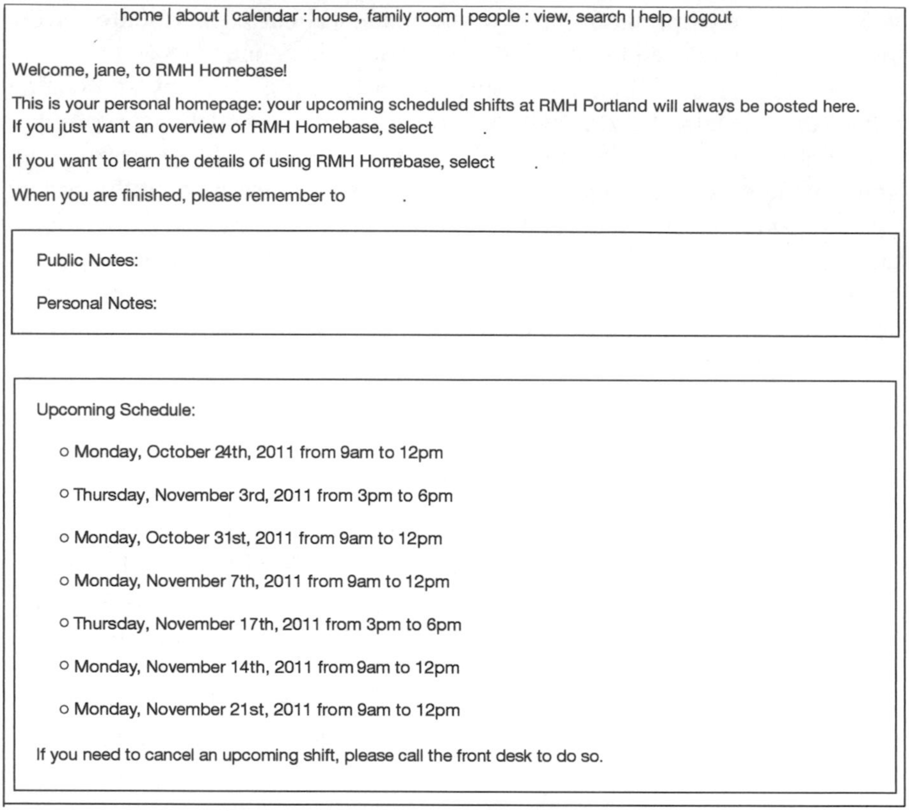

home | about | calendar : house, family room | people : view, search | help | logout

Welcome, jane, to RMH Homebase!

This is your personal homepage: your upcoming scheduled shifts at RMH Portland will always be posted here. If you just want an overview of RMH Homebase, select   .

If you want to learn the details of using RMH Homebase, select   .

When you are finished, please remember to   .

Public Notes:

Personal Notes:

Upcoming Schedule:

   o Monday, October 24th, 2011 from 9am to 12pm

   o Thursday, November 3rd, 2011 from 3pm to 6pm

   o Monday, October 31st, 2011 from 9am to 12pm

   o Monday, November 7th, 2011 from 9am to 12pm

   o Thursday, November 17th, 2011 from 3pm to 6pm

   o Monday, November 14th, 2011 from 9am to 12pm

   o Monday, November 21st, 2011 from 9am to 12pm

If you need to cancel an upcoming shift, please call the front desk to do so.

Figure 8.4. A Volunteer's personal home page.

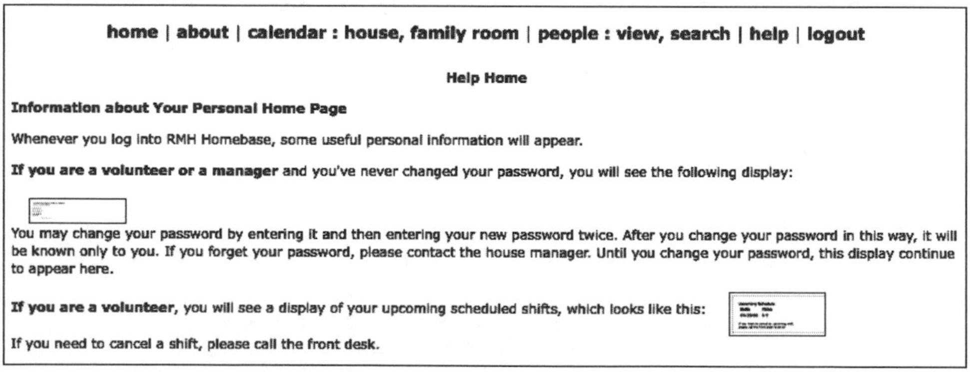

---

home | about | calendar : house, family room | people : view, search | help | logout

Help Home

Information about Your Personal Home Page

Whenever you log into RMH Homebase, some useful personal information will appear.

If you are a volunteer or a manager and you've never changed your password, you will see the following display:

You may change your password by entering it and then entering your new password twice. After you change your password in this way, it will be known only to you. If you forget your password, please contact the house manager. Until you change your password, this display continue to appear here.

If you are a volunteer, you will see a display of your upcoming scheduled shifts, which looks like this:

If you need to cancel a shift, please call the front desk.

Figure 8.5. Help page for the personal home page.

attendees completed a questionnaire whereby they rated the quality of the software and the chances that they would use it and be able to teach it to other volunteers in the future. The questionnaire responses from all eleven participants (originally reported in [6]) are summarized below.

Question	Average response
Evaluate Homebase with regard to:	(1 = poor, 5 = excellent)
1. Logging in	4.7
2. Headings and logo	4.9
3. Searching for volunteers	5
4. Adding, deleting, and changing volunteers	5
5. Viewing the calendar	5
6. Changing the calendar (substitute call lists)	4.7
7. Managing the calendar (generating weeks)	5
8. Editing and managing the master schedule	5
9. Understanding the online help	5
10. Logging out	5
11. Workshop effectiveness	5
12. RMH/Bowdoin collaboration from Jan–May	5

All eleven participants agreed that the software was "extremely user friendly" and that they could see themselves "easily teaching another volunteer" how to use the system. Several commented that the software may be useful at many other Ronald McDonald Houses and similar organizations in the future.

Another way to evaluate the software produced by the Homebase project is to ask how much time and money it would have cost to develop the same software commercially. A crude measure for answering this question is provided by a source-code analyzer called SLOCCount [8]. This tool estimates that a commercial development effort for Homebase would have required 0.98 person-years, or 1.85 full-time developers to complete the project in the given timeline. The total estimated development cost would have been $133,032.

For the Homeroom project, a training session was conducted by the instructor during the summer of 2011 for RMH staff members and social workers who will be using the system. The software currently has a complete client database and complete support for scheduling rooms online. All participants in this training session agreed that the software would be very easy to use and a strong improvement over the manual system that it will be replacing. Since this system is currently so new, it will be important to conduct a follow-up evaluation several months in the future. Maintaining the system in the future will also be a challenge (see Section 8.4 for more discussion).

8.3   OUTCOMES

This section identifies the specific service-learning experiences that these two projects provided to the students enrolled in CS260. It also describes the impact that these projects have had on the students, instructor, staff, and operations of the Ronald McDonald House and other organizations where the software is now in use, and the larger activities of the HFOSS Project itself.

These two projects achieved their service-learning goals because they had strong support from the HFOSS Project, as well as Bowdoin's Center for Common Good, Computer Science faculty, and Information Technology staff. The particular benefits that these two projects provided to the student participants are:

- An opportunity to participate in a "real" software project that had clear public and humanitarian benefits.
- An opportunity to work as a team and use modern collaboration tools and techniques in a software project.
- An opportunity to earn course and major credit while learning the principles and practices of software engineering.
- An opportunity to leave a "legacy" in the form of software artifacts that other students (and professional developers) could use in their future studies (and work assignments).

One of the most important outcomes for a software development course is to enable students to participate in a successful software experience. Software projects always benefit from a team approach in which different team members play different roles during the life of the project. A high level of communication among team members enhances the likelihood of project success. The fact that CS260 provided students with this experience was a major factor in the success of its two projects.

Collaboration of this sort counters the prevailing notion, often promoted in other computer science courses, that successful software comes from a clever individual programmer working alone. In CS260, as in real software projects, an individual working alone cannot usually accomplish what an effective team effort can accomplish. A key challenge of a software development course is to leave each student with an understanding of these different roles and a sense of personal ownership in the final product no matter what particular role he/she played.

At the end of the 2008 semester, the Homebase software and documentation became a Sourceforge project (https://sourceforge.net/projects/rmh-homebase/). Similarly, the Homeroom software is now a Google project (httpsL//code.google.com/p/rmh-homeroom) with a complete code base and user documentation. Because Homebase and Homeroom both share the HFOSS Project's philosophy, their code bases and user interfaces prominently display the GNU GPL notice (see Figure 8.6).

This licensing choice allows the software to be freely copied and adapted to fit the volunteer and/or room scheduling needs of similar organizations. The projects' Sourceforge and Google Code presence also provides other students, instructors, and software developers with a foundation and reference point for future work on related projects.

Finally, these projects provide the RMH Portland staff with a reference point that can be passed on to peers at other RMH locations throughout the world.

8.4   FUTURE CHALLENGES

This section describes specific challenges that accompany embedding a service-learning project within a software development course offering at other undergraduate programs in the information sciences. This section also identifies the unique extracurricular activities and commitments that follow such a project after it is completed.

The challenges are significant. They include instructor preparation, project selection, community support, and the use of open-source code repositories, textbooks, and other Web-based tools that are useful for supporting the collaboration and code development activities at the heart of any such project.

How can the CS260 course's principles and practices be replicated elsewhere without reinventing it from scratch? Here are some suggestions for interested instructors that might help facilitate team projects like Homebase and Homeroom in other software development courses:

```
/*
 *Copyright 2008 by Oliver Radwan, Maxwell Palmer, Nolan McNair,
 * Taylor Talmage, and Allen Tucker. This program is part of RMH Homebase.
 * RMH Homebase is free software. It comes with absolutely no warranty.
 * You can redistribute it and/or modify it under the terms of the GNU
 * General Public License as published by the Free Software Foundation
 * (see <http://www.gnu.org/licenses/ for more information).
 */
```

Figure 8.6. Copyright and GPL notice.

- Select a project early and engage a real client with the goals of the project. Be sure that the project can be accomplished in a one-semester course, or else prepare to divide the project into chunks that bridge over a series of semesters and development teams. One alternative here is to pick an ongoing live project (several are available at http://hfoss.org), contact its developers, and see if contributions to it can be made by students in a software development course.

- For a new project, develop (with help from the client) a design document that clearly describes the client's current (manual) system, identifies the new system's desired use cases, and sketches its domain classes.

- Form a team that includes student developers, client users, and IT staff members as needed for technical support. At this time, there are many good open-source tools available on the Web that support collaboration and synchronization of code development, and so the need for IT staff support may be minimal. The key requirement here is to be sure that student-developed code can be hosted on a live server that can be accessed by the client as well as the developers themselves. This is an important vehicle for obtaining client feedback, especially during the user-interface phase of the development project.

- Allow student developers to assume different roles according to their individual strengths and preferences. Encourage different students to take the lead in different aspects of the project: programming, user-interface development, testing, help-page authoring, and client training. Stress that all roles are essential to the success of the project.

- Use an effective collaboration medium, such as Google Groups, and require all team members to use it for all discussions related to the project. The use of regular e-mail, without such a collaboration medium, should be discouraged.

- Use a source program repository, such as Mercurial, and require all student developers to learn how to clone the code base, commit changes, and perform other tasks that are required to synchronize their work.

- If appropriate and if there is time at the end of the semester, require students to conduct one or two training sessions so that clients may learn to use the system and evaluate its strengths and weaknesses. Use these results to help define future projects.

- Commit to open source (using the GPL or a similar license) as a medium of dissemination and sharing the code base. This will help the project bridge across semesters, development teams, and future projects at other institutions. Sourceforge, Google Code, and Git are three contemporary media for storing and sharing open-source code.

- Disseminate the software widely, especially if it appears to be useful in other software engineering courses with the same goals.

As mentioned above, the new textbook Software Development: An Open-Source Approach [7] provides detailed guidance on these ideas, focusing on project selection, course organization, and the principles of software development that would be found in a software engineering course. Both Homebase and Homeroom are used throughout this textbook as sources of detailed examples of the various aspects of the course.

The online supporting materials for this textbook, along with its table of contents and sample syllabus, are posted at http://myopensoftware.org/textsbook. Because these materials are Creative Commons licensed, they can be freely downloaded and distributed to other student groups as needed. These materials include detailed guidance for such activities as:

- Setting up collaboration tools
- Setting up a local server and database
- Setting up an IDE and a VCS
- Setting up documentation tools
- Setting up debugging and unit-testing tools

The long-term commitment for such service-learning projects can be substantial. That is, if the students in a course develop useful software for a humanitarian organization, arrangements must be made to maintain that software throughout the remainder of its useful life. After the course is over, however, students move on to other commitments in their lives and may not have time or inclination to continue working on the project.

In the case of Homebase, all four student developers were second-semester seniors when they completed the project. After graduation, none was able to continue working on the project, though two have stayed in touch and expressed interest in helping with future improvements. In the case of Homeroom, the two students were a sophomore and a junior, and both have expressed interest in continuing to work on the project when they return to school in the fall. Meanwhile, the instructor has been providing bug fixing and other support to both projects on an as-needed basis. Luckily, these two projects are of sufficiently high quality so that the need for major technical support has been modest.

Looking forward to the future, these experiences suggest that the greatest challenge for these and similar HFOSS projects is replication. For instance, it is clear that the Homebase and Homeroom projects are eminently replicable at many of the 300 other RMHs that are near undergraduate computer science programs that want to engage in service-learning activities with local nonprofit organizations. In fact, these two projects were cited in a 2011 MBA thesis as a potential "business best practice" [9]. That thesis proposed a model by which this software, with support from Ronald McDonald House Charities (RMHC), could be replicated across the country to help other RMHs automate their volunteer and room-scheduling operations.

If such replication can be achieved, not only would it yield great benefit to a large number of nonprofit organizations, it would also provide excellent service-learning experiences for a large and diverse group of computer science students throughout the nation. The authors have been thinking about this particular challenge for some time, and would welcome suggestions from readers for moving this idea forward.

8.5   CONCLUSIONS

In conclusion, the major successes and ongoing challenges that accompany the refocusing of a software development course around an HFOSS project as a service-learning activity can be summarized as follows.

First, such a course retains all the academic integrity of a standard software engineering course in the undergraduate computing curriculum. It provides students with complete topic coverage and prepares them for advanced study in software engineering at the undergraduate or graduate level.

Second, such a course is rich in service-learning content. It provides students an opportunity to engage in relevant and meaningful community-focused activities that advance the common good. Students in the two offerings of the CS260 course unanimously cite that experience as one of the most meaningful in their undergraduate careers. Clients who are the beneficiaries of the Homeroom and Homebase projects also unanimously praise its value to the community.

Third, such a course can be replicated at other undergraduate programs in the computing and information sciences. New teaching materials—a textbook and other online lab support materials—are now available online. Moreover, an abundance of HFOSS projects are available to students and instructors who are interested in developing such a course. A ready source of example projects can be found at the website http://hfoss.org.

We hope that these examples will inspire many other instructors and students to consider offering a service-learning-oriented software engineering course at their own institutions. Anyone interested in talking further about this idea can feel free to contact the first author at allen@bowdoin.edu.

REFERENCES

1. Standish: Project Success Rates Improved Over 10 Years. *Software Magazine,* January 15, 2004. DOI = http://www.softwaremag.com/L.cfm?Doc=newsletter/2004-01-15/Standish.

2. Morelli, R., de Lanerolle, T., Ellis, H., Danner, N. and Iyengar, J., "Teaching and Building Humanitarian Open Source Software." In *Proceedings of the 38th Technical Symposium on Computer Science Education* (SIGCSE 2008). March 2008. DOI = http://hfoss.org.

3. Morelli, R. et al., "Revitalizing Computing Education through Free and Open Source Software for Humanity," *Communications of the ACM,* Vol. 52, No. 8 (August 2009), pp. 67–75.

4. Allen Tucker, Oliver Radwan, Maxwell Palmer, Nolan McNair, and Taylor Talmadge, *Homebase: An Online Volunteer Scheduling System for the Ronald McDonald House in Portland, ME.* April 30, 2008, 42 pages. DOI = https://sourceforge.net/projects/rmhhomebase/.

5. *Homeroom: A New Software Project. Requirements and Initial Design,* October 15, 2010. DOI = https://sourceforge.net/projects/rmhhomeroom/.

6. Tucker, A., "Teaching Client-Driven Software Development," In *Proceedings of the ACM CCSC South Central Conference* (April 2009).

7. Tucker, A., R. Morelli, and C. de Silva, *Software Development: an Open Source Approach,* CRC Press, 2011. DOI = http://myopensoftware.org/textbook and http://www.crcpress.com/product/isbn/9781439812907

8. Wheeler, D. More Than a Gigabuck: Estimating GNU/Linux's Size. July 29, 2002. DOI = http://www.dwheeler.com/sloccount/.

9. Apresa, G., To, T., Parker, S., and Loomis, T. *Operational Excellence at RMHC,* MBA Thesis, Arizona State University, Spring 2011.

CHAPTER 9

SERVICE-LEARNING AND PROJECT MANAGEMENT
The Capstone Course in Information Technology Leadership

Charles Hannon

ABSTRACT

The Information Technology Leadership (ITL) department at Washington & Jefferson College uses service-learning pedagogy to teach a required capstone course in project management. The department uses students' work in the course for overall program assessment. The course challenges students to define and satisfy information technology (IT) project requirements in collaboration with the leadership of local nonprofit community organizations. Establishing this course as a graduation requirement for all ITL majors has raised a number of issues that have required creative solutions over the years. Despite these challenges, the course's focus on service to the community reinforces the meaning of liberal arts education and helps make real the mission of Washington & Jefferson College.

9.1 INTRODUCTION

The Information Technology Leadership (ITL) department at Washington & Jefferson College was created in 2002 to provide an interdisciplinary, liberal-arts-based approach to the study of information technology (IT). We offer a curriculum that is both practical and theoretical, with opportunities to learn advanced applications as well as to understand their role in human society. The department has the dual mission of preparing students to take a leadership role in the area of information technology independent of the career or graduate education paths they pursue, and of advancing the uses of information technology across the Washington & Jefferson curriculum. We accomplish the second part of this mission through our close teaching collaborations with other departments; our participation in interdisciplinary programs in professional writing, graphic design, and film (among others); our early adoption and dissemination of educational technologies on campus; and our volunteering of our expertise to our faculty colleagues. This paper, however, is focused on the use of service-learning pedagogy to accomplish the first part of the department's mission: preparing our students for leadership roles in the areas of information technology throughout their academic and professional lives.

9.2 ITL CURRICULUM SUMMARY, LEARNING OUTCOMES, AND ASSESSMENT

The ITL major requires ten courses: five core courses (IT & Society, Java Programming, Database Concepts, Human Computer Interaction, and Service-Learning Project Management), and five additional courses chosen from one of three areas of emphasis (Computer Science; New Media Technologies; and Data Discovery). The major is designed to provide breadth through the core courses, and depth through the emphasis courses. Students can enter the major in a variety of ways: the first three core courses have no prerequisites, and each emphasis has at least one entry course, which, likewise, requires no prior course work. In addition, we teach a variety of lower-level courses during our three-week January term, and technology-themed First Year Seminars, which tend to bring new students into the department. With approximately 1400 students at the College overall, we graduate 7–15 majors each year. We have four full-time tenure-track faculty and, occasionally, additional temporary full- or part-time positions.

As we began to define a process for assessing the ITL program, we established a list of program-level learning outcomes, and determined to use the capstone course for the major, Service-Learning Project Management, as the primary vehicle for measuring these outcomes. Thus, the course has two sets of learning outcomes—those for the course, and those related to the overall major, which we use to assess our program-level objectives.

9.2.1 Course-Level Learning Outcomes and Assessment

Every course on our campus has course-level learning outcomes that we assess through a variety of means. The course-level learning outcomes for Service-Learning Project Management read as follows:

STUDENT LEARNING OUTCOMES

At the end of the course, students will be able to do the following:

- Apply skills and concepts learned through the ITL curriculum to real-world situations
- Assess technology needs for a community organization and develop a schedule for addressing them
- Resolve conflicts and solve problems that arise during the implementation of any technology project
- Communicate effectively with community organizations and other clients and vendors
- Effectively present the results of their work to a diverse audience

Anyone who has attempted to match outcomes to assessment mechanisms has confronted the difficulty of doing so. Asking students to apply the skills and concepts they have learned in previous classes to a real-world project is a perfectly reasonable requirement for a capstone class. But how does a teacher formulate a specific assignment or task that can be graded and thus used as a concrete assessment of the required outcome? This kind of outcome, especially in a capstone course, encompasses the work of the entire semester. Similarly, with regard to the fourth bulleted item above, I do not grade students' communications with their clients. That level of micromanagement and evaluation can be paralyzing for the student and onerous for the teacher. But we do look, as a class, at e-mail exchanges between students and clients, and discuss how it is that miscommunications arise. (Inevitably, they do.) One example of this was an early January e-mail communication between a student and a potential client in which they agreed to work together "in the spring." To the student, of course, "spring" meant the beginning of the spring semester, in February. To the client, however, it meant seasonal spring, when things warm up, around late March or early April. As a result of this seemingly minor difference of understanding, an entire project for the class had to be shelved because the client could not adjust his schedule and begin working with the student several months earlier than he had expected. We discussed this exchange in depth as a class, and my instincts as a teacher tell me that the students learned something about effectively communicating with outside audiences. This learning experience for the ITL students was not at all lessened by the fact that there was not a graded assignment on the course syllabus representing this particular learning outcome.

Other learning outcomes for the course do have specific assignments that can be graded more traditionally according to rubrics and concrete requirements. When we ask students to assess technology needs and develop a schedule for addressing them, the results of this work take the form of a scope statement that clearly defines the client's needs and the students' plans for addressing them, and of a Gantt chart that lays out a specific time line for accomplishing the various tasks in the associated work breakdown structure (WBS). We spend a lot of class time reviewing this work as a class, discussing the elements of a WBS that are sometimes difficult to remember to include and plan for. For instance, if the students intend to conduct a survey of users, they might simply add "Survey Users" to a first draft of their WBS. When we parse these lists as a class, it becomes clear that even such a simple task requires several steps, including the drafting (and testing) of survey questions; contacting potential users and scheduling meetings; in some cases, a time period during which users can submit the survey; collecting and analysis of the survey results; and documenting that analysis. What might originally have appeared as a one-day task on the students' Gantt chart quickly becomes a weeks-long endeavor, which then has to be conducted in parallel with several other tasks. These acts of drafting and revision, although different from assignments the students have encountered in other courses, can nevertheless be assessed according to standard practices. I take a similar approach with other documents that the students generate during the course of the projects, such as the project charter, team contract, risk probability matrix and risk register, and project transition documents. Similarly, the outcome that requires students to be able to "effectively communicate the results of their work to a diverse audience" can be assessed through standard rubrics related to oral presentation assignments (clarity of purpose, focus, organization, etc.). This particular assessment occurs at the end of the semester, when the students present their work to the campus; and to the department in their final project defense.

9.2.2 Program-Level Outcomes and Assessment

The focus of the course is a team-based IT project that the students complete on behalf of a local nonprofit organization. It is their performance on this project that we use to assess our program-level outcomes, which are articulated in the course syllabus as follows:

PROGRAM-LEVEL STUDENT LEARNING OUTCOMES
Your work on this project represents the "capstone" of your work in the ITL major. You must, therefore, make every effort to demonstrate through your work on the project the ability to:

- Research and analyze an IT challenge and make sound recommendations regarding its solution
- Implement robust and well-documented IT solutions that respond to specific user requirements and that anticipate future needs

- Work as a productive member of a team to accomplish project goals; to plan and schedule project components effectively; to communicate clearly to a variety of audiences in both written and oral forms about the progress, status, and results of an IT project
- Act ethically in the execution of all these objectives

Although there is some overlap between the course- and program-level outcomes, we assess them in very different ways. Course-level outcomes are related to the day-to-day activities of the course, course assignments, and discussions during class meetings. These program-level outcomes function more as a medium for the members of the department to evaluate whether what we are teaching in our other courses is effectively being learned by the students. Assessment, in this context, is almost entirely the product of the conversations we have with the students informally, as the semester progresses; and formally, during the students' preliminary and final project defenses. The final stage in this process of assessment occurs when the department meets, directly after the final project defenses, to evaluate how well each student was able to demonstrate, through his or her work on the project, the outcomes we have set for the program overall. At this meeting, we review our department-level learning outcomes, and discuss ways in which we might change our courses, or even our overall program requirements, in response.

Using the capstone to review our program-level outcomes has had the advantage of forcing us regularly to review the goals of our other classes and make sure that the threads that tie our courses together are strong. As an interdisciplinary program, we want all or most of our courses to explore computing within a variety of social, historical, economic, and other contexts. We want all or most of our courses to stress the importance of understanding the broader effects of technology—on users, on organizations, and on society. We want all or most of our courses to teach students to work in teams, meet deadlines, and bring projects to completion. Our end-of-semester review of the students' work on their projects, and the overall structure of the capstone course itself, forces us also to review the objectives of all the courses that lead up to the capstone.

One example of a program-level outcome that we measure through the students' work is their ability to research IT-related challenges (first bulleted item above). As with most of the concepts we teach, we find we have to spend a lot of time explaining what we mean by "research" in the first place. Students are always eager to get started on the nuts and bolts of a project, and in this context, "research" can mean learning something new about the required technologies. But what we really want to teach them is the importance of learning about the domain of the project, about past efforts to solve the challenges presented by the project, and about the overall organizational structure that will have to support the project in future years. Year after year, we are reminded of the difficulty of explaining these different approaches to "research" to our students. As we assess the projects at the semester's end, we discuss ways that we can add different kinds of research to our other classes. I spend a lot of time on domain and competitive product research in the project phase of my Human Computer Interaction course, for instance, and my colleague spends additional time on interviewing methods in the development of requirements in her Systems Analysis course.

Another example of the difficulty of defining, let alone achieving, our program-level outcomes is in the area of ethics. "Act ethically in the execution of all these objectives," reads the final bulleted item above. We find a great difference in student responses between discussing ethics (after reading the ACM guidelines on ethics, for instance) and actually behaving ethically when interacting with clients. One example that often comes up is in the recommendations that students make to clients. We want students to see the importance of educating their clients as part of the project. We have all seen firsthand the problems caused by people not knowing what technologies are available to solve their problems and, as a result, selecting the first solution that occurs (or is presented) to them. Within the context of project management, this is too often a criticism that can be leveled at IT contractors who propose solutions based more on their recent projects, skill level, or potential for profit than on what is best for the client. Students, busy with other classes, extracurricular activities, and senior-year emotions and concerns, are equally subject to making choices that are more in their interest than in their clients'. We take seriously the ACM caution that "computer professionals are in a position of special trust and, therefore, have a special responsibility to provide objective, credible evaluations to employers, clients, users, and the public" [1]. But it is one thing to discuss this in a class, and something else entirely (and more effective) to see the students encounter the principle and work through their responses to it in their work with clients.

9.3 CHALLENGES OF USING SERVICE-LEARNING FOR PROGRAM ASSESSMENT

Using the students' work on their projects to assess the overall ITL program presents some difficulties, however. First, it provides additional burden on all faculty in the department. While the course meets with one instructor (like other courses), there is a course blog in which students reflect upon their work and experiences, and all members of the department read and post to this blog as well. Many of our weekly department meetings include discussions of the students' work, and we have formal meetings with the students at midterm (preliminary defense) and at the end of the term (final defense). Students seek technical counsel about their projects from all faculty, and this, too, is a time burden. Finally, the inherent openness of the course can be unsettling for the course instructor, who must at times negotiate conflicting advice from department faculty, resolve internal conflicts, and head off the miscommunications that inevitably result from fragmented or distributed discussions.

Our use of the course for program assessment has also required that we experiment with different ways to meet the public dissemination principle of service-learning pedagogy. Public dissemination means that the students should engage in some activity that reports the results of their service project to a broader community. For the first few years of ITL 400, we met this requirement by opening up the students' final presentation to the campus and also inviting the project clients. The occasion was usually a happy one, because the clients, who receive the benefits of the project at little or no cost to themselves, are almost invariably quite pleased with the results. As we began to use these projects, and the final presentations, for program assessment, and as we began to consider the final reports more like defenses than presentations, it became increasingly more uncomfortable to have the clients and, in some cases, other members of the College community, present. Where the clients and casual observers from the community would see success and accomplishment, we saw opportunities missed, objectives left unfulfilled, and substandard results that we knew we had to be critical of. For a few years, we simply did not invite these other constituencies to the presentations, which allowed us to hold the students to a more rigorous standard, but which also had the effect of minimizing the public-dissemination element of the course. It also deprived the students of much-needed validation for their hard work, and the clients of the opportunity to publicly express their gratitude to the students, the department, and the College. After much experimentation, we have decided on a two-event solution: we have an open house on the last day of the semester, to which we invite the College and the clients to come and learn about the students' projects; and we have a department defense two days later, on the reading day before final exams, when the students defend their work according to the department's program-level learning outcomes.

9.4 CLIENTS AND PROJECTS

Students in the course have taken on a wide variety of projects over the years. The most common request is for help with websites, which the students have created for the local literacy council, farmer's market, public library, a teen pregnancy and adoption agency, a community redevelopment organization, and a youth sports club (among others discussed below). Other projects have included contacts databases, LAN installations and backup systems, research and training projects, and formal course instruction. We make an effort to balance the projects between new and previous clients each year, to expose students to the breadth of need in the community, as well as to the importance of long-term relationships with these organizations.

Our work over the years with just one organization, the Washington Community Arts and Cultural Center (Wash Arts), will illustrate the variety of projects we undertake. Wash Arts was established in 2001 (at approximately the same time the ITL department was being formed) to bring cultural programming and arts instruction to southwestern Pennsylvania children at low cost—free for children on free or reduced lunch programs. In the first year of our relationship with the Center, one of our students, Jamie, facilitated the Center's first offering of a digital music class. The class met once a week in W&J's Technology Center, and Jamie's duties included installing and maintaining the class's specialized software on the lab's computers, meeting with students before and after the class to provide tutorial assistance, and helping students create CDs of the electronic music they created in the class. In our second year working with Wash Arts, two ITL students, Kyle and Chad, taught Wash Arts' first class in Digital Art. Meeting at the arts center two nights per week, the students planned the entire curriculum for the course, and even brought department laptops and digital cameras to the class when necessary. In the third year, ITL students Ashley and Matt made a 20-minute documentary film about a neighborhood arts program run by Wash Arts, assuming all responsibility for filming, editing, and scriptwriting the narration for the film. The Center was able to use this documentary, as well as a 30-second short video that they also produced, for fundraising and additional awareness building. In the fourth year, one of our ITL students created a new website for the center. Subsequent years saw ITL students enhancing the Wash Arts website with video of some of their classes, completing an analysis for a planned expansion of the digital arts offerings of the Center, and most recently, completely revising the website again, this time using a content management system so that it would be easier for center staff to update.

Working with clients such as Wash Arts in an ongoing manner allows these organizations to think strategically about how they want to integrate the service of ITL students for both immediate and long-term IT-related projects. It also allows students to see that their work builds upon the work of previous graduates of the program. But not all clients are long-termers. One-time projects have included such clients as the local county Information

Technology office, to assist with the implementation of HIPPA require-ments; the local hospital, to research and recommend an e-mail encryption program; and a local community/government health partnership, to create a client database and to upgrade its internal network and information manage-ment system. None of these projects was strictly technical; rather, students combined their technical skills with their ability to research solutions to in-formation-related problems and collaboratively implemented them.

Both the long- and short-term relationships with community organiza-tions reinforce in our students the sense of obligation to community inherent in liberal education. These commitments also help us communicate to stu-dents, and to our campus colleagues, the liberal arts nature of our program. This has proved to be a surprisingly difficult effort, largely because of the common assumption that technology-related majors are necessarily prepro-fessional. Our department seeks to define information technology as a liber-al arts discipline by stressing the interdisciplinary uses of information tech-nologies, as well as their social and historical contexts. Rather than preparing students for the IT profession specifically, we (like other liberal arts faculty) counsel students to pursue their passions in life. We hope they will consider ITL as a major that will prepare them to address needs related to information, whether they are directing an art museum, a member of the Peace Corps, or in some other occupation that brings meaning to their lives.

9.5 IT SERVICE-LEARNING AND THE LIBERAL ARTS

Proponents of service-learning know that it is both an effective pedagogy and a way to make real the value claims of liberal arts education. Like many colleges, our institutional mission statement includes the concept of giving back to society: we want our students to become "responsible citizens who are prepared to contribute substantially to the world in which they live." Fo-cusing the projects on the needs of nonprofit community organizations helps students learn about the communities surrounding the College, and to see that their efforts make a real difference to the people served by the organiza-tions. This element of the course never ceases to surprise us. One year, two of our least predictable students eagerly volunteered to work on the website for Genesis of Pittsburgh, a community resource for pregnant women. It lat-er emerged that one of the students had been raised by a single mother, and the other had an aunt who had adopted a child through the agency. The web-site they produced (unlike the original version) was tightly focused on the demographic that would most use the site, largely as a result of the empathy these students brought with them to the project. The students' work on this project allowed them to contribute to society in ways that were meaningful both to them and to their clients. It also helped them realize the College's mission in significant and tangible ways.

Another concept of liberal arts education that the course reinforces is integration: the idea that the interdisciplinary nature of general education requirements reveals connections between disciplines that are otherwise obscured by the formal structures (departments, divisions, etc.) of our institutions. When communicating with clients and other stakeholders, for example, the students need to draw upon principles of rhetoric and communication. Whether analyzing problems of design or infrastructure, they need to consider the systems' users within the context of business practices and the clients' institutional history. When making recommendations, they need to consider the psychological difficulty of changing user habits and behaviors. A seemingly simple redesign of a farmers market website can send the students into researching such topics as sustainable and community-supported agriculture, migrant labor policies, food assistance programs, and public transportation investment. Indeed, one of the challenges of teaching such a class is prodding the students to move beyond their impulse to just get the website done, and to see that research into such topics is a necessary part of the planning and research phase of any project.

Their work in this class helps students understand the liberal arts philosophy behind our ITL major: that information technology is inherently interdisciplinary and that one must bring a wealth of contextual as well as technical understanding to any IT project. To take just one example, nearly every project requires some amount of change management: clients need to rethink how information comes into their organizations, who is responsible for it, what they do with it, and what pieces of it need to be protected, shared, or discarded. This requires a deep ethnographic understanding of the organization's mission, its history, and its relation to similar, competing, or complementary organizations. A project to create a donor database for our local public library is a good example of this. Simply understanding the variety of ways that patrons interact with the library and the variety of channels of communication they use to pledge and fulfill donations required the students to perform multiple interviews, write and rewrite dataflow datagrams, and even go through the process of making a donation in order to fully understand the flow of this seemingly simple operation. Our students often come into our program because they are good with computers, but by the time they finish this capstone course, they know that they need to be good in a variety of areas in order to successfully complete IT projects.

Finally, the class helps students understand the leadership element of their major. Early in the semester, the students read articles about service-learning so that they understand the fundamental point that the community service component of the course is primarily a pedagogical method [2–5]. Despite all the altruistic arguments on behalf of service, service-learning is first and foremost a way to teach academic content. The students learn project management by doing service projects much better than they would learn it from textbooks, lectures, and tests alone. Approximately halfway through the semester, they also read articles and case studies about servant leadership, with the aim of seeing both their clients, and ultimately themselves, as leaders seeking to help others realize their shared aspirations and commonly held goals [6–8]. In many ways, this makes the course a nice bookend to the Human Computer Interaction course that is also required in the ITL major, in which we study principles and methods of goal-directed design. In both courses, the students' focus is on creating systems that are responsive to user needs, and this focus is consistent with the principles of servant leadership that require leaders to share power and information, to include others in decision making, and to make decisions that reflect the collective will of an organization.

9.6 PROJECT MANAGEMENT AS A FRAMEWORK FOR ITL SERVICE-LEARNING

When we first taught this course in 2002, the focus was entirely on the project. Inevitably, this meant there were periods of the semester in which the students were less engaged than at other times. Over time, it became clear that the content we were teaching was project management, and that the course could be improved immensely if project management were more formally an object of study in the class. Consequently, the course is now a project management class, and the students learn the content of project management by working on community projects.

This change has had several benefits. First, the students are learning a discipline that employers find very desirable. Whether they use formal project management processes or not, the companies our students work for after graduation appreciate candidates who know how to schedule projects, work with stakeholders, and operate effectively in teams. Second, the focus on project management allows for a more natural structuring of the course. Although their projects might differ vastly, the students can all be at the same stage of the project life cycle at any given moment, whether it is initiating, researching and planning, implementing, controlling, or closing the project. Third, there is a broad array of project-management literature I can use to contextualize the students' projects, whether case studies from the *Harvard Business Review,* project management novels like Tom Demarco's *The Deadline,* or classic textbooks such as Kathy Schwalbe's *Introduction to Project Management.* Indeed, there is usually a topical case in the news as well, such as the thousands of projects that comprise the Recovery and Reinvestment Act, or just some recent billion-dollar global or corporate event or major software rollout. Finding a focus on the academic/professional content described by project management has allowed the course to come together as an invaluable IT learning experience.

Studying the basic principles of project management early in the semester puts students in a position to define projects for themselves from the beginning. Of course, we do considerable work before the start of the term to identify clients and learn about their IT needs. It is a basic principle of service-learning pedagogy that service projects must be generated from authentic community need, and the amount of work required to make these contacts and hold preliminary meetings makes it unfeasible to start this work from scratch in the first week of classes. Nevertheless, the clients do come in on the first day of classes and tell their stories over again, this time to the students, who need to begin the work of scoping right away. How much work will this entail? Can it be accomplished in roughly twelve weeks? What is it likely to cost, and does the client have a budget? Does the client seem well informed about the technologies that lie behind potential solutions? These initial meetings put the students into the position of research, analysis, and planning that is required at the outset of any well-run project, and show them immediately the value of developing scope statements and work-breakdown structures in order to manage the work ahead.

Another textbook project-management topic that works well early in the semester is the research on group dynamics and the various motivation theories from psychology that seek to explain why people work hard (or don't) to achieve success. Schwalbe's *Introduction to Project Management* contains a section on the Myers–Briggs personality tests. I always have students take a version of this test, and then meet in their project teams to discuss how each of them is likely to perform in partnership with the others, and how others on the team should respond to them, based upon their personality types. This section in the Schwalbe textbook is accompanied by a review of psychologists' theories of motivation, from Maslow's hierarchy of needs, to Frederick Herzberg's theories about motivation and achievement. This becomes a good opportunity to discuss with these near-graduates what they intend to accomplish in their first jobs, and what sorts of rewards will motivate them to be successful. It also helps at this time to consider our clients' motivations. For the most part, the directors of community organizations are not seeking fortune, but rather a way to make the world a better place for their served populations. Considering both the students' and the clients' motivations becomes an exciting way to address otherwise dry considerations of human resource management.

Some of the greatest value in using project management principles to frame the course comes at the end: showing students the importance of training the clients to use and maintain the new technology. Early in the term, the students create Gantt chart timelines for their projects, and inevitably, training initially appears in the final two weeks of the semester. We insist that they rethink such timelines and consider portions of the project that can be trained much earlier in the semester. These discussions are also tied to our quality control discussions and the overall question that we ask students often: How will you know if the project is a success? ("The clients are happy" is not an adequate response.) Although there are many objective and quantitative measures of the quality of a project (system response time, image file sizes and download times, browser compatibility, and time-on-task analyses), one of the most important measures is more subjective: can (and will) the clients use the new system? This can only be measured by early training and by building in a certain amount of time to observe the clients' actual behaviors. If clients do not update a website blog (for instance) a single time in a three-week period, something is wrong—perhaps with the early analysis that determined the clients needed a blog, perhaps with the training in how to log in, open an edit page, and make changes or post a message.

Related to training is also the process of formally closing the projects. Again, this involves many details that the students would not ordinarily consider, such as developing a transition plan that details what work needs to be done, and when, to maintain the new technology (system updates, data entry, the posting of fresh information, etc.). It also involves getting clients to sign a final deliverable acceptance form, where the clients can indicate aspects of the project that they feel remain incomplete. One year, for instance, the students redesigned a website in a content management system, and put off the issue of posting and archiving newsletters until the very end of the term. Although it entailed a relatively simple process of saving newsletter files to PDF format and linking them to a special page in the website, this does involve a lot of steps and considerations of information architecture, and the clients did not feel prepared to manage this aspect of the new site when the students sought a signature for the deliverable acceptance form. Fortunately, there was sufficient time remaining in the term for the students to revisit their training documents, detail the correct process, and then walk the clients through it several times.

Some of the richest classroom discussions have centered on project-management-related case studies from the *Harvard Business Review*. Many of these are focused on the elements that make or break projects. An article by Nadim F. Matta and Ronald N. Ashkenas from 2003, for instance, recommends forming "rapid results initiatives" while projects are ongoing, to test assumptions that led the project to be divided into its subtasks [9]. Such initiatives, they argue, can reveal gaps between tasks that conceal difficult elements of the project, which otherwise would only reveal themselves after it is too late to reschedule the critical elements of work. Another article popular with students sets forth the DICE method of determining whether a project will be successful by measuring how long project tasks can be allowed to take without supervision (**D**uration), how well equipped the project team is to complete a project (**I**ntegrity), how much both the workers and management of a company are invested in a project (**C**ommitment), and how much effort will be required for employees to use a new system that results from the project (**E**ffort) [10]. These topics all relate to the larger field of change management, and they serve to remind students that any project that involves new information technologies will at some level require the affected people to change their current workflows and habits. One final case study that I will mention in this context is "Is the Rookie Ready," which summarizes management decisions about taking on a new project and staffing it, and then critiques some of the errors that are made in the process [11]. This case, which does not even go into the specific work that is required for the project, appeals to students who themselves have been placed into a project team and are just then working out issues of team dynamics and leadership roles.

All of these elements of project management contribute to our department's mission of preparing students to take leadership roles in future academic and professional endeavors. Project planning and execution requires a great deal of foresight and commitment, all characteristics that employers and graduate schools value. The students' experience working with clients also provides them with many narratives to relate in job interviews: how they deal with difficult customers, how they communicate to multiple audiences, and how they respond to criticism. Above all, the integration of project management and readings in the field of servant leadership instills in students the idea that projects are most worth pursuing if they help people (users, employees, and citizens) accomplish shared goals and further an enterprise that is larger than themselves. Our leadership curriculum is not designed to make future managers out of students, but rather to show them that the best leaders are those who champion other people's goals and aspirations, and who inspire others to seek and accept change when it is in the interest of the community or organization.

9.7 CHALLENGE OF SERVICE-LEARNING AS A MAJOR REQUIREMENT

Although project management provides a useful framework for the service projects, it is still the case that requiring a service-learning course in the ITL major presents many challenges. Not least is the fact that we have to put *every one* of our majors in front of clients, and trust them with the reputation of the College and the department. While we respect all our students and see great progress in all of them over the course of their four years with us, it is nevertheless the case that we, like all departments, see a wide range of ability in them. Yet, every student must perform at an acceptable level in the class. We have developed a number of strategies to address this challenge.

First, all the students work in teams of three. Although we experimented earlier in the class's history with having the entire class work on a project, and with students working individually, we have found that three is about the right number for most projects with a time line of one semester. This allows students to distribute the project work according to their talents, and it allows us to provide additional mentoring for students who are struggling, without jeopardizing the project's success. It also helps that we work with some clients year after year; they understand our predicament, and know that if they are willing to take an underperforming team one year, they can look forward to a more productive year the next. Ultimately, such clients understand the pedagogical underpinnings of the class, and are more than willing to tailor project requests to such circumstances.

It can also be a challenge to find community projects for the course. Fortunately, word of mouth is a great publicist. But we take a lot of care to filter the requests that come in according to the basic factors that determine any project: is the project sized correctly for approximately three students for twelve weeks; is the budget for the project minimal, or has the required funding been committed by the client; does the project require skills that the students have or can learn in the amount of time available. Our enrollments vary from year to year; we need anywhere from one to six projects that meet these requirements each spring semester. So another challenge is managing community expectations about the course. We cannot take every project, and the ones we can take need to be a good fit for the students in each graduating class.

As mentioned before, it can also be difficult to ensure that students in any given year will have the technical skill set required for projects. One result is that we have a bias toward projects that involve websites, databases, document design, and basic networking and hardware installation. We also have begun to prepare students better for particular projects that we know are coming up. In 2011, for the first time, we worked with another academic department on our campus instead of with a community nonprofit. Our biology department was looking for a way to capture into electronic format long-term ecological monitoring data from property that has been leased to the College for this purpose. Whereas in the past the biology professor had taken students to the site to collect such information using paper spreadsheets, they wanted a mobile app that could serve the same purpose and eliminate the piles of unused data sheets that were accumulating. Knowing that we had two students interested in this topic but lacking actual experience in mobile development, we created an independent study opportunity for them, for the January term prior to the capstone course. This independent study allowed the students to explore Android and iOS development platforms, as well as the technologies necessary to upload datasets to an on-campus server. With this programming experience behind them, they were well prepared to focus on other difficult issues of the project once the capstone course began, such as domain research, interaction design, and user testing.

9.8 SUMMARY AND CONCLUSIONS

Service-learning pedagogy in the ITL capstone course helps students understand their major within the context of their liberal arts education. It helps faculty in the department explain the philosophy of ITL to our students, our faculty colleagues, and to the local community. It also helps us convey to students the importance of soft technology skills, such as writing, research, analysis, oral communication, teamwork, and working with (sometimes difficult) clients. And it helps us teach the human elements of IT ethics.

The course does, however, have some problems. One issue that resurfaces occasionally is the need for project support after the semester is over. We do require students to develop a transition plan, which details the work that clients need to do to maintain the project in the future. This does not mean that clients always know how to do this work, or that leadership in the client's organization will not change over time, thus leaving a support gap behind them. In just the most recent semester, one client announced her departure from the organization two weeks before the end of the semester; and another announced that funding for her organization was being withdrawn abruptly. We try to make sure clients understand that project support after the close date is their responsibility, but the unfortunate fact is that many of them are so woefully underfunded and understaffed that they are nearly helpless when the project (software, website, backup systems, etc.) needs attention. In rare instances, ITL faculty will step in to assist, but this only adds to faculty workload and risks conveying the message, or building the expectation, that we faculty are the clients' support service of last resort.

Another difficulty is the fact that a commitment to service-learning pedagogy is highly individual. This leaves the course in the hands of just one or at most two faculty in a small department such as ours. Occasional sabbaticals can be accommodated by nimble course scheduling, but if the regular instructor for the course were to leave the College, the department would need to reevaluate the course as a curricular requirement.

Tangentially related to this is the wide availability of noncurricular service and volunteer opportunities on campus. Service-learning is often grouped with these other volunteer and service opportunities, causing confusion among both students and faculty colleagues. Offering the course as a major requirement can necessitate constant explanation of the purpose of the course, in contrast with these other opportunities. This problem can be addressed easily on a campus with a visible and vibrant office supporting true service-learning initiatives. It is more often the case that such offices, structurally organized under Student Life, focus on volunteer and community service programs, thus exacerbating the difficulty of explaining the role of service-learning in the curriculum.

Despite these difficulties, we remain committed to Service-Learning Project Management as the capstone course in the ITL major. ITL is not a pre-professional program like accounting or education; we consciously created the major to be in keeping with the liberal arts identity of the College. As a result, our graduates pursue the same mix of professional and graduate school opportunities as other liberal arts majors. They do so prepared to address the challenges of information in an increasingly diverse and interconnected global environment. We hope that their experience with service-learning also empowers them with a lifelong habit of giving back to their communities.

REFERENCES

1. ACM Code of Ethics and Professional Conduct. http://www.acm.org/about/code-of-ethics.

2. Furco, A. (2003). "Service-Learning: A Balanced Approach to Experiential Education." In *Introduction to Service Learning Toolkit* (2nd ed.) (pp. 11–14). Providence, RI: Campus Compact.

3. Zlotkowski, E. (2003). "Pedagogy and Engagement." In *Introduction to service learning toolkit* (2nd ed.) (pp. 63–77). Providence, RI: Campus Compact.

4. Hilton, T. S. E., and Mowry, D. D. (2005). "Teaching Information Systems Ethics Through Service Learning," *Issues in Information Systems*, 6(1), 35–41.

5. Hannon, C. (2006). Service learning in information technology leadership: A natural connection. *Peer Review*, 8(4), 16–19.

6. Greenleaf, R. K. (1977). *Servant Leadership: A Journey Into the Nature of Legitimate Power and Greatness*. New York: Paulist Press. (Original work published 1977).

7. Burns, J. M. (1982). *Leadership*. Harper & Row. (Original work published 1978).

8. Carlzon, J. (1989). *Moments of Truth*. New York: HarperCollins.

9. Matta, N. F., and Ashkenas, R. N. (2003, September). "Why Good Projects Fail Anyway." *Harvard Business Review*, pp. 109–114.

10. Sirkin, H. L., Keenan, P., and Jackson, A. (2005, October). "The Hard Side of Change Management." *Harvard Business Review*, pp. 108–118.

11. Green, S. (2009, December). "Is the Rookie Ready?" *Harvard Business Review*, pp. 33–40.

CHAPTER 10

SERVICE-LEARNING AND ENTREPRENEURSHIP FOR ENGINEERS

Lisa Zidek

ABSTRACT

Service is a fundamental aspect of engineering. Incorporating service-learning into engineering curricula promotes recruitment and retention. Engineering service learning may be incorporated into traditional engineering courses, or may be introduced as an entrepreneurial engineering venture. This chapter will provide an example of a junior-level, design-based engineering entrepreneurship course.

10.1 INTRODUCTION

The engineering profession is based on the premise of serving the community. The concept of engineers serving the community is strongly reflected in the National Society of Professional Engineering (NSPE) code of conduct. To quote the preamble, "Engineering has a direct and vital impact on the quality of life for all people. Accordingly, the services provided by engineers require honesty, impartiality, fairness, and equity, and must be dedicated to the protection of the public health, safety and welfare" [1]. Furthermore, the NSPE professional obligations state that engineers shall strive to service the public interest; specifically, Section III.2.a states that "Engineers are encouraged to participate in civic affairs; career guidance for youths; and work for the advancement of the safety, health, and well-being of their community" [1].

The need for engineering service is also demonstrated in the student outcomes included in the accreditation standards of The Accreditation Board for Engineering and Technology (ABET). In the general criteria for baccalaureate level programs, student outcomes (criterion 3) include "an ability to function on multidisciplinary teams; an understanding of professional and ethical responsibility; the broad education necessary to understand the impact of engineering solutions in a global, economic, environmental, and societal contexts; and a knowledge of contemporary issues" [2].

Engineering service-learning promotes the concept of social responsibility of the engineering profession and provides an opportunity for engineering programs to assess ABET outcomes in a simple, straightforward manner. Service to the community is considered fundamental to success and growth of the engineering profession, a concept that must be introduced while students are learning fundamental engineering skills. As stated by Lima and Oakes, "engineering is, by nature, a profession with a societal context leading to social responsibility" [3]. Since service is prominent in the Engineering Code of Ethics as well as implied in several ABET student outcomes, incorporating engineering service-learning as a stand-alone course or as a component of core courses is beneficial to students in terms of professional skills development and to engineering programs for the purpose of assessment and accreditation.

10.2 SERVICE, STUDENT ENGAGEMENT, AND RETENTION

Research indicates that service-learning has a direct, positive impact on student engagement and retention. One study found that service-learning motivates students to work harder, be more curious, connect learning to personal experience, and demonstrate deeper understanding of subject matter [4]. Although a complete content analysis is pending, narratives from student reflection papers indicate that student engagement occurs at three different levels: the student, the course, and the community, as depicted in Figure 10.1.

Self-engagement describes the students' perceptions of themselves and their capability with respect to the project and their personal abilities. A student who is self-engaged is developing self-confidence in his/her skills as well as a connection to their chosen career. Examples from an engineering service-learning course include statements in reflection papers such as "I have always been unsure of my ability to really engineer something but now I know I can do it"; "Before this experience, I was thinking about changing majors but now I am really excited about becoming an engineer"; and "I now know I want to be an engineer." The client-based, open-ended nature of service-learning projects promotes self-engagement through the development of critical thinking, problem solving, and the application of content from multiple courses in one project. Unlike many course-based projects,

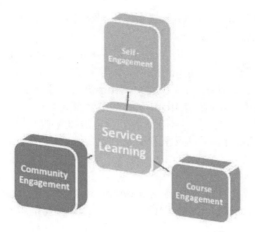

Figure 10.1. Service-learning and engagement.

the "correct" answer is unknown; the emphasis is placed on the process and technique rather than a known entity.

Course engagement occurs when the student no longer asks "when will I ever use this?" Course engagement includes the course in which the service-learning project is initiated as well as other courses the student is, has, or will be taking. In the engineering service-learning course, student reflections such as "I wish I would have paid attention when we covered economics; now I am trying to learn it all on my own"; "After doing this project, I can't wait to take Water Resources"; and "I was amazed to actually use my fluids class in engineering service-learning" are indicators of course engagement. The economics reflection reveals an interesting insight into student perspectives. The Florida Gulf Coast University (FGCU) curriculum does not require engineering economics; economics content is included in the engineering service-learning course. The engineering students often view engineering economics as irrelevant or a topic better suited for business students, and are then surprised by client requests for cost analysis.

Community engagement is the big-picture look at the interaction of engineering in the community or in society. Community ranges from small in scope, such as the college campus, to a large global view. Quotes from reflection papers in engineering service-learning that indicate community engagement include:

- "As engineers, we have the responsibility of providing solutions and alternatives to assist society and its issues."
- "The design process gave us time to think about different aspects of environmental, ethical, and economic considerations. These are all

things that I would have honestly never thought about before this class or this project."

- "This course and project has given me the tools to have a better understanding of us as engineers and our social responsibility to meet the needs of our community by applying the skills and knowledge that has been passed on to us through our education."

Research by Astin and Sax indicate that service-learning students reported greater understanding of community problems, which is echoed in these reflections [5].

Several studies have shown a connection between service-learning and retention. Satisfaction with college, which may result in an increased likelihood that a student will persist at an institution, was positively associated with service-learning [5]. In a study by Muthiah and coworkers, students in service-learning classes indicated the course had an impact with respect to their likelihood of persistence [6]. Gallini and Moely also demonstrated student retention was directly linked to participation in service-learning courses using student self-reports [7].

10.3 BEYOND SERVICE-LEARNING

Service-learning is one pedagogical approach to reaching beyond the classroom in an effort to engage students. Other models include experiential learning theory, experiential education, and the movement into social entrepreneurship.

Experiential learning theory (ELT) is an adult-learning theory that highlights the critical role experience plays in affecting learning and change. Kolb's (1984) formulation of ELT draws on the work of prominent educational and organizational scholars, including John Dewey, Kurt Lewin, and Jean Piaget, who share the common view that learning involves integrating experience with concepts and linking observations to actions [8]. Experiential learning is strongly geared to the adult learner rather than the traditional college student, and encourages students to challenge common theory and approaches based on experiences they have had in similar life situations. This is an indirect method of learning—asking students to recall similar situations and apply lessons learned from those situations to the problem.

Experiential education is a philosophy of education that describes the process that occurs between a teacher and student that infuses direct experience into the learning environment and content. The Association for Experiential Education regards experiential education "as a philosophy and methodology in which educators purposefully engage with learners in direct experience and focused reflection in order to increase knowledge, develop skills, and clarify values" [9,10]. Using experiential education, the instructor incorporates a learning experience, such as a class project, that will be shared by the students and instructor. In other words, the instructor and students are living the project and developing teaching moments from the experience at hand. Experiential learning is an active learning technique, which may or may not include a service-learning component.

Social entrepreneurship is as an emerging trend in the business world, well suited to those already exposed to and excited by service-learning. The concept of social entrepreneurship will be developed later in this chapter as a pedagogical approach to combining service, entrepreneurship, and engineering. Social entrepreneurs are driven by the social mission, and mission-related impact is the central criterion, not making money [11]. Social entrepreneurship is a natural extension of the concepts and theories of service learning. Social entrepreneurship asks students to consider taking the service-learning experience beyond the classroom and instituting social change rather than a one-time classroom event.

10.4 ENGINEERING SERVICE-LEARNING IN THE CLASSROOM

Engineering service-learning promotes the concept of social responsibility of the engineering profession. Service to the community is considered fundamental to success and growth of the engineering profession [12]. A driving factor in the course is to increase student awareness of engineering in society. As stated by Lima and Oakes, "engineering is, by nature, a profession with a societal context leading to social responsibility" [3].

Engineering service-learning models, depicted in Figure 10.2, may range from classroom-based models as described earlier in this chapter, to service-learning in student organizations and larger-scale models such as the engineering-based service-learning curriculum. These models have unique advantages and disadvantages in terms of scale, resource requirements, and scope of projects.

The first model, service-learning in the classroom, has been discussed at length earlier in this chapter. Classroom-based service-learning models offer advantages such as leading the students to an understanding and appreciation of the learning aspect of service-learning. The instructor may select projects that will highlight a particular concept, perhaps designing a bridge for a local nonprofit agency, to reinforce concepts of design, materials, and forces. Disadvantages of such projects include a limited scope (most projects must be completed in an academic semester or quarter), so students

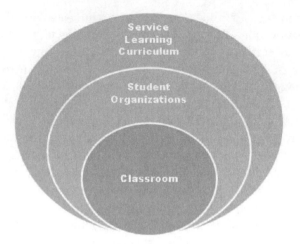

Figure 10.2. Service-learning models.

may not be fully engaged if they are not interested in the project, and limited available resources (typically the course instructor and the liaison at the client site). Of these, the most difficult to overcome is the lack of resources. Properly scoped projects can have an impact on student interest and the learning outcomes for a course. Student engagement may develop over the life of the project, even for those students who were highly disengaged at the start of the course. The disengaged students may be motivated by the application of course work, the hands-on aspect of such a project, or simply by peer pressure, since most service-learning projects take on a team-based approach.

The second model is instigated by students, usually as a requirement of a professional organization. Student organizations such as honor societies, professional societies, and fraternities and sororities all have service requirements. Many student organizations naturally incorporate projects that include a service-learning component. One such example is a student chapter of the American Society of Civil Engineers (ASCE) that works with Habitat for Humanity to provide students learning opportunities within their discipline while under the guidance of an experienced project leader. There are a number of advantages of such programs, including:

- High levels of student engagement
- They are engaged because they want to fulfill their obligation for the professional society and they are at the site as a group representing their society, their program, and their college
- Adequate resources, typically provided by the sponsoring organization

The disadvantage of this model is a lack of connection between the service and learning aspects of the project. Students may not connect the work being done, in particular manual labor aspects, with engineering design, planning, or concepts.

The third model of engineering-based service-learning is large-scale, curriculum-based service-learning. The EPICS model from Purdue University serves as an example [13]. In this model, service-learning is integrated throughout the curriculum, with an opportunity for students to move to different levels of project responsibility as they move through the curriculum. Projects may take on a large-scale, multiyear, multifaceted nature. From a pedagogical standpoint, this model provides active learning, with concepts reinforced in a classroom setting; resources from both faculty and project sponsors; and project ownership for the students. Although a strong model from the student learning perspective, this concept proves difficult to institute in many programs. Credit restrictions, lack of flexibility in the engineering curriculum, and lack of resources to oversee such a curriculum make this model difficult for many engineering programs. For these reasons, the focus of the remainder of this chapter will be on classroom-based engineering service-learning models and the progression from service-learning to social entrepreneurship at one university.

10.5 THE FLORIDA GULF COAST UNIVERSITY STORY

The FGCU mission statement includes the following: "Florida Gulf Coast University continuously pursues academic excellence and practices, promotes environmental sustainability, embraces diversity, nurtures community partnerships, *values public service, encourages civic responsibility,* cultivates habits of lifelong learning, and keeps the advancement of knowledge and pursuit of truth as noble ideals at the heart of the university's purpose" [14] (emphasis added). Note the emphasis on the concepts of public service and civic engagement. The university's commitment to service is included in its graduation requirements. The following excerpt is from the FGCU Academic Catalog:

> **The What and the Why of Service-Learning.** One of the defining characteristics of Florida Gulf Coast University is its institutional commitment to service, put into practice through the civic engagement activities of faculty, staff, and students. Service-learning connects students to the community and the classroom to the real world. Through service-learning, students are both learners and teachers, sharing themselves and their knowledge and, in turn, learning from the clients and the environment where they serve. Because service-learning is such a powerful teaching tool and because service-learning sets the

stage for continued community involvement, University founders established service-learning as an undergraduate requirement. We call our service-learning program EaglesConnect.

How Service-Learning Works. Students admitted to FGCU as first-year students or lower-level transfers must complete 80 hours of service-learning as part of their graduation requirement. Students admitted as upper-level transfers must complete 40 hours of service-learning as part of their graduation requirement. Students who have already completed a bachelor's degree at another institution and are admitted to FGCU to complete a second undergraduate degree must complete 40 hours of service-learning as part of their second degree's graduation requirements. Students who have completed a bachelor's degree at FGCU and are readmitted to FGCU to complete a second undergraduate degree have already fulfilled the degree requirements for service-learning; however, if they register for a class that has a service-learning requirement, they are obligated to complete it as a component of the course's requirements [15].

In addition, the U. A. Whitaker College of Engineering (WCE) mission statement states "The mission of the U. A. Whitaker College of Engineering is to produce graduates and community leaders in selected engineering and computing disciplines with superior technical competence and professional skills to meet the engineering and computing challenges of Southwest Florida and beyond. This is accomplished in an *entrepreneurial and innovative educational and research environment that values diversity, service, integrity, leadership, and collaborations*" [16] (emphasis added).

The WCE began as the U. A. Whitaker School of Engineering in 2005. The engineering program offered an innovative curriculum based on integrated lecture–lab classes and a mission statement that clearly identifies the value of entrepreneurship and service. The initial engineering programs at FGCU were developed with engineering entrepreneurship and engineering service learning as foundation courses for all disciplines (civil, environmental, and bioengineering).

The initial curriculum included a sequence of Engineering Entrepreneurship during the second semester of the sophomore year and Service-Learning in Engineering in the first semester of junior year, with the entrepreneurship course a prerequisite for the service-learning course. The description of Engineering Entrepreneurship was simply to introduce students to entrepreneurship and define a service-learning project. The objective of the course was to have the students define a project that would then be developed during the following semester in the Service Learning in Engineering course. This model was implemented during the spring 2007 semester to the sophomore engineering students. These Engineering Entrepreneurship students were challenged to work with a local high school math department to develop proposals for products or services that would stimulate interest in mathematics, with an ultimate goal of increasing awareness of technology fields such as engineering. The products or services would be developed and implemented as part of the service-learning experience in the fall. During this iteration, Engineering Entrepreneurship was cotaught with a College of Business professor, whereas Service-Learning in Engineering was not cotaught.

Service-Learning in Engineering emphasized team-based community service activity on the business plan developed in Engineering Entrepreneurship. Topics emphasized included the societal context of engineering, the use of the design method and engineering analysis, team skills, project management, communications, engineering standards and liability, and components of critical thinking and self-discovery. This course was taught for the first time during the fall 2007 semester. As a continuation of the Engineering Entrepreneurship course, the projects were centered around the high school math curriculum. Since the projects were an integral aspect of the course grade, the FGCU students put effort into the projects; however, only a few teams exhibited a passion for the project. Examples of the student projects included: an online, real-time tutoring service for specific math classes; an advertising/informational campaign linking math to student interests such as the acoustics of a guitar and the aerodynamics of a race car; a mathematics-based board game; and the development of supplementary teaching materials for the instructor with specific engineering-based examples for every chapter in the high school mathematics textbook. Assessment of the two course sequences (discussed later) resulted in changes to the course sequencing and the topics covered in each course.

Curriculum changes resulted in a revised course sequence for the 2008–2009 academic year. Service-Learning in Engineering was renamed Engineering Service-Learning and was offered during the fall semester. The object of the course was to identify a team-based community service activity that incorporates engineering and has the potential to be developed into a business. Class projects were more diverse than the previous year. The high school was pleased with the results from the previous year and requested additional projects for the 2008–2009 academic year. In addition, community members, including the county parks and a local church, requested project assistance. Finally, students also proposed possible projects. Student teams were assigned based on an application process, with team diversity as a critical factor. The deliverable in Engineering Service-Learning was a modified business plan linked to the team's alternative analysis and proposing the project the team would test, design, and implement in Engineering Entrepreneurship the following semester.

Engineering Entrepreneurship was offered during the spring 2009 semester. The course was intended to be cotaught with a college of business faculty member; however, the business faculty was pulled from the course prior to the start of classes. The objective of the course was to complete the engineering design process started in Engineering Service-Learning, specifically, testing, development, and implementation of the project proposed in the previous course. The various project clients resulted in a diverse set of projects. A sample of the resulting team projects are described below.

Evergreen Energies was a team working on the development of alternative fuel using vegetable oils collected from local restaurants. The purpose was to use the fuel in construction vehicles. This team of students had a working refining system built in the backyard of one of the team members, and a local construction company was using the fuel in their vehicles by the end of the semester. A second team, Natural Footbridge Solutions, worked with a local church to design a footbridge for the church, to be built of all natural materials on land owned by the church and designated as a preserve. A constraint of the project was that all material used were to be recycled, reclaimed, or remanufactured, leading to a consulting organization in sustainable bridge development. A third team worked with a local high school to develop a curriculum for an engineering technology program. The high school had stat-of-the-art facilities designed for an engineering technology program; however, the school district was not successful, in two years, of attracting and retaining an instructor with the appropriate understanding of the equipment and educational relevance. Team Engineering Education developed a complete, semester-long curriculum, approved by the school, that would allow almost any instructor to teach the module. Every lesson had detailed instructions, background information, and lesson plans tied to state standards.

Since both Engineering Service-Learning and Engineering Entrepreneurship are required courses for all FGCU engineering students and the programs were growing steadily, the 2009–2010 academic year brought the challenge of two sections of each course. Due to costs and university policies, the sections could not be offset; therefore, both Engineering Service-Learning sections were offered in fall and Engineering Entrepreneurship during the spring semester. There were no substantial changes to the course. More projects were available from community-based clients, primarily due to publicity and word of mouth from previous semesters. Again, the Engineering Entrepreneurship course was scheduled to be taught with a college of business faculty member but was changed prior to the start of classes. A total of 17 projects were delivered. Projects included students working with Doctors Without Borders to develop a portable surgical suite, solar distillation to convert saltwater to freshwater for kayakers, working to improve pressure vests worn by autistic children, and a methane-based system for grilling, to provide a few examples. As the projects became more complicated, working prototypes became more difficult and many teams were settling for conceptual designs.

During the 2010–2011 academic year, two sections of each class were once again necessary and, again, the business instructor was removed from the schedule at the last minute. Two changes introduced during this academic year were the inclusion of international projects and teaming with a MBA course for one section of Engineering Entrepreneurship.

The international projects were the result of a grant the engineering instructor was involved with during the 2010 summer. Three of the 16 projects had clients from a small Guatemalan village and required the design of assistive devices. Two of the three international projects successfully developed products to be delivered to the Guatemalan clients the following summer. Other projects included student teams working with deaf students to develop a STEM (science, technology, engineering, and math) program to encourage deaf students to follow STEM careers, and a project to address the amount of trash in waterways, primarily the Gulf of Mexico. The water trash project ultimately won a service-learning competition hosted on campus as well as a preliminary business plan competition.

The combined efforts of engineering and business were believed to be important for students to fully grasp how closely these fields work together. Even though the formal coteaching opportunities had been repeatedly thwarted, a business faculty member offered to collaborate with the engineering faculty member. The efforts of the two faculty members resulted in the undergraduate Engineering Entrepreneurship students presenting their proposals to MBA students. The MBA students selected projects of interest and worked with the engineering students to develop the ideas into solid business plans.

The 2011–2012 academic year brought several changes to the programs. Due to program growth, resource constraints, and a desire to provide more in-depth, program-specific courses, the Engineering Service-Learning course has been removed from the curriculum and the Engineering Entrepreneurship course is changing to a course with strong emphasis on social entrepreneurship. The primary driver for this change was due to resource constraints. During the 2011–2012 academic year, four sections of each course would be required. As only one engineering faculty member taught the Engineering Service-Learning and Engineering Entrepreneurship courses, teaching four sections in each semester was unrealistic, and the option to teach at least one of the sections in summer was not available. Also in the 2011–2012 academic year, the U. A. Whitaker School of Engineering became the U. A. Whitaker College of Engineering, and Software Engineering was added to the programs offered. Along with changes to the infrastructure, the curriculum also continued to change. Table 10.1 provides a summary of the significant changes in the two-course sequence.

Table 10.1. Course revision sequence

Year	Course sequence	Project description	Cotaught or cooperative teaching	Number of sections
2007–2008	Engineering Entrepreneurship (spring sophomore year)	Single client, single need	Engineering Entrepreneurship was cotaught	1 each
2008–2009	Engineering Service-Learning (fall junior year)	Carried over from Engineering Entrepreneurship course	No	1 each
2009–2010	Engineering Service-Learning and Engineering Entrepreneurship	Student submissions/client requests, clients throughout the U.S.	No (planned but changed before classes started)	1 each
2010–2011	Engineering Service Learning and Engineering Entrepreneurship	Student submissions/client requests, including international projects	One section of Engineering Entrepreneurship cooperatively taught with MBA Business Planning course	2 each
2011–2012	Engineering Entrepreneurship	Student submissions only	One section of Engineering Entrepreneurship cooperatively taught with undergraduate Business Planning course	2 sections in fall; at least 1, possibly 2 in spring

10.6   COURSE ASSESSMENT

The WCE has strict course assessment procedures that include formal course assessments for every course in the curriculum, every semester. Assessment includes course reports that focus on the learning outcomes for class and course evaluations. Engineering Entrepreneurship was assessed at the end of the 2006–2007 academic year, and Engineering Service-Learning during the 2007–2008 cycle. Although overall the students were meeting the learning objectives of the two courses, course assessment as well as student feedback indicated a need to revise the course offering structure and sequence. Three issues became apparent after the initial course assessment data was collected, and was reaffirmed by student evaluations: first, the course sequencing was not appropriate; second, the project needed to be expanded beyond a single client; and third, the courses needed to be offered in the same academic year.

The need to change the course sequence became obvious during the initial offering of Engineering Entrepreneurship. The course focused on identifying business opportunities, identifying and segmenting customers, financing a business, competitive analysis, and protecting intellectual property. Due to the structure of the course, students had not had the opportunity to identify a customer or the customer's need, rendering discussions on identifying opportunities and needs pointless from a student perspective. Although supporting data is not available due to a technical error in the course evaluations, the students overwhelmingly voiced their opinion regarding the course sequence and the schedule (spring to fall) to both the engineering faculty member and the founding director of the engineering school. Likewise, during the Engineering Service-Learning course, which was offered the following fall semester, topics such as project management and product liability were too late to be relevant for the projects that had been underway since the previous semester. Restructuring the sequence—making Engineering Service Learning a prerequisite to Engineering Entrepreneurship—and running the courses sequentially in a single academic year (Engineering Service Learning in fall and Engineering Entrepreneurship in spring) were addressed by the curriculum committee and implemented for the 2008–2009 academic year.

A second challenge encountered during the initial course offering was the project. The lead engineering instructor was new to campus, arriving from out of state one week prior to the start of classes. The coinstructor, from the College of Business, was not familiar with engineering-based service-learning and entrepreneurship. Due to these limitations, the instructors chose to limit the project to one client with a preidentified need. It was decided that the engineering students would work with a local high school to identify products or services that improved awareness and/or enthusiasm for math, in particular the math skills necessary to study technical fields such as engineering. The impetus for this project stemmed from the severe math deficiency of students entering the FGCU engineering program. This project fit the service-learning definition of Hatcher and Bringle: "students participate in an organized service activity that meets identified community needs" [17]. Furthermore, the project contained the components illustrated by Lima and Oakes, which includes service to underserviced people (identified through the demographics of the high school), academic content (students were using engineering principles to support the high school math program), partnership and reciprocity (this outreach was the beginning of a very good working relationship between the high school and FGCU), mutual learning (the engineering students learned from the high school teachers as the FGCU students taught mathematical applications), and analysis and reflection (analysis is part of the engineering design process and reflection was a required component of the class) [3]. Unfortunately, the project design was not as successful for the entrepreneurial aspects of the design. The primary component missing was passion. Barringer and Ireland state "The number-one characteristic shared by successful entrepreneurs is passion for the business" [18]. The predefined aspects of the project severely limited the chance of any one particular student being passionate about the project, much less a team of students. After several discussions with the students, it became obvious that the challenge was a lack of ownership with respect to the class projects. Students viewed the projects as just "another class assignment" rather than an opportunity to create a business or help a community in need.

A third critical factor in the course design was the timing of the classes. State requirements, program requirements, and prerequisite structures were the original determinants in the decision to place the three-credit Engineering Entrepreneurship course in the spring semester of the sophomore year and the two-credit Engineering Service Learning course in the fall semester of the junior year. In an ideal world, the students would be working diligently on the project all summer and return to classes in fall with a solid prototype. In the real world, students forgot about the project entirely over the summer. A few students decided not to return to classes in fall and the high school had personnel changes that impacted the FGCU student projects. In hindsight, this was simply poor planning. From the initial planning stages, the courses were intended to share a project and the decision was based solely on convenience of scheduling rather than a structure that would enhance student learning. As discussed earlier, the curriculum was modified to allow the courses to be offered in the same academic year, starting with the 2008–2009 academic year.

10.7 COURSE REDESIGN AND JUSTIFICATION, VERSION I

As previously discussed, student input and faculty observations led to redesigning and restructuring the Engineering Service-Leaning and Engineering Entrepreneurship courses.. The Engineering Service-Learning course became the prerequisite for Engineering Entrepreneurship. Both classes were required in the junior year for all engineering students. Students in Engineering Service-Learning were expected to use the engineering design process to identify a community based need, work with a client to identify design criteria and constraints, develop alternative solutions, and develop a basic business plan for one of the solutions. Engineering Entrepreneurship would provide the students with experience in conducting a market analysis and testing and implementation of the design. The students were required to have a product, process, or service that would be given to the client as the final project.

Engineering Service Learning was redesigned with three phases: Need Identification, Engineering Solutions, and Preliminary Business Plan. The justification for this design was pulled from the goal of engineering which is to service the community. Service to the community is considered fundamental to success and growth of the engineering profession. A driving factor of the course was to increase student awareness of engineering in society. As stated by Lima and Oakes, "engineering is, by nature, a profession with a societal context leading to social responsibility."[3] Engineering Service Learning promotes the concepts of social responsibility in the engineering profession. Engineering Entrepreneurship was redesigned to focus on testing alternatives, developing a prototype and delivering a finished product to the client.

The new courses were introduced in the 2008–2009 academic year. In an effort to increase student engagement, the projects were a mix of student proposed projects and project requests from the community. Project concepts were submitted by students and the community at large. All projects were reviewed by the instructor to ensure engineering content and a scope that was acceptable for the academic year. Students were then required to apply for projects, ranking their top three project choices. Interdisciplinary teams were assigned by the instructor. Every effort was made to satisfy a student's first request; however, team demographics were also considered. Project diversity and student engagement were both improved during this iteration.

Another difference in the courses was the method of instruction. Although several attempts to integrate instructors from both the College of Business and the School of Engineering were made, both classes were taught by an engineering instructor only. Engineering Entrepreneurship was scheduled as a cotaught course; however, at the last minute the instructor from the College of Business was reassigned due to scheduling changes in the College of business.

From an assessment perspective, course outcomes continued to be met. Comments on course evaluations no longer reflected significant student dissatisfaction with the course sequence. Student satisfaction with the course projects was also improved.

Engineering Service-Learning course outcomes stated that after completing this course students will have:

- Acquired the skills necessary for public problem solving
- Developed an appreciation for social responsibility
- Developed the skills necessary for interdisciplinary work, including teamwork and conflict resolution
- Developed basic leadership skills
- Demonstrated effective communication skills
- An understanding of the value and impact of engineering solutions in a societal context and the ability to interview potential clients to determine their needs

- An understanding of the value of lifelong learning
- The ability to design a project to meet specific criteria and to carry the project through to completion and delivery to the client

Assessments of these outcomes were tied directly to course work. A sample of the assessment data is illustrated in Tables 10.2 and 10.3, additional assessment data is available in Appendix II. The competency levels (i.e., 40% of the students must score 85% or above) are standard for all senior-level courses in all of the engineering programs. These levels were determined by the faculty and serve as a basis for continuous improvement measures throughout the curriculum. Senior-level metrics are used for these junior-level courses because, in some instances, these courses are the final or only assessment of a student's ability.

In assessing skills for public problem solving, the final project as a whole was used as the benchmark for the student's ability. As indicated from the results in Table 10.2, the students exceeded the course outcome goal.

Table 10.3 illustrates the assessment of the student's appreciation for social responsibility. This outcome was assessed from the rubric results for a reflection paper that students were required to write with respect to their experience in the Engineering Service-Learning course. A copy of the reflection paper rubric is available in Appendix I. As indicated in the Table 10.3, students exceeded the learning outcome goals in terms of developing social responsibility in Engineering Service-Learning.

10.8 COURSE REDESIGN, VERSION II

In the 2010–2011 academic year, additional changes were incorporated into the course sequence. Engineering Service-Learning remained largely unchanged. Project proposals and assignments were completed in the same manner as the previous year; however, international projects were intro-

Table 10.2. Assessment of public problem solving, fall 2008

Assessment tool	The final project—overall results		Results
Course objective	Metric		
Acquired the skills necessary for public problem solving	Goal:	40% of the students score 85% or above on the overall project	67%
		75% score 70% or above	90%
		90% score 65% or above	100%
Action Taken	None needed—performance criteria achieved		

Table 10.3. Social responsibility assessment, fall 2008

Assessment tool	Personal values section of reflection paper		Results
Course objective	Metric		
Developed an appreciation for social responsibility	Goal:	40% of the students score 85% or above on the overall project	77%
		75% score 70% or above	85%
		90% score 65% or above	94%
Action taken	None needed—performance criteria achieved		

duced as potential projects and eagerly pursued by the students. All of the international projects were a result of a summer program that the instructor participated in based in Calhuitz, Guatemala, a village with approximately 1200 residents. A second difference was that program growth made it necessary to offer two sections of both Engineering Service-Learning and Engineering Entrepreneurship. The most significant difference occurred in the spring with the Engineering Entrepreneurship course.

Once again, attempts to coteach the Engineering Entrepreneurship course were derailed at the last minute due to changes in business faculty assignments. The engineering faculty member and a business faculty member were determined to forge a link between the two programs and designed a method to cooperatively teach Engineering Entrepreneurship and an MBA course in Business Plans. The engineering instructor attended the MBA course on the first day and described the projects being pursued in one section of Engineering Entrepreneurship. The MBA students applied for their top project choices and the MBA instructor assigned teams based on student project preference and overall experience of the students. These courses had several differences. The Engineering Entrepreneurship course was an undergraduate-only course offered during the day, two times per week. Many of the students work part time in the evening. The MBA course was primarily for graduate students. The course was offered once a week in the evening and the majority of students were employed full time.

The role of the engineering students was to provide technical details, project updates, client-contact information, and preliminary industry analysis. The MBA students were tasked with completing a marketing survey and a more in-depth industry analysis, and delivering a full business plan at the end of the semester. The students were encouraged, not required, to designate meeting times to exchange information. Space was also provided on the online educational support system (ANGEL) for students in both classes to share documents and have online discussions.

Assessment data, found in Appendix II, from this academic year once again indicate that all course outcomes were being met; students were satisfied with the course overall; and, for the first time, all students successfully completed both courses. No significant differences were detected between the Engineering Entrepreneurship sections with the MBA partner team and the section that was not working with the MBA class. In the future, every attempt will be made to schedule the two courses at the same time, or at least overlapping times. The challenges identified by the engineering students included difficulty in scheduling meetings and little to no involvement in the business plan development. The MBA students also identified meeting times as a challenge as well as a difficult time understanding the projects since the engineering students had already been working on the projects for an entire semester.

10.9 COURSE REDESIGN, VERSION III

The 2011–2012 academic year brought further changes. Due to resource constraints and the desire to offer additional, program-specific electives, the two-credit Engineering Service-Learning course was discontinued and Engineering Entrepreneurship was tasked with assessing learning outcomes formerly associated with Engineering Service-Learning. In addition, multiple sections of Engineering Entrepreneurship will be necessary during both fall and spring semesters. At the time of this writing, assessment data for the classes are not be available.

Changes in the course include student-proposed projects only, an emphasis on social entrepreneurship, and a cooperative educational experience with an undergraduate business process course. The first two changes implemented were related to project determination. The project model was modified from a client/student/faculty-proposed model to student-proposed to attempt to improve student engagement and ownership of the projects. Students are required to complete a project proposal prior to the first class. The faculty member evaluates the proposals for engineering content (the projects must include a tangible deliverable that requires engineering analysis), project scope (must be of reasonable scope to be completed in one academic semester), and additional preference would be given to projects with a social or societal impact. The social aspects of the project were incorporated in an effort to continue the service concepts of the earlier two-sequence course model and introduce engineering students to the concept of social entrepreneurship.

The third change was the collaborative project with undergraduate business students. This model is currently in progress. Currently, there are two sections of Engineering Entrepreneurship running during the fall 2011 academic year for FGCU engineering students. One section is paired with an undergraduate business-planning class. The business students and engineering students are working collaboratively to identify client needs, develop marketing surveys, and propose a final solution. The other Engineering Entrepreneurship section does not have a collaborating business course; however, that is the only difference between the courses.

The model introduced this semester treats the course as the student's job, and their grade as their paycheck. The engineering students and business students received and signed the same agreement referring to expected behavior and contribution. A copy of the contract can be found in Figures 10.3 and 10.4. Although results from this iteration will not be available until the end of the academic year, both the engineering and the business students have expressed excitement regarding the projects and the opportunity to work together.

Contract of Employment

Welcome to EntrepreneurialEngineers, Inc.

As new employees please read the following policies in detail. If you have any questions please ask. When you have finished reading the policies you will be asked to sign the verification form stating that you have read, understand and agree to the stated policies.

Job Description:

You have been accepted as a research and design (R&D) engineer for EntrepreneurialEngineers, Inc. As a member of the R&D team you are expected to perform activities including, but not limited to:

Identifying client needs

Researching current solutions to these needs

Identifying and proposing a minimum of 3 alternative solutions for the client

Designing a feasible solution for the client

Delivery of a working prototype to the client

Documentation of all work

Continuous communication with the client

Communication and meetings with the business planning department.

The R&D team will have multiple projects running simultaneously. Every person will be ASSIGNED to one team and is expected to perform to the best of their abilities. The R&D teams identify needs, develop the concepts, test feasibility, build prototypes and develop the business model. The R&D function is housed in a different location from the business planning department however these two divisions are expected to work closely to identify the feasibility of the R&D prototypes and develop the business model when appropriate. This may require meetings outside the normal business hours, virtual meetings, e-mail communication and other correspondence as necessary to successfully launch the product given constraints such as time and budget.

Your job performance will be evaluated using multiple assessments including:

Mandatory team discussion on ANGEL

Quality of work submitted

Ability to meet deadlines

Figure 10.3. Class contract, page 1.

Ability to function on a team

Ability to follow the engineering design process

Sound engineering concepts

Appropriate research

Reflection of the process/project

Every new employee starts with the rand of R&D Engineer I. Every 4 weeks a competency exam will be available. Successful completion of the competency exam, in addition to appropriate progress on the project, will provide promotion possibilities for the engineering staff. Engineering rank is tied directly to your compensation (in this case, a grade) based on the following scale:

Rank	Maximum % of pay scale	Requirements
Engineer I	72	Be a member of the organization
Engineer II	86	Successfully pass competency exam I (70% or better), have no more than 1 missing or 3 late tasks, evidence of successful project completion*
Engineer III	95	Successfully pass competency exam II (70% or better), have no more than 1 missing or 2 late tasks, evidence of successful project completion*
Senior Engineer	100	Successfully pass competency exam III (70% or better), have no missing or late tasks, evidence of successful project completion*

*Evidence of successful project completion will be assessed using the project milestones developed by the project team. Your individual % effort toward each milestone will indicate your individual project success. % effort will be evaluated by the team.

Figure 10.4. Class contract, page 2.

10.10   CONCLUSIONS

Engineering service and entrepreneurship is a fundamental aspect of the engineering programs at FGCU. As the engineering curriculum has continued to evolve, changes have been implemented in the delivery of courses based engineering service and entrepreneurship. Throughout the development and continued improvement of the courses, course content and project integrity have been of primary concern. The primary tool for assessing content and integrity has been through the formal course reporting system used in the FGCU engineering programs. Not only does this method ensure a continual review of courses and their outcomes, it also provides valuable data on continuous improvement, a necessary component of most accreditation agencies. The inclusion of an entrepreneurial-service-based course has also led to collaborations between the College of Engineering and the College of Business. This collaboration reaches beyond faculty working together, and has facilitated combined course projects, equally engaging both engineering and business students and demonstrating an ability to work on diverse teams and communicate with individuals outside of one's major course of study.

REFERENCES

1. NSPE. "NSPE Code of Ethics for Engineers." Retrieved from http://www.nspe.org/Ethics/CodeofEthics/index.html Aug 26, 2011.

2. ABET. "2011–2012 Criteria for Accrediting Engineering Programs." Retrieved from http://www.abet.org/Linked%20Documents-UPDATE/Program%20Docs/abet-eac-criteria–2011–2012.pdf August 26, 2011.

3. Lima, M. and Oakes W., *Service Learning Engineering in Your Community,* Great Lakes Press, 2006.

4. Jacoby, B., and Assoc. Service Learning in Higher Education. San Francisco: Jossey-Bass, 1996.

5. Astin, A. W. and Sax, L. J. "How Undergraduates are Affected by Service Participation." *Journal of College Student Development,* 39, 251–262, 1998.

6. Muthiah, R. N., Hatcher, J., and Bringle, R. G. "The Role of Service-Learning on Retention of Students: A Multi-Campus study of Service-Learning." Paper presented at the annual meeting of the International Conference on Advances in Service-Learning Research, Berkley, CA, October 2001.

7. Gallini, S. M and Moely, B. E. "Service-Learning, and Engagement, Academic Challenge, and Retention." *Michigan Journal of Community Service Learning,* 10(1), 2003.

8. Ng, K., van Dyne, L., and Ang, S. "From Experience to Experiential Learning: Cultural Intelligence as a Learning Capability for Global Leader Development." *Academy of Management Learning & Education,* Vol. 8(4), 511–526, 2009.

9. Martin, C. M. "Reasserting the Philosophy of Experiential Education as a Vehicle for Change in the 21st Century." *The Journal of Experiential Education,* 22(2), 91–98, 1999.

10. "Experiential Learning and Experiential Education." Wilderdom.com. Retrieved from http://wilderdom.com/experiential/ April 12, 2011.

11. Dees, J.G. (1998) "The Meaning of "Social Entrepreneurship." Retrieved from http://www.redalmarza.com/ing/pdf/TheMeaningofSocialEntrepreneurship.pdf August 28, 2011.

12. Zidek, L. "Engineering Service Learning, Engineering Entrepreneurship an Assessment: Building a Program That Works" Frontier in Education Conference, IEEE, Washington, D.C. October 27–30, 2010.

13. Coyle, E. J., Jamieson, L. H., and Sommers, L. S. (1997) "EPICS: A Model for Integrating Service-Learning into the Engineering Curriculum." *Michigan Journal of Community Service Learning,* Vol 4, 81–89, 1997.

14. "FGCU Mission." Vision, Mission, and Guiding Principles. Florida Gulf Coast University. Retrieved from <http://www.fgcu.edu/info/mission.asp> August 28, 2011.

15. "Service-Learning EaglesConnect 2011–2012 Catalog Year." Florida Gulf Coast University Catalog. Retrieved from http://www.fgcu.edu/Catalog/connect.asp, September 11, 2011.

16. "Engineering Mission." UA Whitaker School of Engineering Vision and Mission. 2008. Retrieved from <http://www.fgcu.edu/cob/eng/vision.html.>, August 28, 2011.

17. Hatcher, J. A. and Bringle, R. G. "Reflection: Bridging the Gap Between Service and Learning." *College Teaching,* 45(4), 153–158, 1997.

18. Barringer, B. R. and Ireland, R. D. *Entrepreneurship: Successfully Launching New Ventures*. Upper Saddle River, NJ: Prentice-Hall, 2008.

APPENDIX I. REFLECTION PAPER RUBRIC

Name: _____

	Accomplished (10-9)	Competent (8-7)	Developing (6-5)	Beginning (4-0)	Your Score
Self-disclosure	Seeks to understand concepts by examining *openly* your own experiences in the past as they relate to the topic, to illustrate points you are making. Demonstrates an *open, non-defensive ability to self-appraise*, discussing both growth and frustrations as they related to learning in class. Risks asking probing questions about self and seeks to answer these.	Seeks to understand concepts by examining *somewhat cautiously* your own experiences in the past as they relate to the topic. Sometimes defensive or one-sided in your analysis. Asks some probing questions about self, but do not engage in seeking to answer these.	Seeks to understand concepts by examining *somewhat cautiously* your own experiences in the past as they relate to the topic. Sometimes defensive or one-sided in your analysis.	*Little self-disclosure, minimal risk* in connecting concepts from class to personal experiences. Self-disclosure tends to be superficial and factual, without self-reflection.	
Connection to outside experiences	*In-depth synthesis* of thoughtfully selected aspects of experiences related to the topic. Makes *clear* connections between what is learned from outside experiences and the topic.	Goes into *some detail* explaining some specific ideas or issues from outside experiences related to the topic. Makes *general* connections between what is learned from outside experiences and the topic.	Goes into *some detail* explaining some specific ideas or issues from outside experiences related to the topic..	Identify some *general ideas* or issues from outside experiences related to the topic	
Connection to class topics & course objectives	Synthesize, analyze and evaluate thoughtfully selected aspects of ideas or issues from the class topics/discussion as they relate to this topic.	Synthesize clearly some directly appropriate ideas or issues from the class topics/discussion as they relate to this topic.	Restate some directly appropriate ideas or issues from the class discussion as they relate to this topic.	Restate some general ideas or issues from the class discussion as they relate to this topic.	
Synthesis of engineering courses, in particular the specific two course series	Synthesize, analyze and evaluate thoughtfully the impact of engineering on the topic, in particular the experience in the two course sequence of service learning and engineering entrepreneurship.	Synthesize the impact of engineering on the topic, in particular the experience in the two course sequence of service learning and engineering entrepreneurship.	Discuss some aspects of engineering with respect to the topic, in particular the experience in the two course sequence of service learning and engineering entrepreneurship.	Did not reflect on the entrepreneurship/service learning experience as a whole, little or no inclusion of other engineering courses.	
Grammar and spelling	Appropriate grammar and spelling used throughout document.	Minor grammar OR spelling errors (less than 3) in document.	Minor grammar AND spelling errors in document (less than 5 total).	Significant (more than 5) grammar AND/OR spelling errors in document.	

Additional Comments:

APPENDIX II. ASSESSMENT DATA

Engineering Service Learning, Fall 2008

Course objective \ Assessment tool	Combined scores on questions 1 and 2 from Exam 1 Part 1 and question 1 from Exam 1 Part 2, team contract, and team charter	Results
developed the skills necessary for interdisciplinary work including team work and conflict resolution	Goal: 40 % of the students score 85% or above on the exam questions related to teams	31%
	75% score 70% or above	60%
	90% score 65% or above	63%
	Goal: 40 % of the students score 85% or above on the team contract	81%
	75% score 70% or above	100%
	90% score 65% or above	100%
	Goal: 40 % of the students score 85% or above on the team contract	8%
	75% score 70% or above	58%
	90% score 65% or above	75%
Action Taken	The instructors forgot to include the team assessment form in the syllabus as part of the regular assignments for the course so it was not completed and returned by all students. This problem will be corrected in fall 2009. It is not clear that the correct tools are being used to assess teamwork.	
Course objective \ Assessment tool		Results
developed basic leadership skills;	Goal: 40 % of the students score 85% or above on the	
	75% score 70 or above	
	90% score 65% or above	
Action Taken	This was not assessed in this course and may not be an appropriate learning outcome for EGN 3833C.	

Engineering Service Learning, Fall 2008

Assessment tool / Course objective	Written: Exam questions, pro bono opinion paper, and reflection paper. Oral: Final presentation	Results
demonstrated effective communication skills;	<u>Goal</u>: 40 % of the students score 85% or above on the exam questions	48%
	75% score 70% or above	88%
	90% score 65% or above	94%
	<u>Goal</u>: 40 % of the students score 85% or above on the pro bono opinion paper	79%
	75% score 70% or above	94%
	90% score 65% or above	94%
	<u>Goal</u>: 40 % of the students score 85% or above on the writing aspects of the reflection paper	73%
	75% score 70% or above	90%
	90% score 65% or above	92%
	<u>Goal</u>: 40 % of the students score 85% or above on the executive summary of the final project	85%
	75% score 70% or above	92%
	90% score 65% or above	100%
	<u>Goal</u>: 40 % of the students score 85% or above on the final presentation grading rubric	100%
	75% score 70% or above	100%
	90% score 65% or above	100%
Action Taken	None needed – performance criteria achieved.	

Engineering Service Learning, Fall 2008

Assessment tool / Course objective	Exam 1 part 2 question 3 content The final project – overall results	Results
Have an understanding of the value and impact of engineering solutions in a societal context	Goal: 40 % of the students score 85% or above on the exam question	46%
	75% score 70 or above	73%
	90% score 65% or above	75%
	Goal: 40 % of the students score 85% or above on the overall project	67%
	75% score 70% or above	90%
	90% score 65% or above	100%
Action Taken	None. All performance criteria were achieved except for one.	
Assessment tool / Course objective	Submission of a resume Background research done to support market for project.	Results
an understanding of the value of lifelong learning	Goal: 40 % of the students score 85% or above on the resume	73%
	75% score 70% or above	83%
	90% score 65% or above	83%
	Goal: 40 % of the students score 85% or above on the market research	60%
	75% score 70% or above	69%
	90% score 65% or above	77%
Action Taken	Nine of the students (17%) failed to turn in resumes, perhaps because the point value (10) was so low. Several of the teams failed to do substantial market research on their project. Those who did the work did well in terms of this learning outcome.	

Engineering Service Learning, Fall 2008

Assessment tool / Course objective	Final project overall grade	Results
the ability to design a project to meet specific criteria and to carry the project through to completion and delivery to the client.	Goal: 40 % of the students score 85% or above on the overall project	67%
	75% score 70% or above	90%
	90% score 65% or above	100%
Action Taken	None needed – performance criteria achieved.	

Assessment tool / Course Learning Outcome	The final project – overall results	Results
acquired the skills necessary for public problem solving;	Goal: 40 % of the students score 85% or above on the overall project	44%
	75% score 70% or above	95%
	90% score 65% or above	95%
Action Taken	None needed – performance criteria achieved.	

Assessment tool / Course Learning Outcome	Reflection paper	Results
developed an appreciation for social responsibility	Goal: 40 % of the students score 85% or above on the personal values section of the reflection paper	75%
	75% score 70% or above	95%
	90% score 65% or above	97%
Action Taken	None needed – performance criteria achieved.	

Engineering Service Learning, Fall 2008

Assessment tool / Course Learning Outcome	Each team was required to have a team contract that included expected behavior, team guidelines and course of action of contract is violated.	Results
developed the skills necessary for interdisciplinary work including team work and conflict resolution	Goal: 40 % of the students score 85% (34 /40) or above on the team contract	91%
	75% score 70% (28/40) or above on the team contract	100%
	90% score 65% (26/40)or above on the team contract	100%
Action Taken	None needed – the performance criteria are achieved. The instructor did facilitate a few teams through conflict resolution, in particular as the semester came to an end. This process is seen as a positive indicator of learning since the students have taken steps to resolve the conflict rather than to carry extra burden if a team member is not contributing.	
Assessment tool / Course Learning Outcome	Chapter 5 addresses leadership skill. The Chapter 5 reading quiz is used to assess student understanding of leadership skills	Results
developed basic leadership skills;	Goal: 40 % of the students score 85% (34 /40) or above on the peer evaluation	75%
	75% score 70% (28/40) or above on peer evaluation	95%
	90% score 65% (26/40)or above on peer evaluation	97%
Action Taken	The previous course report indicated that this course may not be appropriate for assessing leadership skills. Since this was the final offering, changes were not implemented in the learning outcomes, however a better measure of leadership skills was used to assess this outcome.	

Engineering Service Learning, Fall 2008

Assessment tool / Course Learning Outcome	Written: opinion paper, and reflection paper, final documentation. / Oral: Final presentation	Results
demonstrated effective communication skills;	Goal: 40 % of the students score 85% or above on the final documentation	31%
	75% score 70% or above on the final documentation	91%
	90% score 65% or above on the final documentation	97%
	Goal: 40 % of the students score 85% or above on the opinion paper	64%
	75% score 70% or above on the opinion paper	92%
	90% score 65% or above on the opinion paper	97%
	Goal: 40 % of the students score 85% or above on the reflection paper	75%
	75% score 70% or above on the reflection paper	95%
	90% score 65% or above on the reflection paper	97%
	Goal: 40 % of the students score 85% or above on the final presentation grading rubric	69%
	75% score 70% or above	98%
	90% score 65% or above	98%
Action Taken	None. Although the goal of 40% of the students' scores on the final documentation did not exceed 85%, when considering the additional assessment tools this outcome was met.	

Engineering Service Learning, Fall 2008

Assessment tool / Course Learning Outcome	Milestone 1 provides a needs justification for the proposed project / Milestone 2 identifies constraints and criteria	Results
Have an understanding of the value and impact of engineering solutions in a societal context	Goal: 40 % of the students score 85% or above on milestone 1	100%
	75% score 70 or above on milestone 1	100%
	90% score 65% or above on milestone 1	100%
	Goal: 40 % of the students score 85% or above on milestone 2	77%
	75% score 70% or above on milestone 2	100%
	90% score 65% or above on milestone 2	100%
Action Taken	None. All performance criteria were achieved.	
Assessment tool / Course Learning Outcome	Milestone 1 – needs assessment and justification	Results
Have the ability to interview potential clients to determine their needs	Goal: 40 % of the students score 85% or above on milestone 1	77%
	75% score 70 or above on milestone 1	100%
	90% score 65% or above on milestone 1	100%
Action Taken	None needed – performance criteria achieved.	

Engineering Service Learning, Fall 2008

Assessment tool / Course Learning Outcome	The project application included researching the project, completing a resume and writing a cover letter	Results
an understanding of the value of lifelong learning	Goal: 40 % of the students score 85% or above on the project application	64%
	75% score 70% or above	98%
	90% score 65% or above	100%
Action Taken	None needed – performance criteria achieved.	
Assessment tool / Course Learning Outcome	Final project overall grade	Results
the ability to design a project to meet specific criteria and to carry the project through to completion and delivery to the client.	Goal: 40 % of the students score 85% or above on the overall project	44%
	75% score 70% or above	95%
	90% score 65% or above	95%
Action Taken	None needed – performance criteria achieved.	

CHAPTER 11

TEACHING INFORMATION SYSTEMS ETHICS THROUGH SERVICE-LEARNING

Thomas S. E. Hilton and Donald D. Mowry

ABSTRACT

Information system (IS) ethics education has two parts: (1) teaching the rules and (2) evoking ethical behavior. Behavior acquisition is arguably the more difficult of the two. Skinner's behavioral reinforcement and Bandura's social learning can both strongly influence behavior acquisition, so they are incorporated via service-learning projects into an IS senior capstone course. IS majors at University of Wisconsin–Eau Claire work in supervised teams to develop information systems for non-profit clients in the community. Clients model ethical behavior and raise ethics issues, and student efforts are publicly recognized by campus and community leaders. In the face of their obvious impact on community life and the tremendous gratitude of clients, students awaken from a state of anomie to a sense of involvement with the community that evokes ethical behavior. They experience the positive influence they can have when conducting themselves appropriately. Indications are that this experience facilitates student commitment to ethical behavior. The use of service-learning as a tool to practice ethical decision making through experiential learning presents an additional layer of applied ethics and risk management that complicates the equation. However, it can also support very rich engaged learning experiences during the undergraduate years as well as contribute to the goal of preparing undergraduates for a lifetime of informed, responsible, engaged, and ethical citizenship.

11.1 INTRODUCTION

Ethical behavior among information systems (IS) professionals has long been a crucial topic of higher education [27, 38, 46]. Presently, it is particularly important for several reasons. High-profile ethics breaches among influential business leaders have shown yet again both the need for ethical behavior and the sad fact that some people choose to behave unethically [12]. Additionally, increasing IS responsibility for reporting compliance with policies and regulations such as the Health Information Portability and Accountability Act (HIPAA) and the Sarbanes–Oxley Act has made IS ethics more important by establishing civil and criminal penalties for behavior that had previously been merely frowned upon [37]. For example, the ability to transfer a patient's health information electronically from one healthcare provider to another as needed for the patient's welfare is an ethically sound idea, but HIPAA makes it a legal requirement and establishes fines for noncompliance. Similarly, the ability to view electronically the source documents behind a publicly traded company's annual report has long been good practice, but Sarbanes–Oxley makes it a legal requirement and establishes both fines and incarceration terms for noncompliance.

Finally, increasing emphasis by accrediting bodies such as the Association to Advance Collegiate Schools of Business (AACSB) [9, 41] and the Accreditation Board for Engineering and Technology (ABET) [1] has raised the profile of collegiate IS ethics education. AACSB accreditation standards define four broad themes as cornerstones of a viable ethics education curriculum in business schools: responsibility of business in society, ethical decision making, ethical leadership, and corporate governance [41, page 10]. Similarly, ABET requires that accredited computing programs "enable students to attain, by the time of graduation, an understanding of professional, ethical, legal, security, and social issues and responsibilities" [1, page 3].

Ethics in regard to service-learning revolves around two main dimensions that are interdependent. First, service-learning in the ideal sense is a process of working with all concerned as equal parties to the service-learning agreement—all parties participate equally and all benefit. Second, because the learning takes place in the community and there is always a degree of risk of injury or harm to the student, universities must be concerned with the management of risk and the minimization of exposure to liability [23]. Although a bit late in coming, the service-learning movement has generated resources for these dimensions such as *Service-Learning Code of Ethics* [11] and California Campus Compact's publication, *Serving Safely: A Risk Management Resource for College Service Programs* [23].

11.2   TWO-PART IS ETHICS EDUCATION UTILIZING SERVICE-LEARNING

IS ethics education is often thought to consist of content transmission or teaching the rules of using information systems ethically. However, the indisputably more important and arguably more difficult objective of IS ethics instruction is to evoke commitment to career-long ethical behavior among students [18].

In addition, service-learning differs in substantial ways from other experiential education types, such as internships and community service or volunteering, and integrating the community partner as an equal partner in the service and learning enterprise involves a change in values, beliefs, and practices.

11.2.1 Content Transmission

Much research surrounds the development of IS ethics content. Four foundation theories of ethics are commonly referenced: Kant's duty [24], Mill's utilitarianism [34], Rawls' justice/fairness/rights [43], and Aristotle's virtue (more recently by MacIntyre) [31]. From this foundation, more specific bodies of business ethics [45] are developed, and then principles of ethical behavior among IS users and developers are explicated [3, 5, 22].

Prime movers in the development of IS ethics principles are professional societies such as the Association for Computing Machinery (ACM) [3], the Association of Information Technology Professionals (AITP) [5], and the Institute of Electrical and Electronics Engineers (IEEE) [22]. The ACM code of ethics contains 24 statements of personal responsibility, one example being "As an ACM computing professional, I will access computing and communication resources only when authorized to do so" [5]. The AITP code of ethics is couched as a set of six obligations and associated responses, one example being "I acknowledge that I have an obligation to management; therefore, I shall promote the understanding of information processing methods and procedures to management using every resource at my command" [5]. The IEEE code of ethics consists of 10 commitments, one example being "We, the members of IEEE ... agree to maintain and improve our technical competence and to undertake technological tasks for others only if qualified by training or experience, or after full disclosure of pertinent limitations" [22].

Other topics often addressed in IS ethics education are variation in IS ethics norms across cultures [17] and ways to actively participate in developing and maintaining ethics guidelines [25, 20].

In line with content development, much research surrounds the transmission of IS ethics principles. For example, much has been written about teaching a stand-alone IS ethics course, integrating ethics content throughout the IS curriculum, or doing some combination of the two [21]. Mechanisms for communicating the content in memorable ways have also received a generous share of attention [35], as have methods of assessing content retention among students [16].

11.2.2 Behavior Acquisition

Rule learning is worthless without rule using, but theory and practice [26] both indicate that knowing standards of ethical behavior by no means guarantees adherence to them. There is evidence that this is true for college students as well as the general population. The documented prevalence of illegal file sharing among university students [39], presumably including IS students, is one indication that student behavior does not always jibe with the rules. Another indication of this is the prevalence among university students (particularly business students if Pino and Smith [42] are to be believed) of more ordinary academic dishonesty. Add research findings on the prevalence of software piracy among college students [19] and anecdotal conversations with our own students, and a significant gap emerges between what students understand as ethical computing on the one hand and how they behave on the other.

11.2.2.1 Current IS Ethics Pedagogy Vis-à-vis Behavior Acquisition. Although a gap between what we know and how we act is general to the human race, still a goal of IS ethics instruction must be to narrow that gap as much as possible [32]. Various means of inculcating into IS students an inclination to behave ethically have been advanced. Some typical techniques used in this effort to persuade are in-class discussion of IS ethics cases [28], personal reflection essays [7], penalties for academic dishonesty [42], and testimonials from guest speakers [30]. Yet research findings show mixed results from these efforts, at least partly because many college students apparently operate in a state of anomie, the largely subliminal and, hence, unexamined assumption that they are not really members of society, that society offers no place for them, or that they do not want the place it does offer [10]. Student anomie is recognizable by in-class behaviors such as boredom, few remarks or questions, lack of insight, self-centeredness, and narrow perspective [10].

11.2.2.2 Another Approach to Behavior Acquisition. Review of psychological literature reveals a well-developed body of research on methods of effecting behavior acquisition. Many historically common methods of effectively persuading people to adopt a desired behavior are no longer regarded as ethical (see Peters [40] if you don't mind nightmares), but two approaches appear both socially acceptable and remarkably effective: behavioral reinforcement and social learning.

Developed by the famous twentieth-century psychologist B. F. Skinner, Behaviorism indicates that repeatedly rewarding a behavior strongly influences reward recipients to adopt the behavior permanently [44]. Asserting that unobservable internal states such as motivation or cognition are virtually irrelevant to teaching, Skinner advocated a process emphasizing attention to external behaviors that is summarized by the following steps:

1. Define for the learner the action or performance to be learned.
2. Present the action or performance in small, achievable steps from simple to complex.
3. Have the learner perform each step, reinforcing correct actions.
4. Dynamically adjust the requested performance to maximize learner success (and reinforcement), moving the learner toward the goal as competency increases.
5. Continue intermittent reinforcement to maintain learner performance.

Developed by the great Stanford psychologist Albert Bandura, Social Learning Theory indicates that repeatedly observing a "credible model" (i.e., a respected and trusted person) rewarded for engaging in a behavior strongly influences observers to adopt the behavior [6]. In deliberate contrast to Skinner, Bandura defines learners chiefly in terms of their unobservable internal states: as self-organizing, proactive, self-reflecting, and self-regulating agents who interact intelligently with their environments rather than simply responding to stimuli. Bandura summarized his approach to inculcating a skill or behavior in four steps:

1. Introduce the learner to a credible model.
2. Have the learner observe the model engaging in the desired behavior.
3. Have the learner observe the model being rewarded for engaging in the behavior.
4. Repeat steps 1–3 ad infinitum.

Skinner's Behaviorism and Bandura's Social Learning Theory are quite disparate in their foundations, methods, and goals, but they both agree that virtually any skill or behavior can be taught, the key commonality between the two being personal reinforcement or vicarious reward. Thus, it appears that reinforcement/reward, either personal or vicarious, could be key to instilling ethical behavior in IS students. Indeed, something beyond traditional content transmission appears necessary.

11.2.2.3 Is Such Manipulation Ethical? The astute reader will note that the line between education and indoctrination begins to blur at this point in the discussion. Educators accustomed to teaching truth (or its closest available approximation) may regard the reinforcement described above as mere operant conditioning fit only for lab rats. We admit to similar misgivings that this line of reasoning risks reducing instruction to propaganda: the potential for abuse is significant [15]. However, we find that such reinforcement occurs almost continuously both in and out of class on virtually every conceivable topic, obvious examples coming from the world of TV advertising where beautiful people gain fame, fortune, respect, power, love, and so on by buying whatever is being advertised [13]. We also note innumerable precedents in U.S. public education dating at least from John Dewey's transformation of K–12 schools from content transmission tools to institutions of socialization [14]. Thus, we assert that the concept of an instructor using behaviorist or social learning techniques to persuade IS students to behave ethically is not unethical, per se.

11.2.2.4 Service-Learning As a Milking Stool. Garry Hesser, who at the time of this quote was a professor in the departments of Sociology and Urban Studies and Director of Experiential Education at Augsburg College, said that "service-learning is minimally a three-legged stool in which the interests and needs of the community, the student, and the academic institution must be balanced. Each entity must be given and must take an equitable responsibility for the service and learning [personal communication, August 1995]." Thus, the ethics and values of the pedagogy of service-learning dramatically change the educational process and experience for all parties to the agreement. Faculty often find that they move to a more facilitative role and that they share instructional roles with community partners. Faculty also tend to be much more engaged and involved with community partners throughout the process and may even commit more than one semester's class so that both academic and community needs can be best served. Because service-learning is also utilized as a means to the end of preparing students to be active citizens in a democracy, and because it is also a movement in higher education, it has transformed colleges and universities and resulted in a revaluing of engagement with the greater community.

11.3 CASE STUDY: A SENIOR CAPSTONE COURSE

The above rationale led us to the opinion that once IS ethics rules have been taught a major remaining impediment to following them is student anomie. Moreover, we predicted that decreased student anomie would correlate with increased ethical student behavior. Finally, we hypothesized that (a) engaging students in ethically significant service directly to the visible community and (b) providing reinforcement for their service would result in decreased anomie and increased motivation to obey the rules of IS ethics. We therefore set up a situation in which we could make some initial observations of the level of anomie and ethics motivation by interviewing the students periodically.

11.3.1 Capstone Course and Community Service-Learning Requirement

These concepts were implemented in our capstone course for IS seniors. The capstone is a three-semester-credit course required of all graduating seniors in which they are called upon to show that they have integrated the bodies of content taught in the various courses in their program into a holistic ability to meet the information needs of clients.

To satisfy a university graduation requirement that students engage in at least 30 clock hours of approved service to the community, ten three-student teams in the capstone course each conducted a complete information system development project for a community client that otherwise would not be able to afford needed information infrastructure. Some projects and clients were as follows: setting up an office network for the local Epilepsy Foundation, generating an information systems strategic plan for the local chapter of the National Alliance for the Mentally Ill, developing an event-scheduling database system for the local YMCA, and developing a funding application website and database for the local United Way.

11.3.2 Process

The faculty instructor for the course, the director of the Center for Service-Learning, and the community agency partners started meeting months before the course started to plan the project. At the beginning of the effort, the group agreed to work together as true partners with equal status and mutually agreed upon goals. Although the original planning phase was funded by a planning grant from a consortium of Minnesota and Wisconsin Campus Compacts, the full implementation grant was not selected for funding. However, it is significant that in spite of this disappointment, the group unanimously agreed to forge ahead with the plan. At the very beginning, it became apparent that these agencies, with the student team assistance, would not be able to bridge the digital divide in just one semester, and a longer commitment of up to two years was extended by all parties to the contract. The risk of legal liability for the projects anticipated in this longer-term commitment was judged to be low, but all parties to the agreement, including the students, were briefed and signed a contract that listed specific responsibilities and expectations, as well as acknowledgment that support and consultation after project completion would be independently negotiated.

11.3.3 Projects

A variety of projects were completed in the areas of IS strategic planning, network development, hardware/software acquisition and deployment, website development, database development, system security audit/upgrade, and end-user training. Funding for the projects came from client budgets and/or from the community development planning grant awarded to the campus Center for Service-Learning. All projects were conducted within a project-management framework based on the systems-development life cycle (SDLC, also called the systems life cycle) [29].

The student teams managed and executed the projects in cooperation with client representatives and with instructor oversight. Students worked directly on-site, interviewing client staff, interacting with customers of the client, and testing and deploying the systems they developed. They met periodically with the instructor throughout the semester. They made formal project management and design walkthrough presentations to the class and to client representatives. They also reported the final completion of the project at semester's end. A formal letter of acceptance from the client indicating satisfactory system completion was required for a grade in the course. Table 11.1 lists the major project components in order.

11.3.4   Ethically Significant Engagement

All participants unavoidably modeled ethical (or, perhaps, unethical) behaviors in numerous ways. Phone calls and e-mail messages were (or were not)

Table 11.1. Approximate project timeline

Date	Activity	Deliverable
Week 1	Course/project introduction	Student buy-in
Week 1	Team formation	Meeting with instructor
Week 1	Client assignment	Meeting with instructor
Weeks 2–4	IS instruction and review in strategic planning, project management, system development, ethics	Class attendance and discussion
Weeks 2–4	Project definition	Meeting with client
Week 6	Project plan approval	Meeting with instructor
Week 8	Project design approval	Meeting with client and instructor
Week 9	Project plan presentation	Interactive powerpoint presentation to class, client, and instructor on project definition/scope, project staffing plan, project budget plan, project schedule
Week 9	Project design presentation	Interactive powerpoint presentation to class, client, and instructor on existing system analysis, new system design, cost–benefit analysis, coding plan, testing plan, deployment plan, training plan, maintenance plan
Weeks 10–15	Project execution	Project implemented for client
Week 15	Project completion debriefing	Project demonstration to class and instructor
Week 15	Final project approval	Project approval letter from client

returned in a timely manner. Meeting appointments were kept (or not). Students strove to understand user requirements even when the users were physically disabled, mentally compromised, or emotionally unstable. The importance of developing honest, reasonably accurate budgets and time lines and then adhering to them became clear. Setting reasonable product expectations and managing scope creep were significant issues in every project. Clients and students had to practice maintaining effective interpersonal communication in the face of delays, malfunctions, or misunderstandings. Students discovered that client business processes were materially affected by project progress. They also found that a maintenance plan to assure successful system functioning after semester's end was crucial as client needs did not evaporate when the course ended.

11.3.5 Reinforcement

In addition to the customary reinforcement of a course grade, student efforts were recognized by campus and community leaders. The United Way hosted all participating students at its annual Gold Awards breakfast and had them stand to receive the applause of local community leaders. The campus annual report featured a multipage article on the projects and color photos of students working with clients. Students were presented with tokens of esteem from the campus Center for Service-Learning in front of the annual Information Technology Seminar.

The clients and the people the clients serve also reinforced the students' ethical behavior. Client staff members were generous and sincere in their praise of student skills. They were gentle and quick with forgiveness of student mistakes, and they were vocal and frequent in expressing their gratitude for student contributions.

11.4 RESULTS AND DISCUSSION

The effects of the experience on the students appear to have been ethically quite salutary. Table 11.2 is a general qualitative description of ethics-related statements by the students at three points in the semester.

11.4.1 The Good News

At the end of the project, every student commented on the obvious impact of the projects on the local community. Every student reported pleasant surprise at the expressions of gratitude from clients and other community and campus members. Many students commented on a new sense of involvement and connectedness; here are a few examples:

Table 11.2. Qualitative temporal analysis of ethics-related student statements

Date	Activity	Remarks	
Week 4	IS ethics review	Quantity:	Few
		Insight:	Shallow, bored
		Altruism:	Low
		Topics:	Defense of music-file trading
Week 9	Project design presentation	Quantity:	Many
		Insight:	Moderate
		Altruism:	Moderate
		Topics:	Varied, project-related
Week 15	Project completion debriefing	Quantity:	Many
		Insight:	Deep
		Altruism:	High
		Topics:	Varied, client-related

- "I never knew how much I was needed."
- "I didn't know how much I knew."
- "I hadn't realized how different it is for a handicapped person to use a computer."
- "They really depended on us to do what we said we'd do."
- "This has been my best experience in college."

About half the students reported ethically significant experiences that surprised even the instructor. Here are a few examples:

- A project team had to educate the client on the illegality of installing Microsoft Office™ software from bootlegged media.
- A project team had to explain why it would not connect a client computer to a peer-to-peer file-trading network.
- More than one project team discovered the need to explain hardware purchase conditions or software license agreements to their clients.
- A project team gave their client a USB flash drive and trained them in its use midway through the project when it was discovered that the entire customer database, without which the organization could not function, had never been backed up.
- Several individual students developed such a committed relationship with their client that they established gratis after-project maintenance agreements that extended for weeks or months.
- Most students spoke warmly of lasting friendships they had developed.

11.4.2 The Bad News

Not all the news was good. One team did not complete their project until several weeks after the end of the semester, and even then their primary motivation seemed to be their course grade rather than the commitments they had made to their client. Moreover, the product they created, while workable, was of marginal quality. The client was justifiably frustrated with the subpar performance but, thankfully, did still conclude, once the project was complete, that the organization was further ahead than before.

While we hope not to repeat an experience like this, we still believe it was good ethics education for the students. They and the instructor discussed several times the risks of exaggerating one's technical prowess and minimizing the importance of meetings, deadlines, requirements analysis, and project management. They did not initially accept the instructor's counsel sufficiently to change their relationship with their client, and so they ended up receiving more pointed feedback later. In their final meeting with the instructor, two of the three students did give some indication that they had begun to appreciate the need for more honesty, humility, responsiveness, attention to administrative detail, careful communication, and other ethical behaviors in their IS work.

11.5 CONCLUSIONS

We finished the experience with the strong impression that this is a much-needed component of IS ethics education. We continued the project for four semesters, and it continued to yield excellent results. Students continued to experience firsthand the positive influence they can have when conducting themselves appropriately, and most do. On the other hand, they also experience firsthand the disappointment associated with unethical behavior, which has so far been blessedly rare.

It is worth noting that this community-oriented project work has spread to other parts of our IS curriculum. Two additional faculty members incorporated similar team-based community projects into several other courses and report similar results to this day.

The planning group continued to meet over the first and subsequent semesters, and when it was time for dissemination of the results of the collaboration, the group submitted and was selected to present the project at the national annual conference of Community Campus Partnerships for Health. The group also published an invited article in the proceedings for this conference [2]. One of the original community partner agencies essentially withdrew from the project when the Executive Director left and the agency essentially closed. One team was shifted to one of the larger nonprofits that had enough work to keep two teams busy.

Laziness and naïveté rather than malice or sociopathy seem to be emerging as the primary effects of student anomie leading to unethical behavior. We choose to regard this as relatively good news both because things are not as bad as they might be and because we see the project experience as an ideal treatment for laziness and naïveté, whereas it would be a decidedly inappropriate context for addressing malice or sociopathy.

We are left with a number of questions about our experience that we hope to investigate further in the future. However, we conclude here with three on which we most desire help from our colleagues:

1. Given that IS student behavior conformed in large measure to accepted ethics norms throughout the project, should we conclude that, contrary to much of the literature, ethical behavior is actually quite easy to inculcate? Or should we look for a variable other than the class experiences to account for the result? For instance, might students' ethics-related behavior reflect their perceptions of expectations; that is, if the university communicated the same clear expectation of ethical behavior on campus that society communicates in the workplace, might the students respond by behaving as ethically on campus as they did off campus?

2. In addition, if service-learning is a useful pedagogy for supporting the acquisition of ethical behavior, and if it also contributes to a hands-on cementing of IS knowledge and preparation for citizenship, how can it be encouraged and supported by the university and community? It did require more time commitment than a standard lecture-based class, and dealing with real-life issues was inherently messier that a canned case study or an assignment in which the students had easy access to up-to-date computing and software resources (not the case for the nonprofits in this project). Do the ends justify the means in this case?

3. How can service-learning be integrated into the IS curriculum, and other curricula, so that students realize the maximum benefits? Is it best left for a capstone experience or, from a developmental perspective, should students be exposed to civic engagement experiences early on to promote the goal of graduating students who have internalized the liberal education learning goal of personal and social responsibility?

Faculty and community partners interested in developing service-learning collaborations can draw upon the accumulated wisdom in the field as housed in the National Service-Learning Clearinghouse [36] and national Campus Compact [8]. Fact sheets, sample syllabi, best practices, and more can be found quickly by searching on key terms.

Information is arguably the most intimate thing a human being can produce or consume, as both its source and aim are the very mind of humanity. Thus, to treat information ethically is the very heart of treating humanity ethically. We, therefore, hope that IS faculty universally accept the obligation inherent in our field to manage information ethically and to do all in their power to persuade their students to do likewise. Once this obligation is internalized, we encourage IS faculty to take the next step by giving their students personal experiences with the positive power of their profession. Ask community acquaintances for a chance to let IS students ply their nascent craft where it matters, and chances will come.

11.6   REFERENCES

1. ABET (2011). *Criteria for Accrediting Computing Programs.* Baltimore: Computing Accreditation Commission of the Accreditation Board for Engineering and Technology. Retrieved August 21, 2011 from http://www.abet.org/Linked%20Documents-UPDATE/Program%20Docs/abet-cac-criteria-2011-2012.pdf.

2. Armstrong, C., Becker, K., Berg, K., Hilton, T.S., Mowry, D., and Quinlan, C. (2007). "Community–University Partnerships to Bridge the Non-Profit Digital Divide." *Partnership Perspectives: A Publication of Community Campus Partnerships for Health,* 2007, 4(3), 53–61.

3. Association for Computing Machinery (1992). *ACM Code of Ethics and Professional Conduct.* Retrieved August 23, 2011 from http://www.acm.org/about/code-of-ethics.

4. Association for Computing Machinery (1999). *Software Engineering Code of Ethics and Professional Practice.* Retrieved August 23, 2011 from http://www.acm.org/about/se-code.

5. Association of Information Technology Professionals (2002). *Code of Ethics.* Retrieved August 23, 2011 from http://www.aitp.org/?page=Ethics.

6. Bandura, A. (1985). *Social Foundations of Thought and Action.* Upper Saddle River, NJ: Pearson Prentice-Hall.

7. Brinkmann, J. and Sims, R. R. (2001). "Stakeholder-Sensitive Business Ethics Teaching." *Teaching Business Ethics,* Vol. 5, No. 2, May 2001, 171–193.

8. Campus Compact. Retrieved August 21, 2011 from http://www.compact.org/.

9. Carroll, A. B. (2005). "An Ethical Education." *BizEd,* January/February 2005, 26–40.

10. Caruana A., Ramaseshan, B., and Ewing, M. T. (2000). "The Effect of Anomie on Academic Dishonesty Among University Students." *The International Journal of Educational Management,* January 2000, Vol. 14, No. 1, 2–3.

11. Chapdelaine, A., Ruiz, A., Warchal, J., and Wells, C. (2005). *Service-Learning Code of Ethics.* Bolton, MA: Anker Publishing Company, Inc.

12. *Corporate Ethics* (2005). Retrieved August 23, 2011, from http://www.washingtonpost.com/wp-dyn/business/specials/corporateethics/.

13. Croteau, D. and Hoynes, W. (2002). *Media/Society: Industries, Images and Audiences* (3rd ed.). Thousand Oaks, CA: Pine Forge Press.

14. Dewey, J. (1916). *Democracy and Education.* New York: The Macmillan Company. Copyright renewed 1944 by Macmillan Company, 1994 by ILT Digital.

15. Goldiamond, I. (2002). "Toward a Constructional Approach to Social Problems: Ethical and Constitutional Issues Raised by Applied Behavior Analysis." *Behavior and Social Issues,* Vol. 11, 108–197.

16. Hill, A. L. (2004). "Ethics Education: Recommendations for an Evolving Discipline." *Counseling and Values,* Vol. 48, No. 3, April 2004, 183–203.

17. Hilton, T., Oh, S., and Al-Lawati, H. (2007). "Information Systems Ethics in Oman, South Korea, and the USA." *Information Systems Education Journal.* Vol. 5, No. 32, 3–29.

18. Hilton, T. S. (1999). "A Model for Internet-Enhanced Education Systems Derived From History and Experiment." *Journal of Computer Information Systems,* Vol. 39, No. 3, 6–17.

19. Hinduja, S. (2003). "Trends and Patterns Among Online Software Pirates." *Ethics and Information Technology,* Vol. 5, No. 1, March 2003, 49–61.

20. Husted, B. W. (1999). "A Critique of the Empirical Methods of Integrative Social Contracts Theory." *Journal of Business Ethics.* Vol. 20, No. 3, 227–236.

21. Hutchison, L. L. (2002). "Teaching Ethics Across the Public Relations Curriculum." *Public Relations Review,* Vol. 28, No. 3, 301.

22. IEEE Code of Ethics (1990). Retrieved August 23, 2011 from http://www.ieee.org/portal/pages/iportals/aboutus/ethics/code.html.

23. Joyce, S. A. and Ikeda, E. K. (2002). *Serving Safely: A Resource Guide for College Service Programs.* California Campus Compact. Retrieved August 23, 2011 from http://www.servicelearning.org/library/resource/5196.

24. Kant, I. (1959). *The Foundations of the Metaphysics of Morals* (L. W. Beck, Trans.). New York: Liberal Arts Press. (Original work published 1785.)

25. Kaptein, M. and Wempe, J. (1998). "Twelve Gordian Knots When Developing an Organizational Code of Ethics. *Journal of Business Ethics.* Vol. 17, No. 8, 853–870.

26. Keans, C. and Kearns, C. (2004). *Value-Centered Ethics.* Amherst, MA: HRD Press.

27. Ladd, J. (1989). "Computers and Moral Responsibility: A Framework for Ethical Analysis." In C. Gould (Ed.), *The Information Web: Ethical and Social Implications of Computer Networking* (pp. 207–227). Boulder, CO: Westview Press.

28. Lampe, M. (1997). "Increasing Effectiveness in Teaching Ethics to Undergraduate Business Students." *Teaching Business Ethics,* Vol. 1, No. 1, 3–19.

29. Laudon, K. C. and Laudon, J. P. (2011). "Building Information Systems." In *Management Information Systems: Managing the Digital Firm* (12th ed.). Upper Saddle River, NJ: Pearson Prentice-Hall.

30. Loeb, S. E. and Ostas, D. T. (2000). "The Team Teaching of Business Ethics in a Weekly Semester Long Format." *Teaching Business Ethics.* Vol. 4, No. 3, 225–238.

31. MacIntyre, A. C. (1999). *Dependent Rational Animals: Why Human Beings Need the Virtues.* Chicago: Open Court.

32. Marino, G. (2004). "Before Teaching Ethics, Stop Kidding Yourself." *Chronicle of Higher Education.* Vol. 50, No. 24, B5.

33. McCarthy, E. (2005). "BearingPoint Ctes SEC Inquiry, Warns Investors." *Washington Post.* April 21, 2005, E01.

34. Mill, J. S. (1863). *Utilitarianism.* Raleigh, N.C.: Alex Catalogue.

35. Morrell, K. (2004). "Socratic Dialogue as a Tool for Teaching Business Ethics." *Journal of Business Ethics.* Vol. 53, No. 4, 383.

36. National Service-Learning Clearinghouse. Retrieved August 21, 2011 from http://www.servicelearning.org/.

37. "New Reporting and Compliance Rules Challenge Systems at Most Large U.S. Companies, PricewaterhouseCoopers Finds." (2004). *Management Barometer.* Retrieved August 23, 2011 from http://www.barometersurveys.com/production/barsurv.nsf/1cf326 4823a1149c85256b84006d2696/2d661c6b82d4391185256ee0006eed74?OpenDocument.

38. Oz, E. (1992). "Ethical Standards for Information Systems Professionals: A Case for a Unified Code." *MIS Quarterly.* Vol. 16, No. 4, 423–433.

39. Peer-to-Peer piracy on university campuses: Hearing before the Subcommittee on Courts, the Internet, and Intellectual Property of the Committee on the Judiciary, House of Representatives, 108a Cong., 1 (2003).

40. Peters, E. (1997). *Torture.* Philadelphia: University of Pennsylvania Press.

41. Phillips, S. M., Blood, M., Bosland, N., Burke, L., Conrad, C. F., Fernandes, J., et al. (2004). *Ethics Education in Business Schools: Report of the Ethics Education Task Force to AACSB International's Board of Directors.* St. Louis: AACSB International.

42. Pino, N. W. and Smith, W. L. (2003). "College Students and Academic Dishonesty." *College Student Journal,* December 2003.

43. Rawls, J. (1971). *A Theory of Justice.* Boston: The Belknap Press of Harvard University Press.

44. Skinner, B. F. (1953). *Science and Human Behavior.* New York: Macmillan.

45. Vardi, Y. and Weitz, E. (2004). *Misbehavior in Organizations: Theory, Research, and Management.* Mahwah, NJ: L. Erlbaum.

46. Weizenbaum, J. (1976). *Computer Power and Human Reason,* San Francisco: W. H. Freeman and Company.

CHAPTER 12

COMPUTER LITERACY SERVICE-LEARNING PROJECT IN BRAZIL

Wen-Jung Hsin and Olga Ganzen

ABSTRACT

In the globalized twenty-first century, internationalization through global learning has become one of the most important priorities for many universities in the United States. In 2002, with the leadership from its past president, Park University identified internationalization as one of its main goals. As such, part of the mission statement of Park University was to prepare students to "engage in lifelong learning while serving a global community." To achieve this mission, Park University has developed several strategies in international education, including service-learning projects infused in the curriculum. The Department of Information and Computer Science was one of the first departments at Park University leading the way for service-learning projects. This chapter describes the computer literacy service-learning project performed in Brazil.

12.1 INTRODUCTION

In the new era of globalization, many universities worldwide have decided that *internationalization,* defined as "the process of integrating international, intercultural, or global dimensions into the purpose, functions, or delivery of post-secondary education" [1], should become a priority for their future development. According to the results of the research on global education published in 1999 in the *American Educational Research Journal,* the most important strategy for dealing with issues such as economic inequality and environmental degradation was "to look at and approach problems as a member of a global society" [2].

In 2002, Park University's past president, Dr. Byers-Pevitts, initiated a strategic planning process [3] and launched the Global Education Task Force as the first task force for the Strategic Planning Committee. This task force actively participated in all discussions of the future strategic plan. Members of the Strategic Planning Committee came from administration, alumni, community leaders, trustees, faculty, staff, and students, and they developed a planning document, *Explorations and Transformations 2012: Access to Excellence,* in which internationalization of the university was identified as one of the main goals. International service-learning was at the same time determined to be an important priority for a study abroad program [3]. "International service-learning projects could be infused into the existing courses within disciplines and include collaboration with local communities as well as local universities. Participation in international service-learning projects helps students, faculty, and staff understand the interconnectedness of the globalized world and the importance of sustainable development on the planet" [4]. "Service-learning is a teaching and learning strategy that integrates meaningful community service with instruction and reflection to enrich the learning experience, teach civic responsibility, and strengthen communities" (http://www.servicelearning.org).

The Department of Information and Computer Science (ICS) has supported global education and internationalization through the international service-learning project in Brazil conducted by Park University in 2006. Three computer literacy international service-learning projects have been completed by the department since then [3, 5].

This chapter describes several aspects of the project such as its initiation, background, history, management, workshop content, and feedback from the participating students and the community. It is an extension of the short version of the papers published in [3, 5].

This chapter is organized as follows: Section 12.2 describes the service learning project in Brazil, Section 12.3 describes the computer literacy service-learning project, and Section 12.4 gives a summary and conclusion.

12.2 PARK UNIVERSITY'S SERVICE-LEARNING PROJECT IN BRAZIL

This section describes Park University's international service-learning project, including the reason behind the selected partners and destination, the planning process, and the historical background of the project.

12.2.1 Why Undertake Short-Term International Service-Learning In Recife, Brazil?

There are several reasons influencing the decision to develop the Park University international service-learning project with the Pau Amarelo Community in Recife, Brazil.

In 2003, the Alliance for International Education and Cultural Exchange and the National Association of International Educators (NAFSA), in an updated policy statement, stressed that it is

... vital that the number of United States students studying abroad be vastly increased. Simultaneously, the proportion of students studying in non-European areas that are of growing importance to United States interests, in academic and professional fields outside liberal arts, and in languages other than English, should be increased. Enhancing the study-abroad experience by incorporating out-of-classroom experiences that bring students into closer and broader contact with host country people and culture must be a priority. [6]

Park University's International Education Task Force considered other priorities such as a desire to increase the study abroad program within the curriculum, faculty involvement in development of study abroad, and inclusion of an international service-learning component into study abroad.

During the Association of International Educators Conference in Rio de Janeiro (2003), several Brazilian universities approached Park University representatives for international exchange collaboration. Additionally, Park University was invited to collaborate with a Kansas City nonprofit organization, Transformational Journeys, on a service-learning project in the Pau Amarelo community located in Recife, Brazil. The Pau Amarelo community works closely with local favelas (slums) [3]. "Recife is the fourth largest metropolitan area in Brazil" (www.recife.com). It has a populations of 1.3 million people approximately (http://www.recife.info). The combined existence of potential community and academic partners in both Kansas City, Missouri, and Recife, Brazil, helped in the selection of this destination.

Park University selected two local Brazilian universities in the area for collaboration: Facilidade de Boa Viagem (FBV) and Faculdade de Ciencias Humanas de Olinda (FACHO). FBV was selected because locals perceive the university as one of the best business schools in the region, with excellent quality in undergraduate and graduate courses. FACHO was selected because its mission concentrates on working with local communities in the area of education, and the university is very committed to service-learning. These universities also expressed interest in collaborating with Park University on the project with the Pau Amarelo community. This collaboration was essential because it would potentially provide sustainability to the projects when Park University participants were not in Brazil and would help Park University utilize local expertise as well as university facilities for educational training of community members.

Another important factor for selecting a Brazilian community as a partner was the fact that Park University's home campus in Parkville, Missouri had around 25 Brazilian students then. Through the interaction with the Brazilian students, Park University's students and faculty became familiar with their culture. Thus, it was relatively easy to attract students and faculty to Brazil. In addition, potential participants often perceived Brazil as an exotic country with appealing culture, food, and weather [3].

12.2.2   Historical and Philosophical Background of the Program (March 2003 to October 2007)

The international service-learning project in Brazil started with an assessment of community needs for the purpose of appropriately designing the program. Several members of Park University faculty and staff joined service missions of Transformational Journeys, which provided the opportunity to meet with local community members in Brazil. Faculty from the school of Business and Education, and the College of Arts and Sciences interviewed several members of Pau Amarelo community. They found that the community as a whole had a strong interest in obtaining education training [3]. This interest was consistent with the Pau Amarelo community's mission: "to act in poor communities through service, promoting education, generation of income, and improvement in basic needs" [7]. The Pau Amarelo community selected the following priorities for service-learning: small-business development, computer literacy, English as a second language (ESL), hygiene for children and adults, nonprofit management, education, and art [3]. Therefore, after the needs assessment, Park University faculty from various disciplines, such as business, information and computer science, English and linguistics, nursing, public administration, education, and art, were invited to participate in the project.

During the early stage of the program design, Park University took into consideration that the achievement of global competencies (skills, attitudes, and values) for participants of the projects should be a central piece of the program. Coordinators created a long-term sustainable plan for the program in collaboration with local universities and the community. After returning from a service-learning project, faculty and students were encouraged to share their experience with others during their class time in Parkville and through publications and conference presentations.

Several faculty members from the Business Management, Information and Computer Science, Education, English and Linguistics, Communication Arts, Nursing, and Public Administration departments expressed an interest in adding a component about service-learning in Brazil into the existing classes in the 2006 spring semester. Thus, the students who were enrolled in these classes had a service-learning component infused into the curriculum. Subsequently, several students applied for study abroad in Brazil during the spring break. All together, thirty-five representatives from Park University (eighteen undergraduates, three graduate students, and fourteen faculty and staff members) traveled to Recife, Brazil for the international service-learning project in March of 2006 [3]. Students paid for their travel and other expenses. Several student scholarships, and faculty and staff professional-development grants were available through the university resources allocated for internationalization. In order to further assess community needs in the future, several faculty members went to Brazil without students. Later they returned to Brazil with students from their classes in smaller groups.

During a ten-day visit to Brazil, Park University students under faculty supervision put what they learned in class into practice while conducting training workshops for the community [3]. For example, Park University students from the Clinical Nursing Practical Application course taught the community participants how to maintain a healthy lifestyle (such as oral hygiene and first aid basics) in addition to visiting local public and private hospitals. Students from the Business/Management's Global Future and International Marketing course delivered presentations on different aspects of new business development. Graduate students from the Public Affairs' International Service course (Nonprofit Management) provided training in community leadership, with an emphasis on strategic planning, financial management, board development, fund-raising, and volunteer management. Faculty from Information and Computer Science taught basic computer skills including how to use e-mail, the Internet, and a word processor. The School of Education faculty taught basic literacy skills to the community participants by using children's games, songs, and stories. In addition, students and faculty from the Communication Arts' Journalism course helped the local community with its website and videotaped and documented the service-learning experience. Upon returning from Brazil, students and faculty reported on their experience to other students who had chosen to perform their service-learning projects in Kansas City.

After this successful experience, an international service-learning component was included by other faculty in their classes. During 2006 and 2007 spring and fall breaks, all together, four groups of students and faculty participated in the Brazil service-learning projects. The participating academic programs were Business, Communication Arts, Criminal Justice, Education,

English and Linguistics, Graphic Design, Nursing, Information and Computer Science, Psychology, and Public Affairs [3].

12.3 COMPUTER LITERACY SERVICE-LEARNING

Since spring 2006, the Information and Computer Science (ICS) department has conducted the Brazil service-learning project in the area of computer literacy three times. In the following, Section 12.3.1 describes the background information related to information technology in Brazil and the Pau Amarelo community, Section 12.3.2 gives a report on the computer literacy service-learning projects, Section 12.3.3 describes the course at Park University selected to participate in the project, Section 12.3.4 describes the computer literacy workshop content, Section 12.3.5 reports on the feedback from Park University student participants, and Section 12.3.6 reports on the feedback from the Pau Amarelo community participants. Section 12.3.7 describes the future computer plan for the community.

12.3.1 Information Technology in Brazil and the Pau Amarelo Community

According to [8, 9], because the Brazilian government was hoping to encourage information technology (IT) growth within the country, the government imposed heavy tariffs in early 1980s. In early 1990s, as compared to other free-trade countries such as Taiwan, Brazil's IT was lagging behind. Learning from this experience, Brazilian government had since tried to improve the growth of its IT field by lowering the tariffs and adding other incentives and investments [8, 9].

As the IT field in Brazil improved over the years, the Pau Amarelo community perceived a need to know how to use computers [3], not only to catch the wave of the information technology trend, but also simply to make a living. Although local colleges and high schools teach computer courses to their own students, the community residents did not have easy access to computers. The Pau Amarelo community wholeheartedly welcomed our help in educating their citizens. Since the demand for learning how to use computers was very high, ICS was one of the first departments requested to participate in the service-learning project in the Pau Amarelo community, and had been requested repeatedly in the following trips. All together, ICS has conducted three service-learning projects in the Pau Amarelo community since spring 2006.

12.3.2   Computer Literacy Service-Learning Project Report

This section gives a report on three computer literacy service-learning projects conducted by ICS. Section 12.3.2.1 explains how the literacy content was determined. Section 12.3.2.2 describes the workshop logistics and planning. Section 12.3.2.3 describes the characteristics of the participants from Pau Amarelo community. Section 12.3.2.4 describes the Brazilian translators who transferred to Park University as a result of the projects.

12.3.2.1   The Needed Skills in Computer Literacy. During the 2005 fall semester, two leaders from the Pau Amarelo community came to Park University to plan the trip for the spring of 2006. Prior to coming to Park University, the community leaders assessed the need of the community's computer skills based on the needs of the businesses surrounding the community and trends of the global market. They determined the applicable software that was dominant in the market at the time and the foreseeable future, and decided that the community would benefit most by learning to use the Internet, e-mail, and Microsoft® Word® and Excel®.

In the meeting at Park University, the community leaders requested a five-day workshop designed to increase computer literacy. Workshop topics included an introduction to computers, typing, Internet, e-mail, Microsoft® Word®, and Excel® [3]. Typing was critical because most people in the community did not know how to type.

In an effort to stimulate an interest to the field of information and computer science, ICS faculty proposed Alice and robotic design and programming [10, 11]. Although the ideas were interesting to the community leaders, they rejected these proposals because they considered these ideas as luxuries that did not meet the community's needs at the time [3].

12.3.2.2   Workshop Logistics. During the planning meeting in 2005, other logistic issues were also discussed and planned out. For example, the Pau Amarelo community did not have computers for conducting the workshop [3]. Additionally, the transportation of teachers and students to and from a rented facility as well as the provision of lunch meals could pose challenges. The leaders from both Pau Amarelo community and Park University worked diligently in resolving these critical issues.

In the end, for the spring and fall 2006 trips, Faculdade de Ciencias Humanas de Olinda (FACHO), a university collaborating with Park University (see Section 12.2.1), generously contributed a computer lab for the workshops. For the fall 2007 trip, a computer lab from a high school was rented. However, both the university and the high school were not in the close vicinity of the community. Park University arranged rented vehicles to transport both teachers and students to the morning workshop, back to the community for lunch, to the afternoon workshop, and back to the community in the evening [3].

12.3.2.3   Pau Amarelo Community Participants. Fifty community members participated in the computer literacy workshop in the spring 2006 trip, thirty-eight members in the fall 2006 trip, and thirty members in the fall 2007 trip. These numbers were necessarily limited by the number of working computers available in the computer lab. As a result, in all workshops conducted, there were more people who wished to participate but were turned away due to the computer limitation.

The community members who participated in the workshops ranged from preteens to the elderly. The diversity in computer experience among the participating members posed a challenge in the workshop. Although the majority of the community members did not know much about computers, some members knew how to send e-mails and had used a word processor before. By carefully planning ahead, we were able to accommodate advanced participating members with additional materials and projects.

At the conclusion of each workshop, a certificate of achievement was given to each participating member. Many community members received little or no schooling prior to the workshop. Such a certificate was considered as valuable as a diploma by many participants.

12.3.2.4   Brazilian Translators to Study at Park University. In all three workshops, Park University hired two translators who were college students majoring in computer science. In the fall of 2008, these students transferred to the United States to continue their education in ICS at Park University. One student graduated from Park University in the spring of 2011 and continued his studies in the Master of Business Administration (MBA) program with an emphasis in Management Information Systems at Park University in fall 2011. The other student graduated in fall 2011 and had a career in the field of information technology.

During their years at Park University, these students regularly performed service-learning projects outside of the regular classroom. One student became the president of the Association for Computing Machinery (ACM) student club for two years and led the club to perform various ICS-related service-learning projects for Park University and its local community. The other student worked and helped out at the offices of International Students, International Education, and Study Abroad. The following describes the service-learning projects conducted by the ACM student club president.

Fright Night is an annual event hosted by Park University to celebrate

Halloween with the local community. The Office of Student Life is in charge of the event and solicits activities from the student clubs. Most student clubs usually provide a haunted carnival, scary stories, Halloween games, costume contests, and treats. The ACM club president, wanting an activity to be computer-oriented, decided to gather the club students to design and implement computer games for the annual Fright Night event. The learning objectives that he had in mind for this service-learning project were to help ACM students (1) apply what they learned in class in a local community context, and (2) practice teamwork and analytical and problem-solving skills within the ACM student club.

During the 2008–2009 academic year, the club president and nine other students in the ACM student club designed and implemented a VHockey computer program game for the students at Park University to play. In the VHockey computer game, just as in a regular hockey game, there is a puck, represented by a solid circle, in the middle of the computer screen. Two players, positioned on the opposite sides of the computer screen, alternatively use their hands to push the puck toward each other's goal. The hand position, direction, and force are captured by a webcam. The computer game makes calculations based on the puck's position and the direction and the speed of the hand pushing the puck, and then moves the puck to a calculated position. The winner is the person who can push the puck into the goal. The VHockey computer game was set up in the social common for Park students to play and was well received by the students. The club students presented the project at the Fourth Annual Student Research and Creative Arts Symposium at Park University on April 1, 2009 [12]. For the annual Halloween Fright Night at Park University on October 23, 2009, the VHockey game was set up and played by the community youngsters.

Since VHockey was well received by the Park University students as well as the local community youngsters, the ACM club president conducted another computer project, Park Racer, within the ACM club that following academic year, 2009–2010. Park Racer is a computer program that allows a user to drive an animated car through Park University campus as fast as he wishes. The club students first digitalized the the Park University campus as the background for the game. A user controls the animated car via a mouse. Taking the speed and direction of the car in relation to the road conditions (hill, narrow, wide, bump) with accompanying sound effects, Park Racer allows a user to drive the car on a road, to stall on a bump, or to crash by the roadside. During the annual Halloween Fright Night at Park University on October 22, 2010, the Park Racer game was set up and played by the community youngsters. The club students presented the project at the sixth Annual Student Research and Creative Arts Symposium at Park University on April 11, 2011 [13].

Both the VHockey and Park Racer games were led and designed by the ACM student club president. The computer programs were implemented by the club members as well as the club president. The participating students volunteered their time and energy for the projects with no ties to any course work.

12.3.3 Park University Course Selection and Design

This section describes how the course at Park University was selected to participate in the service-learning project in Brazil. Additionally, it explains how the service-learning components were embedded in the course.

12.3.3.1 Why Implement the CS365 Computer Networking Course? During the planning meeting in 2005, the community leaders requested not only the specific workshop content, but also the expertise for consultation in building a networked computer laboratory for the community in the future. This included a computer networking topology design, electrical power requirement, computer equipment, and cable specification. From the meeting, it became clear that CS365, a Computer Networking course, would be the best fit for this service-learning project for several reasons:

1. The students in CS365 had already taken the required general education course CS140, Introduction to Computers, which covered most of the requested workshop content.
2. By taking CS365, the students would have the expertise to provide advices for the future networked computer laboratory in the Pau Amarelo community.
3. Most students in CS365 were juniors or seniors at Park University. Therefore, by the time the students took this course, they would have basic knowledge in the field of ICS such that they could share their knowledge with the people who were less computer literate than they were.
4. More importantly, CS365 students, being juniors or seniors, would be mature enough to act as ambassadors for Park University.

12.3.3.2 Service-Learning Projects in CS365. As there was a cost incurred in the service-learning project in Brazil, CS365 was designed to incorporate other service-learning projects for the students who could not afford to participate in the project in Brazil. In 2006, the service-learning projects were:

1. Brazil service-learning project. The participating students under faculty guidance prepared the workshop content based on the request from the community leaders, conducted the workshop in the Pau Amarelo

community, provided the consultation for the future networked laboratory in the community, participated in the culture-sharing events, and, upon returning from the trip, reported on the experience to classmates back at Park University. This project was conducted three times in 2006 and 2007 [3, 5].

2. Writing a computer networking animation project. Computer networking animations are used to illustrate how various computer networking applications work. The computer networking textbook [14] had a collection of networking animations that were freely available to all computer networking students around the world. The first author observed that her computer networking students had benefited tremendously from watching the animations. To contribute to the computer networking community, the first author had the students write networking animations as a service-learning project [5, 15]. From 2005 to 2008, four students produced four animations. Two of the four animations were published in the student resource website for the textbook [14]. The other two animations were published in the ICS website (http://www.park.edu/ics). These animations have been used by the first author in subsequent computer networking classes to demonstrate the computer networking concepts to ICS students at Park University [5, 15, 16].

Through the generosity of Missouri Campus Compact, in 2007, the first author received a grant to add service-learning projects in the computer networking course [5]. With this grant, students could perform a service-learning project within the information and computer science discipline. Partnered with a local science store near Park University, the third service-learning project, described below, was added.

3. Mentoring a First Lego League (http://www.firstlegoleague.org/) team. The team was composed of ten local community youngsters, aged 9 to 14 years old. The team's mission was to build a robot to conquer 13 obstacles in a challenge course. The student volunteers from CS365 served as mentors, (1) providing general advice in computer-science-related skills, (2) helping to solve any communication problems between the robot and the computer, and (3) serving as role models for the younger generation. There were nine students from CS365 participating in this project. During the entire 2007 fall semester, the team and the mentors met regularly at Park University's home campus. The First Lego League team participated in the Kansas City regional performance competition in February, 2008 [5].

In summary, CS365 has included service-learning projects that spanned from local to world communities over the years. The participating students were able to apply their cumulative information and computer-science-related skills to the communities they served [5].

12.3.4   Computer Literacy Workshop

ICS had conducted three computer literacy workshops since 2006. Each workshop was five days long. The workshop length for each day varied from workshop to workshop depending on the community participants' schedule. In general, the workshop lasted between five and six hours, with a two-hour lunch break. Also, depending on the participants' level, interest, and learning speed, different workshops covered different sets of material. The following describes the overall workshop content.

Unit on Introduction to Computers and Typing, and Preparation of an E-mail Account. In the introduction to computers unit, community participants were introduced to (a) various computer hardware components, (b) general computer system layout and operations, (c) various software applications such as word processor, spreadsheet, presentation, paint utility, Web browsing, audio and video utility, and games [3].

In the typing unit, the community participants were introduced to a proper typing technique with a color-coded diagram showing a typing finger-placement chart. Typing instruction included locating the home row of the keyboard, resting the fingers on the home row when not pressing a key, returning the finger to the home key after pressing a key, and so on. After the proper typing instruction was shown, participants used various websites and typing tools such as Typer Shark on Yahoo!® (http://games.yahoo.com/console/tps), TypeOnline.co.uk, and Tux Typing (http://tux4kids.aliot.debian.org/tuxtype/index.php) to practice typing.

In the next unit, community participants practiced sending and receiving e-mails. The e-mail system provided by www.yahoo.com.br was chosen for the workshop. This e-mail system was recommended by the Brazilian translators because it was popular in Brazil at the time. Getting e-mail accounts for thirty or more participants at the same time in a workshop setting could be very time-consuming, largely because most participants required assistance in entering their personal information for obtaining the e-mail accounts. Also, when several computers from the same network tried to access the same e-mail server at the same time, the server tended to block certain computers for acting on the defense side of denial-of-service (DOS) attack. Thus, getting an e-mail account was performed at the beginning of the workshop so that while some participants practiced typing, others could try to obtain e-mail accounts. The instructor kept track of the participants' e-mail addresses for use in a later unit.

Unit on E-mail and the Internet. Before conducting the e-mail unit, the instructor sent an introductory e-mail message to everyone in the workshop. This introductory e-mail served as a starting point for introducing how to receive and read an e-mail. From here, the participants learned how to respond and send an e-mail. It was a fun activity to have the participants practice sending e-mails to each other [3]. Toward the end of the unit, the participants were shown how to manage the e-mail account, including deleting any unwanted e-mails and saving an e-mail by moving it to a save folder.

In the Internet unit, participants were introduced to Google® or Yahoo!® search engines. By and large, this was a very interesting unit because everyone had a chance to explore the information he/she was interested in. Participants automatically shared their discovery informally during the session. Most participants were excited to find out detailed information about their home towns, countries, and cultures [3].

Unit on Microsoft Word. In this unit, because of varying typing speeds, participants were first given an unformatted letter as an example to load into Microsoft® Word®. Various utilities in Microsoft® Word® such as cut, paste, save, font, size, bold, paragraph spacing, and left-right-center alignment were introduced to the participants so that they could format the sample letter. The Microsoft® Word® Wizard was then introduced to help participants create a resume, a cover letter, and an announcement for a business advertisement [3]. Usually, by the end of the session most participants had documents that were readily available for them to use.

Unit on Microsoft® Excel®. In this unit, participants were first given an unformatted spreadsheet as an example to load into the Microsoft® Excel®. Besides the utilities (such as save, bold, alignment) taught in Microsoft® Word®, the auto-sum, equation, and cell-referencing utilities in Microsoft® Excel® were introduced. This unit was, in general, more challenging to teach than other units because many participants lacked basic mathematical skills. Nonetheless, for some participants, particularly the ones who were self-employed (such as a farmer or a seamstress), this unit broadened their views as to what they could do for their businesses.

Unit on Project. The Project unit was aimed toward the group's interest. The participants were polled to find a general interest of the group. A project was then conducted accordingly. In the first workshop, participants learned Microsoft® PowerPoint® presentations. In the second workshop, participants learned advanced functions such as fancy bolder, WordArt, and graphs in Microsoft Word®. In the third workshop, participants wrote their resumes using the resume template in Microsoft® Word® Resume Wizard.

12.3.5   Service-Learning Feedback from Park University Student Participants

In the first workshop, there was no student from CS365 who could afford the money and time to go to Brazil. The students from the class helped the first author prepare the material to be taught at the community.

For each of the following two workshops, one student participated in the project. A service-learning survey, composed by Professor Brian Cowley, Ph.D. from the Department of Psychology and Sociology at Park University, was given to the students.

Data gathered from the student survey indicated that the students thought that it was important and very effective to apply classroom learning to other communities around the world. They felt very comfortable traveling to different countries and meeting people from other parts of the world. For the questions on culture diversity ("What do you know about the culture of Brazil?"), one student responded, "They are very friendly, thankful, patient, willing to learn, and do not take things for granted." For the question, "What are the benefits of meeting people in other parts of the world?", one student responded, "You can learn from each other. It gives you an opportunity to reflect on your life back home and have a finer appreciation for what you have."

Overall, the students who participated in the project appreciated the opportunity to serve the community and learn from the people in Brazil.

Aside from teaching, the students and faculty toured the internationally famous Brazil Digital Port (http://www.portodigital.org, http://www.physorg.com/news/2011-04-brazil-haven-high-tech-investors.html.   2011). They also toured a local start-up company, which helped broaden the students' view of the computer industry outside the United States.

12.3.6   Feedback from Pau Amarelo Community Participants

At the end of the first two workshops, the Pau Amarelo community participants were asked to write feedback for what they learned in the workshop and what they wished to learn in the future. The participants liked the e-mail and the Internet the most. They overwhelmingly wanted us to come back to teach them more about computers and useful applications. Some community participants obtained computer- and networking-related jobs as a result of taking our workshops. The following is an excerpt from an e-mail sent by a Pau Amarelo community leader after the first trip:

> It's with a lot of joy that we give you this great news. A student from the Pau Amarelo Community got his first internship on a government program. He submitted to a test with mainly computer questions. He said that he was able

to answer most of them because of Park's Computer workshop at FACHO. So now he is going to be a computer assistant and will be able to receive his first salary. So we would like to share this great achievement of your great work and say thank you once again!

In the third workshop, the same pre- and postsurveys were given to the community participants. The surveys asked each participant to assess his comfort level in typing, using a computer, e-mail, Internet, Microsoft® Word®, and Microsoft® Excel®. The survey result showed that twenty-six out of thirty participants knew very little about the computers and the software before the workshop. By the end of the workshop, only three out of thirty participants still did not feel comfortable using computers. The rest of the twenty-seven participants showed varying comfort levels in using different software. Overall, most participants were more comfortable in using e-mail, Internet, and Microsoft Word than Microsoft® Excel®. For the four community participants who were familiar with the computers and the software before the workshop, we deliberately had them do more advanced materials, such as advanced typing challenges in Tux Typing, and advanced Microsoft® Word® utilities. Thus, overall, the community participants benefited from taking the computer literacy workshops.

Aside from the computer literacy training, the community participants actively participated in the cultural exchange through lunch hours and evening culture-sharing events.

12.3.7   Future Computer Plan for the Pau Amarelo Community

Through the generosity of a Kansas City based company, the Pau Amarelo community received a grant to purchase computers for use in the community [3]. The community leaders were looking to construct a computer laboratory for regular community use as well as for the computer literacy training.

Because of the benefits that the community participants received through our computer literacy workshops, it is expected that this workshop will continue as long as the funding is available and there are Park University students who will participate. We also plan to train teachers in teaching computer literacy in the community so that the community can better utilize the computer equipment year round [3].

12.4   SUMMARY AND CONCLUSION

In 2005, the Park University Internationalization Taskforce developed a statement on the Park University globally competent graduate:

Park University graduates will display knowledge of global interconnectedness, world events, cultures, and ideas. They will possess an open, empathetic, and sensitive attitude toward different nations, peoples, cultures, and ways of thinking. Park University graduates will learn about and effectively communicate with those of different cultural identities and experiences. They will work to serve the global community. [17]

The Department of Information and Computer Science (ICS) at Park University has performed a computer literacy service-learning projects in the Pau Amarelo community of Brazil three times since 2006. It has been a wonderful and rewarding experience for the participants from both Park University and Pau Amarelo community. The Park University students were able to utilize their cumulative information and computer-science-related skills to help the Pau Amarelo community become more computer literate. Additionally, both Park University students and the Pau Amarelo community participants were able to embrace the opportunities in cultural exchange [5]. This international service-learning exhibited the traits of "the ability to work cooperatively with others and the ability to understand, accept, appreciate, and tolerate cultural differences" as described in [2] and helped students on their journey to become globally competent graduates.Acknowledgement

ACKNOWLEDGMENTS

The authors wish to thank the following people for making this service-learning project possible: Dr. Byers-Pevitts, former president of Park University; the participating students at Park University; the members of International Education and Study Abroad at Park University; the members of the Pau Amarelo community and the translators in Recife, Brazil.

REFERENCES

1. Knight, J. (2003). Internationalization: Developing an Institutional Self-Portrait. Toronto, Canada: Ontario Institute for Studies in Education. Readings for EOTU Project. Retrieved October 9, 2005 from http://www.eotu.uiuc.edu/events/Illinoisnovfinal.pdf.

2. Parker, W. C, Ninomiva, A., and Cogan, J. (1999). "Educating World Citizens: Toward Multinational Curriculum Development." *American Educational Research Journal,* Vol. 36, No. 2, 117–145.

3. Hsin, W.-J. and Ganzen, O. (2008, April). Computer Literacy in International Service Learning at Park University. *The Journal of Computing Sciences in Colleges,* Vol. 23, No. 4.

4. Ganzen, O. (2007). *Educating Global Citizens: Internationalization of Park University,*

Kansas City, Missouri. (Doctoral dissertation). Cincinnati, Ohio: Union Institute and University.

5. Hsin, W.-J. (2008, October). Service Learning in Computer Networking Course, In *Annual Midwest Academy of Management Conference,* St. Louis, MO.

6. Making Opportunities from challenges. (2003). [Editorial]. *International Educator*, Vol. 12, No. 3, 2–5.

7. Youngblood, S. (2006). Park University website. Reporting II: The International Experience. http://captain.park.edu/digitalpirate/international.

8. Yates, A. (2003, December). Brazil: National ICT Policy. Kogod School of Business, American University. http://www1/american/edu/initeb/ay5376a/nationalpolicy.htm.

9. Botelho, A., Dedrick, J., Kraemer, K., and Tigre, P. (1999, October). From Industry Protection to Industry Promotion: IT Policy in Brazil. Center for Research on Information Technology and Organizations, University of California, Irvine. http://escholarship.org/uc/item/62n7x74x.

10. Dann, W., Cooper, S., and Pausch, R. (2011). *Learning to Program with Alice.* 3rd ed. Prentice-Hall, http://www.alice.org.

11. Institute for Personal Robots in Education. (2008). www.robotcducation.org.

12. Sa, L., Hojimatov, N., Houtum, R., Faivre, F., Tuckness, S., Stahr, N., Degrace, P., Pittman, A., Kinnard, B., and Labitoko, K. (2009, April 1). ACM Club Game Project. 4th Annual Student Research and Creative Arts Symposium at Park University.

13. Sa, L., Van Houtum, R., and Pease, J. (2011, April 11). A 3D Racing Game Through Park University. Sixth Annual Undergraduate Research and Creative Arts Symposium at Park University.

14. Kurose, J., and Ross, K. (2009). *Computer Networking—A Top-Down Approach.* Addison-Wesley, 2009. Computer Networking Animation collection in http://wps.aw.com/aw_kurose_network_5/111/28536/7305312.cw/index.html.

15. Hsin, W.-J. (2010, May). Animations for Computer Networking Protocols. *The Journal of Computing Sciences in Colleges*, Vol. 25, No. 5.

16. Hsin, W.-J. (2007). Student Motivation in Computer Networking Courses. Insight, Center for Excellence in Teaching and Learning. Park University. Vol. 2: Student Motivation.

17. Internationalization Task Force. (2005). Minutes. Parkville, MO: Park University.

CHAPTER 13

SERVICE-LEARNING THROUGH AGILE SOFTWARE DEVELOPMENT

Joseph T. Chao and Jennifer B. Warnke

ABSTRACT

Service-learning is a pedagogical approach that has been used by many in software engineering courses to provide students with a real-world approach to learning software-development skills. This chapter describes an approach to service-learning in the software engineering classroom that involves a central clearinghouse and maintenance center for service-learning project requests, use of agile methods, and collaboration with a technical communication course. The chapter describes the benefits and drawbacks to service-learning in a software engineering course, rationale behind using agile methods, the course layout, specifics of the collaboration, the final feedback of the community partners and students involved, and a discussion of lessons learned.

13.1 INTRODUCTION

Bringle and Hatcher [1] define service-learning as a "course-based, credit bearing educational experience in which students (a) participate in an organized service activity that meets identified community needs, and (b) reflect on the service activity in such a way as to gain further understanding of curricular content, a broader appreciation of the discipline, and an enhanced sense of personal values and civic responsibility."

Service-learning as a pedagogy approach to software engineering and other computer science courses has been embraced by many [2, 3, 4, 5, 6], and its benefits include not only providing students with real-world experience in technical and social skills, but also developing in students a sense of responsibility and ownership. This service-learning approach to software engineering courses contrasts with the traditional approach in which students learn software-development skills by working in a lab on instructor-provided projects. Although more tightly controlled projects allow students the opportunity to practice crucial development skills, they do not provide the experience of working with a client to develop a software solution that meets the task-specific needs of the client, as the service-learning approach does.

Some [7, 8] suggest that the service-learning approach to software engineering courses can prove advantageous to computer science departments that incorporate it, and it can prove advantageous to the entire computer science discipline. It has been suggested that the service-learning approach may attract better-performing students to the computer science discipline, which has been perceived with less interest by potential students in recent years [9].

Though the service-learning approach to software engineering courses has been embraced by many, instructors are often reluctant to incorporate service-learning into their courses because of the inherent drawbacks. Incorporating service-learning projects into a software engineering course requires extra time and organization from the instructor (e.g., soliciting non-profit organizations to serve as community partners, ensuring that the partners are satisfied with their collaboration with the students). It takes a significant amount of time to find suitable software projects for the course. An ideal project should contain enough complexity for student learning, and its size should be reasonable so that student teams are capable of producing a quality system in a restricted time frame. Some methods of providing maintenance and technical support once the students who developed the software systems have completed the course are also necessary.

Another challenge to incorporating service-learning projects into software engineering courses is the time limitations of a typical semester in an educational institution. Most students do not have any prior knowledge of software development before enrolling in the course, and typical semesters are limited to 16 weeks, which provides little time to teach students the building blocks they need to develop quality software systems. Moreover, a typical semester provides little time for students to meet with their teams, develop the software, meet with clients, and write documentation to accompany the software.

In this chapter, we describe the benefits and challenges to service-learning in a software engineering course and present a new approach to mediate the challenges. The outcomes of implementing the approach, including both student feedback and community partner feedback, are also provided. The chapter concludes by giving a list of lessons learned with positive results for future improvements.

13.2 IMPLEMENTING SERVICE-LEARNING IN THE SOFTWARE ENGINEERING COURSE

Aware of the benefits and drawbacks of service-learning in software engineering courses, one instructor recently implemented a new approach that mediated the main challenges of service-learning in a software engineering course. This approach required three steps:

1. Creation of the Agile Software Factory. The Agile Software Factory is a program within the Department of Computer Science that serves as a clearinghouse for software-development requests from nonprofit organizations and continues to provide maintenance and technical support for completed software systems.
2. Collaboration with a technical communication class. The students in the technical communication class practice their skills by developing the documentation for the software, which frees more time for the software engineering students to develop the software and also provides both classes the opportunity to work within a real-world industry scenario.
3. Teaching and incorporation of agile methods. Using agile methods to teach software engineering allows for better product development in a short time period.

Although this approach does not solve all the difficulties in implementing a service-learning software engineering course, it relieves some major challenges, as depicted in Figure 13.1. The three steps are discussed in further detail in this section.

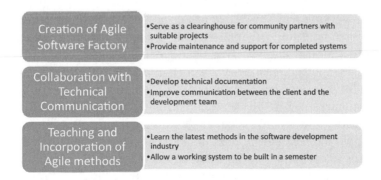

Figure 13.1. Three steps toward implementing a service-learning software engineering course.

13.2.1   Involvement of the Agile Software Factory

The first step in incorporating the service-learning approach in the software engineering course was to establish the Agile Software Factory [10]. Founded in 2008, the Agile Software Factory (ASF) was begun with a grant from the Agile Alliance (http://www.agilealliance.org) and sponsorship from the Bowling Green State University Computer Science (CS) department in which the ASF is housed, as well as sponsorship from the university's Information Technology Services (ITS). The Factory is under the supervision of the Department of Computer Science in the College of Arts and Sciences. The initial personnel of ASF consist of a Director and a grant-funded graduate assistant. The Director, a faculty volunteer approved by the CS department, oversees the daily operations of the Factory and reports to the computer science faculty on the activities of the Factory. Minimum secretarial support is provided by the CS department. ASF also hires student developers to work on software projects. The student developers are funded by project sponsors. For the last three years, ASF has provided employment opportunities for more than twenty student developers, and worked on more than ten internal and external projects.

The ASF exists to accomplish four main goals:

1. Provide computer science students with real-world, hands-on learning opportunities that increase the students' value to future employers.
2. Serve community partners by developing software systems that meet their specific needs and by providing ongoing software support.
3. Further the cause of service-learning as a part of the University's mission to become the premier learning community in Ohio.
4. Promote agile methods of software development, which focus on collaboration, adaptability, and user needs.

The ASF, working with the Office of Service-Learning at the university, actively locates nonprofit organizations that need software solutions developed. Oftentimes, it also receives unsolicited software requests from nonprofit organizations. Once the ASF receives a software request, it evaluates its feasibility as a service-learning project for students in the software engineering courses. A suitable service-learning project should be large and complex enough to provide adequate learning opportunities for the students in the software development class, and should be small enough for the student groups to deliver a useful product in a semester for the community partners. Once students complete the software system, the ASF provides ongoing maintenance and technical support services for the nonprofit organization (i.e., the community partner). This reduces the burden on the instructor to provide maintenance for software systems developed in the courses taught by that instructor.

After students are finished with their service-learning experience, whether for a class or as an independent project, they submit their work back to the Agile Software Factory. When projects are submitted back to the Factory, they are evaluated to determine the quality and future of the project. The quality of our projects is of the utmost concern to the Factory. Because much of our strategy is built on maintaining good relationships with our community partners, we strive to ensure that we provide them with the best software possible. Figure 13.2 illustrates how projects are managed within the Factory and how students and faculty interact with Factory projects.

In addition to providing and supporting service-learning projects for software engineering courses, the ASF offers part-time student employment for undergraduate students and independent projects for graduate students.

In the fall of 2008, the ASF located six service-learning projects from community partners. These projects were assigned to teams of six to ten students, who were mostly undergraduate seniors and first-year graduate students.

13.2.2 Collaboration with the Technical Communication Class

As mentioned previously, a major challenge in service-learning software engineering is the maintenance needs after project completion. One solution is

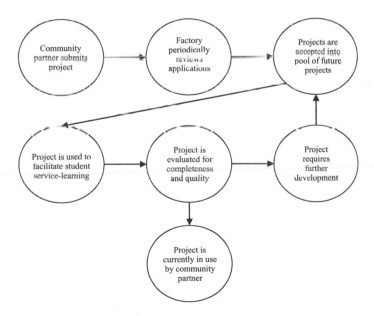

Figure 13.2. Project flow at the ASF.

to have a support center, as suggested by [11]. As another solution, our approach suggests that better user documentation might ease the burden of maintenance.

Based on our past experience in service-learning software development, user documentation produced by the student software developers was typically low quality and/or scarce. There are two main reasons for not having quality documentation:

1. There is limited time for software development itself, which implies limited time for creating documents.
2. Students in computer science or software engineering are not trained in technical communication.

Therefore, to achieve better documentation, the computer science instructor sought collaboration with a technical communication instructor who was teaching a senior-level, undergraduate technical communication course focused on online documentation.

The instructors worked together and designed a curriculum that encompassed technical communication in software development. They determined the basic responsibilities of the computer science students and the technical communication students and then assigned one or two (depending on the scope of the project and the size of the software engineering team) technical communication students to each of the software engineering teams. The software engineering students were responsible for producing programmer-oriented release notes that the technical communication students rewrote for the intended clients. At the end of the semester, the technical communication students compiled and organized the release notes into a complete online help file for the user.

The collaboration involved fifty-six students (forty-six from two software development classes and ten from the technical communication class), and was structured around the idea of providing the students from both courses a real-world learning experience. In planning the collaboration, we identified our goals for and anticipated benefits from the project, outlined the process for the collaboration, addressed any predictable challenges or limitations, and established assessment criteria to determine the success of the collaboration. The goals were identified as:

- Solve the initial problem that instigated the collaboration (poor end-user documentation).
- Provide our students with a hands-on learning experience that allowed them the opportunity to manipulate the tools they would be using in

their careers and to learn to navigate the production processes in their respective fields.

- Provide our students with a collaboration/communication experience similar to what they will have in their careers (working with clients and client needs, collaborating with peers, and navigating communication channels).
- Secure more time for software development.
- Enhance the usability of the software.

To determine the success of the collaboration, the instructors also established a set of assessment criteria that include quality of documentation, usability issues addressed earlier in the development process, and student feedback. More details about the collaboration and the two courses involved can be found in [12].

13.2.3 Use of Agile Methods

The instructor of the software engineering course decided upon teaching and using agile methods for the service-learning project for three main reasons:

1. The growing use of agile methods in industry
2. The focus on clients in the agile approach
3. The iterative and incremental nature of agile methods that would allow a working system to be built by the students in 16 weeks

The agile method used in the course is iterative and incremental based on eXtreme Programming [13] and Scrum [14]. This agile process model was applied successfully by student teams in a similar course taught previously by the same instructor [15], and was recommended by many other educators [16, 17, 18, 19].

Semester Schedule. Before the beginning of the semester, the instructor developed an iteration schedule that took advantage of agile's focus on clients, as well as its iterative and incremental nature. The semester schedule was divided into five iterations, I0–I4, each consisting of two to three weeks (see Table 13.1).

Since most students were not familiar with software development methodologies and were not aware of XP or other agile methods, the first three weeks were designed to provide a quick overview of software engineering background and methods. Throughout the semester, several agile methods and XP practices were also introduced in detail. The XP practices

Table 13.1.: Semester schedule

Week(s)	Service-learning project task
1 and 2	Introduction to software engineering and the projects.
3	Formation of software development project teams and role assignments, as well as the software development and technical communication combined teams.
4	First customer meeting and Iteration 0 (I_0), which consisted of planning and a requirements analysis.
5	Second customer meeting to review requirements and project plan.
6 and 7	Work on I_1 and accompanying documentation.
8	Deliver I_1 (a working system) with accompanying release notes and updated project plan to client.
9	Work on I_2 and accompanying documentation.
10	Deliver I_2 (a working system) with accompanying release notes and updated project plan to client.
11	Work on I_3 and accompanying documentation.
12	Deliver I_3 (a working system) with accompanying release notes and updated project plan to client.
13–15	Work on I_4. Perform qualitative usability test.
16	Deliver final software product and accompanying documentation (as a compiled help file) to client.

used in the course included the whole team, planning game, pair programming, coding standard, test-driven development, refactoring, and continuous integration. More details concerning these XP practices can be found in [13].

Iteration Components. Iteration 0 consisted of project preparation, which included an initial meeting with the community partners, research on technologies, and preliminary project planning and estimation. The student teams were responsible for determining what they could commit to completing for the client by the end of the semester, based on client needs, team skills, and time limitations. At the completion of iteration 0, the project team would have produced a project plan that included a list of user stories (system requirements) to be completed in each of the following four iterations.

Iterations 1 through 4 required the student teams to complete user stories for each iteration and deliver a functioning product (a portion of the larger system) to the community partner at the end of the iteration. Each team arranged a meeting with their community partner at the end of each iteration to deliver the product and documentation.

The technical communication students were responsible for producing release notes to accompany the functioning product of each iteration. The release notes served as reference documentation for the community partner after the software engineering students installed the product and taught the partner how to use it.

Student Responsibilities. At the beginning of the semester, the students were provided the semester schedule shown above, developed by the instructor. Class sessions consisted of lectures that taught students the skills they would need to develop software. Only three class sessions were used for in-class work time, which meant that students would have to work on the majority of their projects outside of class and schedule team meetings outside of class.

All students in a team were to be developers with a shared role in project management. Individual software development roles, such as Coach (Team Leader), Tracker, End User (student customer), Tester, Designer, Tool Guy, Integrator, Presenter, Documenter, and Installer, were elected within each team in order to instill some personal responsibilities in students, as recommended by Dubinsky and Hazzan [20]. To complete each iteration, the teams were responsible for determining among themselves which team members would fulfill which roles. The teams were also responsible for determining who would complete which tasks on which days to ensure that they completed the iterations by the deadlines and were meeting the needs of the community partner.

13.3 OUTCOMES

In the fall semester of 2008, 46 students in two sections of the software engineering course were assigned to one of six teams to complete one of the six service-learning projects. By the end of the semester, the teams had completed the following projects (see Table 13.2):

As with any new approach to teaching, and especially one that requires the coordination of multiple groups of people within a limited time frame, this new approach to service-learning in the software engineering classroom posed a number of challenges (e.g., difficulty coordinating team member schedules, difficulty maintaining consistent communication with the technical communication students, and difficulty completing iterations in a short period of time); however, the majority of the feedback from the community partners and students validated this approach and justified continuing it in future classes.

13.3.1 Student Feedback

It is clear that the software development students valued the service-learning project as a means of providing them an experience similar to what they will

Table 13.2. Service-learning software development projects

Project List	Description
Victim case-tracking system	A system that tracks victim cases that are supported by a grant-funded agency. The agency helps individuals who are victims of circumstances such as sexual assault, domestic violence, stalking, and sexual harassment. The main features include: efficient and speedy data entry, easy retrieval and tracking of records, enabling statistical calculations and reporting.
Employee database system	A client and server database system that tracks employee records. The main features include user authentication and various employee reports.
Service reporting system	A database system that stores agency and grant-related information and produces various required agency reports. The main features include data entry for various agency report forms and automatically producing required management reports periodically.
Service-learning information system	A database system that stores service-learning course and community partner information to facilitate the paring of service-learning courses on campus with community-based clients. The main features include: online data entry of course and project information, course and community partner management reports, and sophisticated online search.
Student activity matching system	An intelligent system that matches students' preference with cabin and roommate availabilities. This system uses an optimization algorithm to match students with their desired choices. Each student will pick four other students that he or she wishes to be cabin mates with. The teacher will have the option to edit or rerun the matchmaking process to obtain a desirable cabin list. Using this program, the teachers will save the time of matching students' preferences while also considering the parents who may chaperone.
Speech league e-voting system	A secured online voting system for a high school speech league. The main features include: user authentication, a streamline voting process, and secured database contains personal and voting information.

undertake in their careers. In the end-of-semester survey, the students agreed that they had learned valuable skills from the service-learning project; in fact, 100% of the 46 students agreed that they had learned skills in the class that were applicable to the real world. Table 13.3 shows the results of an anonymous survey asking the students to rank their level of agreement with a series of statements about the course.

In response to an open-ended question asking whether or not the students thought their participation in the course would improve their chances of

Table 13.3. Student survey results

Survey Statement	SA	A	N	D	SD
• The agile methodology used in this class was a good approach for completing my project.	27	13	5	1	0
• My team project this semester is a good project to fulfill the purpose of this course. (45 respondents)	31	13	0	1	0
• I enjoyed working on the service-learning project in this course.	27	13	3	3	0
• I am satisfied with the project progress this semester.	14	24	3	4	1
• I understand the customer needs for the system.	24	21	0	1	0
• My team has produced a quality system that meets the customer needs.	18	24	3	0	1
• My team has worked with/interacted with the customer as professional service providers would.	15	22	7	2	0
• The communication between my team and the customer has been prompt and painless.	11	23	7	4	1
• My communication skills have improved this semester. (45 respondents)	15	24	4	2	0
• My teamwork skills have improved this semester.	16	25	4	1	0
• The skills I learned in this class are applicable to the real world.	35	11	0	0	0
• Our collaboration with the technical communicators on our team has been effective, purposeful, and useful.	12	13	17	2	2
• The technical communicators on my team have made a valuable contribution to our project.	14	17	10	4	1
• Collaboration with the technical communicators was a good idea and should be continued for this course in the future. (45 respondents)	15	17	11	0	2

Notes: SA = strongly agree; A = agree; N = neutral; D = disagree; SD = strongly disagree.

landing a job after graduation, 34 of the 39 respondents to the question agreed that they indeed thought it would improve their chances of employment. In response to another open-ended question that asked "Name one thing you do not want to see changed about this course," 26 of the 36 question respondents listed the service-learning component. A number of students even mentioned the agile approach itself. In fact, 31 of the 36 respondents to the question listed either (sometimes both) the service-learning or agile components, or everything about the course.

Here are just a few of the students' actual comments, which reinforce their appreciation of the service-learning and agile components of the course:

- "I thought I [could] never be a part of big projects like these."
- "I have learned that teamwork is more important than individual talent."

- "I think this class would not be nearly as effective without being a service-learning project. Going through the motions in a real-life situation is something that I think all [university] CS majors should be a part of."
- "I liked [using] the agile method in a real-life project."
- "I had not heard of agile software development before, but I am now glad I have. It is a great tool that I plan to use in the future."
- "I have gotten to see the other side of development, which is agile. I also finally got to work on a project that matters in the real world."
- "Prior to this class, I was not sold on the idea of software development as a potential career. But after seeing all of the aspects of the process, I would love to go into development."
- "This is one of the most valuable courses in the entire CS department."

The students expressed a sense of fulfillment and pride in completing their projects because the systems they created would actually be used. Additionally, they expressed a feeling of worth and satisfaction in being able to contribute to a nonprofit organization to help better a community.

In questions regarding the collaboration with the technical communication students, only 25 out of 46 software development students agreed (17 were neutral) that "Our collaboration with the technical communicators on our team has been effective, purposeful, and useful." However, 32 out of 45 students agreed (11 neutral) with "Collaboration with the technical communicators was a good idea and should be continued for this course in the future."

The technical communication students were less likely to say that they found the overall project useful to them. For the end-of-semester survey questions listed below, only five of the seven students who completed the survey agreed with the statements:

- I believe this collaboration has given me an experience similar to collaborating in a work setting.
- I believe that what I have learned from this collaboration will be useful in my future career.

However, six of the seven students agreed with the statement "I have gained beneficial skills in working with a team through this collaboration."

These responses could be due to a number of factors, but the technical communication students unanimously agreed on four aspects, indicating these aspects could be major contributors to their disappointment with the project:

1. They were uncertain of their roles and responsibilities, and the understanding they did have oftentimes was not the same understanding that the software development students had of the technical communication students' roles and responsibilities.
2. They often did not feel they were an integral part of the team.
3. The software development students often completed their portion of work the night before it was due, leaving the technical communication students to stay up all night to complete the documentation.
4. Having the Online Docs class delivered completely online was not the ideal delivery method for working with this collaboration. (The delivery method was established prior to the conception of the collaboration.)

13.3.2 Community Partner Feedback

All five of the community partners who responded to an anonymous survey (out of six who participated in the collaboration) reported that they enjoyed working with the team (see Table 13.4). Four of the five strongly agreed that they had received the same quality of software as professional developers would produce and that they would recommend the service-learning collaboration to other non-profit organizations.

In response to the survey question "Name one thing you like about your finished product," the community partners responded with the following:

Table 13.4. Community partner survey results

Survey statement	SA	A	N	D	SD
• The student team has worked with/interacted with me as professional service providers would	1	3	0	1	0
• The communication between the team and me has been prompt and painless.	3	1	0	1	0
• I am satisfied with the project progress throughout the semester.	3	1	0	1	0
• The project was planned well and was carried out as planned.	4	0	0	1	0
• I enjoyed working with the team.	5	0	0	0	0
• The team has produced a useable system that meets my needs. (Only 4 responses)	3	0	0	1	0
• I feel that I received the same quality of software from this project as I would from professional developers.	4	0	0	1	0
• It was worthwhile for me to participate in this service-learning project.	4	0	1	0	0
• I will recommend this service-learning collaboration to other potential organizations.	4	0	1	0	0

Notes: SA = strongly agree; A = agree; N = neutral; D = disagree; SD = strongly disagree.

- "It was an excellent experience and we have a really useful system that we will implement in January. We would not be in a position to do this without the support of the team."
- "This is an excellent piece of software that will be useable by all employees of [organization]. It's fully functional, well thought out, and exceeds [our] expectations."
- "(1) How easy it is to use. (2) The physical appearance is appealing to the eye."
- "It delivered the product that was promised. The product is not intimidating to the end users."
- "It is user friendly and it clearly shows the incredible progress the students made on this project."

The community partners were also asked to name one thing they disliked about their finished product, and answered with the following:

- "N/A"
- "We did not have time to adequately field test the system before the end of the project; but the team did agree to tidy up some final items."
- "Nothing"
- "The installation of the finished product should have been coordinated better on our end using our IT support contractor."
- "It does not allow us to do what we need as hoped. It doesn't allow for the complexity of reporting information needed; it doesn't have any dynamic areas that can grow with agency needs. All of these are things we asked for and students committed to early on. It was clear by the last iteration that this was not possible. Despite this, the remarkable progress students made on this difficult group task is impressive."

When asked what they would like to see changed about the collaboration in the future, the community partners' responses fell into three basic categories:

1. Clearer expectations at the beginning (e.g., required number of meetings, definitions of the documentation they would be receiving, structure of the collaboration)
2. Allowing for more than one semester of work
3. Improved student dynamics

When the community partners were asked what they would like to see unchanged about the collaboration, they responded with the following:

- "I would like everything to remain as it was. There was great communication between team members and the agency and the time line was acceptable."
- "The focus on the final product and the focus on nonprofit partners."
- "Everything."
- "I thought the assignment of clear responsibilities of the team members appeared to be a good group learning exercise and valuable experience in the real world."
- "The amazing talent of most of the students working toward a collective good and the dedication of the instructor to the learning of the students."

We have also received the following testimonial from three community partners:

"Collaboration with the team was excellent and the team remained client-centered, continually working with Victims Services, ensuring that the program developed suited the needs of the agency. We are very happy with the results and look forward to future opportunities such as this one."
—Program Advocate, Victims Services of Behavioral Connections, Bowling Green, Ohio

"It was an excellent experience and we have a really useful system that we will implement in January. We would not be in a position to do this without the collaboration with the student developers."
—Executive Director, Neighborhood Properties, Inc., Toledo, Ohio

"The matching system is wonderful. It is very usable and user-friendly. I spend hours each year matching students in cabins by hand. This computer system will allow me to do the same task in less than an hour. This is what technology is supposed to be used for, to make life easier. The Bowling Green State University students did an outstanding job."
—Teacher, Eastwood Middle School, Pemberville, Ohio

Both sets of feedback provide valuable insight into what can be improved upon in the future of this service-learning collaboration, which is discussed in the Lessons Learned section below.

13.4 LESSONS LEARNED AND FUTURE IMPROVEMENTS

Based on the project results, and the feedback from both students and community partners, this service-learning software engineering approach was a success. In addition to achieving better management of all student projects, the instructor has gained insight in several other areas and will take the following steps into the future:

- Consider the availability of the clients when evaluating the suitability of the projects for the course. It would be valuable to have the clients sign an agreement for their time commitments. Ideally, the customer would be on-site, but because "customer on-site" is not possible, the instructor will ensure that the clients understand that customer availability is required before committing to the project.

- Schedule release meetings, if applicable, early in the semester. One problem encountered in the course was that one of the clients did not have time to meet and provide feedback at the end of each iteration.

- Use class time often, or at least at the end of each iteration, for retrospectives. The instructor has found that it is important to keep abreast of the progress of the projects and keep risk management in mind.

- Participate in customer meetings, especially the first meeting when finding out requirements is essential. In several meetings the instructor attended, students did not always ask probing questions that would allow them to figure out the needs of the client, and they were often confused with system requirements. Although it is not possible for the instructor to attend all meetings for all projects, it is crucial to attend the first meetings.

- Enforce some agile practices such as pair programming and test-driven development. The instructor has found that pair programming not only improves the quality of the system, but also prevents students from procrastinating.

Concerning the collaborations between the software development class and the technical communication class, we found that it offered many surprises that provide new insights for future attempts at this collaboration.

The collaboration was initiated to solve the problem of poor end-user documentation developed by Software Development students to accompany their service-learning software projects. Assessing the quality of the produced documentation through something of a "technical-communication heuristic evaluation," including task-oriented writing, contextual introductions, results of actions, and so on, as well as basic elements such as grammar, usage, and syntax, the documentation produced by the technical communication students was indeed better written than the documentation of the software developers in previous semesters. In terms of addressing usability issues early in development, we found that the technical communication students, not completely convinced of their credibility in playing the role of "user as expert," were hesitant to present their "subjective" usability concerns to the developers. They did, however, help enhance system usability through objective means, such as completing validity testing, or by discovering that a system did not work in Internet browsers other than Microsoft Internet Explorer.

To address the issues in future collaborations between the software development class and the technical communication class, the instructors plan to do the following:

- Visit each other's classes to present how their own students will be interacting with the teams and what role they will play.
- Allow the software development students a portion of class time to work with their team members, and assign the technical communication students into teams partially according to their schedules to ensure that at least one of them from each group can attend the teamwork time.
- Provide each group with a list of discussion points at the beginning of their collaboration. One of those points will be on the students' roles to ensure that both groups of students within the team have the same understanding of everyone's roles.
- Require a two-day window between development completion deadline and the iteration due date with accompanying documentation.
- Incorporate the technical communication students into the initial client meeting so they have a better big-picture understanding of the goals of their team's project and so they feel more comfortable providing input, based upon that better understanding.

13.5 CONCLUSION

This chapter has described a three-step approach to implementing a service-learning software engineering course that involves creating a project clearing house (Agile Software Factory), collaborating with a technical communication class, and incorporating agile methods. We have also discussed in detail the rationale behind using agile methods, the course layout, specifics of the collaboration, and the feedback from the students and community partners involved. The student feedback from a recently implemented course indicates that students valued the service-learning experience and the real-world skills they gained from their involvement in it, and the feedback from the community partners showed that they enjoyed working with the students and appreciated the services provided by the students.

While the implementation is a success, some lessons were learned and future improvements were identified. In terms of the workload for the instructors, each project requires a great deal of preparation, monitoring, and grading, all of which are time-consuming. The incorporation of service-learning projects entails maintaining customer relationships, coordinating meetings, and ensuring quality products. It is inevitable that more projects and more collaboration will imply higher instructor workload. However, we feel that the outcomes in both student learning and community partner satisfaction made the additional workload worthwhile.

With these new insights, the instructor will continue with this agile service-learning approach to software engineering education. We are confident this approach is producing better-prepared software developers.

REFERENCES

1. R.G. Bringle, R. G., and Hatcher, J. A. (1995). "A Service-Learning Curriculum for Faculty." *Michigan Journal of Community Service Learning,* Vol. 2, 112–122.

2. Ferguson, R., Liu, C., Last, M., and Mertz, J. (2006). "Service-Learning Projects: Opportunities and Challenges." SIGCSE Bulletin 38, Houston, TX, March 1–5, 2006, pp. 127–128.

3. Linos, P. K., Herman. S., and Lally, J. (2003). "A Service-Learning Program for Computer Science and Software Engineering." In *ITiCSE'03,* June 30–July 2, 2003, Thessaloniki, Greece, pp. 30–34.

4. Liu, C. (2005). "Enriching Software Engineering Course with Service-Learning Projects and the Open-Source Approach." In *Proceedings of the 27th International Conference on Software Engineering,* pp. 613–614.

5. Sanderson, P. and Vollmar, K. (2000). "A Primer for Applying Service Learning to Computer Science." In *SIGCSE 2000,* Austin, TX, March, 2000, pp. 222–226.

6. Webster, L. D., and Mirielli, E. J. (2007). "Student Reflections on an Academic Service Learning Experience in a Computer Science Classroom." In *SIGITE'07,* Destin, FL, October 18–20, 2007, pp. 207–211.

7. Purewal T. S., Bennett C., and Maier, F. (2007). "Embracing the Social Relevance: Computing, Ethics and the Community." In *Proceedings of the 38th SIGCSE Technical Symposium on Computer Science Education Conference*, SIGCSE'07, Covington, Kentucky, USA.

8. Rosmaita B. J. (2007). "Making Service Learning Accessible to Computer Scientists." In *Proceedings of the 38th SIGCSE Technical Symposium on Computer Science Education Conference,* SIGCSE'07, Covington, Kentucky, USA.

9. Carter, L. (2006). "Why Students with an Apparent Aptitude for Computer Science Don't Choose to Major in Computer Science." In *Proceedings of the 37th SIGCSE technical symposium on Computer science education,* SIGCSE'06, Houston, Texas, USA.

10. Chao, J. and Randles, M. (2009). "Agile Software Factory for Student Service Learning." In *The 22nd IEEE-CS Conference on Software Engineering Education and Training (CSEE&T'09),* February 17–19, 2009, Hyderabad, India.

11. Chase, J. D., Oakes, E., and Ramsey, S. (2007). "Using Live Projects Without Pain: The Development of the Small Project Support Center at Radford University." In *Proceedings of the 38th SIGCSE Technical Symposium on Computer Science Education Conference,* SIGCSE'07, Covington, Kentucky.

12. Brown, J., and Chao, J. (2010). "Collaboration of Two Service-Learning Courses: Software Development and Technical Communication." *Issues in Informing Science and Information Technology (IISIT)*, Vol. 7, 403–412.

13. Beck, K. (2000). *Extreme Programming Explained: Embrace Change.* Addison-Wesley.

14. Schwaber, K., and Beedle, M. (2001). *Agile Project Management with Scrum,* Prentice-Hall.

15. Chao, J. (2005). "Balancing Hands-on and Research Activities: A Graduate Level Agile Software Development Course." In *Proceedings of the Agile Development Conference (ADC'05).*

16. Alfonso, M. I., and Botía, A. (2005). "An Iterative and Agile Process Model for Teaching Software Engineering." In *Proceedings of the 18th Conference on Software Engineering Education and Training (CSEET'05)*, Ottawa, Canada, April 18–20, pp. 9–16.

17. Fenwick, J. (2003). "Adapting XP to an Academic Environment by Phasing-In Practices." In *XP/Agile Universe,* New Orleans, LA, USA, August 2003.

18. Wainer, M. (2003). "Adaptations for Teaching Software Development with Extreme Programming: An Experience Report." In *XP/Agile Universe,* New Orleans, LA, USA, August 2003.

19. Williams, L., and Upchurch, R. (2001). "Extreme Programming for Software Engineering Education." In *31st ASEE/IEEE Frontiers in Education Conference,* Reno, NV, USA, 2001.

20. Dubinsky, Y., and Hazzan, O. (2004). "Roles in Agile Software Development Teams." In *XP/Agile Universe,* Calgary, Canada, August 2004, pp. 32–42.

CHAPTER 14

EMPOWERMENT THROUGH SERVICE-LEARNING
Teaching Technology to Senior Citizens

Sally R. Beisser, Ph.D.

ABSTRACT

This case study describes a two-year (five semester) analysis of service-learning lab reflections from 87 university students in a mid-sized private Midwest university. These students tutored senior citizens in computer and technology skills on a weekly basis, in order to empower seniors as digital citizens. Consequentially, the students themselves reported empowerment as participatory citizens in the larger campus community. Findings revealed that students held increased social competencies, strong levels of engagement in information technology (IT) literacy instruction, and positive values with an expressed desire to continue to volunteer in the future. Conclusions support service-learning pedagogy as a way to empower both students as participatory citizens and seniors as digital citizens.

14.1 INTRODUCTION

The emergence of service-learning in higher education, with renewed emphasis on developing citizenship and community involvement, presents colleges and universities with unique opportunities for campus–community partnerships. Today's service-learning movement extends the traditional interpretation of service to include "participatory citizenship." According to Maxim (1), participatory citizenship is a way to "fully involve individuals possessing the knowledge, skills, and attitudes to participate in and maintain our democratic nation" (p. 15), thus challenging students to build community relationships and analyze social issues and community-based needs. The junction of service and learning go beyond the independent contributions of each.

Service is valued as a civic responsibility whereby service is with, rather than for, the community partner or agency. *Learning* about critical issues in one's own campus community develops ethical grounding, intellectual facility, and resourcefulness required to meet the needs of others experientially. Therefore, service-learning in this study is viewed as a pedagogy that promotes mutually beneficial partnerships between academic institutions and communities. This partnership requires reflection on particular challenges posed in the delivery of service, in this case information technology literacy to an underserved, elderly population.

According to Jacoby (2), "Service-learning is a form of experiential education in which students engage in activities that address human and community needs" (p. 5). One university student in this study, Katie, stated, "Service-learning is not something that is easily explained. On paper it means one thing, yet when you actually do it there is a totally different feeling to the whole thing." Battistoni (3) gives perhaps the most extensive structural suggestions for integrating an effective experiential learning program. He believes the following must be foundational goals of a service-learning program. *Intellectual understanding* must accompany service, with cognitive development creating a "thinking citizen" (p. 151) capable of making assumptions regarding human nature, society, and justice. *Civic skills and attitudes* are developed through persuasive thinking, writing, and listening skills. Such skills are attributes for communicating and deliberating in the public setting that democracy embodies. Finally, civic action within the service should engage students in direct, not passive, problem solving and discussion. Engagement in service to others holds the utmost potential to motivate college students' lifelong participation as citizens in their communities. This study supports service-learning pedagogy as a way to empower both students as participatory citizens who can make a difference and seniors as digital citizens whose technology skills are heightened.

Students in their Digital Citizenship course learned that citizenship is increasingly mediated by digital communication. For example, political parties interact with members online, interest groups use Internet sites and e-mail to woo the public, media organizations perpetually update the news on their information-rich sites, and government makes vital information and documents available online. These are aspects of emerging digital citizenship, yet participation is inequitable as there are disenfranchised populations. Digital disparity exists among populations who differ in socioeconomic status, educational background, gender, minority status, and age (4). Access to home computers is dependent on income and education, with increased use among males (5, 6, 7, 8, 9,10). The "gray gap" population (i.e., senior citizens over the age of sixty-five) are less likely to use digital technology due to concerns about privacy, irrelevance, cost, and perceptions of the steep learning curve required to use computers and the Internet (11, 12). As an often economically vulnerable group lacking disposable income to purchase hardware and software, seniors are not equipped or experienced in using technology. As new technologies emerge exponentially, elderly persons, who did not grow up in the Information Age, are unable to draw on the existing skills and competencies required to learn new digital computer applications. However, this study reveals two findings. First, senior citizens are eager clients in acquiring technology competencies. Second, university students are willing tutors who can empower seniors and thereby contribute as citizens in their campus communities (13).

The Digital Citizenship course prepared students for the service engagement by exploring critical concepts of technology-enhanced empowerment and IT instruction (14). They faced a challenge to confront the "digital divide" and to explore the impact of digital communication on citizenship. They learned that as a group, the elderly are not highly represented as "e-citizens."

In addition to the three-hour Digital Citizenship course, students took a one-hour required service-learning lab, in order to study the ethics of volunteerism, different types of service, and the meaningful delivery of service-learning (15, 16, 17). Lab objectives included comparative definitions of service-learning, distinction between service-learning and volunteerism, ethics and motivation of service, components of high-impact service, and levels of engagement (i.e., direct service, indirect service, and advocacy).

Students learned how to teach computer skills then practiced those skills weekly by tutoring senior citizens in the campus area. Seniors, recruited by the lab instructor from local senior centers close to the university campus, were given information flyers and site visits to answer questions about the tutoring experience. Logistics, such as transportation and parking or handicapped access were handled on a case-by-case basis. Since each senior had different skill sets, each college student prepared an individual lesson in the lab for the tutorial sessions held on campus. The students kept narrative journals throughout the semester highlighting the content, process, and insights from their service experiences. Each student wrote a summative reflection paper at the end of the semester. The reflection paper was worth 80 percent of the lab grade. Other points were given for participation and contributions in class.

A rubric was used to require students to respond to the following:

- Describe your clients and your teaching interactions.
- In what ways were your clients underresourced?
- To what degree did you lead them toward digital citizenship?
- What do you now know about the digital divide that you did not know before?

- What impact did this course have on you?
- If it changed you, what are the new choices you will make?
- If it had no impact or you did not learn anything, what could have been better?
- How does this lab course compare to other service experiences?
- How does this lab course compare with the service-learning examples provided in the handouts and with the "perfect service-learning" environments described in the literature?

Throughout the entire paper, not as a separate section, students were challenged to demonstrate knowledge of the principles of service-learning. They were required to make references to literature and assigned readings, lecture notes, and class discussions. They did not have to agree with those writings, but needed to demonstrate that they had read them and whether they applied or did not apply to experiences in class. Finally, they had to demonstrate understanding of the issues of the digital divide in their final reflection paper.

In summary, student reflection following the service-learning lab experiences invited feedback linking the community intervention to an analysis of theory and practice (18). Importantly, students learned that they were citizens within the community, beyond campus, and were challenged to understand local social issues. They universally benefited as citizens as a result of their interpersonal interactions with senior citizens.

14.2 METHODOLOGY

Three research questions driving this study were:

1. As a result of a service-learning lab with a disenfranchised group such as elderly citizens, did participating university students reflect on social injustice?
2. Do known building blocks for development of healthy, caring, responsible children (e.g., external and internal developmental assets) manifest themselves in the adult development of college students?
3. What indications were there that either the university students or the seniors experienced a sense of empowerment?

All university students ($N = 87$) participating in the service-learning lab sessions completed an end-of-semester reflection paper sharing multiple anecdotes and analytical examples to summarize experiences in the computer lab, offer explanations for the digital divide, and provide evidence of understanding principles of service-learning. After compiling five semesters of students' reflective journals across six classes, reflections were analyzed with ATLAS.ti© qualitative software (19). Using the Search Institute 40 Development Assets (20) as a lens for evaluating the reflections, researchers looked for twenty external and twenty internal developmental assets of healthy, caring, and responsible young adults. The framework of developmental assets offers a way of understanding the strengths young people need in order to be productive members of society. Criteria for analysis were built on core principles in the Search Institute's research-based (20) framework of twenty external assets such as family, neighborhood, school, and community support, and influence, along with twenty internal assets such as commitment to learning through motivation and engagement, positive values through promoting social justice and caring, social competencies such as interpersonal competence and positive identity through personal power, and positive view of the future. The intent of the study was to measure the presence, or absence, of assets in young people's lives as they continue in their postsecondary development. The developmental asset framework and terminology, first introduced in 1990, surveyed over 350,000 sixth-through twelfth-graders in over six hundred communities to learn about risks and resiliency. Findings suggest that these assets encourage prosocial behaviors and decrease risky activities (21, 22). On one level, the forty developmental assets represent everyday wisdom about positive developmental outcomes. On another level, experiential learning through volunteer service empowered college students to reach out to elder citizens.

While *external assets* of college students' backgrounds (e.g., support and empowerment from family, neighborhood, school, or peers activities) were not critically evaluated, students' reflective papers were scanned for representation of *internal assets* (e.g., social competencies, commitment to learning, positive values, and positive identity) in response to their service activity. Multiple readers categorized incidence of the following themes from approximately 700 pages of electronic data: social competencies, commitment to learning, and positive values. Because the Digital Citizenship course fundamentally focused on the digital divide, responses for equality and social justice, appearing under the positive values asset category, were coded separately. For the five categories, a total of 624 quotations were coded (See Appendix A). Results indicate that 30% of responses reflected social competencies, 23% commitment to learning, 20% social justice, 16% general positive values, and 11% positive identity (See Figure 14.1).

In their papers, some respondents demonstrated an appreciation of multiple asset categories.

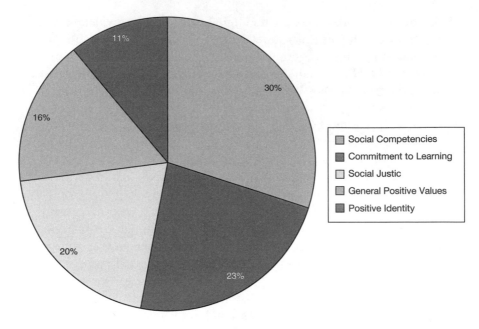

Figure 14.1.

14.3   QUALITATIVE ANALYSIS

The internal asset categories were collapsed into four areas of importance. Student narratives revealed the importance of social competencies, commitment to learning, and positive values with expressed desire to continue to future volunteerism. As a result, the university students viewed themselves as engaged citizens capable of closing the digital divide by empowering those who are disenfranchised from IT communication and information applications.

14.3.1   Social Competencies

Nearly one-third of student responses focused on social competence through planning and decision making, interpersonal competence, and cultural competence. They demonstrated a commitment to empowering people different from themselves. Student comments are represented by pseudonyms.

14.3.1.1   Planning and Decision Making. University students were engaged in planning social connections as tutors. One student planned lessons to teach her senior citizen to learn to use e-mail to "keep in touch with her grandbabies." Another helped her client understand the distinction between ".com and .net sites." Christy wrote, "When our session was complete, we had begun to use search engines. I planned time for us to meet after class, and I could continue lessons. Mary (the senior citizen) was ecstatic. I found by writing procedures for her, she could more easily use computer functions."

Andi explained to her client that she needed a password for her e-mail that protected her identity. She told her not to use her real name. Andi wrote, "The concept that there were millions of other people online with the same first name (Edith) or last name (Smart) was unbelievable to her."

Doug's client went home happy with new information prepared for him. Doug stated, "I made sure she had my e-mail address in case she ever decided she wanted me to answer more questions."

One student learned how to help a client who wanted to "look up public records to see who owned the house that she and her husband had owned for many years."

Rebecca prepared ways for her senior to find websites in her own language, Chinese.

Students had to plan differently for different seniors. "It is here that we were forced to scrutinize ourselves," Josh noted. "Not only did we have to question what we would teach, but how to teach it, and the impact it may have." Josh summarized that planning needed to be intentional. He stated, "I found that the techniques I had used for Glenda and Lewis were no longer adequate for Howard."

14.3.1.2 Interpersonal Competence. Respondents expressed unexpected social interaction within the tutoring relationship as a result of mutual experiences. Kathryn said, "We cared about many of the same things. I taught them computer and Internet skills in exchange for their life experiences and further training in communication and teaching." One student said, "It was not only his first experience with a computer, it was my first experience tutoring. I was quite uncomfortable at first, not sure exactly what to say or do. I was overly conscious of our age difference and afraid of offending him. By the end, however, I worked up to a level of comfort."

Michael reported, "Delilah was unsure how to use search engines. I showed her Google, Yahoo, Go, AltaVista, and AskJeeves. We focused on political and governmental searches. We eventually visited the websites of Iowa Senators and the government homepage for Social Security. She loved these sites and planned on emailing her Senators. Delilah came back the next week all excited to learn about copying pictures from the Internet and putting them in e-mails. As she went to the URL to drag it down to Google, she accidentally clicked on an Asian pornography site. We burst out laughing uncontrollably and I had quite a time explaining that we were not the only group that used these computers and that our class was definitely not responsible for putting that site on the computer. At the end of the semester, Delilah slipped me a $5 bill and told me to 'get myself lunch.' I tried to refuse and told her that taking money might violate the spirit of the project, but she would have none of it and she demanded that I take it. I'll always remember this." Another student said, "I have formed relationships that I would have otherwise never sought. I was able to influence their lives in a small way just as they have influenced mine."

14.3.1.3 Cultural Competence. One aspect of learning across cultures involves intergenerational empathy, sensitivity, and friendship skills. Students need to experience comfort with people of backgrounds different than theirs. A student mused, "I learned a lot about the lives of people who are a couple of generations older than I. I learned about the history that these people experienced before I was even born!" Amber said, "Ideally, service-learning is a two-way street, with both student and client gaining." Rebecca stated, "Not only did students teach senior citizens, but the senior citizens were partners in showing us how the community needed a project like this. With each client, we spoke about our lives and experiences, and created a bond that provided a sense of trust and comfort in ways that transformed my thinking. Arsen and I exchanged school assignment problems and he told me about the woman he wanted to date. Joyann and I talked about our families and she explained where to go for the best shopping deals in town, while Chuck told me about his experience in World War II. I learned about my clients as people and went beyond our original relationship as teacher-client."

Nicole shared, "These six people and their life stories have changed the way I think about technology and they have changed me. Wherever I end up after graduation, I hope to find a program similar to ours to assist people in becoming better citizens and bettering themselves while opening my horizons about groups I incorrectly stereotype." One student summarized, "All of my experiences with clients showed that service-learning provides more than learning for students and a service to the community." Indeed, it is an opportunity for college students to increase knowledge and comfort with people different than themselves.

14.3.2 Commitment to Learning

Nearly one-fourth (23%) of the students reflected on their deliberate preparation for the lab experiences, including the importance of the role as tutor, as well as their awareness of building skills of the seniors with whom they worked. Most students in this study were not education majors, yet were committed to the pedagogy of the tutoring experiences as well as to the learning success of their senior partners. Adam stated, "In teaching the seniors I used many methods. When I first met with my senior partners, I got to know their hobbies in an attempt to mold their learning experience. With Lee, I used a parallel to golf, one of his passions. I told him that Internet explorer was like the cart, used to explore the course." Jake noted that many of his clients came with specific questions pertaining to their own computers and some of their own software. He said, "Mr. Cayom wanted to learn how to make a web page with Microsoft FrontPage© and even brought his unopened CD package to our first session. Luckily I could answer his questions." One senior asked for help with Internet and Photoshop, whereas others learned to use spreadsheets and Microsoft Office. Remarkably, students went beyond what was expected in the learning relationship. One student added, "In addition to the classes offered in the lab, I met with Priscilla once at her home to help her use her own computer." Kyle summarized, "Moreover, through the classes, the clients began understanding the value of computers and their impact on everyday life. Additionally, the appreciation for information technology grew. For example, Mr. Wong had no experience with computers. However, by attending this class, I was able to teach him simple skills so that he might navigate on his own in the future. No matter the experience or expertise of the clients, all were able to understand and value the skills, benefits, and disadvantages of computer and information technology."

14.3.3 Positive Values

Overall, students exhibited positive values toward interaction with the seniors and indicated intentions to continue volunteering. It was clear that this experience was not just about teaching technology to a group of elderly people. This was about getting in touch, connecting through a mutual medium (technology), and keeping in touch. One student said, "My client asked me about my hobbies." Kathryn said, "We keep in contact. I've e-mailed her and she emails back." Abby wrote, "An important role I played was to build her self-esteem through my encouragement." Rebecca declared, "The great thing about e-mail is that if my senior buddies have has future troubles with computers, they can reach me no matter where my career takes me after graduation!"

Jake said, "A very important part of the Digital Citizenship lab experience is relationships between student and client. It is crucial that students treat the senior citizens with the respect they deserve." Jason summed it up, "I feel as though I have a better understanding of a whole new population of people within the community I already live in." Adam realized he had a common bond with his client. Adam said, "I learned that Lewis was a member of Delta Sigma Pi, my business fraternity. One of our key teachings is to help a brother in need if they call upon you, to the best of your ability. He wanted to know how to use chat rooms and search engines. I started by teaching him about Yahoo, Ask.com, and Google. He found them easy to use so we proceeded to set up a profile on Yahoo so that he might chat for free. We chatted with different business people for the rest of the hour." Finally, Vern stated, "The bottom line is that service-learning is an amazing experience for anybody, and it's more than just teaching—it's improving lives."

14.4   CONCLUSIONS

Clearly, this case study found that college students experienced a sense of empowerment as participatory citizens in the greater campus community who were capable of closing the "gray gap" through technology assistance for senior citizens. Students were not only committed to closing the digital divide through technology tutoring, they better understood multiple issues influencing senior citizens and their technology literacy. The benefits were reciprocal. As students viewed themselves as citizens in their university community to assist others, the seniors themselves heightened their technological skills.

This study supports college student engagement in service-learning in order to build internal assets that empower them as citizens to build relationships between campus and community. Results show that students built social competencies through planning and decision making, interpersonal competence, and cultural competence—all aspects of engaged citizenship. Service-learning can influence emerging citizenship of university students and technological empowerment of seniors.

ACKNOWLEDGMENT

The author acknowledges Dr. Stuart Shulman, who was an assistant professor of Environmental Science and Policy at Drake University at the time of the service-learning Digital Citizenship course. Dr. Shulman, Principle Investigator, was instrumental in acquiring a National Science Foundation (NSF) grant for course development and research directing the project under NSF Award Number 0113718. He is a member of the NSF-funded Digital Government Organization. While at Drake, his research focused on the role of electronic rulemaking in citizen–government interaction. He can currently be reached at stu@polsci.umass.edu.

REFERENCES

1. Maxim, G. W. (2010). *Dynamic Social Studies for Constructivist Classrooms: Inspiring Tomorrow's Social Scientists* (9th ed.). Boston, MA: Allyn and Bacon.

2. Jacoby, B. (1996). "Service-learning in today's higher education." In B. Jacoby (Ed.), *Service-Learning in Higher Education: Concepts and Practices* (pp. 3–25). San Francisco, CA: Jossey-Bass.

3. Battistoni, R. M. (1997). "Service-Learning and Democratic Citizenship." *Theory into Practice,* Vol. 36, No. 3, 150–156.

4. Wilson, K., Wallin, J., and Reiser, C. (2003). "Social Stratification and the Digital Divide." *Social Science Computer Review,* Vol. 21,133–143.

5. Beisser, S. R. (1999). *Constructivist Environments Inviting Computer Technology for Problem Solving: New Junctures for Female Students.* Unpublished doctoral dissertation, Iowa State University, Ames, IA.

6. National Telecommunications and Information Administration. (2000). *Falling Through the Net: Toward Digital Inclusion.* Retrieved from http://search.ntia.doc.gov/pdf/fttn00.pdf.

7. National Telecommunications and Information Administration. (2002). *A Nation Online: How Americans are Expanding Their Use of the Internet.* Retrieved from http://www.ntia.doc.gov/ntiahome/dn/anationonline2.pdf.

8. UCLA Internet Report. (2000). *Surveying the Digital Future.* UCLA Center for Communication Policy. Retrieved from http://www.digitalcenter.org/pdf/InternetReportYear One.

9. Roblyer, M. D. (May 2000). "Digital Desperation: Reports on a Growing Technology and Equity Crisis." *Learning and Leading with Technology,* Vol. 27, No. 8, 50–53.

10. Wilhelm, A. G. (2000). *Democracy in the Digital Age: Challenges to Political Life in Cyberspace.* New York, NY: Routledge.

11. Lenhart, A. (2000). *Who's Not Online.* Retrieved from http://www.pcwinternet.org/Reports/2000/Whos-Not-Online.

12. Seiden, P. A. (2000, Summer). Bridging the Digital Divide. *Reference and User Services Quarterly,* 39(4), (accessed via "Infotrac" Expanded Academic Index Copyright © 2000, Gale).

13. Beisser, S. R., Shulman, S. W., and Larson, T. B. (Spring 2005). "Closing the Digital Divide with Service-Learning." *Academic Exchange Quarterly,* Vol. 9, No. 1, 31–36.

14. National Research Council. (1999). *Being Fluent with Information Technology.* Washington, DC: National Academy Press.

15. Beisser, S. R. (2002). "An Electronic Resource for Service-Learning: A Collaborative Project Between Higher Education and a State Department of Education." Paper presented at the 2002 American Educational Research Association Annual Meeting, New Orleans, LA.

16. Beisser, S. R., and Schmidt, D. (2001). "Service-Learning and Community-Based Teaching and Learning: Developing Citizenship through Social Action." In M. Christenson, M. Johnson, and J. Norris (Eds.), *Teaching Together: School and University Collaboration to Improve Social Studies Education* (pp. 31–38). Silver Spring, MD: National Council for the Social Studies.

17. Conrad, D. and Hedin, D. (June 1991). "School-Based Community Service: What We Know From Research and Theory." *Phi Delta Kappan,* Vol. 72, No. 10, 743–749.

18. Shulman, S. W., Beisser, S. R., Larson, T. B., Shelley, M. C., II, and Thrane, L. (2003). "Service-Learning and the Digital Divide." Paper presented at the International Conference on Civic Education Research, November 16–18, 2003, New Orleans, LA.

19. Muhr, T. (1997). *ATLAS.ti©* Short User's Guide. Berlin, Germany: Scientific Software Development.

20. Search Institute (1996). "The Updated Profiles Of Student Life: Attitudes and Behaviors—40 Development Assets Dataset." Retrieved from http://www.search-institute.org/research.

21. Lerner, R., and Benson, P. (Eds.) (2003). *Developmental Assets and Asset-Building Communities: Implications for Research, Policy, and Practice.* New York, NY: Kluwer Academic/Plenum Publishers.

22. Scales, P., and Leffert, N. (1999). *Developmental Assets: A Synthesis of the Scientific Research on Adolescent Development.* Minneapolis, MN: Search Institute.

APPENDIX A—CODING GUIDELINES 40 DEVELOPMENTAL ASSETS©*

The Search Institute has developed the following building blocks of healthy development that help young people grow up healthy, caring, and responsible. From the Internal Asset list, the reflection papers were analyzed. Those defined as External Assets (e.g.; family, school, and community backgrounds or individual experiences) could not be identified in the service learning lab reflection papers from university students.

Internal Assets			
General asset category	Asset #	Name of asset	Description of behavior in the reflection paper that service-learning reflects the asset descriptor
Commitment to learning	21	Achievement motivation	Motivated to do well in school (shows motivation to do well in the service activity or general studies at the university level)
	22	"School" engagement	Actively engaged in learning (shows participatory engagement in service-learning lab)
	23	Homework	Does 1 hr+ of homework daily (an expectation of college level academics-but unobserved here)
	24	Bonding to school	Cares about his/her school (shows attachment to service-learning)

*Reflection Papers from Service Learning Lab. Adapted from the ©1998 Search Institute, 700 S. Third St., Ste 210 Minneapolis, MN 55415.

Internal Assets			
General asset category	Asset #	Name of asset	Description of behavior in the reflection paper that service-learning reflects the asset descriptor
Commitment to learning (*cont.*)	25	Reading for pleasure	Reads for please 3+ hrs per week (unable to be determined in the reflection paper)
Positive values	26	Caring	Places high value on helping other people (indication of valuing the service)
	27*	Equality and social justice	Places high value on promoting equality (relates value in reducing inequities)
	28	Integrity	Acts on convictions and stands up for his or her beliefs (reports on convictions)
	29	Honesty	Tells the truth when it is not easy (indicates honesty as important to decision making)
	30	Responsibility	Accepts and takes responsibility (shows responsibility or initiative in service to seniors)
	31	Restraint	Important to not be sexually active or on drugs (not revealed in these papers)
Social competencies	32	Planning and decision making	Knows how to plan and make choices (shows planning for the service experiences with the senior citizens with whom they worked and tutored)
	33	Interpersonal competence	Empathy, sensitivity, friendship skills (shows empathy, sensitivity, friendliness to seniors—seniors reciprocation of kindness, etc, back to the students)
	34*	Cultural competence (with regard to age)	Knowledge or comfort with people of different cultural/racial/ethnic backgrounds (shows knowledge and comfort with cultural/racial/ethnic or elderly citizens or people different than themselves)
	35	Resistance skills	Resist negative peer pressure and dangerous situations (not observed in these papers)
	36	Peaceful conflict resolution	Seeks to resolve conflict nonviolently (if conflict IS reported, has a positive outlook)
Positive identity	37	Personal power	Feels they have control over "what happens to me" (shares a feeling of personal control or power in the service activity with the senior citizens)

(continues)

Internal Assets			
General asset category	Asset #	Name of asset	Description of behavior in the reflection paper that service-learning reflects the asset descriptor
Violet	38	Self-esteem	Reports a high level of self-esteem (reveals or indicates positive self-esteem)
	39	Sense of purpose	Reports that "my life has a purpose" (shows service as purposeful in the present or the future)
	40	Positive view of personal future	Optimistic about her/her personal future (shows optimism in future life or service to others in their future experiences—sense of reciprocity)

CHAPTER 15

HYBRIDIZING VIRTUAL AND FIELD-BASED SERVICE-LEARNING IN GREEN IT

K. Branker and J. M. Pearce

ABSTRACT

Historically, service-learning (SL) projects can be classified two ways: (1) collaborations with a community group or nonprofit organization to provide specific problem solving around a community need, or (2) an internship-like experience with industry to address work requested by a client (e.g., in engineering service-learning). The limitation of both of these traditional SL approaches is that they do not prepare students to implement unprescribed projects. In contrast, in this chapter a pedagogical experiment is outlined in which students chose both the project and the partner for a self-directed SL experience. This chapter presents the findings of an ongoing investigation of this novel pedagogical exercise in which students acted as change agents for industry by implementing unsolicited energy-conservation measures (ECMs) in order to improve the organizations' environmental and economic performance. The ECMs were largely focused on green information technology (IT), but could be applied to any form of environmentally beneficial technical or behavioral change. The hybrid SL projects described had both virtual and field-work SL components. For the virtual component, the Appropedia Foundation provided an open-source education tool on Appropedia.org for the project so that faculty anywhere in the world can have free access. The student teams developed and published open-source ECM calculators on Appropedia.org, which is a free, open-source, wiki-based tool for collaborative solutions in such areas as sustainability, poverty reduction, and international development. For the field-work component, the teams self-selected industry clients and performed energy audits and IT audits. Applicable ECMs, which had been developed during the virtual component of the project, were then selected and tailored, forming the basis of recommendations to the organizations. The results of this pedagogical exercise not only resulted in overwhelming positive responses from the client organizations and verbal or written commitments to improve their performance following the recommendations of the students, but they also demonstrated the effectiveness of such hybrid SL projects in terms of improving student motivation, learning, and quality of work.

15.1   INTRODUCTION

It is well established that linking community service and academic work strengthens both [1]. Thus, "experience-based education creates a powerful learning environment, which results in new educational outcomes" [2], and such education can be facilitated by service-learning (SL). There is a vast amount of literature evidencing the positive outcomes of SL for students, faculty, educational institutions, and community partners [3–5]. For example, service-learning has beneficial impacts on students' academic learning, course-objective development, moral development, and ability to apply academic knowledge to real-world applications [6, 7]. Students are, therefore, the largest benefactors as they gain increased motivation, better academic outcomes, and real-world experiences [5–12].

Traditional service-learning projects can be classified as: (1) collaborations with a community group or nonprofit organization (NPO) to provide specific engineering design or construction to meet a specific need, or (2) an internship-like experience with industry in which students provide requested work for a client. That is, in traditional SL approaches, students are assigned projects, which are commissioned by the supporting organization. Typically, traditional SL projects involve structured fieldwork in physical locations. More recently, these types of projects have also been completed at a distance, or *virtually*, by students, through the use of the Internet and software (see first row of Table 15.1). Although such SL projects enjoy the benefits listed above, the clear limitation of both of these traditional approaches is that they do not prepare students to implement projects in industry that are not prescribed (i.e., where the identification of the project or problem is determined by the student). This is a problem,

Table 15.1. Traditional versus self-directed service-learning

	Physical location	Virtual location
Traditional (assigned) SL	Field work + commissioned	Web/software + commissioned
Self-directed SL	Field work + uncommissioned	Web/software + uncommissioned

particularly for environmental issues, because they are often periphery problems not given adequate attention from management even when economically profitable [11]. In contrast, this chapter presents the findings for a novel pedagogical approach that allows for self-directed SL (e.g., the second row of Table 15.1). Specifically, this inquiry represents a hybrid approach, in which students (a) create open-source energy conservation measure (ECM) calculators to improve the environmental and economic performance of organizations in general, and then (b) recruit specific organizations and act as change agents by providing audits and recommendations for unsolicited appropriate ECMs. Consequently, the projects contained a hybridization of virtual and field-based engineering service-learning. For the virtual SL component, students created products that are openly available on the Web, whereas for the field-based SL portion, students engaged in field work with organizations. These projects were not commissioned or solicited by organizations; rather, students chose which ECMs to develop, the method to develop them, and the organizations in which to study them (i.e., self-directed SL). Examples of such SL projects were integrated into a fourth-year mechanical engineering elective called Engineering for Sustainable Development. These projects focused on ECMs related to green information technology and systems (IT/S), which refers to software and hardware initiatives to address energy efficiency and improve the organization's ecological impact or environmental footprint.

This chapter is a continued investigation of a virtual and field-hybrid SL project [13]. First, the structure of the project is outlined. Then the results are presented and discussed, and conclusions are drawn regarding the effectiveness of such SL projects for both improving environmental performance and engineering pedagogy.

15.2 SERVICE-LEARNING PROJECTS STUDIED

Organizations are beginning to look beyond short-term economic indicators as their sole focus and instead focus on the triple bottom line of financial, social, and environmental outcomes [14]. It is also becoming increasingly apparent that environmental responsibility can support organizations' financial goals, particularly for energy-consuming businesses [15]. Thus, businesses are under increasing pressure to address issues related to global sustainability, especially environmental responsibility [16], and one of the areas that is being explored is IT/S, because of its relatively fast growth. In the context of a fourth-year university engineering course, the SL project entailed using service-learning in studying and utilizing IT/S resources to address the two business issues of financial and environmental performance.

The SL project was designed to be accomplished by engineering students using a combined approach of both service-learning and commissioned assignments [12, 17]. This type of project complements established engineering design programs because of the focus on students performing interdisciplinary research to find solutions to environmental problems. As described earlier, it has proven extremely motivational for students and is associated with positive learning outcomes [3, 12, 18]. For the projects, students were organized into groups of five, allowing audits to be performed for eight companies. The SL projects were broken down into five parts, as summarized in Figure 15.1.

As can be seen in Figure 15.1, Parts 1–4 were student tasks and Part 5 was completed by a representative of the client company. Parts 1 and 2 represent virtual service-learning objectives, whereas Parts 3–5 represent service-learning objectives that occurred in a physical (field-based) organizational location.

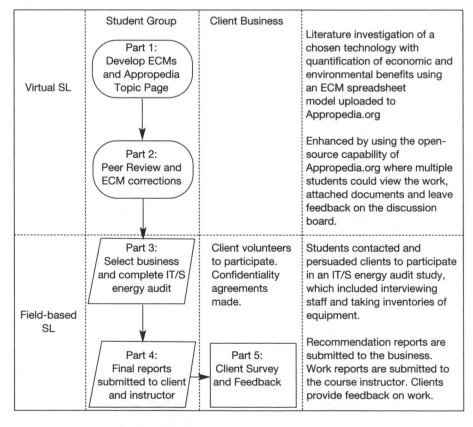

Figure 15.1. Summary of service-learning components of self-directed SL project.

In the SL projects, students developed ECMs and then acted as change agents for industry by auditing recruited organizations and recommending unsolicited ECMs to improve the organizations' environmental and economic performance. These initiatives ranged from incremental techniques (e.g., replacing laptops with more energy-efficient models) to more innovative solutions (e.g., using solar photovoltaic electricity to power data centers). Prior to student involvement, templates for the projects were designed by a multidisciplinary team made up of representatives from economics, engineering, environmental studies, and management information systems [19]. For the virtual SL component, student teams chose and researched a topic and developed an ECM spreadsheet calculator that would evaluate the economic and environmental impact of the ECM. These ECMs were then reviewed to ensure quality and accuracy, and open sourced on Appropedia.org. For the field-based SL component, the student teams performed basic IT/S audits of participating organizations, highlighting areas that would benefit most from recommended ECMs.

15.2.1   Virtual Service Learning

Parts 1 and 2 of the projects entailed using Appropedia.org as a repository and collaboration tool. Appropedia.org is a free wiki-based tool developed by the Appropedia Foundation for collaborative solutions in such areas as sustainability, poverty reduction, and international development. It can be used for SL especially geared toward applied sustainability [20]. As a group collaboration tool, multiple users can contribute (as with a team) on different sections and the wiki file-manager interface allows for the spreadsheet model to be uploaded with a record of changes made and work to be done for other team members. Electronic time stamps and signatures are used, providing a valuable historical record of how students contributed to the work outcome for grading purposes. Lastly, a discussion page, attached to the main page, allows for peers to review the work and make comments and suggestions to improve their work. Collaborators globally could comment as well. Thus, instead of the traditional classroom, in which assignments and projects are generally undertaken for grades and likely unused thereafter, Appropedia enables the work to be part of a useful knowledge database [20] to enable any organization to improve the energy efficiency of their IT/S.

To prepare for the projects, Appropedia template pages and ECM spreadsheet templates were available on the main project website (http://www.appropedia.org/Mech425_GreenIT_Project). The following were pre-designed ECMS:

1. Double-sided printing (saving paper over single-side printing)
2. More efficient printers (e.g., Energy Star for energy savings)

3. Power bars/smart strips (reduces wasted energy with automatic shut-offs, etc.)

4. Substituting digital videoconferencing (DVC) and document sharing for travel

5. Solar photovoltaic power (as cleaner energy source for data centers)

Students were given the opportunity to choose their own project from the lists below or develop a completely novel ECM from both hardware- or software-based topics.

Hardware-based topics:
- Carbon management systems. (Used to improve performance via monitoring of greenhouse gas emissions.)
- Cartridge-free printers and copiers (Waste reduction encourages use of printers and copiers that have ink without physical containment, e.g., Xerox ColorQube.)
- Consolidated printers/copiers/faxes/scanners. (Reduces the number of electronics and energy use via multifunction equipment.)
- Cleaning up storage: disk cleanup, defragment, and so on. (More efficient file storage reduces processing time and reduces overall energy use.)
- Consolidation of data center hardware. (Reduce energy use in data centers.)
- Document-management systems. (Replacement of paper-based communications that are often couriered.)
- Energy-efficient monitors. (Energy reduction compared to existing equipment.)
- Energy-efficient PC/workstations. (Energy reduction compared to existing equipment.)
- Environmental management systems. (Used to manage overall environmental impact of the company, including the IT department.)
- Linear fluorescent retrofit (uppgrading to T8 from T12). (Lighting retrofit for energy reduction.)
- Motion-sensor-controlled vending machines. (Energy reduction compared to existing equipment.)
- Move from thick-client to thin-client computers. (Energy reduction compared to existing equipment.)
- Phantom power reducing power bars. (Reduces wasted energy in idling or inactive equipment.)
- Power-off copiers. (Energy reduction compared to existing equipment.)

- Recycle eWaste and donation (end of life). (Product responsibility at end of life of electronics.)
- Replace incandescent light bulbs with CFL. (Energy reduction compared to existing equipment.)
- Telecommuting. (Energy reduction compared to existing equipment.)
- Turning off lights, motion sensors. (Energy reduction compared to existing equipment.)
- Use of rechargeable batteries. (Waste reduction compared to buying more batteries.)

Software-based topics:
- Automatic shut-down (off) of computers, monitors, and hardware. (Energy reduction compared to existing settings.)
- Electronic document collaboration. (Using electronic document sharing and communication as a paperless option.)
- Energy-efficient software. (Software and metering for efficient management of energy use in IT and buildings.)
- Energy monitoring. (Improve performance by monitoring and analyzing energy use and patterns.)
- Online training. (As opposed to the need for travel and physical class space and resources.)
- Putting screens and computers on standby. (Energy reduction through timers.)
- Server virtualization. (The use of one physical server divided into multiple isolated virtual environments allows more efficient resource management.)
- Virtualization of data center. (Using server virtualization in data centers.)

On the wiki, students chose their project topics, updates were made, and their questions were answered. Projects were categorized and monitored by the course instructor and teaching assistants. Resources were also made available to help with background information on engineering economics and green IT. To ensure that external parties did not edit the work in progress, the template code {{425inprogress|Month Day, Year}} was designed by the course instructor. Using this code on a wiki page (pasted into the script) resulted in a box with the heading "MECH 425 Project Page in Progress" at the top of the given project page with a message not to alter the page if it was external to the project group, but to leave comments on the discussion page.

After choosing a specific green IT technology, system, or methodology, students created a topic page wherein they presented a literature review on the subject, explaining the economic and environmental benefits and how they would incorporate them into an ECM Excel spreadsheet model. Conducting the background research allowed the students to better understand the topic from different perspectives (i.e., financial and technological) and provided references for assumptions and key data used in the ECM calculators. The ECMs were structured similarly to financial investments, such that the costs, savings, and environmental benefits had to be evaluated and quantified. For example, using a more energy-efficient printer would require an investment to purchase it, but the returns would include reduced energy used, resulting in lower electricity costs and greenhouse gas emissions. Thus, in the ECM spreadsheet models, students were able to utilize simple payback, internal rate of return (IRR), and net present value (NPV) as economic measures to evaluate the proposed projects. A simple payback represents the time taken for the project to recover the investment. The IRR is often used to compare investments and is the discount rate at which the net present value of all cash flows (costs and benefits) equal zero. The net present value is the sum of the present values of all cash flows, using the discount rate to convert future cash flows. Finally, the discount rate (like an interest rate) represents an organization's time preference for money. Thus, a positive discount rate indicated preference for money today over the future, and the higher it is, the more the preference is to the present. Quantifiable environmental benefits were mainly due to reduced emissions (from electricity reduction) and conserved trees (by reducing paper use), although other benefits were also mentioned. Students were graded on the communication (adequate description of the topic), presentation (clarity and flow), and accuracy (appropriate citations and thoroughness) of their submissions. Further, students were asked to peer review another group's work. The discussion page on the project wiki enabled this feedback, and signed time stamps assisted in tracking the contributions. Students were graded on the usefulness of their peer reviews and were given the opportunity to incorporate feedback from the reviews into their ECMs before grading. The ECMs created were to be used by various groups for Parts 3 and 4, which meant that the work had to be correct and understandable for all other students. In addition, since the ECMs were to be made available worldwide in the public domain, students were held to a higher standard than might be used in traditional course assignments. In total, thirteen ECM calculators were developed (some teams created more than one ECM for their topic) and approved for use by the eight student teams.

15.2.2 Field-Based Service-Learning

Parts 3 and 4 entailed SL objectives at a physical location where student teams undertook green IT audits at participating companies of various kinds, both public and private (field work). As a precursor to this, students had to identify a company that would be interested in this work and obtain the appropriate consents from company representatives. The volunteering companies tended to have a vision to increase environmentally responsible behaviors in general, but faced implementation challenges. Students performed energy and IT/S audits at the participating company facilities, focusing on the IT/S resources, but also considering other ECMs applicable to the company. Students were required to use at least two of the thirteen available ECM models created by the class or the research team.

Once at the organizational sites, students performed audits. They used surveys, conducted interviews, collated appliance specifications, and used electricity and solar-resource-measuring equipment to obtain the data required for inputs to potential ECMs and to improve assumptions and default values in the ECMs. They also collected important information regarding the company's current and proposed sustainability goals, current initiatives and past implementations, and sustainability program information. All data were collected with signed consent from company representatives.

The final stage of the project for the students involved the preparation of two reports: a recommendation report for the company and a work report for the course instructor. The recommendation report detailed the recommended ECMs, with economic and environmental justifications for each ECM. Students also indicated implementation considerations and potential behavioral changes required for certain initiatives. All assumptions and limitations were addressed and summarized calculations were presented. The work report provided a brief overview of the company and its green initiatives, all measurements made and data collected by the students (including surveys), why the specific ECMs were chosen, and an assessment as to whether the company was a good candidate for future work. A reflection on whether learning objectives were met and the overall project experience were also included.

Following completion of the students' work, a client survey was distributed by the course teaching assistant to each participating company. Clients were asked to comment on the professionalism of the students, general evaluation of the recommendations made (including limitations and improvements), and their desire to continue participation in the green IT research.

15.3   OUTCOMES OF THE STUDENT IT/S PROJECTS

Both virtual and field-based service components of the SL project were successful from both implementation and education perspectives.

15.3.1 Virtual Service-Learning Work

Appropedia.org provided an effective platform for collaboration, allowing students to contribute useful tools for society and providing records of student contributions. In particular, students were able to produce a working advanced spreadsheet and Appropedia.org topic page, and demonstrated evidence of collaboration and peer review via history of student pages. The virtual SL enabled the topic pages and ECMs to be publicly accessible to anyone. Because the students' work contributed to an online knowledge base, unlike traditional assignments, there seemed to be a greater sense of responsibility and commitment to their work that motivated most teams to exceed expectations. Table 15.2 shows the number of views each of the various pages received during the four-month period of the course, and then 13 months later. Given that individual groups made between 50 and 150 edits, the number of views shows that these pages and the associated ECMs were accessed by many more individuals than just the immediate project team. These projects are thus clearly viewed more than traditional projects (which would generally be viewed only by individuals associated with the course and a partner organization). In addition, it is interesting to note that the more popular project pages viewed online tended to be the projects that were also popular with clients, such as lighting retrofits, energy mentoring, and motion-sensor-controlled vending machines. This might have been due to ease of implementation and/or novelty of the given energy conservation topic.

Although some students naturally contribute more than others, a common problem in group work is the occurrence of freeloaders who obtain, with little cost or effort, the benefit of grades earned by industrious members of the

Table 15.2. Summary of views of SL project pages on Appropedia at end of semester of course and a year later

Appropedia page name	Number of views		Ratio of June 2011 to May 2010
	May 14, 2010	June 20, 2011	
Main course green IT page	2832	3922	1.4
Collaborating documents electronically	522	972	1.9
Energy monitoring	1044	2092	2.0
Energy-efficient PC/workstations (3 ECMs)	751	1558	2.1
Linear fluorescent retrofit (upgrading to T8 from T12)	923	3204	3.5
Motion-sensor-controlled vending machines	1039	2763	2.7
Phantom-power-reducing power bars	681	1734	2.5
Server virtualization	666	1333	2.0
Telecommuting	709	1575	2.2

group. This challenge was addressed in a number of ways. The time stamp and signature features and the ability to see the page-edit history in Appropedia were a means of monitoring the level of contribution of each student. These features were highlighted for the students in order to actively discourage freeloading. Because students were aware of this monitoring, there was evidence of reasonable contribution from all group members. Figure 15.2 shows a screen shot of the edit history of a page on Appropedia where two versions can be compared and the frequency and authorship of edits can be found. Figures 15.3a and b show an example of comparisons chosen. In Figure 15.3a, the category tag in wiki-markup language has been added by one of the coauthors in order to put the page in the category of "Green IT". Thus, when Appropedia users search for "Green IT" the page "Phantom power reducing power bars" will be listed as one of the topics. In Figure 15.3b, the second author has added in some text and a reference for a given paragraph. Figure 15.4 shows the result of using the custom wiki template for the project pages to ensure that there were no edits for the public external to the group or premature usage of the information. Finally, Figure 15.5 shows a peer review on a discussion page with the signature and time stamp features.

Each ECM spreadsheet calculator had the following sheets:

- Introduction: ECM overview, disclaimer
- Inputs: User inputs required for analysis
- Executive Summary: Summary of financial and environmental savings projection, including net present value (NPV), internal rate of return (IRR), payback, emissions reduction, tree use (paper) and so on (see Figure 15.3)

Figure 15.2. Tool to enable comparing edit history of pages.

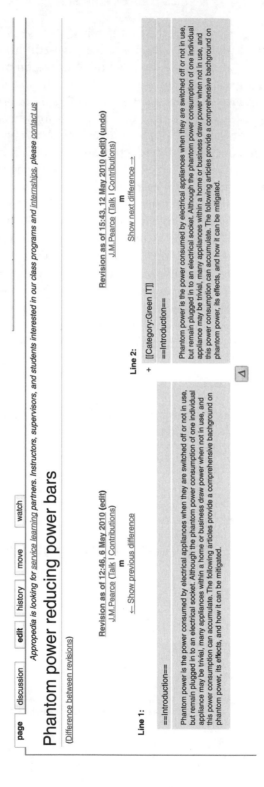

Figure 15.3a. Comparing two versions of a page using the edit history of a page.

322

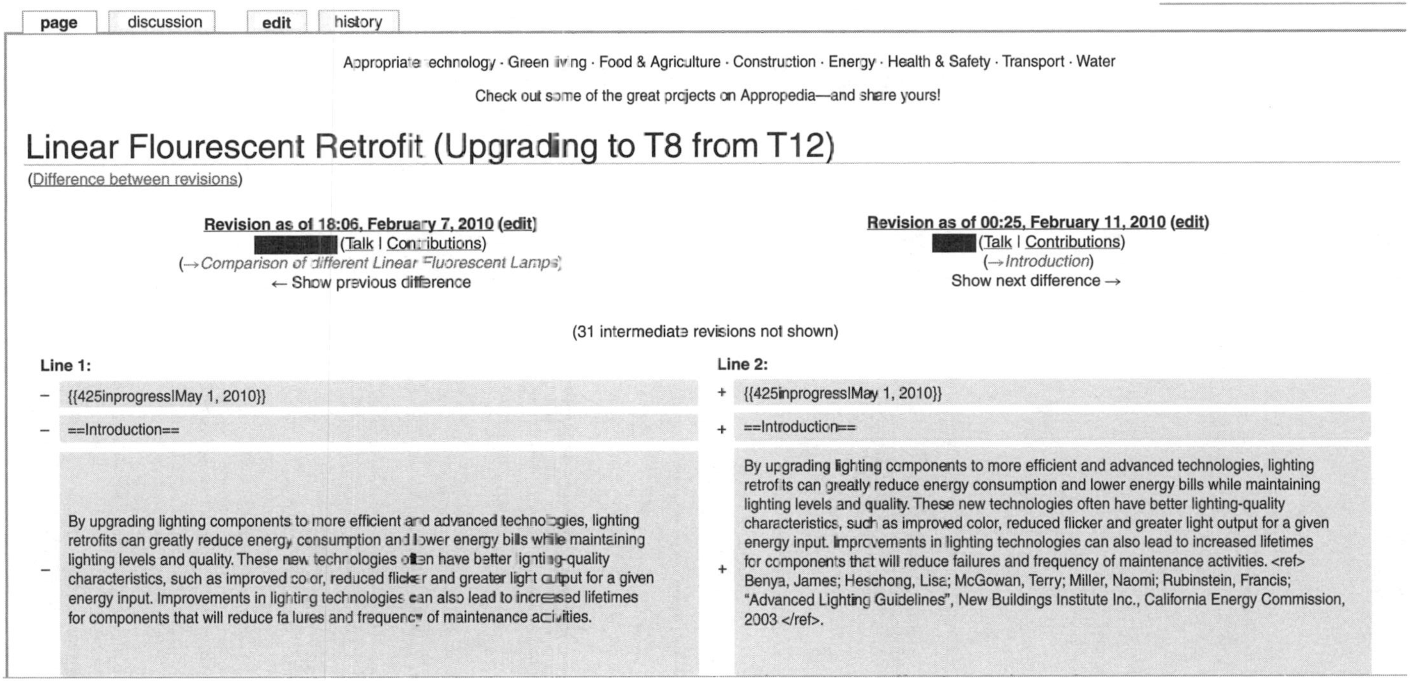

page | discussion | edit | history

Appropriate technology · Green living · Food & Agriculture · Construction · Energy · Health & Safety · Transport · Water

Check out some of the great projects on Appropedia—and share yours!

Linear Flourescent Retrofit (Upgrading to T8 from T12)

(Difference between revisions)

Revision as of 18:06, February 7, 2010 (edit)
░░░░ (Talk | Contributions)
(→ *Comparison of different Linear Fluorescent Lamps*)
← Show previous difference

Revision as of 00:25, February 11, 2010 (edit)
░░░░ (Talk | Contributions)
(→*Introduction*)
Show next difference →

(31 intermediate revisions not shown)

Line 1:

− {{425inprogress|May 1, 2010}}

− ==Introduction==

−

By upgrading lighting components to more efficient and advanced technologies, lighting retrofits can greatly reduce energy consumption and lower energy bills while maintaining lighting levels and quality. These new technologies often have better lighting-quality characteristics, such as improved color, reduced flicker and greater light output for a given energy input. Improvements in lighting technologies can also lead to increased lifetimes for components that will reduce failures and frequency of maintenance activities.

Line 2:

+ {{425inprogress|May 1, 2010}}

+ ==Introduction==

+

By upgrading lighting components to more efficient and advanced technologies, lighting retrofits can greatly reduce energy consumption and lower energy bills while maintaining lighting levels and quality. These new technologies often have better lighting-quality characteristics, such as improved color, reduced flicker and greater light output for a given energy input. Improvements in lighting technologies can also lead to increased lifetimes for components that will reduce failures and frequency of maintenance activities. <ref> Benya, James; Heschong, Lisa; McGowan, Terry; Miller, Naomi; Rubinstein, Francis; "Advanced Lighting Guidelines", New Buildings Institute Inc., California Energy Commission, 2003 </ref>.

Figure 15.3b. Comparing two versions of a page using the edit history of a page.

MECH425 Project Page in Progress

This page is a project page in progress by students in Mech425. Please refrain from making edits unless you are a member of the project team, but feel free to make comments using the discussion tab. Check back for the finished version on May 1, 2010.

Figure 15.4. Result of putting in the custom template wiki code {{425inprogress|May 1, 2010}}. This appears at the top of every project page and the code is visible in Figure 15.3b.

- Project Savings: All calculation analysis including transparent calculation methods
- Assumptions and Sources: Citations for sourced information and assumptions used

With most team members actively engaged in the projects, there was an opportunity for peer-to-peer learning. One area in which this was most apparent was in respect to the students' expertise in using spreadsheets. As students worked to create comprehensive and transparent ECM calculators, course instructors and teaching assistants observed them improving their spreadsheet skills. The open-source nature of the ECMs uploaded to Appropedia meant that students could view each other's work and adopt best practices. Higher-level skills, like the use of conditional sorting, macros, and drop-down lists, which were originally used by some groups, were later adopted by others. Figure 15.6 demonstrates a drop-down list feature used in one ECM calculator that enables the user to choose between options. Again, because the calculators were transparent, the user could add additional items to the option repository for the drop-down list as needed. Figure 15.7 illustrates the Executive Summary page in one of the ECMs with a well-defined layout. Figure 15.8 shows how equations and citations were made apparent

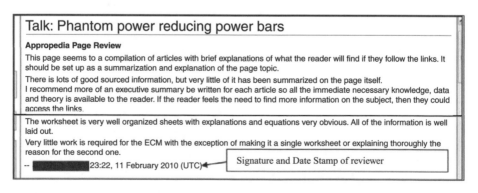

Figure 15.5. Topic page peer review on the discussion page.

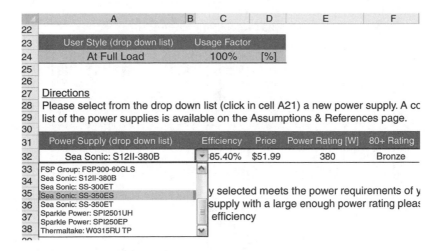

Figure 15.6. Exhibit of higher-level spreadsheet functions. Drop-down list enables users to choose between various options.

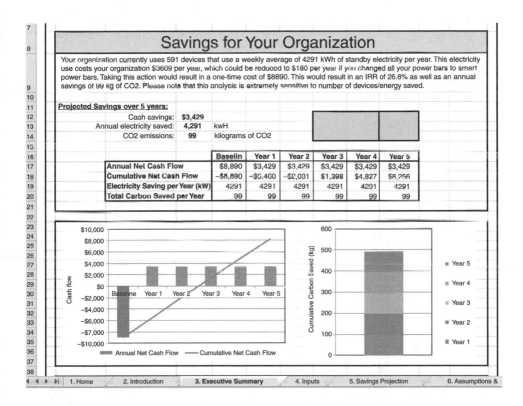

Figure 15.7. Layout of a portion of an ECM executive summary page summarizing the results of the ECM calculations. The tabs indicate the different pages in the ECM calculator.

Projected Savings

	Calculation	Baseline	Year 1	Year 2
No Change in Double-Sided Printing				
Number of impressions printed	A	100,000	100,000	100,000
Continuing current frequency of double-sided print jobs	B	10%	10%	10%
Number of sheets from single-sided print jobs	$C = A \cdot (1 - B)$	90,000	90,000	90,000
Total impressions set to double-sided	$D = A \cdot B$	10,000	10,000	10,000
Double-sided effectiveness (Note4)	E	50%	50%	50%
Number of single-sided sheets printed for double-sided jobs	$F = D \cdot (1 - E)$	5,000	5,000	5,000
Number of double-sided sheets printed for double-sided jobs	$G = 0.5 \cdot (D \cdot E)$	2,500	2,500	2,500
Total number of sheets used	$H = C + F + G$	97,500	97,500	97,500
Percentage of sheets used relative to number of impressions printed	$H/A \cdot 100$	97.5%	97.5%	97.5%
Estimated annual paper savings %	$1 \cdot (H/A \cdot 100)$	2.5%	2.5%	2.5%
Increase in Double-Sided Printing				
Estimated % of double-sided print jobs	I	10%	70%	70%
Number of sheets from single-sided print jobs	$J = A \cdot (1 - I)$	90,000	30,000	30,000
Total impressions set to double-sided	$K = A \cdot I$	10,000	70,000	70,000
Number of single-sided sheets printed for double-sided jobs (Note4)	$L = K \cdot (1 - E)$	5,000	35,000	35,000
Number of double-sided sheets printed for double-sided jobs (Note4)	$M = 0.5 \cdot (K \cdot E)$	2,500	17,500	17,500
Total sheets used	$N = J + L + M$	97,500	82,500	82,500
Percentage of sheets used relative to number of impressions printed	$N/A \cdot 100$	97.5%	82.5%	82.5%
Number of sheets saved by increasing double sided printing	$O = H \cdot N$	0	15,000	15,000
Cumulative # of sheets of paper saved by increasing double sided printing	—	0	15,000	15,000
Estimated annual paper savings %	$1 \cdot (N/A \cdot 100)$	2.5%	17.5%	17.5%
Cost of a single sheet of paper	P	$.0.010	$0.0101	$0.010

2. Introduction | 3. Executive Summary | 4. Input Page | 5. Projected Savings | 6. As…

Figure 15.8. Layout of a portion of an ECM project-savings page showing the citations and formulas used in the ECM calculations.

on the Projected Savings page so that users could understand the underlying methodology of the calculations.

15.3.2   Field Service-Learning Work

Eight companies participated in the field work (the number dictated by the number of teams). Companies, both private and public, of various sizes (market capitalization), from single branches to multiple branches (local, regional and/or international), represented various industry sectors, including services, technology (engineering), manufacturing, telecommunications, hotel and hospitality, and public service. Company experience with green initiatives also varied.

Overall reflections on the project suggest that the field SL method motivated students to demonstrate high commitment, with some students going beyond course expectations. This was evident in student feedback and demonstrated by students completing more work than required for the course objectives. Only one group used the minimum two ECMs for the field work, whereas the other seven teams recommended three or more to their client organizations. Many groups performed additional calculations in order to recommend initiatives tailored to their organization. One group went as far as conducting the analysis using all thirteen ECMs before evaluating which created the greatest impact for the company in terms of energy-consumption reduction. Students commented that their project work felt like a real industry job and that they believed they were actually contributing to being change agents.

All participating companies remarked that the project was a good initiative and valued the recommendations of the student teams, which represented an outside academic source. With the exception of one financially constrained client, all companies offered to participate in future studies. With most companies based in a city with a community sustainability plan, there seemed to be heightened interest to meet sustainability goals. Companies with regional and international operations (half of the companies) indicated that they would consider piloting the recommendations locally before expanding them to their entire organization, as proper evaluations and protocol had to be followed. The major limitations of the study were time and resources. Since there were only thirteen ECMs developed, the range of available initiatives was limited. Further, since the focus was on green IT, most applications were in service industries and within specific departments in these organizations. Thus, as one company indicated, green IT alone would not meet its aggressive energy reduction target. Finally, the client organizations stated that they would prefer a longer period of time spent on conducting the audit, plus a follow-up with a future study. In this case, the academic semester structure of the course was a constraint. Table 15.3 summarizes some of the general feedback from the clients.

15.4 LESSONS FROM THE SL PROJECT

The results recorded from conducting the projects can be used to draw useful benefits and lessons for further improvement of the hybrid service-learning concept.

15.4.1 ECM Development—Virtual Service-Learning Work

In general, developing realistic ECM calculators is a nontrivial task. However, the open-source platform of Appropedia enabled rapid notification of edits and corrections that needed to be made. In addition, using a collaborative online platform is not unlike software used in industry. Although general templates were created, there was still considerable freedom for student innovation in developing ECMs. Some technical difficulties were encountered during the course, such as the use of different versions of the spreadsheet software, which tended to corrupt some of the files. This was managed by assessing and correcting the flaws in the file and using a more robust file-upload interface that could be linked to Appropedia. In the future, it is recommended that a standard open-source data processor be used, such as those available in Open Office [21]. As this was an initial attempt at constructing ECMs, significant learning occurred and the resulting development provided a ledger of improvements that can be applied to provide better templates and ECMs in the future.

Table 15.3. Summary of common organization feedback

Client statement	Number*†	Percentage
Professional	7	100%
Liked the project	7	100%
Would continue the work	7	100%
Wanted a follow-up presentation	3	43%
Foresee cost as an issue to implementation	3	43%
Foresee technical difficulty in implementation	3	43%
Students should spend more time on site	1	14%
Recommendations not sufficient to meet company targets	1	14%

Notes: *One client did not complete the survey.
†The sample size is not large enough for statistical analysis.

This project enabled a useful application of the basics of engineering economics, not just from a business point of view in project evaluation, but also as a tool in sustainability. Although basic engineering economics is covered in another fourth-year engineering course, many students lacked an understanding of fundamental concepts and calculations, and were unsure of how to apply them in real-world projects. This was an initial hurdle to developing the ECMs. Another difficulty from an engineering perspective was determining realistic assumptions for business inputs, such as utility pricing, which differ by commercial size, labor costs, inflation estimates, risk-free rate of return, capital-cost allowance, financial leveraging considerations, and so on. Students were encouraged to improve ECMs used in the audits through interviews with the clients to ensure that assumptions were appropriate. Overall, this project forced students out of their comfort zone in engineering to think about what motivates businesses and what sorts of presentations and discussion would be needed to promote their chosen ECMs.

15.4.2 Field-Service Learning Work

Students developed several useful skills and learned important procedural protocols through their participation in the field work. This project was designed to provide students with the opportunity to add a vital skill set and knowledge base to their present degrees. The audits strengthened their basic understanding of energy, electricity, and applied sustainability. Also, students learned to work with rate equations, basic life-cycle analysis, cost–benefit analysis, and managerial economics. The lessons can be broadly classified into ethics, business interactions, and technical and safety issues, three areas generally not taught in the classroom.

In addition to ensuring proper citations for references in their work, ethical lessons included navigating social-science-based research practices such as acquiring permissions from the clients for conducting the work and collecting data, ensuring client confidentiality, and preparing value-added reports for clients in a professional manner.

In terms of business interactions, securing an appropriate client proved to be a challenge for some student teams and highlighted the importance of industry experience, networking, and communication. This is different from other SL projects on campus that find clients for the students. In addition, in dealing with the companies, students gained an understanding of company protocol in terms of internal turnaround time needed for acquiring permissions, sustainability programs, visitor procedures, and business organizational structures. Interviews taught students what considerations are important to a business for choosing viable projects, including the concept of using debt financing to improve the return on an investment. In general, students gained an understanding of how they would need to communicate and promote their green initiatives from technological, environmental, and financial viewpoints.

Students were astonished by the level of sustainable initiatives already being undertaken by some companies. They were also surprised by what drove the implementation of green initiatives in a number of organizations: three of the clients indicated that financial metrics were not the main motivation for implementation, but, rather, environmental benefits drove initiatives.

Companies voluntarily participated in the study to enhance their sustainability goals and to help overcome current roadblocks with green implementations. As mentioned previously, there was a range of companies in terms of industry sector, market capitalization, and experience with green initiatives. Companies with multiple facilities could scale up benefits so that they would be more beneficial. Moreover, companies with larger IT/S or device use, such as those in the services and hospitality industries, benefited more from the green IT initiatives developed. Thus, students gained a realistic view of corporate social responsibility in regard to the environment.

Students acted as change agents to improve the environmental and economic performance of companies. The company-selection process provided some insights into the challenges of implementing ECM initiatives. For example, students found that companies leasing offices often had no control over their energy use (utilities were included in the rent). This is a hurdle, since green IT projects present both an economic and environmental impact. From an economic standpoint, investing in technology to reduce environmental footprints through the ECMs requires some sort of return. However, if the utilities are included in the rent, a company cannot offset the initial financial investment—the cost of energy would not change if the landlord did not choose to share the savings. Realizing this drawback, one company indicated that it was considering renegotiating its leases or finding new offices where they could separately control their utility bills. Another company declined participation in the project as their management anticipated that the initiatives would not have any financial impact because the energy bills were unavailable to them. This is a lesson of paramount importance to sustainability initiatives and indicates the need for information transparency and a more direct connection between the energy companies use and who is responsible for payment.

Finally, the technical learning objectives achieved during the SL project included using equipment to do basic energy audits, using engineering economics for a real project, and applying conventional measurement skills with proper data-acquisition methodologies. The importance of safety was emphasized for the field work, and students were required to complete

Workplace Hazardous Materials Information System training as mandated by the Occupation Safety and Health Act. Furthermore, off-campus risk-assessment forms were completed that demonstrate student willingness to participate and knowledge of the risks of doing the audit. This experience will also be applicable to true field work in industry.

15.4.3 Traditional Versus Hybrid Service-Learning

Although traditional service-learning may incorporate field and/or virtual work, the hybrid SL project presented in this chapter extended previous approaches by involving a self-directed project. Unlike traditional SL, students approached companies with opportunities to improve their environmental performance through green IT and identified and developed the problem and solution details around efficient IT management. Students needed to effectively market the work they could accomplish for the companies, an additional challenge as compared with traditional SL. Although participating companies generally wanted to reduce their energy consumption, most had not considered green IT projects previously; thus, students presented new solutions for these organizations. Another benefit of the project was the student initiative to find volunteer companies, without arranging for organizational engagements before the term began. These actions further support companies' willingness to improve their environmental footprints, despite many challenges in doing so.

15.4.4 Beyond the SL Project

It is interesting to consider the impacts of the SL project on the students and the green IT research after the project. Many of the students pursued fields that closely related to the SL project. For example, after graduation, many students went on to pursue jobs or further studies in related fields such as renewable energy, energy auditing, management consulting, green building design and modeling, and energy analysis. In addition, after the course was over, other students chose to continue working on ECMs with the green IT research group or working with companies that do similar work to their SL project (e.g., Canada Green ESCO). Finally, two students started their own businesses making their own online ECM calculators and services: Envirolytics (www.envirolytics.ca) and Carbon Savings. This indicates how the experience in the project motivated and perhaps inspired the students to continue in the future.

As shown in Table 15.2, the project pages continue to be viewed online even after the project completed. Since the project, the research team has continued to develop the ECMs using the lessons developed from the student projects and to engage with the companies. Future work will involve the continued expansion of the ECM repository at a dedicated website: www.green-its-research.com.

15.5 CONCLUSIONS

This chapter presented the findings for a novel pedagogical exercise in which students conducted service-learning projects that required them to act as change agents for industry by developing and recommending green information technology and systems and energy conservation measures. Unlike traditional service-learning, both self-directed virtual and field components were included. The preliminary results of this study indicate that the use of a free open-source tool like Appropedia.org for virtual service-learning combined with a field-work-based SL component can be an effective means of achieving the dual goals of education and organizational change directed toward environmental sustainability. Future work is needed to quantify the impact on learning and the effectiveness of such an approach to catalyzing environmentally beneficial changes in organizations.

ACKNOWLEDGMENTS

The authors would like to acknowledge K. Sayili, J. Corbett, J. Webster, and I. Zelenika for their work on the development of the ECM templates and discussion of this work, and A. Nosrat and the Appropedia Foundation for technical assistance regarding Appropedia.org. Further thanks go to the companies and students who participated in this study (confidentiality respected). This work was supported by a SSHRC Strategic Research Grant on Environmental Issues and a Queen's University Service-Learning Grant. An earlier version of this work was presented at the Canadian Engineering Education Association 2010 Conference and published by the *International Journal for Service-Learning and Engineering*. The final edited versions of the ECM templates are at http://www.green-its.research.cc.

REFERENCES

1. B. Jacoby (Ed.), *Service-Learning in Higher Education: Concepts and Practices,* San Francisco, CA, Jossey-Bass, 1996.
2. L. Harrisberger, R. Heydinger, J. Seely, and M. Talburtt, *Experiential Learning in Engineering Education American Society for Engineering Education,* Washington, DC, 1976, p. 121.

3. A. Driscoll, B. Holland, S. Gelmon, and S. Kerrigan, "An Assessment for Service-Learning: Comprehensive Case Studies of Impact on Faculty, Students, Community and Institution," *Michigan Journal of Community Service Learning,* Vol. 3, 66–71, 1996.

4. D. Riley and A. H. Bloomgarden, "Learning and Service in Engineering and Global Development," *International Journal for Service Learning in Engineering,* Vol. 2, No. 1, 48–59, 2006.

5. S. M. Gallini and B. E. Moely, "Service-Learning and Engagement, Academic Challenge, and Retention," *Michigan Journal of Community Service Learning,* Vol. 10, No. 1, 5–14, 2003.

6. J. Eyler and D. E. Giles, *Where's the Learning in Service-Learning?,* San Francisco, CA, Jossey-Bass, 1999.

7. C. Keen, and K. Hall, "Post-Graduation Service and Civic Outcomes for High Financial Need Students of a Multi-Campus, Co-Curricular Service-Learning College Program," *Journal of College and Character,* Vol. 10, No. 2, 2008.

8. J. Eyler, S. Root, and D. E. Giles, "Service Learning and the Development of Expert Citizens: Service Learning and Cognitive Science," In R. Bringle and D. Duffy (Eds.), *With Service in Mind,* Washington, D.C.: American Association of Higher Education, 1998.

9. J. A. Boss, "The Effects of Community Service Work on the Moral Development of College Ethics Students," *Journal of Moral Education* Vol. 23, 183–198, 1994.

10. J. Miller, "Linking Traditional and Service Learning Courses: Outcome Evaluations Utilizing Two Pedagogically Distinct Models," *Michigan Journal of Community Service Learning* Vol. 1, No. 1, 29–36, 1994.

11. J. Pearce and C. Russill, "Student Inquiries into Neglected Research for A Sustainable Society: Communication and Application," *Bulletin of Science, Technology & Society,* Vol. 23, No. 4, 311–320, 2003.

12. J. Pearce and C. Russill, "Interdisciplinary Environmental Education: Communicating and Applying Energy Efficiency for Sustainability," *Applied Environmental Education and Communication,* Vol. 4, No. 1, 65–72, 2005.

13. K. Branker, J. M. Pearce, J. Corbett, and J. Webster, "Hybrid Virtual- and Field-Work-based Service Learning with Green Information Technology and Systems Projects," *International Journal for Service Learning in Engineering,* Vol. 5, No. 2, 44–59, 2010.

14 A. McWilliams and D. Siegel, "Corporate Social Responsibility: A Theory of the Firm Perspective," *The Academy of Management Review,* Vol. 26, No. 1, 117–127, 2001.

15. J.M. Pearce, D. Denkenberger, and H. Zielonka, "Energy Conservation Measures as Investments," in Spadoni, G. (Ed.), *Energy Conservation: New Research,* Nova Science Publishers: New York, 2009, pp. 67–85.

16. H. C. de Bettignies, "Developing Leadership and Responsibility: No Alternative for Business Schools," in P. H. Dembinski, C. Lager, A. Cornford, and J.-M. Bonvin (Eds.), *Enron and World Finance: A Case Study in Ethics,* Palgrave, Macmillan: 2006, pp. 217–225.

17. J. M. Pearce, L. Grafman, T. Colledge, and R. Legg, "Leveraging Information Technology, Social Entrepreneurship and Global Collaboration for Just Sustainable Development," in *Proceedings of the 12th Annual NCIIA Conference,* 2008, pp. 201–210.

18. R. G. Bringle and J. A. Hatcher, "Implementing Service Learning in Higher Education," *Journal of Higher Education,* Vol. 67, 67–73, 1996.

19. J. Corbett, J. Webster, K. Sayili, I. Zelenika, and J. M. Pearce, "Developing and Justifying Energy Conservation Measures: Green IT under Construction," in *Proceedings of the 16th Americas Conference on Information Systems,* Lima, Peru, August 12–15, 2010.

20. J. M. Pearce, "Appropedia as a Tool for Service Learning in Sustainable Development," *Journal of Education for Sustainable Development,* Vol. 3, No. 1, 45–53, 2009.

21. Open Office, http://www.openoffice.org/.

CHAPTER 16

ENGAGING ENGINEERING STUDENTS IN A DEVELOPMENT PROGRAM FOR A GLOBAL SOUTH NATION THROUGH SERVICE-LEARNING

Willie K. Ofosu, Francois Sekyere, and James Oppong

ABSTRACT

Commerce and industry have been two of the main drivers of progress in global north nations (developed nations), placing them in leading positions in the world economy. Global south nations (developing nations) seek to be equal partners with global north nations in the global economy. They view education as the means to achieve this objective. They appreciate that education underpins both commerce and industry, and is the main driver in development.

Education can be combined with service to society through research projects at the tertiary level to advance development via service-learning. The research projects yield credits that count toward graduation. Tertiary level in this context includes vocational education and training, undergraduate and postgraduate education. Service-learning (SL) is any educational activity that integrates meaningful community service with instruction and reflection to enrich the learning experience while teaching civic responsibility. Service-learning is one of the approaches being used in the Master of Science (M.Sc.) program in Telecommunication Engineering at Kwame Nkrumah University of Science and Technology (KNUST) in Ghana.

In this chapter, the project being used in the service-learning format is on power-line communication (PLC). PLC is a technology in which data transmission is overlaid on electric power transmission; hence, all areas that are connected to the national grid can have access to the Internet. Analysis and simulations of the problem are done using the Numerical Electromagnetic Code (NEC-4), and the results are compared to experimental measurements.

16.1   INTRODUCTION

Education has been the main source of supply of manpower in all spheres of endeavor and, therefore, has been a contributor to the development of all global north nations. Although all levels of progress within the education system are important, the tertiary level [1, 2] has a major role to play in the development of global south nations such as Ghana through research. Research topics can be judiciously selected to provide solutions to the needs of the society. Even though the project may be planned based on local needs, the service can grow beyond the bounds of a local community to involve the whole nation [3]. This is particularly important because in a developing nation such as Ghana, obvious gaps exist between extremes such as the rich and the poor, the educated and the less educated, and politicians are bringing such divides to light as part of their agenda for achievement [4]. Viewing such needs as circumstances for providing service to the community gives the universities the opportunity to introduce their students to giving back to their communities. This helps the students to develop the attributes that drive and sustain the impulse to provide service.

To ensure that the development of a nation is sustained, it is necessary that all sectors of the society are engaged in the development process. This is particularly necessary in global south nations such as Ghana, where there are wide gaps in development between urban and rural regions. To accelerate the progress of development, it is useful to have all citizens participate. In this sense, university students have a role to play.

Universities in Ghana are populated with students who come from all sectors of the society. The sectors may be extremes such as urban and rural, rich and poor, across the whole nation, and in some cases from outside of Ghana. This mix of backgrounds of the students provides an appropriate setting for discussions on different rates of development in the different regions within the country. Such discussions lead to discussions on the levels of development between global north and global south nations, and what may be done to bridge the technology divide between them. In seeking a solution to this problem, two things are readily apparent. The first of these is the need to improve technology across the whole nation, in both urban and rural regions, for both rich and poor. The second is to close the technology divide between Ghana and the developed nations [5, 6]. Achieving this developmental stage will also help Ghana in achieving the objective of becoming an equal participant in the global community and help the nation to take advantage of the global economy [7].

The Science Education Resource Center (SERC) [8] at Carleton College lists numerous teaching methods that are relevant to different teaching styles, each of which has proved to be an effective technique in its application. Technology has a place in the classroom and one approach based on current technology is electronic learning (e-learning) [9]. The Internet supports this mode of learning whereby students can receive lessons in a remote setting from an instructor at a different location. This is emphasized by the Ghanaian government's interest to promote information and communication technology (ICT) in schools [10]. E-learning offers students the opportunity to access educational material by use of the computer, and allows each individual to learn at his or her own pace, and also do extra work on their own.

Appropriate teaching content is always an issue in education, and one concept is to write the curriculum such that it incorporates ideas that the students will find easy to identify with. In other words, the content should be based on the environment in which the student lives [11]. It may be argued that the students will find the material useful if it pertains to them and that would make the learning process easier, as the content will not appear to be abstract. The African environment is replete with objects, events, and concepts that the students will be aware of in their daily lives and, hence, involving such material in the classroom will provide a rich local content that will induce the students to learn.

Currently in Ghana, the Internet is provided by applications such as cable and DSL, mostly in urban areas. Subscribers are mostly people who can afford it. The use of the Internet in the Ghanaian environment can be made available to more people by lowering the cost to the user through broadband powerline communication (BPL) [or power-line communication (PLC)] in which data is transmitted on the power line [12]. This is a viable approach because Ghana has an electrical grid that covers most of the country. The Chief Executive Officer of the national electricity generation company, Volta River Authority (VRA), stated that "access to electricity in the urban areas was 70% and for the rural areas it was a little above 30%" [13]. This technology will ensure that most of the schools in the nation can have access to the educational programs that may be available on the Internet. Another approach is by wireless, and this will ensure that the parts of the nation that are not connected to the national electric grid can be reached through the radio spectrum. In trying to reach remote rural areas that are not connected to the national grid by wireless, equipment needed at such places can be powered by converting solar energy to electric power [14]. Whichever approach is taken to extend the use of the Internet, provision of the equipment in deploying the technology will require an initial capital outlay.

The selection of PLC was based primarily on cost [15]. There are systems such as cable, DSL, and satellite already in operation in Ghana, as stated above. But these are all in their initial stages of application. As such, the infrastructure for each of these systems is at the minimum and only in selected places, mostly in urban areas. To use any of these systems will, therefore, require substantial upgrades in infrastructure if the larger portion (or the whole of the country) is to be covered by the communication system. The cost for this will be prohibitive. On the other hand, PLC is basically data transmission over power lines. In this case, use of the national electrical grid will mean that the infrastructure is already in place, which will minimize the cost of the infrastructure. An added advantage is that wherever the national grid reaches, Internet access will be available. The fact that the grid covers most urban areas and some rural areas means that most of the people will have access to the Internet. As stated by Dr. Joseph Oteng-Adjei, the Energy Minister, "Available figures show that about 72% of Ghanaians have access to electricity" [16]. Although this may be a good start, it does not fulfill the requirement for sustained development, which is ensuring that the nation as a whole engage in the development process. For this reason, a wireless application based on solar technology can be combined with the PLC to accommodate the off-grid areas, as stated above.

16.2   BENEFITS OF A PLC SYSTEM

As stated above, PLC supports Internet access. Thus, all educational institutions that are in areas covered by the national electric grid can have connectivity to educational institutions outside of Ghana that are on the Internet. They can also have connectivity to libraries and research establishments around the world. Access to such educational facilities will lead to an upgrade in education for the students and improve their performance. This will be a positive step toward the economic development that Ghana seeks [3].

In many remote rural areas, there are clinics that do not have easy access to any major hospital and, hence, lack the facilities as well as the specialists that may be found in major hospitals. Internet connectivity between the clinics and the hospitals will at a minimum provide the clinics with the expertise of the specialists, which will reduce, to some measure, the mortality rate in these remote areas.

Entrepreneurial abilities of some Ghanaians came to the forefront with the introduction of cell phones in Ghana. The process started with pay phone cards [17] that turned into a profitable, booming business. This venture became widespread and students engaged in it, selling phone cards [18] among other products. These entrepreneurial activities started from the micro level with the focus on self-employment by the participants, which resulted in a reduction of unemployment in the nation. Professor Teel, a renowned Economist at Oxford University, in his lecture on "Poverty in Ghana: Why Don't Ghanaians Believe it Has Halved?," pointed out that "though education plays a significant role in securing employment and higher pay, self-employment offers higher incomes" [19]. The government of Ghana acknowledges the positive economic impact of microentrepreneurial activities engaged in by some Ghanaians. Such entrepreneurial activities can be realized with the PLC technology as well and will help reduce unemployment further. The need for microentrepreneurship was stated by Mr. Sampson Kwaku Boafo, the Ashanti Regional Minister, in his appeal to the Kumasi Metropolitan Assembly (KMA) concerning promoting business, "especially microentrepreneurship," in the metropolis of Kumasi [20]. As Mr. Boafo noted, this would be "consistent with the Ghana Poverty Reduction Strategy objectives." Such ventures help to take people out of poverty and help to improve the economic status of the nation.

16.3   STUDENT DISCUSSIONS AND PROJECT-BASED SERVICE-LEARNING

A group of students in the Master of Science (M.Sc.) in Telecommunication Engineering program were required to do oral presentations in class on problems and needs faced by their communities. This was done as part of a course in Satellite and Broadcast Networks. It was required that the presentations should be based on problems that have been discussed within the community, and also that they should propose solutions to the problems. The solutions should be based on critical thinking together with the knowledge they had acquired in the program. It was explained to the students that completion of any projects that provided solutions to the needs of a community would count as humanitarian service to the community as well as for 36 of the 70 credits required for the completion of the M.Sc. program [21]. The report on the project was to demonstrate the student's mastery of computer usage in solving problems and also demonstrate skills acquired for solving problems related to antennas and electromagnetic radiation, as discussed in the Antennas and Electromagnetics Propagation component of the course on Satellite and Broadcast Networks. Another expected outcome of the program is for the students to demonstrate their skills in designing and developing a solution to a stated problem. This approach is described as project-based (or problem-based) service-learning, for which the students are advanced in their discipline and have knowledge they can draw upon [22, 23]. This exercise was conducted with the objective of selecting possible sites with problems that could be used for project-based service-learning. The importance of this is based on the fact that the selections should provide the students with opportunities to demonstrate the lessons they had learned in the program. Also, the exercise was intended to determine the extent of involvement of the students in their communities. The cultural context of service-learning is discussed in [24]. In the Ghanaian environment, the people of a community would express happiness for the success of the students and, in conversations with them, would encourage them toward greater achievement. They would express their expectations of contributions the students might bring to the community in the future. It was, therefore, anticipated that the students would be aware of the problems from the community perspective and would have the desire to address such problems. The approach to site selection is based on the students' knowledge of the site plus the culture of the Ghanaian people. An initial site visit by faculty to assess suitability for learning occurred after students made their presentations.

A common theme among the many problems and solutions stated was reliable communication within the country. This included communication between a clinic and a hospital and between people in Ghana and the outside world. Health care is a major issue, particularly in rural areas. In some cases, people have to travel miles to seek appropriate medical care; the sick person may die in transit before medical assistance is offered. The interest in connectivity between Ghana and the outside world was mostly focused on technological developments in global north countries that Ghana could benefit from.

It was generally agreed that the system that combined different applications and would also provide many advantages was the Internet. As discusses above, the idea of using an already existing infrastructure was very attractive. The existing infrastructure would continue to provide the service it was originally intended for and, in addition to that, provide additional service in response to an essential need of the people. As stated above, PLC was the natural choice for two reasons. One is that most of the nation is covered by the national grid and the government intends to extend the coverage to places that do not already have electricity [25]. The second is that electric power systems are normally overlaid with a communication system [26] used for supervisory and control functions, and may also be used for billing purposes. Another point made during the discussion was that the people were already familiar with electricity and electrical appliances, hence, the extension to include the Internet would not lead to major problems for the users.

Discussions with the students resulted in identifying communication as a need in many of the communities the students come from. This was one of the requirements of the oral presentation. The other requirement was fulfilled by arriving at the decision to use PLC to provide a solution to that need. One of the students in the class, Mr. Francois Sekyere, comes from a community that has such need and opted to work on this as his project. As a member of the community for the selected site, he was familiar with that environment and their needs, and his knowledge of the site proved to be accurate, as was later assessed by faculty. It is a policy of the university that each student will work exclusively on his or her own project. Other students elected to work on topics that related to the communications industry.

16.4   STUDENT ACTIVITIES

The M.Sc. program covers two years and the project is usually assigned during the second year. It is expected that each student will complete and submit the project thesis by the end of that year. To ensure that Mr. Sekyere would be in compliance to the time schedule, he was required to plan an activities schedule by allocating periods of time to complete specified targets of activities. The three broad categories of activities for the project were literature review, methodology for analysis, and collection of results. The academic year comprises two semesters, each of about 16 weeks in duration. Literature review and methodology were planned to be done during the first semester, and collection of results and writing of the report in the second semester. The need for flexibility was factored into the time schedule. As part of the expectations, students were advised to maintain a log book of all their activities and this, as noted by Brescia et al. [23], supports the need for reflection. Figure 16.1 shows the components of the program.

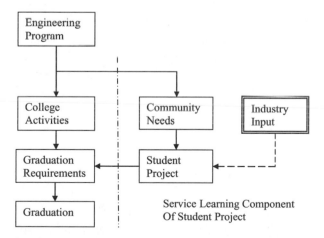

Figure 16.1. Components of program requirements showing input by the community and industry.

16.5   COLLEGE–INDUSTRY COOPERATION

The project is based on development of an existing infrastructure, and that necessitated collaboration with the entity that had oversight of the infrastructure. As stated above, PLC is the transmission of data over electric-power transmission lines. For this project, therefore, it was important to establish a working relationship with the company that generates and distributes power in Ghana, the Volta River Authority (VRA) [27]. VRA is the primary company that supplies most of the generated electric power in Ghana, using hydro generation supplemented by other sources such as the Takoradi Thermal Power Plant [28].

Distribution of electric power is provided by Electricity Corporation of Ghana (ECG) in the southern part of Ghana, and by Northern Electricity Department (NED) in the northern part of Ghana. One of the objectives of VRA is to maintain real-time oversight of the grid to ensure that faults are quickly identified in relation to the type of fault and location within the grid for immediate remedy. The company uses PLC for voice communication across various centers within the perimeter of the national grid. It is also used to transmit signals that initiate protection for the power system. Other essential functions of the PLC are energy management, supervision, and control. The applications that VRA has used PLC for, such as voice transmission, supervision, and control, show that data can be transmitted over the power lines. This functionality can be adopted by entrepreneurs for business activities involving the Internet, as stated above.

The faculty and the student approached VRA concerning this project. A discussion was held with officers of the company and they readily agreed to cooperate with the university on the project. During the course of the project, further visits were made to VRA offices for further discussions with their staff of different aspects of the project, and this formed part of the student activities.

Visits were also made to the site to ensure that the simulation model that would be used for the analytical component of the project was an exact representation of the power lines in the neighborhood. Both VRA and KNUST are public entities; hence, oversight of the cooperation between the two entities falls within the domain of the government of Ghana.

16.6   PLC DEVELOPMENT

The information age is a reality worldwide and the concept of information transmission appeals to many researchers in information technology. The attraction covers all forms of information transmission. The use of power lines to carry data for functions such as billing is indicative of the fact that data for other applications can equally and effectively be carried by power lines. At the user's end, a modem is needed to connect to the PLC and the cost for the modem is not high. The fact that data can be transmitted to many people at low cost has fueled the interest in PLC application and this is happening mostly in Europe [29] and other parts of the world.

It must be stated that PLC technology is not new. Deployment and experimental work on PLC has happened in nations such as Germany, Spain, France, Austria, and Switzerland, and unique challenges were encountered in each country [29]. The frequency spectrum available for communications in the European systems is from 1 to 30 MHz [29], and occasionally up to 50 MHz [30]. In the applications referred to above, the PLC networks have been put into two categories: outdoor for those that cover public areas between the transformer substations and the customer premises, and indoor covering the private area within customer buildings. A point that is noteworthy is that African nations, including Ghana, use voltage levels that are used within the European Union, which is between the limits of 230 V ± 10% at 50 Hz [31]. This makes the examples cited above, collectively, a useful reference point for PLC development in Ghana and Africa in general.

16.7 INDUSTRY INPUT

As previously stated, there was close collaboration between VRA and the research team in the execution of the project. Figure 16.2 shows the system used by VRA. The VRA PLC system consist of a MCD 80 modular coupling device, coupling capacitor (or CVT), and PLC terminal (or PLC equipment). The MCD 80 modular coupling device forms the interface between the HV transmission line and the PLC equipment. It acts as a filter that accepts the carrier frequency signals and rejects the power system frequency. It also protects the PLC terminal from the power system voltage and transient overvoltages caused by switching operations and atmospheric discharges.

A complete coupling comprises a line trap to prevent the PLC signals from being short-circuited by the substation and a coupling filter formed by the coupling capacitor and the coupling device. At VRA, the PLC signals are coupled to two phases of the power system, which is much more reliable than coupling to just one phase. The two-phase mode of coupling is referred to as differential coupling [30]. This results in reduced radiation from the cables because emissions from the "go" path and the "return" path tend to cancel each other's effect.

A two-phase coupling scheme consists of two coupling units, one of which includes a hybrid module, as shown in Figure 16.3. VRA uses low frequency (LF) and medium frequency (MF) for the operation of their PLC system.

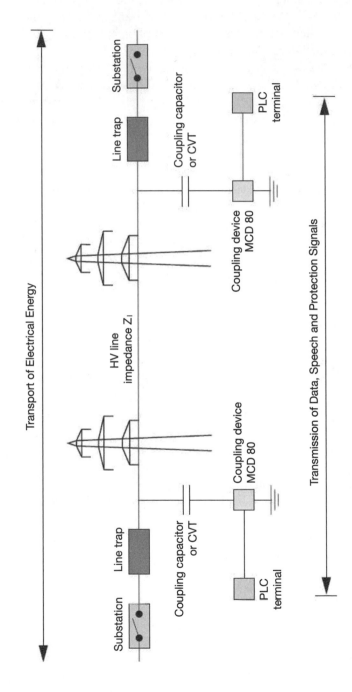

Figure 16.2. Schematic of the PLC system deployed by VRA. (Courtesy of VRA.)

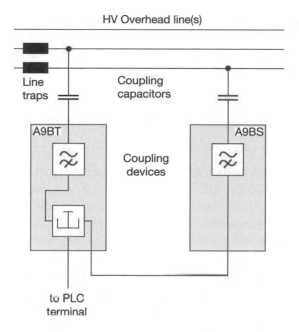

HV Overhead line(s)

Figure 16.3. Two-phase coupling scheme used by VRA. (Courtesy of VRA.)

16.8 COMPUTATIONAL ANALYTICAL APPROACH

Analysis of the technology will provide information on how it behaves, and that will indicate how best to operate it and the different ways in which it can be applied. To do this, the power line with data being transmitted through it is viewed as a traveling-wave antenna. Two activities are evident from this model. First, as the data travels along the cable the signal will be attenuated. Second, transmission of the signal along the cable will cause electromagnetic energy to radiate away from the cable. This manifests as noise and can cause interference in transmissions from communications systems that are in close proximity to the cable.

To characterize the behaviors discussed above, analytical work was done using the Numerical Electromagnetics Code (NEC-4) [32] developed at the Lawrence Livermore National Laboratory. The code uses Fortran 77 and is written for analyzing antennas and other metallic structures. It provides numerical solutions, for example, of currents induced in structures by sources directly connected to the objects under investigation, or in incident fields directly impacting the objects. Other results may be given in electric or magnetic fields. It uses both the electric-field integral equation (EFIE) and the magnetic-field integral equation (MFIE). EFIE can be applied to thin-wire structures of small or vanishing conductor volume, and MFIE is more suited to voluminous structures, especially structures with large, smooth surfaces [32]. Simulations of the VRA PLC system were performed using the NEC-4 package. It was used to model the problem and to calculate the electric-field radiation levels from the power lines.

16.9   SIMULATION AND EXPERIMENTAL RESULTS OF VOICE CHANNEL

The voice communication functionality is operational and in use at frequencies of 444 kHz and 482 kHz, and the initial tests were based on this information. The initial intention was to ensure that the analytical results compared well with experimental results. To do this, computational analysis was done at the frequencies stated. Simulations were done using the NEC-4 code mentioned above and measurements were taken with a Protek 3201 RF Field Analyzer for comparison at the two frequencies of 444 kHz and 482 kHz. The Protek 3201 is a hand-held field-strength analyzer that has wide-band reception ranging from 100 kHz to 2060 MHz. Simulation results and experimental data were collected for transmissions along the lines and radiations off the power lines as a result of the transmissions along the power lines.

The analytical and experimental results for transmission along the power line are shown in Figure 16.4 for 444 kHz and Figure 16.6 for 482 kHz. In both cases, the analytical and experimental results meet at a distance of 200 meters from the source. The near-field condition has not been incorporated

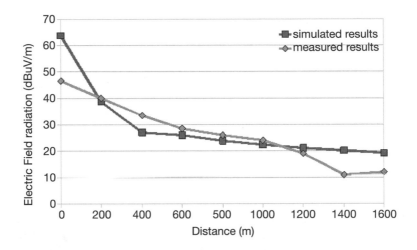

Figure 16.4. Plot of simulated and measured results of signal propagation along the power lines at a frequency of 444 kHz.

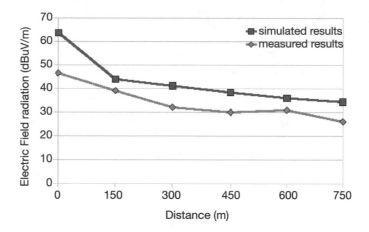

Figure 16.5. Plot of simulated and measured results of electric-field radiation normal to the power lines at a frequency of 444 kHz.

in the results above. This may impact the results presented. From the 200 meter point to 1000 meters, which will fall in the far-field range, the two results show very close agreement. For both frequencies, the two results show a reduction of from −5 to −10 dBuV/m after a distance of 1000 meters from the source point. This suggested that the analytical results compared well with experimental data, which provided confidence in the analytical process employed. The drop in the level of propagation energy after the 1000 meter mark suggested appreciable loss of integrity beyond that point and, hence,

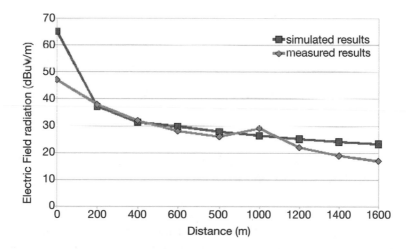

Figure 16.6. Plot of simulated and measured results of signal propagation along the power lines at a frequency of 482 kHz.

couplers may be spaced up to that distance. It is to be expected that data at higher frequencies may present different results.

The radiations of electromagnetic energy away from the power lines for both frequencies are shown in Figures 16.5 and 16.7. An average reduction of –8 to –20 dBuV/m is observed. This can be attributed in part to the level from the ground at which the experimental measurements were performed. The conducting cables are 25 meters above ground and the measurements were taken at 2 meters above ground.

It is expected that the correlation between these results would be closer if the measurements were taken closer to the cables. Measurable results went up to 750 meters. Analysis needs to be done on communications systems that are at different positions within this range to determine the levels of signals that will cause interference from the PLC system. This is stated in light of the fact that filters, rejection systems, and circuits will be built into the communications systems to reject frequencies other than those being used as operational frequencies for these systems.

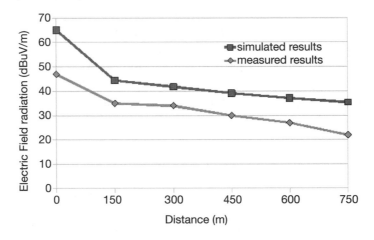

Figure 16.7. Plot of simulated and measured results of electric-field radiation normal to the power lines at a frequency of 482 kHz.

16.10 SIMULATION OF MODEL RESIDENTIAL-NEIGHBORHOOD POWER LINES

As part of the project, frequent visits were made to the site and one of the objectives for the visits was to ensure that the model for distribution would correspond to the map of the site. The section of the national grid used for this study is the VRA substation in Kumasi, where a PLC system is current-

ly being used for line protection and voice communication on the Kumasi–Techiman line. The model used in the NEC-4 simulation was based on
the physical layout of the low-voltage power-distribution system at the
Forestry Research Institute of Ghana residential area in Fumesua near Ejusu
(Figure 16.8). It was designed using power-line maps provided by VRA, and
visits to the site by Mr. Francois Sekyere, the coauthor of the paper, ensured
the accuracy of the maps, as stated above. It should be noted that Mr.
Sekyere actually lived in that vicinity. The project was started and carried
through by Mr. Sekyere when he was an M.Sc. candidate at KNUST.

Residential customers are usually served by single-phase lines; hence, that
is the system assumed for the topology in Figure 16.9. The overall extent of

Figure 16.8. Map of Ghana showing Kumasi and other areas where the measurements were
conducted

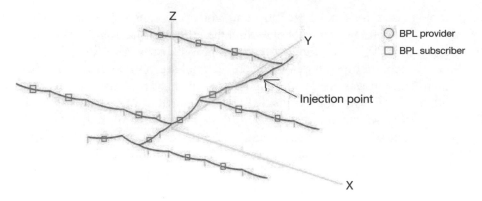

Figure 16.9. Simulation model of the residential neighborhood power line carrying the broadband power-line signal using NEC-4 code.

the model was 900 meters along the x-axis and 800 meters along the y-axis. The modeled power line height was 10 meters and all wires were copper of 12.6 millimeters in diameter and conductivity of 5.8×10^7 S/m. The modeling was done by Mr. Sekyere, as required by the program objectives. He used the wire-modeling technique of the NEC-4 code for a radiating object, such as an antenna that includes a ground. The approach in using this code is to provide command parameters that are called for in the code and select the required outputs. The ground plane for the model was assumed to be a flat earth structure beneath the wire with characteristics of dielectric constant of 13.0 and conductivity of 0.005 S/m. The source power and impedance used for the modeling were 1 W and 150 Ω, respectively. Figure 16.10 shows the horizontal differential format for the feed. As stated above, this technique causes a reduction in the radiations from the lines, as the radiations from one line oppose those from the other line and, hence, tend to cancel each other's effect. The closer the wires, the better would be the effect of cancellation. Differential coupling can also be done vertically between phased lines as well as between a phased line and a neutral. Driving the lines differentially, therefore, helps to suppress radiations from the cables that may be harmful to other applications in the vicinity of the PLC system.

16.11   SIMULATIONS OF DATA TRANSMISSION ON POWER LINES

As stated above, some European nations are engaged in research on the PLC application, and since the electric power system in use in Ghana is patterned after the system that would be found in the European Community, it stands to

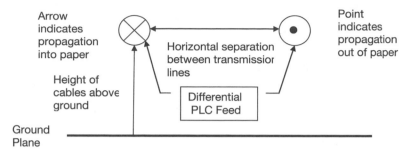

Figure 16.10. Two parallel horizontal power lines above ground, showing directions of signal propagation.

reason that the work being done in Ghana should emulate the research being done in Europe. Ghana may not have the same guidelines for communications systems as Europe or the United States, where regulations have been in place for years, but, considering the need for international standards for communications applications, it was decided that the initial tests should be done around the spectrum employed in Europe and the United States. It is to be expected that the Ghanaian environment will be decidedly different from the U.S. or the European environment with regard to noise present in the radio spectrum, weather conditions, and ambient temperature, for example, and, hence, the impact on the PLC application in Ghana will have its unique problems.

Tests that have been done on European and U.S. systems have been at frequencies typically between 1 and 30 MHz [29, 30], and sometimes at 50 MHz. As stated in the literature [29], that is the frequency spectrum available for communication in Europe, and the European systems use the lower range of the spectrum, from 1–10 MHz for outdoor PLC. This is because lower frequencies have shown less line attenuation due to path loss and local noise. The higher band of 15–30 MHz has been used for indoor PLC because indoor distances are typically shorter and do not greatly impact line attenuation, which is higher for the higher frequency range. In addition, channel noise and power-line noise are much smaller at higher frequencies [29].

Medium-voltage (MV) power lines used by VRA usually consists of three horizontal, parallel, aluminum-conductor, steel-reinforced (ACSR) wires, and low-voltage (LV) power lines consist of four vertical ACSR wires, as shown in Figure 16.11.

In the NEC-4 analysis using differential signal injection for the LV line, one was placed at 7 meters and the other at 7.3 meters above ground, whereas for the MV parallel lines, all were at 10 meters above ground and 500 mm between lines. The ground was modeled with average characteristics with conductivity of 0.005 S/m and dielectric constant of 13.

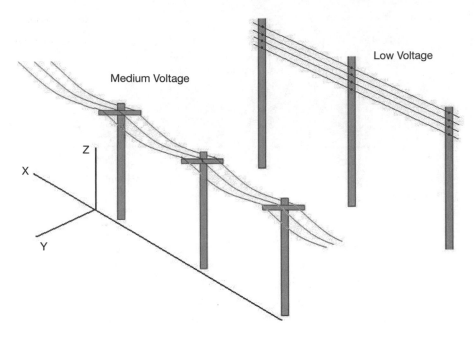

Figure 16.11. Common power-line topologies used in Ghana.

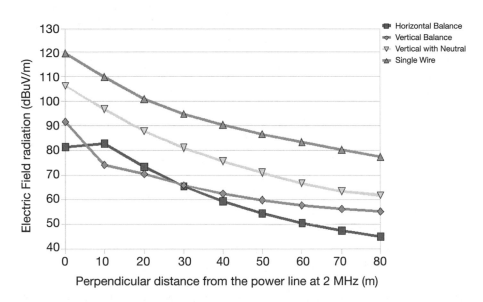

Figure 16.12. Simulation results of electric-field radiation at distances normal to the power line at a frequency of 2 MHz.

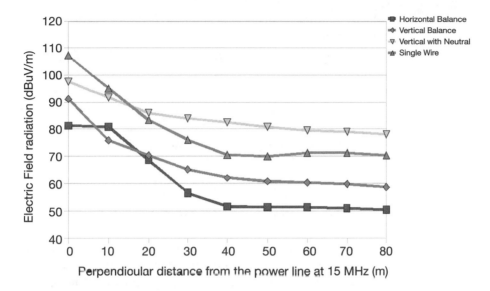

Figure 16.13. Simulation results of electric-field radiation at distances normal to the power line at a frequency of 15 MHz.

For the differential feed between a phase wire and the neutral wire of the vertical power line, the neutral wire was grounded to simulate typical imbalance in the line. The ground connection consisted of four 10 meter radials placed 5 cm above ground. This was used to simulate the typically poor RF (radio frequency) characteristics for the ground. A source impedance of 150 Ω, load impedance of 500 Ω, and source power of 1 W were used. The power-line response for the signal frequencies shown in Figures 16.12 and 16.13 were modeled in the near field, the radiations going away from the power lines for various methods of feed.

The two frequencies of 2 MHz and 15 MHz have been chosen to represent the indoor and outdoor ranges stated above. As expected, the responses for the balanced feed show lower radiations compared to the single- feed responses.

16.12   FUTURE WORK FOR THE PLC PROJECT

Further work needs to be done on this project, including:

- An experimental setup of hardware needs to be constructed to have real-time measurements made for transmission rate of data and radiations from the power lines at realistic frequencies of data transmission.
- Distances between repeater stations have to be determined.

- Number of user stations that can be accommodated on a segment of the line has to be determined.
- Signals captured by the power line will act as interference to the data being transmitted and the levels of signal that will be destructive to the data transmission will have to be determined.
- Experimentation will predict the optimal frequency of transmission that will work best on the lines.
- The number of channels that can be set up on the lines needs to be determined.

16.13   BENEFITS OF SL AND RECOMMENDATIONS

The benefits of service-learning are numerous. The student gets to see the place within society where he becomes a contributor to the development of his people. He gains a real-life experience of using the knowledge he has acquired to solve problems, the solutions of which helps the development of his nation as it improves the quality of life of his people. The faculty experiences the satisfaction that through their efforts, learning has taken place, as a result of which a student, upon graduation, can become a practicing engineer capable of solving real-life problems. By submitting their work to the wider public of academia through publications, the faculty gets the opportunity to share ideas and learn from other practitioners of service-learning. The university demonstrates itself not only capable of furthering but prepared to contribute to the progress of the nation, in this case Ghana. It proves to be a major stakeholder in bringing to fruition the aspirations of the nation. It demonstrates that through its faculty and students, it is prepared to partner with other stakeholders to bring to reality the desires of the nation articulated by the political leadership of the nation.

Though the work presented in this paper was done while Mr. Sekyere was a student at KNUST, as a faculty member at UEW-K (University of Education—Kumasi Campus) he is now in a position to spread the ideas and ideals of service-learning to another university. For this, he and coauthor W. Ofosu plan to partner with the Head of Technology Department of UEW-K, Dr. Amoah, to visit and discuss with different communities their needs, and design topics that, as a team, will engage Masters students of the Technology Department of UEW-K. The service-learning program will be organized the same as has been reported in this paper, and a project-based program and learning expectations will result from the course content of the Masters' program, just as has been demonstrated in this chapter. The service-learning approach is a very visible way for educational institutions in developing nations to demonstrate they can take a leadership role in solving the problems of the people of the nation. It also demonstrates to the taxpayers that their tax funds being paid to public institutions are being used for a useful purpose.

16.14   CONCLUSION

The service-learning format has been used to determine the possibility of setting up a PLC system for a global south nation that can be utilized to support developmental programs. Experimental and analytical results of voice transmission along the lines show close agreement. Computational analyses have shown that both vertical and horizontal differential transmissions along the lines have lower electromagnetic radiations, as has been established by U.S. and European experiments.

REFERENCES

1. General Information, Statistics, Education in Ghana, http://www.ghanaweb.com/Ghana-HomePage/general/statistics.php.
2. National Service-Learning Clearinghouse, http://www.servicelearning.org/what-is-service-learning, 2011.
3. K. Osafo, "Economic Development Plan for Ghana—Osafo," www.ghanaweb.com, General News, Monday, November 5, 2007.
4. F. K. Lartey-Adjei, "CPP Will Push for a Robust District Policy." www.ghanaweb.com, General News Sunday, April 6, 2008.
5. Ghana News Agency (GNAa), "Closing ICT Gap Between Developed and Developing Countries," www.ghanaweb.com, General News Monday, April 28, 2008.
6. Ghana News Agency (GNAb), "Lifting Information Technology Needed to Close Poverty Gap," www.ghanaweb.com, General News Thursday, April 24, 2008.
7. Ghana News Agency (GNAc), "World Economic Power: Where is Africa?," www.ghanaweb.com, Business News, Sunday, June 26, 2011.
8. Science Education Resource Center (SERC) @ Carleton College, http://serc.carleton.edu/sp/library/pedagogies.html.
9. R. L. Martens, J. Gulikers, and T. Bastiaens, "The Impact of Intrinsic Motivation on e-Learning in Authentic Computer Tasks," *Journal of Computer-Assisted Learning*, Vol. 20, 368–376, 2004.
10. Ghana News Agency (GNAd), "Ministry to Promote ICT in Schools," www.ghanaweb.com, General News Friday, December 21, 2007.
11. National Environment Education and Training Foundation (NEETF), "Environmental-based Education: Creating High Performance Schools and Students," http://www.neefusa.org/pdf/NEETF8400.pdf, pp. 3–5, September 2000.
12. P. Amirshahi, and M. Kavehrad, "Medium Voltage Overhead Power-line Broadband Communications; Transmission Capacity and Electromagnetic Interference," in *Proceedings of ISPLC 2005*, Vancouver, Canada, April 2005, pp. 2–6.
13. Ghana News Agency (GNAe), "VRA to Increase Electricity Supply," www.ghanaweb.com, General News Wednesday, April 27, 2011.

14. Ghana News Agency (GNAf), "Communities to Benefit from Solar Electrification Project," www.ghanaweb.com, Regional News Thursday, May 5, 2011.

15. W. K. Ofosu, "Enriching A Curriculum With Local Content," in *2008 American Society for Engineering Education Annual Conference and Exposition,* June 2008.

16. Ghana News Agency (GNAg), "More Ghanaians to Enjoy Electricity by 2015," www.ghanaweb.com, General News, Friday, February 4, 2011.

17. Ghana News Agency (GNAh), "Pay Phone Cards for Hiring," www.ghanaweb.com, General News Tuesday, August 21, 2001.

18. Ghana News Agency (GNAi), "Students Turn Varsity Halls into Markets," www. ghanaweb.com, General News Thursday, October 28, 2004.

19. Ghana News Agency (GNAj), "Ghana Receives High Marks for Reducing Poverty," www.ghanaweb.com, General News Monday, January 10, 2011.

20. Ghana News Agency (GNAk), "Minister Appeals to KMA to Promote Business in the Metropolis," www.ghanaweb.com, Regional News Friday, October 10, 2003.

21. M.Sc. in Telecommunication Program Structure, KNUST, http://www.knust.edu.gh/ pages/sections.php?siteid=ee&mid=337&sid=2986.

22. Northeastern University Service-Learning, http://www.northeastern.edu/servicelearning/about/models.html, 2007.

23. W. Brescia, C. Mullins, and M. Miller, "Project-Based Service-Learning in an Instructional Tecgnology Graduate Program," *International Journal for the Scholarship of Teaching and Learning,* Vol.3, No. 2, July 2009, http://academics.georgiasouthern.edu/ijsotl/v3n2/articles/PDFs/Article_BresciaMullinsMiller.pdf.

24. M. C. Merrill, "The Cultural Context of Service-Learning: Issues to Consider in Importing a Pedagogical Innovation," Indiana University, MC Merrill 2002, http://elibrary.auca.kg:8080/dspace/bitstream/123456789/214/1/Merrill_The%20cultural%20cont ext%20of%20service-learning_Issues%20to%20consider%20in%20importing%20a- %20pedegogical%20innovation.pdf.

25. General News Agency (GNAl) "580 Rural Communities to Benefit from Electrification Project" ,www.ghanaweb.com, Monday, January 7, 2008.

26. Wikipedia Free Encyclopedia, "Power Line Communication," http://en.wikipedia.org/ wiki/Power_line_communication, June 2011.

27. Volta River Authority (VRA), http://www.vra.com, 2007.

28. "Guide to Electric Power in Ghana," Resource Center for Energy Economics and Regulation, Institute of Statistical, Social and Economic Research, University of Ghana, Legon, Accra, Ghana, July 2005.

29. W. Liu, H. Widmer, and P. Raffin, "Broadband PLC Access Systems and Field Deployment in European Power Line Networks," *IEEE Communications Magazine,* May, 114–118, 2003.

30. Paul S. Henry, "Interference Characteristics of Broadband Power Line Communication Systems Using Aerial Medium Voltage Wires," *IEEE Communications Magazine,* April, 92–98, 2005.

31. Wikipedia Free Encyclopedia, "Mains Electricity," http://en.wikipedia.org/wiki/Mains_ electricity, May 2011.

32. Gerald J. Burke, "Numerical Electromagnetics Code—NEC-4, Method of Moments, Part I: User's Manual," January 1992.

CHAPTER 17

LEVERAGING LOCAL RESOURCES TO IMPLEMENT COMMUNITY-ORIENTED, SUSTAINABLE COMPUTER-EDUCATION PROJECTS IN LOS ANGELES

Rohit Mathew, and Christine M. Maxwell

ABSTRACT

BOOTUP is an education and civic-engagement project that was founded in 2005 by members of the UCLA Chapter of Engineers Without Borders (EWB-UCLA). The mission of BOOTUP is to design and implement a sustainable computer education project that provides value to both the local community as well as engineering students at UCLA. Since its inception, BOOTUP has provided over 50 donated/refurbished computers and related equipment to three Los Angeles area schools, as well as individuals and organizations who did not otherwise have consistent access to computers. This project has involved numerous community organizers at UCLA and in Los Angeles as well as UCLA students. We estimate that up to 100 high school students have been impacted by our project. Computer equipment was obtained through donations by a variety of companies and individuals and refurbished for reuse. Unusable equipment was deposited at electronic waste recycling sites including those at UCLA and Goodwill.

17.1   INTRODUCTION

BOOTUP was established as a project through the Engineers Without Borders (EWB) student chapter at UCLA and is geared toward providing a valuable technology-education service and experience to local high schools as well as college student participants at UCLA. To adhere to the core principles of EWB, we also sought to minimize the economic and environmental costs that are often incurred over the lifetime of any undertaking. These costs often manifest in the form of general use equipment and supplies, transportation, advertising, and networking-related costs. Our approach, as a result, incorporates a wide variety of considerations that range from our interactions with schools and partners, the type of service or activity, and the optimizing location.

17.2   CHALLENGES AND CONSIDERATIONS

17.2.1   Activity Selection

Identifying the type of activity to partake in was critical, both in establishing our footing as a new EWB project as well as the success of our community effort. Ultimately, we wanted to provide an engineering or technology-related experience that could be used to target and engage UCLA student volunteers as well as provide a concrete skill-based experience to high school participants.

17.2.2   Volunteers

Recruitment of volunteers was also a challenge, which was made more by the nature of our target volunteer group: engineering undergraduate students. Academics is generally the focus of undergraduate students in engineering and science, and hands-on community-engagement activities are not as strongly emphasized.

17.2.3   Location

Engineers Without Borders-UCLA has successfully planned and partnered with various community groups to implement a technology and education-enhancement space for students. Most notably, Thinklab! was a project in which we refurbished and donated computers to El Buen Samaritano in Jocotenango, Guatemala [1, 2]. It is important to note, however, that limited and unevenly distributed technology resources can also be an issue domestically. From this perspective, we hoped to contribute to the effort to address technology resource inequities in the Los Angeles Unified School District [3, 4].

17.2.4 Sustainability Principles

We wanted to maximize the sustainability of our project by minimizing operations and economic costs as well as impact to the environment. To address this, we managed sustainability from several different angles, including (1) equipment and software, (2) location (transportation and access), and (3) education. These angles tie directly into some of our other motivations and considerations, which will be discussed in further detail.

17.3 METHODOLOGY

17.3.1 Overview of Approach

Our goal was to implement a computer-education project that incorporated the values of education and sustainability. We were able to achieve this by collecting donated computer equipment that would be used in computer-building workshops with high school students. Upon completion of the workshop, high school students were able to keep these computers. Alternate approaches to this project were also taken, including refurbishing donated equipment and then building or enhancing an existing computer-technology lab for local high schools as well as a free-form model of incorporating other types of science and environmental education components (Figure 17.1).

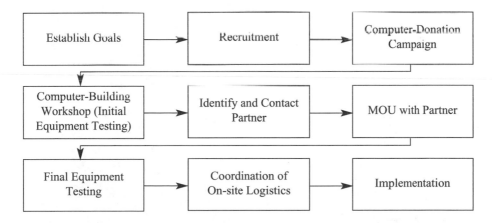

Figure 17.1. Process flow for planning and implementation of computer education project.

17.3.2 Activity Selection

We considered numerous service or activity types, including tutoring in math and science and environmental education. However, there were already several student groups dedicated to tutoring-based activities. Furthermore, we wanted to offer a project that was more hands-on and skills-based. We ultimately resolved to establish a computer-education project, which enabled us the flexibility to hold computer-building workshops that had elements of tutoring and mentorship and facilitated curricula development. We were able to put together concrete reference materials for students with step-by-step instructions. This computer-education project also enabled us to be flexible with respect to timing and schedules; during periods in which we had fewer volunteers, we would opt to donate a computer lab rather than execute a six-week workshop at a high school.

17.3.3 Volunteer Recruitment

The technical nature of this project, namely the incorporation of hands-on workshops, was attractive for many students in the Henry Samueli School of Engineering and Applied Sciences (HSSEAS). We used standard digital and paper media to advertise the project (Figure 17.2). Following an informational session, we organized quarterly college-student workshops that provided instruction on how to assemble/dissemble computers and introduced potential volunteers to the project. After this workshop, we would continue to have weekly meetings to advance the high school component of the project. This model ultimately provided some versatility and resilience to allow for a moderate-to-high rate of student volunteer turnover and also to allow us to maximize the number of students engaged in the project.

Want to get rid of that old computer?

Donate it to Project BOOTUP; we refurbish computer equipment for schools and nonprofits.
You can get a tax write-off receipt!

Please contact Christine at ewbucla@gmail.com or 310.439.9311 if you are interested in donating or helping out with the project. :)

Figure 17.2. Sample flyer posted around UCLA Henry Samueli School of Engineering and Applied Science to advertise for computer donations.

17.3.4 Equipment and Supplies

We established several avenues to obtain hardware.

On-Campus/UCLA-Based Donations. We used standard digital and paper media to advertise the need for donated equipment and worked with department administrators to obtain permanent space to post flyers (Figure 17.2). Flyers typically consisted of project information, including contact (e-mail or phone number) as well as additional incentives. The main incentives, in addition to the environmental and educational benefits, were that computer donations were tax deductible using the 501(c)3 nonprofit status of UCLA (which was later revoked for use with this project due to University policy). We also facilitated donation requests and documentation by generating a Google Form [5] (Figure 17.3).

Off-campus-Based Donations. We also established an account with Tech-Soup [6], which was instrumental in our ability to collect equipment and expand our donor base to the general Southern California region. TechSoup is a nonprofit that is dedicated to providing other nonprofits with technology resources to help them fulfill their civic engagement goals. Through our partnership with TechSoup, we were able to be added to a database of projects that seek to refurbish computers for community-oriented projects. Essentially, when a potential donor wants to find a project to donate their computer equipment to, they can use the TechSoup map–database application to facilitate their decision. Computers were provided by a wide variety of donors, including Boeing, MACTEC Engineering and Consulting, Inc., and many private individuals.

Software. We used a combination of open-source and Microsoft software programs to populate our refurbished computers.

1. Open-source. We leveraged the vast array of open-source software to populate our donated computers, installing Linux and Open Office as the base components of many computers.
2. Microsoft Refurbishers Program (MAP) [7]. To affordably obtain Microsoft programs, we applied to be a Microsoft Authorized Refurbisher, which allowed us to purchase Microsoft software at discounted prices. This approach eliminated many of the costs associated with nonopen-source software and gave us flexibility and variety in the types of programs that could be installed and used by our students. This process involved obtaining reference letters from our community partners and submitting an application. Through the MAR program, we were able to obtain Microsoft Office XP for $5.00 per key and

BOOTUP Request to Donate

Thanks for considering us! If you can fill out this form, that would be really helpful. We refurbish and donate the desktop computers for schools. The laptops are primarily used for international projects—such as a computer lab (Thinklab for El Buen Samaritano in Jocotenango, Guatemala) or health clinic (telemedicine laptops for a clinic in Ndoni, Nigeria—this is 2008 and onwards effort).

Please feel free to email me at chrlee@gmail.com or call at 310.439.9311.

*Required

Name

Contact Information (email preferred)

What kind of equipment are you donating?

How old is equipment?

Do you need a 501c3 receipt?
☐ Yes
☐ No

Will you be able to drop off the computer at UCLA?*
☐ Yes
☐ No

What time is generally convenient for you to meet to donate?

(Submit)

Powered by Google Docs

Report Abuse · Terms of Service · Additional Terms

Figure 17.3. Google Form template was used to facilitate donation applications and documentation.

Windows XP Professional for $5.00 per key (2007 prices). This program has since been reconfigured to the Microsoft Register Refurbishers Program [7].

17.3.5 Identifying a Site

We worked closely with the UCLA Center for Community Learning (CCL) and their partners to determine which schools would benefit from an after-school computer-education program and/or computer-equipment donations. Through CCL, we were able to work with the Children Youth Family Collaborative in Los Angeles (CYFCLA), through which we identified multiple candidates, including Dorsey High School, View Park Preparatory Accelerated High School (VPPAHS), and New Los Angeles Charter School. In other instances, we were contacted by potential partners to work together, as was the case with Central High School in the Mar Vista Gardens Housing Projects. Schools were all located in Los Angeles, CA (Figure 17.4). In this chapter, we discuss our experiences at three schools—Dorsey High, View Park Prep, New Los Angeles Charter, and Central High School Mar Vista— and the lessons learned from different approaches applied at each school.

17.3.6 Dorsey High School (Computer-Building Workshop)

The students who were eligible for the after-school workshop did not have computers at home and signed up to participate in the program out of inter-

Figure 17.4. A map of Los Angeles schools with whom BOOTUP has partnered.

est. In 2006, Dorsey High School was largely African-American (57%) and Hispanic (42.1%) [8]. All of the ten participants in the BOOTUP after-school program were African-American.

17.3.7   View Park Preparatory Accelerated High School and New Los Angeles Charter (Donated Computer Lab)

We donated a computer lab to these schools. We were informed during our discussions with the school-site partner that students at View Park Prep typically had to walk to a library using a route that included Crenshaw and Slauson, which is considered one of the most crime-ridden intersections in Los Angeles. In 2006, 97.3% of students were African-American [9]; however, we did not work directly with students during the implementation of this project. New Los Angeles High School serves 300 middle school (grades 6–8) students and is comprised of 38% African-American students, 35% Hispanic or Latino students, and 36% Caucasian students [9]; however, during this project we also did not work directly with students under this project model.

17.3.8.   Central High School Mar Vista (Computer Lab Donation and Free-Form Seminars)

We began this project as a computer workshop and lab donation and our partnership with the school gradually evolved to include a variety of additional activities. All grade levels were combined into one classroom; on average, there were approximately 15–20 students in attendance. Of those enrolled, 5% were African-American and 95% were Mexican, Salvadorian, Guatemalan, or Honduran [10]. Rather than following a fixed approach, we continued to work together with Central High School to organize seminars, guest speakers, and field trips. In the next section, we will discuss one of our specific environmental education research activities, entitled "Student Waterkeepers in Action." This latter project was essentially the product of a natural progression of our partnership, whereby we organized a field-research project about water pollution for high school students to participate in.

17.4   RESULTS

17.4.1   Dorsey High School Computer-Building Workshop

Project coleads were C. M. Maxwell and H. Pai. During the course of the after-school workshops, which spanned four quarters, we paired 30 high school students to ten UCLA student volunteers (primarily engineering students). High school students enrolled in these workshops as an after-school program and worked with their UCLA mentors to build computers (through dissembling and reassembling) and install and troubleshoot various programs on these computers. Upon completion of the program, they were able to retain the computers upon agreement that they would be used for academic purposes only.

17.4.2 View Park Preparatory Accelerated High School—Computer Lab Donation

Project coleads were C. M. Maxwell and L. Balzano. On June 9, 2007, we went to View Park Prep Accelerated High School (VPPAHS) to set up and donate a computer lab. During this effort, we successfully refurbished 10 computers for use in a classroom that was secured by the school. The time commitment associated with the project was considerably less than that required in the computer-building workshop model and included preparation spanning about 5–10 hours per week for four weeks and 3–4 hours of setting up the lab on one Saturday morning. Prep work included collecting and wiping computers, swapping parts as appropriate, and installing software to be used.

17.4.3 New Los Angeles Charter— Computer Lab Donation

Project lead was R. Mathew. On April 10, 2011, a group of volunteers donated ten working computers (equipped with Windows XP) to the New Los Angeles Charter School, a charter K–8 school in downtown Los Angeles. The computer lab was established in a classroom and will be used in a class of sixth-grade students. The computers were also loaded with essential software before the donation, making them more useful to the students. Internet access was made available through the purchase of USB wi-fi adapters.

17.4.4 Central High School—Computer Donations, Seminars, and Environmental Education

Project coleads were C. M. Maxwell and V. Vasquez. In early winter of 2008, we began visiting Central High School as part of an effort to put together a technology lab for the students. A research scholar (Dr. Young Cho) at UCLA was interested in conducting computer programming classes and needed equipment to establish this workshop. As a result, we have donated five computers (and additional equipment over the following years) to their classroom. We also let the partnership grow more organically, continuing to work together to host guest speakers and activity leaders and diversify the types of learning activities the students were exposed to. Rather than playing a fixed role of being technology providers, the partnership developed such that we felt more personally invested in the students' learning and growth. In 2009, two Ph.D. students [Christine M. Maxwell (formerly Lee) and Victor Vasquez in Civil and Environmental Engineering and the Environmental Science and Engineering programs, respectively] established "Student Waterkeepers in Action." This field-research project was geared toward engaging students in learning about the effects of pollution and conducting water quality testing at the Ballona Creek Watershed in Southern California. The students used the equipment we donated and utilized Microsoft Office tools to put together poster presentations that were held at UCLA. We fulfilled both our original vision of providing technology-based experiences and instructionand also broadened our scope to provide additional science and environmental education experiences.

17.5 DISCUSSION: LESSONS LEARNED

17.5.1 Computer-Education Workshops and After-School Program Model

We found that engaging interested students during an after-school program was a highly effective way to conduct our program. Efforts to use classroom time were more difficult to justify and having an enrollment period ensured that students who were present were interested in participating, as they have a choice of various after school activities to sign up for. We also found that the having the same mentor paired with a student week after week provided consistency and allowed for continued progress between sessions. This approach was time-intensive, as it required a quarter-long, continuous commitment from our volunteers. The experience was also very enriching for our volunteers and, during this time, we had the highest rate of return volunteers compared to the other approaches.

17.5.2 Computer Lab Donation Model

This project was not as time-intensive as the after-school program. The majority of meetings and site-contact discussions were established through meetings between BOOTUP coordinators and schools. The primary time commitment was refurbishing the computers with one site-engagement day required. The lab implementation required only one weekend morning for a few hours and, in general, was much more flexible in terms of time and effort. Student volunteers who were interested in participating in the project were able to do so according to their respective schedules. As a result, we generally had more students who were willing to donate a small amount of time to the project.

17.5.3   Computer Lab Donation, Workshop, and Free-Form Model

This project was the most time-intensive effort of the three presented. However, it was also extremely fulfilling for the UCLA participants, as we were able to fold in additional activities that leveraged our respective areas of expertise during our partnership with the school. One reason we were able to exercise more freedom in the way we developed on-site activities is that the teaching format at Central High School was less restrictive. Many of the other schools we worked with allowed us to visit only during after-school hours or had very strict criteria for activity types. Central High School allowed us to establish activities that took advantage of the larger blocks of time that were available. We were also able to engage the community and develop important leadership and communication skills as a result. The planning and fundraising needed to execute Student Waterkeepers in Action (and other similar activities) represented an additional time and energy commitment because it diverged from our traditional, planned approach. We also had to develop a lesson each week that built on the previous weeks and coordinate with the Ballona Creek Wetlands to plan a trip and water-testing period. Finally, we coordinated a poster session at UCLA that required bringing together different interested parties who were willing to host and sponsor the event (i.e., transportation for the students, poster printing, space requirements, etc.)

17.6   CONCLUSION

From the perspective of time commitment, the computer lab donation model is more sustainable than the after-school workshops model and the free form-model because volunteers are often only able to participate in BOOT-UP in a limited and sometimes sporadic fashion. However, from a holistic standpoint, the leadership and communication skills and experiences obtained from the workshop and free-form models were much more meaningful and impactful to personal growth and civic engagement for the high school students as well as the college students. This long-term impact may contribute more significantly to sustainability, as such experiences are often what drive additional projects and community-engagement efforts. Although a combination of approaches would be ideal, it is important to note that, as a student group project, the sustainability of just the project itself must account for both the student leaders' respective time commitments and constraints. It is critical to evaluate the relative constrains of student group leaders and plan/implement a project that fits reasonably within these constraints and that promotes a balance between academic obligations and civic engagement efforts.

ACKNOWLEDGMENTS

We would like to acknowledge and thank Engineers without Borders-UCLA, high school student participants, and site coordinators. A special thanks to Vitaly at Central High Mar Vista and Drs. Karen Kim and Young Cho at the Center for Embedded Networked Sensing at UCLA. We also gratefully acknowlege Laura Balzano, Hank Pai, and Victor Vasquez for their leadership and initiative in BOOTUP projects.

REFERENCES

1. E. Chisman, K. Laungluknavalai, C. Lee, D. Massaguer, and J. Ros-Giralt, "Labdoo: Re-Inventing International Cooperation Toward Bridging the Digital Divide," in *Information Technology and Service Learning,* Wiley–IEEE, 2012.

2. J. Ros, C. Lee, M. Bruce, and C. Fan, "A Portable and Sustainable Computer Education Project for Developing Countries–Phase I," *International Journal for Service Learning in Engineering,* Vol. 1, 27–47, 2006.

3. K. V. Dominguez, "Discussion of Computer Donations for View Park Prep," View Park Prep Accelerated Charter High School, Los Angeles, 2007.

4. Los Angeles Unified School District and Center for Education Leadership and Technology, "Instructional Technology Plan," 2000.

5. Engineers without Borders-UCLA, *BOOTUP Donations Form and Google Forms.* Available from https://docs.google.com/spreadsheet/viewform?key=0Ai_KBQCVNv-81cEdncW1 BSm9Cd3ZpWTRBRXJ0Y0Q5ZGc&hl=en_US#gid=0, 2008.

6. TechSoup.org. (Online). Available from http://home.techsoup.org/pages/default.aspx.

7. Microsoft Refurbisher Program, *Microsoft Authorized or Registered Refurbisher Program.* Available from http://www.microsoft.com/oem/en/licensing/sblicensing/pages/refurbisher_progra ms.aspx, 2003.

8. Los Angeles Unified School District, *Demographics—School Profile Page (Dorsey High School).* Available from http://search.lausd.k12.ca.us/cgibin/ fccgi.exe?w3exec=school.profile.content&which=8600, 2005–2006.

9. Los Angeles Unified School District, "Demographics—School Profile Page (View Park Preparatory Accelerated High School)," 2006.

10. Vitaly (Central High School Mar Vista teacher), "Student Demographics," 2011.

CHAPTER 18

USING LABDOO TO BRIDGE THE DIGITAL DIVIDE
A New Form of International Cooperation

Jordi Ros-Giralt, Kevin Launglucknavalai, Daniel Massaguer,
Julieta Casanova, and Christine M. Lee

ABSTRACT

With the advent of ubiquitous wireless access to the Internet, computers take an essential role in the fight against global education inequalities. The objective of Labdoo is simple: to provide laptops for every school on the planet so that children can gain free access to sources of education. Although this is not a new concept, what differentiates Labdoo from a traditional nongovernmental organization (NGO) is the approach it takes. A key concept behind Labdoo resides in the notion of solving a mission without incurring additional economic or environmental costs, because the acquisition of such costs implies, by definition, a disinvestment in other crucial humanitarian aid programs such as the provisioning of food and health care. Three current factors make this idea viable: (1) the massive amounts of excess capacity generated in the developed world, (2) the maturity of our information systems, and (3) the wealth of networks or our new capability to break down a very large task into millions of smaller subtasks and execute them ad hoc from different parts of the globe. To maximize the gains from each of these factors, the Labdoo Project is built on the notion of a fully distributed NGO: instead of building a centralized organization, our effort focuses on building the social-network tools needed so that every laptop owner on the planet can take upon the "minimission" of bringing his or her own unused laptop to a child.

This paper describes the socioeconomic factors that make the Labdoo Project possible and how its implementation can help us to understand a new breed of international aid organizations capable of solving global problems by using global means.

18.1   INTRODUCTION

In 2002, William Kamkwamba was a fourteen year old child from Malawi when his country experienced the worst famine in fifty years. He was forced to drop out of secondary school as his parents could no longer afford the $80 tuition [1]. Instead of going to school, William had to stay home and work to help his family. William however loved books and whenever he had a chance, he biked to the village's library to read. On one of these trips, William encountered an American textbook of physics that explained how to build a windmill. He figured out that he could use a windmill to light a bulb in his room to read at night. According to William, "Once the sun goes down, and if there's no moon, everyone stops what they're doing, brushes their teeth, and just goes to sleep. Not at 10:00 P.M., or even nine o'clock, but seven in the evening! Who goes to bed at seven in the evening? Well, I can tell you, most of Africa." [1] So he built a windmill following the indications in the textbook, out of strips of PVC pipe, rusty cars, bicycle parts, and gum trees. And since the windmill worked, he went on and built another one for his neighbors, enough to generate electricity to pump water to irrigate the entire village's fields.

As remarkable William's story is, behind it some crucial socioeconomic lessons ought to be noted. In situations of severe poverty, the traditional model of education based on unidirectional offloading of knowledge from teachers to students may not be affordable. (William's family, once famine hit the village, could no longer afford the school fees.) The self-driven, distributed-education model provided William a powerful, affordable, and sustainable alternative.

In light of this story, an intriguing and somehow troublesome question arises: how many "Williams" are currently in Africa and around the globe who never had the opportunity to encounter a physics textbook and, hence, how many villages and communities lost the chance of benefiting from the true potential capabilities of their people? This question is intimately related to what is commonly referred as the digital divide problem, a situation that arises because people having free access to information gain knowledge at a pace much higher than people that lack such access, creating an ever increasing gap between the two groups.

Consider first, as a framework to guide our discussion, the following experiment. Imagine that we set up a project to bring physics textbooks to all the children's homes in Africa. What impact would such a project have in the development of African villages? Children have a variety of interests. Some may love music, some soccer, some the arts, and others math. As in William's story, our physics textbook experiment would likely attract the attention of those children who enjoy engineering designs, and amongst them, those that have a sense for entrepreneurship (like William) would go as far as developing the skills taught in the textbook and put them into practice, becoming new leaders and helping to ignite a development path within their own communities. This hypothetical experiment illustrates how access to information (the textbook) constitutes a key link in a chain of opportunity-driven events that can potentially spur economic development (Figure 18.1).

Project Labdoo's mission centers around the question of how we as a society can provide such opportunities to all the children in the globe. Although the hypothetical textbook experiment does not constitute a realistic approach (we would need to cut many trees and spend a lot of dollars to bring textbooks to all the children, money and resources that would likely be more efficiently invested in other types of aid, such as medicines and food), we argue that the world in which we live provides enough excess capacity and its state of the art is sufficiently mature that we are in a position to "provide a physics textbook" to every child on the planet without the need to cut any additional trees or use any other type of resources with an opportunity cost larger than zero (such as money, inventory costs, transportation costs, etc.).

The idea of Labdoo is simple. First, the role of the textbook in our fictitious experiment can be emulated using a computer with access to free sources of education such as Wikipedia or any of the open-source educational content already available online. Second, consider the following fact: in 2010 we bought about 170 million laptops world-wide, a number that continues to grow every year (Figure 18.2). Most of these computers will be replaced by new ones in three or four years. On the other hand, in Africa alone, there are 109 million children between the ages of fifteen and nineteen years old. Hence, in just one year, the developed world acquires and

Figure 18.1. Self-driven education model: the textbook, providing free access to information, is the first step of a linked chain of events that can lead to grassroots development. Combined with their curiosity and will to learn, some children become entrepreneurs and help bootstrap their communities.

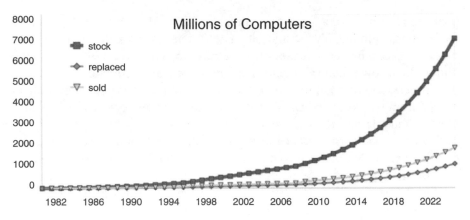

Figure 18.2. In 2010 there were about 170 million laptops sold world-wide. Some of these laptops were used to replace older ones, leading to an ever increasing stock of unused laptops [2, 3].

displaces enough laptops to potentially equip every African child in high school.

Labdoo's mission statement focuses on the concept of providing laptops to every school on the planet so that children can gain free access to education and, as a consequence, help unlock the true potential of every child the same way William unlocked his when he encountered the physics textbook. Although the idea of equipping children with computers to gain access to education is not a new one—there exist a good number of NGOs and organizations that focus on the same concept—the difference resides in the way Labdoo approaches its mission.

The core argument of Labdoo is that our current state-of-the-art technology allows us to solve the problem of the digital divide without the need to cut another tree or use any additional dollars. We believe and argue that this is a crucial concept in the design of sustainable aid projects. In the world of international cooperation, an embedded assumption has been that players (e.g., volunteers, project leads, investors, and beneficiaries) operate under a zero-sum-game regime; that is to say, to provide aid to a certain project P1, one needs to invest a certain amount of resources and, as a consequence, the same amount of resources need to be disinvested from some other project P2. For instance, if we invest our money in buying a new laptop for a school, then we are implicitly disinvesting the same amount of money in all other possible aid projects, such as provisioning of food, clean water, or medicines. This leads us to what can be referred as the *opportunity cost dilemma:* in international cooperation, what is the optimal basket of aid investments? For instance, what is more important, health care or education? And by what fraction? Do we really need to make such tough choices?

In Labdoo, we argue that current technological advances can liberate us from having to make such choices. The core idea is that today it is possible to create global organizations that operate under a non-zero-sum game regime by which all players gain a net benefit or at least are not worse off. It is important to note that by players we here mean the set of all benefactors and beneficiaries that are part of all international aid programs, and we include in that list planet earth. An objective of this chapter is to show that the digital divide problem can be fought without cutting any additional trees nor generating more CO_2 emissions.

The idea of building aid organizations that avoid both economic and environmental costs finds its foundation in the following three observations:

1. *Excess capacity.* We live in a world with plenty of excess capacity; for instance, we continuously acquire new goods and displace older ones that are still in perfect condition. This process of ever-increasing levels of excess capacity is driven by a Schumpeterian process of creative destruction [4], which explains how technology replacement is not driven by the rate of depreciation of our existing technological stock, but rather the creation of new technology that displaces (destroys) the existing one. For instance, we do not tend to replace our computer because it has broken but rather because a new product has appeared in the market that is superior to our current one. The process of creative destruction is specially acute for the case of computers because of the exponential effect Moore's Law, which states that computing capacity doubles every 18 months [5].

2. *Information age.* Our current state-of-the-art technology (e.g., Internet, search engines, and geolocation platforms) is mature enough that it is possible to know at practically no marginal cost where the sources of supply and demand are located, and organize such knowledge to make better informed decisions, lowering the economic and environmental costs of our mission.

3. *Wealth of networks.* As explained by some economists [6], the same current state-of-the-art technology allows us for the first time to resolve large problems by dividing them into millions of very small pieces, so small that each piece has a practically zero opportunity cost.

A key design parameter in the building of a sustainable organization is its degree of decentralization. We argue that the concept of decentralization is intimately related to the notion of larger-than-zero-sum-game organizations, that is, international aid programs in which all players, including planet earth, are not worse off and at least one player is better off. We use this design parameter to create a comparative framework with two types of models: the *centralized model,* which for the most part has been the traditional approach to international aid; and the *distributed model,* which we believe is a type of organization in emergence that will play a key role in the design of a new breed of sustainable aid programs. Distributed organizations are, in fact, not new; for instance, the Wikipedia Project [7] serves as a well-known example of how a decentralized approach has allowed society to solve the problem of building and maintaining a massive encyclopedia much more efficiently. In this context, the Labdoo Project can be understood as a collaborative framework using the same type of distributed tools, albeit applied to help solve the digital divide.

This chapter is organized as follows. We start our discussion in Section 18.2, describing our first project carried out in Guatemala. This initial project, which followed the structure of a traditional centralized approach, will provide a reference model in subsequent sections when describing our new distributed approach. Section 18.3 provides the basic Labdoo framework. We start by discussing how we migrated from a centralized approach to a distributed approach, and follow with a more detailed description of the socioeconomic drivers that make the distributed model sustainable and scalable. To illustrate how Labdoo operates, Section 18.4 provides some brief study cases of minimissions carried out by several groups of volunteers distributed across the globe. In Section 18.5, we describe the benefits of Labdoo from a service-learning perspective, focusing on the specific perspective of the volunteers participating in the project. We add in Section 18.6 a discussion of the role that Labdoo takes within each of the primary factors of production (natural resources, physical and human capital), and then provide a brief introduction to Project Wiki-Kids, a spin-off project from Labdoo that aims at connecting children of different nations by overlaying a network of knowledge sharing on top of Labdoo's physical network of laptops. Conclusions are included in Section 18.7.

18.2 THE ORIGINS OF AN IDEA: PROJECT THINKLAB!, GUATEMALA, 2005

In 2005, our team consisting of four members from Engineers Without Borders-UCLA travelled to Jocotenango, Guatemala to carry out the implementation of project Thinklab! The mission of this project was to partner with the local community of Jocotenango in the construction of a computer lab made of refurbished laptops obtained from various personal and corporate donors in the area of Southern California. The laptops were installed with open-source Linux software, loaded with a variety of education applications, and connected to the Internet. A four-teacher-week course was held at the community organization to instruct the local students on basic computing skills and maintenance.

In this section, we summarize the operations involved in project ThinkLab! with the purpose of illustrating a model—the centralized model—that we will later use as a base reference against the new model provided by Labdoo—the distributed model. (For a thorough description of project ThinkLab! refer to [8].)

18.2.1   Principles and Brief Summary of Project ThinkLab!

In ThinkLab!, we sought to develop and implement a computer-education and technology lab for a community center. This project was conducted in concert with the core principles of Engineers Without Borders—essentially, to be sustainable as well as conscientious of the potential environmental and socioeconomic impacts that the project may incur.

The first considerations, after developing our mission statement, were *location* and *partners*. This decision involved both geographical considerations as well as the people with whom we would be working. The team reviewed the socioeconomic indices for several Latin American countries prior to outreaching to organizations and selected a few. The immediate connection with and enthusiasm of a local school in Jocotenango, Guatemala led the team to focus on the school. This center served an important function for approximately ninety children of all ages in their home, family, and school environments. As was demonstrated, the close partnership with the school was instrumental to the success of the project.

Hardware and software also represented an important challenge to the project. This was largely because of potential costs involved in collecting and maintaining the computers. We achieved this by working with local Southern California partners and Techsoup.* These partners connected us with potential computer donors, enabling us to collect eleven IBM laptops. To minimize upfront and maintenance costs, we also used open-source software to populate the machines, including OpenOffice (alternative to Microsoft Office Suite) and Linux RedHat (alternative to Microsoft Windows). Computers that were not repairable were recycled at the UCLA electronic waste recycling facility.

For the implementation of the actual computer lab, the four EWB-UCLA members travelled to Jocotenango, Guatemala. The team helped prepare one

---

*Techsoup is a nonprofit organization that focuses on providing other nonprofits with technology that empowers them to fulfil their missions and serve their communities. See www.techsoup.org.

of the rooms in the school for the installation of the computers, negotiated with the local telecommunications operator a discounted rate for ADSL Internet access at 256 Kbps, installed and configured the laptops and the network, and held a four-week course on basic computing and maintenance skills for teachers. This phase of the project allowed us to meet our partners and establish new longer term goals with respect to technology education as well as take in other important considerations, such as the energy costs of a computer lab.

18.2.2 The Thinklab! Approach

In accord with many Engineers Without Borders projects, in our first project we sought to establish our work from the ground up, by coordinating and organizing all aspects of each planning task. This centralized approach concentrated the diverse tasks required for the project's implementation to the group, including planning, campaigning for funds and resources, partnership and outreach, and implementation, on the core team. This was a highly educational experience, as each member of the team became highly involved in each stage of the project, learning a wide variety of skills, including leadership, communication and negotiation, and hardware/software skills.

From a sustainability standpoint, however, the turnover rate of EWB members, particularly at the student-chapter level, is typically high. Students who develop the skills to continue advancing the implementation of a project eventually graduate and the capability to redevelop these skills in the next generation team depends heavily on the new members, funding availability, project requirements, and so forth.

The emergence of a new, decentralized approach, becomes key to the sustainability of internationally reaching computer-education projects. This idea will be the focus of the following sections. Essentially, with the new model, the responsibility for on-the-ground tasks is distributed, allowing the specific skills or value of each person or organization to be efficiently leveraged. For instance, companies and individual laptop owners that are able to donate computers are also given the tools for removing, formatting, and installing the units with the specified software, rather than relying on EWB members to do so. Furthermore, this approach empowers donors, allowing them to be a part of the solution, and enabling a mechanism to solve global issues through global means.

With the new model, distributed hubs are operated by teams such as EWB and other NGO groups in such a way that the important personal development skills that accompanied the original centralized approach can still be cultivated. This approach has proved to be highly successful. Whereas it took us one year to implement a single computer lab in Guatemala with a centralized approach, with the new decentralized approach and in a little more than a year, project Labdoo is now servicing fourteen different projects in ten different countries distributed across Central and South America, Africa, and Asia, all made possible by mobilizing a network of grassroots volunteers from California, Taiwan, New York, Barcelona, Madrid, and Rome. Perhaps what is more relevant than these numbers is that the Labdoo network has been designed from the ground up as a project that can grow organically with the grassroots, empowering each of us who owns a laptop to be a part of the solution.

18.3 APPLYING THE WEALTH OF A NETWORK TO BRIDGE THE DIGITAL DIVIDE

18.3.1 Debating Our Original Approach

The core idea motivating the work carried out during the first school project in Guatemala was that by providing free access to education, a computer lab helps unlock the true potential of every child in the school the same way William had unlocked his engineering skills. With a computer lab, the school does not have to put up with the cost of expensive encyclopedias, education games, or even textbooks; instead, it can resort to world-class educational content provided by Wikipedia.org, computer education games from Edubuntu.org, and online course materials from top schools such as MIT's OpenCourseWare.org program [9].

Our initial end-to-end approach—taking care of each and every aspect of the project—had been a great learning experience, and now we had to decide what to do next. We could continue working as a team—perhaps volunteering part of our after-work time as we entered the labor market—building one computer lab at a time and travelling every summer. We were realistic about the impact of such approach, however; it had taken us a full year to plan and implement a single computer lab project to bring just eleven laptops to a school. We had spent years pursuing our degrees in computer science, environmental and civil engineering, and other disciplines, and yet, based on the modus operandi that we had developed in our first project, the best we could do with such approach was to deliver one small computer lab per year. What bottlenecked the capacity of our team and was there a way to unblock it?

The original approach we had taken in the first project was that of a traditional NGO—we would gather a group of volunteers and we would perform every single task by ourselves to complete the project. Such way of operating can be understood as a centralized approach because the execution of each task is confined within a single concentrated domain—a team of volunteers and a set of resources operating from a roughly bounded geographical area, in our case, Southern California. If, for instance, each volunteer had an intrinsic capacity to deliver three laptops a year, then a team consisting of four volunteers would have the capacity to deliver twelve laptops. The question that still remained unanswered was how could we do more than just build one computer lab per year?

18.3.2 The Opposite Approach

We argue that from an operational perspective, the problem of solving the digital divide is structurally very similar to that of writing an encyclopedia such as Wikipedia or that of developing an operating system such as Linux [7]. Consider, for instance, the effort of writing an encyclopedia, a very large task if we consider that it aims at including the most relevant aspects of human knowledge for all times and all civilizations. The traditional approach employed by large publishers has followed a centralized model, employing a small group of experts, each one dedicated to writing a large portion of the encyclopedia. The approach taken by Wikipedia.org can be understood as an antithesis to such a centralized model, relying on a large number of authors each making small contributions (a single article or small adjustments to an article) [10].

A comparably large effort is that of creating a new operating system (OS), the software blueprints that dictate how a computer behaves. To carry out such a mission, Microsoft adopted in the 1980s a centralized approach, hiring a relatively small group of computer scientists, each taking care of the implementation of a specific module of the OS. Years later, the open-source community undertook the same challenge by using a decentralized approach, leveraging small contributions of a large community of computer scientists working from anywhere on the planet and at any time. The result was Linux, which today is known as one of the highest-quality operating systems.

This new way of approaching a problem has revolutionized in three ways the intrinsic nature of the solutions we are now capable of articulating: projects can be executed faster, at a much lower cost, and often with a much higher quality (Table 18.1). Further, these and other examples [7] demonstrate that there is a class of problems that are better solved by employing a very large number of very small and highly distributed resources, rather than a set of few, large, and concentrated resources. In the sections that follow, we argue that the digital divide problem belongs to such class of problems.

Table 18.1. Projects that can be implemented using distributed means tend to enjoy faster deployment times, incur lower costs, and often yield higher quality.

Factor	Rationale	Example
Speed	By tapping into resources that are highly distributed and connected through the network, input resources tend to grow exponentially, quickly reducing output production times.	It took just 5 years for Wikipedia to reach one million articles.
Cost	By unlocking small resources with very little opportunity cost that otherwise would go unused, production costs are drastically reduced.	By unlocking free resources that otherwise would have gone unused, Wikipedia was built at a much reduced economic cost than conventional encyclopedias.
Quality	By having many observers looking at and verifying the various parts of the project, its quality quickly increases with time.	The Linux operating system is regarded by many computer scientists as a fine piece of work.

18.3.3   Building Metagoods, Rather than the Goods Themselves

Suppose that you have a task to carry out. Such task will produce an outcome or good G that will depend on the amount of resources R you have available. We observe that there are two ways to carry out your task (Figure 18.3):

Approach A. You can employ your resources R to directly produce G.

Approach B. You can employ your resources R to produce first an "intermediary good" that others can use to produce G.

There are many examples of projects that have migrated from approach A to approach B. In fact, means of production tend to be in a constant path of

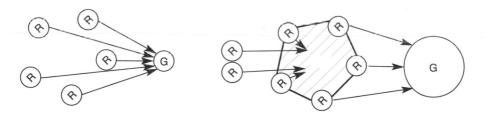

Figure 18.3. Left, a traditional approach to humanitarian aid, in which all resources are directly applied to produce a good G. This is the approach our team took in the first project implemented in Guatemala. Right, an approach based on the wealth of networks, in which resources are first employed to build an intermediary metagood, unlocking a network of resources and yielding a much larger outcome. This is the appoach taken by the Labdoo Project.

migration from A to B, which could also be referred as a process of *virtualization of the means of production*. For instance, in the automobile industry, cars were first assembled manually, with each worker building one car at a time. With the invention of Ford's assembly line, cars were produced using tools (or intermediary goods) that made the production system so efficient that they could be sold for the first time at affordable prices to middle class people. In programming languages, computer scientists use the concept of functions and application programming interfaces (APIs) to implement certain components of a program in a way that others can reuse them without the need to reimplement the whole program.

Concepts like Ford's assembly line, the Internet, or programming APIs can be considered as goods of a special kind, because their function is not to fulfill a final need, but rather to provide the means to produce other goods that fulfill such needs in a much more efficient way. We can call them intermediary goods or *metagoods*.

If metagoods are helping us unlock the true potential of our society, we could ask ourselves, What metagoods are needed to solve the digital divide problem? We started our project wanting to build a computer lab in a disadvantaged school. In our first project, we took approach A, dedicating all our resources to directly build the computer lab. Going forward, we thought that perhaps there was a better way to dedicate our time; instead of building the goods directly, we could take approach B and dedicate our time to develop metagoods to unlock the true potential that we as a society have to solve the digital divide problem. This is how the Labdoo Project was initiated, as an attempt to build metagoods to help solve the digital divide.

18.3.4   The Wealth of Networks, Minimissions, and Drops of Goodwill

Ideas and technologies have the peculiarity of being cumulative—they build on previous ones, and once invented, they cannot be uninvented. This macrotrend is a conduit of other smaller and equally irreversible drivers, one of which has revolutionized twenty-first century production systems—as we invent more technologies, our capability to divide tasks into smaller and smaller subtasks increases. Wikipedia and Linux provide two examples of such phenomena. In the past, the capability of writing an encyclopedia or an operating system was only in the hands of large governments and corporations but now, thanks to technology, we can carry out such large projects by dividing them into a very large number of small subtasks, each carried out by a very small resource.

The extent to which a community or society can divide projects into smaller tasks defines in good degree its capability to undertake and resolve certain problems. This is because of the following simple principle: a resource R cannot resolve any task that requires more than R resources, but it can resolve any task requiring up to R resources. For instance, suppose that a volunteer can offer one hour of her time to help a humanitarian cause. Among all the potential causes, the volunteer would be able to contribute to those projects that have subtasks requiring up to one hour of volunteer work, but not to those for which all subtasks require more than one hour of work. If there is no humanitarian cause with subtasks smaller or equal to one hour, then that volunteer (the resource) will go underutilized. We can say that such resource is locked or wasted due to our inability to divide a large task into small enough subtasks. Based on this principle, we can then argue that, throughout history, to the extent that we have not been able to divide tasks into small enough subtasks, many potential resources have been wasted, deadlocking the real intrinsic potential that we as a society have to solve problems. As technology evolves, our capability to divide tasks into smaller and smaller subtasks increases, and this allows us to unlock massive amounts of potential resources that otherwise would have remained dormant.

Metagoods such as real-time communication and distributed computing have empowered us with an unprecedented capability to divide tasks into nearly arbitrarily small subtasks, allowing us to solve large and challenging projects, such as the development of the Linux operating system or the writing of the Wikipedia, in a very cost-effective manner. As demonstrated by these powerful examples, if the key to unlock the true potential of our community to resolve large problems is the size of the smallest indivisible subtask, then when designing an efficient solution for the digital divide problem we ought to ask ourselves: what are the smallest atomic and indivisible subtasks that need to be carried out to overcome this challenge?

We apply this basic framework to the problem of bringing a large quantity of laptops to children. Four atomic and indivisible subtasks or elements are required to bring a laptop to a child:

AT1. Unused laptop—an unused laptop has to be first donated.

AT2. Sanitization—the laptop has to be sanitized and loaded with the education software.

AT3. Storage and inventory—because supply and demand are not perfectly synchronized, storage is needed to keep the laptop while it waits for demand.

AT4. Shipment—the laptop has to be shipped to a school.

A traditional approach would implement all the tasks above in a centralized manner, preventing us from unlocking the true potential of our community. The wealth of networks principle [6], instead, says that network effect gains can be maximized by (1) identifying first the smallest indivisible sub-tasks (in our case, AT1 through AT4) and (2) carrying them out in a distributed manner, unlocking small resources wherever and whenever they are available.

From this perspective, Labdoo can be understood as a distributed platform to efficiently resolve the problem of sanitizing and bringing large amounts of laptops from one place to another by leveraging a very large number of "drops of goodwill" (small volunteer actions performed asynchronously from anywhere in the world and coordinated through the network) and without imposing any additional costs to planet earth. We elaborate more on the issue of cost in the following section.

18.3.5   Zero-Opportunity-Cost Resources and Sustainable Organizations

We know that every year we replace millions of powerful laptops that are still functional and we know that thousands of schools around the globe could benefit from them. The next question is how we can execute tasks AT1, AT2, AT3, and AT4 on a large scale? A traditional approach would typically work as follows. We would first create a nonprofit organization to establish the legal and operational ground of our project. Next, we would collect funds from investors and friends to pay for its operational costs. Once we had the funding, we would recruit volunteers and employees to execute the project. For the transportation of the laptops, we would pay for a large container and ship the laptops in large batches. Finally, the laptops would be deployed in their final destination.

The traditional approach, however, leads us to the following question: what is the opportunity cost of our project? If we invest money and new planet-earth resources to carry out our mission, then, by definition, we are implicitly disinvesting the same amount of resources in all other possible aid projects, for instance, projects such as the provisioning of food, clean water or medicines. At Labdoo, we argue that, thanks to the current technological state of the art, we can design our organizations in a way that such costs are minimized or even eliminated. The concept of building sustainable organizations that impose no cost to society is made possible thanks to the following three factors:

1. *Excess capacity.* We live in a world with plenty of excess capacity. For instance, we continuously acquire new goods and displace older ones that are still in perfect condition.
2. *Information age.* Our current state-of-the-art technology (e.g., Internet, search engines, and geolocation platforms) is mature enough that

it is possible to know at practically no marginal cost where the sources of supply and demand are located, and organize such knowledge to make better-informed decisions, lowering the economic and environmental costs of our mission.

3. *Wealth of networks.* As explained by some economists [6], the same current state-of-the-art technology allows us for the first time to resolve large problems by dividing them into millions of very small pieces, so small that each piece has a practically zero opportunity cost.

At Labdoo, we set out on the mission to bring laptops to children with the following key requirement: that such mission be carried out without the need for additional funding and without incurring any additional environmental costs to planet earth. The crux of it is to focus on a new generation of innovative ideas and technologies that allow us to leverage our excess capacity, our information systems, and the wealth of the network. These ideas are explained later in more detail in the Cycle of Life box (Box 18.2) and summarized next for each of the atomic tasks.

AT1. Instead of buying or building new laptops (which would lead to both an economic and environmental cost), Labdoo relies on unused but well-conditioned laptops. Since they are unused, their opportunity cost is zero.

AT2. The process of sanitizing a laptop leverages the wealth of networks to decompose the problem into tiny actions, so small that they can be carried out in an unsynchronized, ad hoc manner in any place, at no cost, and out of goodwill. For that, Labdoo provides the tools so that each laptop owner can sanitize his or her own laptop. (It takes about 45 minutes to sanitize a laptop.) We consider that this task is so small that it is cost-free. On the contrary, we argue that it actually brings a net benefit to laptop owners participating in the program as they earn the satisfaction of being part of a global movement solving a global social problem.

AT3. Since supply and demand are not perfectly synchronized, a centralized NGO would require a large warehouse to store all the laptops in stock. At Labdoo, instead, we use social networking tools to coordinate a distributed network of very small inventories provided by drawers and closets located in the homes of each participating laptop owner. In this way, laptops remain in people's homes until demand kicks in, minimizing the need for large, centralized inventories.

AT4. The transportation of a large number of laptops following a traditional approach imposes both an economic cost (the cost of the shipment) and an environmental cost (since the shipment generates new CO_2 emissions to the atmosphere). To avoid such costs, Labdoo has developed another social-network-based tool called *dootrips*. In a dootrip, volunteers traveling to remote locations first register their trip in the Labdoo social network. The dootrip engine makes optimal routing calculations and assigns laptops to travelers. Travelers then carry the laptops in their own luggage. Since travelers need to carry out such trips regardless of project Labdoo, dootrips allow us to effectively transport a large number of computers without incurring any additional costs to planet earth. As you are reading this text, there are probably thousands of humanitarian volunteers traveling in the developing world who can potentially be part of this Web 2.0 transportation system. (In Section 18.4 we describe some of the international dootrip routes that Labdoo has already unlocked.)

18.3.6 Helping Organize the Planet's Information

A recurring question at Labdoo is the value that the new distributed approach brings to the global community. In a centralized approach, it is easy to quantify the impact of a project because each contribution is carried out by a confined team of volunteers. For instance, the bottom-line value of Project ThinkLab! was a computer lab with eleven laptops connected to the Internet in a school in Guatemala. There were few spillover effects using the centralized approach. Measuring the value created by Labdoo is less trivial because, being a fully distributed, network-based, dispersed project, it is more likely to impact the global community in ways that we may still not foresee. (For instance, does the global approach taken by Labdoo help us gain a higher level of global awareness and, hence, make our world more or less sustainable and safe?)

We do believe, however, that Labdoo is contributing in one practical area that the previous centralized approach had little or no impact: on organizing the planet's information.* In particular, thanks to its networked approach, Labdoo allows us to know:

- The location of sources of demand for laptops. What schools need laptops?
- The location of sources of supply for laptops. Who has unused laptops that can be mobilized?
- The location and time availability of dootrips. What travellers can bring laptops in their luggage?

*Notice that this concept is similar to the contribution made by search engines such as Google's.

- The location and time availability of distributed inventory. What rooms, drawers, and closets are available to store laptops while they wait for demand to kick in?
- The location and time availability of volunteers sanitizing laptops. Who has 45 minutes available to sanitize a laptop?

The task of organizing the world's information, though seemingly abstract, is no different than many of the common tasks we usually do on a day-to-day basis. Consider, for instance, a family spending Saturday morning tidying up their home. Besides making home a prettier and more pleasant place in which to live, the main economic value of organizing one's place is *productivity*. A home that is well-organized will allow us to find things (such as a broom, clothes, or dishwasher soap) in a much faster way, helping us carry out our tasks more efficiently.

Similarly, at a global level, knowing with precision where our needs and resources are located ultimately helps us make better-informed decisions and, as a result, helps us achieve our mission in a more efficient way. The bottom line is that to lower the costs of our mission, and, hence deliver it while minimizing the environmental impact to planet earth, it is crucial that we first organize and tidy up our home.

18.3.7 Summary of Properties

To recapitulate the concepts described in the previous section, Table 18.2 summarizes the socioeconomic drivers upon which the Labdoo project is based.

18.4 A GRASSROOTS 2.0 MOVEMENT: BRIEF STUDY CASES

As of this writing, in its first fifteen months of operation, Labdoo has successfully refurbished and "dootripped" spare laptops from five developed countries (United States, Taiwan, Italy, Spain, and Germany) to sixteen communities in ten developing countries (Guatemala, Uganda, Bosnia And Herzegovina, Ecuador, Honduras, Ghana, Kenya, Nigeria, Cambodia, and Tanzania). This has been made possible thanks to the over 400 laptops tagged by volunteers worldwide, the time donated by volunteers in refurbishing laptops, and the spare luggage capacity donated by travelers via their dootrips.

Box 18.1 illustrates some of the international dootrip routes currently being used, including:

- Business people and engineers of a high-tech company who travel between Hsinchu, Taiwan, and San Jose, California

Table 18.2. Summary of Labdoo's socioeconomic drivers

Socioeconomic concept	How it actuates
Wealth of networks	Our current technological state of the art allows us to cut very large tasks into millions of very small subtasks. This, in turn, allows Labdoo to unlock a workforce consisting of a very large number of volunteers each performing a small task.
Goods versus metagoods	Instead of directly executing the tasks required to bring a laptop to a child, Labdoo focuses on developing the metagoods that help every laptop owner deliver his/her laptop to a child.
Zero-opportunity-cost resources	Labdoo's objective is to achieve its mission without the need for funding and without imposing an environmental cost to planet earth. This is made possible thanks to (1) availability of massive amounts of excess capacity, (2) the information age, and (3) the wealth-of-networks concept.
Schumpeter's Creative Destruction and Moore's Law	The process of creative destruction [4] and Moore's law [5] are two sides of the same coin: they mean that most of times we tend to replace a laptop not because it is broken, but because there is a much more powerful substitute available in the market. This process fuels consumption and the generation of large amounts of excess capacity.
Organizing the world's information	Before solving our mission, it is key that we organize the world's information so that we know with precision where the sources of demand and supply are located. This allows us to deliver our mission in a much more efficient manner, helping us to greatly lower the economic and environmental costs of our project.

- NGO staff who travel between New York City and Ndoni, Nigeria
- Volunteers from Engineers Without Borders USA who travel from California to Guatemala and from Massachusetts to Kenya
- A ground-transportation truck company that travels between Barcelona and Rome
- Individual travellers from Madrid visiting Cambodia
- A group of Christian volunteers who frequently travel between Rome and Bosnia
- A software engineer who often travels between Barcelona and New York City

The next two brief study cases illustrate how these occasional and permanent routes are used to complete some of the Labdoo minimissions and empirically demonstrate some of the concepts described in Section 18.3.

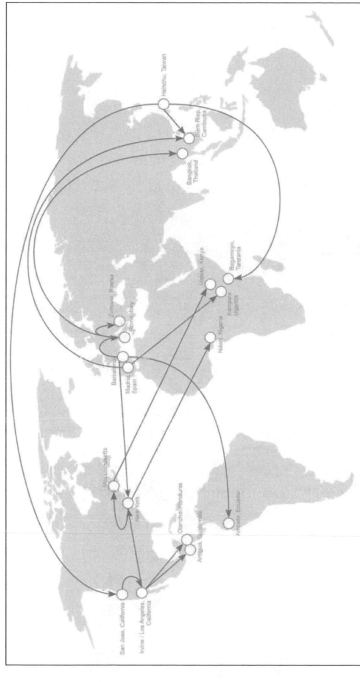

Box 18.1. Dootrips—A Socially Networked Transportation System. Labdoo solves the logistical problem of transporting laptops from one location to another by using a social network to organize information and mobilize dootrippers. Travellers from around the world first register their trips to the Labdoo social network. Then, Labdoo calculates optimal routes to bring laptops to children or to re-cycling factories. Labdoo conveys such information via e-mail, short message service (SMS), or tweets to the volunteers. This mecha-nism effectively provides a logistical transportation system at no economic cost and without incurring additional CO_2 emissions to the atmosphere. The map above displays some of the current mesh of routes that Labdoo is using.

18.4.1   Study Case 1: Matete, Kenya

In Matete, Kenya, a school is establishing a computer lab for their students with the help of Labdoo's social network tools and community. In one of the Labdoo grassroots projects, five idle laptops were located, donated, and collected from an R&D company based in New York. These laptops had been replaced by newer equipment following a Schumpeterian process of creative destruction (Section 18.3.7, and [4]). A Labdoo volunteer collected the laptops and contributed a drop of goodwill (Section 18.3.4) by dedicating some of his time to install Edubuntu in the laptops. The logistics to transport the

Figure 18.4. Students using Labdoo laptops. Who knows where the next William is?

laptops to Matete were coordinated using the dootrip tools, which exposed the inherent knowledge collected by the social network of Labdoo volunteers, mobilizing, in turn, more drops of goodwill from travelers willing to donate excess luggage capacity. In this case, a relative of the volunteer who refurbished the laptops carried them to Boston during one of her usual business trips from New York. Then an NGO volunteer, who travels frequently from Northampton to Boston, picked up the laptops in Boston and brought them to the headquarters of his NGO, which then carried the laptops to Matete, piggybacking on their next project trip.

18.4.2 Study Case 2: Ndoni, Nigeria

In Ndoni, Nigeria, the Saint Agnes School is also building a fifty-laptop computer lab for their 500 students. In another Labdoo grassroots project, Moore's Law [5] had shelved four laptops of four individuals in California. A set of Labdoo dootrips allowed collecting drops of goodwill from travellers who were willing to donate excess luggage capacity to transport the laptops from California to Nigeria. On this occasion, a Labdoo volunteer was traveling from California to Barcelona, stopping by New York for a few days. He carried the four laptops from California to New York. The laptops were then picked up by a representative from an NGO who frequently travels between New York and Ndoni. The NGO representative took the laptops to Ndoni on his following trip, using available space in his luggage. Similarly, six other laptops where carried using dootrips that connected Barcelona, California, New York, and Ndoni. At the time of writing, eleven laptops have also been carried from Hinschu, Taiwan, to San Jose, California, and are now waiting to be dootripped to New York, and from there to Ndoni, Nigeria.

18.5 LABDOO'S SERVICE-LEARNING MODEL

18.5.1 Service-Learning Benefits from the Labdoo Project

In utilizing the wealth of the network, the Labdoo Project is able to critically engage citizens, nonprofit organizations, and industries in the entire process by allowing each group to contribute their unique capabilities. By distributing each subtask in the process, volunteers with different backgrounds and interests are able to enter into and contribute to specific portions of the Labdoo process. As a result, the beneficiaries of the project are not only the recipients of laptops in the developing world, but also every person who participates via a process of service-learning. Further, since the Labdoo network connects everyone who is part of the project, collaboration occurs between groups at every level, across international boundaries and cultures.

Although there are many different types of benefits to both NGOs and industry, in this section we focus on how volunteers benefit through their service in the different aspects of the project.

18.5.2   The Cycle of Life

There are a variety of ways to characterize the benefits of volunteer involvement in Labdoo's service-learning process. In this section, we use three categories: educational, technical, and professional. Although there is overlap between these categories, they still provide a useful framework for understanding the many service-learning opportunities provided by the project. Below, we describe such service-learning opportunities in the context of Labdoo's Cycle of Life Process (Box 18.2), which describes the life cycle of a laptop from the time a laptop is tagged until it is delivered to a child and eventually recycled.

State S0: Tagging. Before participants can even donate an unused laptop, they can contribute to the project by joining the network of Labdooers. This is done by tagging or registering a laptop through the Labdoo website and joining the network. The process of tagging generates a unique identifier that is used to track each laptop as it makes progress toward a child or a recycling factory. People are encouraged to join and tag their laptops after members in the Labdoo project explain that the growing problems of electronic waste and the digital divide between the richer and the poorer countries can be addressed using the Labdoo method. A Labdooer is a person empowered to further spread awareness to other potential volunteers and contribute their individual skills. Due to the distributed approach, volunteers are immediately engaged with the entire process, each one making a small but direct contribution to the overall mission.

By spreading awareness and engaging in a meaningful discussion with others about how Labdoo can achieve its goals, volunteers obtain an advanced understanding of the current unsustainable economics of electronics and challenges of the project. By educating others about issues connected to Labdoo, such as responsible recycling and privacy concerns with donated laptops, volunteers gain a deep understanding of issues in a real world context. In exploring effective methods to carry out Labdoo Project, volunteers also learn various educational and communication methods.

State S1: Donation. When a laptop is no longer needed, its owner can either use the Labdoo online tools to sanitize it for a needed community, dootrip it to another volunteer, or bring it to a Labdoo hub for further processing. In the case that the laptop owner chooses to bring it to a hub, volunteers in the hub arrange the logistics for collecting it, tagging it (if it had not been already tagged), and storing it in the inventory. When arranging the logistics with the local community to collect the laptops, volunteers involved in the project are required to maintain professionalism. Through this process, volunteers learn that such professionalism is key to gaining the trust of the local community.

State S2: Quality Assurance. Once a laptop is donated to the Labdoo Project, the laptop must be checked for sufficient capabilities and sanitized before dootripping it. This includes physical sanitation of the laptop (ensuring that components such as hard drive, wireless card, CD drive, keyboard, and screen are all in good shape), and installation of the open-source operating system (Ubuntu and its education packages, Edubuntu). Although only basic computer skills are required to perform quality assurance, volunteers benefit from further development of technical skills for quicker identification of unsalvageable laptops and for the potential of reusing unused laptop components.

State S3: Maintaining an Inventory. Because, as in any other market economy, demand and supply are not perfectly synchronized, an intermediate storage step between donation of a laptop and its deployment is required. Although seemingly straightforward, volunteers involved in the project are required to secure laptops in a storage room and keep track of the inventory in a manner transparent not only to the Labdoo Project but to the general public. This establishes a firm foundation of trust between the public and the Labdoo volunteers for continued growth. The responsibility of this task gives volunteers maturity, professionalism, and a better understanding of working with a distributed inventory.

State S4: The Laptop is Assigned and Delivered. Once a laptop is fully prepared and a nonprofit organization shows the need for it, the laptop is donated and shipped to the recipient project using the dootrips social network. This provides yet another mechanism by which volunteers from different countries and across different segments (academic, industry, and nonprofit groups) collaborate together toward a common mission.

States S5 and S6: Use and Eventual Recycling. When a deployed Labdoo laptop breaks and is deemed irreparable, it is transported to the closest responsible recycler, using dootrips. Further, since Labdoo accepts laptops in all conditions, certain laptop donations that do not meet the minimum requirements are not suitable for deployment in schools. In such cases, Labdoo volunteers also recycle the laptops via responsible recyclers. The careful selection of recyclers is an important step because of the many different electronic waste recyclers available, some of which do not uphold sustain-

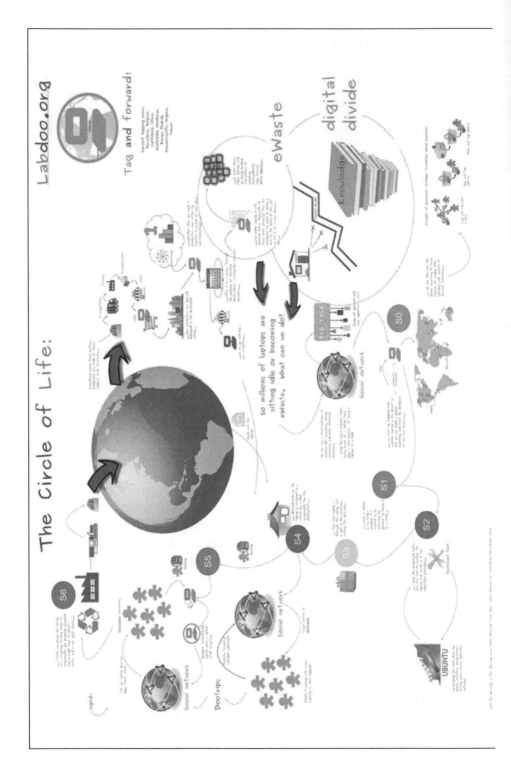

Box 18.1. Labdoo's Cycle of Life Story. The story begins with mother Earth, from which come all the building materials of a laptop. These materials are shipped to a factory where laptops are built. Then a brand-new laptop is sent to a store, waiting for a shopper to take it home. The laptop is used in productive ways, often by scientists in search of new ideas and technologies. Then after 3 or 4 years, through a process of creative destruction, the computer is left unused. It is not that the laptop does not work. It is still thousands of times faster than the computer we used to put a man on the moon. Still, we replace the old laptop with a new one and let the old one sit idly in our home. Large amounts of polluting semiconductor chips become global electronic waste. The paradox lies in that while millions of laptops are sitting idle, millions of children in the impoverished regions of the world still lack access to education. So we have got two globally related challenges: the elimination of e-waste and the provisioning of education to children using technology. How can we solve both of these problems? We can use a social network to mobilize idle resources, heighten awareness, and make informed decisions. With social-network tools, big tasks can be partitioned into very small subtasks with zero opportunity cost. Using social networking, each laptop owner takes upon a minimission to bring a laptop to a child. We start by tagging a laptop. By tagging each available laptop on the planet, we can track the progress of all our minimissions, efficiently matching supply and demand. Once no longer used, a laptop is marked as S1, initiating the process to bring it to a child. At stage S2, volunteers in the social network sanitize the laptop and install education packages such as Edubuntu, leveraging the work of thousands of global volunteer programmers writing open-source education software. Due to time lags between supply and demand, sanitized laptops are kept in the global inventory (Stage S3). When demand kicks in, a recipient school in the developing world is found. At stage S4, this school is assigned the laptop. Labdoo uses also a social network tool called dootrips to transport laptops while minimizing CO_2 emissions. Global travellers with excess capacity in their luggage register their travel via dootrip. The Labdoo social network assigns a laptop to a dootripper and makes a call for laptop pickup via SMS, tweet, or e-mail. A dootripper is found who carries the laptop to the school in the developing world while minimizing impact to the environment. Laptops at this stage are marked as S5. Eventually, deployed laptops break too, and so a plan to recycle them is needed. When that happens, an application called dooplet automatically informs the network, signalling the need for another dootrip. Again, the key is having information at hand to make informed decisions. Once a dootrip is found, the laptop is carried to a recycling factory and marked as S6. The laptop gets disposed at the recycling factory, returning to planet earth and completing another cycle of life. This is the Labdoo story, a story that each of us can be a part of toward making planet earth a sustainable place where every child can have access to education.

393

able practices [11]. At this stage, volunteers learn to perform proper due diligence on potential recyclers, picking only those organizations that follow the highest standards of quality.

Apart from the personal growth that students and other members experience by engaging with global issues and by contributing to a continuously evolving project, the network of volunteers benefit from each other through sharing learned experiences and skills. The network of volunteers benefit both from collaboration across multiple disciplines and from nurturing collaboration in an international setting.

18.6 WIKI-KIDS PROJECT: USING LABDOO TO HELP UNLOCK HUMAN CAPITAL

18.6.1 Physical Capital Versus Human Capital

Suppose that you rent a helicopter full of laptops, travel to a remote area, land the helicopter, install the laptops in a local school, connect them to the Internet (e.g., via a wireless LAN or a satellite station), and, immediately after, depart. What would the impact of such mission be to the local community?

Computers, unlike teachers, are passive devices. By themselves, they do not teach anything. Computers need to be operated by the students themselves, who make their own decisions as to the type of information they access. The metaphorical helicopter experiment helps us understand the difference between physical and human capital. In economics, physical capital refers to any manufactured asset that is applied in production, such as machinery, buildings, vehicles, and so on. In contrast, human capital refers to the stock of competencies, know-how, and personal skills embodied in the ability that humans have to perform labor. Physical capital and human capital are two of the three primary factors of production, the third factor being natural resources [12].

In modern economic history, economists have studied in detail the role of each factor of production in economic growth. The neoclassical growth models attributed economic growth to either the savings rate (e.g., the Harrod–Domar model in the 1940s) or the rate of technical progress (e.g., the Solow model in the 1950s) [13]. Such models are referred also as *exogenous growth* models because the savings rate and the rate of technological progress were assumed to be independent variables (external inputs) to the model and, hence, remained unexplained. They also had limitations in that they failed to take into account factors such as entrepreneurship or knowledge sharing and provided no explanation as to why technological progress occurs. This led in the 1980s to the development of *endogenous growth* models, which provided a framework to explain technological progress through the role of knowledge accumulation.

The endogenous models provide an important framework to economic growth theory because they demonstrate that factors such as the accumulation of knowledge and the generation of new ideas and their immediate spillover effects make increasing returns to scale* possible, a concept that is crucial in explaining sustainable growth over time. For instance, ideas and knowledge are nonrivalrous goods in the sense that once they occur or are acquired, an arbitrarily large number of people can immediately benefit from them. Consider as an example Isaac Newton and the moment he invented and documented the three laws of motion more than three hundred years ago [14]. Once the three laws were known to the public, anyone could start using them, and the value of the laws to society did not diminish as more and more people started to use them. In contrast, consider now the production of a chair. A chair is a rivalrous good because if one person uses it, then another person cannot. Its value depletes with its usage. Because of their exponential/spillover effects, nonrivalrous goods such as ideas, concepts such as knowledge sharing, and human capital in general are intimately related to the notion of sustainable economic growth. As demonstrated by the endogenous growth models, without them, sustainable economic growth of villages and nations as a whole would not be possible.

The helicopter experiment deals exclusively with the building of physical capital, and it neglects the problem of human-capital development. In a context of economic development, we argue that Labdoo is a project that utilizes the wealth of a network and, more specifically, social networking, to help build physical capital, and that that by itself has little to do with the accumulation of knowledge and skills. However, we also argue that the same social networking mechanisms used by Labdoo to build physical capital can be similarly applied to carry out projects on top of the physical infrastructure that will yield human capital growth, and, hence, help unleash the true potential of its spillover effects. Wiki-Kids, described next, is an example of such a project.

18.6.2 Brief Description of the Wiki-Kids Project

Wikipedia[†] is a free, collaborative, multilingual encyclopedia project launched in 2001 that, with 19 million articles and support for 281 languages, has become the largest and most popular general reference work on the

---

*An economic concept that refers to an economy that, when its inputs increase by a factor K, its outputs increase by a factor larger than K.
[†]The name Wikipedia is a combination of wiki (a technology for creating collaborative websites, from the Hawaiian word wiki, meaning "quick") and encyclopedia.

Internet [7]. The Wikipedia project is based on a peer-review process through which articles are first written by a network of participating authors and thereafter exposed to a process of constant review by the same network of participants. This self-regulatory, open mechanism is at the same time responsible for the high-quality standards of the project because, if a mistake is found in an article, an expert in that article's specific field can quickly correct it.

The same mechanism that ensures the quality of the project, however, makes it biased toward a certain type of audience. Because errors are more likely to be detected and corrected by experts in a specific field, articles in the Wikipedia tend to be written by adult, often scientific, writers using a relatively technical language. As a result, the value of Wikipedia to an adult audience is much larger than to a childrens audience. For instance, the Wikipedia article on "gravitation" talks about the General Theory of Relativity, a concept that a twelve-year-old child would normally have trouble understanding. To resolve the conflict between quality and bias toward a certain audience, the Wiki-Kids project is based on the idea that Wikipedia content addressed to a certain cohort should be written by people in that same cohort; for instance, a Wikipedia article addressed to children ages 9 through 12 should be written by children in that same age group.

The Wiki-Kids project is intimately related to Labdoo in that once computers are set up in a school and connected to the Internet, teachers are also offered the option of having their students participate in the Wiki-Kids project. The fundamental idea of Wiki-Kids is simple: essays written in a classroom can be published online so other students in other places of the world can also benefit from that work. Although students can flexibly write their own articles, essays assigned to children typically focus on the definition of a specific concept found in a specific field of science, for instance, "gravity" (in physics), "volcano" (in geography), "octopus" (in natural science), and "Hombres de Maiz" (in literature). Because articles are written in their own words, other students from other nations can also participate and benefit from them.

The ideas behind the Wiki-Kids project lay on top of the following two pillar concepts:

1. **Authorship.** Teachers from a participating school first define a set of topics and assign a topic to each of the participating children. Each child is then responsible for describing in their own words that concept, typically also including a hand drawing of it, and thus becomes the original author of that article in the Wiki-Kids encyclopedia. The concept of authorship provides children with a sense of contribution (giving back) to the global community as well as a sense of ownership of their work (attribution).

2. **Peer review.** Children from anywhere in the planet benefit from the writings of other students and, at the same time, if when accessing an article they find a typo or mistake, they can provide feedback to the author of such article. In a typical Wiki-Kids contribution, peer review is performed by children of two different nations. Consider, for instance, the following example:

Step 1. Children from a school in Guatemala write 10 Wiki-Kids articles. At the same time, children from a school in California write another set of 10 articles, for a total of 20 different articles.

Step 2. The two groups of children swap their articles and revise them. Children from Guatemala review the 10 articles written by the children in California, and vice versa. Then they provide feedback to their peer authors.

Step 3. Each child reviews the feedback received on his/her article and incorporates the changes to it.

These mechanisms allow children to gain a sense of community sharing and global citizenship as, through the collaborative process, they make new friends with children of other nations.

18.6.3   A Repeatable Model

Although from an economic development perspective, we argue that Labdoo focuses solely on the development of physical capital; its platform allows us to overlay on top of it a layer of human-knowledge development. Wiki-Kids serves as an example of a project that leverages physical capital to grow human capital, but there are other types of projects that could follow the same path; for instance, using telemedicine to connect doctors in the developed world with patients in the developing world via the Labdoo network. In the future, Project Labdoo will welcome such types of grassroots initiatives.

18.7   CONCLUSIONS

New technological advances are empowering us with an unprecedented capability to take on global challenges. The key resides in our new capacity to divide very large tasks into a very large number of very small subtasks. This allows us to unlock resources around the globe that up until now have been dormant, effectively elevating the capacity that we as a society have to undertake such challenges.

We propose to use these new technological advances in the design and implementation of a new type of humanitarian nonprofit organization (NPO). Unlike the traditional NPOs, which are based on a centralized model, we use a fully decentralized model, unlocking volunteers from all around the globe and enabling them to make ad hoc contributions by carrying out minitasks.

We apply this model to the challenge of bridging the digital divide and take on the mission of providing a laptop for every child on the planet. The distributed framework tells us that the key to undertake such a large mission resides in identifying the smallest indivisible tasks that can be executed in parallel (atomic tasks). In our simplified model, we identify the four atomic tasks required to bridge the digital divide by using large-scale distribution of laptops: AT1, laptop donation; AT2, laptop sanitization; AT3, inventory; and AT4, laptop transportation.

The idea of Labdoo is simple: instead of building a NPO that takes care of all the tasks involved in the procurement and transportation of laptops to children, we develop the metatools so that every laptop owner on the planet can participate with her or his own minimission. The vehicle to achieve this mission is the Labdoo social network. The social network allows us to (1) identify where the sources of demand and supply are; (2) coordinate and leverage a highly distributed network of small ad hoc volunteers participating from anywhere in the planet; (3) create a human chain to collect, sanitize, store, and transport laptops (tasks AT1 through AT4); and (4) carry out our mission without imposing an additional cost to planet earth.

Being passive devices, computers by themselves do not lead to education. We observe that while Labdoo can potentially make a direct physical-capital contribution to the development of the most impoverished villages of the planet, the project's impact to the building of human capital is limited. To that end, we explain mechanisms by which we can use the Labdoo Project to also help build human capital. One such example is Wiki-Kids, which focuses on the concept of using a network of connected children to build an encyclopedia of the children, by the children, and for the children. Children use the network to write their own articles, perform peer reviews with other children from other nations, and publish their written contributions online to help build a global knowledge base.

Our proposal to fight the digital divide works as follows. Instead of building centralized NPOs, we can use technology to enable every person on the planet to participate by making a small nonmonetary, hands-on contribution. This contribution consists in using the Labdoo tools to recondition and bring a laptop to a child. At Labdoo, every laptop has a story, what will be the story of yours?

ACKNOWLEDGMENTS

This chapter would not have been possible without the work of all the people who are part of the Labdoo network, which includes every person carrying out any of the Labdoo volunteering tasks, whether small or large, such as tagging laptops, sanitizing them, providing mini-storage locations, and dootripping and deploying the laptops to remote schools. To find out more about each of these small stories around the globe, go to www.labdoo.org and www.facebook.com/labdoo.

18.8 REFERENCES

1. William Kamkwamba and Bryan Mealer, *The Boy Who Harnessed the Wind: Creating Currents of Electricity and Hope,* Harper Perennial, 2010.
2. "Market Share of Leading PC Vendors," Gartner Press Release, January 2009.
3. "IDC Projects 19.8% PC Market Growth In 2010," IDC Press Release, June 2010.
4. Joseph Schumpeter, *Capitalism, Socialism and Democracy,* Kessinger Publishing, 2010 (first published in 1942).
5. Moore, Gordon E., "Cramming More Components Onto Integrated Circuits," *Electronics Magazine,* Vol. 38, No. 8, 4, April 1965.
6. Yochai Benkler, *The Wealth of Networks: How Social Production Transforms Markets and Freedom,* Yale University Press, 2007.
7. Anthony D. Williams, "Wikinomics: How Mass Collaboration Changes Everything," *Portfolio Trade,* September 2010.
8. Jordi Ros, Christine Lee, Michael Bruce, and Charlie Fan, "A Portable and Sustainable Computer Education Project for Developing Countries Phase I," *International Journal for Service Learning in Engineering,* April 2006.
9. Project OpenCourseWare, http://ocw.mit.edu/.
10. Aaron Swartz, "Who Writes Wikipedia?" http://www.aaronsw.com/weblog/whowrites-wikipedia, September 2006.
11. "Ghana: Digital Dumping Ground," PBS, *World Stories From a Small Planet,* June 2009.
12. M. P. Todaro and S. C. Smith, *Economic Development,* Prentice-Hall, 11th ed., 2011.
13. R. J. Barro and X. I. Sala-i-Martin, *Economic Growth,* MIT Press, 2nd ed., 2003.
14. Isaac Newton, *Philosophiae Naturalis Principia Mathematica,* 1687.
15. Paul M. Romer, *Economic Growth, in* The Concise Encyclopedia of Economics, 2007.
16. Douglas Rushkoff, *Program or Be Programmed,* OR Books, 2010.

CHAPTER 19

THE CHARMS APPLICATION SUITE
A Community-Based, Mobile Data-Collection and Alerting Environment for HIV/AIDS Orphans and Vulnerable Children in Zambia*

Brian A. Nejmeh and Tyler Dean

ABSTRACT

World Vision (WV) uses the Core HIV and AIDS Response Monitoring System (CHARMS) to track and measure core indicators related to individuals with HIV and AIDS within the communities WV serves. WV uses community care coalitions of volunteer caregivers to care for orphans and vulnerable children (OVC). Current CHARMS data collection involves the registration of caregivers, households, and OVC. Data is manually collected by caregivers about OVC during monthly home visits and manually aggregated semiannually. This research project developed a software application that runs on a low-cost cell phone to automate the CHARMS data collection, alerting and reporting process. The mobile application allows for caregivers to record CHARMS data using the mobile application and transmit the data in real time using an SMS-based wireless communication service. The application also includes real-time Web- and e-mail-based reporting and mobile phone alerting based on key events (food shortage, OVC not visited). During the summer of 2009, a field pilot project was conducted in Zambia involving 10 caregivers. The system allowed for the registration of 300 OVC and 200 households. A total of 145 home visits were recorded via the mobile applica-

*This article originally appeared in the *International Journal of Computing and ICT Research*, Volume 4, Issue No. 2 (December, 2010), pp. 46–63. Reprinted with permission.

tion. Extensive assessment data was collected during the field experience. 100% of the caregivers would recommend the continued use of cell phones to record CHARMS data for reasons ranging from time savings (90%), ease of use (70%), and more interesting to use (40%). The caregivers said the cell phone application either had a very positive (80%) or positive (20%) impact on the quality of their home visit.

19.1   INTRODUCTION

In 2006, World Vision (WV) [2010] introduced CHARMS (**C**ore **H**IV and **A**IDS **R**esponse **M**onitoring **S**ystem) to track and measure core indicators related to HIV/AIDS within the communities they serve. WV uses community care coalitions of volunteer caregivers (herein referred to as caregivers) to care for orphans and vulnerable children (OVC). Current CHARMS data collection involves the manual registration of caregivers, households, and OVC (Figure 19.1). Data is manually collected by caregivers during monthly home visits and manually aggregated semiannually.

A high-level business-process model for the existing CHARMS process follows. It depicts the role of Community Care Coalitions (CCCs) as community-based partners for World Vision and other NGOs to coordinate the HIV/AIDS response effort. World Vision field operations are managed via a hierarchical structure. The world is divided into regions spanning multiple countries. Each country where World Vision is involved is managed via a National Office. The programs within a country National Office are broken down into Area Development Programs (ADPs). ADPs contain community care coalitions (CCCs). Caregivers are volunteers who work in conjunction with a CCC. OVCs are managed as part of an ADP.

The overall purpose of the pilot project was to transform the current manual CHARMS data collection and reporting process into one that was mobile based and real time. The project had the following goals:

- To train WV field staff and volunteer caregivers (CGs) on the use of mobile and Web applications and to see them successfully use the applications
- To test the usability of the mobile and Web applications by WV field staff and caregivers
- To explore and understand the connectivity options (cost, reliability, security, etc.) for transmitting the data from the mobile device to the database
- To develop a cost/benefit analysis to validate the mobile concept

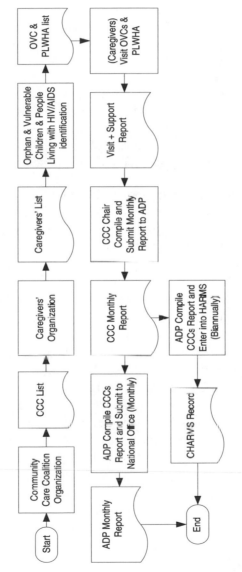

Figure 19.1. CHARMS current process model.

- To validate that the data has been correctly entered and correctly stored in the database
- To explore reports related to CHARMS forms that would be helpful to WV staff
- To define new features to explore for making the applications more valuable to WV
- To record lessons learned about the project

The initial prototype for this project was developed as part of two service-learning courses taught at Messiah College over a twelve-week semester during the spring of 2009. The two courses were a database applications course and a systems analysis and design course. Service-learning is a pedagogical model in which student learning is greatly enhanced through practical, experiential projects. For a course at Messiah College to be considered a service-learning course, it must contain the components of:

- Service. Students must engage in meaningful service that is mutually beneficial. In this case, the development of the mobile and web applications for World Vision to be used in Zambia was the service component of the courses. As part of our understanding of service, the professor and students saw the project as inspired, guided, and directed by James 1:27: "Religion that God our Father accepts as pure and faultless is this: to look after orphans and widows in their distress and to keep oneself from being polluted by the world."
- Content. Students must be exposed to the nonprofit organization and people they are serving so that they may better understand the motivations or the organization and needs of the people they are serving. In this case, World Vision staff lectured in classes at Messiah College and the students were able to interact with field personnel about the nature of their work and those they serve. In addition, World Vision staff showed various videos of their staff interacting with the OVCs.
- Reflection. Students must reflect on their experience in terms of how it informs their notions of vocation and calling in life. In this case, students maintained journals and were prompted throughout the semester by the professor with probing questions that acted as a catalyst for journal entries. At the conclusion of the semester, students submitted a paper that chronicled the nature of their reflections over the semester and summarized the main ways in which this experience informed their notions of vocation.

In addition, several of the students from these classes and the professor worked over the summer of 2009 to complete the project and ready it for field usage. Field trials of the prototype occurred during the latter part of the summer of 2009.

19.2   CHARMS APPLICATION SUITE

19.2.1   Introduction

World Vision has a keen interest in the use of mobile technology to facilitate field data collection and rapid response systems. The convergence and ubiquitous nature of mobile devices and communications technology has created an unprecedented opportunity to reliably, securely, and economically connect remote end points to central repositories of data. World Vision desired to pursue a proof of concept prototype project to explore the efficacy and appropriateness of deploying mobile applications in the developing world.

This research project developed a software application, using the JavaRosa [2010] open-source platform that runs on a low-cost cell phone to automate the CHARMS data collection, alerting, and reporting processes. The mobile application allows for caregivers to record CHARMS data using the mobile application and transmit the data in real time using an SMS-based wireless communication service on a low-cost Nokia phone. The application also includes real-time Web- and e-mail-based reporting and mobile phone alerting based on key events (food shortage, OVC not visited).

There are two different categories of system users. The first category of user is the mobile user. This is likely to be a caregiver or World Vision field staff. The second category of user is the Web user. This is a user who actively uses the Web application to enter agency, household, caregiver, or OVC-related data. This might include a World Vision field manager, a CHARMS manager, World Vision National Office staff, or a World Vision IT manager.

19.2.2   Future State CHARMS Process Model

The major improvement of the CHARMS business process focuses not in eliminating the main business processes, but on the way data is collected, transmitted, stored, analyzed, and reported on. Instead of the caregivers submitting their activity reports to the CCC chairman, they will directly send the data to a central database via the mobile application (Figure 19.2).

Once the data is stored in the CHARMS database, it can be accessed on demand through a Web application containing predefined reports. Unlike the existing CHARMS process in which data is compiled twice (at the CCC level and at the area-development program [ADP] level), data is only captured once in the new CHARMS process. Second, the compilation and aggregation of the data is automatically done in the new CHARMS process; in

Figure 19.2. CHARMS future state process model.

the current CHARMS process, data is manually aggregated. Finally, in the new CHARMS process, detailed individual home-visit data can be easily obtained as there is full traceability from the aggregate reports to the individual records; in the old CHARMS process, data is not automatically traceable once it is aggregated. Though this information is not relevant for high-level data consumers (e.g., for experts at the national, regional, or global level), the existence of data in that traceable, detailed form helps to perform root cause analysis, which is difficult to do in the existing CHARMS process.

19.2.3 CHARMS Application Suite Architecture

Figure 19.3 shows the high-level architecture of the CHARMS application suite. The CHARMS mobile application runs on the Nokia 3110c low-cost cell phone. The phone provides the J2ME platform [2005], which runs the CHARMS application. This mobile application is a customized version of JavaRosa [2010], an open-source data collection tool that runs on J2ME. The JavaRosa framework includes a form engine as the primary means for data collection. After one of these forms is completed on our custom JavaRosa application, the CHARMS data is encoded in XML and transmitted as a series of SMS messages from the mobile phone over the GSM network. This data is sent to the Upside Wireless SMS receiver service [2010]. In turn, the SMS receiver service forwards the SMS messages over HTTP to a custom Web application. The Web application contains a parsing engine that decodes the XML-encoded form data and inserts the data into the MySQL CHARMS database. The CHARMS database allows for various CHARMS-related reports to be produced on demand. The CHARMS database also monitors the data for various critical events identified (i.e., a child in need of food, etc.) and immediately transmits a message over SMS via the SMS receiver service to a mobile phone or e-mail address to alert on a potential emergency. Finally, the desktop/laptop application is a Java program that is used to communicate with the mobile CHARMS application software and database over the Internet. It allows for software and client list updates to be made to each of the mobile phones and for data on the mobile phone that could not be transmitted over SMS to be transmitted to the database over the Internet.

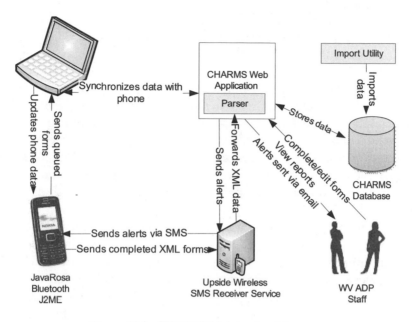

Figure 19.3. CHARMS high-level architecture.

19.2.4 Mobile Application

The process of designing a mobile application that would collect information for the CHARMS dataset originated by identifying an open-source project that was extensible and easily customizable. JavaRosa [2010] was chosen for our mobile component as it is an open source project designed for data collection, analysis, and reporting using a low-cost cell phone. Although JavaRosa proved to be a great fit, our objectives required much modification and customization of this application to support the World Vision CHARMS business process.

After choosing the JavaRosa platform, a cell phone was required to run the mobile application. For our purposes, we required a low-cost cell phone as the primary users would be volunteer caregivers. One of our constraints of the project required keeping the price of cell phone hardware down to reduce the cost of procurement of tens of thousands of phones and potential replacements for theft or damage. In addition, we spoke with the JavaRosa support community for recommendations on compatible cell phones that were known to be able to withstand the conditions of rural areas of Africa. This research pointed to the Nokia 3110c as the phone that would run our customized JavaRosa application.

The CHARMS dataset required a custom menu structure to provide easy interaction by the caregivers. The main menu (Figure 19.4) of the application allows a caregiver to complete a form for a monthly visit, household registration, or OVC registration. Our menu design was driven by the relational aspects of the objects in the CHARMS framework. For example, in CHARMS a household contains one or more children. Therefore, on the main menu, if the caregiver attempts to perform a standard home visit with an OVC, the caregiver must first select the household they are visiting. Once the household is selected, a list of OVCs that reside within the selected household is shown (Figure 19.5). Note that in Figure 19.5, the names are blackened out so as to not disclose the names of actual OVC. This menu structure not only increases the efficiency of the caregiver, but also eliminates the chance of misspelling a name and helps us better track each OVC in the CHARMS database.

The JavaRosa project includes a module that allows for quick creation and deployment of question-and-answer forms by utilizing the industry-standard XForms [2010]. Our team built forms to model the CHARMS dataset by creating simple questions using the various question types supported by XForms. Through these options, XForms allowed our team to focus our design to minimize the amount of typing required by the user to enter data into the system. Thus, we created a more objective approach to CHARMS data collection. For example, the mobile forms were designed to utilize check boxes to allow for easy recording of key indicators by simply selecting items needed by the OVC, or support that was provided from a checklist (food security, social/psychological assistance, abuse/neglect, etc.). Another use of XForms was using conditional questions. For example, CHARMS data collects information about the OVC's parents and whether they are alive or ill. Using conditional questions, if the mother or father is

Figure 19.4. Mobile application main menu.

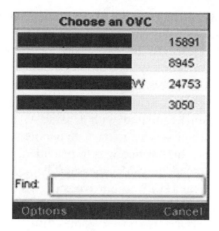

Figure 19.5. Mobile application selection of OVC.

dead, we will not ask if that parent is ill. XForms transparently takes the answer to a previous question and displays an appropriate next question. A key benefit of this design includes reduced costs for data transmission since only selection numbers from a list were transmitted instead of long input text strings. This design also minimized the amount of typing and time required to enter data, thereby reducing the opportunity for erroneous data entry by the caregivers.

19.2.5 Wireless Communications

Once the form has been completed, the JavaRosa application transparently creates an XML structure (from XForms) and sends the data via SMS. Depending on the number of characters in the XML encoded string, JavaRosa splits the XML string into a number of SMS messages in an organized way to deal with the issue of long form data (SMS messages are limited to be no more than 160 characters). Before the message is sent, the caregiver is presented two options based on the perceived level of emergency gained from the home visit.

The first option is "Send Now," which immediately sends the completed form via SMS. In order to keep data transmission costs low and anticipating that the phones may not have great cellular coverage in our target location, our team built the mobile application to save by default a completed form that was unable to be sent. As we indicate later in the chapter, cellular coverage in our target location did not prove to be a problem. However, in the chance of limited or no connectivity, unsent forms would be placed in a queue and could be sent the next time the caregiver entered a coverage area.

For the second option, if the results of the home visit did not appear to indicate an emergency, the caregiver could choose "Send Later," which would allow the completed form to be saved on the phone and sent to the CHARMS database at a later time.

A final piece of the mobile application was the need for an SMS receiver service. This service acted as an intermediary between the text messages and the database. Our team negotiated with Upside Wireless [2010], a large player in the SMS receiver service market, to handle receiving the text messages. The basic role of this service was to provide a phone number for the mobile application to send the SMS message. Upon receipt, the message would be forwarded over HTTP to our website, which parses out the data from the XML and stores it in the CHARMS database.

The SMS receiver service also provided the ability to send a message back to a specific cell phone. This feature was used to send various alert messages back to the caregivers based on specific events generated by the database.

19.2.6   Desktop/Laptop Application

The mobile application's SMS feature is an integral piece to successfully perform mobile data collection. However, while designing the application suite, our team realized in order for our solution to be scalable, a direct communication channel would need to be set up in the CHARMS database. We envisioned the need for OVC client lists to be pushed onto a cell phone issued to a caregiver if the phone was lost or stolen or if OVC data was updated via the Web application. Further, we needed a solution that could drive cost down from solely relying on the GSM wireless network.

Using these requirements, our team determined that an application on an Internet-connected computer would solve these issues. However, a connection between the computer application and the phone would need to be established. Bluetooth became the technology of choice to synchronize the phones with the computer application.

Bluetooth was chosen for a variety of reasons. First, programming libraries and large support communities exist for the standard (compared to proprietary cell phone USB connection cables). Second, Bluetooth was not limited to a specific phone manufacturer and USB connection cable. Rather, the standard can be utilized by any phone that offers Bluetooth capabilities. This was an important consideration as future versions of the mobile application might need to be run on a variety of cell phone makes and models. Therefore, the choice of Bluetooth for data transfer between mobile phone and desktop computer proved to be favorable.

With this design decision, we created the mobile application to perform an initial configuration step that mapped the cell phone number to a caregiver. This operation allows the computer application to download the caregiver's entire client list of OVCs and households from the CHARMS database and sends this information to the phone via Bluetooth. Upon completion of this step, the caregiver could begin using the phone for data collection.

The second purpose of the computer Bluetooth application was to allow any unsent messages or unsynchronized data to be sent to the database from the phone via the computer application. The queued messages could be a completed form for OVC registration, household registration, or a home visit that was not thought to indicate an emergency and the caregiver chose "Send Later."

One issue we ran into was the case in which a caregiver might register a child and would want to complete a home visit form during that visit. However, when the child is added on the phone, she or he does not have a unique key generated by the database. Thus, our team created a method to temporarily assign keys for that child, so the caregiver could perform their home visit. Upon synchronization to the database, these temporary keys would be converted to the database-generated keys, resulting in the synchronization of the CHARMS database and the phone data. In addition, during a synchronization using the computer application, any new or updated households or OVCs created from the Web application would be added to the mobile application.

By incorporating the Bluetooth application on a computer connected to the Internet, we will be able to have much more flexibility in future designs. Additionally, through the benefits of cost savings and updated client lists, we could better manage the data between the cell phone application and the central CHARMS database.

19.2.7 Web Application and Database

A complimentary Web application was designed for quality assurance and viewing data by ADP staff. The Web application is not a vital piece for field data collection; however, it serves as a management window to view the status of an ADP.

The Web application utilizes user management with various rights depending on the needs of the user. For example, an ADP manager might have the ability to create users within their specific ADP, but not in others. Thus, the Web application serves as an interface for the ADP staff to help monitor the program they are managing, review recent updates sent by the mobile phones, and perform corrections and updates as needed. Although not all data would be reviewed, an intuitive interface is available in the case of any needed changes.

The Web application also provides the ability to enter in new data. Each of the forms available on the mobile application is available for the Web application user. The Web application does have additional forms for management of the ADP. For example, a form to add a CCC was created and an "OVC—caregiver assignment" form is available. The latter form allows an ADP staff Web user to change an OVC to a different caregiver if such a circumstance were to come up.

Additionally, the Web application provides the programmatic interface between the SMS receiver service and the database. The Web application includes a robust parsing engine that takes the raw XML messages sent by the mobile phones and reconstructs, decodes, and stores the data in the CHARMS database.

The database back end is created in such a way as to keep data organized and allows for easy reporting. This concept provides great flexibility in not only reporting but also in alerting (discussed later).

The CHARMS dataset, collected manually, includes redundancy within the data that was collected to keep the information organized. However, by storing the information in a database, our team was able to use an entity-relationship model to abstract out supertypes and subtypes to avoid redundancy and keep the information storage more structured and organized. For example, a supertype in our database model was the person class. This class contained three subtypes of WV staff, caregivers, and OVCs (shown in Figure 19.6). Similar to the structure used on the mobile application, the data-

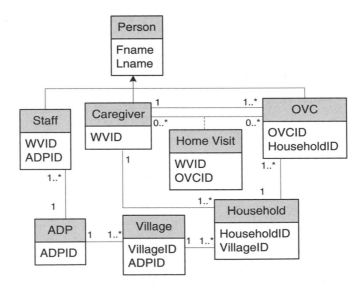

Figure 19.6. High-level database model.

base allows one or more OVCs to be contained in a household unit and a caregiver to care for one or more OVCs. Additionally, the CHARMS dataset hierarchy included groupings by location and by caregiver, allowing relationships to exist that could be leveraged by reports.

19.2.8   Reports

The Web application not only provides the ability for an ADP manager to monitor, edit, and enter new data; one of the more powerful features is the reporting engine. Our team found reports to be easily designed and implemented due to the granularity of the data captured at the database level. These reports provide many new options to World Vision staff compared to the old aggregated-data reports created with the manual method.

The old process of generating reports for stakeholders of World Vision included a tedious process of manual data entry and aggregated data to produce a high-level report. ADP managers and other ADP staff would spend several days aggregating data provided by caregivers from handwritten notebooks. Human error has become an issue in aggregating numbers and misreading entries written by the caregivers. Therefore, the accuracy of data from this manual collection method presents an issue to World Vision, as the reports help decide the amount to invest in the communities.

Additionally, this manual system burdens the larger national directors as they are required to take time to sign off on the data and declare the data valid. Following this action by national directors, a final head of CHARMS would need to prepare final reports to the World Vision stakeholders. By implementing the reporting aspect to the Web application, this time-consuming process is essentially removed.

Utilizing the structured relationships and near-real-time data, the reporting engine leverages the database to provide highly accurate and extremely detailed reports. The central storage provides a streamlined approach to reducing the excess hours needed to complete and aggregate reports. In fact, the reporting section of the Web application provides reports similar to the old reports produced as well as other varieties.

We created a CCC report, annual report, ADP report, indicator report as well as others. The CCC report displays each caregiver, the households, and the OVC for which they tend. The annual report is similar to the aggregated report used by World Vision, with additional options. The ADP report lists all the CCCs in that ADP and the number of caregivers, households, and OVCs in a specific CCC. The indicator report can show percentages for each indicator (food, health, etc.) for a CCC, ADP, or nationally.

These new reports allow managers to drill down into more details if desired. For example, whereas previously reports were rather high level in nature, reports can now look at communities, ADPs, regions, or other levels as well. Due to the structured database, the types of reports can be rather dynamic and easily created to suit future needs for better allocation of funds and staff and other trending. For example, one report displays a caregiver and the number of households, OVCs, and visits that individual made during a specific time period. This report would allow an ADP manager to better identify areas of high volume to help reduce the burden on each volunteer caregiver.

19.2.9   Alerts

Whereas database-driven reporting helps greatly reduce World Vision staff's effort required to produce reports, alerts provide a means to benefit individual communities. Alerting was implemented in several areas. Each application allows for a better quality of service to communities aided by World Vision.

For example, our team set up a trigger that would alert an ADP if an OVC were under an extreme circumstance and needed immediate attention. One of the CHARMS indicators is the amount of food available to a child. In the pilot, if a child had not eaten for more than a day, we instructed the caregiver to mark the "Food" indicator and select the "Send Now" option to send the completed form. Once this form reached the database, a trigger was called and an e-mail was sent to an ADP office where they could take immediate action and instruct staff where to deliver the available aid.

Alerting was also used for accountability reasons. For example, a caregiver is supposed to visit a child at least once a month. However, sometimes caregivers might lose track or neglect to visit a specific child. In such a case, a child might be ill and in dire need of attention. Therefore, the database periodically scans through each child's record and checks to see when the last visit was performed. If the child was not visited for a given length of time, such as 25 days, the database would use the SMS receiver service to forward an SMS message back to the caregiver's phone to remind them of which child needed to be visited and how much time elapsed since the last visit.

19.2.10   Data Import/Export

The features and solutions our application suite provides perform well as data is added to the database. However, initially, our team needed to add preexisting data into the database. For example, for the main menu to work as intended, we needed a list of the households and OVCs each caregiver looked after.

We were able to obtain Excel spreadsheets of the current data for each caregiver in the pilot along with each OVC they cared for and the households they resided in. Our team wrote a custom script to import the data from the spreadsheets into the database.

Although the data import tool proved to be successful, to be scalable, future consideration will be given to a more robust extract–transformation–load (ETL) tool, such as the one Songini describes [2010]. Such a tool could import large amounts of data into the database from a variety of import formats. As a future consideration, it would be useful to allow data to be exported from the database in the form of well-formed Excel files as well.

19.3   PILOT PROJECT

A pilot project of the CHARMS application suit was conducted in Zambia during the summer of 2009. The pilot project involved the participation of various World Vision field staff and ten volunteer caregivers. A faculty member and senior student were involved in the Zambia fieldwork for approximately three weeks. The total pilot project was five weeks in duration. The ten caregivers who participated in the field experience were half male and female. Their education ranged greatly: 30% primary school, 50% secondary school, and 20% college. 80% of the caregivers indicated they used a cell phone to make a call prior to beginning this project. 60% of caregivers indicated they used a cell phone to send a text message prior to beginning this project.

19.3.1   Training

The pilot project began with a three-day training session. The training materials (PowerPoint slides) were written and presented in English. The spoken words of the training were translated (in real time) by one of the caregivers into the local language dialect. The training covered the following topics and audiences:

1. Phone training (primary audience: caregivers)
   a. How to use the phone
   b. Typing on the phone
   c. Creating, editing, and submitting CHARMS forms on the phone
   d. Guidance on how to best use the mobile application
2. CHARMS application training (primary audience: World Vision ADP staff)
   a. Navigating the Web application
   b. Creating, editing, and submitting CHARMS forms via the Web

   c. Guidance on how to best use the Web application

   d. Web administration and IT manager training (primary audient: World Vision ADP staff and IT staff)

   e. Navigating the CHARMS application suite website

   f. Logging into the Web application

   g. Administering users

   h. Forms

   i. Reports

   j. Alerts

   k. Problem reports

   l. Installing the mobile application

   m. Desktop synchronization and updating the mobile application

The primary challenge of the training proved to be linking the manual approach to the mobile phone solution. Walking through each of the forms along with role-play activities proved to be effective. Additionally, pairing caregivers based on comfort level of the application allowed sharing of knowledge and understanding. A field ready-reference guide developed in the native language would have been very beneficial.

19.3.2 Field Activity

Over the five-week pilot project period, 247 OVCs were registered via the import utility and 54 OVCs were registered via the mobile application. One hundred sixty-seven households were registered via the import utility. Thirty-two households were registered via the mobile application. One hundred forty-two home visits and three end home visits were recorded via the mobile application. All ten caregivers were actively involved in using the mobile application throughout the pilot project.

19.3.3 Field Assessment

Surveys given throughout the pilot revealed a positive attitude and experience with the mobile application. All of the caregivers believe the cell phone keeps information safer and more confidential than the paper method. All of the caregivers believe CHARMS forms can be completed quicker using the mobile application than writing down data in a notebook. 100% of the caregivers would recommend the continued use of cell phones to record CHARMS data for reasons ranging from time savings (90%), ease of use (70%), and more interesting to use (40%). The caregivers said the cell phone application either had a very positive (80%) or positive (20%) impact on the quality of their home visit.

For every home visit we observed, there were one to two communication bars on the phone (average of 2.07 bars per visit). However, when caregivers were surveyed, three (30%) of them indicated that they had difficulties sending data because they could not get a communications signal. It is not clear if the caregivers correctly understood the question, as our field work indicated, every one of the 15 household locations we visited had a communications signal.

We devised a data accuracy protocol, but the field staff was unable to complete it for personal reasons. However, the mobile application was designed to minimize typing by displaying more objective style questions. Therefore, we have a high degree of confidence that the information received by the cell phone application is complete and accurate. We have done some high-level spot checking of the data in the database for data accuracy based on our limited knowledge of the OVC and community caregivers. It appears as if data was accurately transmitted from the mobile phone into the database, although some number of typographical errors appear in the data.

In terms of process execution, there are two key metrics to focus on. Process duration (the amount of elapsed time required to complete a process) and process effort (the amount of work effort required to complete a process). During our field experience, we observed a negligible difference between the effort required between the manual approach and the mobile phone process for completing registration and home visits. From observation, the comparative effort required to produce reports using the manual process versus the automated process is dramatically different. With the automated system, producing reports is instantaneous, whereas significant effort and time are required to produce the reports with the manual process. In addition, the report-generation process using the automated system drastically increased both precision and detail and cut the time to compile the reports significantly from the manual approach. Further, the reporting feature of the automated system allows for new reports of greater analysis and provides flexibility of reporting with the specific nature of the stored data. Process effort and duration have both been greatly reduced for producing reports using the automated system. All of the registration processes have duration of 2–4 weeks using the manual system; the registration processes have duration of 15–30 minutes using the mobile phone (given that registrations are instantly available). In short, process duration has been substantially reduced for reporting and getting data into the automated system.

One key aspect of the mobile system is the ability to send data in real time. During the pilot, an alert e-mail was sent to WV staff if a caregiver discovered a food shortage during a home visit. Properly implemented, this system could track other emergency issues to provide immediate response by WV staff. Similarly, an administrative e-mail was sent to WV staff and an SMS message was sent to the caregiver if a child had not been visited within a given number of days to help develop accountability to the caregiver position.

We held focus groups with the caregivers to get their feedback on the system. Below is a summary of their positive comments:

- The automated system has reduced the paperwork and bureaucracy of the manual process.
- Caregivers felt greatly valued by receiving the mobile phone and were encouraged and motivated by it to complete their work.
- Households were intrigued and very positive about the mobile phone application.
- One caregiver reported being able to visit 15 children per day with the mobile application compared to visiting five children per day with the manual system.
- Members of the community are pleased to see their needs being reported directly to authorities.

Negative comments from the focus groups follow:

- One caregiver indicated that the desktop synchronization for the phone failed one time.
- One caregiver reported that the phone battery would run out of power and needed to be charged twice a week.

In terms of the battery charging issue, many of the caregivers paid to have their phones charged at a phone charging station. In a number of cases, the phone charging stations were not conveniently located. In the future, solar charges could be used to charge the phones. This is further discussed in the lessons-learned section of the chapter.

The GSM wireless communications network proved to be widely available and reliable for the regions of Zambia where the field experience was conducted. The average wireless communications cost to complete a mobile transaction was about $0.15. Industry experts, such as Louden [2009], suggest that GPRS/EDGE is more reliable and cost-effective than GSM. However, from our field experience, the availability of SMS appeared to be much greater than GRPS/EDGE. This is based on the fact that our 3G wireless access for the Internet was very spotty in many parts of Zambia compared to the relatively common availability of a GSM signal from the mobile phone.

It should be noted that JavaRosa supports GPRS and the development of GPRS appears more straightforward, given that you can assume the mobile application runs in an IP-addressable space. Thus, there is no need to deal with multiple SMS messages for a single form instance since the data would be sent over the IP network and not as a series of SMS messages. In addition, this means that a GPRS-based system would not require the use of an SMS Receiver Service.

We completed a high-level estimated costing model to deploy the system across a typical World Vision program region. The model includes estimates for the following costs: communication, equipment, software, and support. The model assumes that a typical World Vision program in Zambia will register 4000 OVCs in year one and 600 OVCs per year thereafter. It assumes that the number of end home visits is 5% of the OVC population per year. It also assumes that 50% of OVC registrations will happen on the mobile application and 25% of household registrations will happen on the mobile application. Based on these assumptions, we estimated that the average annual cost to support the CHARMS system would be about $35,000. There would be one-time fixed costs of approximately $60,000 for acquiring the mobile phones, solar charges, servers, and related system software.

19.4 RELATED WORK

There are a variety of platforms available for creating mobile-phone-based applications for rural patient monitoring in the context of community health. By platform, we mean a set of factored-out common services that can be used to construct specific mobile applications to support a particular form of field collection of patient data. These common services include the definition and rendering of data forms, the validation of data during entry, and the transmission of the data over one or more wireless transport protocols. Some of these platforms focus on the development of the client-side mobile application. They require the development of a structured system for persistent storage, reporting, and analysis of the data. Other platforms include a server-side component for managing the data collected via the mobile client applications. In this survey of related work, we focus on open-source platforms as we believe such platforms offer cost-effective options for mobile field data collection among not-for-profit organizations. For each platform, we also reference an example of a community health mobile application written using the platform.

Open Data Kit (ODK), discussed by Anokwa et al. [2009], is an open-source client and server platform for developing mobile applications based on the Google Android operating system. Thus, any Android-enabled device can be supported by the ODK Platform. The ODK is being developed at the University of Washington with support from Google. The platform suite includes three components: ODK Collect, ODK Aggregate and ODK Manage. ODK Collect allows for form design, rendering and navigation, repeating substructures, and data entry validation. Forms are based on the XForms [2010] standard. ODK Collect supports the standard data types such as checkboxes and plain text entry plus a myriad of rich media data types, including photos, audio, video, and barcodes. ODK Collect supports the GPRS wireless transport protocol and Wi-Fi for data transmission. Data can also be transmitted via a USB cable. ODK Aggregate is a Google App Engine cloud-based server that hosts forms and aggregates submitted data results. ODK Manage supports managing the deployment of the forms-based applications to mobile phones. A good number of projects use the ODK platform, including a Kenya-based project focused on mobile data collection for home-based counseling and testing related to the prevention and treatment of HIV.

JavaRosa [2010] is an open-source client platform for developing mobile applications based on the Java Mobile Edition (J2ME) operating system. JavaRosa supports a variety of J2ME-based phones, ranging from the Nokia 3110c to high-end smart phones. It includes support for user authentication, forms definition, rendering, and navigation, as well as data validation. JavaRosa forms are based on the XForms standard. JavaRosa supports the GSM (SMS) and GPRS wireless transport protocols for data transmission. Data can also be transmitted via Bluetooth or a USB cable. No significant server or deployment support is offered by JavaRosa. A number of mobile field data collection applications have been written using JavaRosa, including CommCare, discussed by Svoronos et al. [2010], and GATHERdata [2010]. CommCare is a community health data collection application. GATHERdata uses JavaRosa to deliver a broader platform of support for mobile data-collection applications, including server support for persisting and reporting on transmitted data. Our CHARMS mobile application was also written using JavaRosa.

RapidSMS [2010] is an open-source platform for developing SMS-based mobile applications. RapidSMS uses the notion of specifically defined and formatted text messages as the basis for its data collection. These text messages contain keywords that represent actions interpreted by a back-end Web application to insert data into a database. The platform also includes workflow support that may trigger responses back to the user based on data received by the application. RapidSMS includes a Web interface that allows users to view the data in the system. RapidAndroid [2010] is an implementation of RapidSMS that runs on the Google Android operating system. Several projects have used RapidSMS, including a project in Malawi to collect child nutrition data by Blaschke in 2009, documented by RapidSMS [2010].

FrontLineSMS [2010] is an open-source platform for creating SMS-based mobile applications. It also includes a Java-based simple forms-management capability. FrontLineSMS does not require an Internet connection and allows field data to be stored on a laptop equipped with a SIM card. FrontLineSMS supports a wide variety of phones. It only supports the use of SMS for data transfer. It has been used in a wide variety of projects, including a project discussed by Banks and Nesbit [2008] at St. George's Hospital in Malawi, where it has been used to support a rural healthcare network.

EpiSurveyor [2010] is a cloud-computing-based mobile data-collection and reporting platform. It includes support for the design and deployment of survey forms on mobile phones to collect field data. EpiSurveyor supports a wide array of phones. EpiSurveyor also includes a cloud-based server environment for managing submitted form data and allowing this data to be viewed and analyzed via a Web application. The data can also be exported in various formats. A number of EpiSurveyor community health mobile applications have been developed, including a project focused on containing a polio outbreak in Kenya, described by the BBC News [2008].

OpenXdata [2010] is an open-source client and server platform for the development of mobile applications. It includes support for field survey form design and data collection. It also includes support for data validation. It includes server support for managing data collected via mobile form surveys. OpenXdata supports the GPRS wireless transport protocol. Data can also be transmitted via SMS and Bluetooth. OpenXdata supports a wide variety of phones. Cell-Life [2010] is a significant organization focused on the use of mobile technology to improve the lives of people affected by HIV in South Africa. Cell-Life is leveraging the OpenXdata platform in the development of its mobile community health applications.

The Nokia [2010] Data Gathering platform is open-source and includes client and server components. The platform allows for field survey questionnaires to be created via a Web application and then downloaded to mobile phones for use. The mobile applications can run on any J2ME-enabled phone. Nokia recommends using smart phones such as the Nokia E71 and E72. Data collected via the mobile applications are then transmitted over GPRS or SMS to a MySQL database. A web application allows for reporting and analysis of the submitted data. A number of community health mobile applications have been written using Nokia's [2010] platform.

In the context of the related work, the CHARMS application suite is the first known fielded project that used JavaRosa to transmit mobile form data over SMS. In addition, it is one of the first known community health mobile application projects to be developed as a faculty–student service-learning project at an American undergraduate institution. The CHARMS application suite also contains some novel elements, such as reminder alerts to visit a specific child, that have not been widely reported on in the literature to date. Finally, the lessons learned from the CHARMS application field experience offer other researchers and practitioners insights about mobile field data collection and application development in a rural African setting.

In summary, there are a variety of mobile development platforms available for creating community health applications. These platforms are rapidly evolving and new platforms are likely to emerge in the near future. Care should be taken to select the platform that best suites future mobile application development needs.

19.5   LESSONS LEARNED AND THE FUTURE

19.5.1   Benefits of the CHARMS Application Suite

The benefits of the prototype CHARMS system proved to be numerous:

- World Vision staff and caregivers were genuinely excited about the project and use of mobile phones.
- There were significant improvements in process efficiency and effectiveness (previously discussed) as the system simplified the overall process of data collection and reporting while improving analysis of data.
- It demonstrates World Vision as an appropriate user of technology to donors, government, and community members.
- It provides anytime, anywhere (Web) access to critical CHARMS data for World Vision staff on a global basis. Fully automated, on-demand reporting was also seen as a strong positive. Traceability reports to the individual level were seen as a huge value-add by staff. New reports and analysis are now possible, including trend analysis, comparisons, and so on, based on database-centered report/analysis capability.
- In theory, a donor-facing application can be built to provide donors insight into ADP activity and results.
- By improving the quality, timeliness, and completeness of the CHARMS data process, beneficiaries (OVCs) should be better served via active interventions, follow-up, and analysis.
- It facilitates rapid field response to critical situations based on alerts and making critical information visible to the right people in a timely manner.

19.5.2   CHARMS Application Suite

The pilot in Zambia provided key insights into the benefits and areas of improvement for the CHARMS application suite. The lessons learned from the pilot project demonstrate the feasibility of such a technology to be used to help benefit rural communities and improve the quality of life.

19.5.2.1 Mobile Phone. The mobile device chosen proved to be a good fit; however, additional lessons learned became prevalent. The low-cost phone was a smart choice for both cultural and economic reasons. The rural villages where the caregivers volunteered were in poor standing. Thus, a high-end smart phone might have been insulting to the culture. Additionally, as World Vision is looking into mass deployment of a similar system, cost of tens of thousands of high-end phones might be too drastic and unachievable. Overall, the low-cost Nokia handset proved to work well for the pilot.

A few observations demonstrated areas that would need consideration before a full deployment of the technology. The battery life and additional cell phone features were quickly determined to be potential issues. For example, some of the caregivers used the phone for personal use, including features such as games, the camera, and even music. When the caregivers would use the phone outside of the mobile CHARMS application, the battery appeared to drain quicker. Therefore, one of the lessons learned for the cell phone is to consider locking down the phone and disabling functions to save battery life.

A few solutions to the battery life issue include solar chargers and weekly or biweekly charging at the ADP offices. Solar chargers can greatly benefit the caregivers as they would not be required to send the phones to be charged. The other option could incorporate current ADP staff trips to the villages each week to pick up the cell phones to be charged back at the ADP office.

19.5.2.2 Mobile Application. The mobile application proved to be quite successful in performing the function of a data-collection device. Many design decisions appeared to work well; however, improvements could have been made.

Despite initial worries, the learning curve for the multitap input system proved to be low. Even after the first day of training, most caregivers were inputting data into the fields without much difficulty.

The current XML parsing approach to data transmission and storage proved to be a tedious process. A small change in the forms translated to large overhead on reconfiguring the XML parsing engine. Other avenues exist, including using binary representations of the form data and to serialize and deserialize the objects at the mobile device and the receiving database. Many foreseeable benefits to such an approach exist, including added security, reduction in messages sent, and ease of extracting data from the message.

The actual mobile application's user interface could have been improved for an even shorter learning curve. For example, some of the forms from the CHARMS dataset appeared to be subjective rather than objective. By working with experts in the field, creating objective questions could save caregivers the time of manually inputting letters into the phone by creating dropdown lists to select from. This type of data would also greatly aid in a more granular and consistent analysis by World Vision managers and staff as trends could be more apparent with structured data.

The language barrier became an issue as most caregivers struggled to understand English. Therefore, native language support could greatly improve the data collected and ease of understanding for the caregivers. Additional options could include the use of pictorial icons to represent questions as well to help the caregivers who struggle with reading to better understand the questions as well.

Finally, while the mobile device worked well to transfer data and review it from a Web application, no reporting features existed to do longitudinal analysis in real time during visits. For example, in the manual approach currently used, the caregivers use a paper notebook that tracks their visits. During a visit, a caregiver can easily browse over the past few entries to identify the child's status as better or worse. Thus, a feature to allow a caregiver to look at the past few entries with the mobile device could improve the visit quality.

19.5.2.3 Communications. The communications proved to be better than expected, with satisfactory GSM coverage even in rural villages in Zambia. At every location we visited during our observation of home visits, there was at least one bar of service and in many cases two or more bars of service. In fact, the average signal strength was 2.07 bars out of four.

The Internet access proved to be more of a challenge and may potentially have a negative impact on communications above GSM. In our experience, GPRS coverage was spotty and often unavailable in most locations.

The use of an SMS communications service proved to work well for the application suite. Future considerations could include creating an in-country SMS receiver service to reduce the cost of long-distance text-message fees. Overall, the communications aspect of the project proved to be a positive experience.

19.5.2.4 Computer Application. The desktop application provided a reliable and scalable method for installing the mobile application, distributing client lists, and synchronizing data to the central database.

The phones appeared to provide enough local storage as to not be an issue with saved, unsent forms. Thus, data storage between synchronizations with the computer Bluetooth application did not prove to be a problem.

The desktop application worked rather well for most of the phones. However, one phone out of the ten had an issue with connecting to the computer application via Bluetooth. Additionally, some of the ADP offices do not have Internet availability at all times. This fact demonstrated the need for a queuing functionality for the computer Bluetooth application to hold data before attempting to transmit it over the Internet.

19.5.2.5   Reports. The reporting engine worked well and demonstrated its advantage in the collection and storage of granular data. In fact, the creation of new reports was added to showcase the ease and power of the database and the reporting utility.

The reporting feature also proved to provide better knowledge and information for a variety of individuals. After the pilot project, it became apparent that multiple new reports could greatly aid in decision making for program managers and the community chairperson.

The primary lesson learned with the reporting function was the benefit of structuring the CHARMS dataset into entity relationships. This structured format allowed for a multitude of report possibilities to allow for global-core metrics, national-office metrics, ADP-specific metrics, and even community metrics.

19.5.2.6   Alerts. Alerting seemed to be the function that can potentially have the most impact on communities themselves. By creating intelligent algorithms, automated alerts could be sent to ADP staff based on trends identified by the tracked indicators.

Although the current implementation of the CHARMS forms was rather rudimentary, rules and smart algorithms could replace the human decisions of whether or not to send an alert. By deciding on a standard as to determine when to send an alert, the database can trigger meaningful e-mail alerts to ADP managers who can quickly provide aid to an in-need child.

19.5.3   Service-Learning Impact on Students

All students were required to produce a three-to-five-page paper that chronicles their learning and discovery of community service throughout the semester. The instructor provided prompts throughout the semester for the types of information that should be included in the service-learning and community-engagement reflections document. These student reflection papers clearly demonstrated the profound impact that this service-learning project had on the students. The following excerpts from some of the student papers illustrate the impact of the project on the students.

> "While this has turned out to be one of the greatest learning experiences of my life, it started out as one of the rockiest! I can speak for the team when I say I felt in over my head in a sea of code and technological knowledge that I did not have any awareness of before this past semester. Mobile development was completely foreign to me. Words like open source, GPRS, JavaRosa, Parser, and SMS Receiver Service were being thrown around, and the learning curve seemed steeper and steeper."

> "This project has changed me as a student. I've learned so much in 8 months—I know anything is possible with determination and hard work. It has changed my outlook on the potential of technology to better humanity with the tools necessary to help people in need. This project has also changed me as a person. It has taken my computer science education at Messiah College and completely altered the meaning of it. I now fully understand the importance of using your major to glorify God. In my four years at Messiah, I worked to achieve high grades for my own personal standards. While I worked on this project, all I could think about were children who needed help. The project to me was no longer a letter grade, because you can't attach a letter to a child's life."

19.5.4 The Future

There are many future directions for this project. The current CHARMS prototype system was conceived as a field-facing application with limited regard to the implications of the application and support required by regional offices and national offices in terms of reports, analytics, and so on. In the future, consideration should be given to longitudinal analysis, comparative analysis across individual programs, countries, regions, and so on.

Using the mobile platform opens up a wide range of potential uses in the future. Health clinics could integrate with the system, allowing for OVC referrals, appointments, and rapid response in emergencies. Similar to clinical algorithms is the notion we termed *support algorithms*. Such algorithms would allow caregivers to more objectively answer questions. For example, CHARMS asks the question: "Is the household poor?" Presently, the caregivers do not consistently answer this question using the same criteria. We are exploring the possibility to define criteria that would allow caregivers to consistently and objectively answer questions. Finally, the integration of GPS could allow WV to analyze trends and geographic coverage of programs and OVCs.

This work has been very well received by World Vision. World Vision is currently working with other large NGOs to obtain funding to support the development, deployment, and support for a series of mobile application projects in the future.

ACKNOWLEDGMENTS

We thank World Vision for their financial and operational support to successfully complete this project. We also thank the Messiah College Collaboratory for Strategic Partnerships and Applied Research for their logistical support of the project. We would like to thank several individuals who made significant contributions to the project. Adam Bricker, Maurice Sapiso, Marcia Yu, Ayele Admassu, and Jane Chege of World Vision made very critical contributions to the project. Joy Gallucci, Phil Hess, and Devon Lehman all made substantial contributions to the project. Students from Messiah College's BIS 412 and COSC 333 assisted in the early technical stages of the project. We acknowledge the financial and operational support of Upside Wireless in providing the project SMS receiver service at no cost. Finally, the authors acknowledge the significant contribution of the JavaRosa community in making this project a reality.

REFERENCES

Anokwa, Y., Hartung, C., Brunette, W., Borriello, G., and Lerer, A. 2009. "Open Source Data Collection in the Developing World," *IEEE Computer,* pp. 97–99, October, 2009.

Banks, K. AND Nesbit, J. 2008. "Witnessing the Human Face of Mobile in Malawi," *PC-World,* June 27, 2008, http://www.pcworld.com/businesscenter/article/147679/ witnessing_the_human_face_of mobile_in_malawi.html. (Accessed 12/10/2010)

BBC News. 2008. "Mobiles Combat Kenyan Polio Outbreak," BBC News, September 18, 2008, http://news.bbc.co.uk/2/hi/technology/7619473.stm, (Accessed 12/10/2010)

Cell-Life. 2010. "Cellphones 4 HIV". http://www.cell-life.org/home. (Accessed 12/10/2010)

Episurveyor. 2010. "Global Development 2.0." http://www.datadyne.org/. (Accessed 12/10/2010)

FrontlineSMS, 2010. "FrontlineSMS software". http://www.frontlinesms.com/. (Accessed 12/10/2010)

Gatherdata. 2010. "Center for Health Information and Technology." http://www.healthnet.org/ gather. (Accessed 12/10/2010)

JavaRosa. 2010. "JavaRosa—Open Rosa Consortium." http://www.open-mobile.org/ technologies/javarosa-open-rosa-consortium. (Accessed 9/8/2010)

Loudon, M. 2009. "Mobile Phones for Data Collection." *MobileActive.* http://mobileactive.org/howtos/mobile-phones-data-collection. (Accessed 12/10/2010).

Nejmeh, B. 2010. "Faith Integration through Service-Learning in the Information Sciences," *Christian Business Academy Review,* Spring 3(1), pp. 12—24.

Nokia. "Nokia Data Gathering Solution." http://www.nokia.com/corporate-responsibility/society/nokia-data-gathering/english . (Accessed 12/10/2010)

OpenxData. 2010. "openXdata." http://www.openxdata.org/. (Accessed 12/10/2010)

Rapidandroid. 2010. "RapidSMS for the Android Platform." http://rapidandroid.org/. (Accessed 12/10/2010)

RapidSMS. 2010. "SMS Application Framework." http://www.rapidsms.org/. (Accessed 12/10/2010)

Sing, L., and Knedsen, J. 2005. *Beginning J2ME: From Novice to Professional,* Third Edition, A Press, New York.

Songini, M. 2010. "QuickStudy: Extract, Transform and Load (ETL)." http://www.computerworld.com/s/article/89534/QuickStudy_ETL. (Accessed 9/8/2010)

Svoronos, T., Mjungu, P., Dhadialla, R., Luk, R., Zue, C., Jackson, J., and Lesh, N. 2010. "CommCare: Automated Quality Improvement to Strengthen Community-based Health," http://d-tree.org/wp-content/uploads/2010/05/Svoronos-Medinfo-CommCare-safe-pregnancy1.pdf. (Accessed 12/10/2010)

Upside Wireless. 2010. "Upside Wireless Text Messaging." http://www.upsidewireless.com. (Accessed 9/8/2010)

World Vision. 2010. "Summary Report—CHARMS Africa FY08 Annual Data." http://www.wvi.org/wvi/wviweb.nsf/0CF6565756AEA942882575590061CEAC/$file/CHARMS_FY08_Annual_Summary.Pdf. (Accessed 7/30/2010)

Xforms. 2010. "The Forms Working Group." http://www.w3.org/MarkUp/Forms/. (Accessed 7/30/2010)

LESSONS LEARNED ABOUT SERVICE-LEARNING IN THE COMPUTER AND INFORMATION SCIENCES

The chapters in this part of the book offer significant lessons learned about SL in CIS, including the broad impact of SL in CIS projects on key stakeholders. They also offer perspectives about the future of SL in CIS. The chapters are written by SL in CIS field practitioners.

The first chapter (Chapter 20), entitled "Lessons Learned—Guidance for Building Community-Service Projects," is written by Michael Werner and Lisa MacLean of Wentworth Institute of Technology. This chapter presents key lessons learned from performing SL in CIS in computer science courses. It also discusses some future directions for SL in CIS.

The second chapter (Chapter 21), entitled "Assessing Both the 'Know and Show' in IT Service-Learning," is written by Rick Homkes of Purdue University. It offers insight about the challenges of outcome assessment in SL in CIS projects.

The third chapter (Chapter 22), entitled "From Kudjip to Succotz: The Successes, Lessons, Joys, and Surprises from 25 Years of Service-Learning Projects," is written by James Skon and Doug Karl from Mount Vernon Nazarene University. It chronicles a fifteen-year history of international SL in CIS projects and the many lessons learned along the way.

The fourth chapter (Chapter 23), entitled "Educational Impacts of International Service-Learning Design Project on Project Members and Their Peers," is written by Peter Johnson of Valparaiso University. It examines the impacts international SL engineering projects have on students "who are not directly involved in these projects but are peers of those who are." It also discusses the evolution of international SL engineering courses based on historical lessons learned over time.

The fifth chapter (Chapter 24), entitled "Is the Community Partner Satisfied?", is written by Camille George of the University of Saint Thomas (Minnesota). It develops a collaboration relational structure among a faculty–student team and an NPO partner in an international SL in CIS setting. The author argues that there are some key elements to this relational structure that can have a big influence on the success and impact of SL in CIS projects.

The sixth and final chapter (Chapter 25), entitled "Service-Learning in the Computer and Information Sciences: Lessons Learned and Guidance for the Future," is written by Brian Nejmeh of Messiah College. This chapter highlights the key lessons learned to date about SL in CIS based on the chapters that appear in this book as well as the author's own experiences. In addition, the author suggests a number of imperatives that SL in CIS practitioners should consider in their future work.

CHAPTER 20

LESSONS LEARNED—GUIDANCE FOR BUILDING COMMUNITY-SERVICE PROJECTS

Michael Werner and Lisa MacLean

ABSTRACT

This chapter presents an approach to using real projects for nonprofit agencies in computer science courses. The goals are to deliver a useful service to our nonprofit clients while providing a valuable learning experience to our students. The chapter builds on failures and difficulties encountered in past community-service projects. Risk factors are identified and measures devised to counter them. These measures include developing a systematic approach to managing such projects, enhancing course offerings to better prepare students for working on real projects, and building a repository of practical knowledge within the department. Proper communication between students within and between teams, as well as timely feedback to faculty better preparation and communication on the part of the community agencies is essential for effective projects. We also propose building an application framework, reusing proven design and implementation techniques to exploit the fact that many of our nonprofit clients have similar requirements.

20.1 INTRODUCTION

In an increasingly competitive environment, students must be able to produce commercial-quality applications before they graduate. Our college, Wentworth Institute of Technology in Boston, MA has taken a multipronged approach to this: two mandatory cooperative placements; a required laboratory session for each course so that principles and concepts in the lecture can be applied; and a senior capstone course in which each student is expected to independently conceive, design, program, and document a project of significant quality.

To give our students the edge when seeking employment we decided that real projects, or service-learning, would be injected into all courses that could benefit by this addition. To support these projects, our department has built a new high-availability networking and database laboratory using powerful servers and other state-of-the-art hardware and software. At the institutional level, an office of Service-Learning and Civic Engagement with a full-time staff has been created.

There were successes and failures by students, faculty, and organizations chosen for the service-learning paradigm. Despite initial difficulties, the school remains resolute in its commitment to providing useful software applications for local nonprofit organizations.

Our computer science department currently offers two programs leading to the BS degree: BCOS (Computer Science) and BSCN (Computer Networking). This chapter relates the department's recent experience in service-learning.

Although they are enjoyable and valuable to our students, the community projects have had their frustrations. In part, this was due to the severe financial and time constraints, which are the norm in this type of work, but some frustrations were a product of our own inexperience, particularly regarding project-management issues of planning, time estimation, coordination, and control. In the end, almost all of the projects were completed; our customers were satisfied and are using the systems we developed. Credit for this goes to the dedication and perseverance of our students, who selflessly put in many hours of their own time.

We systematically reexamined our approach to building these projects. We needed to find what delayed projects and devise means to bring them to successful completion. By studying past projects, we have identified a number of risks. Some reflected weaknesses in our curriculum and even in the faculty's preparation. Others were attributed to failures in communication and project management. We identified opportunities for improved approaches by reusing successful techniques from earlier projects. Ultimately, we are working to extract core design and implementation templates into an *application framework* based on the idea that many of the requirements of nonprofits are similar in nature. Looking forward, we have begun preparing for the day when community organizations provide access to their services from personal devices such as smart phones, while at the same time moving their back-end database operations off-site, say to cloud-computing services.

20.2 THE ROLE OF SERVICE-LEARNING

20.2.1 History at our college

In recent years, we have undertaken several successful community-service projects including [1]:

- A database system designed to track and report on the delivery of services to homeless people by a local shelter (St. Francis House)
- An online application process for students seeking training at The Nelson Mandela Training Center
- A database of available day care slots for the Parker Hill/Fenway ABCD
- A Web-enabled application for Christmas gift sponsorship of children for the New England Home for Little Wanderers
- A registration system for courses and other services offered by the Urban League of Eastern Massachusetts

20.2.2 Meeting Program Educational Objectives

As a college, our first duty is to our students. We have defined four educational objectives for our graduates:

1. They will have a solid foundation for engaging in lifelong learning and professional development.
2. They will attain productive and challenging careers in private practice, industry, and government.
3. They will be proficient in applying contemporary computer science theory and practice to problems encountered in their workplace.
4. They will exhibit professionalism and behave in an ethical manner with regard to workplace and societal issues.

Service-learning is one of several means we employ to prepare students to meet these objectives. Perhaps most important, a service-learning project is real; there are real clients to work with and real problems to be solved. A toy project found in a textbook or contrived by a professor is meant to be solved using the methods presented in the book or taught in a class. A real project is much more challenging. Simply defining the problem in terms of requirements is a painstaking process requiring many meetings with clients. Its solution requires integrating techniques presented in several classes and often even this is not enough; the students typically need to go well beyond what they have learned in class. They may seek advice from friends and colleagues, search the Internet, and even visit the library. This directly builds toward objectives 1 and 3 above.

Listing a project on a resume is a conversation opener during a job interview. We regularly meet with our Industrial and Professional Advising Committee (these are the people who hire our graduates). What we hear is that students become animated when they discuss their projects during job interviews; a shy applicant becomes more confident and students who may have difficulty recalling which courses they took the previous semester are able to describe their projects in great detail. Service projects help graduates attain careers (objective 2).

In terms of professionalism (objective 4), working on a service project offers students a chance to behave as responsible adults. In our experience, students are treated with great respect at meetings held with community organizations. They, in turn, tend to dress appropriately, show up on time, and listen carefully. Students are motivated by the idea of involving themselves in societal issues, so much so that we have had numerous instances of students continuing to work on a project after the course was done, even after they graduated, expecting no compensation of any sort.

Projects done for nonprofit organizations can be used to satisfy the community-service requirement that many colleges have for graduation. Participation in the work of nonprofits makes students more aware of the social and ethical implications of computing. Such understanding is now mandated by the ABET, CAC accreditation criteria [2]. Whereas some other schools offer a separate course in service-learning [3], our model is to incorporate it into the project portion of existing courses. Most of this is done in two required senior-level courses, "Software Design and Development" and "Senior Project." The projects are showcased in a design expo sponsored by our College of Engineering, and further publicized on the departmental website cs.wit.edu.

20.2.3   Enhancing Relationships with the Surrounding Community

Wentworth Institute is situated in a dense urban neighborhood. The Longwood Medical area centered on the Harvard Medical School and half a dozen teaching and research hospitals are on one side. There are also a number of institutions of higher education, including Northeastern University and the Massachusetts College of Art and Design. On the other side are the low-income, heavily minority neighborhoods of Roxbury and Mission Hill. These are older, relatively stable urban neighborhoods with a number of well-established nonprofit community-service organizations. These neighborhoods are also politically well organized, with one of their leading concerns being encroachment into neighborhood housing by colleges and hospitals looking for land to build on. We believe that building ties to local community organizations will prove valuable to our institute as we execute our master building plan. Although we do not seek additional land for construction, each project must pass an extensive permitting process in which the community has a voice. We hope that our neighbors will see us in a positive way—that we support the community and work with its institutions.

Our department has entered into several service-learning projects with neighboring hospital research laboratories; however, the nature of these projects has been to provide support to ongoing research rather than to take the lead in developing new applications, as is done with the community projects.

20.2.4 Providing Value to Community Organizations

In our experience, community organizations are often ambitious in their desire to offer services over the Internet; however, they typically lack the expertise to do so on their own. They also tend to have older computer applications for use in carrying out their daily business, providing an audit trail, and other record keeping. Our students, working unpaid, can often update these systems with the only cost to the organization being the time their staff spends in meetings with our team. We have been told that these meetings are often enjoyable for those staff involved. Students bring in a fresh perspective; often, they are just back from four-month cooperative education (co-op) jobs with companies like IBM and EMC, venues where they are exposed to the most recent technologies used in industry. Students are eager to share what they have learned with community organizations. Students are enthusiastic and readily become committed to the community organization's mission.

20.2.5 Difficulties and Constraints

Our semesters last for 15 weeks. Time is needed at the beginning of the semester to organize the student groups and interview the clients about their requirements. We use a standard software engineering approach comprising three phases, with deliverables marking the end of each phase. The phases are:

1. Requirements
2. Design
3. Implementation

The requirements phase tends to drag out, with extensive interviews with the client team to understand their existing system and decide on the features and look and feel of the future one. The students prepare a detailed requirements document, which must be validated by the client. This leaves little time for design and implementation. Only small projects are feasible for completion in a single semester.

The students are undergraduates with limited experience, if any, in building software systems. Although they have already taken programming, database, and systems analysis courses, for the most part they are learning as they go along. A few students are able to use their co-op experience to advantage; this input has proven invaluable in bringing projects to a successful conclusion.

Cooperative education is one of the distinguishing features of our college. Students are required to complete two four-month jobs in industry in order to graduate. Junior students go on co-op in the spring, seniors in the fall. However, significant community-service projects necessarily span more than one semester. With co-op, projects begun by one set of students are continued by an entirely different set the next semester.

20.3   CASE STUDY OF A PROJECT AT RISK—ULEM

This section is an extensive study of a community-service project that serves to illustrate some of the difficulties these projects may engender. The project was for the Urban League of Eastern Massachusetts (ULEM), an interracial, nonprofit, community-based organization, which provides programs of service and advocacy in the areas of education, career/personal development and employment for African Americans and other residents of color [4]. Currently, ULEM's primary focus is Roxbury, a traditionally low-income section of Boston. Community residents are provided with job training and professional skills to start them on a career path.

ULEM depends on financing from a mix of government agencies, foundations, and private donations. The varying reporting requirements of its funding sources require ULEM to carefully track its programs, capturing needed data [5]. Additional data is needed to support day-to-day operations such as enrolling students into courses and tracking attendance and progress. The aim of the project was to replace the former paper-based system with a database system using a Web-based interface.

20.3.1   ULEM Project Initiation

The project was initiated at ULEM's request. ULEM had learned of our community-service program from the director of the Nelson Mandela Learning Center. For the Mandela project, students had programmed five different applications against a large, newly designed relational database [6].

Two faculty members, one a specialist in database design, and the other a specialist in software design, agreed to take on the ULEM project in collaboration. Unlike the Nelson Mandela project, the project would be very large in scale and tie together several different departments. The back-end database design was to fall on students from a junior-level database-management class, whereas the front-end Web interface design, overall analysis, and design tasks were undertaken by a group of six students in a senior-level software design and development class.

20.3.2 Coordinating Development Teams

It was assumed that students would sit in on other team meetings and informally coordinate, with the two professors providing overall coordination. In fact, communications between teams proved to be a problem. Many of our students work outside jobs to pay for college, and the classes' lecture and laboratory dates and times did not allow the two course sections to meet during school hours.

There was also a complete lack of overall project management. The front-end team produced a Gantt project-management chart as part of their course requirements, but this was more a formality than a working document, and was never shared with the other teams. The database teams often disagreed on the design, making it difficult to produce an integrated database.

The two faculty members took different approaches toward incorporating the projects into their curriculums. The database professor was interested in involving every student in the class in the database design. This way, the project could be used as a running example in the lectures and demonstrate the difficulty of large-scale database design. In the software design class, by contrast, this project was only one of a number of projects taken on by various student teams. Some other projects, for example, involved building games and programming handheld devices such as cell phones. This professor's goal was to show that common software-design techniques could be used in building different kinds of applications. He devoted little lecture time to discussing the project, leaving it to the student team to present their work during laboratory periods. The team made three formal presentations as well as several informal progress reports.

20.3.3 ULEM Requirements Definition

To establish requirements, several meetings were held at ULEM's headquarters. Primarily front-end team members attended these meetings, with some representation from back-end teams. On the ULEM side were those most familiar with the programs to be automated and with their existing computer systems. These meetings, though short, were fruitful. Students came prepared with lists of questions as well as use-case diagrams and prototype screens. The ULEM staff supplied existing paper forms and answered questions. Eventually, ULEM identified six programs to be automated:

1. EPST (Employment and Professional Skills Training Program)
2. SCSP (Seniors in Community Service Program)
3. Parent Involvement Program
4. Youth Program
5. Technology Training Program
6. Volunteer Program

The key programs were the training programs. To manage these, ULEM employs four levels of personnel:

1. Front-Line Staff—Clerical staff helping walk-ins fill out request forms for entry to the programs.
2. Coordinators—Managing scheduling and administration of courses, approving enrollment, and recording student attendance and progress.
3. Managers—Responsible for reporting on courses to funding sources.
4. Database Administrators—Responsible for maintaining the integrity and availability of the database and other computer resources.

The software needed to limit access on a need-to-know basis. This concerned both the back-end teams, which needed to limit access to the database tables, and also the single front-end team, which needed to limit access to Web pages.

The front-end team produced a requirements document containing use-case diagrams, scenarios, and a diagram outlining the Web pages to be built and showing navigation between them. This document was made available to the back-end teams and to Urban League staff. To conform to several applications already running at ULEM, the back-end database was to be Microsoft's SQL Server®, and the front-end Web pages would be built using Active Server Pages (ASP) scripting.

20.3.4   ULEM Project Design

The front-end team produced a design document shortly after requirements were set. Among other things, this document spelled out the logic of the processes of requesting entrance to a course, being approved for enrollment, having progress notes added in, and so forth. Appropriate Web forms were designed for accomplishing these tasks. The team was interested in proto-typing the system but, unfortunately, the back-end database was not yet available, so testing a prototype would require the front-end team to create a mock database themselves.

Meanwhile, the back-end teams were dividing the applications up into logical units based on ULEM's six programs. The designs for the smaller units would later be merged to create the global database model. They were also creating data-field names and determining data types and lengths. An entity–relationship diagram (ERD) was produced, depicting over 200 tables. The ERD was clearly unwieldy; there were too many tables and extensive duplication. Furthermore, there was little consistency between the approach-es taken by the various teams. Before merging the databases, they would have to be made to conform to each other, a nontrivial undertaking.

To address these problems, the back-end teams decided to use stored pro-cedures to limit database access. Stored procedures are very secure since they are stored on the centralized back end, and rights to stored procedures can be granted to users even when the user does not have rights to the under-lying tables being accessed [7]. This simplified the front-end task; they could call the stored procedures even while the underlying database was in flux. But the back-end team provided only a few stored procedures. The se-mester was in its final two weeks so the front end had to mock up a database to make its final presentation.

20.3.5   ULEM Project Continues

Even though the spring semester was over and the associated software-de-sign and database management courses had concluded, work on the project continued for more than a year and a half in an ultimately successful effort to provide a workable application to the client. One member of the front-end team agreed to continue the project during the summer as his senior project. He concentrated on the most important program offered by ULEM, namely, the EPST. He wrote and tested ASP scripts to support this program. Howev-er, the stored procedures he used were sometimes unreliable and indicated weaknesses in the design of the base tables.

The following fall, a former member of the back-end team volunteered to work on simplifying and normalizing the database schema, which at this point still had almost 200 tables and a great deal of redundancy due to fail-ure to integrate the efforts of the original teams. Working on his own, he accomplished a much tighter design than had been achieved by some 25 students working in teams. Of course, this also meant recoding the back end of the stored procedures, but this had a big payoff. The interface pro-vided by the stored procedures had not changed (with some exceptions).

The scripts written using the stored procedures could now be tested and de-bugged.

20.3.6 ULEM Project Concludes

A new front-end team was constituted in the spring software-design class. This team was provided with the existing code and documentation, in partic-ular, the ASP scripts and the database design. However the scripts covered only the first level of intake forms. ULEM actually had three stages in their intake process, each with their own forms. So significant additional scripting was required. Also, the database had changed since the scripts were written. This new team had greater expertise in using PHP than ASP. PHP is a free open-source scripting language that is very popular with students [8]. Since the scripts needed to be reworked anyway, the team switched to PHP. By the end of the semester, they had produced a working prototype. It was installed on ULEM's server for on-site testing. ULEM staff now began to provide bug reports on roughly a weekly basis.

However, ULEM now requested a change in the method for authenticat-ing users and assigning privileges to them. Since the project was initiated, ULEM had changed its systems to use Microsoft's Active Directory. Users within the ULEM building are authenticated when they log on to their com-puters. The team was requested to conform its system to Active Directory to avoid the need for a double log-on.

Ultimately, the project was concluded in the summer, 20 months after it started. One of the members of the spring software design team volunteered to continue the work as his senior project. He handled the bug reports that had accumulated from ULEM. He also changed the authentication to align with Active Directory. This made it feasible for ULEM to successfully change over to the new system.

20.3.7 ULEM Postmortem

Although this section is labeled postmortem, it should be emphasized that this was not really a failed project. In the end, a working and tested applica-tion was produced and installed on the client's computer. It was a partial so-lution in the sense that it automated registration and tracking for only one of the client's six programs, albeit the most important one. However, this was in keeping with the client's expectations from the start.

The students generally had a positive view of their experience, as ex-pressed in their course evaluations. One wrote that it felt good to participate in something *meaningful*. Several students felt that they had learned more from the project than from the textbook or classroom lectures. In fact, a common theme was that they wanted to do more service projects, including longer ones stretched over two semesters.

Nevertheless, the project was extremely frustrating for the faculty members involved and seemed to consume more of their energies than warranted. It was a learning experience for us as well as for the students. What went wrong? What are the risks common to service projects of this kind? Here is a short list of risk factors identified in a postproject meeting of the two faculty members joined by two students:

- *Communication can break down, even in a small organization.* That was certainly true at the Wentworth end. The faculty members met with each other on a regular basis but the students from the two classes involved tended to communicate with each other haphazardly. Design documents, including the notorious 200 class entity-relationship diagram were sometimes inaccessible and often out of date. There were also communications failures at the client end. The teams they presented at meetings with us varied from week to week and it is not clear that they communicated with each other outside of our meetings.

- *The development team may lack needed skills.* In our case, the faculty members involved had a background in teaching with little experience between them in actual software development. For example, although an object-oriented design may be an elegant way of describing a software system, it is not entirely clear how to translate the design into a layered system with a back-end relational database. Some of the senior students in the software-design class were able to leverage their experience on co-op jobs to advantage, but even these students were better at carrying out low-level tasks such as writing scripts than at higher-level systems analysis and design.

- *Projects may fail to progress in a timely fashion.* That was certainly true for us, a project meant to complete in four months stretched out to 20. It may simply be that the scope of the project was too large to allow completion in one semester, but there were also lapses in project management, assigning tasks, monitoring milestones, and so on. Too often, team members were stalled waiting for others to complete their parts. We did use tools like Microsoft Project to produce Gantt charts but were remiss in keeping the charts current. In reality, the team leaders tended to make ad-hoc management decisions rather than being informed by the charts.

- *Project participants may have different goals and time schedules.* The most obvious difference was that the development effort conformed to an academic schedule whereas the client followed its normal annual schedule. In some instances, key contacts on the client side became unavailable as staff went on vacation or were otherwise diverted. Meanwhile, the clock was ticking on the developer's side. When the project was initiated, it took until midsemester just to nail down the requirements, leaving little time for design and implementation. Curiously, the client appeared to be infinitely patient, never voicing criticism to us on how long it was taking. In retrospect, the project may have been less important to them than it was to us. The promise was to automate tasks they were currently doing manually on paper; however, the current system worked and there was bound to be some resistance to changing over. On our side, the primary goal was to provide a realistic experience to our students. In the database class, this was carried to an extreme, with every student in the class having a hand in designing the schema. In retrospect, this was not a good way to build a database.

- *Integrating work done by separate groups is problematic.* Going back to the database class, the idea was to get a number of teams going, each one working on one aspect of the problem and then somehow combine the individual schemas into a global one. The client obliged by describing six different programs they eventually wanted to automate, even though some of them were currently inactive. The students were given paper forms used in connection with the six programs, but even these forms were inconsistent with each other since the programs had been developed at different times. Common elements such as names, dates, and social security numbers were represented differently. The teams labored at their tasks with varying success. Some, but not all, managed to produce a normalized (third normal form) schema for their program. The next step, integrating the six schemas into one, was a disaster. Many data fields did not conform to each other in name or type. The chart showing all 200 tables was hand drawn and always out of date. The problem appeared to be intractable and was eventually abandoned when the scope of the problem was narrowed to only one of ULEM's six programs.

- *If projects drag, clients are likely to change their requirements.* As mentioned previously, during the time we were taking to complete the project, the client changed its login procedure to Microsoft's Active Directory. This invalidated some of the authentication work that had already been completed and further delayed the project.

20.4   GEARING UP FOR FUTURE PROJECTS

Following a period of reflection and self-assessment of several recent service-learning projects, including ULEM, we instituted a number of changes in our department with the hope that in the future we will provide a better experience for our clients, our students, and our faculty. These efforts are already bearing fruit as we enter into new community projects and industrial partnerships. This section outlines our current approach.

20.4.1 A Standardized Developer–Client Contract

An ongoing relationship must be maintained with clients starting from the initial contact and project proposal, continuing at least until the project is finished, installed, and tested on the client's machines. Ideally, the relationship should be maintained well after the project is deployed to handle newly discovered bugs and evolution of the client's requirements. On the developer's side, the primary responsibility for maintaining the client relationship necessarily falls on faculty and staff to provide continuity for multisemester projects. Clients are entitled to know that work on their projects will continue if needed after the semester concludes. Similarly, the developers need some assurance that the client will maintain its commitment to a project even if there is some rotation in lower-level personnel. So some senior managers should sign on.

At Wentworth Institute of Technology the Center for Community and Learning Partnerships [9] has developed a template for a Memorandum of Understanding (MOU) for Service-Learning Projects. The MOU is between a faculty member at Wentworth and a community partner. The MOU states the roles and responsibilities for each partner, the agreed-upon scope of the project, and a statement that Wentworth students are subject to the Wentworth code of conduct while on the job.

Our department uses the MOU to define the scope of the project in terms of included features and time line, to define the resources we will commit, and to define the client's commitment in terms of resources and availability of their staff to work with our students.

After the initial meetings, our students supplement the MOU with a detailed proposal sketching the nature of the work and an anticipated time line. Following the detailed proposal, our students begin working with the client team on Phase 1 of software development, namely, drawing up a detailed requirements specification. The functional requirements specify the services to be provided by the software, that is, on-line application forms, data analysis, and reports. The nonfunctional requirements act as constraints on the system, that is, the need to conform to the client's existing software, security, and availability. All requirements need to be testable and the student teams begin creating the acceptance test suite from the requirements, thereby setting a goal for the software to meet. The requirements are also prioritized; the students commit to completing those on the A-list, and B-list requirements are completed if time permits. The students also supply the client with their project plan. Finally, the client representatives and student team sign the requirements document.

To summarize, the developer–client contract is in 3 parts: (1) the MOU between the community organization and the Wentworth faculty members, (2) the detailed project proposal submitted by the student team, and (3) the requirements document signed by the students and client representatives.

20.4.2   Project Management

Much of the risk associated with community-service software development can be mitigated using proper project management. Project management activities include:

- Estimating costs and benefits
- Work breakdown into phases and tasks
- Assigning personnel to tasks
- Coordinating
- Assessing risks
- Managing resources
- Monitoring progress
- Managing artifacts
- Tracking costs and resources

To this end, we now require students in our BSCN program to take a course in project management. Students learn the concepts and also the use of tools such as Microsoft Project. In addition, all projects courses will require student teams to document their use of project management techniques.

20.4.3   Faculty Preparation

Faculty members play key roles in community-service projects:

- They need to make sure they are equipping the students with necessary skills when they plan curricula, devise syllabi, choose textbooks, and so on.
- They directly supervise the projects, providing overall project management. They assess the difficulty of proposed projects, match projects to student capabilities, monitor progress, review documents, enforce deadlines, and provide feedback.

- They act to resolve disputes between team members and between teams and the organization being serviced.
- They provide continuity for projects that span multiple semesters and multiple course offerings.
- They maintain contacts with clients and work with professionals and staff at their institution charged with fostering community service.

To carry out their roles, faculty involved in community-service projects may need to upgrade their own skills in areas such as:

- Current software design techniques
- UML conventions for modeling systems
- Scripting and database languages such as SQL, HTML, JavaScript, and PHP
- Project management, including the use of software such as Microsoft Project

20.4.4   Institutional Support

When our department began doing community-service projects, there was little institutional support. More recently, Wentworth Institute has recognized the importance of such projects and created a fully staffed Center for Community and Learning Partnerships. Students, faculty, and community organizations can submit proposals online. The staff facilitates matching resources to needs.

Within our recently organized College of Engineering, service-learning projects are showcased. They are seen as being an important component of undergraduate education. The College of Engineering is particularly interested in interdisciplinary projects that draw together diverse technical skills.

20.4.5   In-House Applications Laboratory

The Department of Computer Science and Networking is building a state-of-the-art high-availability laboratory capable of supporting a variety of operating systems and programming languages. Suppose a project is being built for a client to conform to their existing hardware, operating system, networking, and database environment. The student team will be able to simulate this environment in our applications laboratory and do most of the development in-house. There are no client concerns that students may inadvertently wreck their systems. After initial testing, the system is then installed on the client's system (and under their supervision) for final acceptance testing.

20.4.6   Application Frameworks

An *application framework* is a reusable partial application that can be specialized to provide custom applications [10]. Application frameworks have been used in industry for almost 25 years, so it is important that computer science students employ this tool in software development. Our department has begun building an application framework for community-service projects. The nonprofits for which these projects are built share certain common traits:

- They provide services to diverse clients, free or at reduced cost.
- They employ both paid staff members and volunteers.
- They receive funds from a combination of government agencies, foundations, and individual contributors, and need to report on how the funds are used.
- They need to manage day-to-day operations such as scheduling classes and appointments.
- They require different levels of access for different groups of users.
- They protect the privacy of those who receive services.
- They prefer common Web interfaces for use internally by the staff, and externally by contributors, clients, and the public.

An application framework can provide partial functionality to meet these common needs. The framework can then be customized with client-specific functionality. Our approach to building an application framework is to start with a well-tested application in use by one of our clients and strip away all the custom features, retaining only the core features used by nearly every organization. To protect the privacy of the original client, names and other identifying references are removed or changed. We believe that by starting with the core application framework we can meet any of our client's requirements in a fraction of the usual time. However, we have not yet conducted a full test of this concept.

We have found it best to use a standard approach to building service projects. We try to use the same languages, currently HTML, JavaScript, PHP, and SQL, for all projects. This way, we can build up an in-house expertise in them.

Key to building an application framework is the use of a layered architecture (see Figure 20.1). This allows decomposition of the total project into subtasks and lessens the need for communication and coordination between the various groups working on different aspects of the problem. Each layer need only coordinate with the one or two layers adjacent to it.

A typical project involves a back-end database component, front-end Web access by different classes of users, and a back-end business logic that

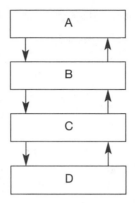

Figure 20.1. A closed layered architecture. Each layer receives services from lower layers and provides services to higher layers.

guides the responses made to requests by users. At the very least, this calls for three layers, as shown in Figure 20.2.

We found that three layers are not enough. We often encountered these problems:

- Database design is difficult. Even a design that is functional in the sense that all queries can be satisfied may not be optimal. It may have redundancy and respond too slowly. Requiring the front-end team to tightly coordinate with the database designers can significantly delay a project.
- Designing professional-looking HTML interfaces is difficult. The Web pages should conform to a common look and feel. Navigation should

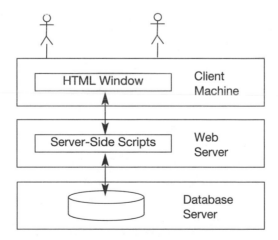

Figure 20.2. A three-layer architecture for Web-based applications.

be intuitive for all classes of user. At the same time, the organization has business rules that indicate how to create responses to user requests. It is a mistake to mix up the processing of business rules with the task of formatting consistent pages.

The solution to these problems is to add two additional layers to the architecture as shown in Figure 20.3.

The Stored-Procedures Layer. Stored procedures are provided by many database-management systems to facilitate data extractions, insertions, updates, and deletions. The user of a stored procedure need not know the actual structure of the underlying base tables in the database. A single insertion via a stored procedure can result in multiple operations on several base tables. Stored procedures can be designed directly from the requirements specification of the project. Once the specified functionality of each stored procedure is agreed upon, the back-end and front-end teams can go their separate ways; the back-end team designs the base tables and implements the stored procedures, and the front-end team calls the stored procedures in its programs and scripts. The ULEM project might have failed had we not used stored procedures.

Here are some added benefits of using stored procedures:

- Limiting database access to stored procedures allows tight security control.

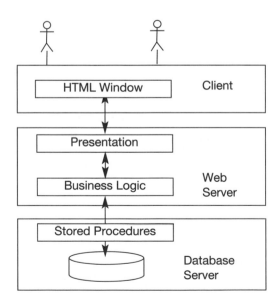

Figure 20.3. A layered architecture with separate layers for presentation and business logic.

- The database can be freely modified as long as the stored procedures are recompiled to continue to meet their specification.
- Users of stored procedures do not need to know how to do complex SQL queries.
- Data rules can be enforced to make sure related base tables are updated in consistent ways.
- Stored procedures are faster than embedded code or scripting, since they are stored in a compiled form with the database.

It should be noted that there are some criticisms of stored procedures [11]. In particular, stored procedures mix business logic with storage considerations and the procedures are vendor dependent. Still, stored procedures have worked well for us. The principal advantage is that they afford separation of concerns, allowing our font-end teams to proceed forward even though the back-end database development is still in flux.

The Business-Logic Layer. Server-side scripting is separated into two layers:

1. Presentation layer. Responsible for formatting HTML pages to convey the response to the user.
2. Business-logic layer [12]. Responsible for determining the content of responses according to the policies and procedures of the organization.

For example, in the ULEM project, there were rules for determining whether a person was eligible to be considered for enrollment in a program. The logic of this determination was somewhat complex and depended both on information submitted by the user requesting enrollment and the user's profile and history stored in the database.

20.5 CONCLUSION AND FUTURE DIRECTIONS

Service-learning projects are an important component in an undergraduate education, particularly in the computer science area. Real projects are always more motivating and challenging than toy ones; they prepare students for their first jobs, either as part of a cooperative education model or as career placement. Projects are added to their portfolios and stand out on their resumes.

Institutions of higher learning exist in communities and absorb resources from them. Examples are increased traffic, parking issues, housing issues, and noise. Colleges can cause resentment within the community. Giving back is not only good policy, but meets a crucial need and exposes students to the positive effects of serving others.

For faculty members, service-learning projects can be challenging. They may find that their own skills need upgrading. Once a project is undertaken, it must be tightly managed and defined, which is time-consuming. Students can grow discouraged when projects fail; so can the users in the community organization. Being aware of conflicts, communication issues, and feature creep is vital. Well-defined roles and deadlines are imperative, as well as keeping lines of communication open between faculty, students, and non-profit technical and other staff.

Section 20.4 outlined our current approach to building service projects. We believe we can minimize the risk of a project failing or becoming too taxing on the time resources of our students and faculty, yet at the same time deliver a quality system to our clients.

Even so, our current approach is not necessarily the last word in development methodology. The next section describes a promising approach we may consider in the future.

20.5.1 Cloud Computing

For most of our community clients, the IT Center provides support services but is not part of the central mission of the organization. For example, at ULEM the computers used to track registration and progress of students in training programs were not themselves used for training; there was a separate lab of teaching computers. The recent invention of publicly available cloud computing services may be an attractive option for off-loading administrative applications.

The cloud provides its customers with adequate hardware, systems software, and database support to run their applications remotely. According to Jinzy Zhu [13],

> We would be able to rent from a virtual storefront the basic necessities needed to build a virtual data center, such as a CPU, memory, and storage, and add on top of that the middleware necessary, such as Web application servers, databases, enterprise server bus, etc., as the platform(s) to support the applications we would like to either rent from an independent software vendor (ISV) or develop ourselves. Together, this is what we call IT as a Service (ITaaS) bundled to us, the end users, as a virtual data center.

This could provide great benefit for our clients. It would relieve them of the burden of acquiring and maintaining their own servers and software licenses. Clients would still need to take the lead in providing security for their data, but could build on the security services provided by the cloud. On the other hand, regular backup and recovery services would be effortlessly provided. No data would ever be lost. The economics of cloud computing seem attractive too. Providers such as Amazon are able to achieve a higher utilization of their hardware resources than can any small organization that allows them to sell cloud services at a reasonable price.

The software architecture shown in Figure 20.3 is easily implemented on a cloud computing platform. End users would only require a minimally equipped computer, notepad, or smart phone to access the system at the top layer. The middle and bottom layers providing Web service, database, and business logic support would operate in the cloud. We are looking forward to building our first cloud-based application.

20.6 REFERENCES

1. L. M. MacLean and M. Werner, "Student Satisfaction Using Real Projects For Object-Oriented and Database Design," in *International Conference on Informatics Education and Research, Seattle, Washington, December 2003.*

2. *Accreditation Board for Engineering and Technology, Item IV-17 in* 2000–2001 Criteria for Accrediting Computer Programs. http://www.abet.org/images/Criteria/cac_criteria_a.pdf.

3. P. Sanderson and K. Vollmar, "A Primer for Applying Service Learning to Computer Science," *SIGCSE Bulletin,* Vol. 32, No. 1, March 2000.

4. ULEM website: http://www.charityamerica.com/charities/infocauseway/CharityAbout.cfm?CharityID=192.

5. R. P. Heine, "Community Services Needs Assessment: An Innovative Approach," *Developments in Business Simulation and Experimental Learning,* Vol. 24, 1997. http://sbaweb.wayne.edu/~absel/bkl/vol24/24an.pdf.

6. L. M. MacLean and T. Pencek, "Benefits and Difficulties in Use of Real Projects for Advanced Database Applications," in *17th Annual Conference of the International Academy of Information Systems, Barcelona, Spain, September 2002.*

7. E. Sommarskog, "Giving Permissions through Stored Procedures." Retrieved Sep 2, 2011 from http://www.sommarskog.se/grantperm.html.

8. PHP home page, retrieved 9 July 2011 from http://www.php.net.

9. Wentworth Institute of Technology: Center for Community and Learning Partnerships, http://www.wit.edu/clp/index.html. Retrieved Oct. 28, 2011.

10. R. Johnson and B. Foot, "Designing Reusable Classes," *Journal of Object-Oriented Programming,* Vol. 1, No. 5, 22–35, 1988.

11. T. Marston, "Stored Procedures are EVIL," retrieved 9-July-2011 from http://www.tony-marston.net/php-mysql/stored-procedures-are-evil.html.

12. Woodger Computing Inc., "General Web Architecture." Retrieved 9-July-2011 from http://www.woodger.ca/archweb.htm.

13. J. Zhu, "Real Cases and Applications of Cloud Computing," in *Cloud Computing and Software Services Theory and Techniques,* Edited by S. A. Ahson and M. Ilyas, CRC Press 2011.

CHAPTER 21

ASSESSING BOTH THE KNOW AND SHOW IN IT SERVICE-LEARNING

Rick Homkes

ABSTRACT

When a faculty member considers creating an information technology service-learning course or module, assessment may not be the first thing that comes to mind. Instead, it is probably a warm feeling of implementing pedagogy that uses experiential learning and promises a service to a community nonprofit organization. It resides halfway between the real world and the classroom, a real-world problem for a real client while still being part of a regular course. Problems, however, can crop up as soon as the instructor starts to develop the course plan. One of the most difficult problems is to determine exactly how the students are going to be assessed. Unlike many courses, a service-learning course requires both hard technical skills and soft skills such as communications and teamwork. Since it is experiential, tests are not an option. Since it is dealing with a new problem every semester, the canned case-study grading rubric does not work. Since the client is real, sometimes issues arise that are beyond the control of the instructor or students. Furthermore, since the problem is real, sometimes a solution simply cannot be found. In response to these problems, this chapter seeks to help an IT service-learning instructor formulate an assessment plan for the course. It starts with some definitions of service-learning and a review of Furco's Continuum so that service-learning can be placed into a context of the several areas of service engagement. It then reports on some of the reasons for service-learning and how the topic of service-learning has become much more common in engineering- and technology-education conferences. Assessment in service-learning, and the requirements of ABET, are next covered. Finally a review of techniques for assessing both the hard and soft skills required of an IT professional is covered. These help us to determine that our students both know and can show the skill set desired.

21.1   INTRODUCTION—WHAT IS SERVICE-LEARNING?

21.1.1   Definition of Service-Learning

Service-learning has several definitions, but one of the most succinct is that from the National Service-Learning Clearinghouse. It is that service-learning is "a teaching and learning strategy that integrates meaningful community service with instruction and reflection to enrich the learning experience, teach civic responsibility, and strengthen communities" [1]. A second definition, from Missouri State University, is that

> Service-learning is a type of experiential education that combines and pursues both academic achievement and community service in a seamless weave, requiring the use of effective reflection exercises. The goal of service-learning, through linking academics to the community, is to develop the skills, sensitivities, and commitments necessary for effective citizenship in a democracy [2].

Another, somewhat longer, definition from Purdue University is that

> Service-learning, a subset of service engagement, is a course-based, credit-bearing educational experience in which students: participate in an organized service activity that meets identified community needs; use knowledge and skills directly related to a course or discipline; and reflect on the service activity in such a way as to gain further understanding of course content, a broader appreciation of the discipline, and an enhanced sense of personal values and civic responsibility [3].

The similarities can be easily seen as individual definitions have evolved, borrowed, and expanded from previous definitions. Each of the definitions above contains the word "service"; in other words, partnership with the community (often through a nonprofit organization) to deliver a service to the community. "Reflection" also appears in all three definitions. The point is that the students not just perform the work, but also think about how the project connects them personally with their plan of study and the outside environment. Likewise, in all three definitions there is a phrase regarding civic responsibility or effective citizenship. This is included to differentiate service-learning from more learning-centered activities such as co-ops or internships. A difference, however, appears in the "credit-bearing" adjective in the Purdue definition. This is included to differentiate service-learning from other forms of volunteer service activities that do not fit into the academic program of study.

21.1.2 Placement of Service-Learning in Furco's Continuum

In order to help explain service-learning in relationship to these other service-engagement activities, Furco [4] developed a continuum of five activities: volunteerism, community service, service-learning, field education, and internships. When placing a program on this continuum, there are two important factors to consider. The first is determining the intended beneficiary of the service work, the recipient or the provider. The second is determining the focus of the activity, either service or learning. Service-learning is balanced between service and leaning, and the program benefits should accrue to both nonprofit recipient and student provider. While placing service-learning in the middle, Furco stressed that any specific activity might move left or right based on its individual merits. Thus, in his example of students volunteering to visit with a patient with Alzheimer's, "as the students begin focusing more on learning about Alzheimer's disease, the program moves toward the center of the continuum to become more like community service (or even service-learning)" [4]. On the other end of the continuum, internships and field experiences have the student receiving the majority of the benefit. In these cases, as with co-op experiences, the focus is on student learning. Again, however, this is a continuum. A required nursing practicum, for example, could be held in a community clinic for patients who would otherwise not receive the medical service. As the nurses start to actually provide the care and learn about the needs of the community, an overlap between field education and service-learning can occur. Overall, however, it is probably less important exactly where a service-learning activity falls on the continuum than that a beneficial service is being provided to the recipient and that real learning is being accomplished by the student.

21.1.3 Service-Learning in Information Technology

For IT programs, the service in service-learning can come in several ways and in several places in the curriculum. Stanley [5] used service-learning in a first year course whereby an introductory class on computer hardware and operating systems set up a computer repair lab. Local residents, who were some distance from any computer repair facilities, had the chance to bring in computers with problems. This was done towards the end of the semester as a lab experience for the students. Students were able to develop their problem-solving skills and communication skills to diagnose and possibly repair the computers. A second type of project could be an infrastructure installation. One of the projects completed by students in the author's junior-level networking course focused on installing a virtual private network (VPN) for the Girl Scouts, connecting a main office in one county with a branch office in another county. This included installing and configuring Windows Server software at the main office, the VPN hardware on both ends, and wireless networking hardware at the branch. Another project completed by students in the junior-level service-learning course included wiring and installing computer networking and projection equipment in classrooms at a local church campus. These classrooms were also used by a neighborhood crime-stoppers group and the local Head Start program. A third type of project could be computer training. Brooks [6] wrote about such a project where, as part of a larger senior-level project on the digital divide, students taught classes in computer use, both in San Francisco and Peru. The most common type of IT service-learning project, however, is probably in the form of an IT product. An example of this is the on-line call logging and reporting system for a women's and children's shelter developed during one of the author's service-learning courses.

There is a basic problem with all service-learning projects, and perhaps especially with service-learning projects in the area of engineering and technology. By its definition, a service-learning project is not a case study or controlled laboratory experience; it is a real project for a real user, often a nonprofit service provider. That is great from an experiential learning point of view, but getting out of the lecture room or laboratory raises new situations that the instructor must handle. The first is that an unstructured problem may not have an answer. One project in which the author assisted could not be completed because a technological problem could not be solved, even by the professor in charge. Real clients also can cause real delays, and at least one client did not see the end of the semester as being a problem. When their month-long delay affected an installation, the response was a simple "... can't they come back in January to finish?" The answer required an explanation of the definition of a semester course and how the instructor had no real control over the students after the final grades were submitted in December. Finally, as a colleague once stated to the author, "It's still just a student project." In other words, our students are on the way to becoming IT professionals, but are not there yet. Some clients have a hard time understanding this, and client expectations must, therefore, be well managed. All of these factors make assessment difficult.

21.2 THE SERVICE-LEARNING MOVEMENT—WHY ARE WE DOING SERVICE-LEARNING?

21.2.1 Results of Service-Learning Workshop Participant Survey

With all of the problems mentioned in a previous section, why would an instructor spend the extra time required to manage a service-learning class?

What is the incentive? Quite simply, proponents believe that it works. In spring 2008, a group of selected service-learning advocates (named Service-Learning Fellows at Purdue University) conducted a service-learning workshop. Forty people were interested enough to show up in the week before class to become more informed about service-learning and the activities of the fellows. A workshop pretest was conducted to determine the attitudes of these attendees. An excerpt of the survey is shown in Table 21.1. The statements on the left were marked by the attendees as strongly agree (SA = 5), agree (A = 4), uncertain (U = 3), disagree (D = 2), and strongly disagree (SD = 1). The AVG column is the average of the responses. As can be seen from the responses, attendees thought that student learning was the most likely outcome of service-learning. However, engagement with the community, assisting societal needs, building relationships, and student leadership development were also high on the list of possible outcomes of service-learning. On the lower end of the responses for possible outcomes were research grant and university student-policy-development opportunities, with the lowest score going to promotion and tenure opportunities.

These data reflect what proponents of service-learning believe: that the active experiential learning allows for better application of concepts; that the required reflective exercises allow for a deeper, more holistic learning; and that the use of real clients allows for the students to practice their professionalism skills. They also show, however, that there are concerns, including grant writing, promotion, and tenure. Especially for untenured faculty, these last concerns, along with problems in assessment, could be a disincentive to do any service-learning projects or courses. This is where a university Engagement Office can be very beneficial to the new professor, helping not

Table 21.1. Workshop participant survey

Statement: Service-learning at Purdue University may be a catalyst for:	SA	A	U	D	SD	AVG
Assisting societal needs	29	11				4.73
Building relationships with community-service organizations	31	6	3			4.70
Course and curriculum change	20	17	3			4.43
Engagement opportunities	32	6	2			4.75
Promotion and tenure	5	10	20	4	1	3.35
Research grant opportunities	12	13	14	1		3.90
Student advocacy policy development	12	12	16			3.90
Student leadership development	29	9	2			4.68
Student learning	33	7				4.83
University recognition	19	18	3			4.40

$N = 40$

only to design and deliver a service-learning module or course, but also to educate the new academic on the value of service-learning to promotion and tenure.

21.2.2   Literature Review—Who is Doing Service-Learning?

With both promise and problems, a question could be asked as to how much service-learning is now occurring in the engineering and technology community, especially in the computing sciences. One way to measure this is to count the number of conference papers with both "service" and "learning" in the title. Four conferences were investigated, as shown in Table 21.2. These were the ASEE summer conference and the yearly conferences for ACM SIGITE (since 2003), ISECON, and ACM SIGCSE. Although not all papers about service-learning were counted because some did not have the keywords in the title, a 15 year trend line is immediately apparent. From very low numbers in the 1990s, the number of conference papers in the topic rose steadily before leveling out in 2010. The interest level in service-learning as pedagogy is demonstrated by these data. Thus, even with the problems resulting from actual projects, and also the perception that service-learning will not help win grants or gain tenure, service-learning has acquired a place in engineering, technology, and information sciences pedagogy. As with any form of experiential learning, however, assessment can be a problem.

Table 21.2. Number of conference papers with "service" and "learning" in title

Year	ASEE	SIGITE	ISECON	SIGCSE	Total
1996	1	NA	0	0	1
1997	1	NA	0	0	1
1998	1	NA	0	0	1
1999	1	NA	0	0	1
2000	7	NA	0	1	8
2001	3	NA	0	0	3
2002	5	NA	1	1	7
2003	3	2	5	0	10
2004	9	1	3	0	13
2005	18	0	2	0	20
2006	17	0	0	2	19
2007	22	1	2	1	26
2008	17	1	1	1	20
2009	19	1	2	0	22
2010	16	1	2	1	20
Total	140	7	18	7	172

21.3 ACCREDITATION AND CQI—WHY IS ASSESSMENT NEEDED?

21.3.1 The Need for Assessment

In education, assessment is the process of determining knowledge and skills, in other words, to document what the students knows and what the student can do—to know and to show. One way to classify assessment is to consider the purpose. Formative assessment is used to determine if the student is learning. Summative assessment is used to determine what the student has learned. Formative assessments are thus useful in regular classroom settings to help the learner find what areas need more work. They can be used to inform and, hopefully, to change learning strategies to lead to better learning. Summative assessments are a summation of the learning experience and are usually given at the end of the course. These are exemplified by the final grade. Both are used in service-learning. Formative assessments can be used to determine if the student or student team is on track to deliver the product on time and with the correct specifications, be it a repaired computer, an installed network, a successful training module, or a software system. Summative assessments, on the other hand, fit in well with outcome-based learning and can be used to determine if the student finished the class with the necessary knowledge and ability. In addition, both types of assessments can be used by the instructor for course improvement. Whereas formative assessments can be used for midterm corrections, summative assessments can be used to modify the course for the next offering. In other words, assessment is "the systematic process used to obtain information about student achievement so that the information can be used to (1) give feedback to students, (2) make education decisions about students, and also (3) make decisions about program/instructional effectiveness" [7]. This last objective is part of the continuous improvement process for which we should all strive, and which ABET requires for accreditation.

21.3.2 CAC of ABET

There are four commissions within ABET, but the one of interest to computing faculty is the Computing Accreditation Commission or CAC. Within the CAC, there are three different program accreditation options: computer science (CS), information systems (IS), and information technology (IT). Even though the author has never been the accreditation lead within a department, he does appreciate the amount of work that is required to prepare for a visit. One of these is to simply understand the terminology. To ABET, the Program Educational Objectives "are broad statements that describe what graduates are expected to attain within a few years of graduation" [8]. These are based on the stakeholders of the programs, for example, the employers of the graduates. Student outcomes, on the other hand, "describe what students are expected to know and be able to do by the time of graduation. These relate to the knowledge, skills, and behaviors that students acquire as they progress through the program" [8]. This is the "knowing and doing" or "knowing and showing" that we must document as part of our assessments. The exact type of assessment is not prescribed directly by ABET, since by ABET's definition assessment can be "direct, indirect, quantitative, and qualitative measures as appropriate to the outcome or objective being measured" [8]. The last important definition to ABET is evaluation. It is defined as "one or more processes for interpreting the data and evidence accumulated through assessment processes" [8]. These are important because they are part of the feedback loop that is used to determine "the extent to which student outcomes and program educational objectives are being attained" and result "in decisions and actions regarding program improvement" [8]. As these definitions show, ABET has moved from an inputs-driven accreditation process to an outputs-driven accreditation process. It now focuses on the extent to which student outcomes and program objectives are being met, along with proposed actions for improvement.

There are a set of student outcomes that are common for all three programs within CAC. These nine outcomes are:

(a) An ability to apply knowledge of computing and mathematics appropriate to the discipline

(b) An ability to analyze a problem, and identify and define the computing requirements appropriate to its solution

(c) An ability to design, implement, and evaluate a computer-based system, process, component, or program to meet desired needs

(d) An ability to function effectively on teams to accomplish a common goal

(e) An understanding of professional, ethical, legal, security, and social issues and responsibilities

(f) An ability to communicate effectively with a range of audiences

(g) An ability to analyze the local and global impact of computing on individuals, organizations, and society

(h) Recognition of the need for and an ability to engage in continuing professional development

(i) An ability to use current techniques, skills, and tools necessary for computing practice [8]

In addition, each program has specific program criteria. For computer science, these are:

(j) An ability to apply mathematical foundations, algorithmic principles, and computer science theory in the modeling and design of computer-based systems in a way that demonstrates comprehension of the tradeoffs involved in design choices

(k) An ability to apply design and development principles in the construction of software systems of varying complexity [8]

Information systems adds a single outcome:

(j) An understanding of processes that support the delivery and management of information systems within a specific application environment [8]

Whereas information technology adds several:

(j) An ability to use and apply current technical concepts and practices in the core information technologies.

(k) An ability to identify and analyze user needs and take them into account in the selection, creation, evaluation and administration of computer-based systems.

(l) An ability to effectively integrate IT-based solutions into the user environment.

(m) An understanding of best practices and standards and their application.

(n) An ability to assist in the creation of an effective project plan [8].

Even for instructors at institutions that are not ABET accredited, these student outcomes can be a guide to what should be assessed as part of any curricular improvement process [9]. For those that are ABET accredited, seeking ABET accreditation, or simply using the ABET outcomes as part of a program assessment process, using the assessment techniques discussed later in the chapter can be used to document the desired outcomes [10, 11].

21.3.3 What Not to Assess—Simple Effort

There is also an item that is often not worth assessing. The first time the author "taught" an IT service-learning course, one of the first class assignments was to develop an online time-card system to keep track of hours invested in the project by the students. The intention was to imitate a consulting company that had its focus on billable hours to the client. This does not, however, fit into the basic definition or objectives of service-learning. Service-learning is not a community service activity in which there are a required number of hours to get credit. Instead it is a learning activity that requires formative and summative assessments. As stated by Bringle et al. [12], "In service-learning classes, students do not receive credit for engaging in community service; they receive academic credit for the learning that occurs as a result of the service experience." There is, however, a nonassessment reason to keep track of hours. During a panel session of the 2006 Engineering Projects in Community Service (EPICS) Conference in Washington, DC, several panel members from outside academe stated that they look more favorably at a grant request that includes metrics on deliverables and hours. Thus, if a reader of this chapter is planning on applying for a grant to continue or expand a service-learning project or course, it may be useful to keep these metrics for the grant request. Otherwise student effort, defined as hours on task, is not usually worth measuring.

21.4 ASSESSMENT OF THE LEARNING AND DOING—IT SKILLS

21.4.1 Planning, Analysis, and Design

It is the author's experience that, when given a task, good planning is not always done by students. Many students take too much to heart our discussions of agile development and agile documentation [13]. This requires, however, the close cooperation of user and developer that is not always available with service-learning projects. Thus, some written documentation is necessary. There are several different documents that can be used to describe the system to be developed, and some of them are pictured in Figure 21.1. These all have standard templates that may have been introduced in previous courses. Using these allows students to see how a real system is documented, and also allows an instructor to assess the planning, analysis, and design of the system.

An initial document could be either a project charter, if viewing from a project management point of view, or a concept of operations (ConOps), if viewing from a systems analysis point of view. One of these documents should be developed so that the student or student team really understands the system to be developed and has communicated this understanding to the client. Both of these documents have a sign-off section whereby the nonprofit client can indicate that they have read and approved of the project plan. In one of the author's courses, a client even marked up the initial document during review with the student team, and requested their initials on the markup before signing and copying. For the project charter, important sections include descriptions of the business need that the project will satisfy, the product that the project will create, and the stakeholders of the project. Other sections of the charter could include scope, duration, constraints, and

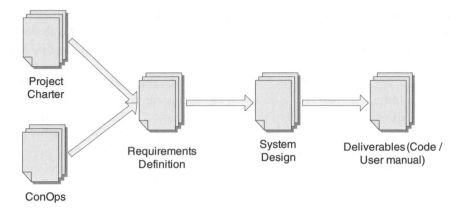

Figure 21.1. System artifacts.

assumptions [14]. Although some parts of a charter may be duplicated in a ConOps, the ConOps "is a user-oriented document that describes system characteristics for a proposed system from the users' viewpoint" [15]. Reasons for completing a ConOps are:

- Get stakeholder agreement in identifying how the system is to be operated, who is responsible for what, and what the lines of communication are
- Define the high-level system concept and justify that it is superior to the other alternatives
- Define the environment in which the system will operate
- Derive high-level requirements, especially user requirements
- Provide the criteria to be used for validation of the completed system [16]

One important and distinctive part of this document describes how the user would actually use the system—a set of operational scenarios. The author has used the ConOps even for networking infrastructure projects in which no programming is completed by the students. Having operational scenarios required the students to actually talk to the users about how the system would be used. For projects that include programming development and additional analysis and design work, the operational scenarios can be used later as a source for the UML use cases. One last point is that both the project charter and the ConOps could have a section on budget. It is sometimes necessary for the nonprofit organization to have some investment in the project in order to make the project real and not just a neat academic exercise, and this is where the budget can be documented. The author has found that a monetary buy-in from the nonprofit client, especially if there is outside grant money supporting the project from the side of the university, results in a much more involved client.

If more analysis is required, some form of requirements-definition document could be assigned and assessed. This document provides "the identification, organization, presentation, and modification of the requirements" [17]. It may also include sections on constraint and assumptions. Useful for any program that has covered UML before the service-learning project would be the incorporation of use-case diagrams and use-case narratives into the document. Students will probably be pleasantly surprised that the number of use cases in a service-learning project is usually less than the case study used in an advanced analysis and design course. If the development of a database is required, this is also the place where the logical database design would be documented.

In the cases in which the project scope requires even more documentation, some form of system design document (SDD) can be required. The U.S. Department of Health and Human Services—Centers for Medicare and Medicaid Services defines a system-design document thusly:

> The System Design Document (SDD) describes how the functional and nonfunctional requirements recorded in the Requirements Document, the preliminary user-oriented functional design recorded in the Concept of Operations (ConOps) , and the preliminary data design documented in the Logical Data Model are transformed into more technical system design specifications from which the system will be built. The SDD is used to document both high-level system design and low-level detailed design specifications [18].

For use in a service learning project, the design document could take the requirements use-case narratives and expand them to actually describe the screen choices seen and taken by the user. In addition, a nonworking screen-face prototype could be developed so that users could comment on the user interface. This type of document is especially useful if the service-learning project is going beyond the scope of a single semester. In one case, the author and a colleague had one student use the fall semester to work up to the point of a set of design-level use-case narratives and a screen prototype. This was done as the senior project of that student, who chose the optional senior project as part of his program of study. In the spring semester, a second student completed his senior project by implementing the design of the first student. In this case, the students did not interact with one another as the instructors were not sure which students would enroll in the optional senior project course and also be interested in completing the project. Thus, the second student had to code the system using only the design document and prototype left by the graduated student. In the same manner, Webster and Mirielli [19] report on one semester whereby "the original student project team drafted initial entity-relationship (E-R) models based on the new data collection forms and prototyped an initial software application user interface." In the second semester, "the initial E-R models were finalized and prototyped using MS-SQL and linked to the prototype user interface application using Web services." Final application development and delivery was then planned for the third semester.

Finally, while a statement of work (SOW) could document many of the items above, the author has not used it for service-learning. In the author's industry experience, a SOW is much more like a contract, not a planning, analysis, or design tool. Since this is a student project, the author has not wished to make this too much like a contracted outsource-development project.

No matter which document or documents are used in planning, analysis, and design, assessment criteria can be the same as was used in the systems-analysis and design courses. This could include completeness and correctness of the document along with its formatting and presentation.

21.4.2 Final Deliverables

As was seen from examples given earlier in the chapter, the products of service-learning projects can be quite varied. For a training module, the final deliverable may be the training itself. In this situation, the training materials along with the course delivery by the student would be the final product. This would have to be assessed for completeness and logical ordering (scope and sequence). For any type of system that includes programming, the actual code can be assessed in much the way that code would be assessed in any regular class. A grading rubric can be created to evaluate the human–computer interface (HCI), time and space efficiency, compliance to requirements, and adherence to coding standards. This last metric, adherence to coding standards, can be stressed, since the coders are probably not going to be the ones completing any maintenance on the system. As a final thought, it is important that the student be prepared for any service-learning project by having experience with the artifacts or standards they will use in the project itself. This means that they should be familiar with the artifacts mentioned above, such as a ConOps or SDD, and even be provided a template for use. These could be modified or expanded versions that were used in an advanced analysis and design class. Coding and HCI standards that were used in previous coursework can also be used for the service-learning project. This has the benefit of using something that the student is familiar with and something that has already had a grading rubric created for it.

21.5   ASSESSMENT OF THE LEARNING AND DOING— PROFESSIONAL SKILLS

One way to assess professional skills is to create a survey that has to be filled out by the community partner. This survey can be easily be set up with one section being a Likert-type scale and a second section being more open-ended questions. Often seen as a five-level scale from "strongly disagree" to "strongly agree," it can also be set up as a four-level scale to force a choice off from the middle. Sample questions and statements that can be put in the survey include:

- Written and oral communications
- Meeting punctuality and involvement
- Appropriate attire and grooming
- Listening to agency representatives regarding needs
- Positive and willing attitude
- Accurate sense of personal capability
- Problem-solving ability
- Overall opinion of the work completed

There is a problem, however, with simply having the community agency fill out this survey. The author has found that the agency representatives vary widely in their responses. Quite simply, some community partners were more interested in having students start a life of volunteerism than in doing an honest appraisal of student appearance and work (or, in one case, even producing a usable product). Thus, a meeting with agency personnel to brief them on the importance of the survey was found to be helpful.

In the author's experience, one of the major problems with any large case or real project is teamwork. Sometimes, the instructor probably wishes that teams would not be used simply to make instruction simpler. CAC of ABET, however, has the ability to work on teams as one of its primary outcomes. In addition, teamwork has been commonly commented on by the Industrial Advisory Board during program reviews. Since teamwork will be used, some form of assessment should be used as well. One favorite method is the peer review. This can be constructed in many ways, but generally results in an evaluation of the student peers on the team, using a percentile, point, or ranking scale. Areas for this peer assessment can be:

- Meeting Attendance and Punctuality
- Participation and Readiness at Meetings

- Work Timeliness and Quality
- Team Spirit and Task Commitment

These are then averaged to provide a value for the teamwork portion of the final grade. The author has expanded this by also including himself in the overall review. This was done for a couple of reasons. One is that some groups automatically give each other high scores as part of a quid pro quo process. The other is that sometimes student behavior is egregious enough that the instructor has to take action. Students should be aware that teamwork is part of the overall evaluation, and there should even be consideration given to adding course policy on a procedure for a team to "fire" a non-performing member.

In project end reviews from the nonprofit clients, one of the most common complaints is that there was a lack of communications with the student team members. The instructor can try to head off this problem by requiring weekly update memos on the project status. This could include a Gantt chart, a risk-management section including problems and possible solutions, and a list of communications with the client. It is important to make the students understand that communications within the team and between the team and client can be the key to a successful project. In addition, the grading rubric for many of the artifacts mentioned in the hard-skills section earlier in the chapter should include a section on grammar. It is important that the students go beyond a good analysis of the proposed solution to also write a readable, professional, coherent, and complete account of that analysis.

There are several ethical and legal issues that the students may encounter as they perform service-learning activities. For the students who created the call log system for a womens and childrens shelter mentioned above, that started with an understanding and acceptance of a nondisclosure agreement (NDA). This had to be reviewed and signed before any work could be done. In addition, the male students were surprised to learn that they had to be "buzzed" into the shelter and were escorted from the door to the IT area by a staff member of the shelter. Movement away from the IT area was forbidden by shelter policy. The general issue of privacy can be an important part of an NDA. This could be legally required if the project were to involve an organization subject to the Family Educational Rights and Privacy Act (FERPA) or the Health Insurance Portability and Accountability Act of 1996 (HIPAA). Finally, there is the important ethical issue of whether the project should be done in the first place. As part of the planning process, the students should be guided into a discussion of whether the nonprofit agency can really use and support the proposed system. It may do more harm than good to deliver a system (e.g., website) that cannot be maintained by the organization. This impact question, along with privacy and other issues, can be included in an early required reflective submission by the students. Lastly, any instructor of a service-learning project should be prepared for the ethical problem to come from a different direction. In one case, a project for a database for a nonprofit agency was never intended to be used. The agency had been promised a system from their national office, but the administrator was concerned that the national office would not be able to deliver. In response, the agency hedged their bets by also having a similar system developed in parallel with the service-learning project (in this case, by an ex-student who wanted to continue in IT service work). It was only after the system was developed and delivered that the instructor found out the complete story.

Student reflection was mentioned in all the service-learning definitions that started this chapter. One assignment used by the author at the beginning of the semester was to require a short paper on the definition and application of service-learning in IT. This assignment, almost a prereflection, was used to make sure that the students understood what was expected during the semester and also to prepare them for a final written reflection at the end of the term. The final reflection can be merged into a project postmortem so that the reflection occurs as part of an accepted IT artifact. This is a good way to end the semester and the project. Students should prepare by reading an article on project success factors, including postmortem preparation [20], and then, on an individual basis, prepare the postmortem. Some prompting questions to the students should include how the project developed, what went right or wrong, what should have been changed, and ethical questions encountered. Another prompting question could be what knowledge or skills were required to complete the project that the student did not have at the start of the semester. This can lead into a discussion of personal growth, and also to the students seeing the need for continuous professional development. If time allows, a discussion of a code of ethics [21] along with the experiences of the semester could set up a separate or included ethics reflection.

Putting some of the above assessment ideas together can form a broad set of assessment mechanisms that avoids having all of the points awarded at the end of the semester. An example is shown in Table 21.3.

21.6   RESEARCH METHODS

Much of the discussion above has been about student and program assessment, but there is also the topic of actually assessing the pedagogy of service-learning itself. Although beyond the scope of this chapter, it is necessary for practitioners of service-learning to compare and contrast it with more traditional pedagogy. Two methods can be used: either qualitative re-

Table 21.3. Sample course assessment weighting

Assessment Mechanism	Total points
Reflective writing assignments (pre and post) @ 100 points each	200
Project update memos, presentations, and discussions (10 @ 10 points each)	100
Client evaluations	50
Peer evaluations	50
Project concept of operations, grant proposal, and design document	100
Project reports and client user documentation	100
Product demonstration and evaluation	100
Total	700

search or quantitative research. Qualitative research is based on inquiry into things such as transcripts, notes, and analog data. Thus, a student reflection can be mined for data. These data can then be coded to organize and classify, looking for themes that are present in multiple reflective papers. Using this, insight into attitudes and values can be gained and also used to gauge the effect of a service-learning experience. Quantitative research is about the analysis of numeric data. Surveys can be used to try to determine attitudes of the students, perhaps before and after a service-learning experience. Using data from research, the efficacy of service-learning to increase learning in the discipline and also feelings of civic responsibility can be attempted to be measured. As stated by Bringle [22], "The best chance for the research to have an impact on the practice of service-learning, on higher education, and on the disciplines and professions is for the research to based on theory, to test theory, and to develop theory." A number of such research-assessment instruments can be found in the book by Bringle et al. [12]. Thus, if the efficacy of service-learning is supported by both theory and research, service-learning will continue to grow.

21.7 SUMMARY

The three pillars of academic responsibility are often condensed to teaching, research, and service. Use of service-learning in the computing disciplines can touch all three of these areas. It is hoped by the author that this reading has enthused the reader about service-learning as pedagogy, and also informed the reader on how assessment can be designed for this type of project. Service-learning has great promise as an experiential learning device that can provide good for a nonprofit organization and the community. This idea must always be tempered, however, with the knowledge that our goal is education, and assessment is a part of education.

21.8   ACKNOWLEDGMENTS

The author would like to thank the staff of the Purdue University Center for Instructional Excellence for their support in helping to develop and implement service-learning, and to Learn & Serve of San Diego for sharing their initial evaluation instrument. This work is based on an earlier work—Assessing IT Service-Learning—in *Proceedings of the 9th ACM SIGITE Conference on Information Technology Education,* © ACM 2008, http://DOI.ACM.ORG,10.1145/1414558.1414564.

21.9   REFERENCES

1. National Service-Learning Clearinghouse (N.D.). "What is service learning?" Retrieved from http://www.servicelearning.org/what-is-service-learning.

2. Missouri State University (N.D.). "Definition of Service-Learning." Retrieved from http:// www.missouristate.edu/casl/4567.htm.

3. Purdue University (N.D.). "About Service-Learning." Retrieved from http://www.purdue.edu/ servicelearning/Service_Learning/about.html.

4. Furco, A. (1996). "Service-Learning: A Balanced Approach to Experiential Education." In B. Taylor (Ed.), *Expanding Boundaries: Serving and Learning*. Washington, DC: Corporation for National and Community Service.

5. Stanley, T., and Colton, D. (2009). "Six Years of Sustainable IT Service." In *10th ACM Conference on SIG-Information Technology Education*. Fairfax, VA: SIGITE. doi:10.1145/1631728.1631755.

6. Brooks, C. (2008). Community Connections: Lessons Learned Developing and Maintaining a Computer Science Service-Learning Program. In *39th SIGCSE Technical Symposium on Computer Science Education*. Portland, OR: SIGCSE. doi: 10.1145/ 1352135.1352256.

7. Dark, M. (2004). Assessing Student Performance Outcomes in an Information Security Risk Assessment, Service-Learning Course. In *5th Conference on Information Technology Education*. Salt Lake City, UT: SIGITE. doi: 10.1145/1029533.1029552.

8. ABET (N.D.) "Criteria for Accrediting Computer Programs, 2012-2013." Retrieved from http://www.abet.org/computing-criteria-2012-2013.

9. Homkes, R. (2008). "Assessing IT Service-Learning." In *9th ACM SIGITE Conference on Information Technology Education*. Cincinnati, OH: SIGITE. doi: 10.1145/ 1414558.1414564.

10. Helps, R., Lunt, B., and Anthony, D. (2005). "ABET Accreditation with IT Criteria." In *6th Conference on Information Technology Education*. Newark, NJ: SIGITE. doi: 10.1145/1095714.1095716.

11. Sanderson, D. (2009). "Revising an Assessment Plan to Conform to the New ABET-CAC Guidelines." In *SIGCSE '09—The 40th ACM Technical Symposium on Computer Science Education*. Chattanooga, TN: SIGCSE. doi:10.1145/1508865.1508993.

12. Bringle, R., Phillips, M., and Hudson, M. (2004). *The Measure of Service-Learning: Research Scales to Assess Student Experiences*. Washington, DC: American Psychological Association.

13. Ambler, S. (2004). *The Object Primer: Agile Model-Driven Development with UML 2.0* (3rd ed.). Cambridge, UK: Cambridge University Press.

14. Centers for Disease Control and Prevention. (N.D.) "Templates." Retrieved from http://www2.cdc.gov/cdcup/library/templates/default.htm.

15. IEEE. IEEE 1362-1998—IEEE Guide for Information Technology—System Definition—Concept of Operations (ConOps) Document. Retrieved from http://standards.ieee.org/findstds/standard/1362-1998.html.

16. U.S. Department of Transportation (N.D.). "Concept of Operations Template." Retrieved from http://www.fhwa.dot.gov/cadiv/segb/views/document/sections/Section8/8_4_5.htm.

17. IEEE. IEEE 1233-1996—IEEE Guide for Developing System Requirements Specifications. Retrieved from http://standards.ieee.org/findstds/standard/1233-1996.html.

18. U.S. Department of Health and Human Services. (N.D.) "System Design Document." Retrieved from http://www.cms.gov/SystemLifecycleFramework/Downloads/SDD.pdf.

19. Webster, L., and Mirielli, E. (2007). "Student Reflections on an Academic Service Learning Experience in a Computer Science Classroom." In *8th ACM SIGITE Conference on Information Technology Education.* Destin, FL: SIGITE. doi: 10.1145/1324302.1324347.

20. Reel, J. (1999). "Critical Success Factors in Software Projects." *IEEE Software.* May/June. 16 (3).

21. IEEE (N.D.). "IEEE Code of Ethics." Retrieved from http://www.ieee.org/about/corporate/governance/p7-8.html.

22. Bringle, R. (2003). "Enhancing Theory-Based Research on Service-Learning." In: S. H. Billig and J. Eyler (eds.), *Deconstructing Service-Learning: Research Exploring Context, Participation, and Impacts.* Greenwich, CT: Information Age Publishing.

CHAPTER 22

FROM KUDJIP TO SUCCOTZ
The Successes, Lessons, Joys, and Surprises from Twenty-Five Years of Service-Learning Projects

James Paul Skon and Doug J. Karl

ABSTRACT

Since 1986, James Skon, professor of computer science, has been engaging in a variety of international technology service-learning projects. This chapter chronicles 25 years of these experiences, examines their effectiveness, and considers what lessons have been learned.

22.1 INTRODUCTION

That the world and its cultures are being transformed by computer technology is, without a doubt, a vast understatement. However, it also seems clear that computer technology not only changes our world, but that these changes almost always result in both winners and losers. Identifying the nature and causes of these phenomena is beyond the scope of this chapter. This concept, however, was one of the key motivating elements that drove the authors of this chapter to engage in the activities described below. This chapter chronicles a personal journey made by the authors in an attempt to find a way to apply the discipline of computer science in this larger setting of a world of need and difficult change, and to include university students in the process.

22.2 BACKGROUND MOTIVATION

In 1984, during the second year as an instructor of computer science, at Mount Vernon Nazarene College (now University; MVNU), I* was handed

*Throughout, "I" refers to James Skon.

a newspaper entitled *In Other Words,* a publication of the Summer Institute of Linguistics. Having an interest in the area of computational linguistics, I read the paper with great interest.

The cover story was about a family that for 17 years had followed a tribe of nomadic Australian aborigines around the central desert plains of Australia. They were attempting to learn their language, so as to begin the process of turning the language into a written form and, thus, to bring literacy to this group of people. Rather than pushing these people to first learn to speak and read English, and in the process cause them to lose the central cohesive component of their culture (their unique language), the goal was to find a way for these people to retain their history and culture first, and then prepare them for the inevitable intersection with the larger world that travel and communication technologies would bring.

I found this notion of using technology (in this case the technology of reading and writing) to better the condition of people intriguing. Like many young academics, I was consumed with the ideal of making a difference with my education. I loved the concept of extending my efforts, and those of my students, beyond the boundaries of the traditional classroom and into situations outside the typical commercial interests. As a young professor, I was not the only one asking the question "what can I do that will really make the world better." I found my students were asking the same questions. As a technologist by education and vocation, the first-blush strategy is to look for technological solutions to all perceived problems. Neil Postman, in the book *Technopoly,* suggests that to someone with a hammer, everything looks like a nail. He goes on to critique the notion that increasing dependence on technology is both positive and desirable, noting that with every new technology there are winners and losers, gains and losses. Postman points out with clarity how much we can lose as we abandon traditional mechanisms of life for newer technological solutions, essentially trading traditional sets of beliefs and values away for the attractive advantages of the new technology. His underlying concern is that we do this without reflection, just assuming that technology is progress.

Such notions were not completely formed in my mind in 1984, and *Technopoly* had not even been published. However, thanks in part to spending several summers in the 1980s studying graduate linguistics and anthropology with the Summer Institute of Linguistics, I was already becoming cognizant of the fact that as cultures collided, and as first-world technology was created and flowed to the third world, changes were inevitable, and not all for the better.

One might posit the suggestion that the best solution is to leave well enough alone, and to avoid the introduction of technology into these more primitive cultural settings. In theory, this concept might have merit, but in practice the notion is absurd. Technology tends to take on a life of its own, and it inevitably trickles down without discrimination.

Thus, the question is not one of protecting far-flung cultures from technologies but, rather, preparing them for its certain arrival. Either educators and volunteers with a motivation of compassion and social justice participate in the process of introducing technology in a culture, or it is left completely to commercial enterprises. And whereas capitalism is a great mechanism for balancing supply and demand, it is rarely a good mechanism for deciding how its wares should be used, or for educating its customers.

22.3 EXPLORING THE POSSIBILITIES

Armed with the vision that I could participate in helping to bridge the technological gap in international settings, I contacted the headquarters of the church denomination affiliated with my college, told them that I was a computer science professor with a free summer and was willing to volunteer. This inquiry led me to spend the summer in Manila, Philippines, where I worked to assist with the computerization of both the denomination's regional offices and a seminary graduate school in the suburbs of Manila.

One year later, a colleague at Mount Vernon Nazarene University (MVNU), a biology professor, approached me and we began to explore expanding this vision of cross-cultural service-learning to the student body. We were joined by a business professor and together found students interested in missions and cross-cultural projects. We started a new official college club, which we named "Mandate," and worked on several projects in the inner cities of Columbus, Cincinnati, and Cleveland, Ohio.

We then began to dream of an international project, and contacted (once again) the central administration of our denomination. They suggested some opportunities in Belize, Central America (formerly British Honduras). Belize is English speaking and less than a two-hour plane flight from the United States. We submitted a proposal to hold a January class in Belize called "Seminar in International Development." The business students would explore the possibility of helping Belizeans start microenterprises and my students and I would bring the first computer ever to a Belizean high school and teach them how to use it. This is how it all started.

22.4 A JOURNEY THROUGH FOUR COUNTRIES: THE EVOLUTION OF A COLLEGIATE SERVICE-LEARNING EXPERIENCE

22.4.1 Manila (Summer 1986)

As I mentioned above, in 1986 I contacted my university's denominational headquarters. I explained my background as a computer science professor, with a modest amount of practical work experience, and waited for a response. Within days I was told the regional offices in both Quito, Ecuador, and Manila, Philippines needed help with networking in 1986 and data computerization. The Manila location also had a graduate seminary, which also needed assistance. My wife and I chose the Manila option, did a bit of fundraising, and were on our way. We spent 80 days in Manila, with our 15-month-old son, living in the regional director's house. While there, I worked with the staff to set up computer systems and software, teach staff how to use them, and help them plan for the future. More importantly, I began to develop many significant relationships with people of the Philippines.

There are so many life-changing experiences that I encountered, but one particularly formative one has helped to shape my vision for service-learning. I had an American friend who worked as a translator in the Philippines. I asked him about the many squatter camps I saw throughout Manila. What were they like? What were the people like? How did they survive? My friend, believing more in experience than in explanation, and having lived and worked in the Philippines for 20 years as a linguist, offered to take my wife and me to visit one. As we entered, all signs of life vanished. Everyone just disappeared. The three of us stood in the midst of mud and squalor; not a person in sight. After several minutes a man approached, obviously angry. My friend interpreted his Tagalog for us. "People come here from the outside, but only to preach and then leave. They never do anything for us! Go away!" I had my friend tell him we had not come to preach, only meet them, and perhaps be friends. After a bit of interaction the man began to cry, saying, "Really, you want to be my friend?" We spent the next hour just talking, he brought out his family and we met them all. I never helped these people, but they sure helped me. They helped me to understand that people want friendship before advice and to be understood more than to be changed. They want to be viewed as friends, equals, and not just as nameless, helpless people.

I returned to the United States from Manila with a long list of unfinished projects and many more ideas. At the time, I had two of my top students (both bound for Ph.D.s in computer science) on my mind. When I saw them, I shared my experience and told them of the need for a computer database system to manage the seminary library in Manila. Perhaps the message was infectious, as both traveled to Manila the next summer as volunteers, one staying for three months before entering graduate school and the other staying for a full year.

22.4.2 Belize (Summer 1988 and 1989)

After I returned from Manila, two other faculty members and I began to meet to discuss the possible creation of meaningful service-learning experiences for students, starting with a variety of local inner-city projects. We soon started to explore the country of Belize. It was close, English speaking, and largely (at the time) unknown. Our first contact was with the principal of a Nazarene high school in Belize City, Dwight, who became (and still is) our lead contact in Belize.

Dwight is a truly exceptional man, and the perfect international collaborator. Belizean born and raised, he had been educated in the United States and was, thus, able to understand both cultures. He was widely respected in Belize, a go-getter, and one of the most trustworthy men I have ever met. Frankly, in our ignorance, we were very lucky! Dwight went on to serve in many other capacities in the school system and the government and is a great partner to this day.

Dwight was able to understand what could and could not be done in Belize, both politically and socially. In addition, being educated in the United States, he understood us, and was able to help us avoid many of the mistakes we might have made if left on our own. I cannot overestimate the value of having such a quality in-country contact.

At MVNU, we had created the class Seminar in International Development, an interdisciplinary course, and offered it as January interim course in Belize. We enrolled 12 students, and a business faculty member, Wayne, and I led the trip.

That first year, $1000 was raised to purchase a single PC to place in a high school. Our team set it up and began to teach the staff how to use it. In packing the PC, I forgot the power cord (the standard kind that seems to breed in data centers). This provides an anecdote as to just how rare a PC was in Belize in 1988. I spent a week in the largest city, Belize City, combing the stores for a cord. In the end I had to fashion my own with a lamp cord and a soldering iron.

During this first trip, I managed to break my foot while trying to kill mosquitoes, resulting in a unique hospital experience and ending with me hopping crutchless from the hospital wrapped in a hospital apron (since I could not pull my pants over the cast!)

We returned again the next year. For this trip, a student group was able to raise $2600 from a fundraiser, allowing us to purchase four more computers to set up a high school computer lab. This was, from my understanding, the first high school computer lab in the country.

In 1990, my third child was born with a significant disability. I decided to curtail my international travel for the near future. Wayne and other faculty continued to offer the MVNU course each January throughout the 1990s and until this day, with me returning to Belize in 2007.

22.4.3 Kudjip, Papua New Guinea (January 2001)

One of my university's 1976 graduates, Jim Radcliffe, continued on to medical school and, after completing his surgical residency, accepted a position as the head surgeon in a small, 100 bed hospital in Kudjip, a small village in the central highland plains of Papua New Guinea. This hospital was started, and is supported, as a mission of my university's denomination.

Dr. Radcliffe was on furlough in the fall of 1999, and spent the semester at my university as a visiting faculty member. He expressed to me the need for a database solution for the hospital, where records were currently kept on paper. The hospital currently stored records on 90,000 treated patients completely on paper!

I was teaching a software engineering course that fall, and I decided to have my class take on the task of designing such a database as the class project. Dr. Radcliffe met with my class every week for two hours explaining what was needed. He provided us with a copy of all the forms used, and we carefully gathered all the information we could pertaining to the information management at the hospital. At the end of the class, we had a database design and a very small prototype implementation.

In the spring of 2001, I was able to find a donor to provide funding for a full-time summer employee to build a complete database system. I was able to collect 15 used computer systems that were being retired from my university, to be installed at the hospital. The hospital was a collection of over 50 small- and medium-sized buildings, about seven of which needed to be networked together immediately. At the time, I was working as a consultant for a developer of some of the very early wireless and WiFi technologies, Doug Karl, the creator of the first wireless Access Point (sold by NCR and Lucent Technologies) and the first residential WiFi router, the Apple Airport. Doug graciously donated several outdoor wireless routers and outdoor antennas to the project.

We arrived in Kudjip in early January 2001, computer equipment amazingly intact after 34 hours of flight. We found ourselves in a beautiful jungle paradise, 15 degrees south of the equator, but at 5000 feet, so the temperature was a perfect 72 degrees virtually every day. This was a valley, 20 by 50 miles, surrounded by a ring of high mountains, with almost one million inhabitants completely cut off from the rest of the world. The culture in this valley was unknown until discovered in 1935 by Australian explorers. This place was literally a single generation away from the stone age, where a majority of the population was still perhaps decades away from having electricity or running water. They lived in grass huts and farmed. Here we were, with boxes of computers and wireless routers!

The project proceeded nicely. The team included 15 students, 12 with another professor, who were working 15 miles away at a college library. My three computer science students immediately began pulling and terminating cables, setting up computers, and installing software, and we discovered one major software flaw. All the dates were in the U.S. format, MM/DD/YYYY. Papua New Guinea (PNG) used DD/MM/YYYY. Of course, every form and report had to be changed.

During the three weeks in PNG, we managed to wire five buildings and interconnect the buildings via outdoor wireless connections (pretty exotic for 2001). We installed an omnidirectional antenna on the central hospital building and then installed directional antennas on four of the other buildings, including the Nursing College building, the administration building, maintenance, and the mission office. It was such a bizarre clash of cultures as we pulled Ethernet cable and tested connections with our laptops, as traditional Papua New Guineans (patients and families) milled around, some wearing grass skirts, nose rings, and huge corks with pierced ears stretched around them. I remember a man walking by as we worked with the wires and laptops out on a breezeway connecting the buildings. He pointed at the laptop, smiled, and simply said "computer," seemingly quite proud to demonstrate his mastery of technology identification. Such interactions were frequent, provided a glimpse into another culture, and encouraged us in our belief that perhaps what we were doing did make a difference.

Perhaps the most poignant moment for me was a day later in the trip when Dr. Radcliffe asked me to accompany him on his morning surgical rounds. As we visited each bed, he assessed the conditions of the patients, and encouraged them and their surrounding family in the room crowded with beds. He explained that each family is responsible to feed the patient, as the hospital could not provide daily food. We came upon two women, co-wives, who had injured each other in a family fight. Then another patient, whose Achilles tendon had been severed when a child while playing with a machete, accidentally hit his mother. This woman had been carried for three days through the jungle on a stretcher made of two long branches with flour sacks stretched between them. Then we came upon a 10-year-old boy, lying in bed, stomach connected to strange red tubes, with a parent sitting on either side. I was struck by this, since my 10-year-old son also lay in a bed, in a body cast from serious back surgery, some 10,000 miles away. Dr. Radcliffe spoke with the boy and his parents, then turned to me as he shook his head, whispering that the boy had cancer and would not survive. I had to leave the room, sobbing. I still cry today as I write this. My son had every advantage at the prestigious Johns Hopkins Hospital in Maryland; this boy had only the compassion of Dr. Radcliffe and his assistants, a man so willing to give of his life for these people. Could my work actually make a difference?

22.4.4   Return to Manila (January 2006)

After taking a few groups to the back areas of the Bahamas in the early 2000s, setting up computer labs for schools, I had a visit from Kevin, a student I had taken to Belize in 1988. Kevin had been a driving force as a student at my school to generate interest in service-learning courses and had subsequently become a full-time worker coordinating various compassion and educational mission projects. He was currently working as the regional business manager, for the denomination, of the Asia Pacific Region, located in a suburb of Manila, and had stopped by to brainstorm about various networking and communication needs in Manila. We decided that a student project could be used to address several needs, including the building of a 1 Gb fiber backbone and associated routers for the seminary. I found a college in Massachusetts (Gordon College) that was upgrading their network and willing to donate their used equipment. Realizing I would need technical help, I approached several of my successful graduates, and they provided the funding so the director of networking at my university could travel with me. Once again, in three weeks, we built the complete backbone and server/ networking room, and fiber connected each building.

22.4.5   Belize (2008–Present)

In 2007, I began to discuss Belize in earnest with my friend Doug Karl. Doug had sold his wireless company in 2004 and was using his time and money in philanthropic pursuits. Initially, I talked with him about the need for schools to have Internet access and we hypothesized about the usefulness of an outdoor wireless system. Doug, still keenly interested in outdoor wireless and doing something meaningful with his life, agreed to visit Belize on a fact-finding mission. Our ten-day exploration of the country turned out to be quite an adventure, and its retelling would require an entire chapter of its own. With our stated goal of getting the Internet into the schools, we began to meet and talk with anyone who might be interested. We talked with school administrators, church leaders, and the directors of both the Ministry of Education and the Public Utilities Commission. We found people eager to find solutions but the telecommunications infrastructure was poor, the terrain was challenging, funding was in short supply, costs were high, and delivery of committed resources was extremely slow.

For example, we found that, officially, BTL (the Belize phone company) was committed to provide free Internet to any school with a computer lab. But we found that this commitment was only useful if there was Internet already available in the area (often not the case), and many schools had met the requirements, applied for service, and were still waiting for their connection years later. BTL was a monopoly with serious operational and expansion challenges. It was subsequently taken over by the government in an effort to further telecommunications infrastructure progress in the country. The future of BTL is still being argued in the courts.

We returned to the United States with a much greater understanding of the technology needs and challenges. We decided the next best step for us would be to help build labs in the schools, as providing Internet connectivity both practically and politically appeared to be a much greater task than we could accomplish on our own. Just prior to this chapter going to press, we met again with BTL, and found that the company was rapidly moving ahead and becoming much better equiped to follow through on their committment to bring internet into schools.

My school was retiring 75 Gateway Pentium 4 desktops with 15″ LCD screens. I had already decided that CRT monitors were not appropriate, their size and weight are prohibitive for transportation but, more importantly, the power consumption and eventual disposal needs were impractical and bad economic and environmental stewardship for a developing country. Transporting this many computers to Belize was a challenge; however, a friend in Belize gave me the number of a Rotary Organization in Findlay, Ohio, called MESA (Medical Equipment and Supplies Abroad). This organization regularly sends full shipping containers of used medical equipment to developing countries. They happened to be preparing a shipment to San Ignacio in Belize! I gave the director a call, and he agreed to include my 75 computers in his shipment at no charge!

We traveled to Belize with several students and installed labs in six schools in Succotz, Belize City, Corozol, and Sarteneja. As we arrived at each school, the children were very excited, and we were told they had been praying for months that the computers would arrive safely. In at least one school, the parents had organized a fundraiser months before our arrival to pay for the renovation of a computer lab room, including the installation of computer tables and proper power.

The following March, we returned to Belize with another group of students, but with only a few computers. I was disappointed as I assessed the previous year's project. We found first that the failure rate of the 75 used computers that we had brought down was high and that the telecommunications company had still not installed the Internet connections.

In January 2011, I returned again with five students and a colleague. As we reviewed our previous work, several weaknesses in our plans become apparent. There was a high rate of failure of the aging systems we had worked so hard to get to Belize and install. These were five-to-six-year old Pentium 4 computers with LCD screens. We found that memory contacts were corroding, hard drives crashing, and CPU fans locking up. We reasoned that the regular power failures and hot, moist sea air were taking their toll on the systems. We also found that most of the working systems had been changed from Linux, as we supplied them, to Windows XP, with varying levels of success. In addition, we found that the schools were struggling to pay the combined cost of the electricity to power the computers, not to mention the cost of air conditioning to cool the rooms. Electricity is seven times more expensive in Belize than in the United States, and this is in a country where the average weekly wage is U.S. $75! Electricity costs take up a majority of the nonsalary operations budget for a typical school that has the good fortune of having a computer lab.

On this trip, I had decided to address the issue of getting inexpensive computers in the hands of the teachers. If the children are to be taught how to use computers, then the teachers need to learn first. I decided to purchase off-lease, ultraportable, enterprise-class laptops. I reasoned that higher-end used laptops might be more durable than newer consumer-grade, lower-priced laptops. I took only one model, reasoning that repair would be simpler if we provided a single model laptop. I personally spent many hours refurbishing these laptops and installing Ubuntu (Linux) and school-related software. I paid the duty on these laptops, since they were not for schools. I was able to get a duty waiver on computers bound for schools. The final cost for the teachers was just over US$200.

While in Belize, we led a series of workshops that included computer literacy for teachers, computer repair and networking for IT people, and school information management for principals. This last proved quite interesting. At the request of the school administration, we demonstrated an open-source school database system called OpenSIS. Virtually all record keeping is still done by hand, and the principals where enthralled! When asked of their level of interest in implementing such a system, on a scale from one to ten, the first said "12," the next "20," and the next "90." In order for OpenSIS to be usable in Belize, it would have to be modified to make it appropriate for the culture of Belize.

We left Belize feeling like our solutions were problematic. Despite my greatest effort to demonstrate the value of Linux over pirated Windows, there was a general belief that Windows was needed for the students and teachers. Used systems were failing too fast and the cost of electricity was prohibitive. We needed to rethink our strategy.

My colleague, Doug Karl, had been on these trips to Belize with me. He is an electrical engineer with a software development and networking background and 20 years of experience installing computer networks and labs at Ohio State University. He began building a spreadsheet model of the total cost of ownership for a computer lab in Belize with a variety of solutions: new, used, desktop, laptop, CRT, and LCD. The model considered procurement, shipping, maintenance, and operation and replacement costs of various approaches. A wattmeter was used to measure the actual consumption of electricity by each solution. We concluded that a small NetBook-style laptop with its lid closed and attached to an LCD screen and a keyboard and mouse, at a total cost of US$300 (new), would save at least that in electricity alone in only three years over the cost of electricity used for a typical desktop computer. The NetBook approach had the advantage of being easy to ship, with a battery backup (a good protection against the frequent power failures), needing much less or no air conditioning, easy to wirelessly network, and came with Windows 7 installed. LCD or, preferably, LED monitors are low power, produce little heat, and have a long lifespan. The wear and tear in this scenario is mostly on the keyboard and mouse, which are easily procured for less than US$5 new and, therefore, a disposable item.

In addition to addressing the design and installation of computer labs, we began to discuss the problem of getting OpenSIS in the schools for the administration. Having installed database systems in a variety of service project settings, I knew that if not done properly, the system would simply never be adopted. The common scenario is that enthusiasm is high at the start, but later, with no support, problems occur, systems fail, discouragement sets in, and the system goes unused. We determined that the system should be rolled out gradually, one or two schools at a time, and within each school, the features should be added incrementally. Rather than set expectations too high and have them do everything on the database, we identified the most useful features and limited initial implementation to those. We decided that a local expert was needed to advise us on adapting the database system to the local needs, and that person could also provide local support. We then identified a talented and hardworking IT teacher in one of the schools and flew him to my University for intensive work in July of 2011. A retired database expert and software engineer in the United States, also named Jim, was recruited, and the two worked to modify OpenSIS for Belize (date formats, local address methods, semester structures, grading styles, reporting standards, etc.).

We will be returning to Belize for the month of January with several more students and plans to continue to roll out OpenSIS, bring more small laptops, do teacher training, see how the systems already installed there are faring, and so on. We also plan to bring a system that we intend to place in the path of the slow, unreliable DSL Internet connection that some schools have. This box, probably a small laptop with battery backup, would have a local DNS server, large Web cache, bandwidth shaper, and layer 3 firewall to make the students' Internet experience much faster and more reliable. A special class in applied networking is working on implementing this approach using pfSense and related open-source software.

22.5 LESSONS LEARNED

We have been doing service-learning projects for many years, made a lot of mistakes, and done a few things right. In this section, I would like to review some of these lessons learned, with the hope that a person planning such a project will adapt some of our successes to their particular target country and avoid some of the mistakes and wrong assumptions that we have made.

22.5.1   Do Not Assume You Know What is Best

First and foremost is the lesson that anyone experienced in taking beliefs, goals, and assumptions to another culture will recognize immediately: a lot of what we know or believe just does not translate across cultural boundaries. My experience in six distinct countries clearly informs me that anything I say will be somewhat anecdotal, it is different in every culture. Certainly, there are generalizations and universals that do cross cultural boundaries, and some of these have to do with common aspects that developing countries share. I am not, however, an anthropologist, so I will not try to overanalyze but, rather, give advice that appears to be somewhat general from my perspective.

This observation brings me to the first point: do not assume that any "typical" notions or assumptions that prove useful in your world will necessarily transfer. This is not to say that some will not, just that it is very good to proceed with caution, conscientiously questioning the normal assumptions and being flexible. As you plan the activity, take time to consider the assumptions you normally use, even ones that seem certain, and consider them as possibly not applicable, or perhaps in need of modification.

From a systems engineering perspective, this is something we already know well: make sure we are building the right solution. Many engineering projects have failed because the stakeholders' perspectives were not fully considered or appreciated, or because the engineer inadequately elicited the needed requirements of the project.

There are a couple of things that can really help here. First is to plan an exploratory trip to the location. A lot can be done by spending some significant time in the country with the people who will be impacted by the project. Taking time to explicitly review your plans and overtly express your assumptions can prove beneficial.

There is a hidden snare here, however, again one we know from systems engineering. In any project, the eventual users are excited and anxious to receive the benefits of the new system and as a result may be hesitant to disagree with the engineer, who is likewise excited and trying to drive the project. They believe the engineer is the expert and do not want to show perceived ignorance or appear uncooperative in a project they believe will greatly benefit them.

This debilitating process can be greatly exacerbated in the typical service-learning project, where a highly educated and relatively wealthy professional appears full of ideas, speaking of solving problems for which no possible local solution is financially or technologically feasible. Then the local person, for example, a school administrator, will be very tempted to simply agree with everything proposed, regardless of internal beliefs about the feasibility or appropriateness of the solution being proposed.

How can this problem be mitigated? One suggestion is to assume a position of humility and transparency. Realize that you do not know what is best or what hidden information may be pivotal, and then let others know that you are uncertain, that this is all new to you, and you really need to hear their perspective. Reassure the host that you are committed to the project regardless of the shape of the solution, and that despite the fact that cost is an issue, you would rather scale the solution to something that would actually work than to over- or underbuild something that will fail to meet the objectives. This is, of course, a difficult process. The cultural distance can be huge, and it is difficult to not appear intimidating with your education and relative wealth.

Another solution I have found to be quite useful is to find local citizens who have traveled and are interested in the success of the project. For example, in my case, early on I developed a relationship with a Belizean principal, Dwight, who had been educated at a U.S. college and had many relatives living in the United States. Dwight had his feet in both cultures and understood that Americans make mistakes, do not have unbounded resources, and do not understand Belizean culture. He also understood many of the specific differences between the underlying assumptions of both cultures, and how Belizeans would respond to various actions of people from the United States.

A couple of examples are in order. As I mentioned above, we began our work by bringing computers down and handing them to schools. As I looked in the various schools, many with 15-year-old computers, I inquired about where they came from and was informed that they had been donated 10 years earlier but had "gone bad." What was not spoken was obvious: they were waiting for the next gift. I started to see that I risked creating a relationship of dependence if I continued to deliver free computers. Later, as I talked to Dwight about another shipment of computers, he mentioned that everyone was waiting for the next visit from "Santa Claus" (me) with his bag of free computers. I knew we were on the wrong track; we needed to find a sustainable solution. Later I will discuss some ideas about the nature of this.

So my next proposed solution was to sell the computers to the schools below cost to help them begin the process of integrating the building of a lab into their long-term financial plan. However, I considered offering microloans to help the schools pay for the systems in a time frame that was feasible. Dwight immediately explained to me that, in Belize, this was unreasonable. If I did not get the payment upfront, the payments would likely never be received. It would just lead to bad feelings. Without Dwight how would I have ever know that this seemingly realistic solution was in fact unrealistic?

Another project was to provide low-cost laptops for teachers. I originally planned to include a one-year warranty in the plan and, thus, in the cost. Dwight informed me that such an idea was absolutely unprecedented, and would not be correctly understood in a country where nothing had a formal warranty. A better plan was to sell the laptops at cost; the teachers would assume they were as-is. Then, without announcing it, we would plan to fix or replace systems that were obviously defective early on, and fix or replace systems at reduced price later in the life cycle if they failed. This was a more Belizean solution, one the people would accept and understand.

So, to summarize, it is wise to not assume you know what will work. Instead, work to cultivate a source of inside, realistic information that you can use to avoid many of the pitfalls of misguided assumptions.

22.5.2   Open-Source Versus Commercial Software

Consider next the conundrum of what software to place or endorse on systems taken. Back in 1986, on my first such trip, I arrived in Manila to find pirated software everywhere. The shops were filled with computer kiosks with every possible popular software package. I heard the workers proudly declare when asked about the latest release, "Oh yes, we are working hard to crack that, it will be available any day." Such software, which could be purchased essentially for the price of the floppy it came on, included a start screen that proudly announced that it was "Cracked by *xxxx*," followed by a real, local phone number! My naive head spun with disbelief. After some internal struggles, I sanctimoniously announced that I would not work with such software.

Now, fortunately, at this time I was working exclusively with American missionaries in Manila and not with local citizens. Thus, possible insensitivity to the local population was not really an issue and, in fact, I feel that, given that I was working with Americans, I did the right thing. These Americans had the funding to buy licensed software and had access to the U.S. marketplace.

Now, in 1986, this position was a real limitation. Very little quality open-source software was available and there was no Internet to search and download from. I was stuck with what little outdated software they had brought from the United States. I developed database applications on outdated versions of Dbase, secretly longing to use the pirated latest releases from the shops.

Fast forward to 2008. As I mentioned earlier, I preloaded all the systems I delivered to Belize with Linux and open-source applications. I traveled around the country, holding seminars and demonstrating the efficacy of such solutions. I handed out Linux open-source CDs and DVDs. I honestly believed in the philosophy.

What I found was that many organizations wanted to continue to use what they were already using: pirated commercial software. Although some of the more well-funded organizations were using open-source solutions, it seemed that most used pirated commercial software, and they seemed very reluctant to change. The biggest concern was that it was not the real thing but some inferior substitute, which would leave them and their students outsiders in the world of relevant technology. Although I generally do not agree with this assessment, and I have even seen evidence in the culture that it is not the case, I believed I must respect their concerns. Change may need to take place slowly or perhaps not at all in a given setting. As I will discuss in the next section, I believe in empowerment over control. If I reflect a bit, I recall that my personal adoption of open-source software took time and is still incomplete. I still run a virtual machine on my Linux machine loaded with the latest version of Windows and Office so that I can open or edit those documents that the latest version of LibreOffice or OpenOffice seems unable to correctly process.

So why not just load up the machines with whatever they want? The answer is cost and international copyright law. United States software companies price software at a level the U.S. market will bear. Buying Microsoft Office for a few hundred dollars is painful for an American, but it is outrageous for a person whose income is at most a tenth of an American's. The same goes for schools and businesses.

To make matters worse, in many countries there is no officially recognized source of most commercial software. No mechanism exists to distribute legitimate licensed versions. Everything must be purchased abroad and brought in. It is as though these countries do not exist in the eyes of the large software firms. There is an apparently true story floating around Belize that Bill Gates brought his yacht to dock at Belize City and checked into the Fort George Hotel, the biggest and best in the city. He was excited to see Windows running on the computers as he checked in and made a big deal of it, not even realizing it was pirated! Did he know that Belize did not even have a single authorized Microsoft reseller actually in the country?

In much of the developing world, particularly in smaller countries, the standard practice is to effectively ignore copyright law. From the perspective of the citizens of these countries, no one appears to care enough to even sell legitimate copies, much less enforce the copyright of the copies they get.

Now, of course it would be wonderful if there were inexpensive distribution systems providing nonexportable versions of software in each country at a price indexed to the local economy, similar to what book, record, and pharmaceutical companies often do. I can only surmise that the cost of such a program is not justified by the expense.

This leaves those of us from developed countries with a dilemma. The cost of new commercial software is almost always prohibitive for a service project, but we cannot, either ethically or legally, participate in the process of disseminating such software in violation of copyright laws. So we are left with several legitimate but still reasonable choices. One is to advocate open-source software, bring it, and let them change it if they see the need to. Another is to always provide new systems preloaded with MS Windows, which will at least solve the operating-system issue. A third is to always get used systems with COAs, and load the systems with the proper dated commercial software. Perhaps a final possibility is to deliver a system without any software and let the local IT people do what they will.

A significant problem, however, emerges if the choice is made to allow the systems to be reimaged with pirated commercial software after we leave. The problem is that any teaching we do and setups we perform are now largely a waste of everyone's time, and much of the remote support we might offer is often moot.

There is no easy, cheap solution. My solution is to be as flexible as possible, explain the differences, and do what I can to support wherever local decisions are made. I still avoid any direct involvement in the dissemination and installation of pirated copyrighted software by either my students or myself, and I privately discuss the matter with my students, explaining the situation as clearly as I understand it, and encourage their comments and discussion within the group.

22.5.3 Empowerment or Dependency: Building a Sustainable Project

In the initial planning phase of how we might get technology into Belizean schools, the idea had emerged to funnel corporate retired or off-lease computers to the schools. Initial research demonstrated that many businesses had a three-year retirement schedule and that at the end they typically got nothing for them, or even had pay to dispose of the computers. One example was a nearby hospital that indicated that they retired 500 three-year-old computers a year. Their leading concern was scrubbing the hard drives to a standard that would satisfy HIPPA laws. We began to explore a system for channeling these desktops to the schools at no cost to the schools. It seemed a good plan to simply build a pipeline from several hospitals to Belize that would keep the school perpetually in technology.

Literature suggests that social welfare increases rather than decreases the levels of perceived need and dependence. What seems like kind charity can in some cases derail not only a belief of self-reliance, but actually ruin chances for the creation of sustainable local industry. One example personally observed by the author is the clothing industry in Papua New Guinea.

Kind-hearted Americans donate hundreds of tons of used clothing, which are compressed into bundles, placed in shipping containers, and sent into the remote areas of the country. Everywhere, people are seen wearing dated American fashion ware, from cartoon-emblazoned pajamas, to beanie hats with "Let it Snow" lettered across the front. Visiting a store reveals these are sold for five cents per item in massive pole-barn "stores."

Now, this might seem wonderful, until you consider the local economy. People can buy clothing cheaply, but with what money? Where can a local citizen earn money if there are no local companies making clothes, or anything else? And what motivation is there to make clothes locally when American clothes can be had for a mere nickel? The process is self-defeating.

By similar reasoning, if computers are available for little or nothing, why save up to buy them? Why plan and budget for computer needs when they simply appear at random times. And what motivation is there for competitive local sales and service of new or used computers if Americans come every few months bearing unreasonably cheap or free computers. In the end, is such a project helping or hurting the local development of technology commerce?

The answer, we are increasingly coming to believe, is to find a fair compromise, not simply giving everything, but partnering. The goal is to search for solutions that are economically feasible within the local economy and then, over time, work toward having local entities become both fiscally and technically involved in the solution.

For example, figure out the real costs of delivering solutions, and increasingly allow the local beneficiaries to pay the cost. If the local beneficiaries of the technologies can begin to pay for appropriately priced solutions, they will begin to consider the costs as expected budget items and, thus, begin to plan for them in the future.

In addition, find ways of creating local support operations for the projects. For example, if used computers are being acquired and brought in, but need refurbishing first, why do the work in the country of origin? Why not create a local enterprise for refurbishing and then maintaining the systems? Not only are you keeping the costs down, and creating local work, but you are also building new marketable skill sets. The organization may be able to expand to other projects and eventually become a commercially viable business.

22.5.4 Volunteer Involvement (Some Comments by Doug Karl)

For the past four years, I* have had the opportunity to partner with a series of service-learning projects in Belize. Now semiretired from decades as a

*In this section "I" refers to Doug Karl.

professional in the computer technology field, I have found an opportunity to apply my education and experience, as well as a new-found passion, in a way that is uniquely satisfying. The ability to tag along as a nonstudent volunteer has, for me, been an amazing experience. I have found that accompanying groups of students on these cross-cultural service-learning projects provides a good context for learning about the true needs and opportunities in a foreign country. In addition, I have found the opportunity to befriend and advise the Belizean people to be richly rewarding. The university affiliation with a local group of schools and churches in the country provides an excellent opportunity to observe and begin to understand the inner workings of a distinctly different culture. This relationship provides a different perspective than a typical tourist sees, or even some well-intentioned business person seeking to find ways to strategically help or partner with another group of people.

Last year, we documented several interviews with people working in the local schools. One U.S. Peace Corps worker who was volunteering in a school where we installed a computer lab stated it most clearly. Her observation was that aid from the United States and Europe was much better utilized when there was an established direct relationship between the local school and the donating organization. Her observation was that the government-to-government aid was not as well utilized. In the case of MVNU (a Nazarene University) and many of the local schools (Nazarene), this relationship included not only monetary aspects but also mentoring, collaboration on various business opportunities, educational exchange, and even Facebook friendships. This same type of collaboration occurs between U.S. universities and the local Belizean universities and also between foreign and local Rotary Clubs and other organizations. Imagine a city school system in the United States adopting a school system in one of Belize's districts. What a great opportunity that would be for cultural exchange and what enriching relationships would follow. What a good use of Internet distance learning, collaboration, conferencing, and video and audio sharing capabilities.

I met Jim Skon when he was a graduate student at Ohio State University and I was on the campus IT staff. I was intimately involved with the installation and management of the first computer labs on campus and then later the installation and growth of the campus Internet network. I am the creative type, always looking for innovative and outside-the-box solutions to the problems we are facing. I left OSU after 22 years of service, started a company, grew it, and then sold it in 2004. After selling my company, Jim kept inviting me to accompany him to Belize. I erroneously thought it was an island in the Pacific. I had no idea it was a short plane flight away. He described to me a country, culture, and people that was hard for me to grasp. I finally decided to go visit with him, when he specifically asked me to assess the Internet infrastructure with an eye toward making recommendations to the various schools on how to connect up. We went there in August, the hottest month of the year, and stayed in the hottest part of the country without any air conditioning. As we traveled around the country that week, meeting people and assessing the telecommunications infrastructure, what was happening to me was that I was falling in love with Belize and the people of Belize. When I returned I was so greatly moved, my wife was not quite sure what was wrong with me. So I had to explain that I had fallen in love with a country and a people. After 35 years of marriage I am blessed with a very patient and understanding wife.

When I was a teen, I had the good fortune of having a great-grandfather who was still living. Grandpa Ponzello had emigrated from Italy in the late 1800s when he was 12 and started working for General Electric, sweeping floors. He later went on to help invent several products for GE, working there all his life. I was in college and beginning my life and wanted to ask him what he thought about as he approached the end of his? What would he do differently and what mattered the most to him? He passed away before I got the opportunity and courage to ask him, but I have pondered that question ever since. Hopefully, if I make it into my eighties and reflect on my life, I want to remember making a real and significant difference in the world. I have had the amazing good fortune to be in the very small percentage of engineers who have made game-changing technological contributions to society. However, that pales in comparison with helping contribute to the betterment of a whole people group. I really want to be included in making a strategic contribution of time, energy, experience, and money to the children of a culture that really needs it.

Less than 5% of the K–12 schools in Belize have any computers for the students to use. The national curriculum, based on the Caribbean standardized curriculum, calls for computer skills to be taught. The reality is that there are very few computers available, limiting the opportunity to actually teach this curriculum. The students want to learn. We visited one school where typing was being taught and the students were using keyboards they had carved out of wood with the letters carefully painted on the keys; they were pretending to type.

There are many challenges in setting up computer labs for the schools in Belize: monetary, of course, but also technical issues such as unreliable and intermittent power, no air conditioning, no insulation even if the room was air conditioned, salty sea air, dust, heat, and unreliable and slow Internet connection (in the few places where Internet is available). Some challenges are related to teacher training and educating the administration on the best design for computer labs. The government of Belize is in debt and heavily relies on tourism for income, which is not doing well after the economic downturn of 2008. The government provides the salary for teachers but nothing else. All the students of Belize have to pay tuition. Big brothers and sisters work to help the family raise tuition for them and their younger siblings who cannot work. Various denominations raise money from relationships they have in the United States and Europe to pay for supplies and operating expenses.

I went to engineering school to learn how to solve problems. I love the people of Belize. Working to help make a difference in Belize is way more fun than sitting around being retired. I like to think Grandpa Ponzello would approve.

22.6   SUMMARY

Service-learning projects have many overt goals, ranging from providing students cross-cultural work and social experiences, gaining meaningful experience while applying skills to solve real-world problems in diverse locations, and providing such experiences while working as a functioning team. In addition, the inclusion of experienced nonstudent volunteers working alongside the students serves to further enhance the possibility of succeeding in these goals and provides valuable mentoring opportunities for the students. But perhaps the most striking phenomena encountered in these projects is the diverse friendships created in the process. Providing opportunities for students and others to work and play side by side with people from a significantly different culture can lead to meaningful refinement and growth of deeply held world-view perspectives for all involved. The author has repeatedly observed in students changed perspectives that are life-altering in terms of vocational and personal choices.

REFERENCES

Niskanen, William A. "Welfare And The Culture Of Poverty," *The CATO Journal,* Vol. 16, No. 1.

Postman, Neil (1993). *Technopoly,* Vintage Press.

CHAPTER 23

EDUCATIONAL IMPACTS OF AN INTERNATIONAL SERVICE-LEARNING DESIGN PROJECT ON PROJECT MEMBERS AND THEIR PEERS

Peter E. Johnson

ABSTRACT

It has been well documented that students involved in international service-learning design projects in engineering receive many educational benefits. This chapter addresses the question of whether or not the benefits gained from international service-learning design projects extend to those students who are not directly involved with these projects but are peers of those who are. To answer this question, graduates of the senior design projects course at Valparaiso University from 2003 to 2011 were surveyed on the course learning objectives, their desire to participate in service-related activities, and their social and cultural awareness. The responses from this survey show that peers of students who experienced an international service-learning design project developed a stronger desire to participate in service-related activities than those alumni who experienced the course prior to the integration of an international service-learning design project into the senior design course sequence. The responses also show that these same peers felt they were more aware of societal issues and other cultures as well. This chapter discusses the senior design course, the international service-learning design project, the survey, the results of this survey, and suggested improvements that will further extend the benefits of an international service-learning design project from those students with direct involvement to their peers.

Service-Learning in Computer and Information Sciences. Edited by Brian A. Nejmeh
Copyright © 2012 John Wiley & Sons, Inc.

23.1 INTRODUCTION

As our world becomes smaller, more engineering educators are introducing international service projects into their curricula [1–10]. The motivations behind these projects are diverse, but many projects are developed to provide a service to a community in need and to provide international exposure and real-world project experiences for their students. Secondary benefits such as increased social and cultural awareness and a stronger desire for service are often expected in these students as well [1].

Valparaiso University is a small, comprehensive university located in northwest Indiana. All electrical, computer, and mechanical engineering students at Valparaiso University must take GE 497/498 Senior Design Project I and II, a two-semester course in which teams of approximately five students complete a design project, resulting in approximately 10 design teams each year. All of the teams meet as a class at times throughout the year, but work solely in their groups on their particular design projects. During each of the academic years of 2005–2006, 2006–2007, 2007–2008, and 2009–2010, one of these teams designed and installed wind turbines in three different communities on Ometepe Island, Nicaragua [2–4]. The Ometepe Project, as it has been called, had a significant effect on the students who participated in designing the wind turbines and traveled to the island to install the systems. Furthermore, it has been theorized that the project may have also had an impact on the peers of the Ometepe Project participants, that is, the students who were involved in other projects in GE 497/498 during the same academic year. In 2008 and again in 2011, a survey was conducted of a total of 161 alumni who had participated in the senior design course sequence from the fall 2002 semester to the spring 2011 semester. During the first two academic years, 2002–2003 to 2003–2004, there were no international service-learning projects. The alumni results from these years have been used as a baseline study. In the next four academic years (2004–2005 to 2007–2008), the Ometepe Project was offered and, therefore, alumni responses have been divided into those students directly involved in the project (the Ometepe Project participants) and those that were not (the peers of the Ometepe Project participants). Of the final three academic years of the survey, the Ometepe Project was only offered during the 2009–2010 academic year. The survey results suggest that the Ometepe Project not only had a positive impact on the students directly involved in the project, but also on their peers who were involved in other projects in this course. The benefits that extend to the peers of the Ometepe Project participants are specifically in their desire to serve and their social and cultural awareness, with no loss in achievement of the course learning objectives.

This article will briefly describe the senior design course at Valparaiso University, including an overview of the Ometepe Project. The survey that was given to the nine graduating classes of alumni who have been involved in the senior design course will also be explained. Finally, it will be shown that the Ometepe Project has not only been influential in the educational development of the students directly involved in the project but also of their peers.

23.2   BACKGROUND

As international service-learning projects in engineering disciplines become more popular, a number of instructors have explored the benefits that these projects provide to the students, including the exposure to new cultures and to different construction practices [1–10]. Some have carefully gathered quantitative information from the students who travel [5, 6]. For example, Phillips and coworkers [5] performed a pre- and a posttrip assessment of students who worked on an international service-learning design project in Bolivia. Changes in the survey responses and entries from journals written during the trip suggest that this service experience helped these students meet ABET Criterion 3, which addresses the skills, knowledge, and behaviors that graduates should have [11]. Similarly, Borg and Zitomer [6] collected data through pre- and posttrip surveys, and they reviewed journal entries of students who worked on an international service-learning project in Guatemala. Various readings were assigned to prepare the students for the cultural and economic adjustment they would experience. The pre- and post-trip survey results showed a surprising decrease in student ratings of four of the 11 learning objectives related to ABET Criterion 3. Borg and Zitomer suggest that the reason behind these decreased ratings was often due to the frustration that can occur when students are thrown into a completely new environment. Teamwork and communication can become challenging when working with simple tools and without the conveniences that are typically available. In these cases, anecdotal evidence in journal entries suggest the significant learning that occurred despite the decrease in the students' ratings.

Other instructors have chronicled their experiences with international service-learning trips from a less quantitative perspective [1, 7–9]. For example, Vader and coworkers [7] qualitatively assessed an international service project in which a student team installed a photovoltaic electric power plant in a village in Burkina Faso. The authors generated opportunities for improvement in the project implementation, including more deliberate instruction in project management, teamwork, and testing. Green and coworkers [8] took a broader approach by assessing the international humanitarian design projects of four faith-based institutions. By determining the similarities in these projects, they were able to provide insight for those looking to optimize the project selection process for team success. Finally, the value of including nonengineers in an international design project was addressed by Freeman and coworkers [9]. The authors compiled journals from team members who experienced a design project for a village in China and found that nonengineers involved in the project provided an added benefit to the team. The authors found that the nonengineers were better able to explain the technology to the villagers. In the assessment of this trip, the authors also recognized that nontraveling members of the team "can have the same team-building experiences, leadership, personal growth, and a feeling of accomplishment as those that traveled." Similarly, Dukhan and coworkers [1] analyzed student responses to questions regarding their levels of social awareness and how their social awareness was affected by the service project they performed, which was to help families in the Detroit area save on heating costs by winterizing their homes and study the thermal effects of these home improvements. The authors found that service-learning increases the student's social awareness and that reflection activities are a valuable component of service-learning projects.

The findings of Dukhan and coworkers [1] are important for the students who are directly involved in the service projects. In contrast, this chapter illustrates that for service projects that are a subset of a larger course, the students who are not directly involved in the service project are also affected in regard to their desire to serve, their cultural awareness, and their knowledge of social issues.

23.3 VALPARAISO UNIVERSITY SENIOR DESIGN PROJECTS I AND II

Students in electrical, computer, and mechanical engineering at Valparaiso University are required to complete a two-semester senior design project experience—GE 497/498 Senior Design Project I and II [2–4, 12–16]. Prior to the start of fall classes, the course instructors compile a list of available projects that typically include a mixture of service-based projects, industry-sponsored projects, faculty research projects, projects for national student design competitions, and other academic projects. Multidisciplinary teams are created based on student preferences. Each student submits her/his top four projects in order and indicates both a preferred team mate and an individual they would prefer not to have on their team. Based on this feedback, the faculty members then create teams of four to six students, resulting in between eight and 12 design teams each year.

Although the students tend to think the course is entirely about fabricating a working prototype, the pedagogical emphasis is on the design process: from problem definition and creation of a conceptual design, through construction and testing of a prototype, to documentation of the project. Due to time constraints, students do not physically close the loop of the design cycle by redesigning their project based on the results of the testing. However, they are required to think through this last phase of the design process in the documentation of their entire project experience. Throughout the two-semester sequence, extensive communication is required, including individual and team presentations, written proposals and final reports, and the creation of team videos and posters, both of which are presented to the local community at the Valparaiso University College of Engineering Design Exposition. The teams meet on a regular basis with their faculty advisor, and all students in the course meet together as a class at various times throughout the school year. The purpose of these latter meetings is for faculty to present information to all of the students simultaneously. These class periods include lessons on such topics as the design process, various documentation and analysis methods, brainstorming techniques, and others. Formal presentations are made by each team to the entire class three times during the year. During these presentations, all students in the course are required to actively participate by listening closely and asking questions. Similarly, individual presentations are made, two by each member of each team. As with the formal team presentations, students are encouraged to pay close attention to the speaker, to ask questions, and to provide feedback.

The course structure and content have gone through incremental changes between 2001 and 2011. The most significant of these occurred during the summers of 2003 and 2007. During these changes, the learning objectives for both semesters of the two-course sequence remained unchanged. Questions regarding alumni achievement of the course learning objectives for GE 498 (the second course) were included in the alumni survey to determine if changes to the course structure resulted in any significant changes to the student self-assessment. These learning objectives state that upon completion of GE 498, students will be able to:

- Function effectively as a member of a multidisciplinary team.
- Build a physical prototype of a design based on engineering drawings, flowcharts, and circuit schematics.
- Effectively present oral progress reports.
- Write a technical document to summarize the design, prototype, and test results.
- Prepare and present an effective technical oral report to summarize the work.

- Use design specifications and a test plan to evaluate the success of a physical prototype.
- Incorporate engineering standards into the design project.
- Create quality audio/visual materials to support oral presentations and written reports.
- Identify important parameters to be measured to check if the design requirements are met.
- Synthesize and integrate previous knowledge in mathematics, science, and engineering to assist in the achievement of a successful design.
- Prepare a budget and cost analysis of the project.

23.3.1 The Ometepe Project

In fall 2004, a project to create an environmentally friendly power supply for a remote community on Ometepe Island in Nicaragua was proposed to the students involved in senior design. Two electrical- and three mechanical-engineering students were assigned to the Ometepe Project in August of 2004. The overall project design goal was to create a wind turbine for the residents of La Palma, a small village on Ometepe Island without available power. The power requirements for this project consisted of generating enough energy for lights in a small health clinic and a classroom for adult education classes and for an emergency radio to call for an ambulance from the nearest hospital on the island. A major design constraint was the project budget. Inexpensive components were required so that the student design could be fabricated by residents of La Palma. Due to budgetary constraints, sending a group of students to Ometepe Island was not introduced as an option during this first attempt at the project. Unfortunately, the system that was developed did not produce enough power to meet the design goals set forth for the project nor was it robust enough to send to the village for implementation.

The strict budgetary constraint for the teams was lifted when the Ometepe Project was offered in 2005–2006, 2006–2007, 2007–2008 [2–4], and 2009–2010. In all four years, teams of two electrical and three mechanical engineering students were assigned to the project. Lifting the budgetary constraint of the project allowed the teams to focus on designing a functional system at the expense of creating a system that was more complex and, therefore, not as easy to maintain by the local residents. This trade-off was deemed necessary to accomplish the primary goal of the project: designing a system that would generate the power needed by the community, or in the 2009–2010 case, designing a data acquisition system to monitor the previous wind turbine installations.

Each year included slight variations to the project goal: the teams went to different locations on the island and the 2007–2008 and 2009–2010 teams were given limited access to designs from the 2005–2006 and 2006–2007 designs. Before they completed their conceptual design, the 2007–2008 team was given access to the final project reports for the 2005–2006 and 2006–2007 teams. This provided the 2007–2008 team with a more explicit chance to close the loop of the design cycle by allowing them to more directly learn from previous implementations. The 2009–2010 team was assigned a much different design problem. This team was given the goal of designing a data acquisition system that could be used to monitor the performance of the systems designed by the previous teams. Therefore, they were given complete access to the earlier design teams' documentation.

Furthermore, in all four projects, a considerable addition to the project budget was the opportunity to travel to the island to install the system if the necessary travel funding could be raised. All four teams raised between $12,000 and $15,000 for costs associated with travel to the island and designed systems that met their design requirements. The 2006–2008 teams were able to install their prototypes on Ometepe Island. The 2010 team was unsuccessful with the design of their data acquisition system but were able to travel to the island and relocate the still functional prototype from the 2007–2008 team. Furthermore, they were able to donate a portion of their data acquisition system, a photovoltaic solar panel, to an additional village on the island.

Each installation met with limited success. In the cases of the 2005–2006, 2006–2007, and 2007–2008 teams, completing the design and fabrication of the prototype by spring break left little time for testing. The shortened schedule and challenges in communication with residents of the island resulted in only minor improvements in the designs from 2005–2006 to 2006–2007 and from 2006–2007 to 2007–2008. Failures seen in the 2005–2006 system were not observed until the 2006–2007 trip, stretching the design cycle into years. During the 2007–2008 and 2009–2010 trips, many improvements were made in the original design and the earlier prototypes were retrofitted to reflect these improvements. Currently, two of the three systems are operable. One is providing power to a family on the island and the other is to be used by an orphanage on the island.

23.3.2 The Alumni Survey

To determine the effects the Ometepe Projects had on the students who were not directly involved in these projects, in July of 2008 a survey was sent to all alumni who experienced the senior design course sequence between the academic years of 2002–2003 and 2007–2008 [2]. In June of 2011, the same survey was distributed to alumni who had experienced GE 498 during the academic years of 2008–2009, 2009–2010, and 2010-11. One question on the surveys separates these alumni responses by the year in which they completed GE 498. From this information, eight categories were created for analyzing the results:

1. Those alumni who completed GE 498 in the two years before the Ometepe Project was proposed (2003 and 2004 graduates)
2. Those alumni who completed GE 498 in 2005, the first year the Ometepe Project was attempted without the option of travel
3. Those alumni who completed GE 498 in the three years that the Ometepe Project students traveled to the island (2006–2008 graduates), excluding those alumni who were directly involved in the Ometepe Project
4. Those alumni who were directly involved in the Ometepe Project and traveled at spring break (2006–2008 graduates)
5. Those alumni who completed GE 498 in 2009, in which the Ometepe Project was not offered
6. Those alumni who completed GE 498 in the year that the Ometepe Project students traveled to the island after completion of the spring semester (2010 graduates), excluding those alumni who were directly involved in the Ometepe Project
7. Those alumni who were directly involved in the Ometepe Project and traveled after completion of the spring semester (2010 graduates)
8. Those alumni who completed GE 498 in 2011, in which the Ometepe Project was not offered

In creating these categories, a distinction has been made between those who were involved directly in the Ometepe Project (for the 2006, 2007, 2008, and 2010 graduates) and those who were not. This ensures that the Ometepe Project alumni responses do not unnecessarily bias the results. The 2005 alumni responses were divided in a similar way; the Ometepe Project alumni from 2005 were not included in the results.

23.4   DISCUSSION OF RESULTS

The alumni were surveyed on their achievement of the course objectives for GE 498, their desire for service-related activities, and their social and cultural awareness. These results can be seen in Table 23.1. In this table, the average survey rating is given for the eight categories discussed previously.

These ratings are on a five-point Likert scale, where 1 = "No" and 5 = "Yes." These categories, including the number of respondents for each are:

1. 2003–2004 graduates (28 respondents—12 respondents from 2003 graduates, 16 from 2004 graduates)
2. 2005 graduates (12 respondents, none from the Ometepe Project)
3. 2006–2008 graduates, excluding the Ometepe Project alumni (79 respondents—22, 26, and 31 respondents from 2006, 2007, and 2008 graduates, respectively)
4. the Ometepe Project alumni from 2006–2008 (14 respondents)
5. 2009 graduates (12 respondents)
6. 2010 graduates, excluding the Ometepe Project alumni (15 respondents)
7. the Ometepe Project alumni from 2010 (5 respondents)
8. 2011 graduates (15 respondents)

Due to the limited number of responses for any single year, it is difficult to statistically distinguish between results from each year. However, it is possible to combine student responses based on the commonalities between them. For example, the 2003 and 2004 alumni both experienced GE 498 without the Ometepe Project and the alumni from 2006–2008 had peers who were involved in the Ometepe Project. These two combinations were analyzed in 2008 following the initial survey and the results were published in [2]. The second survey included alumni from 2009 and 2011, both years in which the Ometepe Project was not offered, and 2010, in which a different type of Ometepe Project was offered. Although 2003 and 2004 alumni and 2009 and 2011 alumni all experienced GE 498 without the Ometepe Project, to combine all four results together is misleading. Prior to the first Ometepe Project in 2005, the idea of international service was just beginning, both at Valparaiso University (Engineers Without Borders-Valparaiso or EWB-Valpo, was established in spring 2003 [17]) and across the United States as well (EWB-USA began in 2002 [18]). By 2009, EWB-Valpo was well established and well known by all engineering students. Many engineering students in EWB-Valpo, including computer-, electrical-, and mechanical-engineering majors, traveled to Kenya (2004–2008) and Tanzania (2008–2011) during the latter part of this study. The university also developed a humanitarian engineering minor in 2008–2009. Due to the potential influence of these programs, the 2009 and 2011 alumni responses have not been combined with the 2003 and 2004 alumni responses.

Table 23.2 shows a more detailed analysis between the 2003–2004 survey ratings and the 2006–2008 survey ratings for those questions that showed a

Table 23.1. Results of the alumni survey divided into eight categories*

#	Course learning objectives	2003–2004	2005	2006–2008	Ometepe Project 2006–2008	2009	2010	Ometepe Project 2010	2011
1	Can you function effectively as a member of a multidisciplinary team?	4.71	4.92	4.81	4.71	5.00	4.80	4.60	4.93
2	Can you build a physical prototype of a product based on engineering drawings, flowcharts, and circuit schematics?	4.00	4.25	4.49	4.36	4.92	4.60	4.60	4.73
3	Can you effectively present oral progress reports?	4.57	4.67	4.60	4.79	4.92	4.80	4.60	4.80
4	Can you write an effective technical document to summarize your work?	4.36	4.50	4.39	4.50	4.50	4.67	4.40	4.47
5	Can you prepare and present an effective technical oral report to summarize your design, prototype, and test results?	4.52	4.67	4.53	4.86	4.92	4.67	4.40	4.50
6	Can you use design specifications and a test plan to evaluate the success of a physical prototype?	4.25	4.75	4.41	4.21	4.75	4.53	4.60	4.33
7	Can you incorporate engineering standards into your design project?	4.07	4.58	4.37	4.07	4.50	4.20	4.40	4.27
8	Can you create quality audio/visual materials to support oral presentations and written reports?	4.46	4.83	4.42	4.43	4.67	4.60	4.60	4.60
9	Can you identify important parameters to be measured to check if your design requirements are met?	4.29	4.75	4.58	4.36	4.75	4.47	4.80	4.64
10	Can you synthesize and integrate previous knowledge in mathematics, science, and engineering to assist in the achievement of a successful design?	4.46	4.67	4.61	4.36	4.67	4.40	4.00	4.60
11	Can you prepare a budget and cost analysis of your project?	4.00	4.17	4.08	4.21	4.42	4.13	4.40	4.40
	Service								
12	Do you feel your senior design project experience inspired you to help others?	1.64	2.67	3.01	4.79	3.50	2.79	3.60	3.13
13	Do you feel your senior design project experience instilled in you or enhanced an existing desire to help others?	1.71	2.58	2.95	4.79	3.55	3.00	4.60	3.00
	Social and cultural awareness								
14	Do you feel your senior design project experience enhanced your knowledge of other cultures?	1.56	1.92	1.98	4.71	2.92	2.33	4.80	3.20

Table 23.1. *Continued*

#	Course learning objectives	2003–2004	2005	2006–2008	Ometepe Project 2006–2008	2009	2010	Ometepe Project 2010	2011
		Social and cultural awareness							
15	Do you feel your senior design project experience opened your eyes to social issues in other countries?	1.19	1.33	1.99	4.79	2.27	1.87	4.80	2.33
16	Do you feel your senior design project experience opened your eyes to social issues more local to you?	1.19	1.75	2.34	4.00	3.25	2.40	3.40	2.40
17	Do you feel your senior design project experience helped connect you to the world around you?	1.48	2.5	2.64	4.71	3.58	2.60	4.20	2.80
18	Do you feel your senior design project experience changed how you interact with the world around you?	1.78	2.67	2.61	4.64	3.50	3.00	3.80	3.40

*Responses to each question were on a five-point Likert scale where 1 = "No" and 5 = "Yes." The shading highlights the course learning objectives that alumni from 2006–2008 rated significantly different from the 2003–2004 alumni.

significant change [2]. In this table, the percentage change from 2003–2004 to 2006–2008 is given as well as the *p*-value from the Student-*t* distribution comparison of means that distinguishes between these two categories.

23.4.1   GE 498 Learning Objectives

The learning objectives from the second semester of the course sequence, GE 498, were included in the alumni survey to determine if changes to the course structure resulted in any significant changes to the alumni self-assessment. As shown in Table 23.1, the 2003–2004 and the 2006–2008 alumni rated their abilities to complete the learning objectives comparable to one another with three notable exceptions (the shaded questions in Table 23.1). Of the three that did see a significant change, all three were improvements, with the largest of these improving by 12% (Table 23.2). The cause of the improvement for these three questions is likely due to incremental changes to the format of the course and to the course content. Figure 23.1 shows an example of a year-to-year progression of the alumni ratings for Question 6, a question that was not rated significantly different from 2003–2004 (4.25 average rating) to 2006–2008 (4.41 average rating). As seen in Figure 23.1, the 2003, 2007, and 2009 changes to the course result in only minor, though noticeable, changes in the alumni ratings. We would expect any larger changes to be outside of the control of the course content and due to other changes such as the types of projects offered.

Table 23.2. Significant results of the alumni survey*

#	Course learning objectives	2003– 2004	2006– 2008	Percent increase in rating	*p*-value
2	Can you build a physical prototype of a product based on engineering drawings, flowcharts, and circuit schematics?	4.00	4.49	12.3%	0.004
7	Can you incorporate engineering standards into your design project?	4.07	4.37	7.4%	0.123
9	Can you identify important parameters to be measured to check if your design requirements are met?	4.29	4.58	6.8%	0.033
	Service				
12	Do you feel your senior design project experience inspired you to help others?	1.64	3.01	83.5%	<0.0001
13	Do you feel your senior design project experience instilled in you or enhanced an existing desire to help others?	1.71	2.95	72.5%	<0.0001
	Social and cultural awareness				
14	Do you feel your senior design project experience enhanced your knowledge of other cultures?	1.56	1.98	26.9%	0.071
15	Do you feel your senior design project experience opened your eyes to social issues in other countries?	1.19	1.99	67.2%	0.001
16	Do you feel your senior design project experience opened your eyes to social issues more local to you?	1.19	2.34	96.6%	<0.0001
17	Do you feel your senior design project experience helped connect you to the world around you?	1.48	2.64	78.4%	<0.0001
18	Do you feel your senior design project experience changed how you interact with the world around you?	1.78	2.61	46.6%	0.001

*This table highlights the notable changes between the 2003–2004 graduates and the 2006–2008 graduates. The percentage increase from 2003–2004 to 2006–2008 is included as well as the *p*-value from the Student-*t* comparison of the means between these two categories. The shaded cells illustrate a *p*-value of less than 5%.

23.4.2   Service

For Questions 12 and 13, the alumni ratings increased significantly between 2003–2004 (1.64 average rating for Question 12 and 1.71 average rating for Question 13) and 2006–2008 (3.01 average rating for Question 12 and 2.95 average rating for Question 13). Year-by-year progressions of the ratings to these two questions for all nine cohorts of alumni can be seen in Figures

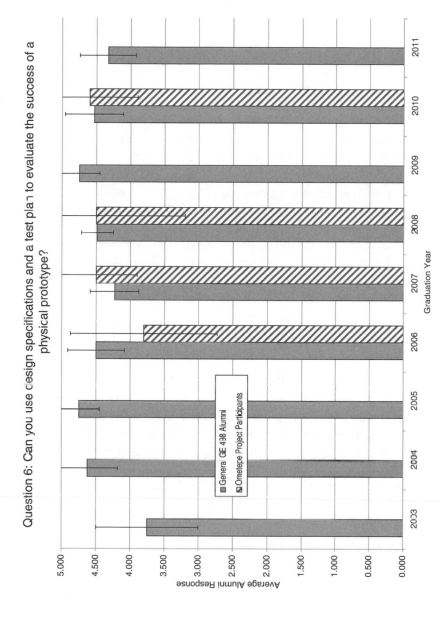

Figure 23.1. A year-by-year progression of the alumni ratings for Question 6, including confidence intervals. This progression excludes the alumni ratings from those students involved directly with the Ometepe Project. The progression highlights the effects of the course changes during the summers of 2003 and 2007.

23.2 and 23.3. Although the separation between average scores is not statistically significant on a year-to-year basis, these progressions allow us to make some hypotheses about why the differences exist between the 2003–2004 and 2006–2008 alumni ratings. In both Figures 23.2 and 23.3, the results tend to increase and level off near the 3.0 level of the Likert scale. It is likely that the alumni ratings for these questions were influenced by the Ometepe Project students' enthusiasm for their project, as illustrated by their high ratings for these questions (4.79 average rating for the 2006–2008 Ometepe Project alumni for both questions). This influence is the result of the dissemination of their energy and insight through the many presentations as well as the close relationship that all 50 (or so) senior design students tend to share.

Another possible explanation is that the increased ratings for Questions 12 and 13 are due to the types of projects offered in a given academic year. Table 23.3 lists the design projects developed during each year of the study. Some projects fulfill multiple categories, such as a fire-fighting robot that was developed for a student competition in 2003–2005. The end goal of the competition was to provide an autonomous system to help save the lives of firefighters. Therefore, this project is categorized as both a service project and a student competition project. As seen in Table 23.3, the number of projects that are service-oriented does not change significantly from year to year and, therefore, it is not likely that the increased ratings for Questions 12 and 13 are due to the types of projects offered.

The alumni from 2009, 2010, and 2011 show an interesting result in that their responses to questions 12 and 13 are comparable to the responses of their 2006–2008 counterparts, despite the fact that the Ometepe Project was only offered during the 2009–2010 academic year. This suggests a change in the culture–a stronger desire for service in Valparaiso University engineering students. Although the trends shown in Figures 23.2 and 23.3 are not definitively due to the Ometepe Project, it is likely that the combination of an international service-learning project in the senior design course, the consistent effort and success of EWB-Valpo, and the implementation of the humanitarian engineering minor all have had an influence on the alumni responses in the later years represented in the survey.

23.4.3   Social and Cultural Awareness

The responses to Questions 14 and 15 show a significant increase in the ratings from the 2003–2004 alumni to the peers of the Ometepe Project in 2006–2008 (Table 23.2). The rating for Question 14 increased by 26.9% and by 67.2% for Question 15. The statistical analysis shows that it is unlikely that either increase is due to random chance.

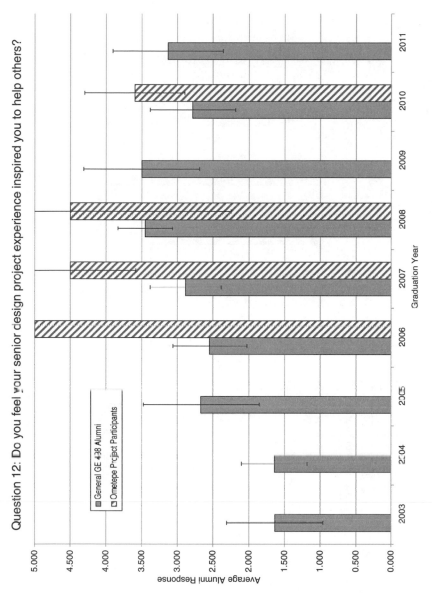

Figure 23.2. A year-by-year progression of the alumni ratings for Question 12, including confidence intervals. This progression excludes the alumni ratings from those students involved directly with the Ometepe Project.

507

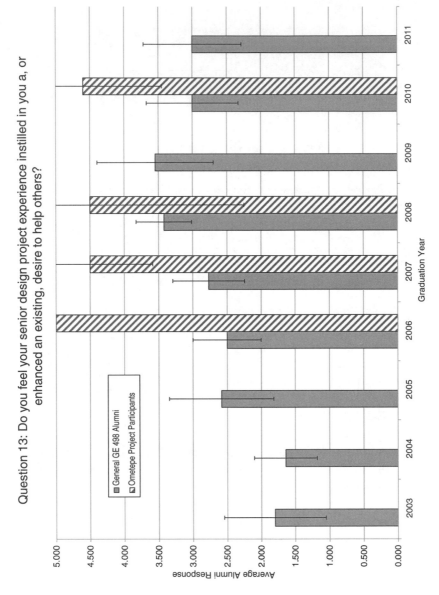

Figure 23.3. A year-by-year progression of the alumni ratings for Question 13, including confidence intervals. This progression excludes the alumni ratings from those students involved directly with the Ometepe Project.

Table 23.3. Types of projects developed in GE 497/498 during the period included in this study

Academic year	Service		Industry	Faculty research	Student competition	Academic/ other	Number of projects
	International	Other					
2002–2003	—	3	—	1	3	5	10
2003–2004	—	2	—	1	2	8	12
2004–2005	1	3	—	—	2	3	8
2005–2006	1	2	—	1	3	3	10
2006–2007	1	1	1	2	3	2	10
2007–2008	1	2	1	1	1	4	10
2008–2009	0	2	0	1	2	3	8
2009–2010	1	0	0	1	1	5	8
2010-2011	0	2	1	1	0	6	10

Another interesting result is that although ratings to both questions increased significantly, the increase in the rating for Question 14 (26.9%) was less than that of Question 15 (67.2%). Figures 23.4 and 23.5 show year-by-year progressions of the alumni responses to these two questions. Also of interest is that the confidence intervals for the 2003–2004 and 2006–2008 ratings overlap more for Question 14 than those for Question 15. In other words, the Student-t distribution p-value of Question 14 (0.071) is higher than that of Question 15 (0.001). This means that there is a 7.1% chance that the increase in rating for Question 14 could be a coincidence, whereas there is only a 0.1% chance that the increased rating for Question 15 would be due to random chance. The results suggest that although having projects similar to the Ometepe Project can increase awareness of social issues in other countries, it does not necessarily mean that these same students will feel more knowledgeable about the cultures. The students involved in the Ometepe Project made many presentations regarding the need of the community and the system that had been designed to address this need. However, these presentations were more focused on the technical aspects of the design and how it was related to the societal need and less on the effect the design would have on the local culture. Furthermore, due to the intensity and shortened schedule, teaching the Ometepe Project students about the local culture was limited to personal experiences from the faculty member who had been to the island. The teams were exposed to the cultural aspects of their project more directly when they traveled to the work site and interacted with the community members. For the 2006–2008 Ometepe Project alumni, this experience occurred in the last half of the second semester of the project. Only one team presentation and two individual presentations followed this trip, thereby limiting the opportunity to disseminate cultural information to the rest of the class. For the 2010 Ometepe Project alumni, travel to the island

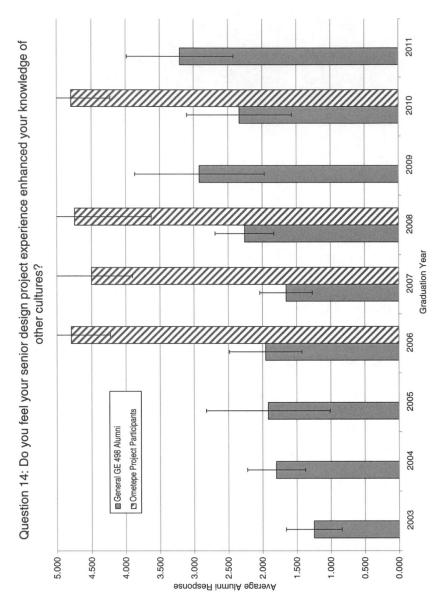

Figure 23.4. A year-by-year progression of the alumni ratings for Question 14, including confidence intervals. This progression excludes the alumni ratings from those students involved directly with the Ometepe Project.

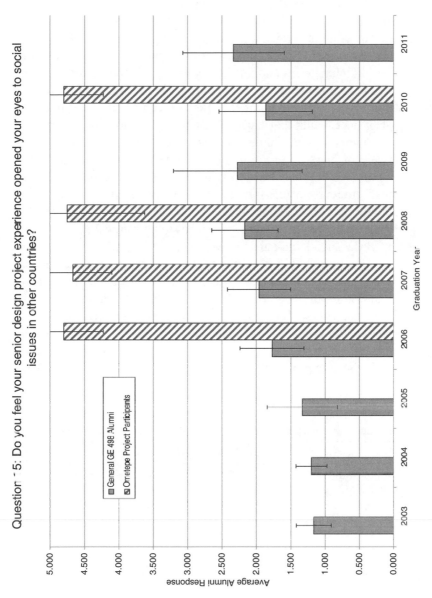

Figure 23.5. A year-by-year progression of the alumni ratings for Question 15, including confidence intervals. This progression excludes the alumni ratings from those students involved directly with the Ometepe Project.

occurred after the completion of the second semester of the project and, therefore, there was no opportunity for the Ometepe students to share their experience with their peers.

Again, the responses from 2009–2011 alumni are high for these two questions. The 2009 and 2011 alumni even give the highest responses to these two questions. As with the service questions, it is likely that the EWB-Valpo influence is present. Furthermore, with regard to Question 14, it is also important to note the change in student demographics. Table 23.4 shows the percentage of international students involved in GE 498 during the time period of this study, as well as the number of project teams and the number and percentage of project teams that had at least one international student as a member. Two points can be made regarding this additional information. First, the significant increase in the number of international students in GE 498 in 2011 is important to note. Second, just as important is that there were no international students in GE 498 in 2009. Because of these opposing facts, it is unlikely that the number of international students in GE 497/498 had a significant impact on the alumni responses to Question 14.

The results of the social and cultural awareness section of the survey suggest that more attention should be given to enhance these students' education by providing more cultural background earlier and to have the team make a presentation on the overarching social issues and culture of the host country to the entire course during their individual updates. Borg and Zitomer [6] assigned reading material for their teams that could provide the necessary background material that would improve the project experience for our students. Furthermore, requiring international service-learning students

Table 23.4. Student demographics in GE 498 during the period included in this study

	2003	2004	2005	2006	2007	2008	2009	2010	2011
Total number of students in GE 498	48	60	39	51	53	53	34	50	51
International students in GE 498 (% of total)	3 (6.3%)	5 (8.3%)	3 (7.7%)	2 (3.9%)	2 (3.8%)	4 (7.5%)	0 (0%)	2 (4.0%)	11 (21.6%)
Total number of project teams in GE 498	10	12	8	10	10	10	8	8	10
Teams with one or more international students (% of total)	2 (20%)	4 (33%)	3 (38%)	3 (30%)	2 (20%)	2 (20%)	0 (0%)	2 (25%)	6 (60%)

to devote presentation time to the social and cultural aspects of their project, both prior to and after their travels, could increase the degree of influence the projects have on the peers of these students in regard to these aspects.

23.5 CONCLUSIONS

A survey of alumni who had experienced the senior design course at Valparaiso University was conducted to determine if an international service-learning design project had positive effects on the peers of those students directly involved in the project. The results of this survey show that:

- Changes made to the course did not result in significant impacts on the course learning objectives.
- Students not directly involved in the Ometepe Project felt a stronger desire to participate in service-related activities than those alumni who experienced the course when an international service-learning design project was not offered.
- Students not directly involved in the Ometepe Project felt an increased awareness of social issues in other countries and an increased knowledge of other cultures than those alumni who experienced the course when an international service-learning design project was not offered.

The results of the questions related to the course learning objectives show that although the course was changed from year to year, this resulted in only minor impacts on the alumni responses. It is, therefore, possible to conclude that the impact on alumni desire to participate in service-related activities, their awareness of social issues in other countries, and their knowledge of other cultures was not impacted considerably by changes made to the course structure.

The alumni who were not directly involved in an international service learning design project felt a stronger desire to participate in service-related activities than their counterparts who experienced the design course in the two years of the survey prior to when such a project was offered. It is unlikely that this could be attributed to any changes made to the course structure or to the number of service-related projects offered. Without any information about these alumni before they took the course, it is impossible to determine if there existed any predisposition to service-related activities. However, the data collected show that a definite increase in the desire to participate in these activities did occur after the international service-learning design project in Nicaragua was first offered. Although not statistically separated, the year-by-year analysis suggests a change in the nature of engineering students at

Valparaiso University. During the time of this study, the average response of Valparaiso University engineering alumni shows an increase in their desire to serve. Although this trend is not definitively due to the Ometepe Project, it is likely that it had an influence on the alumni responses in these years.

A similar finding occurred in the alumni responses to questions regarding their awareness of social issues in other countries and their knowledge of other cultures. Again, it is unknown whether or not these alumni started the course sequence with an increased predisposition. The number of international students involved in senior design and the percentage of teams with international students involved does not appear to have a noticeable influence. The data show that a statistically significant increase in these items occurred during the same years that the Ometepe Project was offered.

A surprising result of the survey showed that although alumni were more aware of social issues in other countries, their increased knowledge of other cultures was less noticeable. This is likely due to the technical focus of the course and it points to an area for improvement in how this type of project is integrated into this course. To better prepare students for immersion in a new culture, a more explicit introduction to this culture should be made. Providing the cultural background to those directly involved in international service-learning projects earlier, as Borg and Zitomer [6] suggest, and providing opportunities for international service-learning students to share this information, will help provide their peers exposure to the culture as well.

In general, international service projects will result in educational benefits to the teams involved in these projects. Based on the survey results, these educational benefits can also impact others in the course if international projects are a subset of a larger course, even if this is not the intended goal. Furthermore, the results of this survey can help others to more consciously direct their international service projects toward those students who are not directly involved in these projects. The emphasis on student presentations keeps everyone in the course updated on the progress of each project, which can help disseminate the experience and, therefore, the benefits, of an international service team to their peers in the same course.

ACKNOWLEDGMENTS

The author would like to acknowledge the alumni who participated in this survey, specifically those alumni enrolled in GE 497/498 during the fall and spring semesters of 2003–2011. Ms. Laura Sanders also deserves thanks for helping implement and organize this survey.

The author would also like to acknowledge the 22 alumni who were involved in the Ometepe Project during the 2005–2008 and 2009–2010 academic years: Tommy Bendlak, Joel Benscoter, Joanne Borchert, Justin Bui, Becca Crocker, Mike Gibbs, Matt Hoovey, Rachel Howell, Sameer Kaul, Daniel Laidig, Michael Lanzerotti, James Nagel, Kyle Olund, Anthony Ortiz, Kristin Painting, Dan Roggendorf, Mike Schallhorn, Tom Shiraki, Erik Smith, Erin Swanson, Kirsten Swanson, and Eric Vurva. Their dedication and willingness to go beyond the course requirements have had a positive impact on the residents of Ometepe Island as well as the Valparaiso University community.

REFERENCES

1. Dukhan, N., Schumack, M. R., and Daniels, J. J. (2009). "Service-Learning as Pedagogy for Promoting Social Awareness of Mechanical Engineering Students." *International Journal of Mechanical Engineering Education,* 37(1), 78–86.

2. Johnson, P. E. (2009). "Direct and Indirect Benefits of an International Service-Learning Design Project: Educational Effects on Project Members and their Peers." *International Journal for Service Learning in Engineering,* 4(1).

3. Johnson, P. E., Sevener, K., Tougaw, D., and Will, J. (2007). "Balancing Learning Objectives and Success in a Multidisciplinary Senior Design Project." In *Proceedings of the 2007 American Society for Engineering Education National Conference,* Honolulu, HI.

4. Johnson, P. E., Budnik, M., Sevener, K., and Will, J. (2007). "Motivation, Inspiration, and Economics of an International Service Project." In *Proceedings of the National Capstone Design Course Conference,* Boulder, CO.

5. Phillips, L., Brady, A., and Jousma, K. (2007). "Interdisciplinary International Senior Design: How Service Learning Projects in Developing Countries Support ABET Accreditation." In *Proceedings of the 2007 American Society for Engineering Education Annual Conference and Exposition,* Honolulu, HO.

6. Burg, J. P., and Zitomer, D. H. (2008). "Dual Team Model for International Service Learning in Engineering: Remote Solar Water Pumping in Guatemala." *Journal of Professional Issues in Engineering Education and Practice,* 134(2), 178–185.

7. Vader, D., Erikson, C. A., and Eby, J. W. (1999). "Cross-Cultural Service Learning for Responsible Engineering Graduates." In *Proceedings of the 1999 American Society for Engineering Education Annual Conference and Exposition,* Charlotte, NC.

8. Green, M. G., Wood, K. L., Vanderleest, S. H., Duda, F. T., Erikson, C., and Van Gaalen, N. (2004). "Service-Learning Approaches to International Humanitarian Design Projects: A Model Based on Experiences of Faith-Based Institutions." In *Proceedings of the 2004 American Society for Engineering Education Annual Conference and Exposition,* Salt Lake City, UT.

9. Freeman, S., Matson, D., Sharpe, G., and Swan, C. (2006). "International Citizenship and Global Service Leadership—The Role of Interdisciplinary Teams in Engineering Education." In *Proceedings of the 2006 American Society for Engineering Education Annual Conference and Exposition,* Chicago, IL.

10. Jiusto, S., and DiBiasio, D. (2006). "Experiential Learning Environments: Do They Prepare Our Students to be Self-Directed, Life-Long Learners?" *Journal of Engineering Education,* 95(3), 195–204.

11. Accreditation Board for Engineering and Technology (ABET). (2004). *Criteria for Accrediting Engineering Programs,* Baltimore, MD.

12. Hagenberger, M., Johnson, P., Tougaw, D., Will, J., Budnik, M., and Sevener, K. (2007). "Managing Senior Projects: Educating Graduates and Undergraduates in a Senior Project Course." In *Proceedings of the 2007 American Society for Engineering Education Annual Conference and Exposition,* Honolulu, HI.

13. Tougaw, D. and Barrett, M. (2002). "Determination of Individual Performance on a Team." In *Proceedings of the 2005 American Society for Engineering Education Illinois/Indiana Sectional Conference,* 124–127, Chicago, IL.

14. Tougaw, D. and Will, J. (2003). "An Innovative Multidisciplinary Capstone Design Course Sequence." In *Proceedings of the 2003 American Society for Engineering Education Annual Conference and Exposition,* Nashville, TN.

15. Tougaw, D. and Will, J. D. (2005). "Integrating National Robotic Competitions into Multidisciplinary Senior Project Courses." In *Proceedings of the 2005 American Society for Engineering Education Illinois/Indiana Sectional Conference,* DeKalb, IL.

16. Tougaw, D., Will, J., Johnson, P., Hagenberger, M., and Budnik, M. (2007). "Integrating Entrepreneurship Into Senior Design Projects." In *Proceedings of the National Collegiate Inventors and Innovators Alliance Annual Conference,* Tampa, FL.

17. Valparaiso University. (2011). *Engineers Without Borders—Valparaiso University.* Retrieved Sept. 6, 2011, from http://www.valpo.edu/student/ewb/ about/index.php.

18. Engineers Without Borders—USA. (2011). *Engineers Without Borders—Our Story.* Retrieved Sept. 6, 2011, from http://www.ewb-usa.org/about-ewb-usa/our-story.

CHAPTER 24

IS THE COMMUNITY PARTNER SATISFIED?

Camille George

ABSTRACT

The chapter proposes that the collaboration structure between a student–faculty team and a community partner in an international service-learning (ISL) project can have an effect on the immediate (short-term) partner's satisfaction, as well as the project's adoption and long-term sustainability. A set of key elements desired in a partnership is compiled by examining insights from international education and study abroad, civic education, participatory development, and cross-cultural studies. They are then applied to two ISL projects to illustrate different collaboration models that resulted in a satisfied and an unsatisfied community partner, and one adopted and one abandoned project.

24.1 INTRODUCTION

Service-learning (SL) projects in science, technology, engineering, and math (STEM) disciplines have been increasing in the past decade. Assessment of these projects is often university-centered and focused on maximizing student learning. Students benefit by applying disciplinary knowledge in a situation that also promotes increased civic participation and social responsibility.

By design, SL experiences are intended to reciprocally benefit communities and their members. However, much less has appeared in the academic literature about the perspective of the community partner: preparing the community for SL visitors, their perspectives on the encounter, or the long-term impact of that encounter on those individuals and communities. George and Shams [1] proposed, as part of the overall strategy in assessing the success of SL projects, three simple straightforward questions to appraise the satisfaction of the community partner:

1. Have the customers' needs been met?
2. Is the project sustainable and maintainable by the customer?
3. Does the project respect the environment and make effective use of local renewable resources?

These three questions can be applied to any service-learning project, local or global; however, it is in cross-cultural projects that the service-learning collaboration structure is particularly important, to ensure that the customers' needs have been met in a responsible and respectful manner.

International service-learning (ISL) combines academic education and community-based service in an international context. ISL has additional goals including increasing participants' global awareness, building intercultural understanding, and improving cross-cultural communication skills. In a well-designed ISL project, the relationship built through the partnership should be mutually beneficial, empowering both the community members and the students.

The discussion in this chapter is relevant to STEM disciplines engaging in ISL efforts that are often done as senior design projects [2]; club projects through Engineers without Borders (EWB) [3], Engineers for a Sustainable World (ESW) [4], or Engineering World Health (EWH) [5]; Master's Degree projects in collaboration with the Peace Corps [6]; information and communication technology projects with nonprofit organizations (NPOs) such as the Geekcorps; or faculty/university efforts to collaborate with institutes of higher education in the developing world to assist in building capacity and global networks [7]. These types of projects have admirably taken on aspects of the U.N. Millennium Development Goals [8] in an effort to reduce poverty and improve health, and promote the role of higher level learning in educating for sustainability as set forth by the U.N. Decade of Education for Sustainable Development [9] and the Association for the Advancement of Sustainability in Higher Education (AASHE) [10].

Technology projects affect a wide array of stakeholders. Even if the project outcomes and deliverables can be viewed as successful from the point of view of an academic institution, the project deliverables may never be adopted or used by the customer, or, worse yet, their implementation may create a negative unintended consequence. This chapter proposes that the collaboration structure between a student–faculty team and a community partner can affect the immediate (short-term) partner's satisfaction, as well as the project's adoption and long-term sustainability.

24.2   ROLE OF REFLECTION

In this paper, ISL refers to American student–faculty teams working on an international project with a partner in the developing world. These kinds of projects have proliferated in the past decade and have exposed students and faculty to new cultures and perspectives, as well as poverty and injustice. ISL is a multifaceted endeavor that has parallels to international education and study abroad, civic education, participatory development, and cross-cultural studies. Crabtree [11] proposed that the foundational research in these related fields could be examined as a way to explore and consider more theoretically grounded approaches to ISL projects and partnerships. Along these lines, this chapter attempts to use an interdisciplinary framework to help inform and improve ISL experiences, but narrows the discussion to the importance of partnership structures.

For the purposes of this chapter, the partnership structure refers to the relational structure between the American student–faculty team and the community partner. It includes the initial introduction, the communication chain, the identification of the decision makers, and the recipients of the project deliverables. Dimensions of the structure that need to be considered when forming a partnership should include who is speaking with whom, who makes decisions for whom, and who is funding the work. For example, one common structure would be that a university team would work with a governmental or nongovernmental organization (NGO) that acts on behalf of a community. In this case, the university team communicates to an intermediary group that makes decisions and accepts the work on behalf of the recipient community. Another structure could partner the university team directly to a committee (elders, teachers, leaders, etc.) in a particular community but the funding for the project could come from a vested third party (e.g., church group or charity organization). Every partnership structure has its own unique configuration. By exploring the best practices of partnership structure from a variety of sources, it is hoped that ISL practitioners from STEM disciplines can learn the methods and strategies that are more likely to produce mutuality in practice.

Reflection is especially relevant for projects involving the STEM disciplines, whereby student–faculty teams use their professional skills for solving applied problems. In these projects, it is exactly the technical expertise being offered that fundamentally affects the relationship. Even if student–faculty teams are committed to serve and work together with the community, the "professionals" are in a position of power. They are knowledge keepers in a divided world of technology have and have-nots, and members of a financially and technologically privileged society. Fiske cautions that "power difference is always part of the cultural difference" [12].

ISL projects should not reinforce for communities that development requires external benefactors, or that national governments need to rely on NGOs to respond to their country's needs. It is important for student–faculty teams to assess and critique the impact on the community to ensure that the work done does in fact benefit the less powerful participants.

This chapter first examines the role of reflection for project members and discusses why purposeful reflection on the collaboration structure provides an opportunity to examine the potential of success of an ISL venture. Ideal partnership structures as suggested by authors in international education, participatory development, and cross-cultural studies are then examined in light of the similarities and differences between ISL and these disciplines, as well as what is realistic for STEM-based ISL projects. In the second half of the chapter, the emergent themes are applied to two ISL projects between the School of Engineering at the University of St. Thomas (UST) and two different service-learning partners in Mali, west Africa. The examples illustrate how different collaboration models may have affected the satisfaction or dissatisfaction of the community partner and the subsequent adoption or abandonment of the project deliverables.

24.3   REFLECTION BY THE STUDENT–FACULTY TEAMS

From academia's perspective, student learning objectives and program outcomes are often assessed by the requirement of the Accreditation Board for Engineering and Technology's Engineering Criteria (ABET EC 2000) [13]. The requirement is to demonstrate clearly that graduates of accredited programs have the broad education necessary to understand the changing needs of our world and have been exposed to a more "humanistic" approach to engineering and technology education. In addition, there is a great need to internationalize American undergraduate education; most educators believe that international experience remains a valuable component of college education [14]. This is especially significant in disciplines such as information science or engineering, which have been encouraged to promote their soft skills and typically have low numbers of students participating in an international undergraduate experience. ISL provides real-life practice in communication and cultural sensitivity in an international setting and has the potential to broaden students' understanding of the needs of our world.

Critical reflection is cited as a fundamental part of all SL experiences and an integral part of the pedagogy. For students, reflections are often integrated into the course milestones through guided activities such as group discussions, journal writing, reflection worksheets, or debriefing interviews [15, 16]. Reflecting on the structure of an ISL collaboration with an explicit examination of the subject positions in relationship to the experience provides opportunities for meaningful discussions that help move students from a charity orientation to one of partner empowerment and social justice. Critical reflection on the partnering process by faculty can lead to a better understanding of our role as project leaders and service-learning facilitators who help students process disconnects in communication and cultural attitudes. Critical reflection can help avoid reinforcing stereotypes [17] and promote constructive engagement in a diverse setting.

Through reflection, students often report that international projects with service components energize them in new ways and affect their worldview [18], underscoring the call by the Association of International Educators (NAFSA) to promote new models of international education and exchange that can help create the conditions for a more peaceful world [19]. Thus, if ISL is an appropriate way to educate and globalize students, then it would be reasonable to explore if there are preferred partnership structures that promote successful ISL collaborations.

One critique of ISL is that students and universities benefit more than the community partners [20]. An examination of the recommendations and warnings from other related disciplines could help guide ISL practitioners to structure a partnership in an informed way in order to maximize the potential of success for all stakeholders.

24.4   PARTNERSHIP RECOMMENDATIONS FROM RELATED FIELDS

The international education and study abroad communities have for decades advocated that ideal structures for international educational experiences include meaningful contacts in a host country [11]. Laubscher [21] argues that it is precisely the out-of-class experiences that bring students into direct contact with the host culture that have the most impact on their study abroad experience, with conversations with host nationals as the most important medium for personal experience, and that both a longer stay and engagement in a work assignment tend to generate greater perceptions of significant impact. Thus, collaboration structures that promote direct contact and conversation over a period of time as well as engagement in a work assignment should be desirable. In a STEM-based ISL project, it is important that the community partner be able to communicate their point of view at the onset of the relationship, during the on-site contact and afterward during the project handoff. However, this may be easier said than done if the community partner and the faculty–student team require multiple language translators or the partner is in a remote location that limits communication options. Practically speaking, the language barriers of the partnership and the frequency of contact must be addressed. A partnership structure should be conducive to frequent correspondence.

Research on intergroup relations has found that cross-cultural contact produces better results when each side shares relatively equal status, when there are shared tasks requiring interdependence and cooperation, and when there are opportunities for interpersonal interaction [22, 23, 24]. For STEM-based ISL collaboration models, this insight suggests partnering with a group that has some technical background, is able to coordinate work assignments, and is accessible enough for one-on-one interactions. Logistically, is there an ideal partner size? ISL practitioners should ask questions such as can a large-scale international or state-sponsored development effort provide interpersonal interaction or can a small rural cooperative share in the technical tasks required of the project.

Both-learning and participatory development are based on the involvement of the community and their determination of their own need. Best practices for partnership models from the participatory-development literature emphasize decentralized, bottom-up development in which the beneficiaries participate in project design, implementation, and assessment [25]. The more the recipient is involved in the planning, design, and implementation of project deliverables, the more likely that they will take ownership of and adopt those deliverables [26]. This suggests that there is a need for consensus, both within the community and between the collaborating partners. There should be opportunities for consultation and decision making throughout planning and implementation, with clearly articulated participant roles, responsibilities, and commitments. The need for consensus suggests that the relationship be built on mutual respect and trust, which takes time. Therefore, the participatory dimension of the relationship needs to be addressed in the partnership structure and may prove to be more difficult in practice then in local or domestic SL relationships.

Reconciling the community's time frame with academia's time frames can prove difficult. Multiyear projects that involve successive student teams also affect the relationship building. Even if a new student group receives an adequate update on the technical status of a project, they must establish their own relationship with the partner. It is difficult to earn trust in an artificial time frame such as a semester, summer term, or short-term visit. Perhaps ISL efforts would be better positioned if STEM-based student–faculty teams partnered with an in-country nonprofit or NGO that works on behalf of a community. The NGO, in turn, engages in facilitating community self-determination and provides for realistic participatory involvement. However, the participatory-development literature also warns that even if an organization's commitment to participatory development seems sincere, the organization may be more concerned with showing effectiveness to an externally determined partner [27] such as a funding agency or political party.

International experiences include cross-cultural contact and immersion. Research from cross-cultural studies and the study abroad community advises that international immersion experiences often involve intense emotional, ideological, and physiological disruptions. Models of intercultural sensitivity map a person's attitude along a continuum from ethnocentric to ethnorelative [28], which may result in a student or faculty member experiencing culture shock or needing cultural-adjustment assistance. Thus, it would be desirable to build a relationship with a bicultural community partner that can act as a cultural liaison.

After reviewing the suggestions from several related disciplines, the emerging ideal ISL partnership structure should

- Facilitate meaningful contact between groups having equal status
- Have a group-consensus system based on partner participation
- Provide sufficient guidance to understand cultural disconnects

Can we use this insight to better design ISL collaboration structures? Or can this insight give any indication of whether some partnership models may be more successful at meeting a customer's needs and producing maintainable and sustainable project deliverables? Certainly, there are many more factors that can be attributed to project success; however, it seems reasonable that something as fundamental as the partnership structure could have a significant and perhaps predictable effect on both partner satisfaction and adoption.

In the next section, two different ISL projects are introduced and discussed in terms of the relative status between the partners and the collaboration structure's potential to provide meaningful contact between groups, have a group-consensus system based on partner participation, and provide sufficient guidance to understand cultural disconnects, with a final reflection on the community partner's acceptance.

24.5   TWO DIFFERENT PARTNERSHIPS

The cases presented here draw on two ISL projects that took place over three years (2004–2007) and involved students from undergraduate courses in engineering at the University of St. Thomas, a midsized private liberal arts school in Minnesota with community partners in Mali, west Africa. The first case involved the design and installation of a low-powered cooling system to cool a computer learning center, and the second case involved the installation of computer aided design (CAD) software at two institutions of higher learning in Mali.

24.5.1   Cooling of a Computer Center: Case History

The author has documented this case in a previous publication and provided theological analysis using the themes of integral human development, solidarity, and resource stewardship [29]. A summary description of the project is presented here in order to analyze the partnership structure with respect to the community partner's satisfaction.

At the beginning of the millennium, one of the developmental aid agreements provided by the United States Agency for International Development (USAID) to Mali in west Africa included a five-year program to hasten development by making information accessible [30]. As a concrete step in achieving their goal, USAID funded Project CLIC and built thirteen Community Learning and Information Centers or Centres Locaux d'Information et de Communication (CLICs), across Mali. These computer-based libraries or "public access tele-centers" were meant to provide useful visual information on topics ranging from health and agriculture to civics and business. The core partners in the implementation of Project CLIC were the Academy for Educational Development (AED), based in Washington, D.C., and the Institut Africain de Gestion et de Formation (INAGEF), an independent Malian nongovernmental organization (NGO). Technical content and expertise for the CLICs was solicited from a variety of organizations such as World Links, the Peace Corps, and various American universities [31].

The University of St. Thomas (UST) became involved in Project CLIC through a United States Department of Agriculture Cooperative State Research, Education, and Extension Service (USDA-CSREES) Higher Education Challenge Program grant involving four universities in a partnership to provide information content for the CLICs by engaging university students through senior-level coursework and independent study. The School of Engineering at UST was subcontracted to examine alternative cooling strategies for the CLICs through its senior design capstone course. The three-year effort designed, tested, and installed a low-powered cooling solution at the largest CLIC in the program, located on the campus of a secondary school in Kangaba, Mali.

24.5.2   Cooling of a Computer Center: Case Analysis

Relative Status of the Partners. INAGEF, the Malian organization charged with running the day-to-day operations of the CLICs, was designated as our community partner and was very helpful in providing technical specifications for the cooling system. They communicated professionally with the engineering students and helped facilitate several structural changes to the CLIC building over the course of three years. The two partners (the UST faculty–student team and the INAGEF staff) had relatively equal status. In fact, there was a Peace Corps volunteer assigned to the CLIC project from St. Paul, MN who added an additional human connection.

The computer center, however, was installed in an existing community, a secondary school for teachers in a mid-sized Malian city. This was the real community partner. USAID/Mali decided that CLICs would be useful institutions for Mali, and the Kangaba Board agreed that the computer center would be useful for their teacher education program. Unfortunately, we were never introduced formally as project participants. As I have noted elsewhere [1], an American academic team can easily undermine current social structures if they enter a community from the outside without proper introductions.

Did the Collaboration Structure Provide Meaningful Contact between Groups? As part of their strategy, the USAID/Mali communication development team purposely leveraged additional resources from various public–private partnerships and alliances. This seems like a good idea, but it made communication difficult. As a small subcontractor distanced by several levels from USAID/Mali, it was difficult for UST to understand the network of development providers. Besides the professional contact with the INAGEF staff members, there was little opportunity for meaningful contact with the Kangaba CLIC staff or Kangaba CLIC board members. In fact, we did not know of each other's existence until the second year of the project. For us, INAGEF was the voice of the Kangaba CLIC.

Did the Collaboration Structure Have a Group Consensus System Based on Partner Participation? There was a group consensus structure at the Kangaba center but it did not include the university team. Some representatives on the CLIC Board were unaware of UST's role in the project and others had an incorrect understanding of what UST would contribute. In the second year of the project, a Peace Corps (PC) volunteer (also, coincidently, from Minnesota) assigned to Kangaba became a member of the CLIC board and explained our role in providing a low-energy cooling strategy for the center. The Kangaba Board did not believe that a cooling strategy was necessary, but allowed the system to be tested and installed.

Did the Partnership Structure Provide Sufficient Guidance to Understand Cultural Disconnects? The partnership structure did not provide sufficient cultural guidance. Obstacles appeared from unexpected places. As time progressed, several PC volunteers and other western foreigners became alarmed at the increase of pornography at the CLIC. One PC volunteer confronted the Kangaba staff, the Kangaba CLIC Board members, and the USAID/Mali director. Since the cooling strategy was presented by her earlier to the staff and Board, by the third year into the project, the cooling strategy became very unpopular among the (mostly male) Board members.

Was the Community Partner Satisfied and is the Project Deliverable Maintainable and Sustainable? Technically, UST delivered a low-power cooling system to the Kangaba CLIC and fulfilled their obligation to INAGEF. Practically, the Kangaba CLIC Board shut down the cooling system as soon as the PC volunteer left Kangaba. The Board did not feel that computer cooling was necessary and that the additional load on the electricity system was unjustified. The Kangaba CLIC Board was unsatisfied with the project and the cooling system is most likely not being used.

In this case, the partnership structure did not provide for meaningful contact or cultural guidance, and the university team was not part of the group consensus system. Despite best intentions, it was not an ISL success.

24.5.3 CAD Installation: Case History

During the same time frame as the previous ISL example, an agribusiness center was envisioned to serve as a permanent home for innovations brought forth by the l'Institut D'Economie Rurale (IER), the agricultural research institute in Bamako, Mali; the Institut Polytechnique Rural de Formation et de Recherche Appliquée (IPR/IFRA), Mali's School of Agriculture and Applied Research; Ecole Nationale d'Ingénieurs (ENI), the country's School of Engineering; and by U.S. faculty–student teams from four institutions working together on service-learning projects with these Malian institutions of higher learning.

The three-year effort identified a group of seven Malian midcareer academics to travel to the United States for extended professional development and to build bridges with American faculty. To support a long-term relationship and to provide a way of transferring deliverables from U.S.–Malian ISL projects, multiple licenses of the CAD software Solid Works™ were to be installed at both ENI and IPR/IFRA. The School of Engineering at UST agreed to partner with the Malian institutions to help install the software and provide some basic training for their faculty. Among the Malian academics who participated in this project was an agricultural engineer who spent one semester at the School of Engineering at UST attending our computer aided design (CAD) course, among other courses. The ISL project partners included faculty and students from the School of Engineering and the graduate program in software, the Malian midcareer academic, and faculty and students from ENI and IPR/IFRA.

24.5.4   CAD Installation: Case Analysis

Relative Status of the Partners. In this case, the partners had equal status and the communication between the universities was professional.

Did the Collaboration Structure Provide Meaningful Contact between Groups? UST invested a significant amount of time and resources in the training of our academic partner to learn the software so that he could become a CAD instructor when he returned to Mali. This relationship provided multiple opportunities for meaningful exchanges and was built on real solidarity between the stakeholders. The partners also invested time and money to have dean-to-dean meetings between the American and Malian universities, further emphasizing mutual respect and collaboration.

Did the Partnership Structure Have a Group Consensus System Based on Partner Participation? The participants did have a group consensus system. Installation issues were solved together on-site with the Malian university IT personnel. Both ENI and IPR/IFRA were prepared to take ownership of the software licenses, and after the first year the respective institutions addressed the licensing and upgrade agreements.

Did The Collaboration Structure Provide Sufficient Guidance to Understand Cultural Disconnects? The Malian midcareer engineering faculty member was able to provide cultural guidance both in terms of setting up the dean-to-dean meetings, hosting the on-site training sessions, and providing a personal view of Malian culture and values. For example, Malians have a "joking cousins" tradition in which people with certain surnames joke about other surnames. In addition, it is common for foreigners to be renamed with a Malian name. When the Dean of Engineering from UST arrived in Mali, he was given a Malian name. The Malian faculty member who had studied at UST told him of the joking cousin tradition and told him which surname he would be expected to joke about. The UST Dean had a good sense of humor and when he would be introduced to someone with his nemesis name, he would playfully add a benign insult and state his Malian name. This would produce an uproar of laughter and goodwill.

Was the Community Partner Satisfied and is the Project Deliverable Maintainable and Sustainable? The universities in Mali were very satisfied with the project and have maintained their software licenses and their CAD training program. In this case, the partnership structure did provide for meaningful contact and cultural guidance, had a functional group consensus system, and could be considered an ISL success.

24.6   FINAL THOUGHTS

I have come to believe that relationships are the centerpiece of ISL projects. We must be actively conscious of our motivations, choices, and the complex impact of our work. The set of key elements desired in a partnership structure compiled by examining insights from international education and study abroad, civic education, participatory development, and cross-cultural studies were largely missing in the cooling of a computer center ISL project and were largely present in the CAD installation ISL project. Partnership structure may not be the only factor in predicting the success of an ISL project, but it can have an effect on the immediate (short-term) partner's satisfaction, as well as the project's adoption and long-term sustainability.

In summary, structures that promote successful projects facilitate meaningful contact between groups having equal status, have a group consensus system based on partner participation, and provide sufficient guidance to understand cultural disconnects. If all these conditions are not present, or an ISL team finds itself in a less than ideal collaboration, the ISL team could begin a dialog with their partner in light of these insights to help ameliorate the situation.

24.7   ACKNOWLEDGMENTS

This material is based upon work supported by the Exploring Ethics Across the Disciplines (EEAD) research initiative at UST and the USDA-CSREES Higher Education Challenge Program Award No. #404-570. Any opinions, findings, conclusions, or recommendations expressed in this publication are those of the author and do not necessarily reflect the view of the U.S. Department of Agriculture. I would also like to thank Florence Dunkel, Sidy Ba, Ashley Shams, Michael Hennessey, Bhabani Misra, Ron Bennett, Christina Ceballos, Dennis Bilodeau, Aminata Maiga Fofana, Jenny Borofka, Clare Caron, Kelly Kanz, Stefan Yanovsky, John Abraham, John Walker, Peter Bulinski, Pete Jacques, Lina Salah, and Ben Dauwalter.

REFERENCES

1. C. George and A. Shams,"The Challenge of Including Customer Satisfaction Into the Assessment Criteria of Overseas Service-Learning Projects," *IJSLE,* vol. 2, no. 2, pp. 64–75, 2007.

2. http://courseweb.stthomas.edu/cmgeorge/.

3. http://www.ewb-usa.org/.

4. http://www.eswusa.org/.

5. http://www.ewh.org/.

6. http://peacecorps.mtu.edu/.

7. http://www.hedprogram.org/.

8. UN Millennium Development Goals. http://www.un.org/millenniumgoals/.

9. Centre for Environment Education. 2008. U.N. Decade of Education for Sustainable Development. http://www.desd.org/About%20ESD.htm.

10. Association for the Advancement of Sustainability in Higher Education. 2010. "Sustainability Curriculum in Higher Education: A Call to Action." http://www.aashe.org/files/A_Call_to_Action_final(2).pdf.

11. Crabtree, R. D. "Theoretical Foundations for International Service-Learning." *Michigan Journ. of Community Service Learning.* pp. 18–36, Fall 2008.

12. J. Fiske. *Power Plays, Power Works.* London: Verso. 1993.

13. ABET (2000). *Criteria for Accrediting Engineering Programs.* The Engineering Accreditation Commission of the Accreditation Board for Engineering and Technology, Inc. http://www.abet.org.

14. An International Education Policy for U.S. Leadership, Competitiveness, and Security http://www.nafsa.org/public_policy.scc/united_states_international/toward_an_internati onal/.

15. L. Klopfenstein, L. Petrasky, V. Winton, and J. Brown, "Addressing Water Quality Issues in Rural Cameroon with Household Biosand Filters," *IJSLE,* vol. 6, no.1, pp. 64–80, Spring 2011.

16. D. DiBiasio. "Outcomes Assessment of an International Engineering Experience." In *ASEE Annual Conference Proceedings,* Albuquerque, NM, 24–27 June 2001.

17. T. Williams and E. McKenna. "Negotiating Subject Positions in a Service-Learning Context: Toward a Feminist Critique of Experiential Learning." In A. A Macdonald & S. Sanchez-Casal (Eds.), *Twenty-First-Century Feminist Classrooms: Pedagogies of Identity and Difference,* pp. 135–154, 2002. New York: Palgrave-Macmillan.

18. A. Shams, and C. George, "Global Competency: An Interdisciplinary Approach." *AEQ,* vol. 10, no. 4, pp. 249–256, Winter 2006.

19. http://www.nafsa.org.

20. N. L. Cruz and D. E. Giles, "Where's the Community in Service-Learning Research?" *Michigan Journal of Community Service Learning,* 7, pp. 28–34, 2000.

21. M. Laubscher, *Encounters with Difference: Student Perceptions of The Role of Out-of-Class Experiences in Education Abroad.* ISSN 0-313-28977-8. 1994. Greenwood Press, Westport, CT.

22. Y. Amir. "Contact Hypothesis in Ethnic Relations." *Psychological Bulletin,* vol. 71, no. 5, pp. 319–342, 1969.

23. S. W. Cook. "Experimenting on Social Issues: The Case of Social Desegregation." *American Psychologist,* vol. 40, pp. 452–460, 1985.

24. W. G. Stephan and C. W. Stephan. *Intergroup Relations.* Dubuque IA: Brown and Benchmark. 1995.

25. G. Bessette. *Involving the Community: A Guide to Participatory Development Communication.* Ottawa: International Development Research Centre. 2004.

26. R. D. Crabtree and D. A. Sapp. "Technical Communication, Participatory Action Research, and Global Civic Engagement: A Teaching, Research and Social Action Collabo-

ration in Kenya." *Reflections: A Journal of Writing, Service-Learning, and Community Literacy,* vol. 4, no. 2, pp. 9–33, 2005.

27. J. Lane. "Non-Governmental Organizations and Participatory Development: The Concept in Theory Versus the Concept in Practice." In N. Nelson and S. Wright (Eds.), *Power and participatory development: Theory and Practice.* pp. 181–191. 1995. London: Intermediate Technologies.

28. M. R. Hammer, M.J. Bennett and R. Wiseman. "Measuring Intercultural Sensitivity: The Intercultural Development Inventory." In R.M. Paige (Guest Ed.) Special Issue on Intercultural Development. *International Journal of Intercultural Relations,* vol. 27, no. 4, pp. 421–443, 2003.

29. C. George and B. Sain, "Human Development and a Senior Project in Mali." In J. Heft and K. Hallinan (Eds.), Engineering Education and Practice: Embracing a Catholic Vision, Chpt 7, pp. 143–168. 2012. University of Notre Dame Press, Notre Dame, Indiana.

30. USAid, Sahelian West Africa—Humanitarian Emergency. Fact Sheet #3, Fiscal Year (FY) 2005. August 23, 2005. http://www.usaid.gov/our_work/humanitarian_assistance/disaster_assistance/countries/sahel/fy2005/Sahel_HE_FS_3_8-23-2005.pdf.

31. Establishing Community Learning and Information Centers (CLICs) in Underserved Malian Communities. Final Report. http://www.eric.ed.gov/PDFS/ED502041.pdf.

32. C. George, A. Shams, and F. Dunkel, "Lessons Learned in an International Service-Learning Collaborative: Shea Butter Case Study," *NACTA Journal,* vol. 55, no. 2, pp. 71–77, June 2011.

SERVICE-LEARNING IN THE COMPUTER AND INFORMATION SCIENCES

Lessons Learned and Guidance for the Future

Brian A. Nejmeh

ABSTRACT

Service-learning in the computer and information sciences (SL in CIS) is still in its infancy. Nonetheless, there are important lessons learned to date from SL in CIS programs and projects to guide others in this practice. This chapter highlights the key lessons learned to date about SL in CIS. These lessons are derived from the chapters that appear in this book and the author's own experiences. In addition, there are a number of open issues and challenges relevant to the future of SL in CIS that are reflected upon in this chapter.

25.1 INTRODUCTION

SL in CIS programs and projects offer much promise, but also present many challenges. The SL in CIS community would benefit from leveraging the lessons learned from past SL in CIS programs and projects. This chapter chronicles key lessons learned about SL in CIS based on the author's personal experiences and from the experiences of the authors who wrote chapters for this book. Section 2 of this chapter outlines the major SL in CIS lessons learned in the following areas:

- Motivation
- Organization

- Partner and project selection and engagement model
- Course structure
- Technology
- Process
- Impact assessment

Given the early stage of SL in CIS development, there are many opportunities to improve the state of SL in CIS practice for the benefit of nonprofit organizations (NPOs), faculty, and students. In Section 3 of this chapter, ten imperatives to be pursued by future SL in CIS practitioners are defined. These imperatives can have a dramatic positive influence on the state of SL in CIS practice and the impact of it.

25.2   SL IN CIS LESSONS LEARNED

25.2.1   Motivation

There are a variety of motivations for engaging in service-learning (SL) in the computer and information sciences (CIS) (herein referred to as SL in CIS). These motivations are different for the various stakeholders (students, faculty, schools, NPOs, and communities served by NPOs). It is useful to understand the motivations for SL in CIS in order to structure SL in CIS programs and projects and to assess the impact of such programs and projects relative to the motivations and objectives for doing them.

The product of any educational institution is a well-rounded and well-educated person who is prepared to be a productive member of the workforce and society. It follows from this that a key motivation for SL in CIS is to better prepare students to more effectively and efficiently transition into the workforce [1, 2]. SL in CIS projects also allow students to develop a broader set of skills beyond the technical [1], including those related to people and project management. For international SL in CIS projects, motivations include "increasing participants' global awareness, building intercultural understanding, and improving cross-cultural communication skills" [3].

For faculty members, SL in CIS projects offer a rich text and context for student learning. Instead of having students solve contrived problems with known solutions as in traditional courses, SL in CIS projects allow students to be challenged in how to best apply their classroom learning to an actual problem facing an NPO. Such projects encourage faculty members to be current on emerging technologies and to better understand the environments in which students will be employed upon graduation. Understanding current technologies allows faculty members to do a better job preparing students for the workforce. Some have argued [4, 5, 6, 7] that SL in CIS projects offer an excellent platform from which to educate students about ethics in the realm of CIS. Certainly, the issues of copyright, software warranties, negotiating with vendors, project status reports, and the like offer rich opportunities for students to understand ethical issues. Finally, SL in CIS projects offer great opportunities for scholarship, including jointly authoring papers with students on project experiences.

In general terms, an underlying motivation for SL in CIS is simply *to do good*. As our world and society face a myriad of challenges, some have argued that "engineering is, by nature, a profession with a societal context leading to social responsibility" [15]. As NPOs are increasingly being asked to do more with less [1], it follows that SL in CIS seeks to remedy this situation. For instance, the overall goal of the Humanitarian Free and Open Software Project (HFOSS) "is to build a collaborative community of individuals, academic computing departments, IT corporations, and humanitarian organizations (local and global) dedicated to the development of socially useful software" [8].

NPOs have a variety of motivations for participating in SL in CIS projects. Simply stated, many NPOs fail to make appropriate use of information technology (IT) simply because they lack the know-how and time required to take advantage of IT. Such projects offer NPOs the opportunity to leverage IT so they may (in turn) better serve their communities. IT also offers tremendous potential to increase organizational efficiency and effectiveness, thereby increasing overall organizational capacity. In addition, by exposing faculty and students to their needs, NPOs may benefit from students and faculty deciding to volunteer their time to aid the organization. Some might even join the organization full-time upon graduation [9].

There is a strong desire of SL in CIS practitioners to want their work to be mutually beneficial to both the student and the community partner. The notion of mutual benefit is well-articulated by David Vader of Messiah College who states: "We understand service to be something that is mutually composed by all participants, members and clients, acknowledging that all have something to share and that everyone receives. Too often, service has been viewed as something that those with knowledge and material wealth do for those without those resources" [9].

For many colleges and universities, the motivation to engage in SL in CIS is *missional*. That is to say, many institutions include the notion of service to mankind as part of their mission statement. As such, SL in CIS can be very consistent with an institutional mission. The institutional missions of some institutions figure prominently in their SL in CIS efforts (Florida Gulf Coast University [10] and Park University [11]). For example, at Messiah College, a Christian institution, "Our mission is to educate men and women toward maturity of intellect, character and Christian faith in preparation for lives of service, leadership, and reconciliation in church and society." The Collaboratory at Messiah College embodies the mission of the college. David Vader, the Director of the Collaboratory, so eloquently states in Chapter 4 of this book,

> Persons maturing in intellect, character, and Christian faith must strive to comprehend both "What must I know?" and "What does it mean?" Those who would live lives of service, leadership, and reconciliation must also seek to understand "What is required of me?" ... [T]he Collaboratory adds value to classroom learning by helping students discover a worthy dream for their lives ... that is worthy of them because it seeks to do good that is larger than them each individually.

Colleges and universities have a variety of motivations for supporting SL in CIS. One motivation is to serve underrepresented groups (minorities and women). Some authors [1, 12, 13] have argued that SL in CIS offers promise in this regard. Others see SL in CIS as a means of revitalizing our dated CIS educational models. For example, a motivation of the HFOSS project is "to answer whether getting students involved in humanitarian FOSS indeed also helps revitalize undergraduate computing education" [13]. Another motivation for universities to do SL in CIS in the local community is the desire for the university to be in good standing and to have a positive reputation in the community [2].

Finally, as reported in Chapter 21, a survey done at Purdue University offers insight into the motivations for SL in CIS:

> As can be seen from the responses, attendees thought that student learning was the most likely outcome from service-learning. However, engagement with the community, assisting societal needs, building relationships, and student leadership development were also high on the list of possible outcomes of service-learning. On the lower end of the responses for possible outcomes were research grant and university student policy development opportunities, with the lowest score going to promotion and tenure opportunities.

25.2.2   Organization

25.2.2.1   SL in CIS Organizational Program Models. There are many different organizational models being used in the SL in CIS community. Below is a summary of several of the SL in CIS programs referenced in this book. Table 25.1 offers a summary and analysis of some of the key aspects of these SL in CIS programs.

The Purdue EPICS Program is among the earliest (established in 1995) and most established SL in CIS programs [1]. "Purdue University has invested in staff to allow EPICS to be implemented at other campuses with more than 20 universities and colleges having adopted programs modeled after EPICS" [1]. EPICS projects are done in the context of EPICS project-based courses. Projects are done across the sectors of "human services, the environment, access and abilities, and education and outreach" [1]. EPICS teams are typically multidisciplinary. Projects typically span multiple semesters. "EPICS has been designated as a separate academic program by the university, housed under the College of Engineering and supported by the provost. EPICS oversees a set of EPICS (EPCS) course numbers, from first-year to senior level and one and two credit options for each year. As an academic program, EPICS has a multidisciplinary faculty curriculum committee that oversees and approves changes to the curriculum. EPICS is housed in dedicated space with labs and offices in the newest of Purdue Engineering's buildings, the Armstrong Hall of Engineering." [1] The EPICS structure is also supported by graduate teaching assistants and local professionals who volunteer as advisors to EPICS projects. A key element in the success of EPICS has been several long-term partnerships with NPOs.

The Butler EPICS Program is an instance of the Purdue EPICS Program that was started at Butler University in 2001 [12]. Butler manages a two-course EPICS sequence that is required of their computer science and software engineering majors. Students can take these two courses at any point in their program of study and may take the courses more than once. Teams are multigenerational. The Butler EPICS Program is a stand-alone program managed exclusively by the Department of Computer Science and Software Engineering. "EPICS courses are endorsed by Butler's Center for Citizenship and Community (CCC) and they are annotated by the Service-Learning (SL) course indicator." [12] Long-term partnerships with NPOs are also a hallmark of this program.

The Collaboratory for Strategic Partnerships and Applied Research at Messiah College began in the early 1990's. The genesis for the Collaboratory was engineering projects [9]. The Collaboratory is a student led organization, wherein students work alongside of faculty and volunteer professionals on engineering problems of significance to NPOs and the communities they serve. "The Collaboratory is a center at Messiah College for applied research and project-based learning in partnership with client nonprofit organizations, businesses, governments, and communities in our region and around the world" [9]. The Collaboratory has a Faculty Director who has a reduced teaching load. The Faculty Director reports to the Dean of the School of Science, Engineering, and Health (SEH). The Collaboratory also has a Student Director. Current thematic areas of focus for the Collaboratory include energy, water, disability resources, communications, transportation, education, and microeconomic development.

The Humanitarian Free and Open Source Software (HFOSS) Project began in 2006 with a consortium of small liberal arts colleges located in the eastern United States [13]. "These two ideas—free and open-source software and its use to serve humanitarian purposes (in the broad sense of the term)—have served as the guiding principles of the HFOSS project since its inception" [13]. HFOSS includes an active outreach program to spread HFOSS practices to other colleges and universities. Today, the project includes involvement from over a dozen U.S.-based colleges and universities. HFOSS has resources that allow their SL in CIS model to be integrated into a number of courses.

The Agile Software Factory (ASF) began at Bowling Green University in 2008 [14]. The ASF is housed in the Department of Computer Science. The ASF "serves as a clearinghouse for software-development requests from nonprofit organizations and continues to provide maintenance and technical support for completed software systems. ... The ASF, working with the Office of Service-Learning at the university, actively locates nonprofit organizations that need software solutions developed" [14]. Once potential projects are vetted by the ASF, some projects are selected and worked on by students in various service-learning project courses. Once completed by the student teams, the results of these projects are evaluated and a determination is made as to the ongoing role the ASF will have in the project.

Table 25.1. Summary of SL in CIS programs

Program	Framework	Thematic areas	Where housed
Purdue EPICS	Course-based	Human services, the environment, access and abilities, and education and outreach	Separate academic program in College of Engineering
Butler EPICS	Course-based	Not explicitly stated	Managed by Department of CS and SE
Messiah College Collaboratory	Cocurricular-based	Energy, water, disability resources, communications, transportation, education, and microeconomic development	School of Science, Engineering, and Health
HFOSS	Course-based	Humanitarian services	Consortium model involving several institutions
Bowling Green ASF	Hybrid	Not explicitly stated	Department of Computer Science

In terms of the SL framework presented in Chapter 1, the different models (course-based, co-curricular-based, and hybrid) are all represented by programs in the book. Three of the five programs summarized above are course-based SL in CIS programs (Purdue EPICS, Butler EPICS, and HFOSS). The Collaboratory at Messiah College is cocurricular-based and the ASF Program at Bowling Green University is a hybrid model, having both a course component and a cocurricular component (the ASF itself). The above programs provide a good mix of options for considering how to go about institutionalizing SL in CIS.

The SL in CIS framework presented in Chapter 1 offers a reasonable place to start as you consider organizational models for SL in CIS. Initially, a decision needs to be made about how to begin doing SL in CIS. In many cases, SL in CIS is started by a single faculty member doing a single project for a local NPO. Once projects are initiated, faculty members begin to realize the need for some organization and structure to manage the SL in CIS process. Over time, this model might evolve to include faculty members and students from the same department, and then other departments. At this point, the various SL in CIS programs in the book offer a variety of patterns that can be used to organize an SL in CIS program. Furthermore, EPICS [1, 12] and HFOSS [13] offer assistance in creating instances of their SL in CIS programs at other campuses. Over time, as the number of projects and NPOs you are working with grows, so does the need to manage the SL in CIS process. In some cases, the administrative support will need to grow to be either a department- or school-level concern. As the chapters in the book suggest, SL in CIS programs evolve over time in order to better manage and scale them. For faculty members beginning to explore SL in CIS, any of the EPICS Programs (Purdue or Butler) or HFOSS Program would be worth contacting for advice.

Many NPOs speak in terms of the sectors or thematic areas they are engaged in with their efforts [59]. A thematic area of focus simply defines an area of society you desire to positively impact. There are multiple advantages for establishing a thematic area of focus for your SL in CIS efforts. Doing so allows for your group to specialize and concentrate on the needs specific to the thematic areas. This allows for the development of subject matter expertise among faculty and multigenerational students that is specific to the areas of focus. Familiarity with the processes, terminology, and issues facing your thematic areas of focus can increase the efficiency and effectiveness of your SL in CIS efforts. Some of the SL in CIS programs chronicled in this book have been explicit about their thematic areas of focus; others have not. It is a sound SL in CIS strategy to explicitly state thematic areas of focus. It is not to say that you will not accept projects outside your thematic areas of focus, but such instances should be rare. Clearly, thematic areas of focus should change over time as the problems NPOs are facing evolve, technology evolves, and the interests of faculty and students evolve.

Some SL in CIS programs are very explicit about their thematic areas of focus. Purdue EPICS [1] has identified education and outreach, access and abilities, human services, and the environment as their areas of focus. The Collaboratory [9] has identified the following thematic areas: energy, water, disability resources, communications, transportation, education and microeconomic development. Computer literacy, digital citizenship and the digital divide [11, 17, 18, 19] are another thematic area for some working in SL in CIS. Green IT and promoting ecofriendly computing is another area of focus [46].

There are a few additional lessons learned worth a brief mention. The importance of student leadership and ownership for SL in CIS projects was highlighted by many authors. For instance, "shared student leadership" is a basic tenet of the Collaboratory [9]. In the experience of this author, he provides his students with a list of possible projects to consider (including those projects sourced by students) and joint faculty–student decisions are made as to which projects to accept. An organizational concept for SL in CIS is the use of professional volunteers as advisors and mentors to projects [1, 4]. In addition, paraprofessionals who are paid staff (either full-time lab assistants or graduate teaching assistants) play an instrumental organizational and support role in some SL in CIS programs [1, 12, 9, 14]. Finally, students are often hired part-time during the school year and full-time in the summer to support ongoing projects, to complete field work, and to aid in the governance of the SL in CIS programs [1, 9, 13].

25.2.2.2   Role of NPOs. The role of NPOs in SL in CIS programs and projects is critically important. At the organizational level, NPO leaders play a key role in committing to work with faculty–student teams in terms of:

- Ensuring that faculty and students involved in the projects understand the mission, vision, and values of the NPO and the plight and challenges facing those in the communities they serve
- Making themselves available and accessible to the SL in CIS project teams
- Helping the SL in CIS teams understand the processes and problems the projects are addressing
- Helping the SL in CIS teams understand the technical environment projects must operate in
- Providing timely feedback about interim and final project results

25.2.2.3   Role of Faculty. Faculty members overseeing SL in CIS projects play the role of player–coach. They are intimately involved in sourcing and selecting projects. Perhaps the most important role faculty members play on SL in CIS projects is that of a high-level project manager. A faculty member's role includes:

- Ensuring that students are focused on a feasible project scope
- Helping to manage conflict among team members
- Ensuring that project risks are appropriately identified and managed
- Providing hands-on technical guidance (based on project type), especially in the areas of requirements, architecture, and design (areas where students typically have very limited experience)
- Reviewing and providing feedback on interim project results to NPO staff and students
- Ensuring effective communication with appropriate NPO staff
- Being knowledgeable about software life cycle models and tools, including Agile methods [14]
- Providing continuity for projects that span multiple teams, courses, or semesters [2, 9]

It helps for faculty members to have had some significant industrial software project experience, either on a full-time or consulting basis. Understanding the realities of industrial-style CIS projects is an important factor in mentoring and guiding students pursuing SL in CIS projects. For faculty members lacking this experience, it might be wise to spend a summer working full-time on an industrial software project.

It is difficult for faculty members who are overseeing multiple SL in CIS projects to master all of the technologies being used by the project teams. The idea of selecting a standard technology stack for all SL in CIS projects will be discussed later in this chapter. Doing so can certainly be of great benefit to all parties; however, there are cases in which there is a need to deviate from a standard technology stack. In the end, faculty members overseeing SL in CIS projects are to be experts in the process of doing SL in CIS projects and in helping students to manage those projects. The detailed technical knowledge needed to complete a diversity of SL in CIS projects must realistically rest with the students. Certainly, the supporting course curriculum at the institution should be equipping students with the prerequisite knowledge needed to complete the projects. Perhaps David Vader of Messiah College said it best in in Chapter 4 when he stated "The third strategic best practice is educators who, in addition to advising and mentoring, connect their scholarship directly to student learning by making hands-on professional contributions to projects" [9].

There can be some tension among faculty members involved in SL in CIS. Faculty members bring different experiences and assumptions to projects. Such tension is seen in the following quote from the work of Hannon at Washington and Jefferson College:

> [T]he inherent openness of the course can be unsettling for the course instructor, who must at times negotiate conflicting advice from department faculty, resolve internal conflicts, and head off the miscommunications that inevitably result from fragmented or distributed discussions. ... These are tough projects with unclear answers and plenty of disagreement" [4].

If the instructor is not caught off-guard, he/she can use such diverging opinions as a real-world teaching tool.

It is useful for faculty members engaging in SL in CIS to stay actively involved in their professional development. This includes their technical knowledge, process and life cycle knowledge, and awareness of current and best SL in CIS practices. It is important for SL in CIS faculty to connect their SL in CIS work to their scholarship. There are ample opportunities for public dissemination of SL in CIS work. Public dissemination venues for SL in CIS scholarship include:

- ACM SIGCSE Technical Symposium on Computer Science Education (SIGCSE) [20]
- ACM SIGCSE ITiCSE (Innovation and Technology in Computer Science Education) (ITCSE) [21]
- ACM SIGCSE ICER (International Computing Education Conference) (ICER) [22]
- ACM SIGITE (Conference on Information Technology Education) (SIGITE) [23]
- American Society for Engineering Education Annual Conference (ASEE) [24]
- CCSC: Northwestern Conference (CCSC) [25]
- InSITE Proceedings of Informing Science and IT Education (InSITE) (INSITE) [26]
- Information Science Educators Conference (ISECON(ISECON) [27]
- Journal of Computing Sciences in Colleges [28]
- Michigan Journal of Community Service Learning (MJCSL) [29]
- International Journal for Service Learning in Engineering (PSU) [30]

Two other areas to briefly discuss are tenure/promotion and faculty loads for those involved in SL in CIS. In terms of tenure and promotion, the informal survey conducted at Purdue [6] indicates that those surveyed did not believe involvement in SL in CIS would strengthen their promotion and tenure opportunities. However, it is reasonable to believe that those institutions whose mission reflects an element of community service are more apt to consider involvement in SL in CIS positively as it relates to tenure and promotion. This is certainly the case at Messiah College. Service and commitment to service are clearly included as part of the term-tenure and promotion process [31]. On a final note related to faculty, it is important that faculty get full course load credit for teaching SL in CIS courses. It is certainly the case that the preplanning (ahead of the semester starting), on-going project involvement inside and outside of the classroom, and the external client nature of SL in CIS projects require at least the same amount of time to be successful as does teaching a traditional course.

25.2.2.4 Funding Models. Funding for SL in CIS is an important topic that has many dimensions. Funding needs include: equipment, support for paraprofessionals and student staff, support for faculty members to find release time to work on projects, student funding for summer work, travel to meet with NPOs and do field work, and professional development to attend conferences and workshops. Funding models include:

- Seeking grants [9, 13]
- Endowment models [9, 12]
- Institutional supported release time [9]
- Corporate sponsorships [9]
- Student fund-raising [9]
- Financial support from alumni [9]

25.2.3 Partner and Project Selection and Engagement Models

25.2.3.1 Sourcing Project Opportunities. The SL in CIS process begins with sourcing candidate projects. A basic tenet of service-learning is the offering of a service in a mutually beneficial relationship to a needy segment of our society. Therefore, it is suggested that only NPOs be considered as candidate project sponsors. The notion of doing an SL in CIS project for a for-profit entity simply does not seem correct. Perhaps an argument could be made for a unique for-profit organization to be a project sponsor, but this should be the rare exception. Furthermore, projects done for a for-profit organization will not likely be central to the main goals of the company (or else their own staff would be working on them). As stated earlier, NPOs often lack the resources, skills, and time to exploit IT. For this reason, NPOs are excellent candidates for SL in CIS projects that are central to the mission of the organization.

Potential project candidates can emerge from a variety of sources. Trustees, administrators, and other faculty members at most institutions are members of NPO boards or are aware of local, regional, or global NPOs. Such individuals can often make an introduction to an NPO executive to begin the SL in CIS courtship process. I have made it a practice to serve on the boards of NPOs, in part, so that I can better understand their needs and how SL in CIS projects could be of service to them. At Messiah College the service-learning office (the Agape Center [32]) hosts an annual luncheon for NPO executives in the region. This luncheon is a thank-you to them for working with our students on SL projects. It is also a time when faculty members talk about their areas of interest and solicit project ideas from NPO executives. As a result of this luncheon, more service project ideas are identified than can realistically be served by the faculty–student population.

Finally, there are a number of NPOs that offer technology and IT assistance to the NPO community at large. These organizations include:

- TechSoup [33]
- Sparked [34]
- Engineers Without Borders [35]
- Engineers for a Sustainable World [36]
- Engineering World Health [37]
- NetHope [38]
- Peace Corps [39]
- Geek Corps [40]

Such organizations often have an inventory of project requests from NPOs that would fit well into an SL in CIS project model.

25.2.3.2 Location. The location of the NPOs and communities they serve is also a consideration when sourcing SL in CIS opportunities. A survey of the chapters in this book reveal a good mix of local, regional, and global NPOs that have been engaged in SL in CIS projects. Conventional wisdom would suggest starting SL in CIS on a local level where faculty and students can be in close proximity to the NPO and the communities they serve. This will facilitate and expedite the discovery, learning, engagement, and feedback processes. However, it is also appropriate to point out that whereas there are legitimate needs local to those working in developed countries, the needs of those in developing countries are far greater. It is generally agreed upon within the SL in CIS community that it is more difficult to succeed at doing SL in CIS projects in developing countries. The reasons for this are many, including cross-cultural and language differences, time differences, technology limitations, accessibility challenges, travel requirements, and required funding. In many ways, however, these challenges make for great learning opportunities for students to experience and learn about the realities of completing projects in the world at large. For these reasons, this author has a personal bias to work with either global NPOs with an office local to his college or NPOs located in developing countries. In the case of this author, about 50% of his SL in CIS projects are connected to the developing world.

Given the emphasis on long-term partnerships with NPOs among the more successful SL in CIS programs [1, 4, 12], it follows that an SL in CIS program should carefully consider working with a select few NPOs in a long-term partnership model. Thus, it might be productive to consider working with an NPO that has multiple projects to be done over a multiyear period or has a single, larger project that can be broken up into a multiyear project.

25.2.3.3 *Thematic Areas of Focus.* Earlier in the chapter, thematic areas of focus were discussed for SL in CIS. A thematic area of focus simply defines an area of society you desire to positively impact. The importance of identifying and working in selected thematic areas was established earlier in this chapter. Once thematic areas of focus are established, it is important to work with NPOs that offer project opportunities in such areas.

25.2.3.4 *Project Types.* One final consideration related to sourcing projects is the type of projects you seek to perform. As delineated in Chapter 1, there are six different SL in CIS project types:

1. Training. Focus on imparting computer and information sciences skills needed by the staff of NPOs.
2. Professional services. Focus on providing advice on computer and information sciences issues facing NPOs.
3. Systems selection. Focus on defining system needs of an NPO, identifying and evaluating candidate solutions, recommending a solution, and (potentially) transitioning the solution to an NPO.
4. Support. Focus on providing customer support related to systems for NPOs.
5. System projects. Focus on developing an information system project for a specific NPO.
6. Products. Focus on developing a common information system product used by many NPOs.

With few exceptions, most of the SL in CIS projects done to date are system projects. That is, they are custom systems developed to the specific needs of a single NPO. Although this is understandable in some respects, it may not be appropriate in many instances. From an educational perspective, a computer science or software engineering course, by its very nature, typically requires the students to develop a system. In these cases, the opportunity is for faculty and students to conceive products that can be used by a variety of NPOs that have the same or similar problems. In such cases, a product should support a degree of configurability that would allow for the individual differences in the needs of the NPOs to be accounted for in the same product. This is in sharp contrast to building a system to support a single NPO with no thought given to how other NPOs might use a similar system. Examples of open-source applications that took a product approach to solving a common NPO problem include CiviCRM [41] and the HFOSS projects Homeroom and Homebase [42]. Clearly, such products impose some limitations on NPOs, but they are likely to have far greater impact in terms of the number of NPOs they would benefit. Obviously, conceiving a product is more difficult than writing a system for a single NPO. Perhaps the best model would be to initially conceive of a project as a systems project for the initial releases of the system. Then, once the problem domain and degrees of freedom needed to support multiple NPOs became clear, a redesign or refactoring of the systems project can be done and migrated over to a product that will serve multiple NPOs.

One final thought related to project type is that for many IT, IS, and systems analysis and design classes, it is totally reasonable for a systems selection project to satisfy the student learning objectives. The advent of open-source models and platforms, such as sourceforge.net, and the many high-quality and affordable commercial-off-the-shelf and SaaS software options suggest that many NPO CIS problems can be addressed with existing solutions. Such an approach also deals well with issues of sustainability and ongoing support requirements. There are clearly not enough systems selection projects being done within the SL in CIS community. This should change for the betterment of student learning objectives and NPOs.

25.2.3.5 Vetting Process. The vetting process is the process used by the faculty–student community to evaluate the merits of candidate SL in CIS projects for selection as actual projects. NPOs should complete a project proposal document. It should include topics such as:

- Name and proposed project liaison contact information for NPO
- Description of problem to be solved
- Constituents benefited
- Users of system
- Relevant existing systems
- Known constraints or considerations related to the problem (i.e., limited Internet access, dated equipment, etc.)

- Timeframe required for completion
- Desired outputs and outcomes
- Budget or funding considerations

Table 25.2 highlights some of the key considerations in vetting a potential project. These project factors should be carefully considered by faculty–student teams deciding on candidate SL in CIS projects to pursue.

25.2.3.6 Initiating a Project. Upon completing the vetting process and selecting one or more viable project candidates, additional work needs to be done. For example, at Butler [12] they indicated that prior to starting a project with a new client, "they make it clear from the beginning that clients are expected to commit the necessary time to mentor our students on a regular basis. In order to facilitate such mentorship, regular meetings are planned both un the client's site and on the Butler campus."

There are certainly legal and ethical issues that must be addressed when doing SL in CIS projects. In addition, the expectations of all involved parties need to be well defined. In most cases, this is done in the form of a memo of understanding (MOU) between an NPO and the faculty involved from the host institution. For example, the Wentworth Institute [44] developed an MOU template structure for SL in CIS projects. In this case, the agreeing parties are the NPO and the faculty members. The MOU outlines project roles and responsibilities, project scope (features, timelines, resources committed, availability of NPO staff, etc.) and states that "Wentworth students are subject to the Wentworth code of conduct while on the job" [2]. As the project progresses, the MOU is extended to include more detailed information about the project and an updated timeline. "To summarize: the developer–client contract is in three parts: (1) the MOU between the community organization and the Wentworth faculty members, (2) the detailed project proposal submitted by the student team, and (3) the requirements document signed by the students and client representatives" [2].

When doing SL in CIS projects, it is important for faculty and students to be humble [7, 9]. For many SL in CIS projects, the best solutions are not always the most obvious and it is important to remain humble and realize that faculty and students have much to learn from their community partners. Skon [7] said it well when he said

Realize that you don't know what is best, what hidden information may be pivotal, and then allow others to know that you are uncertain, that this is all new to you, and you really need to hear their perspective. Reassure the host that you are committed to the project regardless of the shape of the solution, and that despite the fact that cost is an issue, you would rather scale the solu-

Table 25.2. SL in CIS project vetting factors

Factor	Description
Project definition	• Is the project well defined and understood? • Can the project be done in successive phases (perhaps over multiple semesters) to better manage scope? Scope management can be a challenging issue in SL in CIS projects. The notion of the "minimally complete" system should be defined so that something of value can be completed in the allotted project time and effort. Be sure you listen and learn from those who come from the environment the project is intended to benefit [7].
Feasibility	• Is the project technically feasible (with student knowledge, available technology, etc.)? • Is the project organizationally feasible (NPO ready and able to embrace solution and make the changes necessary to do so)? • Is the project financially feasible (sufficient budget to implement and support a solution)?
Accessibility	• Is the NPO accessible in terms of personnel, facilities, and processes and ability to provide timely feedback and review? Consider how Skype and wikis can be used to facilitate communicate with nonlocal NPOs.
Impact	• What potential positive/negative impacts might the proposed project have on the NPO, university (missional fit), faculty (opportunities for scholarship, ability to oversee) and students (learning outcomes, successful project, etc.)?
Commitment and interest	• Is there strong evidence of interest and commitment to the project from the NPO, faculty, and students?
Effort and duration	• Is the project scope consistent with the effort and duration available to the faculty–student team(s)?
Project type	• What type of project [16] (training, professional services, systems selection, support, systems projects, product) is being proposed and how consistent is it with the course objectives? • Can the project be conceived as a systems selection or products project?
Thematic focus	• Is this project consistent with your areas of thematic focus?
Likelihood of success	• Can you define success for this project? • What is the likelihood that this project can be successfully completed to satisfy the objectives of both the NPO and student learning outcomes? • How difficult is this project to complete relative to the student talent that will be working on the project?

Relational structure	• What is the relational structure like between the NPO and the faculty–student team? George [3] defines the relational structure to include "the initial introduction, the communication chain, the identification of the decision makers, and the recipients of the project deliverables." He argues that a partnership structure should:
	  ○ "Facilitate meaningful contact between groups having equal status
	  ○ Have a group consensus system based on partner participation
	  ○ Provide sufficient guidance to understand cultural disconnects."

Table 25.2. *Continued*

Factor	Description
Relational structure (*cont.*)	The notion of collaboration among equals is an important concept that was reinforced by a number of authors [9, 11].
Transition and sustainability	Is there clarity on how the project results will be transitioned to and sustained by the NPO with expectations that can be met by the faculty–student team?

tion to something that would actually work than to over or under build something that will fail to meet the objectives.

It is important that the community partner have a proper sense of what they will be receiving as a result of the project. In many cases, they will be receiving a preproduction prototype for purposes of a field trial. In the case of a field prototype, care must be taken to ensure that all involved in the project understand the temporary nature of the solution and the goal of collecting field feedback. Not doing so can cause serious upheaval when system prototypes are taken from the field and NPO staff and community members do not understand why this is the case or do not know the long-term plan for the system.

25.2.4   Course Structure

For curricular-based approaches to SL in CIS, there are a variety of ways to structure courses. In this section, a number of approaches and considerations are outlined related to SL in CIS. There are a variety of objectives that must be fulfilled by an SL in CIS course. As stated in Chapter 2, "In a project-based course, there are three timescales that must be in synch student learning, project development, and the academic calendar (semester, quarter, or term)." Thus, care must be taken to ensure that any course structure recognizes and synchronizes these timescales.

In order to support the sustainability and ongoing management of an SL in CIS project, it is advisable for courses to be *multigenerational*. A multigenerational course is one in which students who are in different stages (freshman, sophomore, junior, senior) of their college program may participate in the same project at the same time. In the case of the EPICS, students span all four undergraduate years [1]. The roles that EPICS students play in courses evolve over time as expertise and maturing occurs. The multigenerational project model is a best practice of the Collaboratory [9]: "... [a] best practice in the Collaboratory is forming project teams that include students from multiple years of study to enable peer mentoring and sustain transitions between team leaders and members." The Butler EPICS Program supports multigenerational teams as well: "Our EPICS teams are vertically integrated to include students from second-semester freshman to senior year. They earn required (or elective) academic credit that counts toward their graduation. Such teams are also multidisciplinary and are open to any major" [12].

A second element of course structure has to do with *multidisciplinary* teams. This is the idea of students from different fields of study (both within CIS and outside of CIS) becoming members of teams that are collaborating on a project. Such teams can be formed from within the same class or as part of multiple classes who chose to collaborate and work on the same project. Multidisciplinary teams have the advantages of bringing a broader skill set to teams and allowing some level of specialization to occur on the teams. The EPICS experience suggests that "About 25% of the students are from outside of engineering or computing. Multidisciplinary teams add richness to the learning experience and produce more effective designs that can be used by a broad set of users" [1]. In another case [14], a technical communication class collaborated with a software engineering class on the same project. The author points out that "The students in the technical communication class practice their skills by developing the documentation for the software, which frees more time for the software engineering students to develop the software and also provides both classes the opportunity to work within a real-world industry scenario."

Communication can be a problem for teams, even when they are in the same class. For this reason, it is strongly suggested that students establish a regular meeting time one or two days per week outside of class to ensure that they are routinely communicating with each other. Students should also be required to post attendance and meeting notes. A note of caution is in order concerning multidisciplinary teams. As pointed out by Werner [2], "communications between teams proved to be a problem. Many of our students work outside jobs to pay for college, and the classes' lecture and laboratory dates and times did not allow the two course sections to meet during school hours."

Multisemester projects are a cornerstone of some SL in CIS programs. For example, "Having students on the project for multiple semesters is a cornerstone of the EPICS model as it eliminates the restriction of the timing of a semester" [1]. In some cases, SL in CIS programs allow their courses to be taken for a *varying number of credit hours:*

> The rationale behind offering each course as two or three credit hour (e.g., CSSE 482 or CSSE 483) is simply to provide some schedule flexibility to students. For instance, some students only need 2 hours to graduate, or wish to fill their schedule during a specific semester. Initially, we expected less work-

load from students who registered to the two-credit course. However, it quickly became apparent that such distinction was not necessary and that was never
an issue. [12]

In a number of cases, the SL in CIS course model takes the form of either
a capstone senior experience course or a software engineering course. For
example, at the University of Wisconsin–Eau Claire [5], a senior capstone
SL in CIS model is employed in their Information Systems major. This is
similarly the case at Messiah College where a two-course SL in CIS senior
capstone course experience is required for all of our CIS majors. Given that
software engineering is about the creation and evolution of software systems, it follows that courses in software engineering are a good fit for service-learning [1, 12, 13, 14, 45].

There is also the controversial subject of *requiring* students to do a service-learning course to meet graduation requirements. Some would argue
that any notion of required service is itself an oxymoron. Others would argue that required service is a useful construct for those who might not otherwise be exposed to community service. In a number of cases, an SL in CIS
course is a graduation requirement. The list of institutions requiring a service-learning course includes Messiah College [47], Washington and Jefferson [4], Florida Gulf Coast University [10], and the University of Wisconsin–Eau Claire [5]. The Butler EPICS Program went through some evolution
in this respect. Early on, service-learning was an elective, but this changed:

> Since 2010 however, we started requiring all CS and SE majors to take at least
> one semester of EPICS for graduation. This decision was made based on the
> strong recommendations coming from our CSSE advisory board, the positive
> feedback from our students as well as the suggestion of an external reviewer. It
> is worthwhile mentioning that despite the one-semester of EPICS requirement
> for graduation, we have observed that most of the students tend to register to
> our EPICS courses several semesters (some students use the additional hours as
> elective credit for graduation and some simply accrue extra hours). Once stu-
> dents register to EPICS, they soon recognize the opportunity to gain valuable
> experience and balance their technical and soft skills. Also, by taking EPICS
> during consecutive semesters they become experienced and build momentum
> on a specific project which allows them to become leaders of their teams. [12]

In a number of cases, students may require some level of supplemental instruction beyond the normal curriculum to be prepared for an SL in CIS project. In the case of some institutions (Messiah College [9, 47], Butler University [12], and FGCU [10]), this is a motivation for making SL in CIS a
two-course sequence. These courses provide students with prerequisite
knowledge they will need to be successful in a SL in CIS project class. For
example, one author [6] states that

[I]t is important that the student be prepared for any service-learning project by having experience with the artifacts or standards which they will use in the project itself. This means that they should be familiar with artifacts ... such as a ConOps or SDD, and even provided a template for use. These could be modified or expanded versions that were used in an advanced analysis and design class. Coding and HCI standards that were used in previous coursework can also be used for the service-learning project. This has the benefit of using something that the student is familiar with and something that has already had a grading rubric created.

Similarly, students are often not familiar with project management practices [4], defensive coding techniques, scalability issues, and usability concerns for building software to be used by real users. They may have not had prior exposure to life cycle models, agile methods, design techniques, structured analysis, and design or development tools.

25.2.5   Technology

Technology plays a central role in SL in CIS programs. However, technology choices for SL in CIS projects are often constrained by the curriculum and technologies covered in courses taught within the curriculum. For this reason, it is important to make sure that the technology needs of SL in CIS projects and the technologies taught in the curriculum are of mutual influence. Care must be taken not to use technologies in SL in CIS projects that are new to students. There are certain known challenges to learning new technologies concurrent with using them on projects [12].

In many cases, it makes sense to consider standardizing on a *default-technology stack* to be used on all SL in CIS projects. Although there may be exceptions to the default-technology stack for a specific project, it is useful to stipulate a default-technology stack. Typical default-technology stacks include presentation-layer technologies, business-logic-layer technologies, and database-layer technologies. In addition, if there is significant involvement in mobile applications, one may want to standardize on a wireless carrier, mobile-application development environment [47] and mobile device types. Messiah College recently standardized their SL in CIS technology stack to include PHP [48], MySQL [49], and Tomcat [50]. For an example of another technology stack for SL in CIS, see [2]. Clearly, the curriculum should include modules that educate the students about the default-technology stack.

This author provides a cautionary tale on the selection of technology for a particular project. In one of his earlier SL in CIS projects, he was working closely with a software engineer in the area who was volunteering to support the project. From the volunteer's industrial-strength software engineering perspective, he thought the team should use Ruby on Rails [51] as part of their technology stack to build a Web application. This author agreed and required the team to do so. The team really struggled with learning these technologies, despite efforts by this author and his volunteer colleague. With about a third of the semester left, the students had made little demonstrable progress on the system. They insisted that they be allowed to use PHP [48] to rapidly develop the system. Within two weeks, the students had a demonstrable initial version of the system they used to get feedback from the NPO. The point of this story is to make sure you do not select technologies that are ahead of where your students are in their learning and maturity as software engineers.

It is useful to have some form of canonical architecture in mind for applications developed in a SL in CIS setting. Werner and MacLean [2] discuss an example application architecture they use at Wentworth Institute of Technology. In the mobile application space, Nejmeh and Dean [47] discuss a reference architecture they used in developing a mobile-desktop Web application. Much like standardizing a technology stack, defining a standardized application architecture promotes understanding and can accelerate application development.

Environmental factors and technology limitations play a big role in international SL in CIS projects. For example, a recent SL in CIS project was a mobile application project fielded in Zambia [47]. One of the assumptions the project team made, based on discussions with in-country NPO colleagues, was that electricity would be readily available in the villages in order to charge the mobile phones. Unfortunately, when the team got into the countryside, they learned that many people do not have easy access to electricity. Thus, community volunteers using the proposed system had to walk miles and pay a significant fee to get the mobile phones charged at a phone charging station. The project would have been well-served to consider the use of solar chargers for the mobile phones. Similarly, Skon [7] reports on environmental challenges in Belize: "unreliable and intermittent power, no air conditioning, no insulation even if the room was air conditioned, salty sea air, dust, heat, un- reliable and slow Internet (in the few places where Internet is available)" [7].

Earlier in the chapter, the use of open-source technologies for SL in CIS was discussed. This is becoming an increasingly popular option due to the cost, security, availability, and reliability of open-source technologies. These attributes also fit well within the NPO community. In addition to serving the needs of NPOs, using open-source software also prepares students for the workforce where a considerable amount of open-source technology is in use. As stated in Chapter 5, open-source software "in contrast to proprietary software, is software that is licensed to be studied, shared, modified, and redistributed." There are many open-source technologies and applications available at sourceforge.net [43] that should be considered when doing SL in CIS projects. For instance, projects that require virtual collaboration should consider the use of Appropedia.org [52]. This open-source education tool provides "a free and open-source wiki-based tool for collaborative solutions in such areas as sustainability, poverty reduction, and international development" [46].

Finally, for the SL in CIS projects involving the refurbishment and repurposing of computers, consideration should be given to the Microsoft Refurbishers Program (MAP) [53]. The BOOTUP project [18] makes extensive use of this program. It allows organizations to obtain licenses for Microsoft products at discounted prices. The process involves "obtaining reference letters from our community partners and submitting an application. Through the MAR program, we were able to obtain Microsoft Office XP for $5.00 per key (2007 prices)" [18].

25.2.6   Process

This section highlights process lessons learned for SL in CIS.

25.2.6.1   Life Cycle Models. Just as with industrial software projects, there are a variety of life cycle models that can be used in SL in CIS projects. A life cycle model is simply a definition of the steps used to create, design, develop, and sustain a system. In all cases, emphasis should be placed on team life cycle models as SL in CIS projects should be done on a team (as opposed to an individual) basis. A review of the chapters in the book reveals that two primary life cycle models are being used in SL in CIS projects: the waterfall model [54] and some variant of the Agile development model [55].

The waterfall model [54] is depicted in Figure 25.1 and consists of a linear sequence of steps. This model requires that you obtain reasonably accurate and stable requirements for a system early in the process. The traditional artifacts of the waterfall life cycle model [2, 6] include a project charter, requirements document, system design document, code, test cases and reports, user manuals, and so on. Although some SL in CIS projects have successfully used the waterfall model [2, 6], it is not suited for such projects for the following reasons:

- Typically, the requirements of an SL in CIS project are very dynamic and evolve incrementally over the life of the project. In many cases,

Figure 25.1. Waterfall life cycle model.

NPO staff do not fully appreciate the potential of IT until they see some demonstrations of system capability. This often leads to a clearer understanding of requirements. Thus, the waterfall model may not be a good fit for SL in CIS projects.

- For faculty, students, and NPO staff, it is important to show demonstrable progress that can be used to solicit feedback and refine system functionality. Early and frequent demonstration of progress allows for the project to be corrected early on before too much time has elapsed in the semester. NPO staff often provide much better feedback on system mock-ups and prototypes than they do on dry, lengthy requirements documents. Furthermore, requirements documents do not necessarily paint a good picture of system workflows and user interfaces. Since the waterfall model focuses on completely defined requirements before system construction can begin, it is not a good fit for many SL in CIS projects.

- It is also important for students to accelerate their learning of new technologies that they may be using for the first time. The waterfall model often delays hands-on use of the technology until fairly late in the project, when it may be too late to switch technologies.

The agile model [55] is depicted in Figure 25.2 and consists of an iterative set of steps. This model assumes that requirements will be dynamic and evolving over the life of the project. It also requires short-duration (2–3 weeks) sprints that must conclude with a demonstration of a running system. Artifacts for each sprint iteration of the agile model include a prioritized backlog list of brief requirements statements, some design representation, code, test cases/results, and proof-of-concept demonstrations. Many SL in CIS programs [1, 9, 12, 14, 47] employ a variant of the agile method.

Figure 25.2. Agile development method.

When this author uses the Agile development method in his SL in CIS projects, an initial prioritized product backlog list of requirements is established, with inputs from NPO staff members, faculty members, and students. The requirements are briefly described (one or two sentences) and prioritized in terms of relative importance. At the beginning of each sprint, the team holds a sprint planning meeting to determine the items on the sprint backlog list they will work on in the next sprint. This is based on priority, resource capacity, and estimated effort required to complete items on the sprint backlog list. In addition, a work-break down structure (WBS) is created for each item on the sprint backlog list and the work is assigned to team members. The teams then work on the selected sprint backlog list following the WBS. In the above-mentioned classes, sprints are two weeks in duration. During a sprint, no changes are allowed to either the duration or content (items from the backlog list). Each class period during a sprint begins with each team member briefly discussing three things: progress since the last class, planned progress by the next class, and any open issues they are facing. At the conclusion of the sprint, four things occur:

- A demonstration of a running system
- A review and update of the sprint backlog list
- A review of the sprint process to see if anything about it should change
- The next sprint is planned

If possible, we have an NPO representative present (physically or virtually) for the sprint demo at the conclusion of each sprint.

The Agile model addresses the concerns previously cited about the waterfall model, namely:

- It assumes that requirements are constantly evolving and highly dynamic, and readily accommodates this reality.
- Every short-duration sprint (2–3 weeks) concludes with a demonstration of functionality. This allows NPOs to provide early and regular feedback on a true representation of the system (not merely a document).
- Student learning of the technology occurs early and in the actual setting of completing functionality for the NPO system.

25.2.6.2   *Requirements Management.* Any discussion of the SL in CIS process would be incomplete without some discussion of requirements management. Industrial experience demonstrates that the requirements discovery and capture process is among the most difficult and error prone. Poorly defined and understood requirements are a major source of software project failures. Now add to all of this the fact that NPOs are not always able to clearly articulate their needs and students have typically never done requirements discovery. The result is that the requirements part of SL in CIS projects is among the most risky aspects of a project and has certainly led to the failure of many projects. This risk can be greatly reduced by the professor being personally involved (alongside of their students) in the requirements discovery and articulation process. The professional background of this author as a software engineer has been a great asset in this respect. In a number of cases, the author has completed a requirements discovery process with the NPO and developed a draft requirements document prior to the start of the SL in CIS project course. A detailed description of the requirements discovery and articulate process can be found in [56]. In short, this requirements process results in a prioritized list of requirements. Priorities on requirements are critical for SL in CIS projects to ensure that the most important features of the system are completed first.

25.2.6.3   Open Source. Another interesting process concern involves the development of an open-source software product. The HFOSS Program (see Chapter 5) is a great example of an SL in CIS program developing open-source software products for the NPO community. The HFOSS community has published a book [57] on their process model and approach. In addition, those interested in exploring an open-source development model should review the seminal work by Raymond [58] on this subject.

25.2.6.4   Project Roles. Some SL in CIS projects have embraced the idea of explicitly defined roles, whereas others have been informal about role definition. In the case of Bowling Green University (see Chapter 13), they have adopted a model in which

> [A]ll students in a team were to be developers with a shared role in project management. Individual software development roles, such as coach (team leader), tracker, end user (student customer), tester, designer, tool guy, integrator, presenter, documenter, and installer, were elected within each team in order to instill some personal responsibilities in students. ... [T]o complete each iteration, the teams were responsible for determining among themselves which team members would fulfill which roles. The teams were also responsible for determining who would complete which tasks on which days to ensure they completed the iterations by the deadlines and were meeting the needs of the community partner.

When there are multiple teams working on a single project across one or more classes, this author advocates that each team name a technical lead and an integration lead. The technical lead is essentially the team leader on technical matters and facilitates team discussion on key design and technical decisions. The integration lead plays the important role of coordinating with all other teams on everything from file and API naming conventions, to doing integrated nightly builds of source code to ensuring that teams are using the correct versions of components in their software. The integration role has proved to be extremely valuable and it remedies some of the integration challenges faced by other SL in CIS projects [2].

25.2.6.5 Project Management. Project management is the discipline of managing project scope, quality, resources, communication, time, procurement, and risk. For many undergraduate students, project management is a foreign concept. The vast majority of assignments students have completed (prior to enrollment in an SL in CIS course) are single-person projects prescribed in well-defined terms by their professor. SL in CIS projects are anything but prescribed and they are, by definition, team endeavors. Therefore, the discipline of project management must be employed to successfully complete SL in CIS projects.

The importance of communication with NPO partners is emphasized by Hannon [4]. Communication is especially important in SL in CIS projects as NPO staff, faculty and students are learning new terminology and processes and must also manage each other's expectations and schedules. Hannon offers a project management-centered approach to SL in CIS [4].

The issue of timing is addressed in several of the chapters in the book. In Chapter 20, Werner and MacLean make the important point that

> Project participants may have different goals and time schedules. The most obvious difference was that the development effort conformed to an academic schedule whereas the client followed its normal annual schedule. In some instances key contacts on the client side became unavailable as they went on vacation or were otherwise diverted. Meanwhile, the clock was ticking on the developer's side; when the project was initiated it took until midsemester just to nail down the requirements, leaving little time for design and implementation. Curiously, the client appeared to be infinitely patient, never voicing criticism to us on how long it was taking. In retrospect, the project may have been less important to them than it was to us.

Weekly status reports are a common tool used to monitor progress [12]. In some cases, a common complaint among NPO partners in project postmortems is "that there was a lack of communications with the student team members. The instructor can try to head off this problem by requiring weekly update memos on the project status" [6].

Project wiki sites and blogs are beginning to be a common practice among SL in CIS practitioners [9, 45]. Wiki portals allow for work products to be viewed, commented on, and edited by faculty, students, and NPO staff. In some cases [4], a project blog is used, "in which students reflect upon their work and experiences, and all members of the department read and post to this blog as well. Many of our weekly department meetings include discussions of the students' work, and we have formal meetings with the students at midterm (preliminary defense) and at the end of the term (final defense)."

A common practice among SL in CIS practitioners is the use of the final project report and presentation. In the SL in CIS courses taught by this author, all teams make a final project presentation on the final class session. A template for a typical final project presentation follows:

A. Executive summary slide
B. Project introduction
C. Project overview
   - End-to-end project presentation from conception to its completion
   - Phase summary, lessons learned, and issues addressed
D. Application demonstration
E. Application impact: Discuss actual or projected impact of application versus system goals, questions, and metrics.
   - Do you feel the goals will be met and why/why not?
F. Project strengths/weaknesses: Summarize the strengths and weaknesses of the project as a whole.
G. NPO assessment: Discuss NPO's reaction to application and project as a whole (preferably via a video clip on website).
H. Lessons learned: Discuss the significant lessons you learned as a project team in terms of project management, life cycle models, techniques, and ideas you will use in the future.

The Butler EPICS Program offers another view of a final report (see Chapter 3):

Every EPICS group ... submits a comprehensive report at the end of each semester along with a final presentation given to the client and any other interested stakeholders. ... The report typically entails the problem statement, detailed requirements specifications, both short-term (i.e., for the semester) and long-term project goals, a project plan with timeline and milestones, any design, implementation and testing artifacts, and various technical manuals, tutorials, and other related documentation. In addition, the dossier describes each member's role, goals and accomplishments for that semester. Also, it contains copies of all weekly status reports with individual member's detailed contributions and a copy of the final PowerPoint presentation.

25.2.6.6 ***Public Dissemination Models.*** Public presentation and discussion of project results is common practice in SL in CIS. At Messiah College, the school hosts an annual scholarship day during which all SL in CIS projects present their results to the public. For projects that are of high quality, faculty–student teams routinely author and submit papers about the work to journals [47, 59]. Similarly, at the Butler EPICS Program, "all teams are typically expected to prepare and give two separate presentations at the end of each semester; one for the client team (usually nontechnical) and another presentation (which is technical in nature) for the faculty advisor. In some cases, both presentations are combined into a single one (when the client has technical background)" [12].

Hannon (see Chapter 9) points out some of the challenges in public dissemination:

> Public dissemination means that the students should engage in some activity that reports the results of their service project to a broader community. It became increasingly more uncomfortable to have the clients, and in some cases other members of the College community, present. Where the clients and casual observers from the community would see success and accomplishment, we saw opportunities missed, objectives left unfulfilled, and substandard results that we knew we had to be critical of. For a few years, we simply did not invite these other constituencies to the presentations, which allowed us to hold the students to a more rigorous standard, but which also had the effect of minimizing the public dissemination element of the course. It also deprived the students of much-needed validation for their hard work, and the clients of the opportunity to publicly express their gratitude to the students, the department, and the College. After much experimentation, we have decided on a two-event solution: we have an open house on the last day of the semester, when we invite the College and the clients to come and learn about the students' projects; and we have a department defense two days later, on the reading day before final exams, when the students defend their work according to the department's program-level learning outcomes.

25.2.6.7 ***Transition Planning.*** Transition planning for SL in CIS projects is critical. It should start at the beginning of the project and be a consideration in the vetting of a project. Many SL in CIS projects have achieved reasonable student outcomes, but have only temporarily met the needs of NPOs. As the systems age and require changes, the lack of a proper transition and sustainability plan often leads to applications that are either no longer used or are a hindrance to an NPO. As part of transition planning, it is important for NPO staff to understand the status of the project. NPO staff "are entitled to know that work on their projects will continue if needed after the semester concludes. Similarly, the developers need some assurance that the client will maintain its commitment to a project even if there is some rotation in … personnel" [2]. Hannon [4] states that a transition plan "details what work needs to be done, and when, to maintain the new technology (system updates, data entry, the posting of fresh information, etc.). It also involves getting clients to sign a final Deliverable Acceptance Form, whereby the clients can indicate aspects of the project that they feel remain incomplete."

25.2.7 Impact Assessment

There are a variety of impacts envisioned as a result of performing SL in CIS projects. In this section, we outline models for impact assessment related to (1) student outcomes, (2) NPO outcomes, (3) faculty outcomes, and (4) program outcomes.

25.2.7.1 Student Outcome Assessment. An appropriate grading rubric is a key element in assessing student outcomes. Such a rubric is difficult to define for SL in CIS courses. Exams are difficult to give for such courses. Progress can be difficult to measure and assess. In addition, individual student commitment and contribution to projects varies widely. Furthermore, there is a sense in which the team as a whole is being graded on their collective efforts. As Homkes points out [6], a community service grade is simply not a matter of putting in the time. One must really assess the impact that the SL in CIS project is likely to have on the NPO. Thus, clearly, hours put in on a project is not an effective assessment indicator [6].

This author has evolved this grading rubric for his SL in CIS courses over the past eight years. Table 25.3 is a sample grading rubric for an upcoming SL in CIS course this author will be teaching.

A few items are worth highlighting in this grading rubric. First, note that 3% of the student grade is based on an exam about the NPO we are partnering with on the project. This exam covers the basics of the mission of the NPO, communities they serve, their desired outcomes and results to date, and a statement of the problem being addressed by our project. This exam is given within the first two weeks of the semester, after an NPO staff member has presented to our class and students have had a chance to review their website and related materials. The purpose of the exam is to make sure the students have some understanding of the content and mission of the NPO they are supporting.

Second, note that the seven project milestones correspond to each of the two-week sprints during the semester, with an emphasis on the later milestones. The student's individual contribution to the project accounts for 10% of their grade. Students complete peer reviews twice during the semester on each member of their team. Peer reviews allow students to rate and comment on each individual teammate in terms of: contribution to the team, work ethic, timeliness, communication, problem-solving ability, taking initiative to solve problems, and working/communicating effectively within the group. The

Table 25.3. Sample SL in CIS course grading rubric

Component	% of Grade
Class Participation and Preparation. Preparation for and participating in class discussions is an important part of the learning process. Read the prerequisite materials prior to class so you can actively participate in class discussion. In addition, your team will be called on to discuss its results to date in class. Class participation is more than showing up for class prepared and with your assignments done. It also means actively participating in class discussion, challenging ideas, synthesizing new ideas, and being an active listener.	7%
Organization and Project Exam. Students will be examined on their knowledge of the mission of their sponsor organization and the goals of their project.	3%
Team Project. this is the semester-long team project, broken down as follows:	%
• Milestone 1: Product BackLog List	1%
• Milestone 2: Sprint 1	3%
• Milestone 3: Sprint 2	4%
• Milestone 4: Sprint 3	5%
• Milestone 5: Sprint 4	7%
• Milestone 6: Sprint 5	10%
• Milestone 7: Sprint 6	<u>15%</u>
• TOTAL	45%
Individual Contribution to Team Project. I will personally assess your individual contribution to the overall team project based on my personal observations and those of your teammates.	10%
NPO Assessment and Probable Impact. The NPO will assess your overall effort, communication, and project results. In addition, I will work with them to assess the probable impact of the project on the NPO.	30%
Service-Learning Reflections. Each student will be responsible for producing a document that reflects on service-learning and community engagement.	5%

NPO's assessment of the project and team and our collective assessment of the probable impact of the project on the NPO account for 30% of the grade. This is clearly an important component of the grade. Finally, the students are given guided prompts throughout the semester to reflect on regarding service-learning, the NPO we are working with, their notions of service, and so on. At the end of the semester, the students are required to submit a 3–5 page paper on their overall reflections of the project and how they have evolved over the semester. This reflection paper accounts for 5% of their grade.

A sample grading rubric offered by the Butler EPICS Program included "the following criteria: peer reviews, the client's performance evaluation of the team, all project deliverables produced, and, of course, the instructor's ratings" [12]. Another sample grading rubric was offered by Homkes of Purdue [6] and it included reflective writing assignments, project updates and presentations, client evaluations, peer evaluations, concept of operations and design documentation, project reports/user documentation, and product demonstrations.

A number of authors [9, 10, 14, 47] have discussed the importance of reflection. Homkes [6] states:

> [A]t the beginning of the semester [we] require a short paper on the definition and application of service-learning in IT. This assignment, almost a prereflection, was used to make sure that the student understood what was expected during the semester and also to prepare the student for a final written reflection at the end of the term. The final reflection can be merged into a project postmortem so that the reflection occurs as part of an accepted IT artifact. ... Some prompting questions to the students should include how the project developed, what went right or wrong, what should have been changed, ethical questions encountered, and so on. Another prompting question could be on what knowledge or skills were required to complete the project that the student did not have at the start of the semester. This can lead into a discussion of personal growth....

25.2.7.2 NPO Outcome Assessment. A common technique of SL in CIS practitioners is to survey the NPOs they work with to get their assessment of the project [12]. George (see Chapter 24) effectively addressed NPO outcome assessment. The author suggests "three simple straightforward questions to appraise the satisfaction of the community partner:

- Have the customers' needs been met?
- Is the project sustainable and maintainable by the customer?
- Does the project respect the environment and make effective use of local renewable resources?"

Homkes (see Chapter 21) provides a NPO assessment framework regarding topics to be covered on an NPO survey. He suggests that NPO assessment topics include:

- Written and oral communications
- Meeting punctuality and involvement
- Appropriate attire and grooming
- Listening to agency representatives regarding needs
- Positive and willing attitude
- Accurate sense of personal capability
- Problem-solving ability
- Overall opinion of the work completed

He also suggests that it is important to have a conversation with the NPO partner to clarify or amplify their survey responses.

For some projects, it is easy to tangibly see the impact of the project on the NPO [18, 19, 47]. For projects that will be used on an ongoing basis by the NPO, it is good practice to explicitly plan to collect qualitative and quantitative data on project impact.

Noteworthy by its absence was any significant mention of faculty and students assessing an NPO partner. The quality of NPOs as partners varies dramatically. It would be helpful to consider how faculty and students might provide feedback to NPOs on their performance during the project.

25.2.7.3 Faculty Outcome Assessment. It is difficult to assess the impact that SL in CIS projects have on faculty. The faculty assessment framework at Messiah College is informative. All faculty members at Messiah College are assessed in three areas: teaching, institutional service, and scholarship. Remarkably, faculty involvement in SL in CIS positively impacts all three areas. In terms of teaching, student assessments reveal that students greatly value being involved in SL in CIS projects. Much of the anecdotal data and conversations with students indicate that SL in CIS projects positively impact student learning outcomes.

SL in CIS projects have had a very positive impact in the area of institutional service. Some of the SL in CIS projects completed by this author benefited Messiah College [60]. All of the projects completed by this author were very consistent with the mission of the college and, therefore, were seen as acts of institutional service as well.

Finally, regarding scholarship, this author has had ample opportunities to publish papers with students and others about his SL in CIS projects. This book is itself another form of scholarship that has resulted from the work of the SL in CIS community. In all of these areas (teaching, service, and scholarship), the SL in CIS work this author has been involved in has significantly benefited his standing at the institution as reflected by term-tenure renewal and promotion to full professor. Messiah College is a very supportive institution when it comes to its embrace of SL in CIS.

25.2.7.4 Program Outcome Assessment. No discussion of SL in CIS outcomes would be complete without some mention of accreditation. A number of the chapters in the book (e.g., [2, 10, 21]) have addressed the impact of SL in CIS on the accreditation process. The two major accreditation bodies, ABET [61] and AACSB [67], both have elements of their assessment frameworks to which SL in CIS can positively contribute. For example, the ABET accreditation framework [61] includes (under Criteria 3, Student Outcomes) the following elements:

- An ability to function on multidisciplinary teams
- An understanding of professional and ethical responsibility
- The broad education necessary to understand the impact of engineering solutions in global, economic, environmental, and societal contexts
- A knowledge of contemporary issues

25.3 FUTURE DIRECTIONS

My own work on SL in CIS over the past decade, along with the experiences of many others (including the book chapter authors) has informed my view of some important future directions for SL in CIS. There is much to say on this topic. I thought it would be effective to articulate my views of the future of SL in CIS in the form of ten imperatives. I believe that if each of the imperatives were taken seriously, they would dramatically increase the quality and quantity of SL in CIS. This, in turn, would lead to significant benefits to faculty, students, NPOs and the communities served by SL in CIS projects.

1. *The SL in CIS community must be more intentional about pursuing systems selection and products project types.* Many of the SL in CIS projects that have been done to date are custom developed, one-off system projects [16] for a specific NPO. Very few of the projects done to date are either of a systems selection or products product type. The importance of these two project types was discussed earlier in this chapter. In the case of systems selection project types, there are many existing commercial-off-the-shelf and open-source products that can be configured to meet the needs of NPOs. Furthermore, such offerings have defined customer-support models and sustaining engineering models that will serve the long-term needs of NPOs. In the case of products product types, developing a highly configurable solution that can be used by multiple NPOs offers tremendous leverage and impact potential. Even more strategic is the use of open-source software development models for conceiving and evolving products [13]. Such a model also offers the leverage of a global development community to support and advance the capabilities of products. Students benefit greatly by engaging in systems selection projects as much of the commercial and NPO world use configured commercial-off-the-shelf or open source products compared to custom developed systems. In doing so, students will be more equipped for the realities they will be experiencing upon graduation. Similarly, students would benefit greatly by engaging in the development of products that serve multiple NPOs. Issues such as understanding the broad needs of a market and developing configurable products to support them are only truly understood when software is developed

from a product perspective. Such projects will be of great benefit to students and provide faculty rich places from which to teach and mentor.

2. *The sustainability and longevity of projects must be an important consideration in the planning, selection, development and deployment.* In this context, the term sustainability refers to the long-term ability of faculty–student teams and NPO staff to maintain, evolve, and support the software and systems initially developed in a service-learning context over time. A chronic problem facing all SL in CIS programs is what happens when the students who worked on a project complete the SL in CIS course or graduate. Clearly, cocurricular structures aid in the sustainability of projects; however, such cocurricular groups do not exist on all campuses, nor do they always have the capacity to sustain all projects over time. Consideration must be given to improve the models for the sustainability of SL in CIS projects. The ASF model [14] offers promise in this area. NPOs will benefit by having systems that are long-lived and sustainable over time. Faculty and students will benefit by reducing the long-term burden on them for ongoing support for systems they develop. In addition, the practice of effectively transitioning usable systems to NPOs is an important skill to have as students enter the workforce.

3. *The SL in CIS community must develop better methods and tools for assessing the impact and outcomes of projects on NPOs, the communities they serve, faculty, students, and institutions.* The motivation section of this chapter speaks to the desired outcomes and reasons for doing SL in CIS. What is not so evident is how well SL in CIS programs are doing with respect to achieving these desired outcomes and results. Questions such as "Were student learning outcomes improved as a result of teaching a course using a service-learning pedagogy?" and "How is the NPO better able to serve their communities of interest as a result of this project?" are but two of the key questions that must be answered in the future. Consideration should be given to appropriate mechanisms for faculty and students to assess NPO performance. Research needs to be done on how to best measure the impact of SL in CIS across all stakeholder groups, including NPOs, the communities they serve, faculty, students, and institutions of higher education. Impact and outcome assessment tools will provide accountability for and insights on how to improve SL in CIS. This will be of benefit to NPOs, faculty, and students.

4. *Sustainable funding models to support SL in CIS activities must be further developed and advanced to ensure the viability and growth of SL in CIS programs.* There are expenses involved in doing SL in CIS. Such expenses include equipment, travel, paraprofessional support, and release time for faculty administering or managing an SL in CIS program. Although several of the SL in CIS programs in the book discussed funding models [9, 13], it is clear that many of these programs were not well funded. The SL in CIS community would be well served by exploring grants, corporate sponsorship, and oth-

er forms of development fund-raising to support their needs. When SL in CIS programs reach a certain point of maturity, they have a need for funding to sustain their efforts. Such funding will benefit NPOs, faculty, and students; without it, some programs may not be able to continue.

5. *The SL in CIS community must develop guidelines for NPO partner selection and principles for being an effective NPO partner.* Many NPOs lack experience in partnering with academic institutions, especially in the realm of SL in CIS. The SL in CIS community would be well served by the development of guidelines for NPO partner selection. In addition, the development of a set of principles to guide NPO partners in their involvement in projects would be of value to both the NPO and academic communities. A common theme of the chapters in the book is the value of developing a few long-term NPO partnerships. NPOs will benefit from ongoing, long-term project engagement and support. Faculty will benefit from established relationships and understanding of how to best work with select NPOs. Students will benefit from a historical base of knowledge of how to work best with select NPOs by leveraging past projects and existing relationships with an NPO.

6. *The SL in CIS community must be more intentional in developing consortium models for conducting projects.* NPOs such as TechSoup [33] and Engineers Without Borders [35] have been instrumental in raising the awareness and response to NPOs in need of technology. NPO consortium models such as NetHope [38] and SL in CIS consortium models such as HFOSS [13] may well be key to addressing some of the aforementioned imperatives. In the case of NPO consortiums, banding together allows for a better understanding of common problems NPOs are facing and SL in CIS projects that could be developed to address these problems (think in terms of products that would serve the needs of the NPO consortium members). Such NPO consortiums could even be a source of sustainable funding to develop solutions to their problems. Similarly, SL in CIS academic consortiums would allow for more capacity and a diversity of resources to be pooled together to work on projects. Such consortiums could also help address the sustainability challenges by providing a larger resource pool. Such models will provide faculty opportunities for experience sharing and collaboration with other like-minded colleagues. Students will benefit from such consortium models by working in virtual communities that span multiple universities, cultures, and project types.

7. *The SL in CIS community must more aggressively embrace the principles of Agile processes and methods when developing projects.* The merits of Agile processes and methods in the context of SL in CIS were discussed earlier in the chapter. SL in CIS practitioners would be well served to embrace and employ Agile processes and methods in projects. The incremental and evolutionary development style of Agile methods fits well

with SL in CIS projects in which requirements are being constantly discovered and it is important to demonstrate regular and rapid progress. NPOs will benefit by having processes used on projects that provide early and frequent opportunities for feedback and readily accommodate an evolutionary requirements-discovery process. Faculty will benefit by having projects that proceed more smoothly due to using a development model that is a good fit for SL in CIS projects. Students will benefit by using a development model (Agile) that is widely used in the workforce. They will be better prepared to enter the workforce because of their experiences in using Agile methods.

8. *The SL in CIS community must more intentionally focus on the use of mobile technologies, especially in the developing world.* Mobile technologies, including wireless networks, devices, content, and applications, offer tremendous potential to global NPOs. This is especially true in the developing world where wireless networks and devices are ubiquitous and transportation is challenging [47]. Furthermore, the benefits of cost-effective, real-time mobile data collection in the developing world are becoming well established [47]. Virtually all sectors of interest to the NPO community can be impacted by mobile technologies, including health and human services, microfinance, agriculture, education, and commerce. MobileActive.org is a global network of people using mobile technology for social impact [62]. The SL in CIS community must more intentionally focus on the mobile platform. This might require the development of new courses and the acquisition of new equipment. For the past two years, I have focused my SL in CIS projects on mobile technologies. The students have warmly embraced this focus as their personal lives are also deeply vested in the mobile space (texting, twitter, and other forms of social media). Furthermore, the workforce has significant needs for people with skills in mobile technologies. This imperative also allows faculty to remain current in an important area of technology development—the mobile space.

9. *SL in CIS programs must embrace a curriculum and course model that supports multigenerational teams, multisemester courses and projects, and reentrant courses.* Speaking from first-hand experience, SL in CIS courses taught in the context of a single-semester course may be among the most constraining and difficult to manage of all SL in CIS courses. Typically, students can take such courses only once and they tend to be juniors or seniors. SL in CIS courses that are multigenerational allow for mentoring to occur between upper- and lower-level students. They also allow for a variety of skill and experience levels to exist in the class, thereby making it easier for a variety of project roles to be fulfilled. Multisemester courses allow for prerequisite skills to be developed in the initial course (an understanding of the NPO and their needs, project management, specific technology skills needed

to complete a given project, etc.) so that the focus of the sequel course can be on hands-on project development. Multisemester projects simply allow for larger projects that will require more than a single semester of development to be undertaken. In this case, care must be taken to manage project scope and ensure that the resulting work products (requirements, design, code, etc.) from one team can be used by the members of a successor team. Finally, as pointed out by the EPICS Programs [1, 12], the notion of allowing a student to take an SL in CIS project course multiple times is significant in terms of project sustainability and the ability of students to experience a variety of project roles as they mature.

10. *The SL in CIS community must more explicitly incorporate the cloud and SaaS deployment models as a means of lowering TCO and better serving NPOs.* NPOs often lack the IT resources and time to effectively use and manage IT. The advent of cloud computing and the SaaS model offer real promise as delivery and deployment vehicles for NPO-based solutions. The cloud computing offerings of Amazon EC2 [63], SalesForce.com's Force.com [64], Google's App Engine [65] and Oracle's public cloud offering [66] all provide meaningful cloud environments (database, application, and Web-server enabled) that are cost-effective and friendly to academic and NPO partners. The ability to remotely manage such applications and infrastructure (i.e., capacity on demand) can offer lower total cost of ownership (TCO) for fielding NPO solutions. Student exposure to cloud computing and SaaS delivery models will well equip them to deal with these ever-present solution models in the workforce. This imperative also allows faculty to remain current on an important area of technology development—cloud computing.

25.4 SUMMARY

This chapter summarizes many important lessons learned based on the collective experiences of the various chapter authors. These lessons learned should serve to guide new and established SL in CIS practitioners in their future project endeavors. In addition, the future directions section of this chapter should serve to motivate SL in CIS practitioners to think differently about how they conceive and perform SL in CIS projects moving forward.

ACKNOWLEDGMENTS

The author would like to acknowledge the contributions that many of his current and former CSC 333 and BIS 412 students have made to the ideas in this chapter. The author also wishes to acknowledge the authors of the chapters in this book whose work has improved this framework. The author is grateful to Messiah College and the Collaboratory for Strategic Partnerships and Applied Research, and the support they provided for this work. The author is also indebted to his many colleagues at Messiah College who have informed and influenced his understanding of SL in CIS. These colleagues include David Vader, Ray Norman, Chad Frey, and Scott Weaver. The author would like to thank Ian Thomas and Laurie Nejmeh for their reviews of earlier drafts of this chapter.

REFERENCES

1. Oakes, W., and Zoltowski, C. Chapter 2 in this volume.
2. Werner, M., and MacLean, L. Chapter 20 in this volume.
3. George, C. Chapter 24 in this volume.
4. Hannon, C. Chapter 9 in this volume.
5. Hilton, T., and Mowry, D. Chapter 11 in this volume.
6. Homkes, R. Chapter 21 in this volume.
7. Skon, J., and Karl, D. Chapter 22 in this volume..
8. Morelli, R., Tucker A., and de Lanerolle. "The Humanitarian FOSS Project." Open Source Business Resource, Talent First Network, Ottawa, December 2010. http://www.osbr.ca/ojs/index.php/osbr/article/view/1225/1173, retrieved November 15, 2011.
9. Vader. D. Chapter 4 in this volume.
10. Zidek, L. Chapter 10 in this volume.
11. Hsin, W., and Ganzen, O. Chapter 12 in this volume.
12. Linos P. Chapter 3 in this volume.
13. Morelli, R., de Lanerolle, T., and Tucker, A. Chapter 5 in this volume.
14. Chao. J., and Warnke, J. Chapter 13 in this volume.
15. Lima, M., and Oakes, W. (2006). *Service Learning Engineering in Your Community.* Wildwood, MO: Great Lakes Press.
16. Nejmeh, B. Chapter 1 in this volume.
17. Beisser, S. Chapter 14 in this volume.
18. Mathew, W., and Maxwell, C. Chapter 17 in this volume.
19. Ros-Giralt, J., Launglucknavalai, K., Casanova, J. and Maxwell, C. Chapter 18 in this volume.
20. SIGCSE, http://www.sigcse.org/events/symposia.
21. ITCSE, http://www.sigcse.org/events/iticse.
22. ICER, http://www.sigcse.org/events/icer.
23. SIGITE, http://www.sigite.org/events/sigite-2011.
24. ASEE, http://www.asee.org/conferences-and-events/conferences.
25. CCSC, http://www.conferencearoundtheworld.com/conference/information_technology_conference/13th_annual_ccsc_northwestern_regional_conference.html
26. INSITE, http://informingscience.org/proceedings/.

27. ISECON, http://isecon.org/.

28. *Journal of Computing Sciences in Colleges,* http://dl.acm.org/citation.cfm?id=J420.

29. *Michigan Journal of Community Service Learning* (MJCSL), http://ginsberg.umich.edu/mjcsl/.

30. *International Journal for Service Learning in Engineering* (PSU), http://sedtapp.psu.edu/humanitarian/article.php?id=5.

31. Messiah College Promotion Policies, http://www.messiah.edu/academics/coe/documents/SECTION-6.pdf.

32. Agape Center, Messiah College http://www.messiah.edu/external_programs/agape/.

33. TechSoup, www.techsoup.org.

34. Sparked, http://www.sparked.com/.

35. Engineers Without Borders, http://www.ewb-usa.org/.

36. Engineers for a Sustainable World (ESW), http://www.eswusa.org/.

37. Engineering World Health (EWH), http://www.ewh.org/.

38. NetHope, http://www.nethope.org/.

39. Peace Corps, http://www.peacecorps.gov/.

40. GeekCorps (GC), http://www.iesc.org/geekcorps.

41. civiCRM, http://civicrm.org/.

42. Tucker A., Morelli, R., and de Lanerolle, R. Chapter 8 in this volume.

43. Sourceforget.net, http://sourceforge.net/.

44. Wentworth Institute of Technology: Center for Community and Learning Partnerships, http://www.wit.edu/clp/index.html.

45. Vollmar, K., and Sanderson, P. Chapter 6 in this volume.

46. Branker. K., and Pearce, J. Chapter 15 in this volume.

47. Nejmeh, B., and Dean, T. Chapter 19 in this volume.

48. PHP, http://www.php.net/.

49. MySQL, http://www.mysql.com/.

50. Tomcat, http://tomcat.apache.org/.

51. Ruby on Rails, http://rubyonrails.org/.

52. appropedia.org, http://www.appropedia.org/Welcome_to_Appropedia.

53. Microsoft Refurbishers Program, http://www.microsoft.com/oem/en/licensing/sblicensing/pages/refurbisher_programs.aspx.

54. Royce, W. "Managing the Development of Large Software Systems." In *Proceedings of IEEE WESCON 26* (August, 1970), pp. 1 9.

55. Agile Alliance, http://www.agilealliance.org/.

56. Nejmeh, B., and Thomas, I. "Business-Driven Product Planning Using Feature Vectors and Increments," *IEEE Software,* Vol. 19, No. 6 (November/December, 2002), pp. 34–42.

57. Tucker, A., Morelli, R., and de Silva, C. (2011). *Software Development: An Open Source Approach.* New York: CRC Press.

58. Raymond, E. "The Catherdral and the Bazaar," http://catb.org/~esr/writings/homesteading/.

59. Nejmeh, B., and Vicary, B. "Lessons Learned about Design, Monitoring and Evaluation

Process Definition and Information Management for International Development Programmes," *Knowledge Management for Development Journal,* Volume 5, Issue 2 (September, 2009), pp. 143–159.

60. Nejmeh, B. "Faith Integration Through Service-Learning in the Information Sciences," *Christian Business Academy Review,* Volume 3, No. 1 (Spring, 2008), pp. 12–24.

61. ABET Accreditation Criteria, http://www.abet.org/uploadedFiles/Accreditation/Accreditation_Process/Accreditation_Documents/Current/asac-criteria-2012-2013.pdf.

62. Mobileactive.org, http://mobileactive.org/.

63. Amazon EC2, http://aws.amazon.com/ec2/.

64. Force.com, www.force.com.

65. Google App Engine, http://code.google.com/appengine/.

66. Oracle Cloud, http://www.oracle.com/us/technologies/cloud/index.html.

67. AACSB, http://www.aacsb.edu/.

INDEX